# MATHEMATICS
## for Business and Social Sciences
### An Applied Approach

# MATHEMATICS
## for Business and Social Sciences
## An Applied Approach

**Abe Mizrahi**
Indiana University Northwest

**Michael Sullivan**
Chicago State University

**John Wiley & Sons, Inc.**
New York · London · Sydney · Toronto

To our families

This book was set in Optima by York Graphic
Services, Inc., and printed and bound by Halliday
Lithographers, Inc. The text was designed by
Nicholas A. Bernini and the cover is by Blaise Zito
Associates Inc.; the drawings were done by the
Wiley Illustration Department; the editor was
Eugene Patti; Reiko Okamura supervised production.

Copyright © 1976, by John Wiley & Sons, Inc.

**Library of Congress Cataloging in Publication Data**

Mizrahi, Abe.
Mathematics for business and the social sciences.

Includes bibliographies and index.
1. Business mathematics.    2. Business mathematics—
Problems, exercises, etc.    I. Sullivan, Michael,
1942–        joint author.    II. Title.
HF5691.M59        513'.93        75-17901
ISBN 0-471-61191-3

Printed in the United States of America

10 9 8 7 6 5 4 3 2 1

For the student majoring in business and social sciences, the emphasis on quantitative methods has increased greatly in recent years. Today, students not only are required to understand and interpret mathematics, but to use this training in subsequent courses in statistics, operations analysis, and econometrics, for example. The purpose of the textbook is to present a balanced approach to the mathematics required, and its applications in the business and social sciences.

For this reason, we present various topics in mathematics by first introducing problems through real-life situations and then developing the mathematics necessary to handle similar situations. That is, we utilize mathematical models and, to emphasize the relevant character of these models, we cite many references to current applications in the business sciences. For example, an entire chapter is devoted to the concept of a mathematical model. Applications are given to various areas including accounting (straight-line depreciation), ecology (pollution control), economics (Leontief model, consumer's surplus), psychological management (learning curves), operations research (queueing theory), and finance (amortization, tax rates), to name a few.

Throughout the book, the language is easy to understand, and the use of intuition to motivate ideas is stressed. Little emphasis is given to theory. For example, in the calculus section, limits are introduced without resorting to the $\epsilon/\delta$ approach, and area is first calculated without using limits of sums. In an Appendix, area is presented as the limit of a sum. Similarly, linear programming is approached both geometrically (two dimensionally) and algebraically. Thus the more difficult simplex method is motivated first by geometric ideas.

This material is truly a collaborative effort, and the order of authorship is merely alphabetical. We assume equal responsibility for the book's strengths and weaknesses and welcome comments and suggestions for its improvement.

The book contains most of the topics that are included in the traditional first-year finite mathematics and short calculus sequence. It is arranged in five blocks:

| | |
|---|---|
| Preliminary Material | Chapters 1–3 and Appendix I |
| Linear Algebra | Chapters 4–6 |
| Calculus | Chapters 7–12 and Appendix II |
| Probability | Chapters 13–16 |
| Mathematics of Finance | Chapter 17 |

Students whose mathematical background is weak can review the required concepts by covering Chapter 1 and Appendix I: A Review of Algebra. The material in Chapter 1 is needed for the linear algebra portion of the book, while Appendix II is required for the calculus portion. Thus

Chapter 1 and Appendix I may be covered concurrently and should be consulted as needed.

Chapter 2 introduces the important concept of a function, and properties of the linear and quadratic functions. Chapter 3, on mathematical models, provides an introduction to modeling and gives examples of some models discussed in the book.

Chapters 4 to 6 comprise the part of the book that deals with linear algebra. Chapter 4 gives a geometric approach to linear programming and utilizes the topics introduced in Chapter 1. Chapter 5 discusses various topics in matrix algebra, including addition and multiplication of matrices, as well as systems of equations and the inverse of a matrix. Applications to economics (Leontief model), demography, and accounting are included in a separate section that can be omitted without loss of continuity. Chapter 6 continues the study of linear programming by introducing the simplex method.

Chapters 7 to 12 and Appendix II comprise the calculus portion of the book. Chapter 10, on the exponential and logarithm functions, is postponed until after the differential calculus is discussed to improve the readability of Chapters 7 to 9 and to emphasize the importance of these functions in business and social science.

Chapters 13–16 deal with probability. Chapter 13 forms the basis for the subsequent study of discrete probability in Chapter 14 by introducing properties of sets and counting principles. Chapter 15 continues the study of probability, applying it to operations research and game theory. Chapter 16 introduces continuous probability and integrates the calculus with probability.

Chapter 17, "Mathematics of Finance," may be covered at any time.

The diagram on the next page illustrates the dependence/independence of each chapter.

Since credit hours for this type of course vary, we suggest various plans below.

| Time | Sections to be Covered |
|------|------------------------|
| 3 semester hours | Chapters 1, 2, 3, 7–12<br>Chapters 1, 2, 4, 5, 13, 14, 15 or 17<br>Chapters 4, 5, 6, 13, 14, 15<br>Chapters 4, 5, 13, 14, 15, 17 |
| 4 semester hours | Chapters 1, 2, 3, 7–12, 17<br>Chapters 1, 2, 4, 5, 6, 13, 14<br>Chapters 1, 2, 4, 5, 13, 14, 15<br>Chapters 4, 5, 6, 13, 14, 15, 17 |
| 6 semester hours | Chapters 1–3, 4, 5, 7–12, 13, 14, 15<br>Chapters 4–17 |
| 8 semester hours | entire text |

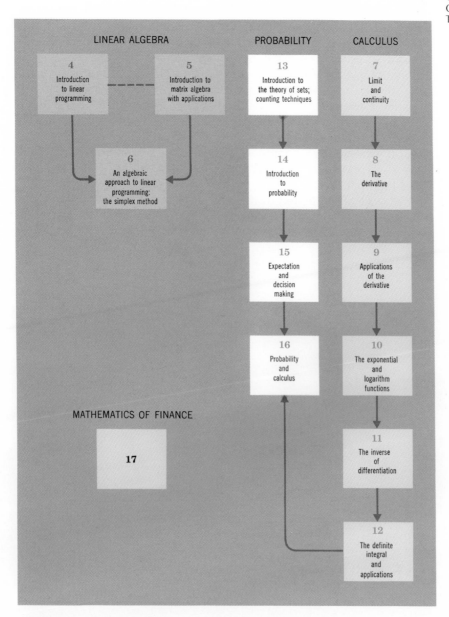

LINEAR ALGEBRA     PROBABILITY     CALCULUS

**4** Introduction to linear programming

**5** Introduction to matrix algebra with applications

**13** Introduction to the theory of sets; counting techniques

**7** Limit and continuity

**6** An algebraic approach to linear programming: the simplex method

**14** Introduction to probability

**8** The derivative

**15** Expectation and decision making

**9** Applications of the derivative

**16** Probability and calculus

**10** The exponential and logarithm functions

MATHEMATICS OF FINANCE

**17**

**11** The inverse of differentiation

**12** The definite integral and applications

Worked-out solutions for approximately 50 percent of the problems are found in the back of the book; answers to all problems are contained in a *Solutions Manual.* Problems with asterisks are considered more challenging.

At the end of each chapter there is a list of important terms and a set of review exercises. In addition, supplementary reading and references are also found after most chapters. Finally, all tables required in the exercises are located at the end of the book.

*A.M.*
*M.S.*

ACKNOWLEDGMENTS    We thank the many students at Indiana University-Northwest and Chicago State University for their comments, criticisms, and, above all, their patience while the manuscript was being class-tested.

We are especially grateful to Professors Larry Schiefelbusch and Howard Silver for their assistance and to Dennis Murphy, Professor of Economics, for his valuable suggestions.

We thank these reviewers for their comments: Professors Harold K. Crowder, Cleveland State University; Edith W. Ainsworth, University of Alabama; David Carlson, Oregon State University; Edward T. Walsh, City College of San Francisco; Joyce Vilseck, Texas A&I University; and Professor B. Linn Soule, Department of Business, Oregon State University.

We also appreciate the patience and skill of Mrs. Marilyn Pappas who typed the final draft.

Finally, we are indebted to the staff of Wiley, whose talent and skill played a significant role in the publication of this book. In particular, we thank Wiley mathematics editor Gary Ostedt, for his patience and help.

*Abe Mizrahi*
*Michael Sullivan*

# 1

# INTRODUCTION

In this section, we briefly introduce the language and notation of sets, since some knowledge of sets is necessary for the terminology in subsequent chapters. A more detailed discussion of sets and their properties can be found in Chapter 13.

There are many examples of sets of which we are already aware. For example, a student may speak of being a member of a certain class, say, Mathematics 101. In this case, Mathematics 101 is a set and the students enrolled in this course are elements of the set. A student *not* enrolled in Mathematics 101 is *not* a member of the set. If no students register for this course, Mathematics 101, then the set is called an *empty set,* that is, a set having *no* elements.

The concepts of *set* and *element of a set* are *described* more precisely in the following paragraphs.

A *set S* is a well-defined collection of objects, where by well-defined    Set
we mean that given any object it can be determined whether or not

**Element**

**Empty Set**

the object belongs to the set. The objects of a set S are called *elements* of S or members of S. A set that has no elements is called the *empty set,* or *null set,* or *vacuous set,* and is denoted by the symbol ∅.

Suppose S is a set and a is an element of the set S. Then we write

$$a \in S$$

read as "a is an element of S" or "a is in S." If a is *not* an element of the set S, then we write

$$a \notin S$$

read as "a is not an element of S" or "a is not in S."

Ordinarily, a set S can be written in one of two ways. These two ways of writing sets are illustrated by the following examples.

**1.1
Example**

Consider the set D of digits. The elements of the set D are

$$0, 1, 2, 3, 4, 5, 6, 7, 8, 9$$

In this case, we write

$$D = \{0, 1, 2, 3, 4, 5, 6, 7, 8, 9\}$$

read as "D is the set consisting of the elements 0, 1, 2, 3, 4, 5, 6, 7, 8, 9." Here, we are actually *listing* or *displaying* the elements of the set D.

Another way of writing this same set D of digits is to write

$$D = \{x \mid x \text{ is a digit}\}$$

read as "D is the set of all x such that x is a digit."

**Set-Builder
Notation**

Here we have described the set D by giving a property that every element of D has and that no element not in D can have: the property of being a digit. This way of writing a set is called *set-builder notation.*

Of course, when it is possible, either of the above two methods of describing a set and its elements may be used. Sometimes, however, it is impossible to list all elements of a set, because of the nature of the set. Examples of such occurrences will appear quite often as we pursue our study of elementary mathematics.

**1.2
Example**

Consider the set W, whose elements are the days in a week. Here we may actually list the elements of W by writing

$$W = \{\text{Monday, Tuesday, Wednesday, Thursday} \\ \text{Friday, Saturday, Sunday}\}$$

In set-builder notation, W is written as

$$W = \{x \mid x \text{ is a day of the week}\}$$

It is important for the student to notice that elements of a set are *not* repeated. A given element is entered as a member of a set only once; there is never a duplication of an element in a set.

Thus, we never write

$$\{3, 2, 2\}$$

Rather we write

$$\{3, 2\}$$

Also, because a set is a collection of objects considered as a whole, when considering a set, the order in which the elements of a set are listed does not make any difference. Thus, the three sets

$$\{2, 3, 4\}, \quad \{2, 4, 3\}, \quad \{3, 4, 2\}$$

are different listings of the *same* set. The *elements* of a set distinguish the set—*not the order* in which the elements are written.

Let us agree, henceforth, to adopt the convention that upper case letters, such as $A$ and $B$, will represent sets and lower case letters, $a$, $b, \ldots, x$, $y$, etc., will represent elements of sets.

If we examine the two sets

$$A = \{1, 2\} \qquad B = \{1, 2, 3, 4\}$$

we see that each element of $A$ is also found in the set $B$. When two sets have this property, we say $A$ *is a subset of B.*

**If every element in a set $A$ is also an element of a set $B$, then** $A$ *is a* **Definition**
*subset of B.* **We use the notation** **of Subset**

$$A \subseteq B$$

**to denote this fact.**

For example,

$$\{1, 3, 5\} \subseteq \{1, 3, 5, 7, 9\}$$
$$\{1, 2, 3\} \subseteq \{1, 2, 3\}$$
$$\emptyset \subseteq \{1, 2, 3\}$$

---

Write each of the following sets in two ways.   1.1
  1. The set $A$ of digits from 6 to 9 inclusive.   Exercise
  2. The set $B$ of vowels in the alphabet.
  3. The set $C$ of digits in your age (in years).
In problems 4–9, replace the * by either $\in$ or $\notin$, whichever is correct.
  4. $3 * \{2, 3, 7\}$
  5. $0 * \{1, 3\}$
  6. $1/2 * \{x \mid x \text{ is a digit}\}$

 7. $1/2 * \{x|x$ is a fraction$\}$
 8. $10 * \{x|x$ is a digit$\}$
 9. $4 * \{2, 1, 6\}$
10. Find a set whose elements cannot be easily listed, but that can be readily described using the set-builder notation.
11. Find a set whose elements can be easily listed, but that cannot be readily described by using set-builder notation.
12. Determine which of the following sets is a subset of $B = \{0, 1, 2, 3, 4, 5, 6\}$
    (a) $A = \{0, 1, 5\}$     (c) $A = \{2, 4, 6, 8\}$
    (b) $A = \emptyset$           (d) $A = \{6\}$

## 1.2 REAL NUMBERS

The numbers we use for listing objects or counting objects, such as the number of members of the House of Representatives or the number of committees that can be formed from a group of five people, are called

#### Whole Numbers

*whole numbers.* In set notation, the whole numbers can be listed as

$$W = \{0, 1, 2, 3, 4 \ldots\}$$

The usefulness of the whole numbers is for counting objects. However, there are many practical situations in which the whole numbers cannot be used.

For example, if your checking account has a balance of $24.00 and you write a check for $30.00, how will you represent the balance in your account (without reverting to red ink)? If the temperature during the day is 5° C (5 degrees Celsius), and that night the temperature falls by 10° C, what is the new outside temperature? How is it represented?

Of course, what we are saying is that we need some new numbers,

#### Negative Numbers

the *negative numbers,* to aid us in representing situations like those described above. In accounting circles, a debit or money owed is generally represented by placing parentheses around the debt. In the checking account example, the balance would be lised as ($6.00). Usually, though, a dash ($-$) before a number means that it is negative. Thus, we could say that the temperature outside in the example above was "minus 5" or "5° below zero", and we would write this temperature as $-5°$ C.

The numbers we use to represent situations such as those given above

#### Integers

are called *integers.* In set notation, the *set of integers* is

$$\{0, 1, -1, 2, -2, 3, -3, \ldots\}$$

The whole numbers 0, 1, 2, ... form a subset of the set of integers, as do the negative (whole) numbers $-1, -2, -3, \ldots$

Often with the set of integers, we run into difficulties in some applications. For example, can we use an integer to answer what part of a dollar is 49¢? Or, can we use an integer to represent the length of a city lot if, when we use a foot-long ruler, we end up with a length more than 125 feet and less than 126 feet?

The answer to both these questions is no! We need a new set of numbers to handle such situations. This new set of numbers is called the *set of rational numbers*.

For example, to answer what part of a dollar is 49¢, we can say 49/100. Rational numbers are thus *ratios of integers*. For a rational number $a/b$, the integer $a$ is called the *numerator,* and the integer $b$, which cannot be zero, is called the *denominator*.

However, in some situations, even a rational number will not accurately describe the situation. For example, if one has an isosceles right triangle in which the two equal sides are of length 1 foot, can the length of the third side be expressed as a rational number? See Figure 1.1. The

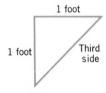

**Figure 1.1**

Greeks first learned that no matter what two circles are used, the ratio of circumference to diameter of the first one is always the same as the ratio of circumference to diameter of the second. Can this common value be represented by a rational number? See Figure 1.2.

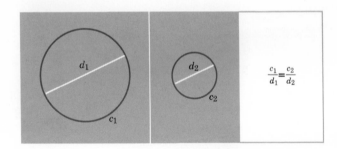

**Figure 1.2**

As it happens, the answer to both these questions is no. For the first question, we know by the Theorem of Pythagoras that the length of the third side is $\sqrt{2}$. However, $\sqrt{2}$ is *not* a rational number—it is not the ratio of two integers. The well-known symbol assigned to the ratio of circumference to diameter of a circle is $\pi$, which also cannot be expressed as the ratio of two integers. Such numbers as $\sqrt{2}$, $\pi$, $\sqrt[3]{5}$, etc. are called *irrational numbers*.

The set of irrational numbers together with the set of rational numbers is called the *set R of real numbers*.

In order to represent real numbers, we use what is commonly called a *decimal representation*. For example, the decimal representation of the rational numbers 3/4, 5/2, 2/3, is

$$\frac{3}{4} = .75, \qquad \frac{5}{2} = 2.5, \qquad \frac{2}{3} = .666\ldots$$

The decimal representations of rational numbers are always of two types: (1) terminating or ending, (3/4, 5/2, etc.) and (2) repeating (2/3, 1/7, etc.) The decimal representation of an irrational number never terminates and never repeats. Thus, for example,

$$\sqrt{2} = 1.414213\ldots, \qquad \pi = 3.14159\ldots$$

That is, if the decimal representation of a real number repeats or terminates, the real number is rational; if the decimal representation neither repeats nor terminates, the real number is irrational.

As an aid to your review of real numbers and their properties, several of the more important concepts involving rules and notation are listed below:

1. *Commutative Laws*
   (a) $a + b = b + a$   (b) $a \cdot b = b \cdot a$ for all real numbers $a$, $b$
2. *Associative Laws*
   (a) $a + b + c = (a + b) + c = a + (b + c)$ for all real numbers $a$, $b$, $c$
   (b) $a \cdot b \cdot c = (a \cdot b) \cdot c = a \cdot (b \cdot c)$ for all real numbers $a$, $b$, $c$
3. *Distributive Law*
   $a \cdot (b + c) = (a \cdot b) + (a \cdot c)$ for all real numbers $a$, $b$, $c$
4. *Arithmetic of Ratios*

   (a) $\dfrac{a}{b} = a \cdot \dfrac{1}{b}$   $b \neq 0$

   (b) $\dfrac{a}{b} + \dfrac{c}{d} = \dfrac{a \cdot d + b \cdot c}{b \cdot d}$   $b \neq 0, d \neq 0$

   (c) $\dfrac{a}{b} \cdot \dfrac{c}{d} = \dfrac{a \cdot c}{b \cdot d}$   $b \neq 0, d \neq 0$

   (d) $\dfrac{a}{b} \div \dfrac{c}{d} = \dfrac{a}{b} \cdot \dfrac{d}{c} = \dfrac{a \cdot d}{b \cdot c}$   $b \neq 0, c \neq 0, d \neq 0$

5. *Rules for Division*

   $0 \div a = 0$   $\dfrac{0}{a} = 0$ for any real number $a$, except 0

   $a \div 0$   $\left(\dfrac{a}{0}\right)$ is undefined for any real number $a$

   $a \div a = 1$   for any real number $a$, except 0
6. *Rules of Signs*
   (a) $a \cdot (-b) = -(a \cdot b)$
   (b) $(-a) \cdot b = -(a \cdot b)$
   (c) $(-a) \cdot (-b) = a \cdot b$
   (d) $-(-a) = a$

7. *Agreements; notations*
   (a) In $a \cdot b + c$, we agree to multiply $a \cdot b$ *first,* and then *add c.*
   (b) A mixed number $3\frac{5}{8}$ means $3 + \frac{5}{8}$; 3 times $\frac{5}{8}$ would be written as $3(\frac{5}{8})$ or $(3)$ $(\frac{5}{8})$ or $3 \cdot \frac{5}{8}$.

---

1. Perform the indicated operation.

   (a) $5 \cdot (-3) + 2$    (h) $\dfrac{1}{2} + \dfrac{3}{8}$

   (b) $6 - 3 \cdot 4$    (i) $\dfrac{7}{8} + \dfrac{3}{4}$

   (c) $(-5) \cdot (6 - 2)$    (j) $\dfrac{4}{3} + \dfrac{2}{3}$

   (d) $-3 - 4 - 5$    (k) $-\dfrac{4}{3} \cdot \dfrac{6}{8}$

   (e) $\dfrac{2}{3} + \dfrac{6}{7}$    (l) $7 + 3 - \dfrac{1}{3} \cdot \dfrac{30}{10}$

   (f) $\dfrac{5}{2} - \dfrac{2}{3}$    (m) $\left(\dfrac{2}{3} - 5\right) \cdot \dfrac{9}{8}$

   (g) $\dfrac{3 - 2}{4 - 2}$

2. Write the decimal representation of the following rational numbers.

   (a) $\dfrac{1}{4}$    (d) $\dfrac{4}{7}$

   (b) $\dfrac{3}{2}$    (e) $\dfrac{5}{12}$

   (c) $\dfrac{3}{5}$    (f) $\dfrac{9}{16}$

---

The set of real numbers can be divided into three subsets that are nonempty and disjoint. These subsets are (1) the set of *positive* real numbers, (2) the set with just 0 as a member, (3) the set of *negative* real numbers.

Some positive real numbers are

$$\frac{2}{3}, 5, \sqrt{2}, \pi, 5\frac{1}{2}, 1, 6.327$$

Some negative real numbers are

$$-\frac{3}{2}, -6, -\frac{1}{2}, -2, -5.219$$

Properties of the positive real numbers include

1. The sum of two positive real numbers is a positive real number.
2. The product of two positive real numbers is a positive real number.

Some properties of negative real numbers are

1. The sum of two negative real numbers is a negative real number.
2. The product of two negative real numbers is a positive real number.

Here is another property of positive and negative real numbers: The product of a negative real number and a positive real number is a negative real number.

Before we begin a review of inequalities, we discuss the *real line*. This will help us understand some of the properties of inequalities used in this chapter and in subsequent chapters.

**Real Line**    The *real line* can be described as a collection of points $P$ so that each point $P$ can be matched with exactly one real number $x$. The real number

**Coordinate**    $x$ is called the *coordinate x* of the point $P$.

Let us see how this matching of points $P$ and real numbers $x$ takes place.

**Origin**    Consider a line $L$. Pick a point $O$ on $L$. Call this point the *origin O*. Suppose we agree to associate to this point $O$, the real number $x = 0$. See Figure 1.3.

**Figure 1.3**

Pick another point $U$, different from the origin $O$, on $L$. Let $x = 1$ be associated with the point $U$. Figure 1.4 depicts this situation in which we agree to pick $U$ to the right of $O$.

**Figure 1.4**

**Scale**    The distance from $O$ to $U$ is called the *scale;* it may be one inch, or one mile, etc. Now, with this scale established, we can associate real numbers $x$ to points on $L$. We agree to abide by the usual convention that points to the *right* of the origin $O$ will be associated with *positive* real numbers and those to the *left* of $O$ to *negative* real numbers. In addition we agree to speak of the point $x$, where $x$ is the coordinate of the point.

For example, the coordinate of the origin $O$ is zero; the coordinate of $U$ is one. Thus, we can represent the real line as in Figure 1.5.

**Figure 1.5**

With these ideas in mind, we are ready to discuss the *arithmetic of inequalities*.

**Let** $a$**,** $b$ **be any real numbers. We say that** $a$ *is less than* $b$ **or that** $b$ *is greater than* $a$**, written as**

Definition
of Less Than
and Greater
Than

$$a < b \qquad \textbf{or} \qquad b > a$$

**if and only if the difference** $b - a$ **is a positive real number.**

For example, $2 < 7$, since $7 - 2 = 5$ is positive. Also, $6 > 3$, since $6 - 3 = 3$ is positive. On the real line, a real number $a$ is *less than* the number $b$, when $a$ is to the *left* of $b$. Thus, $-7 < -3$ since $-7$ lies to the left of $-3$ on the real line.

**Let** $a$**,** $b$ **be real numbers. We say that** $a$ *is less than or equal to* $b$ **or that** $b$ *is greater than or equal to* $a$**, written as**

Definition
of Less Than or
Equal and Greater
Than or Equal

$$a \leq b \qquad \textbf{or} \qquad b \geq a$$

**if and only if the difference** $b - a$ **is either positive or zero.**

For example, $3 \leq 8$ since $8 - 3 = 5$ is positive. Also, $4 \geq 4$ since $4 - 4 = 0$ is zero.

It is easy to see that

$$a \text{ is positive if and only if } a > 0$$
$$a \text{ is negative if and only if } a < 0$$

When it becomes necessary to solve equations, we solve them by certain manipulations. Every time a manipulation is used, it is used subject to the laws or properties of real numbers. For example, when we solve

$$2x - 3 = 6$$

we first add 3 to both members obtaining

$$2x = 9$$

Then we multiply by 1/2 to get

$$x = \frac{9}{2}$$

To solve inequalities (expressions which invole the symbols $<, \leq, \geq$, or $>$), we attack the problem in much the same way. However, as will be seen, some of the laws for inequalities are different from those for equalities.

The laws of inequalities are

1. *Addition Law*
   If $a \leq b$, then $a + c \leq b + c$ for any choice of $c$.
   (That is, addition will not affect the sense or direction of the inequality.)

2. *Multiplication Law*
   (a) If $a \leq b$ and $c > 0$, then $a \cdot c \leq b \cdot c$.
   (b) If $a \leq b$ and $c < 0$, then $a \cdot c \geq b \cdot c$.
   (When multiplying an inequality, the sense or direction of the inequality remains the same if we multiply by a positive number; it is reversed if we multiply by a negative number).

3. *Division Law*
   (a) If $0 < a$, then $1/a > 0$.
   (That is, the reciprocal of a positive number is positive.)
   (b) If $a, b$ are positive and if $a < b$, then $1/a > 1/b$.

**3.1
Example**

Examples of the above laws are

1. Since $2 < 3$, then $2 + 5 < 3 + 5$ or $7 < 8$.
2. (a) Since $2 < 3$ and $6 > 0$, then $2 \cdot 6 < 3 \cdot 6$ or $12 < 18$.
   (b) Since $2 < 3$ and $-4 < 0$, then $2 \cdot (-4) > 3(-4)$ or $-8 > -12$.
3. (a) Since $3 > 0$, then $\frac{1}{3} > 0$.
   (b) Since $2 < 3$, then $\frac{1}{2} > \frac{1}{3}$.

With these laws in mind, we can solve most inequality problems. An inequality is merely an expression in which $<, \leq, >, \geq$ appear. The values of an unknown $x$ that make the inequality a true statement are

**Solution Set**

members of the *solution set* of the inequality.

**3.2
Example**

Find all real numbers $x$ for which

$$2x + 3 \leq 6$$

To solve the inequality, treat it as if it were an equality, but remember that some of the laws are different. Then, if we add $-3$ to both members, we have

$$(2x + 3) + (-3) \leq 6 + (-3)$$
$$2x \leq 3$$

Now we multiply both members by $1/2$. Since $1/2 > 0$, the direction of the inequality will remain the same. Thus,

$$\frac{1}{2}(2x) \leqq \frac{1}{2}(3)$$

$$x \leqq \frac{3}{2}$$

The solution set $X$ is

$$X = \left\{ x \mid x \leqq \frac{3}{2} \right\}$$

The graph of this solution set is given in Figure 1.6 and is indicated in color.

**Figure 1.6**

Find the solution set of

3.3
Example

$$-3x - 2 \leqq 6$$

Again, we proceed as we would for an equality. Adding 2 to both members, we obtain

$$-3x \leqq 8$$

Multiply by $-1/3$. Since $-1/3 < 0$, this operation will reverse the inequality. Thus,

$$\left(-\frac{1}{3}\right)(-3x) \geqq \left(-\frac{1}{3}\right)(8)$$

or

$$x \geqq -\frac{8}{3}$$

The solution set $X$ is

$$X = \left\{ x \mid x \geqq -\frac{8}{3} \right\}$$

The graph of the solution set is given in Figure 1.7.

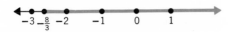

**Figure 1.7**

The cost of publishing each copy of a magazine is $0.22. The revenue from dealer sales is $0.20 per copy and advertising revenue is 15% of the revenue obtained from sales in excess of 15,000 copies. What is the least number of copies that must be sold for a profit to result?

We begin by letting $x$ denote the number of copies sold in excess of 15,000. The revenue from dealer sales is

$$(15{,}000 + x)(0.20)$$

The revenue from advertising is

$$(0.15)(0.20)x$$

The cost of publishing is

$$(15{,}000 + x)(0.22)$$

We require that

$$\text{Profit} = \text{Revenue} - \text{Cost} > 0$$

Thus,

$$(15{,}000 + x)(0.20) + (0.15)(0.20)(x) - (15{,}000 + x)(0.22) > 0$$
$$(0.2x + 0.03x - 0.22x) + (3000 - 3300) > 0$$
$$0.01x > 300$$
$$x > 30{,}000$$

The number of magazines sold must exceed $30{,}000 + 15{,}000$ or 45,000 for a profit to occur.

---

Find and graph the solution set $X$ of the following inequalities.
1. $3x + 5 \leq 2$
2. $3x + 5 \geq 2$
3. $-3x + 5 \leq 2$
4. $6x - 3 \geq 8x + 5$
5. $14x - 21x + 16 \leq 3x - 2$
6. $4 - 5x \geq 3$
7. $8 - 2x \leq 5x - 6$
8. If the publisher in Example 3.4 has a publishing cost of $0.28 per copy, and if the revenue from dealer sales is $0.25 per copy, how many must be sold for a profit to occur? Assume advertising revenue is 20% of revenue obtained from sales in excess of 15,000 copies.

---

Suppose we have two real lines, that are mutually perpendicular. Call the horizontal line the x-axis and the vertical line the y-axis. Coordinatize each of these lines as described earlier using their point of intersection as the origin $O$ and using a convenient scale on each. It is not essential to use the same scale. In fact, for many of our applications, a different scale will be used. If we follow the usual convention that points on the x-axis to the right of O are associated with positive real numbers, those to the left of O to negative numbers, those on the y-axis above O to positive numbers, and those on the y-axis below O to negative real numbers, we obtain Figure 1.8.

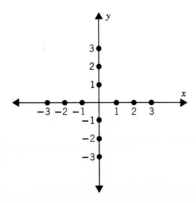

**Figure 1.8**

Any point P in the plane can be located by using an ordered pair $(x, y)$ of real numbers by the following method. Let x denote the signed distance of P from the y-axis (signed in the sense that if P is to the right of the y-axis, then $x > 0$ and if P is to the left of the y-axis, then $x < 0$). Let y denote the signed distance of P from the x-axis. Then, the ordered pair $(x, y)$ gives us enough information to locate the point P. By following this procedure, we can assign ordered pairs of real numbers to every point P. In this way, we can *coordinatize the plane*. See Figure 1.9.

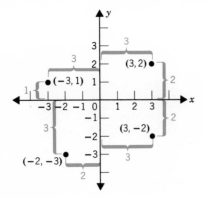

**Figure 1.9**

If $(x, y)$ are the coordinates of a point P, then x is called the *abscissa* of P and y is the *ordinate* of P.

Abscissa

Ordinate

For example, the coordinates of the origin $O$ are $(0,0)$. The abscissa of any point on the $y$-axis is zero.

The type of coordinate system introduced above is a *rectangular coordinate system,* and it divides the plane into four sections. These sections are called *quadrants* and are depicted in Figure 1.10. Notice that in Quadrant One, both the abscissa $x$ and the ordinate $y$ of all points $P$ are positive.

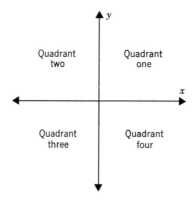

**Figure 1.10**

We now state a formula for finding the distance between two points in the plane.

**Let $(x_1, y_1)$ denote the coordinates of a point $P_1$ and let $(x_2, y_2)$ be the coordinates of a point $P_2$. The distance $d$ between $P_1$ and $P_2$ is given by the formula:**

$$d = \sqrt{(x_2 - x_1)^2 + (y_2 - y_1)^2}$$

See Figure 1.11 for a justification of this result. A proof requires the Pythagorean theorem.

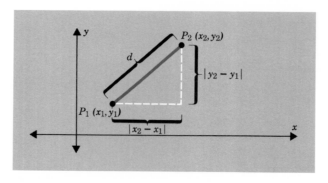

**Figure 1.11**

Thus, to compute the distance between two points, find the difference of their abscissas, square it, and add this to the square of the difference of their ordinates. The square root of this sum is the distance.

The distance $d$ between $P_1$ and $P_2$ is sometimes denoted by

$$d = d(P_1, P_2)$$

Find the distance between the points $(-2, 5)$ and $(3, 2)$. Here

4.1
Example

$$d = \sqrt{(-2 - 3)^2 + (5 - 2)^2} = \sqrt{(-5)^2 + (3)^2}$$
$$= \sqrt{25 + 9} = \sqrt{34}$$

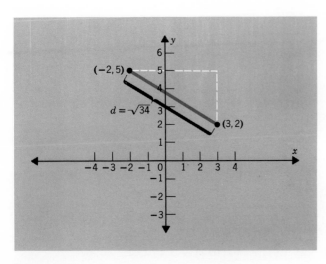

**Figure 1.12**

The distance between two points is never a negative number. Furthermore, the only time a distance of zero can be obtained is when the two points are identical. Finally, it makes no difference whether the distance is computed from $P_1$ to $P_2$ or from $P_2$ to $P_1$; that is, $d(P_1, P_2) = d(P_2, P_1)$.

Next, we review *graphing*.

Graph the set of points $(x, y)$ defined by

4.2
Example

$$y = x$$

Here, we want to locate all points $(x, y)$ for which the abscissa $x$ and ordinate $y$ are equal. Some of these points are

$(0, 0)$, $(0.1, 0.1)$, $(1, 1)$, $(1.5, 1.5)$, $(3, 3)$
$(-3, -3)$, $(-0.2, -0.2)$, $(8, 8)$

The graph is given in Figure 1.13.

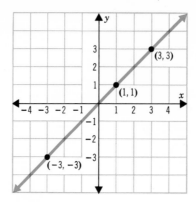

**Figure 1.13**

4.3
Example

Graph the set of points $(x, y)$ given by

$$y = 2x + 5$$

Here, we want to find all points $(x, y)$ for which the ordinate $y$ equals twice the abscissa $x$ plus 5. To locate some of these points (and thus to get an idea of the pattern of the graph), let us *assign* some values to $x$ and find corresponding values for $y$. Thus,

$$\text{if } x = 0, y = 2 \cdot 0 + 5 = 5$$
$$\text{if } x = 1, y = 2 \cdot 1 + 5 = 7$$
$$\text{if } x = -5, y = 2 \cdot (-5) + 5 = -5$$
$$\text{if } x = 10, y = 2 \cdot (10) + 5 = 25$$
$$\text{if } x = 10.1, y = 2(10.1) + 5 = 25.2$$

Connecting some of these points, we obtain Figure 1.14.

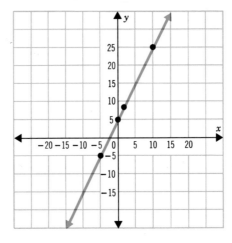

**Figure 1.14**

This method of graphing sets of points is sometimes cumbersome; an important application of differential calculus enables us to graph without locating a lot of points.

1. Locate the following points in a rectangular coordinate system.
   (a) $(3, -2)$    (d) $(6, 0)$
   (b) $(-6, 5)$   (e) $(-3, -5)$
   (c) $(0, 5)$    (f) $(4, 5)$
2. Label the points in Figure 1.15. Assume the coordinates are integers.

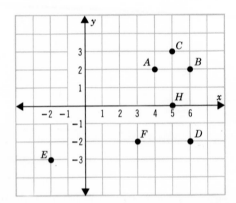

**Figure 1.15**

3. In Figure 1.15, if $A = (a_1, a_2)$, $F = (f_1, f_2)$, $C = (c_1, c_2)$, use the result of problem 2 to compute

   (a) $\dfrac{f_2 - a_2}{f_1 - a_1}$    (c) $\dfrac{a_2 - c_2}{a_1 - c_1}$

   (b) $\dfrac{f_2 - c_2}{f_1 - c_1}$

4. Find the distance between the following pairs of points.
   (a) $P_1(3, -4)$,     $P_2(3, 1)$
   (b) $P_1(-6, 2)$,   $P_2(-4, -2)$
   (c) $P_1(\frac{1}{2}, 0)$,     $P_2(2, 1)$
   (d) $P_1(-5, 1.2)$,  $P_2(0.6, -0.5)$
5. Find the length of each side of the triangle determined by the following triplets of points and state whether the triangle is an isosceles triangle or a right triangle or neither or both. Graph each triangle.
   (a) $P_1(2, 1)$,    $P_2(-4, 1)$,   $P_3(-4, -3)$
   (b) $P_1(-1, 4)$,  $P_2(6, 2)$,    $P_3(4, -5)$
   (c) $P_1(-2, -1)$, $P_2(0, 7)$,    $P_3(3, 2)$

6. Graph the set of points $(x, y)$ for which
   (a) $y = 3x$         (e) $y = -2x - 3$
   (b) $y = 2x - 3$     (f) $y = -2x - 4$
   (c) $3y + 2x + 1 = 0$   (g) $y = -2x - 5$
   (d) $y = 0$           (h) $y = 2x^2$
7. Graph problems 6e, 6f, 6g, in the same coordinate system. Do you notice anything?

**1.5
THE STRAIGHT
LINE**

In this section, we study a certain type of graph, the *straight line*. We begin by recalling a result from plane geometry.

**If $P$ and $Q$ are two distinct points, there is one and only one line $L$ containing $P$ and $Q$.**

**Figure 1.16**

If we coordinatize the plane so that $P$ and $Q$ are both represented by ordered pairs of real numbers, the following definition can be given.

**Definition
of Slope of a
Line**

**Let $P$ and $Q$ be two distinct points with coordinates $(x_1, y_1)$ and $(x_2, y_2)$ respectively. The *slope $m$ of the line $L$* containing $P$ and $Q$ is defined by the formula**

$$m = \frac{y_2 - y_1}{x_2 - x_1} \quad \text{if} \quad x_1 \neq x_2$$

**If $x_1 = x_2$, the slope $m$ of $L$ is said to be *undefined* and $L$ is *vertical*.**

In words, the slope $m$ of the line $L$ measures the ratio of the difference of the ordinates of $P$ and $Q$ to the difference of the abscissas of $P$ and $Q$.

Since

$$\frac{y_2 - y_1}{x_2 - x_1} = \frac{y_1 - y_2}{x_1 - x_2}$$

it will not matter which point is taken first in computing the slope $m$.

Geometrically, the slope $m$ measures the "rise-over-run" of a line $L$. See Figure 1.17.

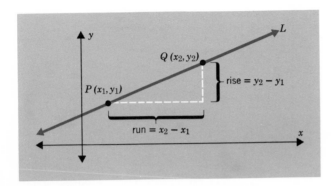

**Figure 1.17**

To get a better idea of the meaning of the slope of a line $L$, consider the following examples.

5.1
Example

Compute the slope of the line containing the following pairs of points. Graph each line.
(a) $P = (2, 3)$, $Q_1 = (-1, -2)$
(b) $P = (2, 3)$, $Q_2 = (3, -1)$
(c) $P = (2, 3)$, $Q_3 = (5, 3)$
(d) $P = (2, 3)$, $Q_4 = (2, 1)$

Let $m_1$, $m_2$, $m_3$, $m_4$ denote the slopes of the lines $L_1$, $L_2$, $L_3$, $L_4$ given by the points $P, Q_1; P, Q_2; P, Q_3; P, Q_4$, respectively. Then

$$m_1 = \frac{-2 - 3}{-1 - 2} = \frac{-5}{-3} = \frac{5}{3} \quad \text{(a rise of 5 over a run of 3)}$$

$$m_2 = \frac{-1 - 3}{3 - 2} = \frac{-4}{1} = -4$$

$$m_3 = \frac{3 - 3}{5 - 2} = \frac{0}{3} = 0$$

$$m_4 \quad \text{is undefined}$$

The graphs of these lines are given in Figure 1.18.

As the illustration indicates, when the slope $m$ of a line is positive, the line *slants upward* from left to right ($L_1$); when the slope $m$ is negative the line *slants downward* from left to right ($L_2$); when the slope $m = 0$, the line is horizontal ($L_3$); and when the slope $m$ is undefined, the line is vertical ($L_4$).

We also recognize something else regarding the slope of a line. Since slope measures the rise-over-run of a line and since a line has a constant

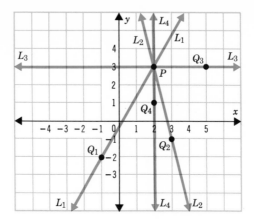

**Figure 1.18**

or never changing rise-over-run, it can be concluded that the slope of a line $L$ will be the same no matter what two distinct points on $L$ are used. That this is indeed true can be verified by using the notion of similar triangles.

Let $L$ be a line joining the two distinct points $P$ and $Q$ and let $X$ and $Y$ be any other two distinct points on $L$. Construct the triangles depicted

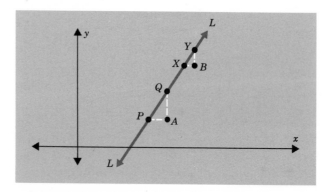

**Figure 1.19**

in Figure 1.19. Since $\triangle PQA$ is similar to $\triangle XYB$ (why?), it follows that corresponding sides are in proportion. That is,

$$\frac{AQ}{BY} = \frac{AP}{BX} \quad \text{or} \quad \frac{AQ}{AP} = \frac{BY}{BX}$$

But the slope $m$ of $L$ is

$$m = \frac{AQ}{AP}$$

By the above equality, we see that

$$m = \frac{BY}{BX}$$

Thus, since $X$, $Y$ were arbitrary, we see that *the slope $m$ of a line $L$ is the same no matter what points on $L$ are used to compute $m$.*

With this fact, we can now proceed to find out what relationship exists between the abscissa $x$ and ordinate $y$ of any point $P = (x, y)$ on a given line $L$.

We begin by asking an easier question. What property will every point $P = (x, y)$ on a vertical line $L$ have? For a vertical line $L$, the abscissa $x$ of every point on $L$ is the same, while the ordinate $y$ varies. Thus,

**Theorem 5.1**
**A vertical line is represented by**

$$x = a$$

**where $a$ is fixed.**

Note that the slope $m$ of a vertical line is undefined.

5.2
Example

Graph all points $(x, y)$ that obey

$$x = 3$$

By Theorem 5.1, this is a vertical line, and its graph is given in Figure 1.20.

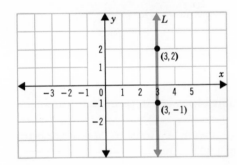

**Figure 1.20**

Next, we consider the question of nonvertical lines. Suppose $P_1 = (x_1, y_1)$ and $P_2 = (x_2, y_2)$ are two distinct points on a line $L$. (Since $L$ is assumed nonvertical, we know that $x_1 \neq x_2$. Why?) Suppose $P = (x, y)$ is *any* point on $L$. Then, since the slope $m$ of $L$ is the same no matter what two points are used, we can compute $m$ by using $P_1$, $P_2$ and by using $P_1$, $P$. Then

$$m = \frac{y_2 - y_1}{x_2 - x_1}, \qquad m = \frac{y - y_1}{x - x_1}$$

Setting the values of $m$ equal gives

$$\frac{y_2 - y_1}{x_2 - x_1} = \frac{y - y_1}{x - x_1}$$

Or, simplifying,

$$y - y_1 = \left(\frac{y_2 - y_1}{x_2 - x_1}\right) \cdot (x - x_1)$$

### Theorem 5.2
**The equation that defines a nonvertical line $L$ passing through $P_1 = (x_1, y_1)$, $P_2 = (x_2, y_2)$ is**

$$y = y_1 + \frac{(y_2 - y_1)}{(x_2 - x_1)} \cdot (x - x_1)$$

Two-Point Form of a Line

**This is called the** *two-point form of the equation of a line $L$.*

### Corollary
**The equation that defines a nonvertical line $L$ of slope $m$ and passing through the point $(x_1, y_1)$ is**

$$y = y_1 + m(x - x_1)$$

Point Slope Form of a Line

**This is called the** *point-slope form of the equation of a line $L$.*

5.3
Example

Find the equation that defines that line $L$ passing through the points $(2, 3)$ and $(-4, 5)$. Graph the line $L$.

Here, since two points are given, we use the two-point form to find the equation of the line $L$. Thus,

$$y - 3 = \frac{(5 - 3)}{(-4 - 2)} \cdot (x - 2)$$

or

$$y - 3 = \frac{2}{-6}(x - 2) \qquad \text{or} \qquad y = -\frac{1}{3}x + \frac{11}{3}$$

The graph of the line $L$ is given in Figure 1.21.

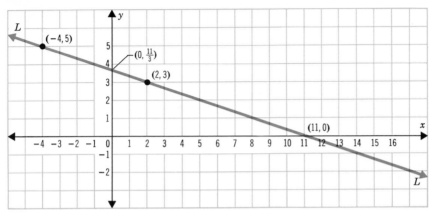

**Figure 1.21**

Find the equation of the line $L$ with slope 4 and passing through the point $(1, 2)$.

Since we know the slope $m$ and a point $P$, we use the point-slope form of a line. Then,

$$y = 2 + 4(x - 1)$$

or

$$y = 4x - 2$$

To graph this line $L$, we need to know two points. To find another point on $L$, we assign an arbitrary value to $x$, say $x = 0$. When $x = 0$, $y = -2 + 4(0) = -2$. Thus, $(0, -2)$ is also on $L$. The graph of $L$ is given in Figure 1.22.

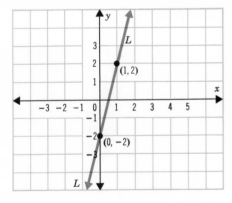

**Figure 1.22**

The fact that the slope $m = 4 > 0$ checks with the fact that $L$ slants upward from left to right.

In Example 5.4, we needed to find another point on $L$ and set $x = 0$

to find this point. Those points at which a line $L$ crosses the axes are of special importance.

**Definition of Intercepts** **Those points at which the graph of a line $L$ crosses the axes are called** *intercepts.* **The** *x-intercept* **is the abscissa of the point at which the line cross the x-axis and the** *y-intercept* **is the ordinate of the point at which the y-axis is crossed.**

For example, the line $L$ of Figure 1.23 has intercepts $(2, 0)$ and $(0, -3)$. The x-intercept is 2 and the y-intercept is $-3$.

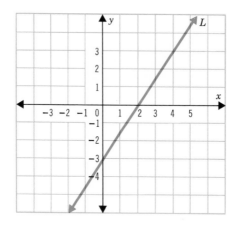

**Figure 1.23**

If we know the slope $m$ of a line $L$ and if we know that its y-intercept is $b$, then we know both the slope $m$ of $L$ and a point of $L$, namely, $(0, b)$, and can find the equation of $L$ by using the point-slope form. Then we obtain

$$y - b = m(x - 0)$$

or

$$y = mx + b$$

**Theorem 5.3**

**The equation of a line $L$ with slope $m$ and y-intercept $b$ is**

$$y = mx + b$$

**Slope-Intercept Form of a Line** **This is called the** *slope-intercept form of the equation of a line L.*

For the line

$$y = -3x + 6$$

the slope is $-3$ and the $y$-intercept is 6. Its graph is given in Figure 1.24.

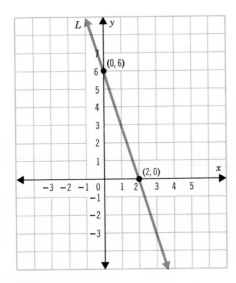

**Figure 1.24**

Sometimes it is more convenient to write the equation of a line $L$ in *general form*, namely,

$$Ax + By + C = 0$$

where $A$, $B$, $C$ are three real numbers and $A$, $B$ are not both zero.

Find the slope $m$ and $y$-intercept $b$ of the line $L$ given by

$$2x + 4y - 8 = 0$$

Graph the line.

Here, we transform the equation so that it looks like the slope-intercept form of a line.

To do this, we solve for $y$. Then,

$$4y = -2x + 8$$

$$y = -\frac{1}{2}x + 2$$

Comparing this to $y = mx + b$, we see that

$$m = -\frac{1}{2}; \quad b = 2$$

Thus, the line $L$ given in Example 5.6 has slope $m = -1/2$ and $y$-intercept $b = 2$.

To graph $L$, we need one other point on $L$ (since we only know that $(0, 2)$ is on $L$). The $x$-intercept of $L$ can be found by setting $y = 0$ and solving for $x$. Then, $2x - 8 = 0$ or $x = 4$.

Thus, the $x$-intercept is 4 and $(4, 0)$ is on $L$. See Figure 1.25.

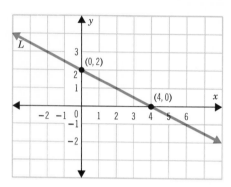

**Figure 1.25**

The theorems given earlier can be used either to find the equation of a line $L$ when information is known about $L$ (such as its slope $m$, etc.) or to find out information about $L$ when its equation is known.

1. Find the slope $m$ of the lines joining the following pairs of points.
   (a) $P_1 = (2, 3)$, $P_2 = (0, 1)$
   (b) $P_1 = (1, 1)$, $P_2 = (5, -6)$
   (c) $P_1 = (-3, 0)$, $P_2 = (-5, -4)$
   (d) $P_1 = (4, -3)$, $P_2 = (0, 0)$
   (e) $P_1 = (.1, .3)$, $P_2 = (1.5, 4.0)$
   (f) $P_1 = (-3, -2)$, $P_2 = (6, -2)$
2. Find the equation of the line passing through the points given in problem 1. Graph these lines.
3. Find the equation of the line with the following properties:
   (a) Slope $m = 1/2$, passing through $(-2, 3)$
   (b) Slope $m = 0$, passing through $(-2, 0)$
   (c) Slope $m = -3$, passing through $(0, 0)$
   (d) Passing through the points $(0, 3)$ and $(1, 1)$
   (e) Slope $m = 2$, $y$-intercept $= 3$
   (f) Slope $m = 3$, $x$-intercept $= -1/2$
   (g) $x$-intercept $= -3$, $y$-intercept $= 1/2$
   Graph each line.

4. Copy and complete the missing values of the given equation.

(a) $y = x - 3$

| $x$ | 0 | 1 | $\frac{-1}{2}$ | | | 5 | |
|---|---|---|---|---|---|---|---|
| $y$ | | | | 3 | 2 | | $-6$ |

(b) $y = \frac{1}{2}x - \frac{1}{17}$

| $x$ | | 2 | | $-3$ | 0 | | $\frac{3}{2}$ | | 18 |
|---|---|---|---|---|---|---|---|---|---|
| $y$ | 0 | | 4 | | | $\frac{1}{2}$ | | 1 | |

(c) $2x - y = 6$

| $x$ | $\frac{1}{2}$ | | | 2 | | $-4$ | |
|---|---|---|---|---|---|---|---|
| $y$ | | 2 | 3 | | $-3$ | | |

5. Find the slope and $y$-intercept of the following lines. Graph each line.
   (a) $3x - 2y = 6$      (b) $x + y = 0$
   (c) $2x + 5y = 10$      (d) $x = 2$
   (e) $y = 5$           (f) $2x - 2y = 1$
   (g) $y = x$          (h) $-2x + y = 6$

6. The annual sales of Motors Incorporated for the past five years are

| Years | Units Sold (in thousands) |
|---|---|
| 1967 | 2200 |
| 1968 | 2800 |
| 1969 | 3100 |
| 1970 | 3200 |
| 1971 | 3400 |

   (a) Graph this information using the $x$-axis for years and the $y$-axis for units sold. (For convenience, use a different scale on each axis.)
   (b) Draw a line $L$ that passes through two of the points and comes close to passing through the remaining points.
   (c) Find the equation of the line $L$.
   (d) Using the equation of the line, what is your estimate for units sold in 1972?

7. The Highland Cab Company charges a fixed fee of $0.50 upon entering a cab and a variable rate of $0.50 per mile. Write an expression for the cost $C$ of a trip of $x$ miles. Graph the result, measuring $C$ along the $y$-axis and $x$ along the $x$-axis.

8. The relationship between Celsius C and Fahrenheit F for measuring temperature is a straight line. Find the equation relating C and F if 0° C corresponds to 32° F and 100° C corresponds to 212° F. Use the equation to find the Celsius measure of 70° F.

9. The profits of the Royal Electric Company are given by the formula

$$P(t) = \$3100t + \$75{,}000$$

where $t$ is measured in years, and $t = 0$ corresponds to the year 1968. Find

(a) $P(0)$

(b) $P(6)$

(c) Profits in 1976

(d) If this trend continues, what would you predict the profit will be in 1980.

1.6
INTERSECTING
LINES

Let $L$ and $M$ be two lines. There are three possible relationships that can exist between two lines $L$ and $M$:

1. Either all the points on $L$ are the same as the points on $M$.
2. Or one point on $L$ is the same as one point on $M$.
3. Or no points on $L$ are also on $M$.

For the first relationship, the lines $L$ and $M$ are called *identical lines*. In this case, their slopes and their intercepts will be the same. Henceforth, we assume the lines $L$ and $M$ are distinct.

Definition
of Intersecting
Lines; Parallel
Lines

**Let $L$ and $M$ be two (distinct) lines. If $L$ and $M$ have exactly one point $P$ in common, then $L$ and $M$ are said to *intersect* and the common point $P$ is called the *point of intersection*. If $L$ and $M$ have no points in common, they are said to be *parallel*.**

First, we discuss the case in which $L$ and $M$ are *parallel*. If $L$ and $M$ are two lines with no points in common, it is clear that the rise-over-run of each must be the same. Otherwise, they would eventually meet. Thus, **Two lines $L$ and $M$ are parallel if and only if their slopes are equal.**

6.1
Example

The two lines

$$L: 2x + 3y - 5 = 0 \qquad M: 4x + 6y - 12 = 0$$

are parallel.

For, the slope of $L$ and the slope of $M$ are both $-2/3$.

Their graphs are given in Figure 1.26.

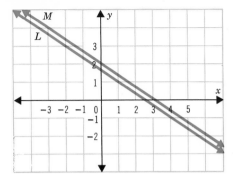

**Figure 1.26**

Next, suppose we have two lines $L$ and $M$ that intersect. Then there is a point $(x, y)$ that is on both $L$ and $M$. This means that some value of $x$ and some value of $y$ will satisfy the equation of $L$ *and* the equation of $M$. The next example shows how this fact is used to find the common point of two intersecting lines.

Find the point $P$ of intersection of the two lines.

$$L: x + y - 5 = 0 \qquad M: 2x + y - 6 = 0$$

6.2
Example

Let the coordinates of the point $P$ of intersection of $L$ and $M$ be $(x_0, y_0)$. Since $(x_0, y_0)$ is on both $L$ and $M$, then

$$x_0 + y_0 - 5 = 0 \qquad 2x_0 + y_0 - 6 = 0$$

Thus,

$$y_0 = 5 - x_0 \qquad y_0 = -2x_0 + 6$$

Setting these equal, we obtain

$$5 - x_0 = 6 - 2x_0$$
$$x_0 = 1$$

If $x_0 = 1$, then $y_0 = 5 - x_0 = 4$. Thus, the point $P$ of intersection of $L$ and $M$ is $(1, 4)$. To check this result, we verify that $(1, 4)$ is on both $L$ and $M$. Since

$$1 + 4 - 5 = 0, \qquad 2 \cdot 1 + 4 - 6 = 0$$

we see that $(1, 4)$ is the point of intersection.

The graph of the situation in Example 6.2 is given by Figure 1.27.

The technique given in the previous example for finding the point $P$ of intersection of two lines is sometimes called the "substitution technique," since in reality the value for $y$ in one equation is substituted for the value of $y$ in the other equation.

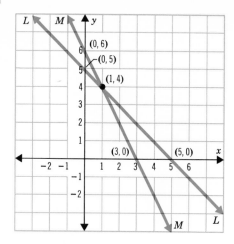

**Figure 1.27**

System of Two
Linear Equations

This technique can also be used to solve a system of two linear equations in two unknowns. A *system of two linear equations in two unknowns x and y* is of the form

$$Ax + By + C = 0$$
$$A_1x + B_1y + C_1 = 0,$$

in which $A$, $B$, $C$, $A_1$, $B_1$, $C_1$ are real numbers.

Solution

A *solution* $(x, y)$ of such a system is an ordered pair of real numbers that satisfies both equations. Finding the solution $(x, y)$ of a system of two linear equations in two unknowns is the same as finding the point $P$ of intersection of the two lines determined by the equation. Of course, if the equations of a system represent parallel lines, there will be no solution; if the equations represent identical lines, any point $P$ of the line will be a solution of the system of equations (in this case there are infinitely many solutions).

6.3
Example

Find the solution, if there is one, of the system of two linear equations in two unknowns.

$$2x + y + 6 = 0$$
$$4x + 2y + 8 = 0$$

If we treat these equations as lines, we can place them in slope-intercept form as

$$y = -2x - 6$$
$$y = -2x - 4$$

Note that each of these lines has a slope of $-2$. Since their $y$-intercepts are different (one is $-6$, the other $-4$), these equations represent two parallel lines. Hence, there are no values $(x, y)$ that satisfy both equations. That is, the system has no solution. See Figure 1.28.

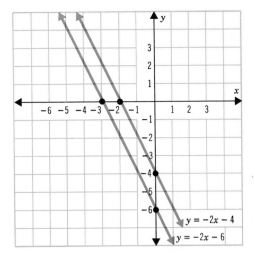

**Figure 1.28**

Nutt's Nuts, a store that specializes in selling nuts, sells cashews for $1.50 per pound and peanuts for $0.80 per pound. At the end of the month it is found that the peanuts are not selling well. In order to sell 30 pounds of peanuts more quickly, Mr. Nutt decides to mix the 30 pounds of peanuts with some cashews and sell the mixture of peanuts and cashews for $1.00 a pound. How many pounds of cashews should be mixed with the peanuts so that his revenue remains the same.

Here, there are two unknowns: the number of pounds of cashews (call this $x$) and the number of pounds of the mixture (call this $y$). Then, we know that the number of pounds of cashews plus 30 pounds of peanuts equals the number of pounds of the mixture. That is,

$$y = x + 30$$

Also, in order to keep revenue the same, we must have

(no. of pounds of cashews)(price per pound)
    + (no. of pounds of peanuts)(price per pound)
        = (no. of pounds of mixture)(price per pound)

That is,

$$(1.50)x + (0.80)(30) = (1.00) \cdot y$$

Thus, we have a system of two linear equations in two unknowns to solve:

$$y = x + 30$$
$$y = \frac{3}{2}x + 24$$

Here

$$\frac{3}{2}x + 24 = x + 30 \qquad x = 12$$

Thus, the owner should mix 12 pounds of cashews with 30 pounds of peanuts. See Figure 1.29.

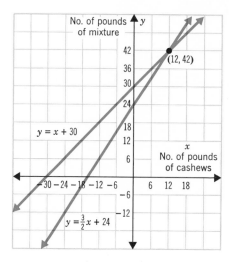

**Figure 1.29**

• 1. Determine whether the following lines are identical, parallel, or intersecting. If they intersect, find the point $P$ of intersection. Graph each pair of lines.

    (a) $L$: $2x - 3y + 6 = 0$     • (d) $L$: $4x - y + 2 = 0$
        $M$: $4x - 6y + 7 = 0$             $M$: $3x + 2y = 0$

    (b) $L$: $-2x + 3y + 6 = 0$    (e) $L$: $2x + 3y - 5 = 0$
        $M$: $4x - 6y - 12 = 0$        $M$: $5x - 6y + 1 = 0$

    (c) $L$: $3x - 3y + 10 = 0$    • (f) $L$: $2x - 5y - 1 = 0$
        $M$: $x + y - 2 = 0$             $M$: $x - 2y - 1 = 0$

• 2. Sweet Delight Candys, Inc., sells boxes of candy consisting of cremes and caramels. Each box sells for $4.00 and holds 50 pieces of candy (all pieces are of the same size). If the caramels cost $0.05 to produce and the cremes cost $0.10 to produce, how many caramels and cremes should be in each box for no profit or loss? Would you increase or decrease the number of caramels in order to obtain a profit?

3. Mr. Nicholson has just retired and needs $4000 per year in income to live on. He has $50,000 to invest and can invest in AAA bonds at 9 percent interest annually or in Savings and Loan Certificates at 7 percent per year. How much

money should be invested in each so that he realizes exactly $4000 in income per year?

- 4. Mr. Nicholson finds after one year that because of inflation he now needs $4200 per year to live on. How should he transfer his funds to achieve this amount? (Use the same data as in Problem 3.)

5. Mr. Nutt, owner of Nutt's Nuts, regularly sells cashews for $1.50 per pound, pecans for $1.80 per pound, and peanuts for $0.80 per pound. How many pounds of cashews and pecans should be mixed with 40 pounds of peanuts to obtain a mixture of 100 pounds that will sell at $1.25 a pound so that the profit or loss is unchanged?

- 6. Mike has $1.65 in his piggy bank. He knows he only placed nickels and quarters in the bank and he knows that he put a total of 13 coins in the bank. Can he find out how many nickels he has without breaking his bank?

7. A coffee manufacturer wants to market a new blend of coffee that will cost $0.90 per pound, by mixing $0.75/pound coffee and $1/pound coffee. What amounts of the $0.75 coffee and $1 coffee should be blended to obtain the desired mixture? *Hint:* Assume the total weight of the desired blend is 100 pounds.

- 8. One solution is 15 percent acid and another is 5 percent acid. How many cubic centimeters of each should be mixed to obtain 100 cc of a solution that is 8 percent acid?

9. A bank loaned $10,000, some at an annual rate of 8 percent and some at an annual rate of 18 percent. If the income from these loans was $1000, how much was loaned at 8 percent? How much at 18 percent?

- 10. The Star Theater wants to know whether the majority of its patrons are adults or children. During a week in July, 5200 tickets were sold and the receipts totaled $11,875. The adult admission is $2.75 and the childrens admission is $1.50. How many adult patrons were there?

11. After one hour of a car ride, 1/3 of the total distance is covered. One hour later, the car is 18 miles past the halfway point. What is the speed of the car (assumed constant for the trip) and what is the total distance to be covered? How long will the trip take? (*Hint:* distance = speed · time.)

We have already discussed linear equations or linear equalities, namely, equations of the form

$$Ax + By + C = 0 \qquad (7.1)$$

where $A$, $B$, $C$ are real numbers. If we replace the equal sign in (7.1) by either $>$, $<$, $\geqq$, or $\leqq$ we obtain a *linear inequality*.

Linear Inequality

Thus,

$$2x + 3y - 6 \geqq 0 \qquad 3x - 4y + 7 < 0$$

are examples of linear inequalities. The following example indicates a technique for graphing linear inequalities.

7.1
Example

Graph the set of points $(x, y)$ obeying

$$2x + 3y - 6 \geqq 0 \qquad (7.2)$$

First, we find the graph of the line

$$L: 2x + 3y - 6 = 0 \qquad (7.3)$$

Since any point on the line $L$ of (7.3) will obey (7.2), these points are in the set of points obeying or satisfying (2). [If the $\geqq$ in (7.2) were replaced by $>$, the points on the line $L$ would *not* be in the set of points obeying (7.2).] See Figure 1.30.

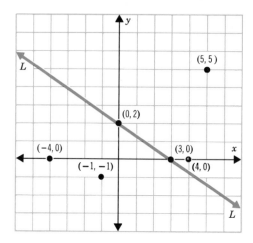

**Figure 1.30**

Let us begin to test a few points, such as $(-1, -1)$, $(5, 5)$, $(4, 0)$, $(-4, 0)$. We do this by substituting the coordinates of each point into the left member of (7.2) and determine if the result is $\geqq 0$ or $< 0$. Then,

$$(-1, -1): 2(-1) + 3(-1) - 6 = -2 - 3 - 6 = -11 < 0$$

Thus, $(-1, -1)$ is not part of the graph. Next

$$(5, 5): 2(5) + 3(5) - 6 = 25 - 6 = 19 > 0$$

Thus, $(5, 5)$ is part of the graph. Also

$$(4, 0): 2(4) + 3(0) - 6 = 8 - 6 = 2 > 0$$
$$(-4, 0): 2(-4) + 3(0) - 6 = -8 - 6 = -14 < 0$$

Thus, $(4,0)$ is on the graph, but $(-4,0)$ is not. Notice that the two points $(4,0)$ and $(5,5)$ that are on the graph both lie on one side of $L$ and the points $(-4,0)$ and $(-1,-1)$ (not on the graph) lie on the other side of $L$. This is not an accident. The graph of (7.2) is the shaded region of Figure 1.31.

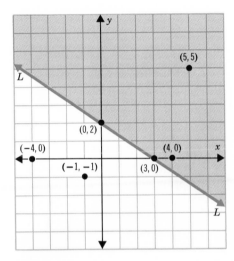

**Figure 1.31**

**The following rules should be used to graph linear inequalities:**

1. **Graph the corresponding linear equality, a line $L$.**
2. **Select a point $P$ not on the line $L$.**
3. **If the coordinates of this point $P$ satisfy the linear inequality, then all points on the same side of $L$ as the point $P$ satisfy the inequality.**
4. **If the coordinates of the point $P$ do not obey the linear inequality, then all points on the opposite side of $L$ from $P$ satisfy the inequality.**
5. **Points on the line $L$ itself may or may not obey the inequality.**

Graph the linear inequality

7.2
Example

$$2x - y + 4 < 0$$

The corresponding linear equation is the line

$$L: 2x - y + 4 = 0$$

For its graph, see Figure 1.32.

We select a point on either side of $L$ to be tested, for example $(0,0)$. Then

$$2(0) - 0 + 4 = 4 > 0$$

Since $(0,0)$ does not obey the inequality, all points on the opposite side of $L$ from $(0,0)$ are on the graph.

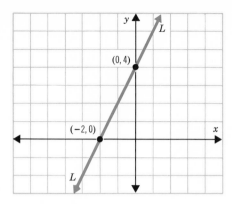

**Figure 1.32**

Since no point on $L$ can be on the graph (why?), the graph is the shaded region of Figure 1.33 in which the line $L$ is dotted to indicate it is not part of the graph.

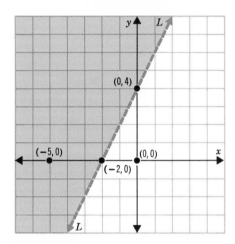

**Figure 1.33**

The set of points belonging to the graph of a linear inequality is sometimes called a *half-plane*.

Half-Plane

In a system of linear inequalities, we want to find all points that simultaneously satisfy each linear inequality of the system.

A system of two distinct linear inequalities in two unknowns, as will be seen, will sometimes have a certain region of the $x, y$ plane as a solution.

That this is the case can be seen by considering two linear inequalities. Let $L$ and $M$ be the lines corresponding to these linear inequalities. Suppose $L$ and $M$ intersect. See Figure 1.34.

The two lines $L$ and $M$ divide the plane into four regions $a$, $b$, $c$, and $d$. One of these regions is the solution of the system. If the lines $L$ and

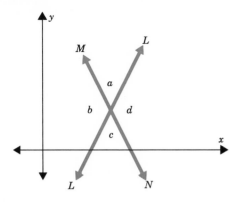

**Figure 1.34**

$M$ are parallel, the system of linear inequalities may or may not have a solution. Examples of such situations are given below.

Graph the system

$$2x - y + 4 < 0$$
$$x + y + 1 \geqq 0 \qquad (7.4)$$

The lines corresponding to each of these linear inequalities are

$$L: 2x - y + 4 = 0$$
$$M: x + y + 1 = 0$$

The graphs of $L$ and $M$ are given in Figure 1.35.

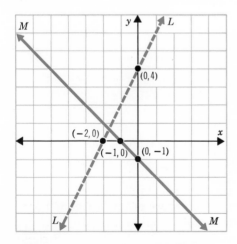

**Figure 1.35**

Now if we graph each linear inequality of (7.4) as a separate problem and then find the region common to the two resulting half-planes, we will have the solution of the system. Thus, we obtain Figure 1.36.

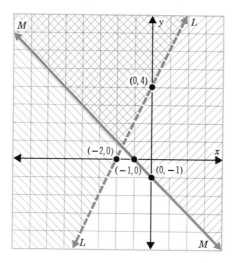

**Figure 1.36**

The checkered region is the solution. The fact that *L* is dotted indicates points on *L* are not part of the solution; *M* is drawn in full since its points are to be included.

It should be pointed out that the checkered region is merely the intersection of the sets $A = \{(x, y) \mid 2x - y + 4 < 0\}$ and $B = \{(x, y) \mid x + y - 1 \geqq 0\}$. It is usually easier, however, to express the solution graphically than to attempt to write it as a single set. As it turns out, we will not need to write out the solution as a single set.

7.4
Example

Graph the system

$$2x - y + 4 < 0$$
$$2x - y + 2 \leqq 0$$

The lines corresponding to each of these linear inequalities are

$$L: 2x - y + 4 = 0$$
$$M: 2x - y + 2 = 0$$

These lines are parallel. Their graphs are given in Figure 1.37.

The solution is given by the checkered region in Figure 1.38. Notice that the solution of the system is the same as that of the single linear inequality $2x - y + 4 < 0$.

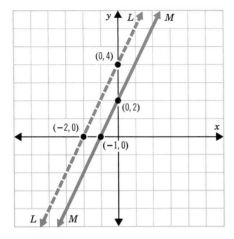

**Figure 1.37**

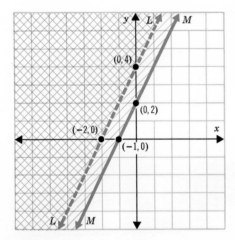

**Figure 1.38**

The graph of the system

$$2x - y + 4 > 0$$
$$2x - y + 2 \leqq 0$$

is given in Figure 1.39.

Such a region is sometimes referred to as a *strip*.

The system

$$2x - y + 4 < 0$$
$$2x - y + 2 \geqq 0$$

has no solution, as Figure 1.40 indicates.

Thus far we have only considered systems of two inequalities in two unknowns. The next example is of a system of four inequalities in two unknowns. As we shall see, the technique for graphing such systems is the same as that used for two inequalities in two unknowns.

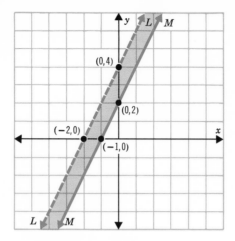

**Figure 1.39**

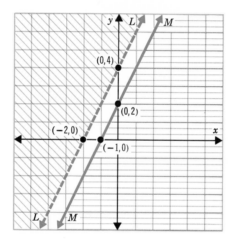

**Figure 1.40**

Graph the system

$$x + y - 2 \geqq 0$$
$$2x + y - 3 > 0$$
$$x \geqq 0$$
$$y \geqq 0$$

Again, we first look at the graphs of the four lines

$$L_1: x + y - 2 = 0$$
$$L_2: 2x + y - 3 = 0$$
$$L_3: x = 0$$
$$L_4: y = 0$$

Figure 1.41 gives the graph of $L_1$, $L_2$, $L_3$, and $L_4$. Notice that $L_3$ and $L_4$ are the $y$-axis and $x$-axis, respectively.

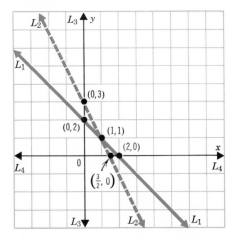

**Figure 1.41**

The graph of the system in Example 7.5 will be the intersection of the four regions determined by each of the four inequalities. The shaded region in Figure 1.42 gives the graph of the system in Example 7.5.

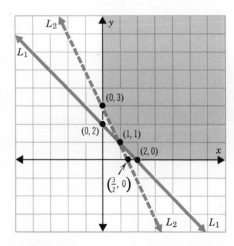

**Figure 1.42**

Graph the system

7.6
Example

$$x + y - 2 < 0$$
$$2x + y - 3 < 0$$
$$x \geqq 0$$
$$y \geqq 0$$

Since the lines associated with these linear inequalities are the same as those of the previous example, we proceed directly to the graph. See Figure 1.43.

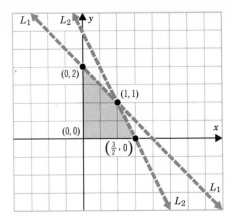

**Figure 1.43**

The region determined by the four linear inequalities in Example 7.6 is a quadrilateral whose vertices are the points $(0, 0)$, $(0, 2)$, $(1, 1)$, and $(3/2, 0)$.

**1.7
Exercise**

1. Graph the regions
   (a) $2x + y + 5 > 0$         (d) $x < 0$,   $y > 0$
   (b) $3x + 4y - 12 \leqq 0$     (e) $x - 5 < 0$
   (c) $x \geqq 0$                 (f) $2x + 3y - 4 \geqq 0$
2. Graph the following systems of inequalities.
   (a) $5x - 12y - 60 > 0$,      $x - y + 2 < 0$
   (b) $3x - 4y < 0$,      $x + y \geqq 0$
   (c) $2x + 2y - 5 > 0$,      $x + y - 2 < 0$
   (d) $3x - y \leqq 0$,      $3x - y > 0$
   (e) $x - y + 2 > 0$,      $2x - 2y + 5 \leqq 0$
   (f) $2x - y + 4 \leqq 0$,      $x \geqq 0$,      $y \geqq 0$
   (g) $2x - y \leqq 0$,      $x + y - 8 < 0$,      $x \geqq 0$,      $y \geqq 0$
   (h) $x + 2y - 4 \geqq 0$,      $x + y \leqq 12$,      $x \geqq 0$,      $y \geqq 0$
   (i) $2x - y - 4 > 0$,      $x - 2y - 10 < 0$,
       $x \geqq 0$,      $y \geqq 0$,      $x + y - 2 < 0$
   (j) $x + 3y - 12 \leqq 0$,      $3x + 2y - 6 < 0$,
       $x \geqq 0$,      $y \geqq 0$
   (k) $3x + 4y - 12 \leqq 0$,      $x - y + 2 > 0$,
       $x \geqq 0$,      $y \geqq 0$

CHAPTER
REVIEW
Important
Terms

set
element of a set
empty set
set-builder notation
subset

counting numbers
whole numbers
negative numbers
integers
numerator

denominator
irrational numbers
real numbers
decimal representation
positive number
negative number
coordinate
inequality
solution set
rectangular coordinates
abscissa
ordinate

distance
graphing
straight line
vertical line
slope of a line
point-slope form of a line
two-point form of a line
intercepts
slope-intercept form of a line
intersecting lines
parallel lines

Review
Exercises

1. Find $x$ in each of the following problems.
   (a) $x = \frac{2}{3} + \frac{3}{4}$
   (b) $x = (-2)^4$
   (c) $x = 2^{-3}$
   (d) $2x + 5 = 8$
   (e) $2x - 4 \leq 8$
   (f) $x + 2 = 6$
   (g) $x + 5 \leq 2$
   (h) $2^x = 8$
   (i) $(2x)^4 = 16$
   (j) $x^4 = 81$
   (k) $4 - 2x \geq 2$
   (l) $2x < 5$
   (m) $-3x + 4 \leq 6x - 3$

2. Graph each of the following lines on a rectangular coordinate system.
   (a) $y = 3x - 4$
   (b) $y = -2x + 4$
   (c) $x = 0$
   (d) $y = 0$

3. Find the slope and $y$-intercept of the following lines. Graph each line.
   (a) $3x - 4y + 12 = 0$
   (b) $-9x - 3y + 5 = 0$
   (c) $4x + 2y - 9 = 0$

4. Find the equation of each of the following lines. Sketch the graph.
   (a) Slope 2, passes through the point $(1, 2)$.
   (b) Passes through the points $(3, 2)$ and $(-4, 0)$.
   (c) Slope $= -3$, $y$-intercept 4.

5. Find the point of intersection, if there is one, of the following pairs of lines.
   (a) $y = 3x + 4$
   $2x + 3y = 6$
   (b) $2y + 4x = 0$
   $y = 3x + 1$
   (c) $2x + 3y - 4 = 0$
   $2x - 2y + 5 = 0$
   (d) $3x - y + 5 = 0$
   $y = 3x - 2$

6. Determine whether the following lines are identical, parallel, or intersect. If they intersect, find the point of intersection. Graph each pair of lines.
   (a) $3x - 4y + 12 = 0$
   $6x - 8y + \phantom{0}9 = 0$

(b) $\quad x - \phantom{4}y + \phantom{1}2 = 0$
$\quad\quad 3x - 4y + 12 = 0$

(c) $\quad x - \phantom{4}y \phantom{+12} = 0$
$\quad\quad 2x + 3y + 6 = 0$

7. Mr. Byrd has just retired and finds that he and his wife need $5000 per year to live on. Fortunately, he has a nest egg of $70,000 that he can invest in somewhat risky A-rated bonds at 9 percent interest per year or in a well-known bank at 4 percent per year. How much money should he invest in each so that he realizes exactly $5000 in income each year?

8. One solution is 20 percent acid and another 12 percent acid. How many cubic centimeters of each should be mixed to obtain 100 cc of a solution which is 15 percent acid?

9. Graph the following linear inequalities.

(a) $x \geqq 0, \quad y \geqq 0$
$\quad 2x + y \leqq 2$

(b) $x \geqq 0, \quad y \geqq 0$
$\quad 3x + y \geqq 4, \quad x + y \geqq 2$

(c) $x \geqq 0, \quad y \geqq 0$
$\quad 3x + 2y \geqq 6, \quad x + y \geqq 4$

(d) $x \geqq 0, \quad y \geqq 0$
$\quad 4x + 3y \leqq 12, \quad x + y \leqq 2, \quad 3x + y \leqq 3$

## Bibliography

*Mathematics*

Wooton and Drooyan, *Intermediate Algebra,* Third Alternate Edition, Wadsworth, 1972. Chapters 1-7.

# 2

# FUNCTIONS

In this chapter we lay the foundation of the forthcoming chapters on mathematical models and calculus by introducing the important concept of a function. Practically every study involving empirical data and practical needs leads to this mathematical concept. To begin, we describe a function intuitively, relying on examples to give an understanding of what functions are. Later, a definition is given.

2.1
THE CONCEPT OF
A FUNCTION

Very simply, a *function f* is a rule that associates to any given number $x$ a single number $f(x)$, read "f of x." Here $f(x)$ is the number that results when $x$ is given; $f(x)$ does not mean $f$ times $x$.

For example, the function $f$ that associates the square of a number to the given number $x$ is

$$f(x) = x^2$$

The given number $x$ is called the *independent variable* and the number associated to it by the function is called the *dependent variable* since it depends for its value on $x$.

Independent
Variable

Dependent
Variable

For the function

$$f(x) = 4x^2 - 5$$

1.1
Example

find the value of the dependent variable $f(x)$ when the independent variable $x$ equals three.

Here the value of the dependent variable is

$$f(3) = 4 \cdot 3^2 - 5 = 4 \cdot 9 - 5 = 36 - 5 = 31$$

For functions such as

$$f(x) = x^2, \qquad g(x) = 2x - 3, \qquad h(x) = \frac{1}{x}$$

we usually denote the dependent variable by $y$, so that we write

$$y = f(x) = x^2, \qquad y = g(x) = 2x - 3, \qquad y = h(x) = \frac{1}{x}$$

We now give a definition of a function.

**Definition of a Function; Domain; Range**

**Let $D$ and $R$ be two given sets. A** *function* **$f$ is a rule that assigns to each element $x$ in $D$ one and only one element $y$ in $R$. The set $D$ is called the** *domain* **of the function $f$ and $R$ is termed its** *range*.

**1.2 Example**

Let the set $D$ consist of students in a class and let $R$ be the set of their final grades. Since each student is associated with exactly one final grade, this is an example of a function.

In the above example, the domain, range, and rule of association are specified. Usually, though, only the rule of association is given so that the domain and range need to be found. Thus, given a function $f$, it is reasonable to ask what is the domain of $f$ and what is the range of $f$? In providing an answer, we confine our studies to cases and situations in which both the domain $D$ and range $R$ are sets of real numbers.

Let us go back to the square function $y = f(x) = x^2$. For what real numbers is it possible to find the square? That is: On what set of real numbers can the operation of squaring be performed? We find that it is always possible to square a real number. Thus, the *domain* of $y = f(x) = x^2$ is the set $R^{\#}$ of real numbers. Now, what happens when a real number is squared? What kind of number results? Since the square of any real number is always non-negative ($\geqq 0$), we see that the set of numbers of the range are the non-negative real numbers. Thus, if $D$ is the domain and $R$ is the range of the function $f(x) = x^2$, then

$$D = \{x \,|\, x \in R^{\#}\}, \qquad R = \{y \,|\, y \geqq 0\}$$

**1.3 Example**

Consider the relationship given by

$$y = f(x) = 20x + 100$$

For what real numbers $x$ is it possible to compute $20x + 100$? That is: When can we add 100 to twenty times a number? The answer is always. Thus the domain of $f$ is

$$D = \{x \mid x \in R^{\#}\}$$

Similarly, the range of $f$, the set of numbers that can be associated to the numbers $x$ in the domain, is

$$R = \{y \mid y \in R^{\#}\}$$

Finally, $f$ is a function, since to each $x$ there corresponds exactly one $y$. The graph of the function consists of all points $(x, y)$ for which $y = 20x + 100$. See Figure 2.1.

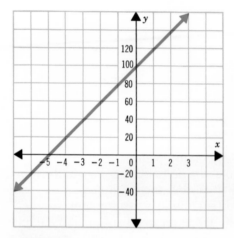

**Figure 2.1**

Suppose the function $f$ of Example 1.3 represents the total expense of production in a factory in which overhead is $100 and the cost for each item manufactured is $20. In this situation, $x$ represents the number of items produced. What is then the domain of $f$ and the range of $f$?

Since the variable $x$ now represents the number of items produced and since it is only meaningful to speak of non-negative integral values for $x$, we see that

$$D = \{0, 1, 2, 3, \ldots\}$$

Now, as the variable $x$ takes on the values $0, 1, 2, 3, \ldots,$ the variable $y$ assumes the values

$$f(0) = 20 \cdot 0 + 100 = 100$$
$$f(1) = 20 \cdot 1 + 100 = 120$$
$$f(2) = 20 \cdot 2 + 100 = 140$$

Thus the range is

$$R = \{100, 120, 140, 160, \ldots\}$$

The graph is given in Figure 2.2.

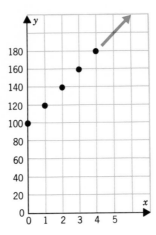

**Figure 2.2**

We will find as we pursue the study of functions that many times practical considerations may alter the domain and range of the function. We observe that in these two situations, the first function may assume any value, whereas the second function may assume only non-negative integral values. The domain and range for the first function are referred to as *continuous,* while for the second; the domain and range are called *discrete.* Time is an example of a variable that is measured continuously; the number of people in a given age bracket must be measured discretely.

*Continuous*

*Discrete*

We have seen that a function *f* associates to real numbers *x* other real numbers *y,* and we have agreed to use the notation

$$y = f(x)$$

to denote the rule that associates *x* and *y.* If we write down all the ordered pairs $(x, y)$, where *y* is the ordinate and *x* the abscissa, the collection of all points $(x, y)$ is called the *graph* of $y = f(x)$.

*Graph of a Function*

Sometimes it is helpful to visualize a function as an apparatus that manipulates numbers; the domain is the input for the apparatus and the range is the output. We can call such an apparatus an *input-output machine.* See Figure 2.3.

The only restrictions on an input-output machine are:

1. It only accepts numbers from the domain of *f,* that is, it only accepts numbers for which there is an output.
2. For each input there is exactly one output (which may be repeated).

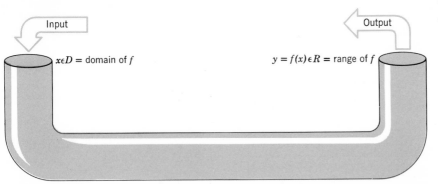

**Figure 2.3**

To illustrate what is meant by restriction (1) consider the following example.

Find the domain $D$ of the function

$$f(x) = \sqrt{1 - x}$$

1.4
Example

To find the domain $D$ of $f$, we ask the question "What are the values of $x$ for which we can compute $\sqrt{1 - x}$?" Now, we know it is impossible (in the set of real numbers) to find the square root of a negative number. Thus, only those values of $x$ for which

$$1 - x \geqq 0 \qquad \text{or} \qquad x \leqq 1$$

can be in the domain. Hence,

$$D = \{x \mid x \leqq 1\}$$

This means that the graph must lie to the left of $x = 1$. Furthermore, notice that to each $x \in D$ there can be associated *exactly one* number $y$. This number $y$ is non-negative because of the definition of the square root. (See the Appendix). The graph is given in Figure 2.4.

Graph the function

$$f(x) = \begin{cases} x + 1, & \text{if} \quad x > 0 \\ 1, & \text{if} \quad x \leqq 0 \end{cases}$$

1.5
Example

In this problem the domain is given to be all real numbers since a value of $y$ can be found for all real values of $x$. Its graph is given in Figure 2.5. Observe that the function $f$ is given by two rules: one for $x > 0$; the other for $x \leqq 0$.

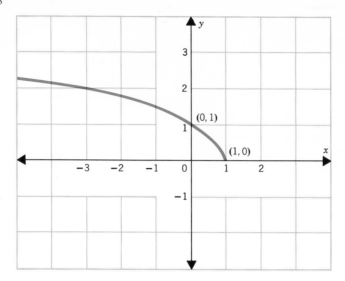

**Figure 2.4**

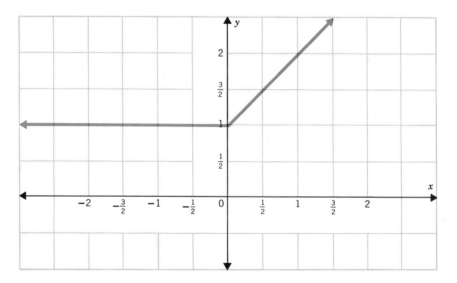

**Figure 2.5**

1.6
Example Graph the function

$$f(x) = \begin{cases} \dfrac{x}{2}, & \text{if} & -1 \leqq x < 1 \\[2mm] 2, & \text{if} & x = 1 \\[2mm] x + \dfrac{1}{2}, & \text{if} & x > 1 \end{cases}$$

Here the domain of $f$ is all real numbers $\geqq -1$. Its graph is given in Figure 2.6. We use a filled circle ● to indicate that at $x = 1$, the value of $f(x)$ is 2; we use an open circle ○ to illustrate that the curves do not assume the values 1/2 and 3/2, respectively, at $x = 1$.

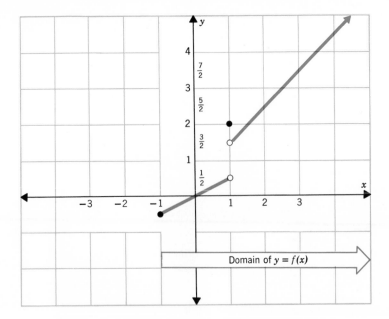

**Figure 2.6**

1.7
Example
Stock
Depletion

A supermarket initially stocks 48 cans of corn on its shelf and finds that each day 12 cans are sold. When stock size reaches 12, they replenish the stock with a case containing 36 cans. Construct a graph that describes this situation measuring time along the horizontal axis and number of cans on the shelf along the vertical axis.

We begin by noting that at time $t = 0$, stock size is 48 so that $(0, 48)$ is a point on the graph. At $t = 1$, stock size is 36; at $t = 2$, it is 24; and at $t = 3$, it is 12. At this point, we add 36 cans to the shelf so that the stock size is back at 48. This pattern is continued as time goes on. See Figure 2.7.

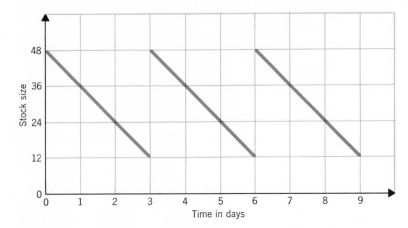

**Figure 2.7**

One of the most important uses of the function notation for later chapters is illustrated in the next two examples.

1.8
Example

For the function

$$f(x) = 3x + 1$$

find
(a) $f(x + h)$
(b) $f(x + h) - f(x)$
(c) $\dfrac{f(x + h) - f(x)}{h}, \; h \neq 0$

(a) The function $f(x) = 3x + 1$ tells us to multiply $x$ by 3 and then add 1. To find $f(x + h)$, we should multiply $(x + h)$ by 3 and then add 1. Thus,

$$f(x + h) = 3(x + h) + 1 = 3x + 3h + 1$$

Notice that $x$ is replaced by the quantity $(x + h)$.
(b) $f(x + h) - f(x) = (3x + 3h + 1) - (3x + 1) = 3h$

(c) $\dfrac{f(x + h) - f(x)}{h} = \dfrac{3h}{h} = 3, \qquad h \neq 0$

1.9
Example

For the function

$$f(x) = \frac{1}{x}$$

find
(a) $f(x + h)$
(b) $f(x + h) - f(x)$
(c) $\dfrac{f(x + h) - f(x)}{h}, \qquad h \neq 0$

(a) The function $f(x) = 1/x$ tells us to find the reciprocal of $x$. Thus, for $f(x + h)$ we should find the reciprocal of $(x + h)$. That is,

$$f(x + h) = \frac{1}{x + h}$$

(b) $f(x + h) - f(x) = \dfrac{1}{x + h} - \dfrac{1}{x} = \dfrac{x - (x + h)}{x(x + h)} = \dfrac{-h}{x(x + h)}$

(c) $\dfrac{f(x + h) - f(x)}{h} = \dfrac{-h}{x(x + h)} \cdot \dfrac{1}{h} = \dfrac{-1}{x(x + h)}$

1. For the function $f(x) = 3x - 2$, find
   (a) $f(3)$      (c) $f(0)$
   (b) $f(-2)$    (d) $f(11)$

2. For the function

$$f(x) = 3x^4 + 1$$

   find
   (a) $f(1)$    (c) $f(0)$
   (b) $f(h)$    (d) $f(h + 1)$

3. For the functions

   (I) $f(x) = 2x + 5$    (II) $f(x) = x^2$    (III) $f(x) = \dfrac{1}{x + 3}$

   find
   (a) $f(x + h)$
   (b) $f(x + h) - f(x)$
   (c) $\dfrac{f(x + h) - f(x)}{h}$, $\quad h \neq 0$

4. Determine which of the following are functions and, for each function, find the domain. Graph each function.
   (a) $y^2 = 1 - x^2$    (d) $y = \pm\sqrt{1 - 2x}$
   (b) $y = \dfrac{2}{x}$         (e) $y = \sqrt{1 + x}$
   (c) $y = x^2 - 1$      (f) $y = \dfrac{1}{x - 2}$

5. Graph each of the following functions and find their domain.
   (a) $f(x) = \begin{cases} 2x - 3, & \text{if} & x < 0 \\ x - 3, & \text{if} & 0 \leq x < 5 \end{cases}$
   (b) $f(x) = \begin{cases} 4x + 5, & \text{if} & -2 \leq x < 0 \\ 4, & \text{if} & x = 0 \\ 2x, & \text{if} & x > 0 \end{cases}$
   (c) $f(x) = \begin{cases} x^2, & \text{if} & x \leq 0 \\ x + 1, & \text{if} & x > 0 \end{cases}$

6. A supermarket initially stocks 72 cans of peas on its shelf and finds that each day 8 cans are sold. When stock size reaches zero, they replenish the stocks with 3 cases of peas containing 24 cans each. Construct a graph that depicts this situation.

Many business situations lead to functions that can be easily classified and discussed. In this section, we give definitions of these functions, determine their domains, and graph them.

The first important function we discuss is one we have already encountered—the linear function or the function whose graph is a non-vertical straight line.

**A** *linear function* **is one of the form**

$$f(x) = mx + b$$

**in which** $m$ **and** $b$ **are real constants.**

It is clear that the linear function has the domain

$$D = \{x \mid x \in R^{\#}\}$$

As for the graph of the linear function, recall that $m$ represents the slope of the line and $b$ is its $y$-intercept.[1]

Another function we need for later use is the quadratic function. Some practical applications of this function are given in Chapter 3.

**A** *quadratic function* **is one of the form**

$$f(x) = ax^2 + bx + c$$

**in which** $a \neq 0$, $b$, $c$ **are three real constants.**

It is clear that no matter what value is assigned to $x$, it is possible to compute $f(x)$. That is, the domain of the quadratic function is

$$D = \{x \mid x \in R^{\#}\}$$

The $x$-intercept of a quadratic function is of particular importance. The $x$-intercept is that point (or points) at which the graph crosses the $x$-axis; that is, the point at which $y = 0$. If such points exist, they satisfy the equation.

$$ax^2 + bx + c = 0,$$

If the quantity $b^2 - 4ac \geq 0$, this equation has two solutions given by the so-called *quadratic formula:*

$$x = \frac{-b + \sqrt{b^2 - 4ac}}{2a} \quad \text{and} \quad x = \frac{-b - \sqrt{b^2 - 4ac}}{2a}$$

The quantity $b^2 - 4ac$ is called the *discriminant* of a quadratic equation, and its value gives information about the solutions of the equation $ax^2 + bx + c = 0$.

$b^2 - 4ac > 0$ **indicates two distinct real solutions. In this case the graph of** $f(x) = ax^2 + bx + c$ **crosses the** $x$-**axis at two points.**
$b^2 - 4ac = 0$ **indicates two equal real solutions. In this case the graph of** $f(x) = ax^2 + bx + c$ **touches the** $x$-**axis at one point.**
$b^2 - 4ax < 0$ **indicates no real number solution. In this case the graph of** $f(x) = ax^2 + bx + c$ **does not cross the** $x$-**axis.**

[1] These concepts are discussed at length in Chapter 1 Section 1.5, page 18.

Graph the quadratic function

$$f(x) = x^2 + x - 2$$

Find the $y$-intercept and the $x$-intercepts, if they exist.

The $y$-intercept is $-2$, obtained by setting $x = 0$.

To find the $x$ intercepts, we need to solve the equation

$$x^2 + x - 2 = 0$$

Since $b^2 - 4ac = 1 - 4 \cdot 1 \cdot (-2) = 1 + 8 = 9 > 0$, the equation has two solutions. By factoring, we find the solutions to be

$$x = -2, \quad x = 1$$

(We could have used the quadratic formula to find the solutions.) Thus, the graph of $f(x) = x^2 + x - 2$ crosses the $x$-axis at $(-2, 0)$ and at $(1, 0)$.

To find other points of the graph we set $x$ equal to various values. Thus,

$$
\begin{aligned}
&\text{if } x = 2, & y = f(2) = 4 + 2 - 2 = 4 \\
&\text{if } x = -1, & y = f(-1) = -2 \\
&\text{if } x = 4, & y = f(4) = 4^2 + 4 - 2 = 18 \\
&\text{if } x = -4, & y = f(-4) = (-4)^2 - 4 - 2 = 10
\end{aligned}
$$

This selection of points, when connected by a smooth curve, should indicate the general nature of the graph. See Figure 2.8.

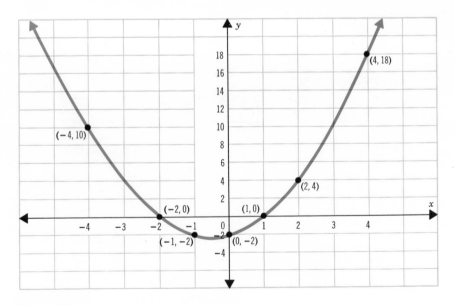

**Figure 2.8**

Parabola   **The graph of a quadratic function is called a** *parabola.* **The minimum or maximum point of a parabola is called the** *vertex.*

Vertex   To analyze the quadratic function more accurately, we proceed to complete the square. Then,

$$y = a\left(x^2 + \frac{b}{a}x + \frac{c}{a}\right)$$

Adding and subtracting $b^2/4a^2$, we obtain

$$y = a\left[\left(x^2 + \frac{b}{a}x + \frac{b^2}{4a^2} + \frac{c}{a} - \frac{b^2}{4a^2}\right)\right]$$

$$y = a\left[\left(x + \frac{b}{2a}\right)^2 + \left(\frac{4ac - b^2}{4a^2}\right)\right]$$

$$y = a\left(x + \frac{b}{2a}\right)^2 + \frac{4ac - b^2}{4a}$$

Now, the value of $y$ depends on the value of $x$ in the term $(x + b/2a)^2$. Since this term is either positive or zero, the smallest value of this term occurs when $x = -b/2a$. Thus, the point on the parabola for which $x = -b/2a$ is the vertex of the parabola.

**It turns out that when** $a > 0$, **the vertex is a minimum point and the graph opens upward; when** $a < 0$, **the vertex is a maximum point and the graph opens downward.**

2.2   Graph the function
Example

$$f(x) = -2x^2 - 5x + 3$$

Find its vertex and the $x$-intercepts, if they exist.

Here we notice that $a = -2 < 0$ so that the vertex is a maximum point and the graph opens downward. To find the vertex we remember that it occurs for $x = -b/2a$. Here $a = -2$ and $b = -5$, so that the abscissa of the vertex is $x = -5/4$. The ordinate of the vertex is

$$y = f\left(\frac{-5}{4}\right) = -2\left(\frac{-5}{4}\right)^2 - 5\left(\frac{-5}{4}\right) + 3$$

$$= -2\left(\frac{25}{16}\right) + \frac{25}{4} + 3 = \frac{-25 + 50 + 24}{8} = \frac{49}{8}$$

Next, since the discriminant $b^2 - 4ac = 25 + 24 = 49$ is positive, the graph crosses the $x$-axis at two points. We locate these points by using the quadratic formula. They are

$$x_1 = \frac{5 + 7}{-4} = -3 \qquad x_2 = \frac{5 - 7}{-4} = \frac{1}{2}$$

With these three points, we can now graph the parabola. See Figure 2.9.

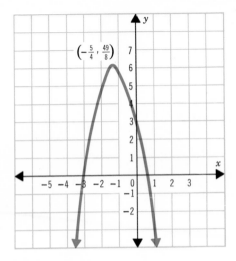

**Figure 2.9**

Both the linear function and quadratic function are examples of a larger class of functions called *polynomial functions*.

A *polynomial function* **is of the form**

$$f(x) = a_n x^n + a_{n-1} x^{n-1} + \cdots + a_2 x^2 + a_1 x + a_0$$

**where** $a_n \neq 0$, $a_{n-1}, \ldots, a_2, a_1, a_0$ **are real constants,** $n \geq 0$ **is a non-negative integer, and** $x$ **is the independent variable.**

Definition
of a Polynomial
Function

For a polynomial function, the real constants $a_n, a_{n-1}, \ldots, a_1, a_0$ are called *coefficients* and $a_n \neq 0$ is called the *leading coefficient*. The exponent $n$ is called the *degree of the polynomial*. Thus, a linear function $f(x) = ax + b$, $a \neq 0$, is a polynomial of degree one and a quadratic function $f(x) = ax^2 + bx + c$, $a \neq 0$, is a polynomial of degree two.

Degree of the
Polynomial

Of course, the domain of a polynomial function is

$$D = \{x \mid x \in R^{\#}\}$$

Notice that for a polynomial function each exponent of the independent variable $x$ must be a non-negative integer. Thus $f(x) = \sqrt{x} + 1$ and $g(x) = 1/x$ are not polynomial functions.

Graph the function

2.3
Example

$$f(x) = x^3$$

This is a polynomial function of degree three and its intercept is $(0, 0)$. Its graph is given in Figure 2.10.

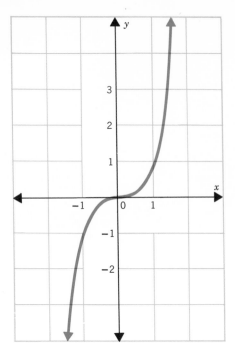

**Figure 2.10**

Definition
of a Rational
Function

Sometimes it is required to form the ratio of two polynomials. Such functions are termed *rational functions* and are of the form

$$f(x) = \frac{P(x)}{Q(x)} = \frac{a_n x^n + \cdots + a_1 x + a_0}{b_m x^m + \cdots + b_1 x + b_0}$$

where $P(x)$ is a polynomial function of degree $n$ and $Q(x)$ is a nonzero polynomial function of degree $m$.

To find the domain of a rational function, remember that the only time we will not be able to compute a value for $f(x)$ is when the $x$ chosen gives a 0 in the denominator. Thus the domain of $f$ is

$$D = \{x \mid Q(x) \neq 0\}$$

2.4
Example

Graph the function

$$f(x) = \frac{1}{x - 1}$$

This is a rational function whose domain is

$$D = \{x \mid x \neq 1\}$$

There is no $x$-intercept, but the $y$-intercept is $-1$. To graph $y = f(x)$, we notice that as $x$ gets very large, the value of $f(x)$ remains positive and gets closer to zero. As $x$ gets close to one, but remains larger than one, then the value of $f(x)$ gets very large and positive. A similar argument gives the graph for $x < 1$. See Figure 2.11.

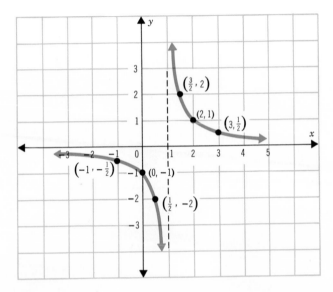

**Figure 2.11**

The cost of eliminating a large part of the pollutants from the atmosphere (or from water) is relatively cheap. However, to remove the remainder of it results in a significant increase in cost. A typical relationship between the cost $C$, in thousands of dollars, for removal and the percent $x$ of pollutant removed is

$$C(x) = \frac{3x}{105 - x}$$

The cost of removing 0 percent of the pollutant is

$$C(0) = 0$$

The cost of removing 50 percent of the pollutant is

$$C(50) = \frac{150}{55} = 2.727 \text{ thousand dollars}$$

The cost of removing 60 percent and 70 percent are

$$C(60) = \frac{180}{45} = 4 \qquad C(70) = \frac{210}{35} = 6 \text{ thousand dollars.}$$

Observe that the cost of removing an additional 10 percent of the pollutant, after 50 percent had been removed, is $1273, while the cost of removing an additional 10 percent after 60 percent is removed is $2000. Figure 2.12 illustrates the graph.

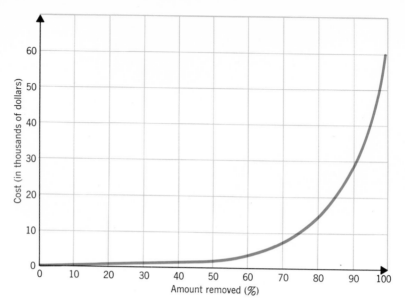

**Figure 2.12**

1. Determine whether the following quadratic functions open upward or open downward. Find the vertex and the intercepts, if they exist. Graph each one.
   (a) $y = f(x) = 2x^2 + x - 3$
   (b) $y = f(x) = -2x^2 - x + 3$
   (c) $y = f(x) = x^2 - 4$
   (d) $y = f(x) = x^2 + 4x + 4$
   (e) $y = f(x) = x^2 + 1$
   (f) $y = f(x) = -3x^2 + 5x + 2$
   (g) $y = f(x) = -x^2 + 1$
   (h) $y = f(x) = x^2 + 2x + 1$

2. Which of the following functions are polynomial functions?

   (a) $f(x) = 2x^5 - 3x + 4$     (d) $f(x) = \dfrac{1}{x}$

   (b) $f(x) = 2x^2 - x$     (e) $f(x) = \dfrac{2x + 3}{x - 2}$

   (c) $f(x) = x - 2$     (f) $f(x) = 3x^2 + 5\sqrt{x}$

3. Find the domain of the following functions.

   (a) $f(x) = \dfrac{3x}{x + 2}$     (c) $f(x) = \dfrac{2x + 1}{3x^2 - 5x - 2}$

   (b) $f(x) = \dfrac{2}{x^2 - 4}$     (d) $f(x) = \dfrac{x^4}{x^3 - 8}$

4. Show that $f(x) = (x^2 - 4)/(x - 2)$, $x \neq 2$ can be reduced to a polynomial function.
5. Graph each of the following functions.
   (a) $f(x) = x^3 + 8$    (c) $f(x) = x^3 - x$
   (b) $f(x) = \dfrac{3}{x - 2}$    (d) $f(x) = \dfrac{1}{x^2 + 1}$

function
dependent variable
independent variable
domain
range
graph of a function
linear function
quadratic function

quadratic formula
discriminant
parabola
vertex of a parabola
polynomial function
degree of a polynomial
rational function

CHAPTER
REVIEW

Important
Terms

1. Determine which of the following are functions and, for those that are, find the domain.
   (a) $y^2 = x$    (c) $y = \sqrt{x - 2}$
   (b) $y = x^2$    (d) $y = \dfrac{1}{\sqrt{x - 1}}$

2. For each of the functions
   (a) $f(x) = 3x + 4$    (b) $f(x) = x^3$
   find $f(x + h)$, $f(x + h) - f(x)$, and $\dfrac{f(x + h) - f(x)}{h}$, $h \neq 0$

3. Graph and find the domain of each of the functions.
   (a) $f(x) = \begin{cases} x^2, & \text{if} \quad x \geq 0 \\ 2x, & \text{if} \quad x < 0 \end{cases}$

   (b) $f(x) = \begin{cases} 2 - x, & \text{if} \quad -1 \leq x \leq 1 \\ \dfrac{1}{x}, & \text{if} \quad x > 1 \end{cases}$

4. Graph each of the following functions.
   (a) $y = f(x) = x^2 - 1$    (d) $y = f(x) = \dfrac{1}{x + 1}$
   (b) $y = f(x) = x^3 - 1$    (e) $y = f(x) = \dfrac{1}{x^2}$
   (c) $y = f(x) = x^2 + x$    (f) $y = f(x) = x^4$

Review
Exercises

## Bibliography

*Mathematics*

Wooton and Drooyan, *Intermediate Algebra,* Third Alternate Edition, Wadsworth, 1972. Chapters 6–8.

# 3

# MATHEMATICAL MODELS

Practical situations usually do not take the form of a mathematical problem since the real world is normally far too complicated and complex to be described precisely. To solve real-world problems, we rely on a simplified formulation, which is called a mathematical model. The purpose of this chapter is to acquaint the reader with mathematical models: what they are, how they are constructed, and how they are interpreted.

After completing this chapter, the reader will be aware of the complex nature of developing models and, as a result, should appreciate the power of mathematics. The Bibliography appearing at the end of the chapter refers the interested reader to books that discuss modeling in greater detail.

We begin this section by considering an application of linear functions to a typical real-world situation.

Suppose a company operates a factory and the fixed cost of operation, the overhead cost for rent, electricity, water, etc., amounts to $150 per workday. Furthermore, suppose the cost for each item manufactured in the factory is $0.50 per day, that is, the unit cost is $0.50. It is clear that the overhead is a fixed cost, the unit cost is variable, and the total cost depends on the number of items produced.

To get a representation for the total cost, we first assign symbols to represent the variable quantities; they are

$$x = \text{number of units produced per day}$$
$$C(x) = \text{total daily cost of producing } x \text{ units}$$

From the data given, there is the following relationship between these variables:

$$C(x) = \$150 + \$0.50x$$

where $150 is the daily fixed cost and $0.50 is the cost for each unit produced.

The above expression represents a simplified version of the actual cost of running the company in question, since in computing the cost we have excluded such items as selling expenses, management overhead, etc. Furthermore, we implicitly assume that the cost function is linear; that is, an increase in production of one unit increases the cost by $0.50. Nothing has been said about whether the cost actually is, or should be, related to the number of items produced in this way. According to the procedure, if the relationship is linear, then certain conclusions can be drawn.

What we have done here is to find a mathematical expression for a business situation in which many assumptions were made; that is, a mathematical model has been designed. The advantage of using a mathematical model is that it allows the full power of mathematics to be utilized in drawing conclusions that may be important for real-world interpretations. The model need not be, and usually is not, an exact duplication of the real world. However, it is adequate for the purpose at hand and will give results that can be used in a practical way.

Deterministic   The model just constructed is an example of a *deterministic model*. It is deterministic in the sense that once the number of items produced is known, the cost is predicted in an *exact* way by the model. This is in contrast to, for example, a model constructed to predict the weather.

Probabilistic   Here, once the input is known, the prediction is given in *probabilistic* terms, such as "There is an 80 percent chance of rain."

Definition   **Mathematical models are thus of two types: probabilistic and deter-**
of a Model   **ministic. A probabilistic model deals with situations that are random in character. A deterministic model is one that, based on certain assumptions and laws, will predict exactly the outcome of a situation.**

Chapters 4 to 12 discuss the mathematics required to handle certain deterministic models, while Chapters 13 to 16 consider probabilistic models.

How does one go about constructing a mathematical model? Once constructed, how can we be sure the model gives an accurate interpretation? How do we test models?

Often, the answers will depend on both the degree of accuracy wanted and on the degree of difficulty of a particular model. That is, a given physical event can sometimes be interpreted mathematically in more than one way, with one way giving more accurate results but, at the same time, requiring more involved computation or deeper mathematical principles.

At other times, two different models for the same physical event may not be so easy to distinguish. In these cases individual or historical biases may decide the "better" model.

Let us follow the historical development of a model from the field of astronomy.[1] Early astronomers were concerned with explaining the behavior of the sun, moon, and planets. They watched both the sun and moon rise in the east and set in the west and concluded that both the sun and moon revolved about the earth in circular orbits. This circular orbiting of the sun and moon about the earth is an interpretation of a physical event—a model. Through the use of this model, various conclusions, many of them valid, most of them false and contradictory, were arrived at.

Because of the many contradictions that arose, the model went through various changes and refinements. Finally, the famous astronomer Kepler proposed a model for planetary motion in which each planet moved about the sun in an elliptical path with the sun fixed at a focus of the ellipse. See Figure 3.1.

[1] A. Mizrahi and M. Sullivan, "Mathematical Models and Applications," *The Mathematics Teacher, 66,* 5(May 1973), pp. 394–402.

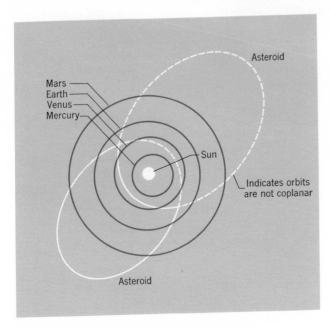

**Figure 3.1**

This model led to results that agreed quite closely with the results due to observation. Thus, a "better" (more accurate) model for explaining planetary motion was discovered.

However, Kepler relied on a theory involving magnetic forces to explain the behavior of planetary motion. Of course, Kepler's magnetic forces were not very satisfactory, and true understanding of universal gravitation awaited Newton two generations later. Newton's contribution was to explain the why of Kepler's model. This paved the way for a much more sophisticated understanding of a large class of happenings.

Still, slight discrepancies with observed fact were noted in the use of the Kepler model. For example, slight aberrations in the orbit of Mercury were observed, and these could not be explained by the Keplerian model. It was Einstein who later refined the Keplerian model so that the Mercury aberration was taken into account. Thus, the construction of a model is often an ongoing process, with continual refinements taking place.

The above example illustrates that, in general, mathematics cannot deal directly with real-world situations. In order to use mathematics to solve problems in the real world, it is necessary to construct a mathematical model in which real-life objects are represented by mathematical objects.

John Synge[2] in 1961 described the modeling process as consisting of three stages:

1. A dive from the world of reality into the world of mathematics.
2. A swim in the world of mathematics.
3. A climb from the world of mathematics back into the world of reality, carrying a prediction in our teeth.

The modeling process can be more concisely defined by using a flow chart, such as computer programmers use. See Figure 3.2.

To summarize, the flow chart in Figure 3.2 consists of the following steps:

1. Remove from the original setting only the bare features of the real-world problem. This requires due examination of the original setting to gain direction in determining what is fundamental. The result of such an effort is a simplified, idealized physical model of the original problem.
2. Make this idealized model the subject of mathematical investigation by direct translation to mathematical terms. Essentially, this translation is a mathematical model of the idealized physical model of the original problem.
3. Through manipulative computation obtain a solution for the mathematical model. In this stage there is no reference to the original setting or to the idealized physical model.
4. Interpret the solution in terms of the idealized physical model.
5. Finally, interpret the solution in terms of the original setting.

The validity of the results must be verified and depends upon the extent to which the model includes all of the pertinent facts.

[2]John Synge, "Mathematical Education Notes," *American Mathematical Monthly* 68 (October 1961), p. 799.

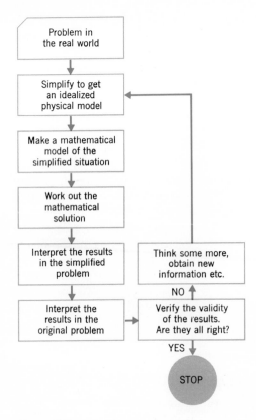

**Figure 3.2**

The following example is presented here to illustrate the first three stages of the modeling process. The fourth stage, working out the mathematical solution, requires knowledge of certain mathematical techniques. The purpose of this book is to provide these techniques; it is not expected that the student be able to construct mathematical models as a result of completing the chapter. Thus, throughout this course, applications, illustrations, examples, and problems of real-world situations will be solved or explained through the use of a model developed for this purpose. Remember that the solutions given are in actuality solutions of a mathematical model, which is merely an interpretation of the real-world situation and may only approximate reality.

Mary's File Cabinet House is a retailer of filing cabinets, having three stores at which the cabinets are sold and two warehouses in which they are stored. The company has solid information going back several years about the cost of shipping cabinets between each warehouse and each store and about the number of files stored in each warehouse and the number needed by each store. However, the company wants to know how many files should be stored in each warehouse so that each store can

2.1
Example

be sufficiently stocked, and at the same time keep shipping costs at a minimum.

The above is a description of the real-world problem. In order to pass to an idealized physical model, the company consults its records and determines how many file cabinets are needed in each store. This, of course, is an estimate based on past experience and may, or may not, accurately reflect current demand for file cabinets.

The company also draws on past experience to estimate the cost of shipping from each warehouse to each store. In fact, the company may, or may not, be able to obtain a commitment from the transporter to ship at a specific rate. Finally, the company assumes that the cost of transporting $n$ file cabinets is $n$ times the cost of transporting a single file cabinet. With these assumptions, we have progressed to step 2 of the modeling process.

To build the mathematical model, we begin by assigning symbols to represent the quantities involved in the problem. Thus,

$S_1$ = stock size needed at store 1
$S_2$ = stock size needed at store 2
$S_3$ = stock size needed at store 3
$W_1$ = number of files kept at warehouse 1
$W_2$ = number of files kept at warehouse 2
$N_{11}$ = number of files shipped from warehouse 1 to store 1
$N_{12}$ = number of files shipped from warehouse 1 to store 2
$N_{13}$ = number of files shipped from warehouse 1 to store 3
$N_{21}$ = number of files shipped from warehouse 2 to store 1
$N_{22}$ = number of files shipped from warehouse 2 to store 2
$N_{23}$ = number of files shipped from warehouse 2 to store 3
$C_{11}$ = cost of shipping a single file from warehouse 1 to store 1
$C_{12}$ = cost of shipping a single file from warehouse 1 to store 2
$C_{13}$ = cost of shipping a single file from warehouse 1 to store 3
$C_{21}$ = cost of shipping a single file from warehouse 2 to store 1
$C_{22}$ = cost of shipping a single file from warehouse 2 to store 2
$C_{23}$ = cost of shipping a single file from warehouse 2 to store 3

Finally, we let $C$ = total cost.

The assumptions of the idealized physical model require that, for example, store 1 received at least $S_1$ files; thus, the number of files shipped to store 1 from warehouse 1 and warehouse 2 must exceed $S_1$. That is

$$N_{11} + N_{21} \geqq S_1$$

Similarly

$$N_{12} + N_{22} \geqq S_2$$
$$N_{13} + N_{23} \geqq S_3$$

**69**
3.3
LINEAR BUSINESS
MODELS;
BREAK-EVEN
ANALYSIS;
STRAIGHT-LINE
DEPRECIATION

Also, the number shipped from warehouse 1 cannot exceed the number stored in warehouse 1. That is

$$N_{11} + N_{12} + N_{13} \leqq W_1$$
$$N_{21} + N_{22} + N_{23} \leqq W_2$$

Finally, the cost function $C$ of shipping is the sum of the number from warehouse 1 to store 1 times the cost $C_{11}$, the number from warehouse 1 to store 2 times the cost $C_{12}$, and so on. That is,

$$C = N_{11} \cdot C_{11} + N_{12} \cdot C_{12} + N_{13} \cdot C_{13}$$
$$+ N_{21} \cdot C_{21} + N_{22} \cdot C_{22} + N_{23} \cdot C_{23}$$

Our problem then is to find the numbers $N_{11}, N_{12}, N_{13}, N_{21}, N_{22}, N_{23}$ so that the cost function $C$ is as small as possible. We have now progressed to the mathematical model.

As stated, the above is called a *transportation problem*. Techniques for solving this and other related problems are considered in Chapters 4 and 6.

Our main goal for the rest of this chapter is to analyze various business situations that lead to models that utilize a linear or quadratic function. In this section we shall discuss real-world situations that lead to functions whose graphs are straight lines. Such functions are of the form

3.3
LINEAR
BUSINESS
MODELS; BREAK-
EVEN ANALYSIS;
STRAIGHT-LINE
DEPRECIATION

$$f(x) = mx + b$$

in which $m$ is the slope of the line and $b$ is the $y$-intercept. Sometimes the analysis of the business situation is of a type that can be most easily handled using the two-point form of a straight line, namely,

$$y = y_1 + \frac{y_2 - y_1}{x_2 - x_1}(x - x_1)$$

The following examples will serve to illustrate the types of situations for which linear models can be used.

A used car dealer determines the selling price of its cars by marking up the cost of the car 60 percent. Find a function or formula that will give the selling price of any car.

Let $c$ represent the cost of the car to the dealer and let $S$ represent the selling price of the car. Since the selling price is a function of the cost $c$, the function we seek is $S(c)$.

The selling price is obtained by adding the cost and markup. That is,

$$S(c) = c + 0.6c = (1 + 0.6)c = 1.6c$$

Thus, if a car costs the dealer $600, its selling price will be

$$S(600) = (1.6)(600) = \$960$$

If a car has a selling price of $995, what is the dealer's profit? Here, we need to find the cost $c$ to the dealer. Thus,

$$S(c) = 995 = 1.6c$$

or

$$c = \frac{995}{1.6} = \$621.88$$

This means the dealer's profit is

$$S(c) - c = \$995 - \$621.88 = \$373.12$$

The graph of the selling price function is given in Figure 3.3. It is a straight line with slope 1.6 and intercept 0.

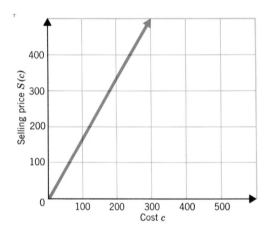

**Figure 3.3**

Harry's Hardware Store has in stock 400 six-inch screwdrivers at the beginning of the year. Past experience indicates that the sales of this type of screwdriver average 8 per sales day. Find a function that describes the number of screwdrivers on hand on any sales day of the year. When will the stock be depleted? If Harry decides to reorder when the stock reaches a level of 100, when should he place the order? (Assume six sales days per week.)

First, we seek a function describing the situation. Let $x$ denote the number of sales days and let $f(x)$ be the number of six-inch screwdrivers in stock. We are given that when $x = 0$, (no sales day has occurred), the number in stock is 400. Also, we know the average reduction in stock is 8 per sales day; that is, the function is linear, and its slope is $m = -8$. Thus, we know the slope $m = -8$ and a point $(0, 400)$ on the line. The function is

$$f(x) = -8x + 400$$

**71**
3.3
LINEAR BUSINESS
MODELS;
BREAK-EVEN
ANALYSIS;
STRAIGHT-LINE
DEPRECIATION

The stock is depleted when $f(x) = 0$. Thus,

$$0 = -8x + 400$$
$$8x = 400$$
$$x = 50$$

After 50 sales days (in the 9th week of the year), the stock will be depleted.

The stock reaches a level of 100 when

$$100 = -8x + 400$$
$$8x = 300$$
$$x = 37.5$$

That is, on the 38th day of the sales year (the 2nd selling day of the 7th week), Harry should order more screwdrivers.

Often, both the cost of production $C$ and the revenue $R$ obtained from sales can be expressed as linear functions of the number $x$ of items produced. If this is the case, it is clear that whenever the cost of production $C$ exceeds the revenue $R$ from sales, the business is operating at a loss; if the revenue $R$ exceeds the cost $C$, there is a profit. When the cost and revenue are equal, there is no profit or loss—this value is usually referred to as the *break-even point*.

Break-Even Point

Sweet Delight Candies, Inc., has a daily fixed cost due to salaries and building operations of $300. Each pound of candy produced costs $1 and is sold for $2 per pound. What is the break-even point? That is, how many pounds of candy must be sold each day to guarantee no loss and no profit?

Here the cost of production $C$ is the fixed cost plus the variable cost of producing $x$ pounds of candy at $1 per pound. Thus,

$$C = \$1 \cdot x + \$300$$

The revenue $R$ obtained from the sale of $x$ pounds of candy at $2 per pound is

$$R = \$2 \cdot x$$

The break-even point is that point at which these two lines meet. Thus, setting $R = C$, we find

$$x + 300 = 2x \qquad \text{or} \qquad x = 300$$

That is, 300 pounds of candy must be sold each day in order to break even.

3.3
Example

In Figure 3.4, we see the graphical interpretation of the break-even point. Note that for $x > 300$, the revenue $R$ always exceeds the cost $C$ so that a profit results. Similarly, for $x < 300$, the cost exceeds the revenue, resulting in a loss.

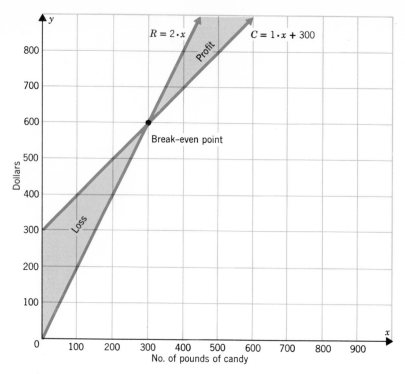

**Figure 3.4**

3.4
Example

After a negotiation with employees of Sweet Delight Candies and an increase in the price of chocolate, the daily cost of production $C$ for $x$ pounds of candy is

$$C = \$1.05x + \$330$$

(a) If each pound is sold for $2, how many must be sold each day to break even?

(b) If the selling price is increased to $2.25 per pound, what is the break-even point?

(c) If it is known that at least 325 pounds of candy can be sold daily, what price should be charged per pound to guarantee no loss?

(a) If each pound is sold for $2, the revenue from sales is

$$R = \$2x$$

where $x$ represents the number of pounds sold. The break-even point obeys

$$2x = 1.05x + 330$$
$$0.95x = 330$$
$$x = \frac{33{,}000}{95} = 347.37$$

**73**
3.3
LINEAR BUSINESS
MODELS;
BREAK-EVEN
ANALYSIS;
STRAIGHT-LINE
DEPRECIATION

Thus, if 347 pounds are sold, a loss is incurred; if 348 pounds are sold, a profit results.

(b) If the selling price is increased to $2.25 per pound, the new revenue due to sales is

$$R = \$2.25x$$

The break-even point obeys

$$2.25x = 1.05x + 330$$
$$1.2x = 330$$
$$x = \frac{3300}{12} = 275$$

With the new selling price, the break-even point is 275 pounds.

(c) If we know at least 325 pounds will be sold daily, the price per pound $p$ needed to guarantee no loss (that is, to guarantee at worst a break-even point) obeys

$$325 \cdot p = (1.05)(325) + 330$$
$$325p = 671.25$$
$$p = \$2.07$$

We should charge approximately $2.07 per pound to guarantee at worst break even if at least 325 pounds will be sold each day.

3.5
Example

A producer sells items for $0.30 each. If his cost for production is

$$C = \$0.15x + \$105$$

where $x$ is the number of items sold, find his break-even point. If he can change his cost to

$$C = \$0.12x + \$110$$

would it be to his advantage to do so?

First, the revenue received is

$$R = \$0.3x$$

The break-even point obeys

$$0.3x = 0.15x + \$105$$
$$0.15x = 105$$
$$x = 700$$

Thus, for the first cost function, the break-even point is 700 items.

To determine the answer to the second part, we find the break-even point that results from the second cost function is $x = 611.11$. The old break-even point was $x = 700$. Thus, the second cost function will require fewer items to be sold in order to break even. Management should probably change over to the new cost function. See Figure 3.5.

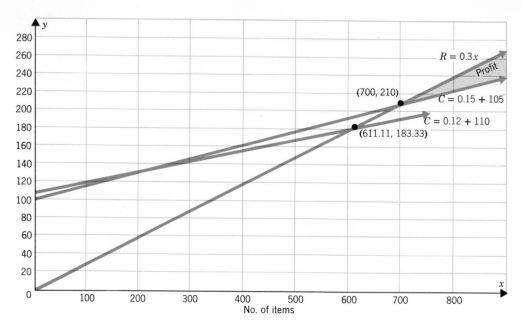

**Figure 3.5**

Supply Function

The *supply function* in economics is used to specify the amount of a particular commodity that sellers have available to offer in the market

Demand Function

at various prices. The *demand function* specifies the amount of a particular commodity that buyers are willing to purchase at various prices. Let $S$ denote the supply at price $p$ and $D$ denote the amount demanded at price $p$.

It is well known that an increase in price usually causes an increase in the supply, but a decrease in demand; on the other hand, a decrease in price brings about a decrease in supply and an increase in demand.

Market Price

The *market price* is defined as the price at which supply and demand are equal.

3.6
Example

The supply and demand functions for flour during the period 1920–1935 were estimated according to the equations

$$S = 0.8p + 0.5, \qquad D = -0.4p + 1.5$$

where $p$ is measured in dollars and $S$, $D$ are measured in 50-lb units of flour. Find the market price and graph the supply and demand functions.

The market price is the point of intersection of the two lines in Figure 3.6. Thus, the market price $p$ is the solution of

$$0.8p + 0.5 = -0.4p + 1.5$$
$$1.2p = 1$$
$$p = 0.83$$

**75**
3.3
LINEAR BUSINESS
MODELS;
BREAK-EVEN
ANALYSIS;
STRAIGHT-LINE
DEPRECIATION

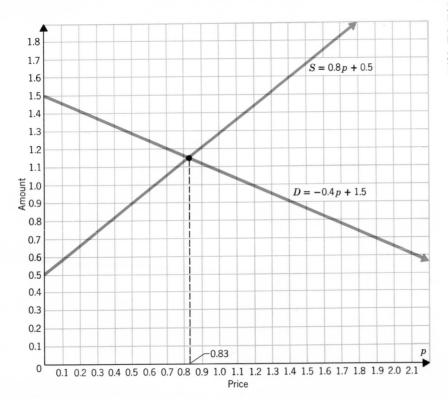

**Figure 3.6**

One of the methods permitted by the Internal Revenue Service for depreciating business property is the *straight-line method.* Under this method of depreciation, an item whose useful life is determined to be *n* years will depreciate in value by $1/n$ each year. For example, if a cash register has an eight-year life, it would loose 1/8th of its value each year under the *straight-line* method.

Straight-Line
Depreciation

In calculating the amount of depreciation allowable, the *scrap value,* that is, the value of the item at the end of its useful life, must be subtracted from its original cost before calculating yearly depreciation. This difference is called the *depreciable value V.* Thus, if the cash register was purchased for $2100 and its scrap value is $100, the depreciable value is $2000 and the yearly allowable depreciation is

Scrap Value

Depreciable Value

$$\frac{1}{8}(2100 - 100) = \frac{1}{8}(2000) = \$250$$

In general, if an item has depreciable value *V,* and a useful life of *n* years, the annual depreciation allowable is

$$\frac{V}{n}$$

After *x* years, the total depreciation taken is

$$x \cdot \frac{V}{n}$$

Undepreciated
Balance The *undepreciated balance B* is the difference between depreciable value
and the total depreciation taken. That is,

$$B = V - \frac{xV}{n}$$

The relationship between undepreciated balance $B$ and the time $x$ is
linear, with slope $-V/n$.

For example, the undepreciated balance after $x$ years for the cash
register is

$$B = 2000 - \frac{2000}{8}x = 2000 - 250x$$

Thus after 5 years, the undepreciated balance is

$$2000 - (250)(5) = \$750$$

There are many examples of business equipment that depreciate
according to the straight-line method. Many others, however, behave
quite differently. Thus, for computing depreciation on cars, clothing, and
the like, the Internal Revenue Service may allow other methods, such
as the sum-of-the-year's-digits method or the double-declining-balance
method. These methods are described in the publications of the IRS.

1. In Example 3.2, (page 70), suppose Harry's Hardware Store
   estimates that the average daily sales of 6-inch screwdrivers
   is 5 per sales day instead of 8 per sales day. What is the
   function describing the number of screwdrivers on hand
   on any sales day of the year? When will the stock be
   depleted? (Assume 6 sales days per week.)

2. A construction worker earns $6.50 per hour. His take-home
   pay, after taxes and other amounts withheld, amounts to
   81 percent of his gross pay. Find a function for determining
   take-home pay. How many hours must he work to take
   home $200?

3. It costs $5.00 to transport one pound of merchandise 100
   miles and $28.50 to transport one pound of merchandise
   700 miles. Assuming the relationship between the cost of
   transportation and mileage is linear, find the function
   describing the relationship. How much does it cost per
   pound to transport merchandise 200 miles? 400 miles?

4. A trucking company transports goods between Chicago and
   New York, a distance of 960 miles. Their policy is to charge
   for each pound $0.50 per mile for the first 100 miles, $0.40
   per mile for the next 300 miles, $0.25 per mile for the next
   400 miles, and no charge for the remaining 160 miles. Graph
   the relationship between the cost of transportation and
   mileage over the entire 960 mile route. Find the cost as a
   function of mileage for hauls between 100 and 400 miles

from Chicago. Find the cost as a function of mileage for hauls between 400 and 800 miles from Chicago.

5. Find the break-even point for the cost of production $C$ and the revenue $R$ received for each of the following; graph each result.

(a) $C = \$10x + \$600,$ $\qquad R = \$30x$
(b) $C = \$5x + \$200,$ $\qquad R = \$8x$
(c) $C = \$0.2x + \$50,$ $\qquad R = \$0.3x$
(d) $C = \$1800x + \$3000,$ $\qquad R = \$2500x$

6. A manufacturer produces items at a daily cost to him of 75¢ per item and sells them for $1 per item. His daily operational overhead is $300. What is his break-even point? Graph your result.

7. If the manufacturer of problem 6 is able to reduce his cost per item to 65¢, but with an increase to $350 in operational overhead, is it to his advantage to do so? Graph your result.

8. The supply and demand functions for sugar from 1890–1915 were estimated by H. Schulz[3] to be given by

$$S = 0.7p + 0.4, \qquad D = -0.5p + 1.6$$

Find the market price. What quantity of supply is demanded at this market price? Graph both the supply function and demand function. Interpret the point of intersection of the two lines.

9. A Milex car repair center purchased a compressor and lift for $2500. Its scrap value is estimated at $100 and its useful life at 20 years. What is the annual allowable depreciation under the straight-line method? What is the undepreciated balance after 12 years? Find the relationship between undepreciated balance and time. Graph this relationship.

10. An apartment building was purchased for $350,000 in 1953. Assuming a useful life of 50 years with a zero scrap value, what is the current (1976) undepreciated balance if the straight-line method of depreciation is used?

In the last section we constructed models that led to linear functions. In this section we treat situations that are slightly more complex and, as might be expected, give rise to slightly more difficult mathematics. For the purposes of this section, we confine ourselves to a discussion of models that require the use of a quadratic function. (A discussion of the quadratic equation can be found in Section 2.2 of Chapter 2.) As the student progresses, he will discover that many of the models solved in this section using algebraic techniques can be more easily handled by utilizing the power of calculus.

3.4
QUADRATIC
BUSINESS
MODELS

[3] H. Schulz, *Statistical Laws of Demand and Supply with Special Applications to Sugar,* University of Chicago Press, Chicago, 1928.

The new owner of an apartment building complex wants to determine the monthly rental on each 50 units. If he charges $120 per month, all the units will be rented. He has reason to believe that, for each $5 increase, a unit will become vacant and remain vacant. Also, the owner's expenses for maintenance are $8 more per month for occupied versus vacant apartments. Find a functional relationship between profit and the number of unoccupied units. What is the monthly rental charge needed to obtain maximum profit? What is the maximum profit?

First, let $x$ denote the number of vacant units and let $P(x)$ denote the profit before fixed maintenance expenses. The rental for each occupied unit is

$$\$120 + \$5 \cdot x$$

and the number of occupied units is

$$50 - x$$

The total rental income is thus

$$(120 + 5x)(50 - x)$$

The additional maintenance expense for each occupied unit is $8 for a total expense of

$$\$8(50 - x)$$

Since the rental income less additional maintenance expense is profit, the profit (in dollars) is

$$P(x) = (120 + 5x)(50 - x) - 8(50 - x)$$

or

$$P(x) = -5x^2 + 138x + 5600$$

The profit function $P$ is a quadratic function with $a = -5 < 0$. Thus, it opens downward and the vertex is the maximum point. This vertex is

$$(13.8, \$6552.20)$$

Thus, when 13.8 units are unoccupied, the profit $6552.20 is largest. However, it is not possible to have 13.8 units unoccupied, so we test the profit for 13 and 14 unoccupied units. See Figure 3.7.

For $x = 13$,     $P(13) = -5(169) + 138(13) + 5600 = \$6549.00$

For $x = 14$,     $P(14) = -5(196) + 138(14) + 5600 = \$6552.00$

Thus, the maximum profit is $6552 obtained when 14 units are left vacant. The monthly rental charge for maximum profit is

$$\$120 + \$5(14) = \$190$$

The Alexander Coffee Pot Company is planning to market a new percolator. Rather than set the selling price of the percolator

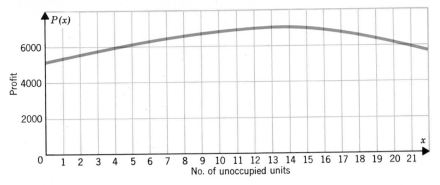

**Figure 3.7**

based only on production cost estimates, management polls the retailers of the percolator to see how many percolators they would buy for various prices. From this survey it is determined that the unit demand function (the relationship between the amount $x$ each retailer would buy and the price $p$ he is willing to pay) is

$$x = -750p + 15{,}000$$

The fixed costs to the company for production of the percolator are found to be \$7000 and the cost for material and labor to produce each percolator is estimated to be \$4.00 per unit. What price should the company charge retailers in order to obtain a maximum profit?

Let $x$ denote the number of units produced, let $C$ denote the cost of production to the Company, and let $p$ denote the price per unit (in dollars). Then, the cost $C$ is given by

$$C = \$4x + \$7000$$

and the unit demand is

$$x = -750p + 15{,}000$$

Substituting, we find that the cost function $C$ in terms of the price $p$ per unit is

$$C = 4 \cdot (-750p + 15{,}000) + 7000$$

or

$$C = -3000p + 67{,}000$$

The money derived from the sale of the percolators as a function of the price $p$ per unit is the product of the number sold by the price per unit. That is, the revenue $R$ is

$$R = (-750p + 15{,}000)p$$

or

$$R = -750p^2 + 15{,}000p$$

The profit $P$ to the company is merely the difference between revenue (money derived from sales) and total cost. That is,

$$P = R - C$$
$$= (-750p^2 + 15,000p) - (-3000p + 67,000)$$
$$= -750p^2 + 18,000p - 67,000$$

Since the profit to the company is a quadratic function, the maximum profit is found when $p = -18,000/-1500 = 12$. The profit for this price is

$$P = -750(144) + 18,000(12) - 67,000 = \$41,000$$

The number of units sold at this price $p$ is

$$x = (-750)(12) + 15,000 = 6000$$

Figure 3.8 shows the relationships between the cost function $C$ and the revenue function $R$.

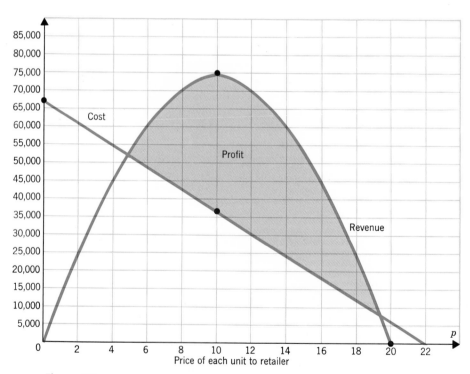

**Figure 3.8**

The reader is cautioned against drawing the conclusion that the mathematical models introduced in the last two sections will solve all management problems. Indeed, even though under the artificial conditions of the examples given, we have found optimal solutions to maximize profit, it may be, and usually is, true that other factors such as sales revenue or good will may play a greater role in the decision-making process than profit to the company.

Subsequent chapters contain developments of additional models as the situation requires.

1. Suppose the owner of the 50-unit apartment building of Example 4.1, page 78, feels that for each $3 increase in rent an apartment will become vacant. Suppose, though, that he estimates the maintenance expense to be $6 more per month for occupied versus vacant apartments. If $120 is the rental charge at which every unit is occupied, find a functional relationship between gross profit and the number of unoccupied units. What number of units should be vacant for gross profit to be a maximum? What is the maximum gross profit? What is the monthly rental charge needed to obtain the maximum gross profit?

2. The unit demand function is $p = 18 - 2x$, where $x$ is the number of units and $p$ is the price. Then the revenue function in terms of number of units is $R = (18 - 2x)x = 18x - 2x^2$. Let the average cost per unit be $6 so that $C = 6x$.
   (a) Find the profit function $P$.
   (b) Find the number of units that maximize the profit.
   (c) Find the maximum profit.
   (d) Graph $R$ and $C$.

3. The unit demand function is $x = \frac{1}{2}(18 - p)$, where $x$ is the number of units and $p$ is the price. Let the average cost per unit be $6.
   (a) Find the revenue function $R$ in terms of price $p$.
   (b) Find the cost function $C$.
   (c) Find the profit function $P$.
   (d) Find the price per unit that maximizes the profit function.
   (e) Find the maximum profit.
   (f) Graph $R$ and $C$.

4. Let the unit demand function be $p = 12 - 3x$ where $x$ is the quantity demanded at price $p$ and let the cost function be $C = x + 4$.
   (a) Find the revenue function $R$.
   (b) Find the cost function $C$.
   (c) Find the profit function $P$.
   (d) Find the quantity $x$ and price $p$ at which there is maximum profit.
   (e) Find the maximum profit.
   (f) Graph $R$ and $C$.

5. Find the break-even point if the revenue and cost are

$$R = 90\sqrt{2x}$$
$$C = 3x + 1200$$

Interpret your answer.

*6. Let the unit demand function be

$$x = ep + b$$

and the cost function be

$$C = vx + f$$

where

$x$ = sales (in units), $p$ = price (in dollars),
$f$ = fixed cost (in dollars),
$v$ = cost per unit, $b$ = demand when $p = 0$,
$e$ = slope of unit demand function

(a) Find the cost $C$ as a function of $p$.
(b) Find the revenue function $R$.
(c) Find the profit function $P$.

**mathematical model**
**deterministic model**
**probabilistic model**
**break-even point**
**supply and demand functions**
**linear business function**

**straight-line depreciation**
**scrap value**
**depreciable value**
**undepreciated balance**
**quadratic business function**

1. Construct a linear cost function to represent a business whose overhead is $1200 per day and whose cost to produce each item is $1.50.
2. For the cost function of problem 1, if the selling price of each item is $5, find the break-even point. How many items need to be sold for a daily profit of $100?
3. For a unit demand function of $p = 12 - 4x$, where $x$ is the number of units in thousands and $p$ is the price in dollars, find the sales function. If the average cost per unit is $4, find
(a) The profit function.
(b) The number of units that maximize the profit function.
(c) The maximum profit.
(d) Graph the cost and revenue functions.
4. The market price for a certain product is $4.50 per unit and occurs when 13,500 units are produced. At a price of $1, no units are manufactured and, at a price of $20, no units will

be purchased. Find the supply and demand functions if each is linear.

5. A church group is planning a dance in the school auditorium to raise money for its school. The band they will hire charges $500; the advertising costs are estimated at $100; and food is supplied at the rate of $2.00 per person. The church group would like to clear at least $900 after expenses.

   (a) Determine how many people need to attend the dance for the group to break even if tickets are sold at $5 each.

   (b) Determine how many need to attend to achieve the desired profit if tickets are sold for $5 each.

   (c) Answer the above two questions if the tickets are sold for $6 each.

## Bibliography

*Mathematics*

Kemeny, J. C. and J. L. Snell, *Mathematical Models in the Social Sciences,* Blaisdell Publishing, Walton, Mass., 1962.

Maki, D. and M. Thompson, *Mathematical Models and Applications with Emphasis on Social, Life, and Management Sciences,* Prentice-Hall, Englewood Cliffs, N.J., 1973.

*Applied*

Springer, Herlihy, Beggs, *Advanced Methods and Models,* Irwin Press, Homewood, Ill., 1965.

# 4

# INTRODUCTION TO LINEAR PROGRAMMING

The flow of resources in a production process or among sectors of the economy involves complex interrelationships between numerous activities. Differences may exist between the processes involved as well as between the goals to be achieved. Nevertheless, in many cases there are essential similarities in the operation of seemingly very different systems.

In order to analyze such systems, it is necessary to construct a statement of the working parts of the system (such as capital, raw materials, and man power) and the goal or objective to be achieved (such as minimum cost or maximum profit). If the system can be represented mathematically (that is, if a *model* for the system can be found) and if the goal can be similarly quantified, it may be possible to devise a computational scheme for determining the *best* program or schedule of actions among alternatives to achieve the goal. Such schemes are called *mathematical programs*.

Mathematical Program

If the system to be analyzed can be represented by a model consisting of linear inequalities, and if the goal or objective can be expressed as the minimization or maximization of a linear expression, the analysis

Linear Program of the structure is known as a *linear program*. A large class of business, economic, and engineering problems can be represented by a linear system. Other times, a linear system constitutes a good approximation of the conditions of the problem. Of course, for any particular application, one must determine whether a linear system constitutes a "good enough" approximation. We shall not concern ourselves here with whether a given approximation is "good enough," but rather we give the student an introduction to the technique of solving *linear programming problems*.

Historically, linear programs for the solution of problems involving resource allocation were developed during World War II by the United States Air Force. Among those who worked on such problems for the Air Force was George Dantzig, who later gave a general formulation of the linear programming problem and offered a method for solving it. His technique, called the *simplex method*, is studied in Chapter 6.

Before studying ways to solve a linear programming problem, we shall give several examples of the types of systems that can be solved using a linear program model.

**1.1
Example**

A producer of chicken feed is required by the United States Department of Agriculture to furnish a certain amount of nutritional elements (such as vitamins and minerals) per hundred pounds of feed. These elements are found in known proportions in various grains and concentrated supplements whose cost is known. What proportions of these grains and concentrated supplements should be mixed so that the desired amount of nutritional elements is found in the feed and, at the same time, the producer's cost for these elements is least?

**Diet or
Mixture
Problem**

Problems like Example 1.1 are called *diet* or *mixture problems*.

**1.2
Example**

A manufacturer has several production facilities and a number of warehouses. Each production facility can ship goods to any of the warehouses requiring goods. Shipments must be such that each warehouse receives at least as much as its requirements, possibly from more than one source. There is a known cost per unit shipped along each route from production facility to warehouse. The manufacturer wishes to devise a shipping scheme that satisfies the requirements of the warehouses at lowest possible total transportation cost.

**Transportation
Problem**

Problems like Example 1.2 are called *transportation problems*.

A company manufactures several different products. In making each product, a certain amount of manpower, skilled and non-skilled, and a known amount of raw material are used. The company sells each product for a known profit. How much of each product should be manufactured in order to maximize profits?

Each of the above examples has certain similarities. All require a linear function (called the *objective function*) to be minimized or maximized. All require this objective function to occur under given conditions or constraints that can be expressed by linear inequalities. Problems with these two characteristics can usually be solved by using a *linear program*.

The importance of linear programming should be quite clear. When many alternative actions are possible, a guessing technique (sometimes referred to as intuition or as a "by the seat of the pants approach") may not give the best solution. The difference between the intuitive solution and a linear programming solution could be millions of dollars.

The next section provides a way of solving certain kinds of linear programming problems by graphical methods. Although such kinds of problems are too simple to be realistic, they are instructional. The simplex method is used to solve more complicated linear programming problems and is adaptable to computer systems for relatively fast solutions.

If we restrict ourselves to a linear programming problem in two variables, it is possible to represent and solve the problem graphically. Although problems in two variables are too simplistic to be of much practical interest, consideration of simple problems will nevertheless illuminate the nature of linear programming problems in general.

4.2
A GEOMETRIC
APPROACH TO
LINEAR
PROGRAMMING
PROBLEMS

The problem consists of two sorts of expressions: (1) a linear objective function, which is to be minimized (or maximized), and (2) a set of linear inequalities, which must be simultaneously satisfied.

Let us first consider the objective function. It is an expression of the form

$$f = Ax + By \qquad (2.1)$$

where $A$ and $B$ are given real numbers. If we fix $f$ at some value, this expression describes a line in the plane. Consider a change in the value of $f$. Then the expression (2.1) describes another line that is *parallel to the first*. If we let $f$ vary through all possible real values, the expression (2.1) represents a family of straight lines all with the same slope $(-A/B)$.

To minimize (maximize) the objective function $f = Ax + By$ means to find points $(x, y)$ that make the corresponding value of $f$ the smallest (largest).

In a certain linear programming problem, the linear objective function is given by the expression

$$f = x + 2y$$

Graph the above linear function for $f = 0$, $f = 1$, $f = 2$, $f = 6$.
   If we rewrite this linear function in slope-intercept form we obtain

$$y = -\frac{1}{2}x + \frac{f}{2}$$

   Notice that no matter what value is assigned to $f$, the slope of the linear objective function is $-1/2$. It should be clear that the possible values that $f$ can take on are unlimited in the absence of some restrictions. See Figure 4.1 for an illustration.

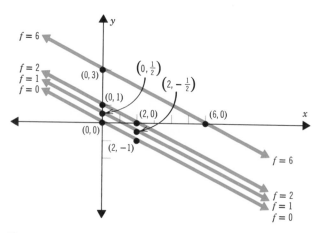

**Figure 4.1**

Definition of a
Linear
Programming
Problem

**A** *linear programming problem* **consists of minimizing (or maximizing) an objective function**

$$f = Ax + By$$

**in which $A$ and $B$ are given real numbers, subject to certain conditions or constraints expressible as linear inequalities in $x$ and $y$.**

Polyhedral Set

Convex Set

   If we graph the linear inequalities (the constraints of the linear programming problem), we obtain a set of points called a *polyhedral set*. This polyhedral set of points is *convex*; that is, it has the property that the line segment that joins any pair of points in the set lies entirely in the set. See Figure 4.2.
   Fortunately, the set resulting from the constraints of a linear programming problem always results in a polyhedral convex set. It is this fact and the fact that the intersection of a finite number of convex sets is

**89**
4.2
A GEOMETRIC
APPROACH TO
LINEAR
PROGRAMMING
PROBLEMS

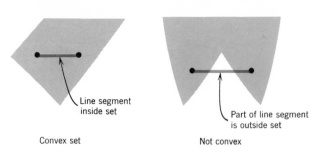

Convex set                    Not convex

**Figure 4.2**

a convex set, that allows us to solve linear programming problems the way we do.

Any point $(x, y)$ in the polyhedral convex set of the constraints of the linear programming problem is called a *feasible solution*. If no such point exists, the linear programming problem has no solution.

Feasible
Solution

In a linear programming problem, we want to find that feasible solution which minimizes (or maximizes) the objective function. If none of the possible feasible solutions minimize (or maximize) the objective function, then the linear programming problem has no solution.

**By** *a solution* **to a linear programming problem is meant a point** $(x, y)$**, together with the value of the objective function at that point, that minimizes (maximizes) the objective function.**

Solution of a
Linear
Programming
Problem

A linear programming problem consists of minimizing the objective function

2.2
Example

$$f = x + 2y$$

subject to the condition that

$$x + y \geqq 1$$

First, we graph the condition $x + y \geqq 1$. See Figure 4.3.[1]

[1] The reader is encouraged to review graphing linear inequalities; see Section 1.7 of Chapter 1, page 33).

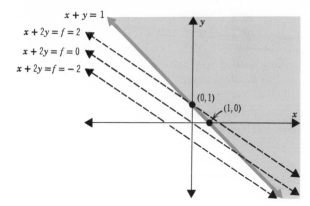

**Figure 4.3**

Notice that any value of $(x, y)$ in the shaded region including the points on the line $x + y = 1$, is a feasible solution. However, since none of these values make $f$ smallest, the linear programming problem has no solution. This can be verified by noticing that, for any value of $f$, no matter how small, the objective function will pass through the shaded region.

2.3
Example

A linear programming problem consists of minimizing the objective function

$$f = x + 2y \tag{2.2}$$

subject to the conditions

$$x + y \geqq 1, \qquad x \geqq 0, \qquad y \geqq 0$$

Again we graph the constraints. See Figure 4.4.

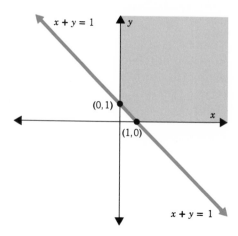

**Figure 4.4**

The shaded region of Figure 4.4 shows the polyhedral convex set of feasible solutions. To see if there is a value that makes $f$ smallest, we graph the line (2.2) and move it parallel to itself. This allows us to observe all values of the objective function. Since we want a minimum value for $f$ we try to move $f = x + 2y$ down as far as possible while keeping some part of the line within the feasible region. The "best" solution is obtained when the line just touches one corner or *vertex* of the feasible region. This situation is shown in Figure 4.5. The "best" solution is $x = 1$, $y = 0$, and $f = 1$. There is no other feasible solution for which $f$ is smaller.

Vertex

Notice that the feasible solution which minimizes $f$ occurs at a vertex. This is not an unusual situation. If there is a feasible solution minimizing

**91**
4.2
A GEOMETRIC
APPROACH TO
LINEAR
PROGRAMMING
PROBLEMS

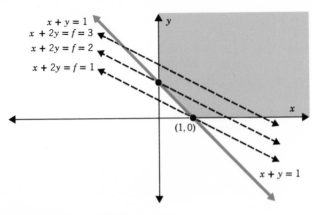

**Figure 4.5**

(or maximizing) the objective function, it is *usually* located at a vertex of the polyhedral convex set of feasible solutions.

However, it is possible for a feasible solution that is not a vertex to minimize (or maximize) the objective function. This occurs when the slope of the objective function is the same as the slope of one side of the set of feasible solutions. The following example illustrates this possibility.

A linear programming problem consists of minimizing the objective function

2.4
Example

$$f = x + 2y \qquad (2.3)$$

subject to the conditions

$$x + y \geqq 1, \qquad 2x + 4y \geqq 3, \qquad x \geqq 0, \qquad y \geqq 0 \qquad (2.4)$$

Again, we first graph the constraints of (2.4). See Figure 4.6. The shaded region of Figure 4.6 shows the polyhedral convex

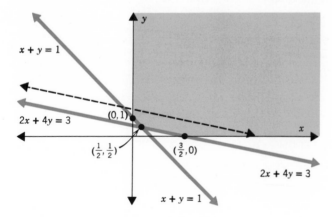

**Figure 4.6**

set of feasible solutions. If we graph the objective function (2.3) and move it down, we see that a minimum is reached when $f = 3/2$. However, any point on the line $2x + 4y = 3$ between $(1/2, 1/2)$ and $(3/2, 0)$ will minimize the objective function. Notice that the points $(3/2, 0)$ and $(1/2, 1/2)$ are at vertices of the polyhedral convex set of feasible solutions. Of course, the reason any point on $2x + 4y = 3$ minimizes the objective function $f = x + 2y$ is that these two lines are parallel (both have slope $-1/2$).

In each example so far that had a solution, *at least one* feasible solution which minimized the objective function is found at a vertex of the set of feasible solutions. We state the following general result.

**If a linear programming problem has a solution, it is located at a vertex of the polyhedral convex set of feasible solutions; if a linear programming problem has multiple solutions, at least one of them is located at a vertex of the polyhedral convex set of feasible solutions. In either case, the corresponding value of the objective function is unique.**

Notice that the above law is valid whether the objective function is to be minimized or maximized. Also, the result is independent of the number of variables involved. Because of this, the solution of a linear programming problem involves finding the vertices of the polyhedral convex set of feasible solutions and then evaluating the objective function for these values. Fortunately, a technique better than graphing has been developed to find those vertices that minimize (or maximize) the objective function. This technique—the simplex method—is discussed in Chapter 6.

Finally, it is important to observe that the above law assumes the existence of a solution of the problem.

It is possible for the set of feasible solutions to be empty or to have only one point. The following example illustrates these possibilities.

2.5
Example

The constraints or restrictions of a linear programming problem consist of

$$x + y \geqq 1, \qquad x - y \geqq 1, \qquad 2x + y \leqq 2$$

Graph the set of feasible solutions.

The set of feasible solutions consists of a single point $(1, 0)$. See Figure 4.7.

If we add the constraint

$$x - y \geqq 2$$

to the constraints of Example 2.5, there is no point in the set of feasible solutions. (The empty set is considered to be a convex set.) In this case, the linear programming problem has no solution.

**93**
4.2
A GEOMETRIC
APPROACH TO
LINEAR
PROGRAMMING
PROBLEMS

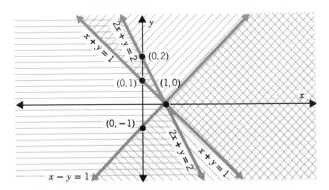

**Figure 4.7**

2.6
Example
Mixture
Problem

Nutt's Nuts has 75 pounds of cashews and 120 pounds of peanuts. These are to be mixed in 1-pound packages as follows: a
low-grade mixture that contains 4 ounces of cashews and 12
ounces of peanuts and a high-grade mixture that contains 8
ounces of cashews and 8 ounces of peanuts. On the low-grade
mixture a profit of $0.25 a package is to be made, while the
high-grade mixture profit is to be $0.45 a package. How many
packages of each mixture should be made to obtain a maximum
profit?

First, we notice there are two variables. Let

$x$ = number of packages of low-grade mixture
$y$ = number of packages of high-grade mixture

The profit $P$ is given by the linear function

$$P = (\$0.25)x + (\$0.45)y$$

The restrictions on $x$ and $y$ are that

$$x \geq 0, \quad y \geq 0$$

since $x$ and $y$ stand for numbers of packages and negative numbers of packages are meaningless. Also, there is a limit to the
number of pounds of cashews and peanuts available. That is,
the total number of pounds of cashews cannot exceed 75 pounds
(1200 ounces) and the number of pounds of peanuts cannot
exceed 120 pounds (1920 ounces). This means that

$$4x + 8y \leq 1200$$
$$12x + 8y \leq 1920$$

The linear programming problem is to maximize the objective
(profit) function

$$P = \$0.25x + \$0.45y \tag{2.5}$$

subject to the conditions

①$x + 2y \leq 300,$ ②$3x + 2y \leq 480,$

③$x \geq 0,$ ④$y \geq 0$ (2.6)

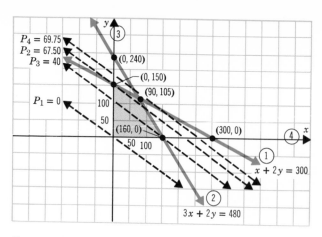

**Figure 4.8**

Since we know the solution, if it exists, is found at a vertex, we need only find the vertices of the set of feasible solution.

To do this, we graph the set of feasible solutions. See Figure 4.8. The vertices of the set of feasible solutions are the points of intersection of lines ③ and ④, ① and ③, ② and ④, and ① and ②. Using methods developed in Section 1.6 of Chapter 1 (page 28), the vertices of the set of feasible solution are, respectively,

$$(0,0), \quad (0,150), \quad (160,0), \quad (90,105)$$

(Notice that the points of intersection of lines ① and ④ and lines ② and ③ are not feasible solutions.) It only remains to test each of the vertices in the profit function (2.5). Then

$$P_1 = (\$0.25)(0) + (\$0.45)(0) = 0$$

Clearly, a profit of $0.00 is not a maximum. Next,

$$P_2 = (\$0.25)(0) + (\$0.45)(150) = \$67.50$$
$$P_3 = (\$0.25)(160) + (\$0.45)(0) = \$40.00$$
$$P_4 = (\$0.25)(90) + (\$0.45)(105) = \$69.75$$

Thus, a maximum profit is obtained if 90 packages of low-grade mixture and 105 packages of high-grade mixture are made. The maximum profit obtainable under the conditions described is $69.75.

We now have a method for solving a linear programming problem, provided it has a solution. We outline this procedure below.

1. **Find an expression for the objective function that is to be maximized or minimized.**

**95**
4.2
A GEOMETRIC
APPROACH TO
LINEAR
PROGRAMMING
PROBLEMS

2. List all the constraints.
3. Find the vertices of the polyhedral convex set of constraints.
4. Determine the value of the objective function at each vertex.

Mike's Famous Toy Trucks manufactures two kinds of toy trucks—a standard model and a deluxe model. In the manufacturing process, each standard model requires 2 hours of grinding and 2 hours of finishing, and each deluxe model needs 2 hours of grinding and 4 hours of finishing. The company has 2 grinders and 3 finishers, each of whom work 40 hours per week. Each standard model toy truck brings a profit of $3 and each deluxe model a profit of $4. Assuming every truck made will be sold, how many of each should be made to maximize profits?

2.7
Example

First, let

$$x = \text{number of standard models made}$$
$$y = \text{number of deluxe models made}$$

The profit $P$ is given by the linear function

$$P = \$3x + \$4y$$

To manufacture 1 standard model requires 2 grinding hours and to make 1 deluxe model requires 2 grinding hours. Thus, the number of grinding hours for $x$ standard and $y$ deluxe models is

$$2x + 2y$$

But there is at most 80 hours per week of grinding. This means we have the constraint

$$2x + 2y \leqq 80$$

associated with this problem. Similarly, we have the constraint

$$2x + 4y \leqq 120$$

for the finishing hours.

The linear programming problem is to maximize the objective (profit) function

$$P = 3x + 4y$$

subject to the conditions

$$2x + 2y \leqq 80, \qquad x \geqq 0$$
$$2x + 4y \leqq 120, \qquad y \geqq 0$$

The vertices of the polyhedral convex set of feasible solutions are

$$(0, 0), \qquad (0, 30), \qquad (40, 0), \qquad (20, 20)$$

See Figure 4.9.

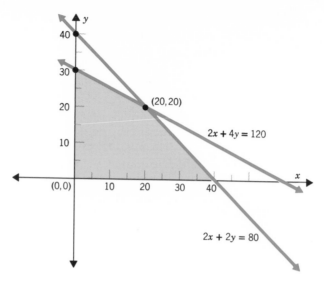

**Figure 4.9**

Testing each of these values, we see that

$$P_1 = 3(0) + 4(0) = \$0$$
$$P_2 = 3(0) + 4(30) = \$120$$
$$P_3 = 3(40) + 4(0) = \$120$$
$$P_4 = 3(20) + 4(20) = \$140$$

Thus, a maximum profit is obtained if 20 standard trucks and 20 deluxe trucks are manufactured. The maximum profit is $140.

The following example is taken from a paper by Robert E. Kohn.[2]

2.8
Example
An Application
to Pollution
Control

In this paper, a linear programming model is proposed that can be useful in determining what air pollution controls should be adopted in an airshed. The methodology is based on the premise that air quality goals should be achieved at the least possible cost. Advantages of the model are its simplicity, its emphasis on economic efficiency, and its appropriateness for the kind of data that is already available.

To illustrate the model, consider a hypothetical airshed with a single industry, cement manufacturing. Annual production is 2,500,000 barrels of cement. Although the kilns are equipped with mechanical collectors for air pollution control, they are still emitting two pounds of dust for every barrel of cement produced. The industry can be required to replace the mechanical collectors with four-field electrostatic precipitators, which would reduce emissions to 0.5 pound of dust per barrel of cement, or with five-field electrostatic precipitators, which would reduce

[2] R. E. Kohn, "A Mathematical Programming Model for Air Pollution Control," *School Science and Mathematics* (June 1969), pp. 487–499.

**97**

4.2
A GEOMETRIC
APPROACH TO
LINEAR
PROGRAMMING
PROBLEMS

emissions to 0.2 pound per barrel. If the capital and operating costs of the four-field precipitator are $0.14 per barrel of cement produced and of the five-field precipitator are $0.18 per barrel, what control methods should be required of this industry? Assume that, for this hypothetical airshed, it has been determined that particulate emissions (which now total 5,000,000 pounds per year) should be reduced by 4,200,000 pounds.

If C represents the cost of control, x is the number of barrels of annual cement production subject to the four-field electrostatic precipitator, whose cost is $0.14 a barrel of cement produced, and with which the pollutant reduction is (2–0.5) or 1.5 pounds of particulates per barrel of cement produced, and y is the number of barrels of annual cement production subject to the five-field electrostatic precipitator control method, whose cost is $0.18 and with which the particulate reduction is (2–0.2) or 1.8 pounds per barrel of cement produced, then the model can be stated as follows:

Minimize

$$C = \$0.14x + \$0.18y$$

subject to

$$x + y \leq 2,500,000$$
$$1.5x + 1.8y \geq 4,200,000$$
$$x \geq 0, \qquad y \geq 0$$

The function C states that our objective is to minimize air pollution control costs; the first inequality states that barrels of cement production subject to the two control methods cannot exceed the annual production; the second that the particulate reduction from the two methods must be greater than or equal to the particulate reduction target. The final expressions preclude a solution of the model with negative quantities of cement.

Figure 4.10 illustrates a graphic solution to the problem. The least cost solution would be to install the four-field precipitator on kilns producing 1,000,000 ($x = 1,000,000$) and the five-field precipitator on kilns producing 1,500,000 barrels of cement ($y = 1,500,000$) at a cost of $C = \$410,000$.

A further analysis of this problem is found in Example 5.5 on page 188.

A further analysis of this problem is found in Example 5.5 on page 188.

The example concerns reclaimed land and its allocation into two major uses—agricultural and urban (or nonagricultural). The

2.9
Example
An Application
to Urban
Economics[3]

[3] Maurice Yeates, *An Introduction to Quantitative Analysis in Economic Geography*, McGraw-Hill, New York, 1968.

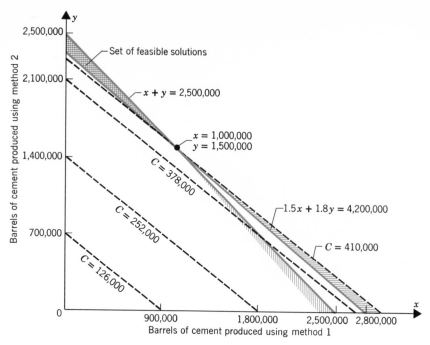

Figure 4.10

reclamation of land for urban purposes costs $400 per acre and for agricultural uses, $300. The primal problem is that the reclamation agency wishes to minimize the total cost $C$ of reclaiming the land

$$C = \$400x + \$300y$$

where $x =$ the number of acres of urban land and $y =$ the number of acres of agricultural land. Obviously this equation can be minimized by setting both $x$ and $y$ at zero, that is, reclaiming nothing, but the problem is subject to a number of constraints derived from three different groups.

The first is an urban group, which insists that at least 4000 acres of land be reclaimed for urban purposes. The second group is concerned with agriculture and says that at least 5000 acres of land must be reclaimed for agricultural uses. Finally, the third group is concerned only with reclamation and is quite disinterested in the use to which the land will be put. The third group, however, says that at least 10,000 acres of land must be reclaimed. The primal problem and the constraints can, therefore, be written in full as follows.

Minimize

$$C = \$400x + \$300y$$

**99**
4.2
A GEOMETRIC
APPROACH TO
LINEAR
PROGRAMMING
PROBLEMS

subject to

$$x \geqq 4000$$
$$y \geqq 5000$$
$$x + y \geqq 10,000$$

The graphic solution to this problem is presented in Figure 4.11.

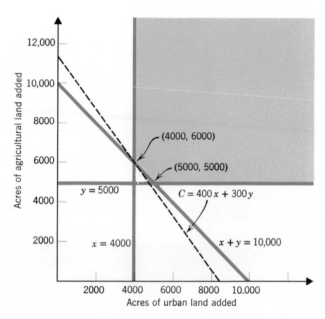

**Figure 4.11**

The combination of urban and agricultural land at the vertex $(4000, 6000)$ reveals that if 4000 acres are devoted to urban purposes and 6000 acres to agricultural purposes, the cost is a minimum and is

$$C = (\$400)(4000) + (\$300)(6000) = \$3,400,000$$

---

1. Maximize (if possible)

$$f = 5x + 7y$$

subject to the constraints
(a) $x \geqq 0, y \geqq 0, x + y \geqq 2$
(b) $x \geqq 0, y \geqq 0, x + y \geqq 2, 2x + 3y \leqq 6$
(c) $x \geqq 0, y \geqq 0, 2x + 3y \geqq 6$
(d) $x \geqq 0, y \geqq 0, x + y \geqq 2, 2x + 3y \leqq 12, 3x + y \leqq 12$
(e) $x \geqq 0, y \geqq 0, 2 \leqq x + y \leqq 8, 2x + y \leqq 10, 3x + y \leqq 12$
(f) $x \geqq 0, y \geqq 0, 2 \leqq x + y \leqq 8, 1 \leqq x + 2y \leqq 10$

2. Minimize (if possible)

$$f = 2x + 3y$$

subject to the constraints

(a) $x \geq 0$, $y \geq 0$

(b) $x \geq 0$, $y \geq 0$, $x + y \geq 2$

(c) $x \geq 0$, $y \geq 0$, $x + y \geq 2$, $2x + 3y \leq 12$, $3x + y \leq 12$

(d) $x \geq 0$, $y \geq 0$, $2 \leq x + y \leq 10$, $2x + 3y \leq 6$

(e) $x \geq 0$, $y \geq 0$, $1 \leq x + 2y \leq 10$

(f) $x \geq 0$, $y \geq 0$, $1 \leq x + 2y \leq 10$, $2 \leq x + y \leq 8$

3. Subject to the constraints

$$x \geq 0, \quad y \geq 0, \quad x + y \leq 10,$$
$$2x + y \geq 10, \quad x + 2y \geq 10$$

Maximize and minimize (if possible)

(a) $f = x + y$        (d) $f = 2x + 3y$

(b) $f = x + 2y$       (e) $f = 5x + 2y$

(c) $f = 3x + 4y$      (f) $f = 3x + 6y$

4. In Example 2.6 (page 93) if the profit on the low-grade mixture is $0.30 per package and the profit on the high-grade mixture is $0.40 per package, how many packages of each mixture should be made for a maximum profit?

5. Using the information supplied in Example 2.7, page 95, suppose the profit on each standard model is $4 and the profit on each deluxe model is $4. How many of each should be manufactured in order to maximize profit?

6. Using the information supplied in Example 2.7, page 95, suppose the profit on each standard model is $4 and on each deluxe model is $3. How many of each should be manufactured in order to maximize profits?

7. A factory manufactures two products, each requiring the use of three machines. The first machine can be used at most 70 hours; the second machine at most 40 hours; and the third machine at most 90 hours. The first product requires 2 hours on Machine 1, 1 hour on Machine 2, and 1 hour on Machine 3; the second product requires 1 hour each on Machines 1 and 2, and 3 hours on the third machine. If the profit is $40 per unit for the first product and is $60 per unit for the second product, how many units of each product should be manufactured to maximize profit?

8. A diet is to contain at least 400 units of vitamins, 500 units of minerals, and 1400 calories. There are available two foods $F_1$ and $F_2$ costing $0.05 per unit and $0.03 per unit, respectively. A unit of food $F_1$ contains 2 units of vitamins, 1 unit of minerals, and 4 calories; a unit of food $F_2$ contains 1 unit of vitamin, 2 units of mineral, and 4 calories. Find

**101**
4.2
A GEOMETRIC
APPROACH TO
LINEAR
PROGRAMMING
PROBLEMS

the minimum cost for a diet consisting of a mixture of these two foods which meets the minimal nutrition requirements.

9. Danny's Chicken Farm is a producer of frying chickens. In order to produce the best fryers possible, he supplements the regular chicken feed by four vitamins. The minimum amount required per 100 ounces of feed of each vitamin is Vitamin 1, 50 units; Vitamin 2, 100 units; Vitamin 3, 60 units; Vitamin 4, 180 units. Two kinds of supplement are available. Supplement I costs $0.03 per ounce and contains 5 units of Vitamin 1 per ounce, 25 units of Vitamin 2 per ounce, 10 units of Vitamin 3 per ounce, and 35 units of Vitamin 4 per ounce. Supplement II costs $0.04 per ounce and contains 25 units of Vitamin 1 per ounce, 10 units of Vitamin 2 per ounce, 10 units of Vitamin 3 per ounce, and 20 units of Vitamin 4 per ounce. How much of each supplement should he buy to add to each 100 ounces of feed in order to minimize his cost, but still have the desired vitamin amounts present?

10. Mr. Thomas, who owns a 100-acre farm, wants to plant crop A and crop B. The seed and other costs for crop A amount to $10 per acre and for crop B amount to $40 per acre. Expected profit from crop A is $40 per acre, and from crop B is $120 per acre. Labor for crop A is 2 man-days per acre and for crop B is 3 man-days per acre. If Mr. Thomas has a capital of $1100 and 160 man-days of labor to invest in his farm, how many acres of each crop should he plant to insure himself maximum profit? How much of his land should remain idle in order to maximize his profit?

*11. The J. B. Rug Manufacturers has available 1200 square yards of wool and 1000 square yards of nylon for the manufacture of two grades of carpeting: high-grade and low-grade that sell for $500 and $300 per roll, respectively. Twenty square yards of wool and 40 square yards of nylon are used in a roll of high-grade carpet and 40 square yards of nylon are used in a roll of low-grade carpet. Forty man-hours are required for each roll of the high-grade carpet and 20 man-hours for each roll of the low-grade carpet are needed, at an average cost of $6.00 per man-hour with a maximum of 800 man-hours available. The cost of wool is $5.00 a square yard and the cost of nylon is $2.00 a square yard. How many rolls of each type of carpet should be manufactured to maximize income?

Hint:

Income = revenue from sale − production cost
(material + labor)

*12. Maximize

$$f = 2x + y + 3z$$

subject to

$$x + 2y + z \leq 25$$
$$3x + 2y + 3z \leq 30$$
$$x \geq 0, \quad y \geq 0, \quad z \geq 0$$

Hint: Solve the constraints three at a time and find those points that are in the set of feasible solutions and test each of them in the objective function. Assume a solution exists.

CHAPTER
REVIEW

Important
Terms

mathematical program
linear program
linear programming problem
objective function
polyhedral set
convex set

feasible solution
constraints
vertex
polyhedral convex set
solution of a linear programming
  problem

Review
Exercises

1. Maximize and minimize (if possible) the objective function

$$f = 15x + 20y$$

subject to the conditions

(a) $3x + 4y \leq 12$
   $x \geq 0, \quad y \geq 0$

(b) $x + 2y \leq 40$
   $x - 3y \geq 20$
   $x \geq 0, \quad y \geq 0$

(c) $5x + 2y \leq 30$
   $x + y \leq 9$
   $x \geq 0, \quad y \geq 0$

(d) $x + y \geq 5$
   $x + y \leq 20$
   $x \geq 0, \quad y \geq 0$

2. Maximize and minimize the objective function

$$f = 5x + 2y$$

subject to the conditions of Problem 1.

3. Katy needs at least 60 units of carbohydrates, 45 units of protein and 30 units of fat each month. From each pound of Food A, she receives 5 units of carbohydrates, 3 of protein and 4 of fat. Food B contains, respectively, 2, 2 and 1 units of carbohydrates, protein and fat per pound. If Food A costs $1.30 per pound and Food B costs $0.80 per pound, how many pounds of each food should Katy buy each month to keep costs at a minimum?

# 5

# INTRODUCTION TO MATRIX ALGEBRA WITH APPLICATIONS

There are many situations in both pure and applied mathematics that deal with rectangular arrays of numbers or functions. In fact in many branches of business, biological and social sciences, it is necessary for scientists to express and use a set of numbers in a rectangular array.

In this chapter we survey briefly a branch of mathematics called *linear algebra*. Linear algebra deals with generalizations of numbers, called *vectors and matrices*. These generalizations are made in such a way that most of the algebraic properties of the real numbers are retained.

| | Sedan Model | Hard-top Model | Convertible Model |
|---|---|---|---|
| Units of material | 23 | 16 | 10 |
| Units of labor | 7 | 9 | 11 |

**Figure 5.1**

1.1<br>Example

Motors Incorporated produces three models of cars: a sedan, a hard-top, and a convertible. If the company wishes to compare the units of raw material and the units of labor involved in one month's production of each of these models, a rectangular array could be used to present the data (see Figure 5.1). If the pattern in which the units and models are recorded in Figure 5.1 is retained, this array may be presented simply by

$$A = \begin{pmatrix} 23 & 16 & 10 \\ 7 & 9 & 11 \end{pmatrix}$$

In this example, the array, called a *matrix*, has two rows (the units) and three columns (the models).

1.2<br>Example

The following are all examples of matrices.

$$A = \begin{pmatrix} 1 & \frac{1}{2} \\ 0 & 2 \end{pmatrix} \qquad B = \begin{pmatrix} 2 \\ -5 \end{pmatrix}$$

$$C = \begin{pmatrix} 0.01 & 0.02 & 0.07 \\ 0.1 & 0.9 & 0 \end{pmatrix} \qquad D = (1.2 \quad 5)$$

The matrix $A$ has two rows and two columns; the matrix $B$ has two rows and one column; $C$ has two rows and three columns; and matrix $D$ has one row and two columns.

**Definition of a Matrix**

**A** *matrix* $A$ **is a rectangular array of elements** $a_{ij}$ **of the form**

$$j\text{th column}$$

$$A = \begin{pmatrix} a_{11} & a_{12} & \cdots & a_{1j} & \cdots & a_{1m} \\ a_{21} & a_{22} & \cdots & a_{2j} & \cdots & a_{2m} \\ \vdots & \vdots & & \vdots & & \vdots \\ a_{i1} & a_{i2} & \cdots & a_{ij} & \cdots & a_{im} \\ \vdots & \vdots & & \vdots & & \vdots \\ a_{n1} & a_{n2} & \cdots & a_{nj} & \cdots & a_{nm} \end{pmatrix} i\text{th row}$$

(1.1)

**in which the** $a_{ij}$ **are** $n \cdot m$ **real numbers.**

Each element $a_{ij}$ of the matrix $A$ has two indices: the *row index, i,* and the *column index, j.* The symbols $a_{i1}, a_{i2}, \ldots, a_{im}$ represent the elements of the *i*th row, and the symbols $a_{1j}, a_{2j}, \ldots, a_{nj}$ represent the elements of the *j*th column.

Row

Column

For convenience, matrices will be denoted by capital letters and the elements (also called *entries* or *components*) will be denoted by small letters corresponding to the capital letter denoting the matrix. Thus, the matrix $A$ of (1.1) can be abbreviated by

$$A = (a_{ij}) \qquad i = 1, 2, \ldots, n; \qquad j = 1, 2, \ldots, m$$

which has $n$ rows and $m$ columns.

**The *dimension of a matrix A* is determined by the number of rows and the number of columns of the matrix. If a matrix $A$ has $n$ rows and $m$ columns, we denote the dimension of $A$ by $n \times m$, read as "n by m."**

Definition
of
Dimension
of a
Matrix

For a $2 \times 3$ matrix, it is important to remember that the first number 2 denotes the number of rows and the second number 3 is the number of columns. A matrix with 3 rows and 2 columns is of dimension $3 \times 2$.

Let $A = (a_{ij})$ be a matrix of dimension $n \times m$, $i = 1, \ldots, n$; $j = 1, \ldots, m$. The entries of $A$ for which $i = j$, namely, $a_{11}, a_{22}, a_{33}, a_{44}$, and so on, form the *diagonal of A.*

Diagonal Entries

**If a matrix $A$ has the same number of rows as it has columns, it is called a *square matrix.***

Definition
of a
Square
Matrix

Examples of square matrices are

$$\begin{pmatrix} 1 & 0 \\ 0 & 1 \end{pmatrix} \qquad \begin{pmatrix} 3 & -5 & 1 \\ 6 & 4 & 0 \\ 1 & 2 & 1 \end{pmatrix} \qquad \begin{pmatrix} 6 & 2 & \frac{1}{2} & 5 \\ 0 & 3 & 1 & 9 \\ 1 & 0 & \frac{3}{4} & 1 \\ 5 & -1 & 0 & 1 \end{pmatrix}$$

$\qquad 2 \times 2 \qquad\qquad 3 \times 3 \qquad\qquad 4 \times 4$

The diagonal entries of the $2 \times 2$ matrix are 1, 1; of the $3 \times 3$ matrix are 3, 4, 1; and the $4 \times 4$ matrix are 6, 3, 3/4, 1.

In a recent U.S. Census, the following figures were obtained with regard to the city of Glenwood. Each year 7 percent of city residents move to the suburbs and 1 percent of the people in the suburbs move to the city. This situation can be represented by the transition matrix

1.3
Example

$$P = \begin{array}{c} \\ \text{City} \\ \text{Suburbs} \end{array} \begin{array}{cc} \text{City} & \text{Suburbs} \\ \begin{pmatrix} 0.93 & 0.07 \\ 0.01 & 0.99 \end{pmatrix} \end{array}$$

Here the entry in row 1, column 2, 0.07, indicates that 7 percent of city residents move to the suburbs. The matrix $P$ is a square matrix and its dimension is $2 \times 2$. The diagonal entries are 0.93 and 0.99.

**Definition of a Row Matrix and Column Matrix**

A *row matrix* **is a matrix with one row of elements. A** *column matrix* **is a matrix with one column of elements.**

**Row Vector**

**Column Vector**

Row matrices and column matrices are usually referred to as *row vectors* and *column vectors,* respectively.

**1.4 Example**

The matrices

$$A = (23 \quad 16 \quad 10) \qquad B = (7 \quad 9)$$

$$C = \begin{pmatrix} 23 \\ -1 \\ 7 \end{pmatrix} \qquad D = \begin{pmatrix} 16 \\ 9 \end{pmatrix} \qquad E = (10)$$

have the dimensions $A$: $1 \times 3$, $B$: $1 \times 2$, $C$: $3 \times 1$, $D$: $2 \times 1$, $E$: $1 \times 1$. Here, $A$, $B$, and $E$ are row vectors and $C$, $D$, and $E$ are column vectors.

The matrix $E = (10)$ is a $1 \times 1$ matrix and, as such, can be treated as merely a real number. That is, $E = (10) = 10$, the real number 10.

As with most mathematical quantities, we now want to ask about relationships between two matrices. We might ask, "When, if at all, are two matrices equal?"

Let us try to arrive at a sound definition for equality of matrices by requiring equal matrices to have certain desirable properties. First, it would seem necessary that two equal matrices have the same dimension, that is, that they both be $n \times m$ matrices. Next, it would seem necessary that their entries be identical numbers. With these two restrictions, we define equality of matrices.

**Definition of Equality of Matrices**

**Two matrices $A$ and $B$ are** *equal* **if they are of the same dimension and if corresponding entries are equal. In this case, we write $A = B$, read as "matrix $A$ is equal to matrix $B$."**

In order for the two matrices

$$A = \begin{pmatrix} p & q \\ 1 & 0 \end{pmatrix} \quad \text{and} \quad B = \begin{pmatrix} \frac{1}{2} & \frac{1}{2} \\ n & 0 \end{pmatrix}$$

to be equal, we must have $p = 1/2$, $q = 1/2$, and $n = 1$.

Let $A$ and $B$ be the two matrices given by

$$A = \begin{pmatrix} x + 2 \\ 3y - 7 \end{pmatrix} \quad B = \begin{pmatrix} 4 - y \\ x - 3 \end{pmatrix}$$

Find $x$ and $y$ so that $A = B$.

It is important to recognize that both $A$ and $B$ are $2 \times 1$ matrices—or column vectors. Thus, the entry $x + 2$ is a single number.

Now, from the Definition of Equality, $A = B$ if and only if

$$x + 2 = 4 - y \quad \text{and} \quad 3y - 7 = x - 3$$

Here we have two equations in two unknowns $x$ and $y$. Solving them, we see that the solutions are

$$x = \frac{1}{2}, \quad y = \frac{3}{2}$$

We check this solution by substituting in $A$ and $B$.

$$A = \begin{pmatrix} \frac{1}{2} + 2 \\ 3 \cdot \frac{3}{2} - 7 \end{pmatrix} = \begin{pmatrix} \frac{5}{2} \\ -\frac{5}{2} \end{pmatrix}, \quad B = \begin{pmatrix} 4 - \frac{3}{2} \\ \frac{1}{2} - 3 \end{pmatrix} = \begin{pmatrix} \frac{5}{2} \\ -\frac{5}{2} \end{pmatrix}$$

Let $A$ and $B$ be two matrices given by

$$A = \begin{pmatrix} x + y & 6 \\ 2x - 3 & 2 - y \end{pmatrix} \quad B = \begin{pmatrix} 5 & 5x + 2 \\ y & x - y \end{pmatrix}$$

Find $x$ and $y$ so that $A$ and $B$ are equal.
$A$ and $B$ are both $2 \times 2$ matrices. Thus, $A = B$ if and only if

(a) $x + y = 5$      (c) $2x - 3 = y$
(b) $5x + 2 = 6$      (d) $2 - y = x - y$

Here we have four equations in the two unknowns $x$ and $y$. From equation (d), we see that $x = 2$. Using this value in equation (a), we obtain $y = 3$. But $x = 2$, $y = 3$ do not satisfy either (b) or (c). Hence, there are *no* values for $x$ and $y$ satisfying all four equations. This means $A$ and $B$ can never be equal. That is,

$$A \neq B.$$

1. Find the dimension of the following matrices:

(a) $A = \begin{pmatrix} 2 & 1 & -3 \\ 1 & 0 & -1 \end{pmatrix}$
(d) $A = \begin{pmatrix} 1 & 2 \\ 2 & 1 \\ 1 & 2 \end{pmatrix}$

(b) $A = \begin{pmatrix} 4 \\ 1 \end{pmatrix}$
(e) $A = \begin{pmatrix} 5 & -7 & 2 & 5 \\ \dfrac{1}{3} & -\dfrac{1}{2} & 6 & 4 \end{pmatrix}$

(c) $A = (2 \ \ 1 \ \ -3)$
(f) $A = (2)$

2. XYZ Company produces steel and aluminum nails. One week, 25 gross 1/2-inch steel nails and 45 gross 1-inch steel nails were produced. Suppose, 13 gross 1/2-inch and 20 gross 1-inch aluminum nails and 35 gross 2-inch steel and 23 gross 2-inch aluminum nails were also made. Write a 2 × 3 matrix depicting this. Could you also write a 3 × 2 matrix for this situation?

3. Katy, Mike, and Danny go to the candy store. Katy buys 5 sticks of gum, 2 ice cream cones, and 10 jelly beans. Mike buys 2 sticks of gum, 15 jelly beans, and 2 candy bars. Danny buys 1 stick of gum, 1 ice cream cone, and 4 candy bars. Write a matrix depicting this situation.

4. Find $x$ so that the matrices

$$A = \begin{pmatrix} x \\ 3 \end{pmatrix} \qquad B = \begin{pmatrix} 4 \\ 3 \end{pmatrix}$$

are equal.

5. Find $x$, $y$, and $z$ so that the matrices

$$A = \begin{pmatrix} x + y & 2 \\ 4 & 0 \end{pmatrix} \qquad B = \begin{pmatrix} 6 & x - y \\ 4 & z \end{pmatrix}$$

are equal.

6. Find $x$ and $y$ so that the matrices

$$A = \begin{pmatrix} x - 2y & 0 \\ -2 & 6 \end{pmatrix} \qquad B = \begin{pmatrix} 3 & 0 \\ -2 & x + y \end{pmatrix}$$

are equal.

7. Find $x$, $y$, and $z$ so that the matrices

$$A = \begin{pmatrix} x - 2 & 3 & 2z \\ 6y & x & 2y \end{pmatrix} \qquad B = \begin{pmatrix} y & z & 6 \\ 18z & y + 2 & 6z \end{pmatrix}$$

are equal.

Thus far we have discussed the concept of equality of matrices. Can two matrices be added? And, if so, what is the rule or law for addition of matrices?

Let us return to Example 1.1, page 104. In that example, we recorded one month's production of Motors Incorporated with the matrix

$$A = \begin{pmatrix} 23 & 16 & 10 \\ 7 & 9 & 11 \end{pmatrix}$$

Suppose the next month's production is

$$B = \begin{pmatrix} 18 & 12 & 9 \\ 14 & 6 & 8 \end{pmatrix}$$

in which the pattern of recording units and models remains the same.
   The total production for the two months can be displayed by the matrix

$$C = \begin{pmatrix} 41 & 28 & 19 \\ 21 & 15 & 19 \end{pmatrix}$$

since the number of units of material for sedan models is $41 = 23 + 18$; the number of units of material for hard-top models is $28 = 16 + 12$; and so on.
   This leads us to define the sum $A + B$ of two matrices $A$ and $B$ as merely that matrix consisting of the sum of corresponding entries from $A$ and $B$.

**Let $A = (a_{ij})$ and $B = (b_{ij})$ be two $n \times m$ matrices. The *sum* $A + B$ is defined as the $n \times m$ matrix $(a_{ij} + b_{ij})$.**

Definition
of Addition of
Matrices

Notice that it is possible to add two matrices only if their dimensions are the same. Also, the dimension of the sum of two matrices is the same as that of the two original matrices.
   Using the matrices given previously, we see that

$$A + B = \begin{pmatrix} 23 & 16 & 10 \\ 7 & 9 & 11 \end{pmatrix} + \begin{pmatrix} 18 & 12 & 9 \\ 14 & 6 & 8 \end{pmatrix}$$

$$= \begin{pmatrix} 23 + 18 & 16 + 12 & 10 + 9 \\ 7 + 14 & 9 + 6 & 11 + 8 \end{pmatrix}$$

$$= \begin{pmatrix} 41 & 28 & 19 \\ 21 & 15 & 19 \end{pmatrix} = C$$

The following pairs of matrices cannot be added since they are of different dimensions.

(a) $A = \begin{pmatrix} 1 & 2 \\ 7 & 2 \end{pmatrix}, \qquad B = \begin{pmatrix} 1 \\ -3 \end{pmatrix}$

(b) $A = (2 \quad 3), \qquad B = (1 \quad 1 \quad 1)$

(c) $A = \begin{pmatrix} -1 & 7 & 0 \\ 2 & \frac{1}{2} & 0 \end{pmatrix}, \qquad B = \begin{pmatrix} -1 & 2 \\ 3 & 0 \\ 1 & 5 \end{pmatrix}$

Now that we have a definition for adding two matrices, we would like to find out whether the usual rules for addition of numbers (e.g., commutative laws, associative laws) are also valid for matrix addition. As it turns out, matrix addition and addition of numbers have the same properties.

### Theorem 2.1
**If $A$ and $B$ are two matrices of the same dimension then**

$$A + B = B + A$$

**That is, matrix addition is** *commutative.*

2.1
Example
Let

$$A = \begin{pmatrix} 1 & 5 \\ 7 & -3 \end{pmatrix}, \qquad B = \begin{pmatrix} 3 & -2 \\ 4 & 1 \end{pmatrix}$$

Then

$$A + B = \begin{pmatrix} 1 & 5 \\ 7 & -3 \end{pmatrix} + \begin{pmatrix} 3 & -2 \\ 4 & 1 \end{pmatrix} = \begin{pmatrix} 1+3 & 5+(-2) \\ 7+4 & -3+1 \end{pmatrix}$$

$$= \begin{pmatrix} 4 & 3 \\ 11 & -2 \end{pmatrix}$$

$$B + A = \begin{pmatrix} 3 & -2 \\ 4 & 1 \end{pmatrix} + \begin{pmatrix} 1 & 5 \\ 7 & -3 \end{pmatrix} = \begin{pmatrix} 4 & 3 \\ 11 & -2 \end{pmatrix}$$

### Theorem 2.2
**If $A, B, C$, are three matrices of the same dimension, then**

$$A + (B + C) = (A + B) + C$$

**That is, matrix addition is** *associative.*

Proof
Let

$$A = (a_{ij}), \qquad B = (b_{ij}), \qquad C = (c_{ij})$$

Then
$$\begin{aligned}
A + [B + C] &= (a_{ij}) + [(b_{ij}) + (c_{ij})] = (a_{ij}) + [(b_{ij} + c_{ij})] \\
&= (a_{ij}) + (b_{ij} + c_{ij}) = (a_{ij} + b_{ij} + c_{ij}) \\
&= [(a_{ij} + b_{ij})] + (c_{ij}) = [(a_{ij}) + (b_{ij})] + (c_{ij}) \\
&= [A + B] + C
\end{aligned}$$

In the proof, we used the fact that addition of real numbers is associative. Where?

The fact that addition of matrices is associative means that the notation $A + B + C$ is *not* ambiguous, since $(A + B) + C = A + (B + C)$.

A matrix in which all entries are zero is called a *zero matrix*. We use the symbol $\theta$ to represent a zero matrix of any dimension.

An important property of a zero matrix $\theta$ is that whenever it is added to a matrix $A$ the result is $A$. In this case, the dimension of $\theta$ must be the same as that of $A$.

Theorem 2.3

**Let $A$ be an $n \times m$ matrix. Then**

$$A + \theta = A$$

Proof

Let $A = (a_{ij})$. Then

$$A + \theta = (a_{ij}) + (0) = (a_{ij} + 0) = (a_{ij}) = A$$

If

2.2
Example

$$A = \begin{pmatrix} 3 & 4 & -\dfrac{1}{2} \\ \sqrt{2} & 0 & 3 \end{pmatrix}$$

$$A + \theta = \begin{pmatrix} 3 & 4 & -\dfrac{1}{2} \\ \sqrt{2} & 0 & 3 \end{pmatrix} + \begin{pmatrix} 0 & 0 & 0 \\ 0 & 0 & 0 \end{pmatrix}$$

$$= \begin{pmatrix} 3+0 & 4+0 & -\dfrac{1}{2}+0 \\ \sqrt{2}+0 & 0+0 & 3+0 \end{pmatrix} = \begin{pmatrix} 3 & 4 & -\dfrac{1}{2} \\ \sqrt{2} & 0 & 3 \end{pmatrix} = A$$

With the sum of two matrices having been defined, it is natural to ask about the *difference* of two matrices. As will be seen, subtracting matrices and subtracting numbers are much the same kind of process.

**Let $A = (a_{ij})$ and $B = (b_{ij})$ be two $n \times m$ matrices. The *difference* $B - A$ is defined as the $n \times m$ matrix $X$ for which**

$$A + X = B$$

Suppose

2.3
Example

$$A = \begin{pmatrix} 2 & 3 & 4 \\ 1 & 0 & 2 \end{pmatrix}, \qquad B = \begin{pmatrix} -2 & 1 & -1 \\ 3 & 0 & 3 \end{pmatrix}$$

To find $X = B - A$, let

$$X = \begin{pmatrix} a & b & c \\ d & e & f \end{pmatrix}$$

Then

$$A + X = \begin{pmatrix} 2 + a & 3 + b & 4 + c \\ 1 + d & e & 2 + f \end{pmatrix} = \begin{pmatrix} -2 & 1 & -1 \\ 3 & 0 & 3 \end{pmatrix}$$

That is

$$
\begin{array}{lll}
2 + a = -2 & \text{or} & a = -4 \\
3 + b = 1 & \text{or} & b = -2 \\
4 + c = -1 & \text{or} & c = -5 \\
1 + d = 3 & \text{or} & d = 2 \\
e = 0 & \text{or} & e = 0 \\
2 + f = 3 & \text{or} & f = 1
\end{array}
$$

Thus

$$X = B - A = \begin{pmatrix} -4 & -2 & -5 \\ 2 & 0 & 1 \end{pmatrix}$$

Notice that $B - A$ is nothing more than the matrix formed by subtracting the entries in $A$ from the corresponding entries in $B$. That is, the easy way to compute $B - A$ is

$$B - A = \begin{pmatrix} -2 & 1 & -1 \\ 3 & 0 & 3 \end{pmatrix} - \begin{pmatrix} 2 & 3 & 4 \\ 1 & 0 & 2 \end{pmatrix}$$

$$= \begin{pmatrix} -2 - 2 & 1 - 3 & -1 - 4 \\ 3 - 1 & 0 - 0 & 3 - 2 \end{pmatrix} = \begin{pmatrix} -4 & -2 & -5 \\ 2 & 0 & 1 \end{pmatrix}$$

**5.2
Exercise**

1. If

$$A = \begin{pmatrix} 2 & -\dfrac{1}{2} & -\dfrac{1}{3} \\ 6 & 4 & \dfrac{2}{3} \end{pmatrix}, \qquad B = \begin{pmatrix} -2 & 6 & 0 \\ 3 & -1 & \dfrac{2}{3} \end{pmatrix}$$

$$C = \begin{pmatrix} -3 & \dfrac{1}{2} & \dfrac{2}{3} \\ -2 & 0 & \dfrac{1}{3} \end{pmatrix},$$

find

(a) $A + B$      (d) $A - B$
(b) $(A + B) + C$      (e) $C - B$
(c) $A + (C + B)$      (f) $(C + A) + B$

2. Find $x$, $y$, and $z$ so that

$$(2 \quad 3 \quad -4) + (x \quad y \quad z) = (6 \quad -8 \quad 2)$$

3. Find $x$ and $y$ so that

$$\begin{pmatrix} 3 & -\frac{1}{2} & 2 \\ 1 & 0 & -1 \end{pmatrix} + \begin{pmatrix} x-y & \frac{1}{2} & -2 \\ 4 & x & 6 \end{pmatrix} = \begin{pmatrix} 6 & 0 & 0 \\ 5 & 2x+y & 5 \end{pmatrix}$$

4. Prove Theorem 2.1.

As we shall see, there will be two kinds of multiplication involving matrices. We can multiply a real number and a matrix, *scalar multiplication;* and we can multiply two matrices, *matrix multiplication.*

Before defining what the meaning of scalar multiplication is, let us return to the production of Motors Incorporated during the month specified in Example 1.1, page 104. You may recall the matrix $A$ describing this production is

$$A = \begin{pmatrix} 23 & 16 & 10 \\ 7 & 9 & 11 \end{pmatrix}$$

Let us assume that for 3 consecutive months, the monthly production remained the same. Then the total production for the 3 months is merely the sum of the matrix $A$ 3 times. If we represent the total production by the matrix $T$, then

$$T = \begin{pmatrix} 23 & 16 & 10 \\ 7 & 9 & 11 \end{pmatrix} + \begin{pmatrix} 23 & 16 & 10 \\ 7 & 9 & 11 \end{pmatrix} + \begin{pmatrix} 23 & 16 & 10 \\ 7 & 9 & 11 \end{pmatrix}$$

$$= \begin{pmatrix} 23 + 23 + 23 & 16 + 16 + 16 & 10 + 10 + 10 \\ 7 + 7 + 7 & 9 + 9 + 9 & 11 + 11 + 11 \end{pmatrix}$$

$$= \begin{pmatrix} 3 \cdot 23 & 3 \cdot 16 & 3 \cdot 10 \\ 3 \cdot 7 & 3 \cdot 9 & 3 \cdot 11 \end{pmatrix} = \begin{pmatrix} 69 & 48 & 30 \\ 21 & 27 & 33 \end{pmatrix}$$

In other words, when we add the matrix $A$ 3 times, we merely multiply each entry of $A$ by 3. This leads to the following definition of scalar multiplication.

**Let $A = (a_{ij})$ be an $n \times m$ matrix and let $c$ be a real number. The** *scalar product $cA$ of the matrix $A$ and the real number $c$* **(called the** *scalar)* **is the $n \times m$ matrix $cA = (ca_{ij})$.**

Definition
of Scalar
Product

Thus, when multiplying a scalar times a matrix, each entry of the matrix is multiplied by the scalar. Notice that the dimension of $A$ and the dimension of the scalar product $cA$ are the same.

Let

$$A = \begin{pmatrix} 2 \\ 5 \\ -7 \end{pmatrix} \qquad B = \begin{pmatrix} 21 & 1 \\ 18 & 8 \end{pmatrix}$$

Then

$$3A = 3 \begin{pmatrix} 2 \\ 5 \\ -7 \end{pmatrix} = \begin{pmatrix} 3 \cdot 2 \\ 3 \cdot 5 \\ 3 \cdot -7 \end{pmatrix} = \begin{pmatrix} 6 \\ 15 \\ -21 \end{pmatrix}$$

and

$$\frac{1}{2}B = \frac{1}{2} \begin{pmatrix} 21 & 1 \\ 18 & 8 \end{pmatrix} = \begin{pmatrix} \frac{1}{2} \cdot 21 & \frac{1}{2} \cdot 1 \\ \frac{1}{2} \cdot 18 & \frac{1}{2} \cdot 8 \end{pmatrix} = \begin{pmatrix} \frac{21}{2} & \frac{1}{2} \\ 9 & 4 \end{pmatrix}$$

Let

$$A = \begin{pmatrix} 3 & 1 \\ 4 & 0 \\ 2 & -3 \end{pmatrix} \qquad B = \begin{pmatrix} 2 & -3 \\ -1 & 1 \\ 1 & 0 \end{pmatrix}$$

Then

$$A - B = \begin{pmatrix} 1 & 4 \\ 5 & -1 \\ 1 & -3 \end{pmatrix}$$

Also

$$A + (-1) \cdot B = \begin{pmatrix} 3 & 1 \\ 4 & 0 \\ 2 & -3 \end{pmatrix} + \begin{pmatrix} -2 & 3 \\ 1 & -1 \\ -1 & 0 \end{pmatrix} = \begin{pmatrix} 1 & 4 \\ 5 & -1 \\ 1 & -3 \end{pmatrix}$$

The above example illustrates the result

$$A - B = A + (-1) \cdot B$$

To arrive at a definition for multiplying two matrices, we consider the following example.

Using the data of one month's production of Motors Incorporated from Example 1.1, page 104, we have

|  | Sedan | Hard-top | Convertible |  |
|---|---|---|---|---|
| $A = $ | 23 | 16 | 10 | Units of material |
|  | 7 | 9 | 11 | Units of labor |

Suppose that in this month's production, the cost for each unit of material is \$45 and the cost for each unit of labor is \$60. What is the total cost to manufacture the sedans, the hard tops, and the convertibles?

For sedans, the cost is 23 units of material at $45 each plus 7 units of labor at $60 each for a total cost of

$$23 \cdot 45 + 7 \cdot 60 = 1035 + 420 = 1455$$

Similarly, for hard tops, the total cost is

$$16 \cdot 45 + 9 \cdot 60 = 720 + 540 = 1260$$

Finally, for convertibles, the total cost is

$$10 \cdot 45 + 11 \cdot 60 = 450 + 660 = 1110$$

We can represent the total cost for sedans, hard tops, and convertibles by the matrix

$$(1455 \quad 1260 \quad 1110)$$

If we represent the cost of units of material and the units of labor by the row vector

$$U = (45 \quad 60)$$

the total cost of units for sedans, hard tops, and convertibles will then be $U \cdot A$. Now $U \cdot A$ is computed as follows.

$$U \cdot A = (45 \quad 60) \cdot \begin{pmatrix} 23 & 16 & 10 \\ 7 & 9 & 11 \end{pmatrix}$$

$$= (45 \cdot 23 + 60 \cdot 7 \quad 45 \cdot 16 + 60 \cdot 9 \quad 45 \cdot 10 + 60 \cdot 11)$$
$$= (1455 \quad 1260 \quad 1110)$$

In this example, notice that the number of columns of $U$ is the same as the number of rows of $A$. Also, the number of rows of $U$ is the same as the number of rows of the product $U \cdot A$ and the number of columns of $A$ is the same as the number of columns of the product $U \cdot A$. With this in mind, we define the product of two matrices.

**Let $A = (a_{ij})$ be a matrix of dimension $n \times m$ and let $B = (b_{jk})$ be a matrix of dimension $m \times p$. The product $A \cdot B$ is the matrix $C = (c_{ik})$ of dimension $n \times p$ where the $ik$th entry of $C$ is**    Definition of Matrix Multiplication

$$c_{ik} = a_{i1}b_{1k} + a_{i2}b_{2k} + a_{i3}b_{3k} + \cdots + a_{im}b_{mk}$$

The element in the $i$th row and $k$th column of $C$, namely, $c_{ik}$, is obtained by summing the products of the elements of the $i$th row of $A$ and the corresponding elements of the $k$th column of $B$.

The rule for multiplication of matrices is best illustrated by examples.

Let    3.4 Example

$$A = \begin{pmatrix} 1 & 3 & -2 \\ 4 & -1 & 5 \end{pmatrix}, \qquad B = \begin{pmatrix} 2 & -3 & 4 & 1 \\ -1 & 2 & 2 & 0 \\ 4 & 5 & 1 & 1 \end{pmatrix}$$

Here $A$ is $2 \times 3$ and $B$ is $3 \times 4$. The product $A \cdot B$ will be $2 \times 4$.

For example, the entry in row 2, column 3 of $A \cdot B$ is obtained by multiplying the entries in row 2 of $A$ by the corresponding entries in column 3 of $B$ and adding. That is,

$$\begin{pmatrix} 1 & 3 & -2 \\ 4 & -1 & 5 \end{pmatrix} \begin{pmatrix} 2 & -3 & 4 & 1 \\ -1 & 2 & 2 & 0 \\ 4 & 5 & 1 & 1 \end{pmatrix}$$

| Row 2 of $A$ | Column 3 of $B$ | Product |
|---|---|---|
| 4 | 4 | 16 |
| $-1$ | 2 | $-2$ |
| 5 | 1 | 5 |
| | | Sum $\overline{\phantom{0}19}$ |

entry in row 2, column 3 of $A \cdot B$.

Thus,

$$A \cdot B = \begin{pmatrix} 1 \cdot 2 + 3(-1) + (-2)4 & 1(-3) + 3 \cdot 2 + (-2)5 \\ 4 \cdot 2 + (-1)(-1) + 5 \cdot 4 & 4(-3) + (-1)2 + 5 \cdot 5 \end{pmatrix}$$

$$\begin{matrix} 1 \cdot 4 + 3 \cdot 2 + (-2)1 & 1 \cdot 1 + 3 \cdot 0 + (-2) \cdot 1 \\ 4 \cdot 4 + (-1)2 + 5 \cdot 1 & 4 \cdot 1 + (-1) \cdot 0 + 5 \cdot 1 \end{matrix}$$

$$= \begin{pmatrix} -9 & -7 & 8 & -1 \\ 29 & 11 & 19 & 9 \end{pmatrix}$$

3.5
Example

Let

$$A = \begin{pmatrix} 2 & -1 & 2 \\ 1 & 2 & -4 \\ 3 & -1 & 1 \end{pmatrix} \qquad B = \begin{pmatrix} x \\ y \\ z \end{pmatrix}$$

Here $A$ is $3 \times 3$ and $B$ is $3 \times 1$. The product $A \cdot B$ is $3 \times 1$ and is

$$A \cdot B = \begin{pmatrix} 2 & -1 & 2 \\ 1 & 2 & -4 \\ 3 & -1 & 1 \end{pmatrix} \begin{pmatrix} x \\ y \\ z \end{pmatrix} = \begin{pmatrix} 2x - y + 2z \\ x + 2y - 4z \\ 3x - y + z \end{pmatrix}$$

If $A$ is a matrix of dimension $n \times m$ (which has $m$ columns) and $B$ is a matrix of dimension $p \times q$ (which has $p$ rows) and if $m \neq p$, there is *no* product $A \cdot B$ defined. That is, multiplication of matrices is possible only if the number of columns of the first equals the number of rows of the second. Otherwise, it is impossible.

If $A$ is of dimension $n \times m$ and if $B$ is of dimension $m \times p$, then the product $A \cdot B$ can be found and the product matrix is of dimension $n \times p$. See Figure 5.2. Because of this requirement for multiplying matrices, it may be possible to find the product $A \cdot B$ of two matrices, although it is impossible to find $B \cdot A$. The matrices in Example 3.4 illustrate this.

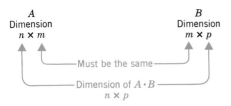

*A*
Dimension
$n \times m$

*B*
Dimension
$m \times p$

Must be the same

Dimension of $A \cdot B$
$n \times p$

**Figure 5.2**

We continue our study of scalar multiplication and matrix multiplication by listing some of the properties obeyed.

Theorem 3.1
**Let $k$ and $h$ be two real numbers and let $A = (a_{ij})$ and $B = (b_{ij})$, $i = 1, \ldots, n, j = 1, \ldots, m$ be matrices of dimension $n \times m$. Then**

| | |
|---|---|
| **(I)** | $k[hA] = [kh]A$ |
| **(II)** | $[k + h]A = kA + hA$ |
| **(III)** | $k[A + B] = kA + kB$ |

Proof
(I) Here

$$k[hA] = k[h(a_{ij})] = k[(ha_{ij})] = k(ha_{ij})$$
$$= (kha_{ij}) = [kh](a_{ij})$$

(II) For this property we have

$$[k + h]A = [k + h](a_{ij}) = ([k + h]a_{ij})$$
$$= (ka_{ij} + ha_{ij}) = (ka_{ij}) + (ha_{ij})$$
$$= k(a_{ij}) + h(a_{ij}) = kA + hA$$

(III) This is left for the student.

The three properties listed above in Theorem 3.1 are illustrated in the following example:

Let

3.6
Example

$$A = \begin{pmatrix} 2 & -3 & -1 \\ 5 & 6 & 4 \end{pmatrix}, \qquad B = \begin{pmatrix} -3 & 0 & 4 \\ 2 & -1 & 5 \end{pmatrix}$$

Then

(I) $\quad 5(2A) = 5\begin{pmatrix} 4 & -6 & -2 \\ 10 & 12 & 8 \end{pmatrix} = \begin{pmatrix} 20 & -30 & -10 \\ 50 & 60 & 40 \end{pmatrix}$

$$10A = \begin{pmatrix} 20 & -30 & -10 \\ 50 & 60 & 40 \end{pmatrix}$$

Also

(II) $\qquad (4 + 3)A = 7A = \begin{pmatrix} 14 & -21 & -7 \\ 35 & 42 & 28 \end{pmatrix}$

$$4A + 3A = \begin{pmatrix} 8 & -12 & -4 \\ 20 & 24 & 16 \end{pmatrix} + \begin{pmatrix} 6 & -9 & -3 \\ 15 & 18 & 12 \end{pmatrix}$$

$$= \begin{pmatrix} 14 & -21 & -7 \\ 35 & 42 & 28 \end{pmatrix}$$

Finally

(III) $\qquad 3(A + B) = 3\begin{pmatrix} -1 & -3 & 3 \\ 7 & 5 & 9 \end{pmatrix} = \begin{pmatrix} -3 & -9 & 9 \\ 21 & 15 & 27 \end{pmatrix}$

$$3A + 3B = \begin{pmatrix} 6 & -9 & -3 \\ 15 & 18 & 12 \end{pmatrix} + \begin{pmatrix} -9 & 0 & 12 \\ 6 & -3 & 15 \end{pmatrix}$$

$$= \begin{pmatrix} -3 & -9 & 9 \\ 21 & 15 & 27 \end{pmatrix}$$

Next, we list some properties of matrix multiplication. We agree to follow the notational convention that $A \cdot B = AB$.

### Theorem 3.2

**Let $A$ be a matrix of dimension $n \times m$, let $B$ be a matrix of dimension $m \times p$, and let $C$ be a matrix of dimension $p \times q$. Then matrix multiplication is** *associative.* **That is**

$$A(BC) = (AB)C$$

**The resulting matrix $ABC$ is of dimension $n \times q$.**

Again, notice the limitations that are placed on the dimensions of the matrices in order for multiplication to be associative.

### Theorem 3.3

**Let $A$ be a matrix of dimension $n \times m$. Let $B$ and $C$ be matrices of dimension $m \times p$. Then** *matrix multiplication distributes over matrix addition.* **That is,**

$$A(B + C) = AB + AC$$

**The resulting matrix $AB + AC$ is of dimension $n \times p$.**

The above theorems indicate that under certain conditions multiplication is associative and multiplication distributes over addition.

Matrix multiplication is not always commutative, that is, $AB \neq BA$. For example, if $A$ is of dimension $2 \times 3$ and $B$ is of dimension $3 \times 2$, the product $AB$ is of dimension $2 \times 2$ and $BA$ is of dimension $3 \times 3$. Problems 5 and 9 in Exercise 5.3 illustrate that multiplication of square matrices is also not always commutative.

A special type of square matrix of great interest to us is the *identity matrix,* which is denoted by $I_n$ and has the property that all its diagonal entries are 1's and all other entries are 0's. It is of the form

$$I_n = \begin{pmatrix} 1 & 0 & \cdots & 0 & 0 \\ 0 & 1 & \cdots & 0 & 0 \\ \vdots & \vdots & \cdots & \vdots & \vdots \\ 0 & 0 & \cdots & 1 & 0 \\ 0 & 0 & \cdots & 0 & 1 \end{pmatrix}$$

where the subscript $n$ denotes the fact that $I_n$ is of dimension $n \times n$.

Let

$$A = \begin{pmatrix} 3 & 2 \\ -4 & \frac{1}{2} \end{pmatrix} \qquad I_2 = \begin{pmatrix} 1 & 0 \\ 0 & 1 \end{pmatrix}$$

Then

$$AI_2 = \begin{pmatrix} 3 & 2 \\ -4 & \frac{1}{2} \end{pmatrix}\begin{pmatrix} 1 & 0 \\ 0 & 1 \end{pmatrix} = \begin{pmatrix} 3 & 2 \\ -4 & \frac{1}{2} \end{pmatrix} = A$$

Also

$$I_2 A = \begin{pmatrix} 1 & 0 \\ 0 & 1 \end{pmatrix}\begin{pmatrix} 3 & 2 \\ -4 & \frac{1}{2} \end{pmatrix} = \begin{pmatrix} 3 & 2 \\ -4 & \frac{1}{2} \end{pmatrix} = A$$

This example can be generalized by the following result.

**Theorem 3.4**
**If $A$ is a square matrix of dimension $n \times n$ and if $I_n$ is an identity matrix of dimension $n \times n$, then**

$$AI_n = I_n A = A$$

Thus far we have only considered identity matrices associated to a *square* matrix $A$. The reason for this is illustrated in the following example.

Let

$$A = \begin{pmatrix} 1 & 2 \\ 3 & 2 \\ 1 & 1 \end{pmatrix}$$

Then

$$A \cdot \begin{pmatrix} 1 & 0 \\ 0 & 1 \end{pmatrix} = \begin{pmatrix} 1 & 2 \\ 3 & 2 \\ 1 & 1 \end{pmatrix} \begin{pmatrix} 1 & 0 \\ 0 & 1 \end{pmatrix} = \begin{pmatrix} 1 & 2 \\ 3 & 2 \\ 1 & 1 \end{pmatrix} = A$$

However, $\begin{pmatrix} 1 & 0 \\ 0 & 1 \end{pmatrix} \cdot A$ is *not* possible. Notice, though, that

$$\begin{pmatrix} 1 & 0 & 0 \\ 0 & 1 & 0 \\ 0 & 0 & 1 \end{pmatrix} \cdot A = \begin{pmatrix} 1 & 0 & 0 \\ 0 & 1 & 0 \\ 0 & 0 & 1 \end{pmatrix} \begin{pmatrix} 1 & 2 \\ 3 & 2 \\ 1 & 1 \end{pmatrix} = \begin{pmatrix} 1 & 2 \\ 3 & 2 \\ 1 & 1 \end{pmatrix} = A$$

That is, for nonsquare matrices, the corresponding identity matrix is *not* unique.

**Definition of an Inverse Matrix**

**Let $A$ be a matrix of dimension $n \times n$. A matrix $B$ of dimension $n \times n$ is called an *inverse* of $A$ if and only if $AB = I_n$. We denote the inverse of a matrix $A$, if it exists, by $A^{-1}$.**

If $A^{-1}$ is an inverse of $A$, then it can be shown that

$$AA^{-1} = A^{-1}A = I_n$$

That is, a matrix and its inverse commute under multiplication. See Problem 18, Exercise 5.3 on page 125.

The next example provides a technique for finding the inverse of a matrix. Although this technique is not the most efficient (see Section 5.5 for an efficient way), it is illustrative.

Find the inverse of the matrix $\begin{pmatrix} 2 & 1 \\ 0 & 1 \end{pmatrix}$.

The inverse $A^{-1}$, if it exists, obeys the relationship

$$\begin{pmatrix} 2 & 1 \\ 0 & 1 \end{pmatrix} \cdot A^{-1} = I_2$$

If we let

$$A^{-1} = \begin{pmatrix} a & b \\ c & d \end{pmatrix}$$

then

$$\begin{pmatrix} 2 & 1 \\ 0 & 1 \end{pmatrix} \begin{pmatrix} a & b \\ c & d \end{pmatrix} = \begin{pmatrix} 1 & 0 \\ 0 & 1 \end{pmatrix}$$

Expanding, we obtain

$$2a + c = 1, 2b + d = 0, c = 0, d = 1$$

Thus,

$$a = \frac{1}{2}, \qquad b = -\frac{1}{2}, \qquad c = 0, \qquad d = 1$$

Hence the inverse of $A = \begin{pmatrix} 2 & 1 \\ 0 & 1 \end{pmatrix}$ is

$$A^{-1} = \begin{pmatrix} \dfrac{1}{2} & -\dfrac{1}{2} \\ 0 & 1 \end{pmatrix}$$

This, indeed, is the inverse since

$$AA^{-1} = \begin{pmatrix} 2 & 1 \\ 0 & 1 \end{pmatrix} \begin{pmatrix} \dfrac{1}{2} & -\dfrac{1}{2} \\ 0 & 1 \end{pmatrix} = \begin{pmatrix} 1 & 0 \\ 0 & 1 \end{pmatrix}$$

The inverse we calculated in Example 3.9 for $A = \begin{pmatrix} 2 & 1 \\ 0 & 1 \end{pmatrix}$ is the only inverse $A$ has. Theorem 3.5 guarantees this.

**Theorem 3.5**
**A square matrix $A$ has at most one inverse. That is, the inverse of a matrix is _unique_ if it exists.**

Proof
Suppose that we have two inverses $B$ and $C$ for a matrix $A$. Then

$$AB = BA = I_n \qquad \text{and} \qquad AC = CA = I_n$$

Multiplying both sides of $AC = I_n$ by $B$, we find

$$B(AC) = BI_n = B$$

Similarly, multiplying both sides of $BA = I_n$ by $C$, we obtain

$$(BA)C = I_nC = C$$

But

$$B(AC) = (BA)C$$

Thus

$$B = C$$

Not all matrices possess inverses. A nonsquare matrix, for example, does not have an inverse since the products $AB$ and $BA$ cannot be equal. Even if a matrix is square its inverse does not always exist. Consider the following example.

Does the matrix

$$A = \begin{pmatrix} 0 & 1 \\ 0 & 0 \end{pmatrix}$$

have an inverse?

Suppose its inverse is

$$B = \begin{pmatrix} x & y \\ z & w \end{pmatrix}$$

Then, we must have

$$A \cdot B = I_2$$

That is,

$$\begin{pmatrix} 0 & 1 \\ 0 & 0 \end{pmatrix} \begin{pmatrix} x & y \\ z & w \end{pmatrix} = \begin{pmatrix} 1 & 0 \\ 0 & 1 \end{pmatrix}$$

Performing the multiplication, we have

$$\begin{pmatrix} z & w \\ 0 & 0 \end{pmatrix} = \begin{pmatrix} 1 & 0 \\ 0 & 1 \end{pmatrix}$$

These two matrices can never be equal. Hence, the matrix $A$ in Example 3.10 has *no* inverse.

1. Perform the matrix multiplications:

(a) $\begin{pmatrix} 1 & -1 & 1 \\ 2 & 0 & 1 \\ 3 & -1 & 1 \end{pmatrix} \begin{pmatrix} 1 & 2 \\ -1 & 1 \\ 1 & 3 \end{pmatrix}$    (c) $\begin{pmatrix} 4 & 0 & 1 \\ 0 & 6 & 0 \\ 0 & -2 & 3 \end{pmatrix} \begin{pmatrix} 5 & 2 \\ -2 & 1 \\ 0 & 3 \end{pmatrix}$

(b) $\begin{pmatrix} 1 & 0 & 0 \\ 0 & 1 & 0 \\ 0 & 0 & 1 \end{pmatrix} \begin{pmatrix} a_1 & a_2 & a_3 \\ b_1 & b_2 & b_3 \\ c_1 & c_2 & c_3 \end{pmatrix}$    (d) $\begin{pmatrix} \frac{1}{4} & 3 \\ 4 & 4 \end{pmatrix} \begin{pmatrix} \frac{1}{2} & \frac{1}{2} \\ \frac{1}{3} & \frac{2}{3} \end{pmatrix}$

2. Let

$$A = \begin{pmatrix} 1 & -1 & 1 \\ 20 & 1 & 0 \end{pmatrix} \quad B = \begin{pmatrix} 1 & -1 & 0 \\ 0 & 1 & -1 \\ 1 & 1 & 1 \end{pmatrix} \quad C = \begin{pmatrix} 1 & 0 \\ 0 & 1 \\ 1 & 1 \end{pmatrix}$$

Test the rule $(AB)C = A(BC)$.

3. If possible find a matrix $A$ such that

$$A \cdot \begin{pmatrix} 0 & 1 \\ 2 & -1 \end{pmatrix} = \begin{pmatrix} 2 & 1 \\ -1 & 0 \end{pmatrix}$$

Hint: Let $A = \begin{pmatrix} a & b \\ c & d \end{pmatrix}$.

4. For what values of $x$ will

$$(x \quad 4 \quad 1) \begin{pmatrix} 2 & 1 & 0 \\ 1 & 0 & 2 \\ 0 & 2 & 4 \end{pmatrix} \begin{pmatrix} x \\ -7 \\ \frac{5}{4} \end{pmatrix} = 0$$

5. If

$$A = \begin{pmatrix} 1 & -1 \\ 2 & 0 \end{pmatrix} \qquad B = \begin{pmatrix} 3 & 2 \\ -1 & 4 \end{pmatrix}$$

find $AB$ and $BA$. Notice that $AB \neq BA$. Could this have been predicted?

6. Let

$$U = \begin{pmatrix} 2 \\ -1 \\ 3 \end{pmatrix} \qquad V = \begin{pmatrix} \frac{1}{2} \\ 0 \\ 1 \end{pmatrix} \qquad W = \begin{pmatrix} -3 \\ -7 \\ 0 \end{pmatrix}$$

Compute the following:
(a) $U + V$          (d) $U + V - W$
(b) $U - V$          (e) $2U - 7V$
(c) $\frac{1}{2}(U + V)$     (f) $\frac{1}{4}U - \frac{1}{4}V - \frac{1}{4}W$

7. Find $a_1$, $a_2$, $a_3$ which satisfy the following:

$$\begin{pmatrix} 2 \\ 1 \\ 0 \end{pmatrix} + \begin{pmatrix} a_1 \\ a_2 \\ a_3 \end{pmatrix} = \begin{pmatrix} 2 \\ -1 \\ 3 \end{pmatrix}$$

8. Consider the two column vectors

$$U = \begin{pmatrix} u_1 \\ u_2 \\ \vdots \\ u_n \end{pmatrix} \qquad V = \begin{pmatrix} v_1 \\ v_2 \\ \vdots \\ v_n \end{pmatrix}$$

Find the vector $\frac{1}{n}(U + V)$.

9. What must be true about $a$, $b$, $c$, and $d$ if we demand $A \cdot B = B \cdot A$, for

$$A = \begin{pmatrix} a & b \\ c & d \end{pmatrix}, \qquad B = \begin{pmatrix} 1 & 1 \\ -1 & 1 \end{pmatrix}$$

Assume that

$$\begin{pmatrix} a & b \\ c & d \end{pmatrix} \neq \begin{pmatrix} 1 & 0 \\ 0 & 1 \end{pmatrix}$$

10. Find the inverse, if it exists, of

(a) $A = \begin{pmatrix} 1 & 1 \\ 0 & 2 \end{pmatrix}$    (c) $A = \begin{pmatrix} 2 & 0 & 0 \\ 0 & 1 & 0 \\ 1 & 1 & 1 \end{pmatrix}$

(b) $A = \begin{pmatrix} 2 & 1 \\ 1 & 1 \end{pmatrix}$

11. If $AB = BA$ the matrices $A$ and $B$ are said to be *commutative*. Show that for all values $a, b, c,$ and $d,$ the matrices

$$A = \begin{pmatrix} a & b \\ -b & a \end{pmatrix} \quad \text{and} \quad B = \begin{pmatrix} c & d \\ -d & c \end{pmatrix}$$

are commutative.

12. Let

$$A = \begin{pmatrix} a & b \\ b & a \end{pmatrix}$$

Find $a$ and $b$ such that $A^2 + A = 0,$ where $A^2 = A \cdot A.$

13. Let

$$A = \begin{pmatrix} 1 & 2 & 5 \\ 2 & 4 & 10 \\ -1 & -2 & -5 \end{pmatrix}$$

Show that $A^2 = 0.$ Thus, the rule in the real number system that if $a^2 = 0,$ then $a = 0$ does not hold for matrices.

14. For the matrix

$$A = \begin{pmatrix} a & 1 - a \\ 1 + a & -a \end{pmatrix}$$

show that $A^2 = A \cdot A = I_2.$ A matrix $A$ with this property is called *involutorial*.

15. Find the vector $(x_1 \quad x_2)$ such that

$$(x_1 \quad x_2) \begin{pmatrix} \dfrac{1}{2} & \dfrac{1}{2} \\ \dfrac{1}{4} & \dfrac{3}{4} \end{pmatrix} = (x_1 \quad x_2)$$

under the condition that $x_1 + x_2 = 1.$
Here the vector $(x_1 \quad x_2)$ is called a fixed vector of the matrix
$$\begin{pmatrix} \dfrac{1}{2} & \dfrac{1}{2} \\ \dfrac{1}{4} & \dfrac{3}{4} \end{pmatrix}$$

16. Let

$$A = \begin{pmatrix} 2 & 3 & 0 \\ 1 & 1 & 0 \\ 2 & 1 & 2 \end{pmatrix}$$

Compute $I_3 - A$ and $A - I_3.$

17. Prove III in Theorem 3.1.

*18. Prove that if $AB = I_n$, then $BA = I_n$, where $A$ and $B$ are of dimension $n \times n$.

19. Mike went to a department store and purchased 6 pants, 8 shirts, and 2 jackets. Danny purchased 2 pants, 5 shirts and 3 jackets. If the pants are $5 each, the shirts $3 each and the jackets $9 each, use matrix multiplication to find the amounts spent by Mike and Danny.

20. Suppose a factory is asked to produce three types of products, which we will call $P_1$, $P_2$, $P_3$. Suppose the following purchasing order was received: $P_1 = 7$, $P_2 = 12$, $P_3 = 5$. Represent this order by a row vector and call it $P$.

$$P = (7 \quad 12 \quad 5)$$

To produce each of the products, raw material of four kinds is needed. Call the raw material $M_1$, $M_2$, $M_3$, and $M_4$. The matrix below gives the amount of material needed corresponding to each product.

$$Q = \begin{array}{c} \\ P_1 \\ P_2 \\ P_3 \end{array} \begin{array}{cccc} M_1 & M_2 & M_3 & M_4 \\ \begin{pmatrix} 2 & 3 & 1 & 12 \\ 7 & 9 & 5 & 20 \\ 8 & 12 & 6 & 15 \end{pmatrix} \end{array}$$

Suppose the cost for each of the materials $M_1$, $M_2$, $M_3$, and $M_4$ is 10, 12, 15, and 20 dollars, respectively. The cost vector is

$$C = \begin{pmatrix} 10 \\ 12 \\ 15 \\ 20 \end{pmatrix}$$

Compute the following

(a) $P \cdot Q$     (c) $P \cdot Q \cdot C$

(b) $Q \cdot C$

Interpret each of these.

*21. For a square matrix $A$, it is always possible to find $A \cdot A = A^2$. It is also clear that we can compute

$$A^n = \underbrace{A \cdot A \cdots A}_{n \text{ times}}$$

Find $A^2$, $A^3$, $A^4$ for the following square matrices:

(a) $A = \begin{pmatrix} 1 & 0 \\ 3 & 2 \end{pmatrix}$     (d) $A = \begin{pmatrix} 1 & 0 \\ 0 & 1 \end{pmatrix}$

(b) $A = \begin{pmatrix} 3 & 1 \\ -2 & -1 \end{pmatrix}$    (e) $\begin{pmatrix} \dfrac{1}{2} & \dfrac{1}{2} \\ \dfrac{1}{4} & \dfrac{3}{4} \end{pmatrix}$

(c) $A = \begin{pmatrix} 0 & 1 & 1 \\ 0 & -1 & 2 \\ 6 & 3 & -2 \end{pmatrix}$

Can you guess what $A^n$ looks like for 21(d)? for 21(e)?

**5.4
SYSTEMS OF
EQUATIONS**

We begin by considering the system of two equations in two unknowns

$$x + 4y = 14$$
$$3x - 2y = 0 \tag{4.1}$$

To find a solution, we multiply the first equation by 3 and subtract from the second. The result is

$$x + 4y = 14$$
$$-14y = -42$$

Dividing the second equation by $-14$, we get

$$x + 4y = 14$$
$$y = 3$$

To find $x$, we multiply the second equation by 4 and subtract from the first. The result is

$$x = 2$$
$$y = 3 \tag{4.2}$$

The above system of equations has the solution $x = 2$, $y = 3$. In addition, this system is equivalent to the system (4.1), so that the solution of the system (4.1) is also $x = 2$, $y = 3$. We obtain the system (4.2) from (4.1) by a series of operations. Although the system (4.1) could have been solved more quickly (because of its simplicity), the pattern of solution given here leads to a general method for solving any system of equations. The purpose of this section is to present this general method.

We begin by classifying the manipulations used to obtain the solution to the system (4.1). When such manipulations are performed on a matrix, they are called *elementary row operations*.

**Elementary row operations are described as follows:**

**(I) The interchange of any two rows of a matrix.**

**(II) The replacement of any row of a matrix by a nonzero scalar product of that same row.**

**(III) The replacement of any row of a matrix by the sum of that row and a scalar multiple of some other row.**

Observe that when we solved the system (4.1), we began by multiplying the first equation by 3 and subtracting this from the second. This is (III) above. Later we divided the second equation by $-14$. This is (II) above.

An example of each elementary row operation is given below.

Consider the matrix

$$A = \begin{pmatrix} 3 & 4 & -3 \\ 7 & -\dfrac{1}{2} & 0 \end{pmatrix}$$

(I) The matrix obtained by interchanging the first and second rows of $A$ is

$$\begin{pmatrix} 7 & -\dfrac{1}{2} & 0 \\ 3 & 4 & -3 \end{pmatrix}$$

(II) The matrix obtained by multiplying row 2 of $A$ by 5 is

$$\begin{pmatrix} 3 & 4 & -3 \\ 35 & -\dfrac{5}{2} & 0 \end{pmatrix}$$

We denote this operation by writing $r_2' = 5r_2$.

(III) The matrix obtained from $A$ by adding 3 times row 1 to row 2 is

$$\begin{pmatrix} 3 & 4 & -3 \\ 7 + 3 \cdot 3 & -\dfrac{1}{2} + 3 \cdot 4 & 0 + 3 \cdot (-3) \end{pmatrix} = \begin{pmatrix} 3 & 4 & -3 \\ 16 & \dfrac{23}{2} & -9 \end{pmatrix}$$

We denote this operation by writing $r_2' = r_2 + 3r_1$.

Of course, the matrix resulting from a row operation is not equal to the original matrix; such matrices are called *row equivalent*.

**Two matrices $A$ and $B$ are *row equivalent*, written as**

$$A \approx B$$

**if and only if $B$ can be obtained from $A$ by using one or more elementary row operations.**

For the matrix $A$

$$A = \begin{pmatrix} 1 & 4 & 14 \\ 3 & -2 & 0 \end{pmatrix}$$

perform the following row operation

(1) $$r'_2 = r_2 - 3r_1$$

(This means to multiply row 1 by 3 and to subtract this result from row 2, obtaining a new row 2, $r'_2$.)

The result is the matrix

$$\begin{pmatrix} 1 & 4 & 14 \\ 0 & -14 & -42 \end{pmatrix}$$

on the above matrix, perform the row operation

(2) $$r'_2 = -\tfrac{1}{14}r_2$$

The result is

$$\begin{pmatrix} 1 & 4 & 14 \\ 0 & 1 & 3 \end{pmatrix}$$

Next on this matrix perform

(3) $$r'_1 = r_1 - 4r_2$$

The result is

$$\begin{pmatrix} 1 & 0 & 2 \\ 0 & 1 & 3 \end{pmatrix}$$

Compare the original matrix $A$ with the final matrix and observe that the entries in $A$ are merely the numbers that appear in the system (4.1), while the entries in the final matrix are those that appear in (4.2).

The final matrix of Example 4.2 is called a *row-reduced matrix* of $A$. What follows is a definition of and an example for finding a row-reduced matrix.

**Definition of a Row-Reduced Matrix** **Let $A$ be a given matrix of dimension $n \times m$. A *row-reduced matrix* $H$ is a matrix row-equivalent to $A$ for which**

1. **The first $k$ rows contain nonzero entries; entries in the remaining rows are all zero.**
2. **The first nonzero entry in each nonzero row is 1 and it appears to the right of the first nonzero entry of any row above it.**
3. **The first nonzero entry in a nonzero row has zeros above it and below it in its column.**

The following matrices are row-reduced.

$$\begin{pmatrix} 1 & 0 & 0 & 3 \\ 0 & 1 & 0 & 8 \\ 0 & 0 & 1 & -4 \end{pmatrix} \quad \begin{pmatrix} 0 & 1 & -2 & 0 & 5 \\ 0 & 0 & 0 & 1 & 2 \\ 0 & 0 & 0 & 0 & 0 \end{pmatrix}$$

$$\begin{pmatrix} 1 & 0 & 0 & 0 \\ 0 & 1 & 0 & 0 \\ 0 & 0 & 0 & 1 \end{pmatrix} \quad \begin{pmatrix} 0 & 0 \\ 0 & 0 \end{pmatrix}$$

The reader should verify that each of the above matrices satisfy the three conditions of the definition of a row-reduced matrix.

The following matrices are not row-reduced.

$$\begin{pmatrix} 1 & 0 & 0 \\ 0 & 0 & 0 \\ 0 & 1 & 0 \end{pmatrix}$$ The second row contains all zeros and the third does not—this violates rule 1.

$$\begin{pmatrix} 1 & 0 & 2 & 4 \\ 0 & 0 & 2 & 3 \\ 0 & 0 & 0 & 1 \end{pmatrix}$$ The first nonzero entry in row 2 is not a 1—this violates rule 2.

$$\begin{pmatrix} 1 & 0 & 5 \\ 0 & 1 & 1 \\ 0 & 2 & 2 \end{pmatrix}$$ The first nonzero entry in the second row does not have above it and below it zeros in its column—this violates rule 3.

Find the row-reduced matrix $H$ of

4.3
Example

$$A = \begin{pmatrix} 1 & -1 & 2 \\ 2 & -3 & 2 \\ 3 & -5 & 2 \end{pmatrix}$$

With $a_{11} = 1$, we want to obtain a row-equivalent matrix in which all the entries in column 1, except $a_{11}$, are zero.

We can obtain such a matrix by

$$r'_2 = r_2 - 2r_1$$
$$r'_3 = r_3 - 3r_1$$

The new matrix is

$$\begin{pmatrix} 1 & -1 & 2 \\ 0 & -1 & -2 \\ 0 & -2 & -4 \end{pmatrix}$$

We want $a_{22} = 1$. By multiplying row 2 by $(-1)$, we obtain

$$\begin{pmatrix} 1 & -1 & 2 \\ 0 & 1 & 2 \\ 0 & -2 & -4 \end{pmatrix}$$

Now column 2 should have zeros, except for $a_{22} = 1$. This can be accomplished by applying the following row operations.

$$r_1' = r_1 + r_2$$
$$r_3' = r_3 + 2r_2$$

The new matrix is

$$\begin{pmatrix} 1 & 0 & 4 \\ 0 & 1 & 2 \\ 0 & 0 & 0 \end{pmatrix}$$

The matrix above is in row-reduced form. Of course, the matrix $A$ given in Example 4.3 is row-equivalent to the matrix given above.

**4.4**
**Example**

Find the row-reduced matrix $H$ of

$$A = \begin{pmatrix} 1 & -1 & 2 & 2 \\ 2 & -3 & 2 & 1 \\ 3 & -5 & 2 & -3 \\ -4 & 12 & 8 & 10 \end{pmatrix}$$

As before, we perform elementary row operations. If we perform

$$r_2' = r_2 - 2r_1, \qquad r_3' = r_3 - 3r_1, \qquad r_4' = r_4 + 4r_1$$

we obtain

$$\begin{pmatrix} 1 & -1 & 2 & 2 \\ 0 & -1 & -2 & -3 \\ 0 & -2 & -4 & -9 \\ 0 & 8 & 16 & 18 \end{pmatrix}$$

If we perform $r_2' = -r_2$, we obtain

$$\begin{pmatrix} 1 & -1 & 2 & 2 \\ 0 & 1 & 2 & 3 \\ 0 & -2 & -4 & -9 \\ 0 & 8 & 16 & 18 \end{pmatrix}$$

If we perform

$$r_1' = r_2 + r_1, \qquad r_3' = r_3 + 2r_2, \qquad r_4' = r_4 - 8r_2$$

we have

$$\begin{pmatrix} 1 & 0 & 4 & 5 \\ 0 & 1 & 2 & 3 \\ 0 & 0 & 0 & -3 \\ 0 & 0 & 0 & -6 \end{pmatrix}$$

Next perform $r_3' = -1/3 r_3$; the result is

$$\begin{pmatrix} 1 & 0 & 4 & 5 \\ 0 & 1 & 2 & 3 \\ 0 & 0 & 0 & 1 \\ 0 & 0 & 0 & -6 \end{pmatrix}$$

To obtain zero's in column 4, perform

$$r_1' = r_1 - 5r_3, \qquad r_2' = r_2 - 3r_3, \qquad r_4' = r_4 + 6r_3$$

The result is a row-reduced matrix:

$$H = \begin{pmatrix} 1 & 0 & 4 & 0 \\ 0 & 1 & 2 & 0 \\ 0 & 0 & 0 & 1 \\ 0 & 0 & 0 & 0 \end{pmatrix}$$

**Let $H$ be a row-reduced matrix. If there are $r$ rows of $H$ that contain nonzero entries and all other rows of $H$ contain zero entries, then $r$ is called the** *rank* **of $H$.**

Rank of a
Row-reduced
Matrix

For example, the matrix $H$ in Example 4.3 is of rank 2. The matrix $H$ of Example 4.4 is of rank 3.

We also use "rank" with regard to any matrix $A$. **A matrix $A$ is of** *rank* **$r$ if and only if its row-reduced matrix $H$ is of rank $r$.**

Rank of a Matrix

This definition is possible because two row equivalent matrices cannot have different ranks.

**It should be clear that the rank $r$ of a matrix $A$ of dimension $n \times m$ can never exceed the smaller of $n$ and $m$. That is,**

$$\text{rank } A \leqq \min(n, m)$$

Thus, if $A$ is of dimension $3 \times 4$, the rank of $A$ is at most 3.

1. State the row operation that justifies the following statements.

5.4.1
Exercise

(a) $\begin{pmatrix} 3 & 2 & 1 \\ 2 & 1 & 0 \end{pmatrix} \approx \begin{pmatrix} 1 & 1 & 1 \\ 2 & 1 & 0 \end{pmatrix}$

(b) $\begin{pmatrix} 3 & 2 & 1 \\ 2 & 1 & 0 \end{pmatrix} \approx \begin{pmatrix} 12 & 8 & 4 \\ 2 & 1 & 0 \end{pmatrix}$

(c) $\begin{pmatrix} 3 & 2 & 1 \\ 2 & 1 & 0 \end{pmatrix} \approx \begin{pmatrix} 3 & 2 & 1 \\ 4 & 2 & 0 \end{pmatrix} \approx \begin{pmatrix} 3 & 2 & 1 \\ 1 & 0 & -1 \end{pmatrix}$

2. Find a row-reduced matrix of the following matrices in order to determine their *rank*.

(a) $\begin{pmatrix} 1 & 2 & 3 & 8 \\ 0 & 5 & -2 & 1 \\ -2 & 0 & -3 & 4 \\ 2 & 2 & 2 & 2 \end{pmatrix}$ 

(e) $\begin{pmatrix} 2 & 4 & 5 & 2 \\ 3 & 4 & 5 & 4 \\ 4 & 4 & 5 & 3 \\ 1 & 4 & 5 & 1 \end{pmatrix}$

(b) $\begin{pmatrix} 2 & 1 & -1 & 2 \\ 7 & 5 & 3 & 2 \end{pmatrix}$ 

(f) $\begin{pmatrix} 1 & 0 & 1 & 0 \\ 1 & 1 & 0 & 0 \\ 0 & 1 & 1 & 1 \end{pmatrix}$

(c) $(1 \quad 1 \quad 1)$ 

(g) $\begin{pmatrix} 0 & 1 \\ 1 & 0 \end{pmatrix}$

(d) $\begin{pmatrix} 1 \\ 1 \\ 1 \end{pmatrix}$

3. Find the rank of the matrices

(a) $\begin{pmatrix} 1 & 1 & 1 \\ 3 & 2 & -1 \\ 3 & 1 & 2 \end{pmatrix}$ 

(b) $\begin{pmatrix} 1 & 1 & 1 & 6 \\ 3 & 2 & -1 & 4 \\ 3 & 1 & 2 & 11 \end{pmatrix}$

Now that we have introduced the concepts of elementary row operations, row equivalence of matrices, and rank of matrices, we can discuss the problem of solving a system of $m$ linear equations in $n$ unknowns.

An example of a system of 3 equations in 4 unknowns is

$$x_1 + 3x_2 + 5x_3 + x_4 = 2$$
$$2x_1 + 3x_2 + 4x_3 + 2x_4 = 1$$
$$x_1 + 2x_2 + 3x_3 + x_4 = 1$$

In general, a system of $m$ linear equations in the $n$ unknowns $x_1, x_2, \ldots, x_n$ is of the form

$$\begin{aligned} a_{11}x_1 + a_{12}x_2 + \cdots + a_{1n}x_n &= b_1 \\ a_{21}x_1 + a_{22}x_2 + \cdots + a_{2n}x_n &= b_2 \\ a_{31}x_1 + a_{32}x_2 + \cdots + a_{3n}x_n &= b_3 \\ \vdots \qquad \vdots \qquad \vdots \qquad \vdots \\ a_{i1}x_1 + a_{i2}x_2 + \cdots + a_{in}x_n &= b_i \\ \vdots \qquad \vdots \qquad \vdots \qquad \vdots \\ a_{m1}x_1 + a_{m2}x_2 + \cdots + a_{mn}x_n &= b_m \end{aligned} \tag{4.3}$$

where $a_{ij}$ and $b_i$ are real numbers, $i = 1, 2, \ldots, m; j = 1, 2, \ldots, n$.

This is a system of *linear* equations because the unknowns $x_1, x_2, \ldots, x_n$ all appear to the power one and there are no products of unknowns.

Keep in mind that the subscript on the $x$ is meant only as a distinguishing symbol—it is *not* an exponent. Finally, if we examine the equations in (4.3), we see that there are $m$ of them, with a total of $n$ unknowns $x_1, x_2, \ldots, x_n$.

By a *solution* of the system of equations (4.3) is meant any ordered $n$-tuple $(x_1, x_2, \ldots, x_n)$ of real numbers for which *each* of the $m$ equations of the system is satisfied.

**Definition of Solution**

For example, it can be verified that the ordered pair $(4/3, 2)$ is a solution to the following system of two linear equations in the two unknowns $x_1$ and $x_2$.

$$3x_1 + 4x_2 = 12$$
$$3x_1 - 2x_2 = 0$$

For

$$3 \cdot \frac{4}{3} + 4 \cdot 2 = 12$$

$$3 \cdot \frac{4}{3} - 2 \cdot 2 = 0$$

Define $X$ and $B$ as the column vectors

$$X = \begin{pmatrix} x_1 \\ \vdots \\ x_n \end{pmatrix} \qquad B = \begin{pmatrix} b_1 \\ \vdots \\ b_m \end{pmatrix}$$

Let $A$ denote the *coefficient matrix* of the system of equations (4.3), namely,

$$A = \begin{pmatrix} a_{11} & a_{12} & \cdots & a_{1n} \\ a_{21} & a_{22} & \cdots & a_{2n} \\ \vdots & \vdots & \cdots & \vdots \\ a_{m1} & a_{m2} & \cdots & a_{mn} \end{pmatrix}$$

The system of equations (4.3) can be written in matrix form as

$$AX = B$$

**The *augmented matrix* of the system of linear equations (4.3) is the matrix $A|B$ formed by appending the column $B$ to the coefficient matrix $A$.**

**Definition of Augmented Matrix**

Consider the following system of three equations in three unknowns:

$$x_1 + x_2 + x_3 = 6$$
$$3x_1 + 2x_2 - x_3 = 4$$
$$3x_1 + x_2 + 2x_3 = 11$$

**4.5 Example**

The matrix form of this system is:

$$\begin{pmatrix} 1 & 1 & 1 \\ 3 & 2 & -1 \\ 3 & 1 & 2 \end{pmatrix} \begin{pmatrix} x_1 \\ x_2 \\ x_3 \end{pmatrix} = \begin{pmatrix} 6 \\ 4 \\ 11 \end{pmatrix}$$

The coefficient matrix $A$ is

$$A = \begin{pmatrix} 1 & 1 & 1 \\ 3 & 2 & -1 \\ 3 & 1 & 2 \end{pmatrix}$$

The augmented matrix $A|B$ is

$$A|B = \begin{pmatrix} 1 & 1 & 1 & 6 \\ 3 & 2 & -1 & 4 \\ 3 & 1 & 2 & 11 \end{pmatrix}$$

Notice that $A$ is of dimension $3 \times 3$, while $A|B$ is of dimension $3 \times 4$.

The reader should verify that (see problem 3, Exercise 5.4.1, page 132)

$$A = \begin{pmatrix} 1 & 1 & 1 \\ 3 & 2 & -1 \\ 3 & 1 & 2 \end{pmatrix} \approx \begin{pmatrix} 1 & 0 & 0 \\ 0 & 1 & 0 \\ 0 & 0 & 1 \end{pmatrix}$$

Thus,

$$\text{rank } A = 3$$

For the augmented matrix $A|B$, the reader should verify that (see problem 3, Exercise 5.4.1, page 132)

$$A|B = \begin{pmatrix} 1 & 1 & 1 & 6 \\ 3 & 2 & -1 & 4 \\ 3 & 1 & 2 & 11 \end{pmatrix} \approx \begin{pmatrix} 1 & 0 & 0 & 1 \\ 0 & 1 & 0 & 2 \\ 0 & 0 & 1 & 3 \end{pmatrix}$$

Thus

$$\text{rank } A|B = 3$$

Since the augmented matrix $A|B$ of a system of equations is formed by adding one column to the coefficient matrix $A$ of the system, it follows that

$$\text{rank } A \leqq \text{rank } A|B$$

The augmented matrix $A|B$ of a system of equations gives us all the essential information we need to know about the system—provided we remember which unknown is associated with which *column* and we remember the significance of the last *column*. If we perform only *row* operations on $A|B$, we obtain a system of equations having the same solution as that of the original system—since *row* operations will not affect the significance we have placed on the *columns*.

This technique for solving a system of equations is illustrated on the following page.

Find the solution of

$$x_1 + x_2 + x_3 = 6$$
$$3x_1 + 2x_2 - x_3 = 4$$
$$3x_1 + x_2 + 2x_3 = 11$$

The augmented matrix $A|B$ of this system is

$$A|B = \begin{pmatrix} 1 & 1 & 1 & | & 6 \\ 3 & 2 & -1 & | & 4 \\ 3 & 1 & 2 & | & 11 \end{pmatrix}$$

Let us approach $A|B$ as if we were to obtain the row-reduced matrix.

Perform the row operations

$$r_2' = -3r_1 + r_2$$
$$r_3' = -3r_1 + r_3$$

Then, we obtain

$$\begin{pmatrix} 1 & 1 & 1 & | & 6 \\ 0 & -1 & -4 & | & -14 \\ 0 & -2 & -1 & | & -7 \end{pmatrix}$$

If we let $r_2' = -r_2$, we have

$$\begin{pmatrix} 1 & 1 & 1 & | & 6 \\ 0 & 1 & 4 & | & 14 \\ 0 & -2 & -1 & | & -7 \end{pmatrix}$$

If the row operations $r_1' = r_1 - r_2$, $r_3' = 2r_2 + r_3$, are performed, we have

$$\begin{pmatrix} 1 & 0 & -3 & | & -8 \\ 0 & 1 & 4 & | & 14 \\ 0 & 0 & 7 & | & 21 \end{pmatrix}$$

The system of equations this matrix represents is

$$x_1 - 3x_3 = -8$$
$$x_2 + 4x_3 = 14$$
$$7x_3 = 21$$

Continuing, let

$$r_3' = \frac{1}{7} r_3$$

Then we obtain

$$\begin{pmatrix} 1 & 0 & -3 & | & -8 \\ 0 & 1 & 4 & | & 14 \\ 0 & 0 & 1 & | & 3 \end{pmatrix} \qquad \begin{aligned} x_1 - 3x_3 &= -8 \\ x_2 + 4x_3 &= 14 \\ x_3 &= 3 \end{aligned}$$

Finally

$$r'_1 = r_1 + 3r_3$$
$$r'_2 = r_2 - 4r_3$$

With these operations, we have

$$\begin{pmatrix} 1 & 0 & 0 & | & 1 \\ 0 & 1 & 0 & | & 2 \\ 0 & 0 & 1 & | & 3 \end{pmatrix} \qquad \begin{matrix} x_1 = 1 \\ x_2 = 2 \\ x_3 = 3 \end{matrix}$$

The solution of the system of Example 4.6 is

$$x_1 = 1, \qquad x_2 = 2, \qquad x_3 = 3$$

Now some systems of equations will not have solutions. Other systems may have more than one solution. If a system of equations has at least one solution, it is called a *consistent system;* otherwise it is said to be *inconsistent.*

The test for whether a system of linear equations has a solution and the test for uniqueness are given below.

Consistent
System

Inconsistent
System

**Test for Consistency**    **A system of equations**

$$AX = B$$

**has at least one solution if and only if**

$$\textbf{rank } A = \textbf{rank } A\,|\,B$$

Otherwise, the system has no solution.

**Test for Uniqueness**    **A system of equations**

$$AX = B$$

**has exactly one solution if and only if**

$$\textbf{rank } A = \textbf{rank } A\,|\,B = \textbf{number of unknowns}$$

**For the system of equations**

$$AX = B$$

**suppose**

$$\textbf{rank } A = \textbf{rank } A\,|\,B = r$$

**and**

$$\textbf{number of unknowns} = m$$

**If $m = r$, the solution is unique.**
**If $m > r$, there are infinitely many solutions.**

The next two examples illustrate the use of matrices in determining the nature of the solution of a system of equations with two unknowns and provide a geometric interpretation for the tests stated above.

Apply the use of matrices to discuss the system

4.7
Example

$$3x_1 + 2x_2 = 7$$
$$x_1 + 6x_2 = 13$$

The coefficient matrix $A$ and the augmented matrix $A|B$ are

$$A = \begin{pmatrix} 3 & 2 \\ 1 & 6 \end{pmatrix} \qquad A|B = \begin{pmatrix} 3 & 2 & | & 7 \\ 1 & 6 & | & 13 \end{pmatrix}$$

The ranks of these matrices are

$$\text{rank } A = 2 \qquad \text{rank } A|B = 2$$

By the Test for Consistency, this system is consistent. Since the number of unknowns is also 2, by the Test for Uniqueness, the solution is unique. By performing row operations on $A|B$, we obtain

$$A|B \approx \begin{pmatrix} 1 & 0 & | & 1 \\ 0 & 1 & | & 2 \end{pmatrix} \qquad \begin{matrix} x_1 = 1 \\ x_2 = 2 \end{matrix}$$

The geometrical significance of the fact that rank $A$ = rank $A|B$ = number of unknowns is that the two lines intersect. See Figure 5.3.

Apply the use of matrices to discuss the system

4.8
Example

$$x_1 + 2x_2 = 6$$
$$2x_1 + 4x_2 = 12$$

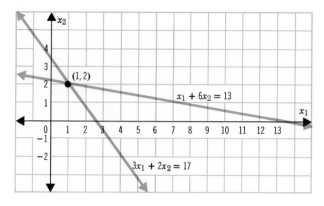

**Figure 5.3**

The coefficient matrix $A$ and the augmented matrix $A|B$ are

$$A = \begin{pmatrix} 1 & 2 \\ 2 & 4 \end{pmatrix} \qquad A|B = \begin{pmatrix} 1 & 2 & 6 \\ 2 & 4 & 12 \end{pmatrix}$$

The ranks of these matrices are

$$\text{rank } A = 1 \qquad \text{rank } A|B = 1$$

By the Test for Consistency, the system is consistent. Since the number of unknowns exceeds the common rank, there are infinitely many solutions. By performing row operations on $A|B$, we obtain

$$A|B \approx \begin{pmatrix} 1 & 2 & | & 6 \\ 0 & 0 & | & 0 \end{pmatrix} \qquad x_1 = 6 - 2x_2$$

The geometrical significance of the fact that rank $A = $ rank $A|B <$ number of unknowns is that the two lines are identical. See Figure 5.4.

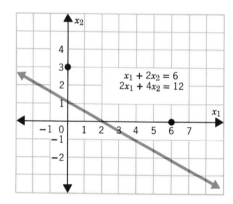

**Figure 5.4**

For systems of two equations in two unknowns, the geometrical significance of rank $A <$ rank $A|B$ is that the lines are parallel. In this case the system is inconsistent.

4.9
Example

Consider the system of equations

$$\begin{aligned}
x_1 + 2x_2 + x_3 &= 1 \\
2x_1 - x_2 + 2x_3 &= 2 \\
3x_1 + x_2 + 3x_3 &= 4
\end{aligned}$$

The coefficient matrix $A$ and the augmented matrix $A|B$ are

$$A = \begin{pmatrix} 1 & 2 & 1 \\ 2 & -1 & 2 \\ 3 & 1 & 3 \end{pmatrix}, \qquad A|B = \begin{pmatrix} 1 & 2 & 1 & | & 1 \\ 2 & -1 & 2 & | & 2 \\ 3 & 1 & 3 & | & 4 \end{pmatrix}$$

The reader should verify that

$$\text{rank } A = 2, \qquad \text{rank } A|B = 3$$

Thus, the system of Example 4.9 has no solution.

Were we to approach this system as we did the one in Example 4.6, we would arrive at

$$\begin{pmatrix} 1 & 0 & 1 & | & 1 \\ 0 & 1 & 0 & | & 0 \\ 0 & 0 & 0 & | & 1 \end{pmatrix} \qquad \begin{aligned} x_1 + x_3 &= 1 \\ x_2 &= 0 \\ 0 \cdot x_1 + 0 \cdot x_2 + 0 \cdot x_3 &= 1 \end{aligned}$$

It is clear from the contradiction of the third equation $(0 = 1)$, that the system has no solution.

Consider the system

4.10
Example

$$\begin{aligned} x_1 + 3x_2 + x_3 &= 6 \\ 3x_1 - 2x_2 - 8x_3 &= 7 \\ 4x_1 + 5x_2 - 3x_3 &= 17 \end{aligned}$$

The coefficient matrix $A$ and the augmented matrix $A|B$ are

$$A = \begin{pmatrix} 1 & 3 & 1 \\ 3 & -2 & -8 \\ 4 & 5 & -3 \end{pmatrix}, \qquad A|B = \begin{pmatrix} 1 & 3 & 1 & | & 6 \\ 3 & -2 & -8 & | & 7 \\ 4 & 5 & -3 & | & 17 \end{pmatrix}$$

The reader should verify that

$$\text{rank } A = 2, \qquad \text{rank } A|B = 2$$

Thus, the system of Example 4.10 has a solution. However

$$\text{number of unknowns} = 3$$

Thus, the solution is *not* unique.

By performing row operations on $A|B$, we obtain

$$\begin{pmatrix} 1 & 0 & -2 & | & 3 \\ 0 & 1 & 1 & | & 1 \\ 0 & 0 & 0 & | & 0 \end{pmatrix} \qquad \begin{aligned} x_1 - 2x_3 &= 3 \\ x_2 + x_3 &= 1 \\ 0 \cdot x_1 + 0 \cdot x_2 + 0 \cdot x_3 &= 0 \end{aligned}$$

There are infinitely many solutions since

$$x_1 = 3 + 2x_3 \qquad x_2 = 1 - x_3$$

and we can allow $x_3$ to take on any value.

For example,

$$\begin{aligned} \text{if } x_3 = 0, && x_1 = 3, && x_2 = 1 \\ \text{if } x_3 = 4, && x_1 = 11, && x_2 = -3 \\ \text{if } x_3 = \tfrac{1}{2}, && x_1 = 4, && x_2 = \tfrac{1}{2} \end{aligned}$$

*Note:* In Example 4.10

$$\text{number of unknowns} - \text{rank } A = 3 - 2 = 1$$

and we solved for two unknowns $x_1$ and $x_2$ in terms of the remaining unknown $x_3$. In general, if $m > r$, then some collection of $r$ unknowns can be determined in terms of the remaining $m - r$ unknowns.

4.11
Example

Consider the system

$$\begin{aligned}
x_1 + 3x_2 + 5x_3 + \ x_4 &= 2 \\
2x_1 + 3x_2 + 4x_3 + 2x_4 &= 1 \\
x_1 + 2x_2 + 3x_3 + \ x_4 &= 1
\end{aligned}$$

The coefficient matrix $A$ and the augmented matrix $A|B$ are

$$A = \begin{pmatrix} 1 & 3 & 5 & 1 \\ 2 & 3 & 4 & 2 \\ 1 & 2 & 3 & 1 \end{pmatrix}, \qquad A|B = \begin{pmatrix} 1 & 3 & 5 & 1 & 2 \\ 2 & 3 & 4 & 2 & 1 \\ 1 & 2 & 3 & 1 & 1 \end{pmatrix}$$

Their ranks are

$$\text{rank } A = 2 \qquad \text{rank } A|B = 2$$

Since there are four unknowns, we know that this system has infinitely many solutions and that we can solve for two of the unknowns in terms of the remaining two.

We proceed to obtain a solution by reducing the augmented matrix $A|B$. Thus,

$$A|B \approx \begin{pmatrix} 1 & 3 & 5 & 1 & 2 \\ 0 & -3 & -6 & 0 & -3 \\ 0 & -1 & -2 & 0 & -1 \end{pmatrix} \approx \begin{pmatrix} 1 & 3 & 5 & 1 & 2 \\ 0 & 1 & 2 & 0 & 1 \\ 0 & -1 & -2 & 0 & -1 \end{pmatrix}$$

$$\approx \begin{pmatrix} 1 & 0 & -1 & 1 & -1 \\ 0 & 1 & -2 & 0 & 1 \\ 0 & 0 & 0 & 0 & 0 \end{pmatrix}$$

Thus, a solution is

$$\begin{aligned}
x_1 &= \ x_3 - x_4 - 1 \\
x_2 &= 2x_3 + 1
\end{aligned}$$

Here we treat $x_3$ and $x_4$ as *parameters,* that is, constants that may be changed at the option of the person handling the system. Of course, we could have written the solution in the form

$$x_3 = -\frac{1}{2}x_2 - \frac{1}{2}, \qquad x_4 = -x_1 + \frac{1}{2}x_2 - \frac{3}{2}$$

in which we have solved for $x_3$, $x_4$ in terms of $x_1$, $x_2$. In this case, $x_1$ and $x_2$ are now treated as parameters.

We point out that in this system, we cannot solve for $x_1$ and $x_4$ in terms of $x_2$ and $x_3$.

4.12 Example

In a chemistry laboratory one solution is 10 percent hydrochloric acid, a second solution contains 20 percent HCl, and a third contains 40 percent HCl. How many liters of each should be mixed to obtain 100 liters of 25 percent HCl?

First, let $x_1$, $x_2$, and $x_3$ represent the number of liters of 10, 20, and 40 percent solutions of HCl, respectively. Then

$$\begin{aligned} x_1 + \quad x_2 + \quad x_3 &= 100 \\ 0.1x_1 + 0.2x_2 + 0.4x_3 &= \ \ 25 \end{aligned}$$

since we want 100 liters in all and the amount of HCl obtained from each solution must sum to 25 percent of 100 or 25 liters. Thus, our problem reduces to two equations in three unknowns and so we must solve for two of the unknowns in terms of the third.

If we decide that $x_3$ is to be the parameter, we have

$$\begin{aligned} x_1 + \ x_2 &= 100 - \ x_3 \\ x_1 + 2x_2 &= 250 - 4x_3 \end{aligned}$$

Thus

$$\begin{aligned} x_1 &= \ \ 2x_3 - \ 50 \\ x_2 &= -3x_3 + 150 \end{aligned}$$

where $x_3$ can represent any real number. Now the practical considerations of this problem lead us to the conditions that $x_1 \geqq 0$, $x_2 \geqq 0$, $x_3 \geqq 0$. Thus, we must have $x_3 \geqq 25$ and $x_3 \leqq 50$, since otherwise $x_1 < 0$ or $x_2 < 0$. Some possible solutions are listed in Figure 5.5. The final determination by the chemistry laboratory will more than likely be based on the amount and availability of one acid solution versus others.

| No. liters 10% Solution | No. liters 20% Solution | No. liters 40% Solution |
|---|---|---|
| 0 | 75 | 25 |
| 10 | 60 | 30 |
| 12 | 57 | 31 |
| 16 | 51 | 33 |
| 20 | 45 | 35 |
| 25 | 37.5 | 37.5 |
| 26 | 36 | 38 |
| 30 | 30 | 40 |
| 36 | 21 | 43 |
| 38 | 18 | 44 |
| 46 | 6 | 48 |
| 50 | 0 | 50 |

**Figure 5.5**

1. Find solutions, if they exist, for the following systems of equations.

(a) $2x_1 + 3x_2 - x_3 = 8$
$x_1 + x_2 + x_3 = 7$
$2x_2 - x_3 = 3$

(b) $2x_1 + 3x_2 = 8$
$2x_1 - x_2 = 12$

(c) $x_1 + x_2 - x_3 = 12$
$3x_1 - x_2 = 1$
$2x_1 - 3x_2 + 4x_3 = 3$

(d) $x_1 + x_2 = 7$
$x_2 - x_3 + x_4 = 5$
$x_1 - x_2 + x_3 + x_4 = 6$
$x_2 - x_4 = 10$

(e) $x_1 + 2x_2 - x_3 = 1$
$2x_1 - x_2 = -3$
$x_2 + 2x_3 = 5$

(f) $3x_1 - 4x_2 = 7$
$6x_1 - 8x_2 = 13$

(g) $x_1 + 2x_2 + 3x_3 - x_4 = 0$
$3x_1 - x_3 = 4$
$x_2 - x_3 - x_4 = 2$

(h) $2x_1 - 3x_2 + 4x_3 = 7$
$x_1 - 2x_2 + 3x_3 = 2$

(i) $x_1 + x_2 + x_3 + x_4 = 0$
$2x_1 - x_2 - x_3 + x_4 = 0$
$x_1 - x_2 - x_3 + x_4 = 0$
$x_1 + x_2 - x_3 - x_4 = 0$

2. Follow the directions of Problem 1, in which the left-hand side of problems (a), (b), (c), (d) remain the same and the right-hand side changes to

(a) 3
   7
   8

(b) 5
   7

(c) 0
   0
   0

(d) 0
   1
   0
   1

3. Find a matrix $A$ such that

$$\begin{pmatrix} 1 & 2 \\ 3 & 4 \end{pmatrix} A = \begin{pmatrix} 9 & 1 \\ 0 & 7 \end{pmatrix}$$

4. Show that one solution to

$$\begin{pmatrix} 1 & 1 \\ 1 & 1 \end{pmatrix}\begin{pmatrix} x_1 \\ x_2 \end{pmatrix} = \begin{pmatrix} 1 \\ 1 \end{pmatrix}$$

is

$$\begin{pmatrix} x_1 \\ x_2 \end{pmatrix} = \begin{pmatrix} \frac{1}{2} \\ \frac{1}{2} \end{pmatrix}$$

Find all the solutions of this system.

5. An amount of $5000 is put into three investments at rates of 6, 7, and 8 percent per annum, respectively. The total annual income is $358. The combined income from the first two investments is $70 more than the income from the third investment. Find the amount of each investment. Let $x_1, x_2,$

and $x_3$ denote the amount invested at 6, 7, and 8 percent, respectively. Then

$$0.06x_1 + 0.07x_2 + 0.08x_3 = 358$$
$$0.06x_1 + 0.07x_2 - 0.08x_3 = 70$$
$$x_1 + x_2 + x_3 = 5000$$

These three equations can be written in a matrix form as

$$AX = B$$

where

$$A = \begin{pmatrix} 0.06 & 0.07 & 0.08 \\ 0.06 & 0.07 & -0.08 \\ 1 & 1 & 1 \end{pmatrix}, \quad X = \begin{pmatrix} x_1 \\ x_2 \\ x_3 \end{pmatrix}, \quad B = \begin{pmatrix} 358 \\ 70 \\ 5000 \end{pmatrix}$$

Find $X$.

---

In this section, we discuss a technique for finding the inverse of a matrix. Recall that if $A$, $B$, and $I_n$ are square matrices of dimension $n \times n$, then $B$ is an inverse of $A$ if and only if $AB = I_n$, where $I_n$ is the identity matrix.
  Suppose we want to find the inverse of a matrix $A$ given by

$$A = \begin{pmatrix} 2 & 1 \\ 0 & 1 \end{pmatrix}$$

Let

$$X = \begin{pmatrix} x_1 & x_2 \\ x_3 & x_4 \end{pmatrix}$$

be an inverse of $A$, if such an inverse exists. Then

$$AX = I_2$$

This matrix equation can be written as the following system of equations

$$2x_1 + x_3 = 1, \qquad 2x_2 + x_4 = 0$$
$$x_3 = 0, \qquad x_4 = 1 \tag{5.1}$$

Solving these equations, using previous techniques, we find that

$$x_1 = \frac{1}{2}, \qquad x_2 = -\frac{1}{2}, \qquad x_3 = 0, \qquad x_4 = 1$$

Thus, the inverse of $A$ is

$$A^{-1} = \begin{pmatrix} \frac{1}{2} & -\frac{1}{2} \\ 0 & 1 \end{pmatrix}$$

The four equations in (5.1) can be written in two blocks as

(a) $\begin{aligned} 2x_1 + x_3 &= 1 \\ x_3 &= 0 \end{aligned}$    (b) $\begin{aligned} 2x_2 + x_4 &= 0 \\ x_4 &= 1 \end{aligned}$

Their augmented matrices are

$$\text{(a)} \begin{pmatrix} 2 & 1 & | & 1 \\ 0 & 1 & | & 0 \end{pmatrix} \quad \text{and} \quad \text{(b)} \begin{pmatrix} 2 & 1 & | & 0 \\ 0 & 1 & | & 1 \end{pmatrix}$$

Since the matrix $A$ appears in both (a) and (b), any row operations we perform can more easily be performed on the augmented matrix that combines the two right-hand columns. We denote this matrix by $A|I_2$ and we write

$$A|I_2 = \begin{pmatrix} 2 & 1 & | & 1 & 0 \\ 0 & 1 & | & 0 & 1 \end{pmatrix}$$

If we perform row operations on $A|I_2$, obtaining the matrix

$$\begin{pmatrix} 1 & 0 & | & \frac{1}{2} & -\frac{1}{2} \\ 0 & 1 & | & 0 & 1 \end{pmatrix}$$

we observe that the $2 \times 2$ matrix on the right-hand side of the above matrix is $A^{-1}$. This example illustrates the following general principle:

**Let $A$ be a matrix of dimension $n \times n$ having an inverse. Let $A|I_n$ denote its augmented matrix. If $I_n|B$ is a matrix row-equivalent to $A|I_n$, then $B$ is an inverse of $A$.**

5.1
Example

Find the inverse of

$$A = \begin{pmatrix} 1 & 1 & 2 \\ 2 & 1 & 0 \\ 1 & 2 & 2 \end{pmatrix}$$

Since $A$ is of dimension $3 \times 3$, we use the identity matrix $I_3$. The augmented matrix $A|I_3$ is

$$\begin{pmatrix} 1 & 1 & 2 & | & 1 & 0 & 0 \\ 2 & 1 & 0 & | & 0 & 1 & 0 \\ 1 & 2 & 2 & | & 0 & 0 & 1 \end{pmatrix}$$

Now

$$\begin{pmatrix} 1 & 1 & 2 & | & 1 & 0 & 0 \\ 2 & 1 & 0 & | & 0 & 1 & 0 \\ 1 & 2 & 2 & | & 0 & 0 & 1 \end{pmatrix} \approx \begin{pmatrix} 1 & 1 & 2 & | & 1 & 0 & 0 \\ 0 & -1 & -4 & | & -2 & 1 & 0 \\ 0 & 1 & 0 & | & -1 & 0 & 1 \end{pmatrix}$$

$$\approx \begin{pmatrix} 1 & 0 & 2 & | & 2 & 0 & -1 \\ 0 & 0 & -4 & | & -3 & 1 & 1 \\ 0 & 1 & 0 & | & -1 & 0 & 1 \end{pmatrix} \approx \begin{pmatrix} 1 & 0 & 2 & | & 2 & 0 & -1 \\ 0 & 1 & 0 & | & -1 & 0 & 1 \\ 0 & 0 & 1 & | & \frac{3}{4} & -\frac{1}{4} & -\frac{1}{4} \end{pmatrix}$$

$$\approx \begin{pmatrix} 1 & 0 & 0 & | & \frac{1}{2} & \frac{1}{2} & -\frac{1}{2} \\ 0 & 1 & 0 & | & -1 & 0 & 1 \\ 0 & 0 & 1 & | & \frac{3}{4} & -\frac{1}{4} & -\frac{1}{4} \end{pmatrix}$$

Thus, the inverse of $A$ is

$$A^{-1} = \begin{pmatrix} \frac{1}{2} & \frac{1}{2} & -\frac{1}{2} \\ -1 & 0 & 1 \\ \frac{3}{4} & -\frac{1}{4} & -\frac{1}{4} \end{pmatrix}$$

The student should verify that $AA^{-1} = I_3$.

The following result gives the condition under which a matrix $A$ has an inverse. We omit the proof.

**A matrix $A$ of dimension $n \times n$ has an inverse $A^{-1}$ if and only if the rank of $A = n$.**

A matrix $A$ that has an inverse is said to be *nonsingular*.  Nonsingular Matrix

An application of the use of inverse matrices to the solution of systems of equations in which the coefficient matrix is nonsingular is given below.

Solve the system of equations  5.2
Example

$$\begin{aligned} x_1 + x_2 + 2x_3 &= 1 \\ 2x_1 + x_2 \quad\quad &= 2 \\ x_1 + 2x_2 + 2x_3 &= 3 \end{aligned}$$

If we let

$$A = \begin{pmatrix} 1 & 1 & 2 \\ 2 & 1 & 0 \\ 1 & 2 & 2 \end{pmatrix}, \quad X = \begin{pmatrix} x_1 \\ x_2 \\ x_3 \end{pmatrix}, \quad B = \begin{pmatrix} 1 \\ 2 \\ 3 \end{pmatrix}$$

the above system can be written as

$$AX = B \tag{5.2}$$

in which $A$ is the coefficient matrix. Since $A$ is nonsingular (see Example 5.1), its inverse $A^{-1}$ exists. If we multiply equation 5.2 by $A^{-1}$, we obtain

$$\begin{aligned} A^{-1}(AX) &= A^{-1}B \\ (A^{-1}A)X &= A^{-1}B \\ I_3X &= A^{-1}B \\ X &= A^{-1}B \end{aligned}$$

$$X = \begin{pmatrix} \frac{1}{2} & \frac{1}{2} & -\frac{1}{2} \\ -1 & 0 & 1 \\ \frac{3}{4} & -\frac{1}{4} & -\frac{1}{4} \end{pmatrix} \begin{pmatrix} 1 \\ 2 \\ 3 \end{pmatrix}$$

$$= \begin{pmatrix} 0 \\ 2 \\ -\frac{1}{2} \end{pmatrix}$$

Thus the solution is

$$x_1 = 0, \qquad x_2 = 2, \qquad x_3 = -\frac{1}{2}$$

1. Find the inverse, if it exists, of each of the following matrices

(a) $\begin{pmatrix} 0 & 0 & 1 \\ 0 & 1 & 0 \\ 1 & 0 & 0 \end{pmatrix}$

(f) $\begin{pmatrix} 1 & 1 & 0 & 0 \\ 0 & 1 & -1 & 1 \\ 1 & -1 & 1 & 1 \\ 0 & 1 & 0 & -1 \end{pmatrix}$

(b) $\begin{pmatrix} -1 & 1 & 0 \\ 1 & 0 & 2 \\ 3 & 1 & 0 \end{pmatrix}$

(g) $\begin{pmatrix} 2 & 1 \\ 4 & 3 \end{pmatrix}$

(c) $\begin{pmatrix} 2 & 3 & -1 \\ 1 & 1 & 1 \\ 0 & 2 & -1 \end{pmatrix}$

(h) $\begin{pmatrix} 1 & 1 & -1 \\ 2 & 1 & 1 \\ 1 & 0 & 1 \end{pmatrix}$

(d) $\begin{pmatrix} 2 & 3 \\ 2 & -1 \end{pmatrix}$

(i) $\begin{pmatrix} 1 & 1 & 1 \\ 2 & 1 & 1 \\ 1 & 1 & 2 \end{pmatrix}$

(e) $\begin{pmatrix} 1 & 1 & -1 \\ 3 & -1 & 0 \\ 2 & -3 & 4 \end{pmatrix}$

2. Find a matrix $A$ such that

$$A \begin{pmatrix} 1 & 4 \\ 2 & 3 \end{pmatrix} = I_2$$

3. If $A = \begin{pmatrix} 1 & 2 \\ 7 & 9 \end{pmatrix}$, find $(I_2 - A)^{-1}$.

4. Show that

(a) $(A^{-1})^{-1} = A$ for $A = \begin{pmatrix} 3 & -2 \\ 2 & 4 \end{pmatrix}$

(b) $(AB)^{-1} = B^{-1}A^{-1}$ for $A = \begin{pmatrix} 3 & -2 \\ 2 & 4 \end{pmatrix}$, $B = \begin{pmatrix} 4 & -1 \\ 5 & 2 \end{pmatrix}$

*5. What is the necessary and sufficient condition for

$$A = \begin{pmatrix} a & b \\ c & d \end{pmatrix}$$

to have an inverse?

## Economics: The Leontief Input-Output Model

The Leontief input-output model in economics is named after Wassily Leontief, a recipient of the Nobel Prize in Economics in 1973. (See the October 29, 1973 issue of *Newsweek*, p. 94.) The input-output model can be characterized as a description of an economy in which input equals output or, in other words, production equals consumption. That is, the model assumes that whatever is produced is always consumed.

Input-output models are of two types: closed, in which the entire production is consumed by those participating in the production; and open, in which some of the production is consumed by those who produce it and the rest of the production is consumed by external bodies.

We begin with a study of a closed input-output model. For example, consider a very simple society that consists only of a farmer (who provides food), a builder (who constructs homes), and a tailor (who provides clothing, shoes, etc.). Suppose the farmer consumes one-half of the food he grows, while the remainder is consumed equally by the builder and the tailor. Suppose the production of the builder is shared equally by the farmer, builder and tailor. Finally, suppose all of the clothing is consumed so that 40 percent is consumed by both the farmer and builder and 20 percent by the tailor.

The Closed
Model

Of importance is the fact that all production is consumed internally, a characteristic of the closed model.

We can represent the information of the example by a $3 \times 3$ matrix:

$$
\begin{array}{c}
 & \text{Food} \quad \text{Shelter} \quad \text{Clothing} \\
\begin{array}{c}
\text{Farmer} \\
\text{Builder} \\
\text{Tailor}
\end{array}
\begin{pmatrix}
\dfrac{1}{2} & \dfrac{1}{3} & \dfrac{2}{5} \\
\dfrac{1}{4} & \dfrac{1}{3} & \dfrac{2}{5} \\
\dfrac{1}{4} & \dfrac{1}{3} & \dfrac{1}{5}
\end{pmatrix}
\end{array}
$$

This matrix is termed an *input-output matrix*.

Input-Output
Matrix

**In general, an input-output matrix for a closed Leontief model is of the form**

$$A = (a_{ij}) \qquad i, j = 1, 2, \ldots, n$$

**where the $a_{ij}$ represent the fractional amount of goods used by $i$ and produced by $j$. For a closed model, the sum of each column equals one (this is the condition that all production is consumed internally) and $0 \leq a_{ij} \leq 1$ for all entries (this is the restriction that each entry is a fraction).**

If $x_1$ represents the income that the farmer receives for selling food, and $x_2$ and $x_3$ are the incomes received by the builder and tailor, respectively, then, since the system is closed, we must have

$$x_1 = \frac{1}{2}x_1 + \frac{1}{3}x_2 + \frac{2}{5}x_3$$

$$x_2 = \frac{1}{4}x_1 + \frac{1}{3}x_2 + \frac{2}{5}x_3 \qquad (6.1)$$

$$x_3 = \frac{1}{4}x_1 + \frac{1}{3}x_2 + \frac{1}{5}x_3$$

What we can say about each one's income?

**In general, if $A$ is the input-output matrix of a closed system with $n$ participants and $X$ is a column vector representing the income of each participant in the system, then**

$$X = AX \qquad \text{or} \qquad (I_n - A)X = \theta \qquad (6.2)$$

A matrix equation like (6.2) is called a homogeneous system, since the matrix on the right side is the zero matrix. This system of equations has a solution since

$$\text{rank}\,(I_n - A) = \text{rank}\,((I_n - A)\,|\,\theta)$$

(Refer to section 5.4 of this chapter.)

The matrix $I_n - A$ is of rank $(n - 1)$, provided all the entries in $A$ are positive. (This fact is not to be derived and is offered without proof.) Since the number of unknowns is $n$, this means the system (6.2) has infinitely many solutions. Furthermore, we can solve for $(n - 1)$ of the unknowns in terms of exactly one of them.

For example, if we solve the system (6.1), we find that

$$x_1 = \frac{8}{5}x_3$$

$$x_2 = \frac{6}{5}x_3$$

Thus the incomes of the farmer, builder, and tailor are in the ratio 8:6:5.

**The Open Model**    For an open input-output model, in addition to internal consumption of goods produced, there is an outside demand for the goods produced. This outside demand may take the form of exportation of goods or may be the goods needed to support consumer demand. Again, however, we make the assumption that whatever is produced is also consumed.

For example, suppose an economy consists of three industries $R$, $S$, and $T$, and suppose each one produces a single product. We assume that a portion of $R$'s production is used by each of the three industries, while the remainder is used up by consumers. The same is true of the production of $S$ and $T$. To fix our ideas, we construct a table that describes this interaction of the use of $R$, $S$, and $T$'s production over some fixed period of time.

|   | R | S | T | Consumer | Total |
|---|---|---|---|----------|-------|
| R | 50 | 20 | 40 | 70 | 180 |
| S | 20 | 30 | 20 | 90 | 160 |
| T | 30 | 20 | 20 | 50 | 120 |

All entries of the table are in appropriate units, say dollars. Then, the first row (row $R$) represents the production in dollars of industry $R$ (input). Out of the total of $180 worth of goods produced by $R$, the industries $R$, $S$, and $T$ use $50, $20, and $40, respectively, for the production of their goods while consumers purchase the remaining $70 for their consumption (output). Observe that input equals output since everything produced by $R$ is used up by $R$, $S$, $T$, and consumers.

The second and third rows are interpreted in the same way.

An important observation is that the goal of $R$'s production is to produce $70 worth of goods, since this is the demand of consumers. In order to meet this demand, $R$ must produce a total of $180, since the difference $110 is required internally by $R$, $S$, and $T$.

Suppose, however, that consumer demand is expected to change. To anticipate this change, how much should each industry produce? For example, in the table above, current demand for $R$, $S$, $T$ can be represented by a *demand vector*

Demand Vector

$$D_0 = \begin{pmatrix} 70 \\ 90 \\ 50 \end{pmatrix}$$

But suppose marketing forecasts predict that in three years the demand vector will be

$$D_3 = \begin{pmatrix} 60 \\ 110 \\ 60 \end{pmatrix}$$

Here the demand for item $R$ has decreased; the demand for item $S$ has increased significantly, and the demand for item $T$ is slightly higher. Given the current total output of $R$, $S$, and $T$ at $180, $160, and $120, respectively, what must it be in three years to meet this projected demand?

In using input-output analysis to obtain a solution to such a forecasting problem, we take into account the fact that the output of one of these industries is affected by changes in the two others, since the total demand for $R$, say, in three years depends not only on consumer demand for $R$, but also on consumer demand for $S$ and $T$. That is, the industries are interrelated.

This type of forecasting problem is called the *open Leontief model* in input-output analysis.

To obtain the input-output matrix, we determine how much of each of the three products $R$, $S$, and $T$ is required to produce one unit of $R$. For example, to obtain 180 units of $R$ requires the use of 50 units of $R$, 20 units of $S$ and 30 units of $T$ (the entries in column one). Forming the ratios, we find that to produce 1 unit of $R$ requires $50/180 = 0.278$ of $R$, $20/180 = 0.111$ of $S$, and $30/180 = 0.167$ of $T$. If we want, say, $x_1$ units of $R$, we will require $0.278x_1$ units of $R$, $0.111x_1$ units of $S$, and $0.167x_1$ units of $T$.

Continuing in this way, we can construct the input-output matrix

$$A = \begin{array}{c} \\ R \\ S \\ T \end{array} \begin{pmatrix} R & S & T \\ 0.278 & 0.125 & 0.333 \\ 0.111 & 0.188 & 0.167 \\ 0.167 & 0.125 & 0.167 \end{pmatrix}$$

For example, the entry 0.125 in row 3, column 2 represents the amount of $T$ needed to produce 1 unit of $S$.

Suppose we wish to forecast total output required for a given demand vector $D$. For example, for the demand vector

$$D_0 = \begin{pmatrix} 70 \\ 90 \\ 50 \end{pmatrix}$$

the total output vector is

$$X = \begin{pmatrix} 180 \\ 160 \\ 120 \end{pmatrix}$$

To find the total output $X = \begin{pmatrix} x_1 \\ x_2 \\ x_3 \end{pmatrix}$ required for the demand vector

$$D_3 = \begin{pmatrix} 60 \\ 110 \\ 60 \end{pmatrix}$$

we observe that the production of industry $R$ must be

$$0.278x_1 + 0.125x_2 + 0.333x_3 + 60 = x_1$$

Here the first three terms represent the amount of product $R$ required by industries $R$, $S$, and $T$, respectively; and the number 60 represents the forecast demand for $R$. Thus, the sum of these must equal the total output of product $R$, namely, $x_1$.

By the same reasoning, for products $S$ and $T$, we have

$$0.111x_1 + 0.188x_2 + 0.167x_3 + 110 = x_2$$
$$0.167x_1 + 0.125x_2 + 0.167x_3 + 60 = x_3$$

Using matrix notation, these equations become

$$\begin{pmatrix} 0.278 & 0.125 & 0.333 \\ 0.111 & 0.188 & 0.167 \\ 0.167 & 0.125 & 0.167 \end{pmatrix} \begin{pmatrix} x_1 \\ x_2 \\ x_3 \end{pmatrix} + \begin{pmatrix} 60 \\ 110 \\ 60 \end{pmatrix} = \begin{pmatrix} x_1 \\ x_2 \\ x_3 \end{pmatrix}$$

or

$$AX + D_3 = X$$

or

$$(I_3 - A)X = D_3$$

151
5.6
APPLICATIONS TO
ECONOMICS,
DEMOGRAPHY, AND
ACCOUNTING

Solving for $X$, we have

$$X = (I_3 - A)^{-1} \cdot D_3$$

$$= \begin{pmatrix} 0.722 & -0.125 & -0.333 \\ -0.111 & 0.812 & -0.167 \\ -0.167 & -0.125 & 0.833 \end{pmatrix}^{-1} \begin{pmatrix} 60 \\ 110 \\ 60 \end{pmatrix}$$

$$= \begin{pmatrix} 1.6048 & 0.3568 & 0.7131 \\ 0.2946 & 1.3363 & 0.3857 \\ 0.3660 & 0.2721 & 1.4013 \end{pmatrix} \begin{pmatrix} 60 \\ 110 \\ 60 \end{pmatrix}$$

$$= \begin{pmatrix} 178.322 \\ 187.811 \\ 135.969 \end{pmatrix}$$

Thus, the total output of $R$, $S$, and $T$ required three years from now for the forecast demand $D_3$, is

$$x_1 = 178.322 \qquad x_2 = 187.811 \qquad x_3 = 135.969$$

**In general if $A$ is the input-output matrix of an open Leontief model with $n$ industries, $X$ is a column vector representing the production of each industry in the system, and $D$ is a column vector representing future demand for goods produced in the system, then**

$$X = AX + D \qquad \text{or} \qquad (I_n - A)X = D \qquad (6.3)$$

This matrix equation represents a system of $n$ equations in $n$ unknowns and will have a solution provided

$$\text{rank}\,(I_n - A) = n$$

It can be shown that the matrix $I_n - A$ is always of rank $n$, provided the column sums of $A$ are less than one and $A$ has all positive entries. Thus, the matrix solution of (6.3) is

$$X = (I_n - A)^{-1}D$$

We conclude by noting that the use of an input-output matrix to solve forecasting problems assumes that each industry produces a single commodity or good and that no technological advances take place in the period of time under investigation (in other words, the proportions found in the input-output matrix are fixed).

1. A society consists of four individuals, a farmer, a builder, a tailor, and a rancher (who produces meat products). Of the food produced by the farmer, he uses 3/10 of it, the builder 2/10, the tailor 2/10, and the rancher 3/10. The builder's production is utilized 30 percent by the farmer, 30 percent by the builder, 10 percent by the tailor, and 30 percent by the rancher. The tailor's production is used in

5.6.1
Exercise

the ratios 3/10, 3/10, 1/10, and 3/10 by the farmer, builder, tailor, and rancher. Finally, meat products are used 20 percent by each of the farmer, builder, and tailor and 40 percent by the rancher. In what ratios are their incomes?

2. If in Problem 1, the meat production utilization changes so that it is used equally by all four individuals, while everyone else's production utilization remains the same, in what ratios are their incomes?

3. For the three industries $R$, $S$, and $T$ in the open Leontief model on page 148, compute the total output vector $X$ if the forecast demand vector is

$$D_2 = \begin{pmatrix} 80 \\ 90 \\ 60 \end{pmatrix}$$

4. Suppose the interrelationships between the production of two industries $R$ and $S$ in a given year is

|   | $R$ | $S$ | Current Consumer Demand | Total output |
|---|---|---|---|---|
| $R$ | 30 | 40 | 60 | 130 |
| $S$ | 20 | 10 | 40 | 70 |

If the forecast demand in two years is

$$D_2 = \begin{pmatrix} 80 \\ 40 \end{pmatrix}$$

what should the total output $X$ be?

## Demography[1]

A further application of matrices can be made to demography, a science of vital statistics, which deals with birth rates, death rates, and population trends.

To project population trends, three sets of data are needed: (1) the number of people living in different age categories on a given date, (2) the number of people surviving in these age categories over a time interval from that date, (3) the number of people born in the time interval to people in a given age category.

In order to simplify the data involved in such a study, (1) we shall assign daughters born according to the age category of their mother,

[1] Richard Stone, "Mathematics in the Social Sciences," *Scientific American* (September 1964).

**153**
5.6
APPLICATIONS TO
ECONOMICS,
DEMOGRAPHY, AND
ACCOUNTING

| Age | No. Females Alive in 1940 | Females Alive 15 Years Later (in 1955) | Daughters Born in 15-Year Interval (1940–1955) |
|---|---|---|---|
| 0–14 | 14,459 | 16,428 | 4,651 |
| 15–29 | 15,264 | 14,258 | 10,403 |
| 30–44 | 11,346 | 14,836 | 1,374 |

**Figure 5.6**

and (2) we shall assume a constant pattern of birth and death for the time interval studied.

Based on the 1940 United States Census, we obtain the data matrix for the time interval 1940–1955. See Figure 5.6.

The entries in column one represent the number of females alive in 1940 for the three age groups specified. The entries in column two represent the number of females that are alive in 1955 for each of the three age brackets. For example, the entry in row two, column two, 14,258, represents the survivors from the age group 0–14 alive in 1940 (14,459). Similarly, 14,836 represents the number of females alive in 1955 that survived from the 15,264 alive in 1940. The entries in column three represent the number of daughters born to females from the three age groups during the 15 year period 1940–1955.

Now, divide the number of daughters born in the 15-year interval (as shown in the third column) by the total number of females (as shown in the first column). The resulting ratios give the frequency for births in a given age group. These ratios are inserted in the first row of the frequency matrix shown in Figure 5.7. To obtain the second row, we need to know the survival frequency from the 0–14 age group to the 15–29 age group. Those females in the 0–14 age group (14,459) who survived 15 years later number 14,258. Thus, the ratio of survival is $14258 \div 14,459$. We use zeros for the remaining entries of row 2, since it is not possible to speak of a survival frequency in these age groups. Similarly, row 3 is obtained.

The product of the frequency matrix $F$ by the column matrix for

|  | 0–14 | 15–29 | 30–44 |
|---|---|---|---|
| Frequency for birth | $\dfrac{4651}{14459}$ | $\dfrac{10403}{15264}$ | $\dfrac{1374}{11346}$ |
| Survival frequency 0–14 to 15–29 | $\dfrac{14258}{14459}$ | 0 | 0 |
| Survival frequency 15–29 to 30–44 | 0 | $\dfrac{14836}{15264}$ | 0 |

**Figure 5.7**

females alive in 1940 gives the number of females alive in 1955. That is

$$
\begin{array}{ccc}
\text{Frequency matrix } F & \text{Females (1940)} & \begin{array}{c}\text{Females alive 15}\\\text{years later (1955)}\end{array}
\end{array}
$$

$$
\begin{pmatrix} 0.32167 & 0.68154 & 0.12110 \\ 0.98610 & 0 & 0 \\ 0 & 0.97196 & 0 \end{pmatrix}
\begin{pmatrix} 14459 \\ 15264 \\ 11346 \end{pmatrix}
=
\begin{pmatrix} 16428 \\ 14258 \\ 14836 \end{pmatrix}
$$

Since this is in agreement with the information in Figure 5.6, it indicates that our frequency matrix $F$ has been correctly calculated.

To obtain a projection for 1970, which is 15 years later than 1955, merely find the product of the square of the frequency matrix $F$ times the column matrix for females in 1940. Thus

$$
\begin{array}{c}\text{Females}\\(1940)\end{array}
$$

$$
F^2 \cdot \begin{pmatrix} 14459 \\ 15264 \\ 11346 \end{pmatrix}
= \begin{pmatrix} 0.77554 & 0.33694 & 0.03895 \\ 0.31719 & 0.67207 & 0.11942 \\ 0.95852 & 0 & 0 \end{pmatrix}
\begin{pmatrix} 14459 \\ 15264 \\ 11346 \end{pmatrix}
= \begin{pmatrix} 16{,}799 \\ 16{,}200 \\ 13{,}863 \end{pmatrix}
$$

To obtain a projection for 1985 (30 years past 1955), find the product of the cube of the frequency matrix times the column matrix for females in 1940. Then

$$
\begin{array}{c}\text{Females}\\(1940)\end{array}
$$

$$
F^3 \cdot \begin{pmatrix} 14459 \\ 15264 \\ 11346 \end{pmatrix}
= \begin{pmatrix} 0.58172 & 0.56643 & 0.09392 \\ 0.76476 & 0.33226 & 0.03841 \\ 0.30832 & 0.65327 & 0.11608 \end{pmatrix}
\begin{pmatrix} 14459 \\ 15264 \\ 11346 \end{pmatrix}
= \begin{pmatrix} 18{,}123 \\ 16{,}565 \\ 15{,}747 \end{pmatrix}
$$

5.6.2
Exercise

1. Using the 1950 United States Census, and data from 1965, develop a projection for females in the 0–14, 15–29, and 30–44 age groups for the years 1980 and 1995.
2. Make the same sort of projection as in Problem 1 using data from the 1955 and the 1970 United States Census as a base. How does this projection compare with that found in the text for the year 1985?

## Accounting

Consider a firm which has two types of departments, production and service. The production departments produce goods that can be sold in the market, and the service departments provide services to the production departments.

The price of the final product must include direct costs (salaries, wages, cost of materials) and indirect costs (charges for the services the pro-

**155**
5.6
APPLICATIONS TO
ECONOMICS,
DEMOGRAPHY, AND
ACCOUNTING

duction departments receive from the service departments). Moreover, the service departments also provide services for the service departments themselves. For example, an accounting department usually provides accounting services for service departments as well as for the production departments. Thus the cost of services rendered by a service department must be determined in order to correctly assess the cost of operating the production departments. The total costs of a service department consist of its direct costs (salaries, wages, and materials) and its indirect costs (charges for the services it receives from the service departments). The nature of the problem and its solution are illustrated by the following example.

6.2
Example

Consider a firm with two production departments $P_1$ and $P_2$ and three service departments $S_1$, $S_2$, and $S_3$. These five departments are shown in the first column of the table in Figure 5.8. The total monthly costs of these departments are unknown and are denoted by $x_1, x_2, x_3, x_4, x_5$. The direct monthly costs of the five departments are shown in the third column. The fourth, fifth, and sixth columns show the allocation of charges for the services of $S_1$, $S_2$, and $S_3$ to the various departments. Since the total cost of a department is the direct plus indirect costs, the first three rows of the table yield the total costs for the three service departments. Thus

$$\begin{aligned} x_1 &= 600 + 0.25x_1 + 0.15x_2 + 0.15x_3 \\ x_2 &= 1100 + 0.35x_1 + 0.20x_2 + 0.25x_3 \\ x_3 &= 600 + 0.10x_1 + 0.10x_2 + 0.35x_3 \end{aligned} \tag{6.5}$$

Let $X$, $C$, and $D$ denote the following matrices:

$$X = \begin{pmatrix} x_1 \\ x_2 \\ x_3 \end{pmatrix}, \qquad C = \begin{pmatrix} 0.25 & 0.15 & 0.15 \\ 0.35 & 0.20 & 0.25 \\ 0.10 & 0.10 & 0.35 \end{pmatrix}, \qquad D = \begin{pmatrix} 600 \\ 1100 \\ 600 \end{pmatrix}$$

| Department | Total Costs | Direct Costs, dollars | Indirect Costs for Services from Departments | | |
|---|---|---|---|---|---|
| | | | $S_1$ | $S_2$ | $S_3$ |
| $S_1$ | $x_1$ | 600 | $0.25x_1$ | $0.15x_2$ | $0.15x_3$ |
| $S_2$ | $x_2$ | 1100 | $0.35x_1$ | $0.20x_2$ | $0.25x_3$ |
| $S_3$ | $x_3$ | 600 | $0.10x_1$ | $0.10x_2$ | $0.35x_3$ |
| $P_1$ | $x_4$ | 2100 | $0.15x_1$ | $0.25x_2$ | $0.15x_3$ |
| $P_2$ | $x_5$ | 1500 | $0.15x_1$ | $0.30x_2$ | $0.10x_3$ |
| Totals | | | $x_1$ | $x_2$ | $x_3$ |

**Figure 5.8**

Then the set of equations (6.5) can be written in matrix notation

$$X = D + C \cdot X$$

This is equivalent to

$$(I_3 - C) \cdot X = D \tag{6.6}$$

The total costs of the three service departments can be obtained by solving the matrix equation (6.6) for $X$. The solution is

$$X = (I_3 - C)^{-1} \cdot D \tag{6.7}$$

Now

$$I_3 - C = \begin{pmatrix} 0.75 & -0.15 & -0.15 \\ -0.35 & 0.80 & -0.25 \\ -0.10 & -0.10 & 0.65 \end{pmatrix}$$

It can be verified that

$$(I_3 - C)^{-1} = \begin{pmatrix} 1.57 & 0.36 & 0.50 \\ 0.79 & 1.49 & 0.76 \\ 0.36 & 0.28 & 1.73 \end{pmatrix} \tag{6.8}$$

It is significant that the inverse of $(I_3 - C)$ exists, and that all of its entries are nonnegative. Because of this, and the fact that the matrix $D$ contains only nonnegative entries, the matrix $X$ computed from (6.7) will also have only nonnegative entries. This means there is a meaningful solution to the accounting problem.

From Equations (6.7) and (6.8), the matrix $X$ is

$$X = \begin{pmatrix} 1638.00 \\ 2569.00 \\ 1562.00 \end{pmatrix}$$

Thus $x_1 = \$1638.00$, $x_2 = \$2569.00$, and $x_3 = \$1562.00$. All direct and indirect costs can now be determined by substituting these values in the table of Figure 5.8. See Figure 5.9.

From Figure 5.9 we learn that department $P_1$ pays \$1122.25 for the services it receives from $S_1$, $S_2$, $S_3$, and $P_2$ pays \$1172.60 for the services it receives from these departments. The procedure we have followed charges the direct costs of the service departments to the production departments, and each production department is charged according to the services it utilizes. Furthermore, the total cost for $P_1$ and $P_2$ is \$5894.85, and this figure approximates the sum of the direct costs of the three service departments and the two production departments. The results are consistent with conventional accounting procedure. Discrepancies that occur are due to rounding off.

Finally, a comment should be made about the allocation of charges for services as shown in Figure 5.8. How is it determined that 25 percent of the total cost $x_1$ of $S_1$ should be charged to $S_1$, 35 percent to $S_2$, 10 percent to $S_3$, 15 percent to $P_1$, and 15 percent to $P_2$? There are two possible answers. First, it may be an arbitrary decision. Second, the

**157**
5.6
APPLICATIONS TO
ECONOMICS,
DEMOGRAPHY, AND
ACCOUNTING

| Department | Total Costs, dollars | Direct Costs dollars | Indirect Costs for Services from Departments, dollars | | |
|---|---|---|---|---|---|
| | | | $S_1$ | $S_2$ | $S_3$ |
| $S_1$ | 1629.15 | 600 | 409.50 | 385.35 | 234.30 |
| $S_2$ | 2577.60 | 1100 | 573.30 | 513.80 | 390.50 |
| $S_3$ | 1567.40 | 600 | 163.80 | 256.90 | 546.70 |
| $P_1$ | 3222.25 | 2100 | 245.70 | 642.25 | 234.30 |
| $P_2$ | 2672.60 | 1500 | 245.70 | 770.70 | 156.20 |
| | | | | | |

**Figure 5.9** *Monthly costs corresponding to the information in Figure 5.8.*

services of each department may be measured in some suitable unit, and each department may be charged according to the number of these units of service it receives. If 20 percent of the accounting items concern a given department, that department is charged 20 percent of the total cost of the accounting department.

Consider a firm for which the departments, direct costs, and allocations of indirect costs are those shown in the table of Figure 5.10. It should be observed that the total costs of the service departments $S_1$ and $S_2$ are allocated to these same two departments.

6.3
Example

| Department | Total Costs | Direct Costs, dollars | Indirect Costs for Services from Departments | | | |
|---|---|---|---|---|---|---|
| | | | $S_1$ | $S_2$ | $S_3$ | $S_4$ |
| $S_1$ | $x_1$ | 1600 | $0.35x_1$ | $0.40x_2$ | $0.15x_3$ | $0.05x_4$ |
| $S_2$ | $x_2$ | 1000 | $0.65x_1$ | $0.60x_2$ | $0.20x_3$ | $0.10x_4$ |
| $S_3$ | $x_3$ | 800 | 0 | 0 | $0.20x_3$ | $0.05x_4$ |
| $S_4$ | $x_4$ | 1700 | 0 | 0 | $0.15x_3$ | $0.15x_4$ |
| $P_1$ | $x_5$ | 5000 | 0 | 0 | $0.10x_3$ | $0.20x_4$ |
| $P_2$ | $x_6$ | 4000 | 0 | 0 | $0.10x_3$ | $0.25x_4$ |
| $P_3$ | $x_7$ | 2500 | 0 | 0 | $0.10x_3$ | $0.20x_4$ |
| Totals | | | $x_1$ | $x_2$ | $x_3$ | $x_4$ |

**Figure 5.10**

Proceeding as in Example 6.2, we obtain the following equations for determining the total costs $x_1$, $x_2$, $x_3$, $x_4$ of the four service departments $S_1$, $S_2$, $S_3$, $S_4$.

$$x_1 = 1600 + 0.35x_1 + 0.40x_2 + 0.15x_3 + 0.05x_4$$
$$x_2 = 1000 + 0.65x_1 + 0.60x_2 + 0.20x_3 + 0.10x_4$$
$$x_3 = \phantom{1}800 \phantom{+ 0.65x_1 + 0.60x_2} + 0.20x_3 + 0.05x_4$$
$$x_4 = 1700 \phantom{+ 0.65x_1 + 0.60x_2} + 0.15x_3 + 0.15x_4$$

If we add the first two of these four equations, we find that $x_3$ and $x_4$ cannot both be positive. Thus it is clear that no set $x_1$, $x_2$, $x_3$, $x_4$ of nonnegative numbers satisfies these equations. Clearly, a practical constraint for the $x$'s is that they must be nonnegative. Therefore, the accounting problem specified by the data in the table in Figure 5.10 has no solution.

1. Consider the accounting problem described by the data in the table in Figure 5.11. Determine whether this accounting problem has a solution. If it does, find the total costs.

   Make a table that corresponds to the one in Figure 5.9. Show that the total of the service charges allocated to $P_1$, $P_2$, $P_3$ is equal to the sum of the direct costs of the service departments $S_1$, $S_2$.

2. Midwestern University has a School of Arts and Sciences, a School of Education, and a School of Business. The direct costs (in thousands of dollars) of operating the three schools are shown in the third column of the table in Figure 5.12. The costs of operating the three schools are charged to the schools themselves (they provide services for one another) and to legislative appropriations, student fees, and endowment income. The Board of Trustees decides that the costs of the three schools shall be allocated as shown in the fourth, fifth, and sixth columns in the table in Figure 5.12. Observe

| Department | Total Costs | Direct Costs, dollars | Indirect Costs $S_1$ | $S_2$ |
|---|---|---|---|---|
| $S_1$ | $x_1$ | 2000 | $1/9\ x_1$ | $3/9\ x_2$ |
| $S_2$ | $x_2$ | 1000 | $3/9\ x_1$ | $1/9\ x_2$ |
| $P_1$ | $x_3$ | 2500 | $1/9\ x_1$ | $2/9\ x_2$ |
| $P_2$ | $x_4$ | 1500 | $3/9\ x_1$ | $1/9\ x_2$ |
| $P_3$ | $x_5$ | 3000 | $1/9\ x_1$ | $2/9\ x_2$ |
| Totals | | | $x_1$ | $x_2$ |

**Figure 5.11**

| School | Total Costs | Direct Costs, thousands of dollars | Allocation of Costs: Arts and Sciences | Engineering | Business |
|---|---|---|---|---|---|
| Arts and Sciences | $x_1$ | 3000 | $0.05x_1$ | $0.10x_2$ | $0.15x_3$ |
| Education | $x_2$ | 3000 | $0.06x_1$ | $0.06x_2$ | $0.15x_3$ |
| Business | $x_3$ | 1500 | $0.05x_1$ | $0.10x_2$ | $0.15x_3$ |
| Legislative appropriations | $x_4$ | | $0.50x_1$ | $0.55x_2$ | $0.20x_3$ |
| Student fees | $x_5$ | | $0.25x_1$ | $0.12x_2$ | $0.15x_3$ |
| Endowment | $x_6$ | | $0.09x_1$ | $0.07x_2$ | $0.20x_3$ |
| Totals | | | $x_1$ | $x_2$ | $x_3$ |

**Figure 5.12**

that $x_4 + x_5 + x_6$ (the sum of the outside funds required to operate the three schools) is exactly equal to the sum of the direct costs of operating the three schools. Determine whether this accounting problem has a solution, and, if it does, find the total costs.

## CHAPTER REVIEW

### Important Terms

**dimension of a matrix**
**diagonal of a matrix**
**square matrix**
**vector**
**zero matrix**
**scalar**
**identity matrix**
**inverse of a matrix**
**coefficient matrix**
**augmented matrix**
**row-equivalent matrices**
**row-reduced matrix**
**rank of a matrix**
**row operation**
**nonsingular matrix**
**parameter**
**Leontief model (open and closed)**

### Review Exercises

1. Let $A$, $B$, $C$, denote the matrices:

$$A = \begin{pmatrix} -2 & 0 & 7 \\ 1 & 8 & 3 \\ 2 & 4 & 21 \end{pmatrix} \quad B = \begin{pmatrix} 1 & 3 & 9 \\ 2 & 7 & 5 \\ 3 & 6 & 8 \end{pmatrix} \quad C = \begin{pmatrix} 0 & 1 & 2 \\ 0 & 5 & 1 \\ 8 & 7 & 9 \end{pmatrix}$$

Find the following matrices:

(a) $A + B$
(b) $B + A$
(c) $3(A + B)$
(d) $3A + 3B$
(e) $3A - 3B$
(f) $2(5A)$
(g) $\frac{3}{2}A$
(h) $B - C$
(i) $C - B$
(j) $2A + \frac{1}{2}B - 3C$
(k) $AB$
(l) $BA$
(m) $(B - A) \cdot C$

2. What must be true about $x$, $y$, $z$, $w$, if the matrices

$$A = \begin{pmatrix} x & y \\ z & w \end{pmatrix} \quad \text{and} \quad B = \begin{pmatrix} 1 & 1 \\ -1 & 1 \end{pmatrix}$$

are to commute? That is, $AB = BA$.

3. Let $t = (t_1 \quad t_2)$, with $t_1 + t_2 = 1$, and let $A = \begin{pmatrix} \dfrac{1}{4} & \dfrac{3}{4} \\ \dfrac{2}{3} & \dfrac{1}{3} \end{pmatrix}$

Find $t$ such that $tA = t$.

4. Find the inverse of the matrices

(a) $\begin{pmatrix} 3 & 0 \\ -2 & 1 \end{pmatrix}$    (b) $\begin{pmatrix} 1 & 2 & 3 \\ 2 & 4 & 5 \\ 3 & 5 & 6 \end{pmatrix}$

5. Find the row-reduced matrix of each of the following matrices and determine the rank of each.

(a) $\begin{pmatrix} 2 & 0 & 1 \\ 3 & 7 & -1 \\ 1 & 0 & 2 \end{pmatrix}$    (b) $\begin{pmatrix} 1 \\ 1 \\ 1 \end{pmatrix}$

6. Find the solution of

$$\begin{aligned} 2x_1 - x_2 + x_3 &= 1 \\ x_1 + x_2 - x_3 &= 2 \\ 3x_1 - x_2 + x_3 &= 0 \end{aligned}$$

using the matrix technique introduced in this chapter.

## Bibliography

### Mathematics

Johnston, J., G. Price, and F. VanVleck, *Linear Equations and Matrices*, Addison-Wesley, Reading, Mass., 1966.

Knopp, Paul J., *Linear Algebra*, Hamilton Publishing, Santa Barbara, Calif., 1974.

### Applied

Boot, Johannes, *Mathematical Reasoning in Economics and Management Science*, Prentice-Hall, Englewood Cliffs, N.J., 1967.

Gale, D., *The Theory of Linear Economic Models*, McGraw-Hill, New York, 1960.

Leontief, Wassily, "Quantitative Input and Output Relations in the Economic System of the United States," *Review of Economic Statistics*, **18** (1936), pp. 105–125.

Leontief, Wassily, *The Structure of the American Economy 1919–1939*, 2nd Edition, Oxford University Press, New York, 1951.

Leontief, Wassily, *Input-Output Analysis,* Oxford University Press, New York, 1966.

Vazsonyi, A., "The Use of Mathematics in Production and Inventory Control," *Management Science,* **1** (1954), pp. 70–75.

Yan, C. S., *Introduction to Input-Output Economics,* Holt, Rinehart and Winston, New York, 1969.

# 6

# AN ALGEBRAIC APPROACH TO LINEAR PROGRAMMING: THE SIMPLEX METHOD

The graphical method, introduced in Chapter 4, for solving a linear programming problem is useful only when the number of variables is two and when the number of constraints is small.

When the number of variables is three or more, the graphical method cannot be used to find the vertices of the polyhedral convex set of constraints (see step 3 of the linear programming solution procedure described on page 95 in Chapter 4). However, these vertices can be found by first finding the points of intersection of all possible combinations of equations corresponding to the constraint inequalities, and then discarding those points of intersection which are not feasible, that is, which do not satisfy all of the other constraint inequalities. Thus, to solve

**164**
AN ALGEBRAIC
APPROACH TO
LINEAR
PROGRAMMING: THE
SIMPLEX METHOD

even a linear programming problem with only four variables and seven constraint equations by the procedure given in Chapter 4, we would need to select any four of the seven equations and solve them simultaneously (this gives a total of $\binom{7}{4} = 35$ potential vertices). Then we would have to test each solution (point of intersection) in the set of constraints to determine which of these points of intersection are feasible and, consequently, are vertices of the polyhedral convex set of feasible solutions.

The computational difficulties of solving a system of several equations in several unknowns, and then discarding the solutions that are not feasible, can be overcome by using a systematic approach that allows us to proceed from one solution to another. As we proceed, the objective function is improved until a solution is found at which the objective function is minimized (maximized) or until it is determined that no solution exists. This systematic approach, which is suitable for computer application, is called the *simplex method*.

Since the simplex method is directly related to the solution of systems of equations, we shall find that row operations on matrices play a major role. Before proceeding, we illustrate how to convert the set of constraints of a maximum linear programming problem to a system of equations.

Return to Example 2.7 of Chapter 4 (page 95). The linear programming problem consists of maximizing

$$P = 3x_1 + 4x_2$$

subject to the conditions

$$
\begin{array}{ll}
(1)\ \ 2x_1 + 2x_2 \leqq 80 & (3)\ \ x_1 \geqq 0 \\
(2)\ \ 2x_1 + 4x_2 \leqq 120 & (4)\ \ x_2 \geqq 0
\end{array}
$$

We look at the constraints with a view to changing them to a system of linear equations.

The constraints (1) and (2) arise because the grinding time cannot exceed 80 hours and finishing time cannot exceed 120 hours. If, for instance, the actual grinding time used is 70 hours, there is a slack of 10 hours of unused time. Let $x_3$ represent the unused grinding time. ($x_3$ is a non-negative variable since we do not know how much grinding time is unused.) Thus to make the inequality (1) into an equation; we add $x_3$ to the left side obtaining

$$2x_1 + 2x_2 + x_3 = 80 \qquad x_3 \geqq 0$$

Slack Variable  Here $x_3$ is called a *slack variable*. Similarly, we introduce a non-negative slack variable $x_4$ to convert the inequality (2) into an equation.

$$2x_1 + 4x_2 + x_4 = 120 \qquad x_4 \geqq 0$$

The linear programming problem can now be restated as follows: Find $x_1$, $x_2$, $x_3$, and $x_4$ in order to maximize

$$P = 3x_1 + 4x_2$$

subject to the conditions

$$2x_1 + 2x_2 + x_3 = 80 \qquad x_1 \geqq 0,\ x_2 \geqq 0$$
$$2x_1 + 4x_2 + x_4 = 120 \qquad x_3 \geqq 0,\ x_4 \geqq 0$$

We shall continue this problem in Section 6.3.

The next example illustrates the procedure to follow if the constraints of a maximum linear programming problem are not all of the $\leqq$ variety.

The constraints of a maximum linear programming problem are

(1) $3x_1 + 4x_2 + 4x_3 \leqq 24 \qquad x_1 \geqq 0$
(2) $4x_1 + 3x_2 + x_3 \leqq 12 \qquad x_2 \geqq 0$
(3) $x_1 + x_2 + 5x_3 \geqq 15 \qquad x_3 \geqq 0$

Convert them into a system of equations by introducing slack variables.

To make the inequalities (1) and (2) into equations, we introduce non-negative slack variables $x_4$ and $x_5$. Then (1) and (2) become

$$3x_1 + 4x_2 + 4x_3 + x_4 = 24 \qquad x_4 \geqq 0$$
$$4x_1 + 3x_2 + x_3 + x_5 = 12 \qquad x_5 \geqq 0$$

The simplex method requires that the constraints of a maximum linear programming problem appear as inequalities with a $\leqq$ symbol. Thus, we change the inequality (3) from $\geqq$ to $\leqq$ by multiplying by $-1$. This gives

$$-x_1 - x_2 - 5x_3 \leqq -15$$

Now we add a non-negative slack variable $x_6$ to the left side. Then, we have

$$-x_1 - x_2 - 5x_3 + x_6 = -15 \qquad x_6 \geqq 0$$

Convert each of the following sets of constraints of a maximum linear programming problem into a system of equations by introducing slack variables.

1. $5x_1 + 2x_2 + x_3 \leqq 20$
   $6x_1 + x_2 + 4x_3 \leqq 24$
   $x_1 + x_2 + 4x_3 \leqq 16$
   $x_1 \geqq 0,\ x_2 \geqq 0,\ x_3 \geqq 0$

2. $2.2x_1 + 1.8x_2 \leqq 5$
   $0.8x_1 + 1.2x_2 \leqq 2.5$
   $x_1 + x_2 \geqq 0.1$
   $x_1 \geqq 0,\ x_2 \geqq 0$

3. $x_1 + x_2 + x_3 \leqq 50$
   $3x_1 + 2x_2 + x_3 \geqq 10$
   $x_1 \geqq 0,\ x_2 \geqq 0,\ x_3 \geqq 0$

Before we introduce the simplex method for solving a linear programming problem, we need to discuss a procedure called a *pivot operation*.

**166**

AN ALGEBRAIC
APPROACH TO
LINEAR
PROGRAMMING: THE
SIMPLEX METHOD

In a linear programming problem, a pivot operation enables us to move from one feasible solution to another by using row operations in such a way that each new feasible solution improves the value of the objective function. In this section the pivot element is prescribed and only the pivoting procedure is discussed; in Section 6.3 a procedure for selecting the pivot element is given.

We illustrate a pivot operation in the following example.

2.1
Example

Perform a pivot operation on the equations

$$2x_1 + 2x_2 + x_3 = 80$$
$$2x_1 + \text{④}x_2 + x_4 = 120$$

in which the circled entry is the pivot element.

We begin by writing the above equations as the augmented matrix

$$
\begin{array}{cccc}
x_1 & x_2 & x_3 & x_4
\end{array}
$$
$$
\begin{pmatrix}
2 & 2 & 1 & 0 & | & 80 \\
2 & ④ & 0 & 1 & | & 120
\end{pmatrix}
\begin{array}{c}
x_3 \\
x_4
\end{array}
$$

in which the circled entry is the pivot element.

Observe that the entries in column $x_3$ and column $x_4$ form the identity matrix $I_2$. The significance of this is that it is easy to solve for $x_3$ and $x_4$ in terms of $x_1$ and $x_2$. That is,

$$
\begin{array}{lll}
2x_1 + 2x_2 + x_3 = 80 & \text{or} & x_3 = 80 - 2x_1 - 2x_2 \\
2x_1 + 4x_2 + x_4 = 120 & & x_4 = 120 - 2x_1 - 4x_2
\end{array}
$$

The fact that we have solved for $x_3$ and $x_4$ in terms of the other variables is exhibited by placing $x_3$ and $x_4$ to the right of the augmented matrix.

**To pivot means to use row operations so that the pivot element becomes one and all other entries in its column become zero.**

This requires that the vector $\begin{pmatrix} 0 \\ 1 \end{pmatrix}$ appear in the $x_2$ column. We use a row operation to accomplish this and begin by dividing row two by 4. Then

$$
\begin{array}{cccc}
x_1 & x_2 & x_3 & x_4
\end{array}
$$
$$
\begin{pmatrix}
2 & 2 & 1 & 0 & | & 80 \\
\dfrac{1}{2} & 1 & 0 & \dfrac{1}{4} & | & 30
\end{pmatrix}
\qquad
\begin{array}{l}
2x_1 + 2x_2 + \quad x_3 = 80 \\
\dfrac{1}{2}x_1 + \quad x_2 + \dfrac{1}{4}x_4 = 30
\end{array}
$$

Now multiply row two by 2 and subtract from row one. Then

$$
\begin{array}{cccc}
x_1 & x_2 & x_3 & x_4
\end{array}
$$
$$
\begin{pmatrix}
1 & 0 & 1 & -\dfrac{1}{2} & | & 20 \\
\dfrac{1}{2} & 1 & 0 & \dfrac{1}{4} & | & 30
\end{pmatrix}
\begin{array}{c}
x_3 \\
x_2
\end{array}
\qquad
\begin{array}{l}
x_3 = 20 - \quad x_1 + \dfrac{1}{2}x_4 \\
x_2 = 30 - \dfrac{1}{2}x_1 - \dfrac{1}{4}x_4
\end{array}
$$

In the above augmented matrix we notice that the identity matrix $I_2$ has been shifted and its columns now appear in column $x_3$ and column $x_2$. This means it is easy to solve for $x_3$ and $x_2$ in terms of $x_1$ and $x_4$. This is the result of pivoting, and we indicate this by writing $x_3$ and $x_2$ to the right of the augmented matrix.

2.2
Example

Perform a pivot operation on the system of equations

$$
\begin{array}{ccccc}
x_1 & x_2 & x_3 & x_4 & x_5
\end{array}
$$
$$
\left(\begin{array}{ccccc|c}
3 & 2 & 1 & 0 & 0 & 4 \\
-1 & ① & 0 & 1 & 0 & 2 \\
1 & -2 & 0 & 0 & 1 & -3
\end{array}\right)
\begin{array}{l}
x_3 \\ x_4 \\ x_5
\end{array}
\qquad
\begin{array}{l}
3x_1 + 2x_2 + x_3 = 4 \\
-x_1 + x_2 + x_4 = 2 \\
x_1 - 2x_2 + x_5 = -3
\end{array}
$$

in which the circled entry in the augmented matrix is the pivot element.

To obtain zeros in the column $x_2$, we multiply row two by $-2$ and add it to row one and multiply row two by 2 and add it to row three. The result is

$$
\begin{array}{ccccc}
x_1 & x_2 & x_3 & x_4 & x_5
\end{array}
$$
$$
\left(\begin{array}{ccccc|c}
5 & 0 & 1 & -2 & 0 & 0 \\
-1 & 1 & 0 & 1 & 0 & 2 \\
-1 & 0 & 0 & 2 & 1 & 1
\end{array}\right)
\begin{array}{l}
x_3 \\ x_2 \\ x_5
\end{array}
$$

Since the column of $x_2$ is $\begin{pmatrix}0\\1\\0\end{pmatrix}$, the pivoting process is complete.

Notice that the variables $x_3$, $x_2$, $x_5$ appear to the right of the augmented matrix, indicating we have interchanged the role of $x_4$ and $x_2$.

6.2
Exercise

Perform a pivot operation on each of the following augmented matrices. The pivot element is circled. Write the original system of equations and the final system of equations.

1. 
$$
\begin{array}{cccc}
x_1 & x_2 & x_3 & x_4
\end{array}
$$
$$
\left(\begin{array}{cccc|c}
1 & ② & 1 & 0 & 300 \\
3 & 2 & 0 & 1 & 480
\end{array}\right)
\begin{array}{l}
x_3 \\ x_4
\end{array}
$$

2. 
$$
\begin{array}{ccccc}
x_1 & x_2 & x_3 & x_4 & x_5
\end{array}
$$
$$
\left(\begin{array}{ccccc|c}
1 & 2 & 4 & 1 & 0 & 24 \\
3 & ② & 4 & 0 & 1 & 36
\end{array}\right)
\begin{array}{l}
x_4 \\ x_5
\end{array}
$$

3. 
$$
\begin{array}{cccccccc}
x_1 & x_2 & x_3 & x_4 & x_5 & x_6 & x_7 & x_8
\end{array}
$$
$$
\left(\begin{array}{cccccccc|c}
-3 & 0 & 1 & 0 & 1 & 0 & 0 & 0 & 20 \\
-2 & 0 & 0 & 1 & 0 & 1 & 0 & 0 & 24 \\
0 & -3 & 1 & 0 & 0 & 0 & 1 & 0 & 28 \\
0 & -3 & 0 & 1 & 0 & 0 & 0 & 1 & 24
\end{array}\right)
\begin{array}{l}
x_5 \\ x_6 \\ x_7 \\ x_8
\end{array}
$$

6.3
THE SIMPLEX
METHOD FOR
MAXIMIZING A
LINEAR
PROGRAMMING
PROBLEM

Return once more to Example 2.7 of Chapter 4 (page 95). When the linear programming problem is rewritten using slack variables, so that the constraints are expressed as a system of equations, the problem becomes:

Maximize

$$P = 3x_1 + 4x_2$$

subject to

$$2x_1 + 2x_2 + x_3 = 80 \qquad x_1 \geq 0,\ x_2 \geq 0$$
$$2x_1 + 4x_2 + x_4 = 120 \qquad x_3 \geq 0,\ x_4 \geq 0$$

*Simplex Tableau*

Since we utilize a pivot operation in the simplex method, we organize the problem in a matrix, called the *simplex tableau*. This is merely a shorthand notation for representing both the objective function and the set of constraints. For the problem above, the tableau is

$$
\begin{array}{cccc}
x_1 & x_2 & x_3 & x_4 \\
\end{array}
$$

$$
\left(
\begin{array}{cccc|c}
2 & 2 & 1 & 0 & 80 \\
2 & \boxed{4} & 0 & 1 & 120 \\
\hline
-3 & -4 & 0 & 0 & 0 \\
\end{array}
\right)
\begin{array}{l}
x_3 \\
x_4 \\
\\
P = 0 + 3x_1 + 4x_2
\end{array}
$$

Notice that the bottom row of the tableau

$$-3 \quad -4 \quad 0 \quad 0 \mid 0$$

contains the negative of the coefficients of the objective function.

To help us remember that the last row represents the objective function, we separate the last row from the other rows by a dotted line.

The simplex method consists of pivoting from one tableau to another by selecting an "appropriate" pivot element. The main questions are

1. How is the pivot element chosen?
2. When does the process end?

We begin by observing that an obvious solution of the system of constraint equations is

$$x_1 = 0, \qquad x_2 = 0, \qquad x_3 = 80, \qquad x_4 = 120$$

Clearly, this feasible solution is not optimal, since $P = 0$. However, we can increase $P = 3x_1 + 4x_2$ by increasing either $x_1$ or $x_2$. We observe that increasing $x_2$ will increase $P$ faster since its coefficient (4) is larger. (Note that this coefficient appears as $-4$ in the last row of the simplex tableau and is the smallest negative entry in this row.)

We cannot increase $x_2$ indefinitely since, for $x_2$ large enough, the value of a slack variable will become negative. Recall that the conditions are

$$x_1 = 0, \qquad x_3 = 80 - 2x_2, \qquad x_4 = 120 - 4x_2$$

Thus, if we increase $x_2$ beyond 30, the slack variable $x_4$ becomes negative. (Observe that $x_2$ cannot exceed the smaller of the ratios 80/2 and 120/4.)

**169**
6.3
THE SIMPLEX
METHOD FOR
MAXIMIZING A
LINEAR
PROGRAMMING
PROBLEM

With $x_1 = 0$ and $x_2 = 120/4 = 30$, we have the new feasible solution

$$x_1 = 0, \qquad x_2 = 30, \qquad x_3 = 20, \qquad x_4 = 0$$

For this solution, $P = 120$—an obvious improvement over the first solution.

If we continue this process, we improve $P$ until a maximum value is obtained.

Looking over this process, we see that in the first solution we solved for $x_3$ and $x_4$, whereas in the second solution, we solved for $x_3$ and $x_2$. That is, we pivoted, using the entry in the column $x_2$ and row $x_4$ as pivot element. The choice of this pivot element was made as follows:

1. **The column of the pivot element is selected by locating the smallest negative entry in the last row. This is called the** *pivot column.*

Pivot Column

2. **Divide each entry in the last column by its corresponding entry in the pivot column. The** *pivot row* **is the row for which the smallest positive ratio is obtained. The pivot element is never in the last row.**

Pivot Row

In our example, $-4$ is the smallest negative entry in the last row, so the pivot column is column two. When we divide 80 by 2 and 120 by 4, the smallest positive ratio is 30. Thus, row two is the pivot row. The pivot element, 4, is circled in the original simplex tableau.

Pivoting, we obtain the tableau,

$$
\begin{array}{cccc}
x_1 & x_2 & x_3 & x_4 \\
\end{array}
$$

$$
\left(
\begin{array}{cccc|c}
① & 0 & 1 & -\dfrac{1}{2} & 20 \\
\dfrac{1}{2} & 1 & 0 & \dfrac{1}{4} & 30 \\
\hline
-1 & 0 & 0 & 1 & 120 \\
\end{array}
\right)
\begin{array}{l}
x_3 \\
x_2 \\
\\
P = 120 + x_1 - x_4
\end{array}
$$

Since the last row contains a negative entry, we can improve the value of $P$; thus, we pivot again selecting the pivot element as before. In this case the pivot element is 1. The new tableau is

$$
\begin{array}{cccc}
x_1 & x_2 & x_3 & x_4 \\
\end{array}
$$

$$
\left(
\begin{array}{cccc|c}
1 & 0 & 1 & -\dfrac{1}{2} & 20 \\
0 & 1 & -\dfrac{1}{2} & \dfrac{1}{2} & 20 \\
\hline
0 & 0 & 1 & \dfrac{1}{2} & 140 \\
\end{array}
\right)
\begin{array}{l}
x_1 \\
x_2 \\
\\
P = 140 - x_3 - \dfrac{1}{2}x_4
\end{array}
$$

Since there are no negative entries in the last row, no further improvement in $P$ is possible. In fact, the last row represents the equation

$$P = 140 - x_3 - \frac{1}{2}x_4$$

Since $x_3$ and $x_4$ are each nonnegative, the largest value for $P$ is 140. This

**170**
AN ALGEBRAIC
APPROACH TO
LINEAR
PROGRAMMING: THE
SIMPLEX METHOD

value occurs when $x_3 = 0$ and $x_4 = 0$. If we write the equation represented by the second and third row of the tableau, we find that

$$x_1 + x_3 - \frac{1}{2}x_4 = 20$$

$$x_2 - \frac{1}{2}x_3 + \frac{1}{2}x_4 = 20$$

When $x_3 = x_4 = 0$, we have the optimal solution

$$x_1 = 20, \qquad x_2 = 20, \qquad x_3 = 0, \qquad x_4 = 0, \qquad P = 140$$

We interpret the final tableau by associating the values in the last column with the variables that appear next to each entry. Thus, from the final tableau, we read that

$$x_1 = 20, \qquad x_2 = 20$$

This represents the optimal solution. The maximum value of $P$ appears in the lower right-hand corner and has the value $P = 140$.

This solution is in agreement with the one found by geometric techniques in Section 4.2, page 96.

**3.1**
**Example**

Maximize

$$P = 6x_1 + 8x_2 + x_3$$

subject to

$$3x_1 + 5x_2 + 3x_3 \leq 20 \qquad x_1 \geq 0, \qquad x_2 \geq 0, \qquad x_3 \geq 0$$
$$x_1 + 3x_2 + 2x_3 \leq 9$$
$$6x_1 + 2x_2 + 5x_3 \leq 30$$

First, we introduce the slack variables $x_4$, $x_5$, and $x_6$. The system of constraints becomes

$$3x_1 + 5x_2 + 3x_3 + x_4 = 20 \qquad x_1 \geq 0, \qquad x_2 \geq 0, \qquad x_3 \geq 0$$
$$x_1 + 3x_2 + 2x_3 + x_5 = 9 \qquad x_4 \geq 0, \qquad x_5 \geq 0, \qquad x_6 \geq 0$$
$$6x_1 + 2x_2 + 5x_3 + x_6 = 30$$

The simplex tableau for this problem is

$$\begin{array}{cccccc} x_1 & x_2 & x_3 & x_4 & x_5 & x_6 \\ \end{array}$$

$$\left( \begin{array}{cccccc|c} 3 & 5 & 3 & 1 & 0 & 0 & 20 \\ 1 & ③ & 2 & 0 & 1 & 0 & 9 \\ 6 & 2 & 5 & 0 & 0 & 1 & 30 \\ \hline -6 & -8 & -1 & 0 & 0 & 0 & 0 \end{array} \right) \begin{array}{l} x_4 \\ x_5 \\ x_6 \\ \\ P = 0 + 6x_1 + 8x_2 + x_3 \end{array}$$

The pivot column is obtained by locating the column containing the smallest entry in the last row ($-8$ in column two).

The pivot row is obtained by dividing each entry in the last column by its corresponding entry in this pivot column and selecting the smallest positive ratio. Thus, the second row is the pivot row and the pivot element is 3. The new tableau is

171
6.3
THE SIMPLEX
METHOD FOR
MAXIMIZING A
LINEAR
PROGRAMMING
PROBLEM

$$\begin{array}{cccccc} x_1 & x_2 & x_3 & x_4 & x_5 & x_6 \end{array}$$

$$\left(\begin{array}{cccccc|c} \boxed{\dfrac{4}{3}} & 0 & -\dfrac{1}{3} & 1 & -\dfrac{5}{3} & 0 & 5 \\[2mm] \dfrac{1}{3} & 1 & \dfrac{2}{3} & 0 & \dfrac{1}{3} & 0 & 3 \\[2mm] \dfrac{16}{3} & 0 & \dfrac{11}{3} & 0 & -\dfrac{2}{3} & 1 & 24 \\[2mm] \hdashline -\dfrac{10}{3} & 0 & \dfrac{13}{3} & 0 & \dfrac{8}{3} & 0 & 24 \end{array}\right) \begin{array}{l} x_4 \\[2mm] x_2 \\[2mm] x_6 \\[2mm] \\ \end{array}$$

$$P = 24 + \frac{10}{3}x_1 - \frac{13}{3}x_3 - \frac{8}{3}x_5$$

Again, by using the same procedure, we determine the pivot element to be 4/3. The new tableau is

$$\begin{array}{cccccc} x_1 & x_2 & x_3 & x_4 & x_5 & x_6 \end{array}$$

$$\left(\begin{array}{cccccc|c} 1 & 0 & -\dfrac{1}{4} & \dfrac{3}{4} & -\dfrac{5}{4} & 0 & \dfrac{15}{4} \\[2mm] 0 & 1 & \dfrac{3}{4} & -\dfrac{1}{4} & \dfrac{3}{4} & 0 & \dfrac{7}{4} \\[2mm] 0 & 0 & 5 & -4 & \boxed{6} & 1 & 4 \\[2mm] \hdashline 0 & 0 & \dfrac{7}{2} & \dfrac{5}{2} & -\dfrac{3}{2} & 0 & \dfrac{73}{2} \end{array}\right) \begin{array}{l} x_1 \\[2mm] x_2 \\[2mm] x_6 \\[2mm] \\ \end{array}$$

$$P = \frac{73}{2} - \frac{7}{2}x_3 - \frac{5}{2}x_4 + \frac{3}{2}x_5$$

Since the last row contains a negative entry, we have not yet obtained a maximum solution. The pivot column is $x_5$ and the pivot row is $x_6$. (Remember that the pivot row is obtained by dividing the last column by the entries in the pivot column and selecting the smallest positive ratio.) The new tableau is

$$\begin{array}{cccccc} x_1 & x_2 & x_3 & x_4 & x_5 & x_6 \end{array}$$

$$\left(\begin{array}{cccccc|c} 1 & 0 & \dfrac{19}{24} & -\dfrac{1}{12} & 0 & \dfrac{5}{24} & \dfrac{165}{36} \\[2mm] 0 & 1 & \dfrac{1}{8} & \dfrac{1}{4} & 0 & -\dfrac{1}{8} & \dfrac{5}{4} \\[2mm] 0 & 0 & \dfrac{5}{6} & -\dfrac{2}{3} & 1 & \dfrac{1}{6} & \dfrac{2}{3} \\[2mm] \hdashline 0 & 0 & \dfrac{19}{4} & \dfrac{3}{2} & 0 & \dfrac{1}{4} & \dfrac{75}{2} \end{array}\right) \begin{array}{l} x_1 \\[2mm] x_2 \\[2mm] x_5 \\[2mm] \\ \end{array}$$

$$P = \frac{75}{2} - \frac{19}{4}x_3 - \frac{3}{2}x_4 - \frac{1}{4}x_6$$

**172**

AN ALGEBRAIC
APPROACH TO
LINEAR
PROGRAMMING: THE
SIMPLEX METHOD

This is a final tableau and we read the solution to be

$$P = \frac{75}{2}, \quad x_1 = \frac{165}{36}, \quad x_2 = \frac{5}{4}, \quad x_3 = 0$$

(We read that $x_3 = 0$ because it does not appear to the right of the tableau.)

We conclude this section by emphasizing that the techniques introduced in this chapter do not handle all possible situations. Many difficulties may arise. One of the more important is *cycling*, a phenomenon in which the pivot operation produces a tableau that gives a solution that has occurred previously, resulting in a vicious circle. This situation is called a *degenerate case* and special techniques must be used to handle it.

Another difficulty occurs when the smallest ratio is zero. In this case, the pivot operation gives no improvement in the value of the objective function. Finally, it may happen that a pivot column is selected in which all the ratios are negative. In this situation the linear programming problem has no solution.

The interested student should consult the Bibliography in the Chapter Review for sources that treat these situations in some detail.

---

6.3
Exercise

Use the simplex method to solve the following maximum linear programming problems.

1. Maximize

$$P = 5x_1 + 7x_2$$

subject to

$$2x_1 + 3x_2 \leq 12, \quad 3x_1 + x_2 \leq 12, \quad x_1 \geq 0, \quad x_2 \geq 0$$

2. Maximize

$$P = x_1 + 5x_2$$

subject to

$$2x_1 + x_2 \leq 10, \quad x_1 + 2x_2 \leq 10, \quad x_1 \geq 0, \quad x_2 \geq 0$$

3. Maximize

$$P = 2x_1 + x_2 + x_3$$

subject to

$$-2x_1 + x_2 - 2x_3 \leq 4, \quad x_1 \geq 0, \quad x_2 \geq 0, \quad x_3 \geq 0$$
$$x_1 - 2x_2 + x_3 \leq 2$$

4. Maximize

$$P = 4x_1 + 2x_2 + 5x_3$$

**173**
6.4
THE SIMPLEX
METHOD FOR
MINIMIZING A
LINEAR
PROGRAMMING
PROBLEM

subject to

$$x_1 + 3x_2 + 2x_3 \leq 30, \qquad x_1 \geq 0, \quad x_2 \geq 0, \quad x_3 \geq 0$$
$$2x_1 + x_2 + 3x_3 \leq 12$$

5. Maximize

$$P = 2x_1 + x_2 + 3x_3$$

subject to

$$x_1 + 2x_2 + x_3 \leq 25, \qquad x_1 \geq 0, \quad x_2 \geq 0, \quad x_3 \geq 0$$
$$3x_1 + 2x_2 + 3x_3 \leq 30$$

6. Maximize

$$P = 6x_1 + 6x_2 + 2x_3$$

subject to

$$2x_1 + 2x_2 + 3x_3 \leq 30, \qquad x_1 \geq 0, \quad x_2 \geq 0, \quad x_3 \geq 0$$
$$2x_1 + 2x_2 + x_3 \leq 12$$

7. Maximize

$$P = 2x_1 + 4x_2 + x_3 + x_4$$

subject to

$$2x_1 + x_2 + 2x_3 + 3x_4 \leq 12, \quad x_1 \geq 0, \quad x_2 \geq 0$$
$$2x_2 + x_3 + 2x_4 \leq 20, \qquad x_3 \geq 0, \quad x_4 \geq 0$$
$$2x_1 + x_2 + 4x_3 \leq 16$$

Up to now, the linear programming problems we have encountered were of the maximizing variety. In this section we discuss a technique for solving linear programming problems where the objective function is to be minimized. A theorem of Von Neumann states that the solution, if it exists, of a minimum linear programming problem is the same as the solution of a corresponding maximum linear programming problem, called the *dual program*.

We illustrate how to obtain the dual program by example.

6.4
THE SIMPLEX
METHOD FOR
MINIMIZING A
LINEAR
PROGRAMMING
PROBLEM

Minimize

$$C = 300x_1 + 480x_2$$

subject to the conditions

$$x_1 + 3x_2 \geq 0.25 \qquad x_1 \geq 0$$
$$2x_1 + 2x_2 \geq 0.45 \qquad x_2 \geq 0$$

We begin by constructing an augmented matrix for the coefficients of the constraints of this problem without introducing

**174**
AN ALGEBRAIC
APPROACH TO
LINEAR
PROGRAMMING: THE
SIMPLEX METHOD

slack variables. As before, we place the objective function in the last row. The result is

$$
\begin{array}{cc}
x_1 & x_2 \\
\end{array}
$$

$$
\left(
\begin{array}{cc|c}
1 & 3 & 0.25 \\
2 & 2 & 0.45 \\
\hline
300 & 480 & 0
\end{array}
\right)
$$

The corresponding augmented matrix for the data of Example 2.6 of Chapter 4, page 93, is

$$
\left(
\begin{array}{cc|c}
1 & 2 & 300 \\
3 & 2 & 480 \\
\hline
0.25 & 0.45 & 0
\end{array}
\right)
$$

We observe upon comparing these two matrices that the rows of the first matrix, which represents the minimum problem, are the columns of the second matrix, which represents a maximum problem. When a maximum and a minimum linear programming problem have this characteristic, they are termed *dual programs*.

Dual Program

This relationship between a minimum linear programming problem and the dual program is significant as shown by the theorem stated below.

### Theorem: Von Neumann Duality Principle

**The solution of a minimum linear programming problem, if it exists, has the same value as the solution of its dual program, a maximum linear programming problem.**

This result tells us that to solve a minimum linear programming problem requires that we solve the dual program, a maximum linear programming problem.

To obtain the dual program of a minimum linear programming problem, we proceed as follows:

1. **Construct the augmented matrix of the constraint equations and the objective function without introducing slack variables.**
2. **Interchange the rows and columns to form the augmented matrix of the dual problem.**
3. **Write the maximum linear programming problem for this matrix.**

The next example illustrates this procedure.

4.2
Example

Obtain the dual program for the minimum linear programming problem:

Minimize

$$
C = 2x_1 + 3x_2
$$

175
6.4
THE SIMPLEX
METHOD FOR
MINIMIZING A
LINEAR
PROGRAMMING
PROBLEM

subject to

$$2x_1 + x_2 \geq 6 \qquad x_1 \geq 0$$
$$x_1 + 2x_2 \geq 4 \qquad x_2 \geq 0$$
$$x_1 + x_2 \geq 5$$

The augmented matrix for this problem is

$$\begin{pmatrix} 2 & 1 & | & 6 \\ 1 & 2 & | & 4 \\ 1 & 1 & | & 5 \\ \hline 2 & 3 & | & 0 \end{pmatrix}$$

Interchanging rows and columns, we obtain the matrix

$$\begin{pmatrix} 2 & 1 & 1 & | & 2 \\ 1 & 2 & 1 & | & 3 \\ \hline 6 & 4 & 5 & | & 0 \end{pmatrix}$$

This matrix corresponds to the maximum linear programming problem:

Maximize

$$P = 6y_1 + 4y_2 + 5y_3$$

subject to

$$2y_1 + y_2 + y_3 \leq 2, \qquad y_1 + 2y_2 + y_3 \leq 3$$
$$y_1 \geq 0, \qquad y_2 \geq 0, \qquad y_3 \geq 0$$

Observe the following features in the above example:

1. The variables of the minimum problem are $x_1$ and $x_2$, and the variables of the maximum problem are $y_1$, $y_2$, and $y_3$.
2. The inequalities describing the constraints are $\geq$ for the minimum problem and $\leq$ for the maximum problem.
3. We use $C$ to denote the quantity to be minimized and $P$ to denote the quantity to be maximized.

We continue with this example by solving the maximum problem using the techniques introduced in the previous section.
We begin by writing the simplex tableau for this problem.

$$\begin{array}{ccccc} y_1 & y_2 & y_3 & y_4 & y_5 \\ \begin{pmatrix} ② & 1 & 1 & 1 & 0 & | & 2 \\ 1 & 2 & 1 & 0 & 1 & | & 3 \\ \hline -6 & -4 & -5 & 0 & 0 & | & 0 \end{pmatrix} & \begin{array}{l} y_4 \\ y_5 \end{array} \end{array}$$

**176**
AN ALGEBRAIC
APPROACH TO
LINEAR
PROGRAMMING: THE
SIMPLEX METHOD

Here, $y_4$ and $y_5$ represent the slack variables. Using 2 as a pivot element, we obtain the tableau

$$
\begin{array}{ccccc}
y_1 & y_2 & y_3 & y_4 & y_5 \\
\end{array}
$$

$$
\left(
\begin{array}{ccccc|c}
1 & \dfrac{1}{2} & \boxed{\dfrac{1}{2}} & \dfrac{1}{2} & 0 & 1 \\[2mm]
0 & \dfrac{3}{2} & \dfrac{1}{2} & -\dfrac{1}{2} & 1 & 2 \\[2mm]
\hline
0 & -1 & -2 & 3 & 0 & 6
\end{array}
\right)
\begin{array}{l}
y_1 \\[4mm]
y_5 \\[4mm]
\\
\end{array}
$$

Again we must pivot, this time using $1/2$ as pivot element. The result is the tableau

$$
\begin{array}{ccccc}
y_1 & y_2 & y_3 & y_4 & y_5 \\
\end{array}
$$

$$
\left(
\begin{array}{ccccc|c}
2 & 1 & 1 & 1 & 0 & 2 \\
-1 & 1 & 0 & -1 & 1 & 1 \\
\hline
4 & 1 & 0 & 5 & 0 & 10
\end{array}
\right)
\begin{array}{l}
y_3 \\
y_5 \\
\\
\end{array}
$$

Since all the entries in the last row are non-negative, this represents a final tableau. We read from it that the solution to the maximum problem is

$$
P = 10, \qquad y_1 = 0, \qquad y_2 = 0, \qquad y_3 = 2
$$

Because of the Duality Principle, the solution to the minimum problem is the same as that of the maximum problem; that is,

$$
C = 10
$$

To determine the values of $x_1$, $x_2$ that give this minimum value, we must return to the relationship that exists between the $x$ variables and $y$ variables. The slack variable $y_4$ was introduced in the first row of the tableau of the maximum problem. But this row corresponds to the first column of the minimum problem, which lists the coefficients of $x_1$. Thus, we identify $y_4$ with $x_1$ and read the value of $x_1$ as the last entry under $y_4$ in the final tableau; namely, $x_1 = 5$. Similarly, we read the value of $x_2$ as the last entry under $y_5$ in the final tableau. Thus, the solution to the minimum linear programming problem is

$$
x_1 = 5, \qquad x_2 = 0, \qquad C = 10
$$

We outline below the steps required to solve a minimum linear programming problem.

1. **Obtain the dual program (a maximum linear programming problem).**
2. **Solve this maximum linear programming problem by obtaining a final tableau for it.**
3. **The minimum value of the objective function $C$ is the maximum value of the objective function $P$.**

**177**
6.4
THE SIMPLEX
METHOD FOR
MINIMIZING A
LINEAR
PROGRAMMING
PROBLEM

4. **The optimum solution of the minimum linear programming problem is given by the last entry in the columns under the slack variables in the final tableau.**

Minimize

$$C = 6x_1 + 8x_2 + x_3$$

subject to

$$
\begin{array}{ll}
3x_1 + 5x_2 + 3x_3 \geq 20 & x_1 \geq 0 \\
x_1 + 3x_2 + 2x_3 \geq 9 & x_2 \geq 0 \\
6x_1 + 2x_2 + 5x_3 \geq 30 & x_3 \geq 0
\end{array}
$$

The augmented matrix of this program is

$$
\left(\begin{array}{ccc|c}
3 & 5 & 3 & 20 \\
1 & 3 & 2 & 9 \\
6 & 2 & 5 & 30 \\
\hline
6 & 8 & 1 & 0
\end{array}\right)
$$

Interchanging rows and columns, we obtain

$$
\left(\begin{array}{ccc|c}
3 & 1 & 6 & 6 \\
5 & 3 & 2 & 8 \\
3 & 2 & 5 & 1 \\
\hline
20 & 9 & 30 & 0
\end{array}\right)
$$

The dual program is
  Maximize

$$P = 20y_1 + 9y_2 + 30y_3$$

subject to

$$
\begin{array}{ll}
3y_1 + y_2 + 6y_3 \leq 6 & y_1 \geq 0 \\
5y_1 + 3y_2 + 2y_3 \leq 8 & y_2 \geq 0 \\
3y_1 + 2y_2 + 5y_3 \leq 1 & y_3 \geq 0
\end{array}
$$

If we introduce slack variables $y_4, y_5, y_6$, the simplex tableau for this problem is

$$
\begin{array}{cccccc}
y_1 & y_2 & y_3 & y_4 & y_5 & y_6 & \\
\left(\begin{array}{cccccc|c}
3 & 1 & 6 & 1 & 0 & 0 & 6 \\
5 & 3 & 2 & 0 & 1 & 0 & 8 \\
3 & 2 & ⑤ & 0 & 0 & 1 & 1 \\
\hline
-20 & -9 & -30 & 0 & 0 & 0 & 0
\end{array}\right)
& \begin{array}{c} \\ y_4 \\ y_5 \\ y_6 \\ \\ \end{array}
\end{array}
$$

**178**
AN ALGEBRAIC
APPROACH TO
LINEAR
PROGRAMMING: THE
SIMPLEX METHOD

The final tableau (as the reader should verify) is

$$
\begin{array}{c}
\begin{array}{cccccc}
y_1 & y_2 & y_3 & y_4 & y_5 & y_6
\end{array} \\
\left(
\begin{array}{cccccc|c}
0 & -1 & 1 & 1 & 0 & -1 & 5 \\
0 & -\dfrac{1}{3} & -\dfrac{19}{3} & 0 & 1 & -\dfrac{5}{3} & \dfrac{19}{3} \\
1 & \dfrac{2}{3} & \dfrac{5}{3} & 0 & 0 & \dfrac{1}{3} & \dfrac{1}{3} \\
\hline
0 & \dfrac{13}{3} & \dfrac{10}{3} & 0 & 0 & \dfrac{20}{3} & \dfrac{20}{3}
\end{array}
\right)
\begin{array}{l}
y_4 \\
y_5 \\
y_1 \\
\\
\end{array}
\end{array}
$$

From this, we read that the solution to the minimum problem is

$$
x_1 = 0, \qquad x_2 = 0, \qquad x_3 = \frac{20}{3}
$$

and the minimum value is $C = 20/3$.

---

**6.4**
**Exercise**

Solve the following minimum linear programming problems by using the simplex method.

1. Minimize

$$
C = 6x_1 + 3x_2
$$

subject to

$$
\begin{array}{ll}
x_1 + x_2 \geqq 4 & x_1 \geqq 0 \\
3x_1 + 4x_2 \geqq 12 & x_2 \geqq 0
\end{array}
$$

2. Minimize

$$
C = 2x_1 + 3x_2 + 4x_3
$$

subject to

$$
\begin{array}{ll}
x_1 - 2x_2 - 2x_3 \geqq -2 & x_1 \geqq 0 \\
x_1 + x_2 + x_3 \geqq 2 & x_2 \geqq 0 \\
2x_1 + x_3 \geqq 3 & x_3 \geqq 0
\end{array}
$$

3. Minimize

$$
C = x_1 + 2x_2 + x_3
$$

subject to

$$
\begin{array}{ll}
x_1 - 3x_2 + 4x_3 \geqq 12 & x_1 \geqq 0 \\
3x_1 + x_2 + 2x_3 \geqq 10 & x_2 \geqq 0 \\
x_1 - x_2 - x_3 \leqq -8 & x_3 \geqq 0
\end{array}
$$

---

**6.5**
**APPLICATIONS**

In Chapter 4, we gave examples of practical situations that lead to linear programming problems, such as the mixture problem and the transportation problem. In this section, we give further examples of applications of linear programming, in which the number of variables exceeds two.

The first example is typical of a *transportation problem*.

The Red Tomato Company operates two plants for canning their tomatoes and has three warehouses for storing the finished products until they are purchased by retailers. The Company wants to arrange its shipments from the plants to the warehouses so that the requirements of the warehouses are met and so that shipping costs are kept at a minimum. The schedule in Figure 6.1 represents the per case shipping cost from plant to ware-

| | | Warehouse | | |
|---|---|---|---|---|
| | | A | B | C |
| Plant | I | $0.25 | $0.17 | $0.18 |
| | II | $0.25 | $0.18 | $0.14 |

**Figure 6.1**

house. Each week, plant I can produce at least 850 cases and plant II can produce at least 650 cases of tomatoes. Also, each week warehouse A requires at least 300 cases, warehouse B at least 400 cases, and warehouse C at least 500 cases. If we represent the number of cases shipped from plant I to warehouse A by $x_1$, from plant I to warehouse B by $x_2$, and so on, the above data can be represented by the table in Figure 6.2.

| | | Warehouse | | | Minimum Available |
|---|---|---|---|---|---|
| | | A | B | C | |
| Plant | I | $x_1$ | $x_2$ | $x_3$ | 850 |
| | II | $x_4$ | $x_5$ | $x_6$ | 650 |
| Min. Demand | | 300 | 400 | 500 | |

**Figure 6.2**

The linear programming problem is stated as follows:
Minimize the cost function

$$C = 0.25x_1 + 0.17x_2 + 0.18x_3 + 0.25x_4 + 0.18x_5 + 0.14x_6 \quad (6.1)$$

subject to

$$\begin{aligned}
x_1 + x_2 + x_3 &\geq 850 & x_1 &\geq 0, & x_2 &\geq 0 \\
x_4 + x_5 + x_6 &\geq 650 & x_3 &\geq 0, & x_4 &\geq 0 \\
x_1 + x_4 &\geq 300 & x_5 &\geq 0, & x_6 &\geq 0 & \quad (6.2) \\
x_2 + x_5 &\geq 400 \\
x_3 + x_6 &\geq 500
\end{aligned}$$

**180**
AN ALGEBRAIC
APPROACH TO
LINEAR
PROGRAMMING: THE
SIMPLEX METHOD

Since this is a minimum linear programming problem, we proceed to find the dual program. The augmented matrix for the minimum program is

$$\begin{pmatrix} 1 & 1 & 1 & 0 & 0 & 0 & | & 850 \\ 0 & 0 & 0 & 1 & 1 & 1 & | & 650 \\ 1 & 0 & 0 & 1 & 0 & 0 & | & 300 \\ 0 & 1 & 0 & 0 & 1 & 0 & | & 400 \\ 0 & 0 & 1 & 0 & 0 & 1 & | & 500 \\ \hline 0.25 & 0.17 & 0.18 & 0.25 & 0.18 & 0.14 & | & 0 \end{pmatrix}$$

The augmented matrix of the dual program is

$$\begin{pmatrix} 1 & 0 & 1 & 0 & 0 & | & 0.25 \\ 1 & 0 & 0 & 1 & 0 & | & 0.17 \\ 1 & 0 & 0 & 0 & 1 & | & 0.18 \\ 0 & 1 & 1 & 0 & 0 & | & 0.25 \\ 0 & 1 & 0 & 1 & 0 & | & 0.18 \\ 0 & 1 & 0 & 0 & 1 & | & 0.14 \\ \hline 850 & 650 & 300 & 400 & 500 & | & 0 \end{pmatrix}$$

The maximum problem is
  Maximize

$$P = 850y_1 + 650y_2 + 300y_3 + 400y_4 + 500y_5$$

subject to

(1) $y_1 + y_3 \leq 0.25$   (4) $y_2 + y_3 \leq 0.25$   $y_1 \geq 0, y_2 \geq 0$
(2) $y_1 + y_4 \leq 0.17$   (5) $y_2 + y_4 \leq 0.18$   $y_3 \geq 0, y_4 \geq 0$
(3) $y_1 + y_5 \leq 0.18$   (6) $y_2 + y_5 \leq 0.14$   $y_5 \geq 0$

Introducing the slack variables $u_1, u_2, u_3, u_4, u_5, u_6$ (the subscripts correspond to the numbers assigned the inequalities), we construct the original simplex tableau and list each tableau leading to the final tableau.

| $y_1$ | $y_2$ | $y_3$ | $y_4$ | $y_5$ | $u_1$ | $u_2$ | $u_3$ | $u_4$ | $u_5$ | $u_6$ | | |
|---|---|---|---|---|---|---|---|---|---|---|---|---|
| 1 | 0 | 1 | 0 | 0 | 1 | 0 | 0 | 0 | 0 | 0 | 0.25 | $u_1$ |
| ① | 0 | 0 | 1 | 0 | 0 | 1 | 0 | 0 | 0 | 0 | 0.17 | $u_2$ |
| 1 | 0 | 0 | 0 | 1 | 0 | 0 | 1 | 0 | 0 | 0 | 0.18 | $u_3$ |
| 0 | 1 | 1 | 0 | 0 | 0 | 0 | 0 | 1 | 0 | 0 | 0.25 | $u_4$ |
| 0 | 1 | 0 | 1 | 0 | 0 | 0 | 0 | 0 | 1 | 0 | 0.18 | $u_5$ |
| 0 | 1 | 0 | 0 | 1 | 0 | 0 | 0 | 0 | 0 | 1 | 0.14 | $u_6$ |
| $-850$ | $-650$ | $-300$ | $-400$ | $-500$ | 0 | 0 | 0 | 0 | 0 | 0 | 0 | |

$$\begin{array}{ccccccccccc}
y_1 & y_2 & y_3 & y_4 & y_5 & u_1 & u_2 & u_3 & u_4 & u_5 & u_6 \\
\end{array}$$

$$\left(\begin{array}{ccccccccccc|cl}
0 & 0 & 1 & -1 & 0 & 1 & -1 & 0 & 0 & 0 & 0 & 0.08 & u_1 \\
1 & 0 & 0 & 1 & 0 & 0 & 1 & 0 & 0 & 0 & 0 & 0.17 & y_1 \\
0 & 0 & 0 & -1 & 1 & 0 & -1 & 1 & 0 & 0 & 0 & 0.01 & u_3 \\
0 & 1 & 1 & 0 & 0 & 0 & 0 & 0 & 1 & 0 & 0 & 0.25 & u_4 \\
0 & 1 & 0 & 1 & 0 & 0 & 0 & 0 & 0 & 1 & 0 & 0.18 & u_5 \\
0 & ① & 0 & 0 & 1 & 0 & 0 & 0 & 0 & 0 & 1 & 0.14 & u_6 \\
\hline
0 & -650 & -300 & 450 & -500 & 0 & 850 & 0 & 0 & 0 & 0 & 144.50 &
\end{array}\right)$$

$$\begin{array}{ccccccccccc}
y_1 & y_2 & y_3 & y_4 & y_5 & u_1 & u_2 & u_3 & u_4 & u_5 & u_6 \\
\end{array}$$

$$\left(\begin{array}{ccccccccccc|cl}
0 & 0 & ① & -1 & 0 & 1 & -1 & 0 & 0 & 0 & 0 & 0.08 & u_1 \\
1 & 0 & 0 & 1 & 0 & 0 & 1 & 0 & 0 & 0 & 0 & 0.17 & y_1 \\
0 & 0 & 0 & -1 & 1 & 0 & -1 & 1 & 0 & 0 & 0 & 0.01 & u_3 \\
0 & 0 & 1 & 0 & -1 & 0 & 0 & 0 & 1 & 0 & -1 & 0.11 & u_4 \\
0 & 0 & 0 & 1 & -1 & 0 & 0 & 0 & 0 & 1 & -1 & 0.04 & u_5 \\
0 & 1 & 0 & 0 & 1 & 0 & 0 & 0 & 0 & 0 & 1 & 0.14 & y_2 \\
\hline
0 & 0 & -300 & 450 & 150 & 0 & 850 & 0 & 0 & 0 & 650 & 235.50 &
\end{array}\right)$$

$$\begin{array}{ccccccccccc}
y_1 & y_2 & y_3 & y_4 & y_5 & u_1 & u_2 & u_3 & u_4 & u_5 & u_6 \\
\end{array}$$

$$\left(\begin{array}{ccccccccccc|cl}
0 & 0 & 1 & -1 & 0 & 1 & -1 & 0 & 0 & 0 & 0 & 0.08 & y_3 \\
1 & 0 & 0 & 1 & 0 & 0 & 1 & 0 & 0 & 0 & 0 & 0.17 & y_1 \\
0 & 0 & 0 & -1 & 1 & 0 & -1 & 1 & 0 & 0 & 0 & 0.01 & u_3 \\
0 & 0 & 0 & 1 & -1 & -1 & 1 & 0 & 1 & 0 & -1 & 0.03 & u_4 \\
0 & 0 & 0 & 1 & -1 & 0 & 0 & 0 & 0 & 1 & -1 & 0.04 & u_5 \\
0 & 1 & 0 & 0 & 1 & 0 & 0 & 0 & 0 & 0 & 1 & 0.14 & y_2 \\
\hline
0 & 0 & 0 & 150 & 150 & 300 & 550 & 0 & 0 & 0 & 650 & 259.50 &
\end{array}\right)$$

This is a final tableau. The solution to the minimum linear programming problem is

$$C = \$259.50, \qquad x_1 = 300, \qquad x_2 = 550, \qquad x_3 = 0,$$
$$x_4 = 0, \qquad x_5 = 0, \qquad x_6 = 650$$

Mike's Famous Toy Trucks specializes in making four kinds of toy trucks: a delivery truck, a dump truck, a garbage truck, and a gasoline truck. Three machines—a metal casting machine, a paint spray machine, and a packaging machine—are used in the production of these trucks. The time, in hours, each machine works to make each type of truck and the profit for each truck are given in Figure 6.3. The maximum time available per week for each machine is: metal casting 4000 hours; paint spray 1800

5.2
Example

182
AN ALGEBRAIC
APPROACH TO
LINEAR
PROGRAMMING: THE
SIMPLEX METHOD

| | Metal Casting | Paint Spray | Packaging | Profit |
|---|---|---|---|---|
| Delivery truck | 2.0 | 1.0 | 0.5 | $0.50 |
| Dump truck | 2.5 | 1.5 | 0.5 | $1.00 |
| Garbage truck | 2.0 | 1.0 | 1.0 | $1.50 |
| Gasoline truck | 2.0 | 2.0 | 1.0 | $2.00 |

**Figure 6.3**

hours; and packaging 1000 hours. How many of each type truck should be produced to maximize profit? Assume every truck made is sold.

First let $x_1$, $x_2$, $x_3$, and $x_4$ denote the number of delivery trucks, dump trucks, garbage trucks, and gasoline trucks, respectively, to be made. If $P$ denotes the profit to be maximized, we have the problem:

Maximize

$$P = 0.5x_1 + x_2 + 1.5x_3 + 2x_4$$

subject to the conditions

$$2x_1 + 2.5x_2 + 2x_3 + 2x_4 \leq 4000 \qquad x_1 \geq 0$$
$$x_1 + 1.5x_2 + x_3 + 2x_4 \leq 1800 \qquad x_2 \geq 0$$
$$0.5x_1 + 0.5x_2 + x_3 + x_4 \leq 1000 \qquad x_3 \geq 0, \qquad x_4 \geq 0$$

We introduce the slack variables $x_5$, $x_6$, $x_7$ and, since this is a maximizing problem, we immediately write the simplex tableau, namely,

$$
\begin{array}{ccccccc}
x_1 & x_2 & x_3 & x_4 & x_5 & x_6 & x_7 \\
\end{array}
$$

$$
\left(
\begin{array}{ccccccc|c}
2 & 2.5 & 2 & 2 & 1 & 0 & 0 & 4000 \\
1 & 1.5 & 1 & ② & 0 & 1 & 0 & 1800 \\
0.5 & 0.5 & 1 & 1 & 0 & 0 & 1 & 1000 \\
\hline
-0.5 & -1 & -1.5 & -2 & 0 & 0 & 0 & 0 \\
\end{array}
\right)
\begin{array}{c}
x_5 \\ x_6 \\ x_7 \\ \\ \\
\end{array}
$$

$$
\begin{array}{ccccccc}
x_1 & x_2 & x_3 & x_4 & x_5 & x_6 & x_7 \\
\end{array}
$$

$$
\left(
\begin{array}{ccccccc|c}
1 & 1 & 1 & 0 & 1 & -1 & 0 & 2200 \\
0.5 & 0.75 & 0.5 & 1 & 0 & 0.5 & 0 & 900 \\
0 & -0.25 & ⓪.5 & 0 & 0 & -0.5 & 1 & 100 \\
\hline
0.5 & 0.5 & -0.5 & 0 & 0 & 1 & 0 & 1800 \\
\end{array}
\right)
\begin{array}{c}
x_5 \\ x_4 \\ x_7 \\ \\ \\
\end{array}
$$

$$
\begin{array}{ccccccc}
x_1 & x_2 & x_3 & x_4 & x_5 & x_6 & x_7 \\
\end{array}
$$

$$
\left(
\begin{array}{ccccccc|c}
1 & 1.5 & 0 & 0 & 1 & 0 & -2 & 2000 \\
0.5 & 1 & 0 & 1 & 0 & 1 & -1 & 800 \\
0 & -0.5 & 1 & 0 & 0 & -1 & 2 & 200 \\
\hline
0.5 & 0.25 & 0 & 0 & 0 & 0.5 & 1 & 1900 \\
\end{array}
\right)
\begin{array}{c}
x_5 \\ x_4 \\ x_3 \\ \\ \\
\end{array}
$$

This is a final tableau. The maximum profit is $P = \$1900$ and it is attained for

$$x_1 = 0 \qquad x_2 = 0 \qquad x_3 = 200 \qquad x_4 = 800$$

The practical considerations of this situation are that delivery trucks and dump trucks are either too costly to produce or too little profit is being gained from their sale. Since the slack variable $x_5$ has a value of 2000 for maximum $P$ and since $x_5$ represents the number of hours the metal casting machine is printing no truck (that is, the time the machine is idle), it may be possible to release this machine for other duties.

Katy's Hand-Made Dolls must decide how many of two types of dolls to produce in order to maximize profits. One type is a Crying Doll that requires 15 minutes in machine production and 1 3/4 hours in hand finishing; the other type is a Laughing and Crying Doll requiring 30 minutes for machine production and 3 hours in hand finishing. The profit on the Crying Doll is $8 and on the Laughing and Crying Doll $12. Machine production is limited to 10 hours per day and hand finishing is limited to 8 hours per day.

5.3
Example

Let $x_1$ represent the number of Crying Dolls and $x_2$ the number of Laughing and Crying Dolls to be produced. Our problem is to maximize

$$P = 8x_1 + 12x_2$$

subject to the conditions

$$\frac{1}{4}x_1 + \frac{1}{2}x_2 \leq 10, \qquad \frac{7}{4}x_1 + 3x_2 \leq 8, \qquad x_1 \geq 0, \qquad x_2 \geq 0$$

The simplex tableau for this problem is

$$
\begin{array}{cccc|c}
x_1 & x_2 & x_3 & x_4 & \\
\frac{1}{4} & \frac{1}{2} & 1 & 0 & 10 \quad x_3 \\
\frac{7}{4} & ③ & 0 & 1 & 8 \quad x_4 \\
\hline
-8 & -12 & 0 & 0 & 0
\end{array}
$$

$$
\begin{array}{ccc|c}
x_1 & x_2 & x_3 & x_4 & \\
-\frac{1}{24} & 0 & 1 & -\frac{1}{6} & \frac{26}{3} \quad x_3 \\
\frac{7}{12} & 1 & 0 & \frac{1}{3} & \frac{8}{3} \quad x_2 \\
\hline
-1 & 0 & 0 & 4 & 32
\end{array}
$$

**184**

AN ALGEBRAIC
APPROACH TO
LINEAR
PROGRAMMING: THE
SIMPLEX METHOD

$$
\begin{array}{cccc}
x_1 & x_2 & x_3 & x_4 \\
\end{array}
$$

$$
\left(
\begin{array}{cccc|c}
0 & \dfrac{1}{14} & 1 & -\dfrac{1}{7} & \dfrac{62}{7} \\[2mm]
1 & \dfrac{12}{7} & 0 & \dfrac{4}{7} & \dfrac{32}{7} \\[2mm]
\hline
0 & \dfrac{12}{7} & 0 & \dfrac{32}{7} & \dfrac{256}{7}
\end{array}
\right)
\begin{array}{l}
x_3 \\[6mm]
x_1 \\[10mm]
\phantom{x}
\end{array}
$$

Thus, we can approximate the maximum profit at $P = \$32.00$ per day when 4 Crying Dolls are made and no Laughing and Crying Dolls are made.

The fact that the slack variable $x_3$ is positive is indicative of idle machine time.

The approximate solution given to the problem in Example 5.3 illustrates a common situation in which only integers are really appropriate as an answer. One may come to the conclusion that the "best integer solution" is found nearest the fractional solution. Unfortunately, this may not be the case. Thus, the solution $x_1 = 4$, $x_2 = 0$ is found by a trial-and-error method rather than a simplex method.

We refer the interested reader to recent publications on Integer Programming.

The next example is taken *verbatim* from the publication *Some Mathematical Models in Biology*,[1] and is presented to illustrate the use of the simplex method in linear programming and to provide experience in reading journal articles. This model is an interesting application of linear programming to a bio-economic situation; it gives a graphic illustration of how it is necessary to sift and interpret the given information in order to formulate a useful mathematical model.

| 5.4 | |
|---|---|
| Example | |
| Ecology | |
| Model | |

In the Edwards Plateau country of west Texas the vegetation is easily modified by grazing animals from a mixed vegetation to a dominance of grasses, or forbs, or browse or various combinations of these. It is common to see in pastures in this area herds of cattle, bands of sheep, and flocks of mohair goats. Whitetail deer and wild turkey are common if there is sufficient browse and mixed vegetation. Catfish will thrive in ponds if there is suitable vegetation cover to prevent siltation. Ranchers sell beef, wool, mutton, mohair and lease deer and turkey hunting and catfishing rights. The relative monetary income values per animal are: cattle, 10.; goats, 1.; sheep, 1. (wool and mutton combined); deer, 0.5; turkey, 0.05; and fish, 0.001. A rancher owns 10 sections of such land which has a maximum carrying capacity of 10 animal units per section per year. The animal unit equivalents for the various species per animal are: cattle, 1.; sheep, 0.2; goats, 0.25; deer, 0.3; and essentially zero for turkeys and fish. To properly organize his operation for livestock production he has to have at least 20 cattle and at least 20 goats on his ranch. The rancher wants at least some sheep and

[1]G. M. Van Dyne and Kenneth R. Rebman, "Maintaining a Profitable Ecological Balance," *Some Mathematical Models in Biology*, Robert M. Thrall, ed., University of Michigan Press, 1967.

some deer on his ranch. He can maintain the desired vegetation cover for turkey and fish if he has (a) cattle, sheep, goats, and deer, (b) cattle, sheep, and goats, or (c) cattle, goats and deer, but no more than 75% of the grazing load (measured in animal units) may be due to cattle and goats combined. Of course, he wants his total stocking rate of all organisms combined to be equal to or less than the carrying capacity of the range. Furthermore, he can put in no more than one pond per section each of which will support no more than 500 fish each, and can harvest no more than 25% of the catfish per pond per year. The requirements and habits of the wild turkey are such that he cannot maintain more than 2 flocks of 10 birds per flock per section and he cannot harvest more than 20% of the population per year. He keeps only castrated male goats for mohair and shears them once each year. His cattle, sheep, and deer harvests which will maintain a given population are respectively about 25, 35, and 15% of the population per year. For simplification, the 35% for sheep includes both wool and mutton.

The first step is to isolate the salient points from this description. They are:

1) The relative monetary income values per animal are:

| | |
|---|---|
| cattle | 10 |
| goats | 1 |
| sheep | 1 |
| deer | .5 |
| turkey | .05 |
| fish | .001 |

2) There are 10 sections of land, each with a maximum carrying capacity of 10 animal units per year.
3) Animal unit equivalents for the species are:

| | |
|---|---|
| cattle | 1 |
| goats | .25 |
| sheep | .2 |
| deer | .3 |
| turkey | 0 |
| fish | 0 |

4) The ranch must have at least 20 cattle and 20 goats.
5) There must be some sheep and some deer.
6) If there are to be any turkey and fish, there must be
  a) cattle, sheep and goats
    or
  b) cattle, goats, and deer.
7) Cattle and goats can comprise no more than 75% of the animal units.
8) Total animal units cannot exceed the carrying capacity.
9) A maximum of 500 fish per section, with a 25% annual harvest.
10) A maximum of 20 birds per section, with a 20% annual harvest.
11) Harvest percentages:

| | |
|---|---|
| cattle | 25% |
| goats | 100% |
| sheep | 35% |
| deer | 15% |

12) How many individuals of each species should the rancher have in order to maximize annual profit?

The next step is to quantify these conditions.

In the first place the rancher is hoping for an answer that is something like: have 30 cattle, 22 sheep, etc. He will be understandably upset if he is told that to realize a maximum profit, he requires 33.25 cattle and 21.7 sheep. The rancher is certainly anticipating the answer to be in integers. However, any programming

186
AN ALGEBRAIC
APPROACH TO
LINEAR
PROGRAMMING: THE
SIMPLEX METHOD

problem that imposes integer constraints on the variables is apt to be extremely difficult to solve. Thus, the first simplification is to treat the problem as a continuous programming problem. It may even turn out that all or some of the optimal values of the variables of this problem *are* actually integers. If not, the solution can be rounded to the nearest integer solution. It is important to realize that this rounded solution may *not* be the best integer solution. However, if

$p_0$ is the maximum profit for the continuous problem,
$p_1$ is the profit obtained by rounding the optimal solution
$p_2$ is the maximum profit to the integer problem

then clearly $p_1 \leqslant p_2 \leqslant p_0$. If $p_0 - p_1$ is very small, the rancher will not care anyway.

The next step is to determine the variables. Since he has 10 parcels of land, each being able to support 6 different species, the first inclination is to use 60 variables $x_{ij}$, $i = 1 \ldots 6, j = 1 \ldots 10$. Then $x_{ij}$ will represent the number of species $i$ to be placed on parcel $j$. However, since the conditions for survival are the same in any parcel, it is much simpler to consider the entire ten parcels as a single unit. Then only 6 variables $x_i$, $i = 1 \ldots 6$ are needed, where $x_i$ represents the total number of species $i$. In the final solution, $1/10$ of $x_i$ can be placed in each parcel. (Or other adjustments can be made, at the rancher's preference.) (Note that we cannot just maximize profit over a single parcel. The constraints would require *some* deer on *every* parcel, which is not required in the given problem.)

Thus we have the following 6 variables:

$x_1$: number of cattle
$x_2$: number of goats
$x_3$: number of sheep
$x_4$: number of deer
$x_5$: number of turkey
$x_6$: number of fish

The conditions then give the following constraints:
Condition 2) says the maximum carrying capacity available is 100 units. Condition 3) gives the animal units for each species. Then, condition 7) gives the constraint:

$$1x_1 + .25x_2 \leqslant 75$$

Condition 8) becomes:

$$1x_1 + .25x_2 + .2x_3 + .3x_4 \leqslant 100$$

Condition 4) is:

$$x_1 \geqslant 20$$
$$x_2 \geqslant 20$$

Condition 5) is:

$$x_3 \geqslant \text{"some"}$$
$$x_4 \geqslant \text{"some"}$$

where "some" is the minimum number of sheep and deer the rancher wants. Since the rancher is vague about this, let us assume that "some" = 1. So lower bound constraints are:

$$x_1 \geqslant 20$$
$$x_2 \geqslant 20$$
$$x_3 \geqslant 1$$
$$x_4 \geqslant 1$$

Now we see that condition 6) is irrelevant. The lower bound constraints guarantee that 7) a) and b) will *always* be satisfied. Hence, it will always be possible to have turkey ($x_5 > 0$) and fish ($x_6 > 0$). Condition 9) gives

$$x_6 \leqslant 5000$$
$$x_5 \leqslant 200$$

Finally, it is only needed to calculate the profit. Condition 1) gives profit per animal. Not all animals can be harvested, however. Harvest percentages are given in 9), 10), and 11). The annual profit from each species is:

| | |
|---|---|
| cattle | $(10)(.25x_1)$ |
| goat | $(1)(x_2)$ |
| sheep | $(1)(.35x_3)$ |
| deer | $(.5)(.15x_4)$ |
| turkey | $(.05)(.20x_5)$ |
| fish | $(.001)(.25x_6)$ |

Thus the rancher's problem is:
Subject to the constraints

$$x_1 + .25x_2 \leqslant 75$$
$$x_1 + .25x_2 + .2x_3 + .3x_4 \leqslant 100$$
$$x_1 \geqslant 20$$
$$x_2 \geqslant 20$$
$$x_3 \geqslant 1$$
$$x_4 \geqslant 1$$
$$0 \leqslant x_5 \leqslant 200$$
$$0 \leqslant x_6 \leqslant 5000$$

maximize the objective function

$$z = 2.5x_1 + x_2 + .35x_3 + .075x_4 + .01x_5 + .00025x_6.$$

[The reader should solve this problem using the simplex method.]
For maximum annual profit, the rancher's selection should be:

| | | |
|---|---|---|
| 70 | cattle for a profit of | 175. |
| 20 | goats for a profit of | 20. |
| 123.5 | sheep for a profit of | 43.225 |
| 1 | deer for a profit of | .075 |
| 200 | turkeys for a profit of | 2. |
| 5000 | fish for a profit of | 1.25 |

giving a profit of 241.55 units.

Of course, the rancher will have to have only 123 sheep, reducing his profit by .175. He will not be able to realize any profit on his single deer, which he insisted on having. So his profit is further reduced by .075.

Thus, his total profit, with an integral number of species, is 241.30.

Since the *best* integral solution can give no more than 241.55 profit, it is probably not worth finding it. (In fact this is very likely it.)

If the rancher now decides that one deer does not constitute "some", then the problem can be re-done, giving a larger lower bound for $x_4$.

It only remains to distribute the species over the 10 parcels if each parcel must have an integral number of species to itself. Each parcel then will have

7 cattle
2 goats
2 flocks of 10 birds each
1 pond with 500 fish

Putting an integral number of sheep on each parcel means that only 12 sheep can be on any parcel. This further reduces the profit by 1.05, since only 120 sheep are present. (*Now*, the total profit is only 240.25, but the *best* integral solution can give a profit no greater than 241.55.)

**188**

AN ALGEBRAIC
APPROACH TO
LINEAR
PROGRAMMING: THE
SIMPLEX METHOD

Note that the 7 cattle, 2 goats, and 12 sheep on each parcel use a total of 9.9 land units. Thus, no single parcel can support the deer. However, the deer can presumably roam over all 10 parcels, in which case there are enough land units to support three deer, which are still not enough for a deer "harvest".

In Example 2.8 of Chapter 4 (page 96), we considered an application to air pollution control. A more realistic continuation is given in Example 5.5. In this example we merely indicate the complicated nature of attempting to solve a real-world problem. Thus, the linear programming problem is set up, but no solution is actually given.

5.5
Example
Air Pollution
Model

Now consider a more realistic model. There are many pollution sources and not one, but five major pollutants. In the larger model, the required pollutant reductions in the Saint Louis airshed for the year 1970 are as follows:

| | |
|---|---|
| sulfur dioxide | 485,000,000 pounds |
| carbon monoxide | 1,300,000,000 pounds |
| hydrocarbons | 280,000,000 pounds |
| nitrogen oxides | 75,000,000 pounds |
| particulate matter | 180,000,000 pounds |

The model includes a wide variety of possible control methods. Among them are the installation of exhaust and crankcase devices on used as well as new automobiles, the substitution of natural gas for coal, the catalytic oxidation system to convert sulfur dioxide in the stacks of power plants to salable sulfuric acid, even the municipal collection of leaves as an alternative to burning.

The most contested control method in the Saint Louis airshed has been a restriction on the sulfur content of coal. Consider a particular category of traveling grate stokers that burn 3.1 percent sulfur coal. Let control method 3 be the substitution of 1.8 percent sulfur coal for the high sulfur coal in these stokers. The variable $X_3$ represents the number of tons of 3.1 percent sulfur coal replaced with low sulfur coal.

Total cost of this control method is

$$C = (\$2.50)X_3$$

where $2.50 is an estimate of the incremental cost of the low sulfur coal.

Just as the number of barrels of cement controlled by any process was constrained in our simple example, so

$$X_3 \leqq 200,000$$

where 200,000 tons is the estimate of the quantity of coal that will be burned in this category of traveling grate stokers in 1970.

For every ton of 3.1 percent sulfur coal replaced by 1.8 percent sulfur coal, sulfur dioxide emissions are reduced by

[(0.031 sulfur content)
(2000 pounds per ton of coal)(0.95 complete burning)(2)]
$-$ [(0.944)(0.018 sulfur content)(2000 pounds)(0.95)(2)]
$= 53.2$ pounds

where the factor (2) doubles the weight of sulfur burned to get the weight of sulfur dioxide; where the factor (0.944) accounts for the higher BTU content of the low sulfur coal, which permits 0.944 ton of it to replace one ton of the high sulfur coal; and where (0.95) incorporates an assumption of 95 percent complete burning. The two square bracketed terms represent emission of sulfur dioxide from 3.1 percent and 1.8 percent sulfur coal, respectively. Thus we have

$(53.2)X_3 =$ pounds of sulfur dioxide reduced

The remaining pollutant reductions are

$(0.2)X_3 =$ pounds of carbon monoxide reduced
$(0.1)X_3 =$ pounds of hydrocarbons reduced
$(1.1)X_3 =$ pounds of nitrogen oxide reduced
$(12.2)X_3 =$ pounds of particulates reduced

The relatively high reduction in particulates reflects not only the fact that 0.944 ton of the 1.8 percent sulfur coal is burned in place of one whole ton, but also the lower ash content of the substituted coal. (Reduction coefficients are not always positive; low sulfur coal in a pulverized coal boiler, which has a high efficiency electrostatic precipitator, can cause an increase in particulate emissions. The presence of less sulfur dioxide in the flue gas reduces the chargeability of the particles so that the benefits of the lower ash and higher BTU content may be offset by the reduced efficiency of the electrostatic precipitator.)

Figure 6.4 illustrates the mathematical programming model for 1970. Notice that control methods $X_1$ and $X_2$ for the cement industry are included, as well as control method $X_3$. The dots represent the remaining 200 to 300 control methods.

The pollution reduction requirements mentioned above appear in the model given in Figure 6.4. In summing the pollutant reductions contributed by the various control methods, we are assuming that all pounds of any pollutant are homogeneous, regardless of where or when they are emitted. This is a limitation of the model because it is dependent on a close correspondence between a pollutant reduction and a specific concentration measured in parts per million or micrograms per cubic meter of that pollutant in the ambient air.

However, where necessary, meteorological sophistication can be incorporated in the model by selective weighting of those

$$\text{Minimize } C = \$0.14X_1 + \$0.18X_2 + \$2.50X_3 + \cdots$$

$$
\begin{array}{llll}
\text{Subject to} & X_1 + & X_2 & \leqslant 2{,}500{,}000 \\
& & X_3 + \cdots & \leqslant 200{,}000 \\
& & & \leqslant \quad . \\
& & & \leqslant \quad . \\
& & & \leqslant \quad . \\
& & & \leqslant \quad . \\
& & 53.2X_3 + \cdots & \geqslant 485{,}000{,}000 \text{ pounds of sulfur dioxide} \\
& & 0.2X_3 + \cdots & \geqslant 1{,}300{,}000{,}000 \text{ pounds of carbon monoxide} \\
& & 0.1X_3 + \cdots & \geqslant 280{,}000{,}000 \text{ pounds of hydrocarbons} \\
& & 1.1X_3 + \cdots & \geqslant 75{,}000{,}000 \text{ pounds of nitrogen oxides} \\
1.5X_1 + & 1.8X_2 + & 12.2X_3 + \cdots & \geqq 180{,}000 \text{ pounds of particulates} \\
X_1, & X_2, & X_3, \quad \cdots & \geqslant 0
\end{array}
$$

**Figure 6.4**

sources that seem to have a greater or lesser proportional effect on air quality than others.

When the number of variables is large, it is best to use a computer to obtain a solution.

1. Minimize the cost of preparing the following mixture of foods if the mixture is made up of three foods I, II, III in which food I costs $2 per unit, food II costs $1 per unit, and food III costs $3 per unit. Also, each unit of food I contains 2 ounces of protein and 4 ounces carbohydrate; each unit of food II has 3 ounces of protein and 2 ounces of carbohydrate; each unit of food III has 4 ounces of protein and 2 ounces of carbohydrate. The mixture must contain at least 20 ounces of protein and 15 ounces of carbohydrate.

2. Nutt's Nut Company has 500 pounds of cashews, 100 pounds of pecans and 50 pounds of peanuts on hand. They package three 5-pound cans of nuts consisting of

   can I: 3 pounds cashews, 1 pound pecans, 1 pound peanuts
   can II: 4 pounds cashews, 1/2 pound pecans, 1/2 pound peanuts
   can III: 5 pounds cashews

   The selling price for each can is $5, $4, and $6, respectively. How many cans of each kind should be made to maximize revenue?

3. By hiring additional help, Katy's Hand Made Dolls finds that its Crying Dolls can be made with 15 minutes of machine production and 1 hour of hand finishing, and its Laughing and Crying Doll requires 30 minutes of machine production and 2 hours of hand finishing. The profit on the Crying Doll is $8; on the Laughing and Crying Doll, $12. Machine pro-

duction is limited to 10 hours per day, while hand finishing is limited to 50 hours per day (about 6 full-time people). What number of each type doll will give a maximum profit?

4. One of the methods used by the Alexander Company to separate copper, lead, and zinc from ores is the flotation separation process. This process consists of three steps: oiling, mixing and separation, which must be applied for 2, 2, and 1 hour, respectively, to produce 1 unit of copper; 2, 3, and 1 hour respectively, to produce 1 unit of lead; and 1, 1, and 3 hours, respectively, to produce 1 unit of zinc. The oiling and separation phases of the process can be in operation for a maximum of 10 hours a day, while the mixing phase can be in operation for a maximum of 11 hours a day. The Alexander Company makes a profit of $45 per unit of copper, $30 per unit lead, and $35 per unit zinc. The demand for these metals is unlimited. How many units of each metal should be produced daily by use of the flotation process to achieve the highest profit?

<table>
<tr><td>

**pivot operation**
**pivot element**
**pivot row**
**pivot column**
**simplex method**
</td><td>

**slack variables**
**dual program**
**simplex tableau**
**duality principle**
</td><td>

CHAPTER
REVIEW

Important
Terms
</td></tr>
</table>

1. Convert the set of constraints of a maximum linear programming problem

$$3x_1 + 5x_2 \leqq 12$$
$$x_1 + 7x_2 \leqq 8$$
$$x_1 + 2x_2 \leqq 5$$

into a system of equations.

2. Maximize the objective function

$$P = 40x_1 + 60x_2 + 50x_3$$

subject to the constraints

$$x_1 + x_2 + x_3 \leqq 30$$
$$- x_1 + 2x_3 \leqq 0$$
$$x_1 + x_3 - x_2 \geqq 0$$
$$x_1 \geqq 0, \quad x_2 \geqq 0, \quad x_3 \geqq 0$$

3. Minimize the objective function

$$C = 5x_1 + 4x_2 + 3x_3$$

Review
Exercises

**192**
AN ALGEBRAIC
APPROACH TO
LINEAR
PROGRAMMING: THE
SIMPLEX METHOD

subject to the constraints

$$
\begin{aligned}
x_1 + x_2 + x_3 &\leq 30 \\
-x_1 + 2x_3 &\geq 0 \\
x_1 - x_2 + x_3 &\geq 0 \\
x_1 + x_2 + x_3 &\geq 20 \\
x_1 \geq 0, \qquad x_2 \geq 0, \qquad x_3 &\geq 0
\end{aligned}
$$

### Bibliography

*Applied*

Dantzig, George B., *Linear Programming and Extensions,* Princeton University Press, Princeton, N.J., 1963.

Ferguson, C. E., *Microeconomic Theory,* Richard D. Irwin, Homewood, Ill., 1969.

Samuelson, Paul, Robert Dorfman, and Robert Solow, *Linear Programming and Economic Analysis,* McGraw-Hill, New York, 1958.

Vazsonyi, Andrew, *Scientific Programming in Business and Industry,* Wiley, New York, 1958.

# 7

# LIMIT AND CONTINUITY

With this chapter we begin our study of the calculus, which can be divided in two parts: the differential calculus and the integral calculus. In keeping with the goals set forth in the preface, our main objective in studying these chapters is to gain an understanding of the use and application of the calculus and not to get too involved with its theory.

Calculus is an extension of elementary mathematics. To gain some idea of the kind of extension calculus provides, we consider some examples from elementary mathematics and the corresponding extension in calculus. See diagram on page 194.

In pursuing the study of differential calculus, we rely heavily on the function concept that is introduced in Chapter 2. However, before we can talk about the derivative and some of its applications, we need to understand the concepts of limit and continuity, the subjects of this chapter.

Imagine an object and further imagine a solid wall. Suppose we think of our object as being at a fixed distance from the wall and moving

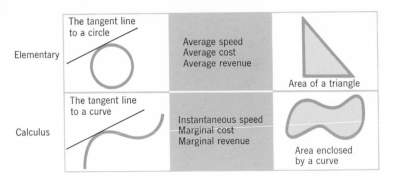

**Graphical Approach**  halfway to the wall every minute. It is clear that the object is getting "closer and closer" to the wall as time passes. We might even say the object is "approaching" the wall. That is, the distance of the object from the wall is getting "smaller and smaller." In calculus, we say that the distance of the object from the wall approaches zero.

Now suppose we think of this object as a projectile traveling along a path toward the wall. See Figure 7.1.

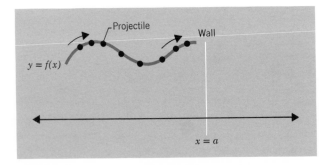

**Figure 7.1**

It is convenient to denote the path of the projectile by the graph of a function $y = f(x)$ and the wall by a vertical line $x = a$. Based on the motion of the projectile along its path, we want to predict at what height it will strike the wall. This prediction of the height the projectile strikes **Limit from the** the wall $x = a$, as it proceeds along the path $y = f(x)$, is called the *limit* **Left** *of $f(x)$ as $x$ approaches $a$ from the left* (since the projectile is moving toward the wall from the left side). We use the notation

$$\lim_{x \to a^-} f(x) = L$$

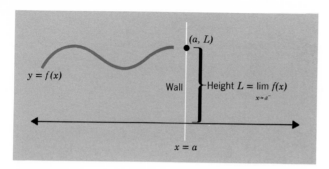

**Figure 7.2**

read as "the limit of $f(x)$ as $x$ approaches $a$ from the left equals $L$," to denote the fact that we predict the projectile hits the wall at the height $L$. See Figure 7.2.

We use the notation $x \to a^-$ with the ($-$) sign to show that $x$ is always a little less than $a$, that is, that something must be "subtracted" from $a$ to yield $x$. This follows from choosing $x$ to the left of $a$.

If it is impossible to predict at what height the projectile might strike the wall (due to erratic behavior near the wall), then the limit of $f(x)$ as $x$ approaches $a$ from the left does not exist. See Figure 7.3.

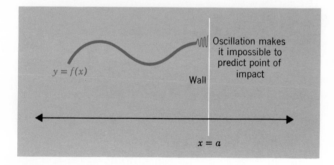

**Figure 7.3**

If we envision a projectile approaching the wall (line $x = a$) from the right side, then the prediction of where the projectile strikes the wall is the *limit of $f(x)$ as $x$ approaches $a$ from the right*. We use the notation

Limit from the Right

$$\lim_{x \to a^+} f(x) = R$$

to denote the fact that we predict the projectile will strike the wall at a height $R$. See Figure 7.4.

Here the notation $x \to a^+$ is used because $x$ is always to the right of $a$, that is, a little larger than $a$.

If it is impossible to make this prediction, then $\lim_{x \to a^+} f(x)$ does not exist.

Now combine the two situations of a projectile traveling toward the wall from the left and another toward the same wall from the right and

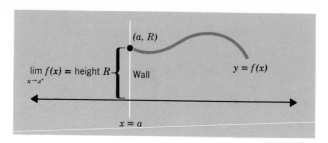

**Figure 7.4**

think of the union of the two paths as being a function $y = f(x)$. If we predict the two projectiles strike the wall at exactly the same height, (i.e. $R = L$), we say that the *limit of $f(x)$ as x approaches a exists and equals the common height $(R = L)$*; that is,

$$\lim_{x \to a} f(x) = R = L$$

If the two projectiles strike the wall at different heights, or if it is impossible to predict where one or both of them strike the wall, then we say that the limit of $f(x)$ as x approaches a does not exist.

Thus, we have the following definition.

**Definition of a Limit**

**Let $y = f(x)$ be a function. If**

**1.** $\lim_{x \to a^-} f(x) = L$    **2.** $\lim_{x \to a^+} f(x) = R$    **3.** $L = R$

**then the limit of $f(x)$ as x approaches a exists and is denoted by**

$$\lim_{x \to a} f(x) = L = R$$

Notice that the definition requires three conditions to hold simultaneously in order for the limit of a function at a point to exist. If any one of the conditions is not satisfied, the limit does not exist at the point.

In Figures 7.5, 7.6, 7.7, and 7.8 we illustrate some geometrical examples of situations involving limits of functions.

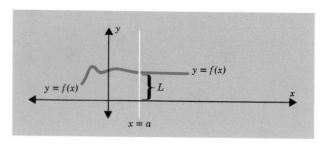

**Figure 7.5**

Since $\lim_{x \to a^-} f(x) = L$ and $\lim_{x \to a^+} f(x) = L$, then $\lim_{x \to a} f(x) = L$.

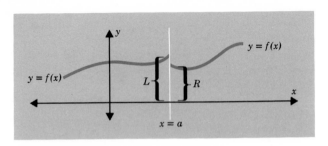

**Figure 7.6**

Here $\lim_{x \to a^-} f(x) = L$ and $\lim_{x \to a^+} f(x) = R$. Since $L \neq R$, $\lim_{x \to a} f(x)$ does not exist.

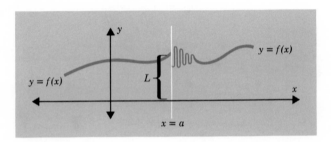

**Figure 7.7**

Here $\lim_{x \to a^-} f(x) = L$, but the oscillation of $f(x)$ to the right of $x = a$ makes it impossible to predict where it will strike the line $x = a$ so that $\lim_{x \to a^+} f(x)$ does not exist. Hence, $\lim_{x \to a} f(x)$ cannot exist either.

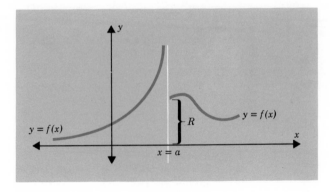

**Figure 7.8**

Here it is clear that $\lim\limits_{x \to a^+} f(x) = R$. However, if we ask ourselves where the graph of the function to the left of $x = a$ strikes the line $x = a$, we are hard pressed to answer since it looks like it *never* strikes the line $x = a$. In this case we write $\lim\limits_{x \to a^-} f(x) = +\infty$. Here we use the symbol $+\infty$ to denote that the value $f(x)$ of the function increases without bound (that is, it keeps getting larger and larger) as $x$ approaches $a$ from the left. Thus, in this case, $\lim\limits_{x \to a} f(x)$ does not exist.

To summarize

$$\lim_{x \to a} f(x) = L = R$$

is a statement that describes how a function behaves for values of $x$ near, but not equal to, $a$. [That is, $\lim\limits_{x \to a} f(x)$ describes the value of $f(x)$ around the value $a$.] Of course, we already know that $f(a)$ describes the value of the function at $x = a$, provided the function is defined at $x = a$.

**Numerical Approach**    Let us see how this interpretation of the meaning of $\lim\limits_{x \to a} f(x)$ can be used to find limits of functions without using the graph of the function as a predictor. For our example, we use the function

$$f(x) = x^3$$

and ask about

$$\lim_{x \to 2} f(x)$$

The following table gives values of $f(x) = x^3$ at points close to 2.

| From the left | $x$ | 1 | 1.5 | 1.6 | 1.75 | 1.8 | 1.9 | 1.99 | 1.999 | 1.9999 |
|---|---|---|---|---|---|---|---|---|---|---|
| | $f(x)$ | 1 | 3.375 | 4.096 | 5.359 | 5.832 | 6.859 | 7.8806 | 7.988 | 7.9988 |
| From the right | $x$ | 3 | 2.5 | 2.4 | 2.25 | 2.2 | 2.1 | 2.01 | 2.001 | 2.0001 |
| | $f(x)$ | 27 | 15.625 | 13.824 | 11.3906 | 10.648 | 9.261 | 8.1206 | 8.012 | 8.0012 |

We can conclude that, as $x$ approaches 2 from the left or from the right, the function $f(x) = x^3$ gets closer to 8. That is,

$$\lim_{x \to 2} x^3 = 8$$

In this example, we see that $\lim\limits_{x \to 2} x^3$ is the same as the value of $f(x)$ at $x = 2$, namely, $2^3 = 8$. Although this is not unusual, the next example serves to illustrate that this need not always be the case.

It is possible for a function to have a limit at $x = a$ but not have a value at $x = a$. For example, consider the function

$$f(x) = \frac{x^2 - 1}{x - 1}$$

and take $a = 1$.

Here $f(1)$ does not exist since division by zero is not defined. If $x \neq 1$, then $f(x) = (x + 1)(x - 1)/(x - 1) = x + 1$, a straight line. See Figure 7.9. We conclude from the graph that

$$\lim_{x \to 1} \frac{x^2 - 1}{x - 1} = 2.$$

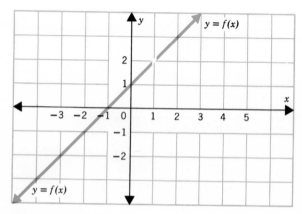

**Figure 7.9**

We can also arrive at this result by constructing a table of values for $f(x) = (x^2 - 1)/(x - 1)$ for values of $x$ around 1.

| | $x$ | 0 | 0.5 | 0.75 | 0.9 | 0.99 |
|---|---|---|---|---|---|---|
| From the left | $f(x) = \dfrac{x^2 - 1}{x - 1}$ | 1 | 1.5 | 1.75 | 1.9 | 1.99 |
| From the right | $x$ | 2 | 1.5 | 1.25 | 1.1 | 1.01 |
| | $f(x) = \dfrac{x^2 - 1}{x - 1}$ | 3 | 2.5 | 2.25 | 2.1 | 2.01 |

By constructing a table of values, determine whether $\lim\limits_{x \to 0^-} 1/x$, $\lim\limits_{x \to 0^+} 1/x$, and $\lim\limits_{x \to 0} 1/x$ exists.

We begin by constructing a table of values for negative values of $x$ that are close to 0.

| From the left | $x$ | $-1$ | $-0.1$ | $-0.01$ | $-0.001$ | $-0.0001$ | $-0.00001$ |
|---|---|---|---|---|---|---|---|
| | $f(x) = \dfrac{1}{x}$ | $-1$ | $-10$ | $-100$ | $-1000$ | $-10,000$ | $-100,000$ |

It is easy to see that as $x$ gets closer to zero from the left, the value of $1/x$ becomes a smaller and smaller negative number. In this situation, we say that

$$\lim_{x \to 0^-} \frac{1}{x} = -\infty$$

That is, we use the symbol $-\infty$ to denote that as $x$ approaches zero from the left, the value of the function takes on negative values increasingly further away from zero.

To determine $\lim\limits_{x \to 0^+} 1/x$, we construct a table for positive values of $x$ nearby 0.

| From the right | $x$ | 1 | 0.1 | 0.01 | 0.001 | 0.0001 | 0.00001 |
|---|---|---|---|---|---|---|---|
| | $f(x) = \dfrac{1}{x}$ | 1 | 10 | 100 | 1000 | 10,000 | 100,000 |

Observe that as $x$ gets closer to zero from the right, the function $1/x$ is increasing without bound, that is, $1/x$ becomes a larger and larger positive number. In this case,

$$\lim_{x \to 0^+} \frac{1}{x} = +\infty$$

Since the left-hand limit of $1/x$ does not equal the right-hand limit of $1/x$, then $\lim\limits_{x \to 0} 1/x$ does not exist.

Until now, we have only considered the behavior of a function near finite values of $x$. We can also ask about the behavior of a function for arbitrarily large positive values of $x$. That is, we can ask for the limit of a function as $x$ approaches $+\infty$. We may also be interested in determining the behavior of a function when $x$ becomes negative without bound ($x \to -\infty$).

**2.3
Example**

Determine $\lim\limits_{x \to +\infty} 1/x$ and $\lim\limits_{x \to -\infty} 1/x$.

Again we rely on a table of values to determine the behavior of $1/x$ for extreme values of $x$, large positive values in the case where $x \to +\infty$ and increasingly negative values in the case where $x \to -\infty$.

| x | 1 | 10 | 100 | 1000 | 10,000 | 100,000 |
|---|---|----|-----|------|--------|---------|
| $f(x) = \dfrac{1}{x}$ | 1 | 0.1 | 0.01 | 0.001 | 0.0001 | 0.00001 |

This table indicates that as x gets large and positive, the values of 1/x get closer and closer to 0. That is,

$$\lim_{x \to +\infty} \frac{1}{x} = 0$$

| x | −1 | −10 | −100 | −1000 | −10,000 | −100,000 |
|---|----|-----|------|-------|---------|----------|
| $f(x) = \dfrac{1}{x}$ | −1 | −0.1 | −0.01 | −0.001 | −0.0001 | −0.00001 |

Similarly, as x assumes increasingly negative values, the value of 1/x gets closer and closer to 0. That is,

$$\lim_{x \to -\infty} \frac{1}{x} = 0$$

As a result of this information, we can graph $f(x) = 1/x$. See Figure 7.10, below.

Notice how the information that $\lim_{x \to -\infty} 1/x = 0$, $\lim_{x \to 0^-} 1/x = -\infty$, $\lim_{x \to 0^+} 1/x = +\infty$ and $\lim_{x \to +\infty} 1/x = 0$ helps to determine the graph of $f(x) = 1/x$. Of course, some well-chosen points such as $(1,1)$ and $(-1, -1)$ are also used.

Thus far we have relied either on geometric intuition or on cumbersome computation to determine whether or not a function has a limit

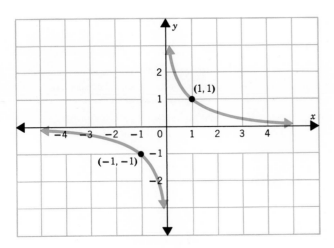

**Figure 7.10**

at a point $x = a$. Since functions are usually described by equations and not by graphs, we will want to develop techniques for finding the limit of a function by looking at its equation. Methods for computing limits without relying either on geometric techniques or on difficult computation are given in the next section.

1. For each of the graphs below, determine by observation whether $\lim\limits_{x \to a^-} f(x)$, $\lim\limits_{x \to a^+} f(x)$ and $\lim\limits_{x \to a} f(x)$ exist.

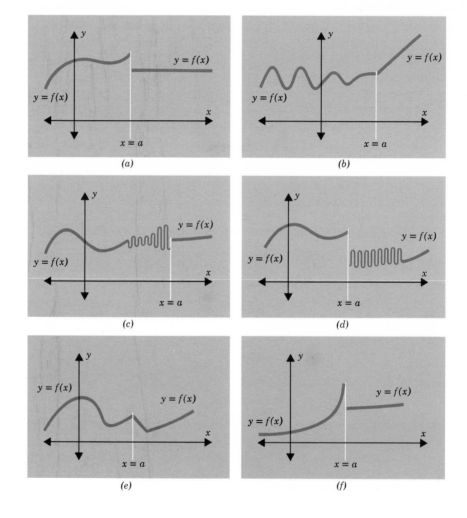

2. Graph each of the following functions and determine whether $\lim\limits_{x \to a^-} f(x)$, $\lim\limits_{x \to a^+} f(x)$, and $\lim\limits_{x \to a} f(x)$ exist for the given value of $a$.

(a) $f(x) = \begin{cases} 2x + 5 & \text{if} \quad x \leq 2 \\ 4x + 1 & \text{if} \quad x > 2 \end{cases} \qquad a = 2$

(b) $f(x) = \begin{cases} 2x + 1 & \text{if} \quad x \leq 0 \\ 2x & \text{if} \quad x > 0 \end{cases}$     $a = 0$

(c) $f(x) = \begin{cases} 3x - 1 & \text{if} \quad x < 1 \\ 4 & \text{if} \quad x = 1 \\ 2x & \text{if} \quad x > 1 \end{cases}$     $a = 1$

(d) $f(x) = \begin{cases} 3x - 1 & \text{if} \quad x < 1 \\ 2 & \text{if} \quad x = 1 \\ 2x & \text{if} \quad x > 1 \end{cases}$     $a = 1$

(e) $f(x) = \begin{cases} 3x - 1 & \text{if} \quad x < 1 \\ \text{not defined} & \text{if} \quad x = 1 \\ 2x & \text{if} \quad x > 1 \end{cases}$     $a = 1$

(f) $f(x) = \begin{cases} 3x - 1 & \text{if} \quad x < 1 \\ 2 & \text{if} \quad x = 1 \\ 3x & \text{if} \quad x > 1 \end{cases}$     $a = 1$

(g) $f(x) = \begin{cases} x^2 & \text{if} \quad x \leq 0 \\ 2x & \text{if} \quad x > 0 \end{cases}$     $a = 0$

(h) $f(x) = \begin{cases} x^2 & \text{if} \quad x < -1 \\ 2 & \text{if} \quad x = -1 \\ -3x + 2 & \text{if} \quad x > -1 \end{cases}$     $a = -1$

3. For the absolute value function

$$f(x) = |x|$$

(a) Graph the function.
(b) Determine whether $\lim_{x \to 0^-} f(x)$ exists.

(c) Determine whether $\lim_{x \to 0^+} f(x)$ exists.

(d) Determine whether $\lim_{x \to 0} f(x)$ exists.

4. For the function

$$f(x) = 2x + 1, \qquad 0 \leq x \leq 1$$

(a) Graph the function.
(b) Determine whether $\lim_{x \to 0^+} f(x)$ exists.

(c) Determine whether $\lim_{x \to 1^-} f(x)$ exists.

(d) Why can't you find $\lim_{x \to 0^-} f(x)$ or $\lim_{x \to 1^+} f(x)$?

5. For the function $f(x) = x^2$, use the values 2.8, 2.9, 2.99, 3.2, 3.1, 3.01 for $x$ to convince yourself that $\lim_{x \to 3} x^2 = 9$.

6. Use a numerical approach to find the following limits (if they exist).

(a) $\lim_{x \to 0} \dfrac{1}{x^2}$       (d) $\lim_{x \to 2} \dfrac{1}{(x - 2)^2}$

(b) $\lim\limits_{x \to 5} (2x + 3)$      (e) $\lim\limits_{x \to +\infty} \dfrac{1}{x^2}$

(c) $\lim\limits_{x \to 2} \dfrac{1}{x - 2}$      (f) $\lim\limits_{x \to -\infty} \dfrac{2}{x}$

**7.3**
**ALGEBRAIC**
**TECHNIQUES FOR**
**EVALUATING**
**LIMITS**

In this section, we establish some useful algebraic properties of limits. These, in turn, we use later to discuss continuity and differentiation. In addition, these properties allow us to find limits without using numerical or graphical approaches.

Limit of a
Constant

**(I) For the constant function $f(x) = c$, $c$ is a constant, we have**

$$\lim_{x \to a} f(x) = \lim_{x \to a} c = c$$

**for any value of $a$.**

The graph of the constant function $f(x) = c$ is merely a horizontal straight line. Clearly, no matter what the value of $x$ is, the height of $f(x)$ is always $c$. Thus, as we approach $x = a$ from either the right or the left, we hit the line $x = a$ at a height of $c$. That is, $\lim\limits_{x \to a} f(x) = c$. See Figure 7.11.

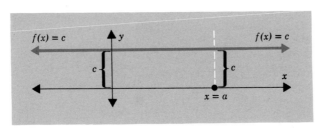

**Figure 7.11**

For example,

$$\lim_{x \to 3} 5 = 5$$

Limit of
$f(x) = x$

**(II) For the function $f(x) = x$, we have**

$$\lim_{x \to a} f(x) = \lim_{x \to a} x = a$$

**for any value of $a$.**

The graph of the function $f(x) = x$ is a straight line with slope 1, passing through the origin. See Figure 7.12. No matter what value of $a$ is

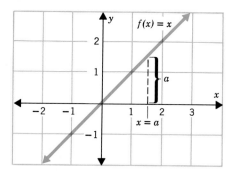

**Figure 7.12**

chosen, as we approach the line $x = a$ from either the left or the right, the function approaches the line $x = a$ at a height of $a$. That is,

$$\lim_{x \to a} f(x) = \lim_{x \to a} x = a$$

For example,

$$\lim_{x \to 4} x = 4$$

The next four properties are of fundamental importance for evaluating limits of functions. We state these properties and rely on examples to give a working knowledge of their many uses.

**(III) Let $f$ and $g$ be two functions whose limits at $x = a$ exist; that is,**    Limit of a Sum
**suppose $\lim_{x \to a} f(x)$ and $\lim_{x \to a} g(x)$ are both known real numbers. Then the**
**limit of the function $f + g$ also exists at $x = a$ and**

$$\lim_{x \to a} [f(x) + g(x)] = \lim_{x \to a} f(x) + \lim_{x \to a} g(x)$$

**Thus, the limit of the sum of two functions equals the sum of their limits.**

Because of the relationship between addition and subtraction, the condition stated in Property III leads us to the result

$$\lim_{x \to a} [f(x) - g(x)] = \lim_{x \to a} f(x) - \lim_{x \to a} g(x)$$

**That is, the limit of the difference of two functions equals the difference of their limits.**

Find

$$\lim_{x \to 3} (2 + x)$$

3.1
Example

Here we are asked to compute the limit of a function $h(x) = 2 + x$, which is really the sum of two other functions,

$f(x) = 2$ and $g(x) = x$. From Properties I and II, we know that

$$\lim_{x \to 3} 2 = 2, \qquad \lim_{x \to 3} x = 3$$

Then, using Property III,

$$\lim_{x \to 3} (2 + x) = \lim_{x \to 3} 2 + \lim_{x \to 3} x = 2 + 3 = 5$$

**Limit of a Product**

**(IV) Let $f$ and $g$ be two functions whose limits at $x = a$ exist; that is, suppose $\lim_{x \to a} f(x)$ and $\lim_{x \to a} g(x)$ are both known real numbers. Then the limit of the function $f \cdot g$ also exists at $x = a$ and**

$$\lim_{x \to a} [f(x) \cdot g(x)] = \left[ \lim_{x \to a} f(x) \right] \cdot \left[ \lim_{x \to a} g(x) \right]$$

**Thus, the limit of the product of two functions equals the product of their limits.**

The next example illustrates this result.

**3.2 Example**

Find

$$\lim_{x \to -2} 3x$$

Here we are being asked to find the limit of a function $h(x) = 3x$ that is the product of two other functions, $f(x) = 3$ and $g(x) = x$. From Properties (I) and (II), we know

$$\lim_{x \to -2} 3 = 3 \qquad \lim_{x \to -2} x = -2$$

Then,

$$\lim_{x \to -2} 3x = \left[ \lim_{x \to -2} 3 \right] \cdot \left[ \lim_{x \to -2} x \right] = (3) \cdot (-2) = -6$$

**3.3 Example**

Find

$$\lim_{x \to 3} (4x + 5)$$

Here we use Properties I, II, III, and IV, and write

$$\lim_{x \to 3} (4x + 5) = \lim_{x \to 3} 4x + \lim_{x \to 3} 5$$
$$= \left( \lim_{x \to 3} 4 \right) \left( \lim_{x \to 3} x \right) + 5$$
$$= (4)(3) + 5 = 12 + 5 = 17$$

**3.4 Example**

Find

$$\lim_{x \to 4} x^2$$

Here,

$$\lim_{x \to 4} x^2 = \left[\lim_{x \to 4} x\right]\left[\lim_{x \to 4} x\right] = (4)(4) = 16$$

The previous example leads us to state an additional property of limits which is a consequence of Property II and the repeated use of Property IV.

**(V) If $n \geq 1$ is a positive integer,**

$$\lim_{x \to a} x^n = \left[\lim_{x \to a} x\right] \cdot \left[\lim_{x \to a} x\right] \cdot \text{-----} \cdot \left[\lim_{x \to a} x\right]$$

$$= \underbrace{a \cdot a \cdot \text{-----} \cdot a}_{n \text{ times}} = a^n$$

The last property of limits we take up involves division of functions.

**(VI) Let $f$ and $g$ be two functions whose limits at $x = a$ exist; that is, suppose $\lim_{x \to a} f(x)$ and $\lim_{x \to a} g(x)$ are both known real numbers. If $\lim_{x \to a} g(x) \neq 0$, then the limit of the function $f/g$ at $x = a$ also exists and**

$$\lim_{x \to a} \frac{f(x)}{g(x)} = \frac{\lim_{x \to a} f(x)}{\lim_{x \to a} g(x)}$$

**Thus, if the limit of the denominator function is not zero, the limit of the ratio of two functions equals the ratio of their limits.**

Find

$$\lim_{x \to 3} \frac{2x^2 + 1}{x^3 - 2}$$

First, we look at the denominator function $g(x) = x^3 - 2$ to see if $\lim_{x \to 3} (x^3 - 2)$ exists and is not zero. Now

$$\lim_{x \to 3} (x^3 - 2) = \lim_{x \to 3} x^3 - \lim_{x \to 3} 2 = 3^3 - 2 = 25$$

Since the limit of the denominator function is not zero, we proceed to compute the limit of the numerator function. Then,

$$\lim_{x \to 3} (2x^2 + 1) = \lim_{x \to 3} 2x^2 + \lim_{x \to 3} 1 = (2)(9) + 1 = 19$$

Thus,

$$\lim_{x \to 3} \frac{2x^2 + 1}{x^3 - 2} = \frac{19}{25}$$

The previous examples might lead us to think that the evaluation of limits is simply a question of substituting the value that x approaches into the function. The next few examples are a reminder that this approach cannot always be used.

Find

$$\lim_{x \to -2} \frac{x^2 + 5x + 6}{x^2 - 4}$$

Here,

$$\lim_{x \to -2} (x^2 - 4) = \lim_{x \to -2} x^2 - \lim_{x \to -2} 4 = 4 - 4 = 0$$

Since the limit of the denominator function is zero, we cannot use Property VI. This does not mean, however, that the limit in Example 3.6 does not exist! Instead we use algebraic techniques and factor. Then,

$$\frac{x^2 + 5x + 6}{x^2 - 4} = \frac{(x + 3)(x + 2)}{(x - 2)(x + 2)}$$

Since we are interested only in the limit as x *approaches* −2, and *not* in the value when x *equals* −2, the quantity (x + 2) is not zero. Hence, we can cancel the (x + 2)'s. Then

$$\lim_{x \to -2} \frac{x^2 + 5x + 6}{x^2 - 4} = \lim_{x \to -2} \frac{x + 3}{x - 2} = \frac{\lim_{x \to -2}(x + 3)}{\lim_{x \to -2}(x - 2)}$$

$$= \frac{-2 + 3}{-2 - 2} = \frac{1}{-4} = -\frac{1}{4}$$

For the function

$$f(x) = x^3$$

find

$$\lim_{x \to a} \frac{f(x) - f(a)}{x - a}$$

Since the limit of the denominator function equals zero, we shall attempt to algebraically eliminate the troublesome term (in this case, x − a). Thus, since x ≠ a,

$$\frac{f(x) - f(a)}{x - a} = \frac{x^3 - a^3}{x - a} = \frac{(x - a)(x^2 + ax + a^2)}{x - a}$$

$$= x^2 + ax + a^2$$

Then,

$$\lim_{x \to a} \frac{f(x) - f(a)}{x - a} = \lim_{x \to a} (x^2 + ax + a^2)$$

$$= a^2 + a^2 + a^2 = 3a^2$$

Notice that we used Properties I, II, III, and IV to arrive at the result.

We conclude this section with a discussion of limits at infinity. Recall from page 201 that

$$\lim_{x \to +\infty} \frac{1}{x} = 0 \qquad \lim_{x \to -\infty} \frac{1}{x} = 0$$

The arguments used to establish these results can be used to evaluate limits of ratios in which the numerator is a constant. For example, to find

$$\lim_{x \to +\infty} \frac{4}{2x + 5}$$

We argue that as $x$ gets very large, the numerator is fixed at 4, while the denominator increases without bound. Hence, the ratio must tend to zero.

When the ratio has variables in both numerator and denominator, we perform an algebraic manipulation like the one illustrated in the next example.

Find

3.8
Example

$$\lim_{x \to +\infty} \frac{3x}{4x^4 + 1}$$

To compute this limit, look at the highest power of $x$ in the numerator and the highest power of $x$ in the denominator. Then divide by the larger of these. In this example, we divide by $x^4$. Then

$$\lim_{x \to +\infty} \frac{3x}{4x^4 + 1} = \lim_{x \to +\infty} \frac{3/x^3}{4 + 1/x^4}$$

Examining the new limit, we observe that the numerator tends to 0, the $1/x^4$ term tends to zero, while the 4 is fixed. Thus we argue that the ratio tends to zero.

1. Find the following limits and state the name of the Property (ies) used.

7.3
Exercise

(a) $\lim_{x \to 6} (6x^2 + 1)$

(e) $\lim_{x \to 5} \left( x^3 - \frac{1}{x^3} \right)$

(b) $\lim_{x \to -2} (2x + 7)$

(f) $\lim_{x \to 4} \frac{x^5}{x^2 - 1}$

(c) $\lim_{x \to 1} (5x^3 + 2x^2 - 1)$

(g) $\lim_{x \to 3} 4$

(d) $\lim_{x \to 0} \left( \frac{3x - 2}{x^3 - 1} \right)$

(h) $\lim_{x \to -3} (x + 2)$

2. Find

(a) $\lim_{x \to 3} \dfrac{x^2 - 9}{x - 3}$

(d) $\lim_{x \to 1} \left( x^3 - \dfrac{1}{x} \right)$

(b) $\lim_{x \to -4} \dfrac{x^2 + 7x + 12}{x^2 + 6x + 8}$

(e) $\lim_{x \to 0} \dfrac{3x}{x^3 - x}$

(c) $\lim_{x \to 2} \dfrac{x^2 - 4}{x^2 + 4}$

(f) $\lim_{x \to -1} \dfrac{x^2 - 1}{x^2 + x}$

3. Find

(a) $\lim_{x \to +\infty} \dfrac{x + 1}{x - 1}$

(d) $\lim_{x \to +\infty} \dfrac{x^3}{x^2 + 1}$

(b) $\lim_{x \to +\infty} \dfrac{7x^2 + 5}{x^2 - 2}$

(e) $\lim_{x \to +\infty} \dfrac{3x^{5/2} + 2}{x^2 + \sqrt{x}}$

(c) $\lim_{x \to +\infty} \dfrac{x}{x^2 + 1}$

4. If $f(x) = x^2$, find (a) $\lim_{x \to 3} \dfrac{f(x) - f(3)}{x - 3}$ (b) $\lim_{x \to a} \dfrac{f(x) - f(a)}{x - a}$

5. If $f(x) = \dfrac{1}{x}$, find $\lim_{x \to a} \dfrac{f(x) - f(a)}{x - a}$, $a \neq 0$.

6. For the polynomial

$$f(x) = a_n \cdot x^n + a_{n-1} \cdot x^{n-1} + \cdots + a_1 \cdot x + a_0$$

find $\lim_{x \to a} f(x)$.

*7. If $n \geq 1$ is a positive integer, find

$$\lim_{x \to a} \dfrac{x^n - a^n}{x - a}$$

Hint: $x^n - a^n = (x - a)(x^{n-1} + ax^{n-2} + \cdots + a^{n-2}x + a^{n-1})$.

---

**7.4
CONTINUOUS
FUNCTIONS**

Thus far, we have considered whether the limit of a function exists at some value $x = a$. We have not been concerned at all with the value of the function at $x = a$, namely, $f(a)$; in fact, $f(a)$ need not even be defined in order to discuss the limit of $f(x)$ at $x = a$.

What is the relationship between $\lim_{x \to a} f(x)$ and $f(a)$? There are five possibilities that can occur involving $\lim_{x \to a} f(x)$ and $f(a)$, namely,

(a) $\lim_{x \to a} f(x)$ exists and equals $f(a)$

(b) $\lim_{x \to a} f(x)$ exists and does not equal $f(a)$

(c) $\lim_{x \to a} f(x)$ exists and $f(a)$ is not defined

(d) $\lim_{x \to a} f(x)$ does not exist and $f(a)$ is defined

(e) $\lim\limits_{x\to a} f(x)$ does not exist and $f(a)$ is not defined

These situations are illustrated in Figure 7.13.

(a)

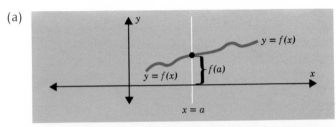

(b)

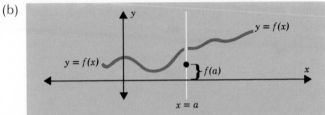

(c)

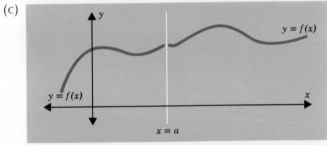

(d)

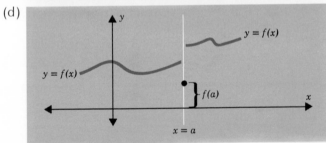

(e)

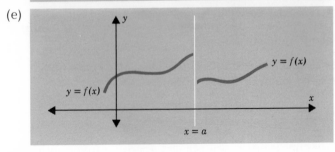

**Figure 7.13**

From the five situations illustrated above, the "nicest" one is that given in (a) of Figure 7.13 since there, not only does $\lim\limits_{x \to a} f(x)$ exist, but it is equal to $f(a)$. Functions that have this particular quality are said to be *continuous at x = a*. This is in agreement with the intuitive notion usually given in elementary courses that states "a function is continuous if its graph can be drawn without lifting the pencil." The functions in (b), (c), (d), and (e) are not continuous at $x = a$, since each has a "break" in the graph at $x = a$. This leads us to make the following definition.

**Definition of a Continuous Function** Let $y = f(x)$ **be a function. If**

$$\lim_{x \to a^-} f(x) = f(a) = \lim_{x \to a^+} f(x)$$

**then the function is said to be** *continuous at the point x = a*. **A function is called** *continuous on an interval* **if it is continuous at every point of the interval.**

At first, it may seem that the definition of continuity and the intuitive concept of continuity have little in common. To see that they are indeed equivalent, let's look at the Definition of a Continuous Function more closely.

The condition for a function to be continuous at $x = a$ is that

$$\lim_{x \to a^-} f(x) = f(a) = \lim_{x \to a^+} f(x)$$

We interpret $\lim\limits_{x \to a^-} f(x) = f(a)$ to say that as we travel along the function approaching $x = a$ from the left, we expect to hit the line $x = a$ at the height $f(a)$. This means there is no break in the graph as we proceed from values near $a$ (but to the left of $a$) to the value at $a$ itself. The fact that $\lim\limits_{x \to a^+} f(x) = f(a)$ says that when we proceed to values to the right of $x = a$, we are still at a height $f(a)$, so that again there is no jump or break in the graph. Thus the condition for continuity is that the values of the function for $x$ near $a$ should be very close to the value of the function at $x = a$.

To summarize, a function is continuous at a point $a$ provided that three conditions are simultaneously satisfied:

1. $x = a$ is in the domain of the function so that $f(a)$ is defined,
2. $\lim\limits_{x \to a} f(x)$ is a real number,

3. $\lim\limits_{x \to a} f(x) = f(a)$

**Discontinuous Function** If any one of these conditions is not obeyed, then the function is said to be *discontinuous at x = a*.

Discuss the continuity of $f(x) = |x|$ at $x = 0$.

First $x = 0$ is in the domain of $f$ and $f(0) = 0$. Next, using the result found in problem 3, Exercise 7.2, page 203, we find that $\lim_{x \to 0^-} f(x) = \lim_{x \to 0^+} f(x) = 0$. Thus, $f(x) = |x|$ is continuous at $x = 0$.

See Figure 7.14.

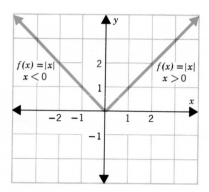

**Figure 7.14**

Determine whether $f(x) = \dfrac{|x|}{x}$ is continuous at $x = 0$.

Since the function has no value when $x = 0$, the first condition for continuity is not obeyed and so the function is discontinuous at $x = 0$. The graph of the function is given in Figure 7.15.

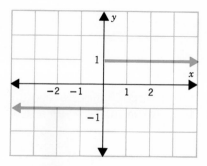

**Figure 7.15**

Notice that the function of Example 4.2 is continuous for all $x < 0$ and for all $x > 0$. The function is discontinuous only at $x = 0$ where a *jump* occurs.

Discuss the continuity of the function

$$f(x) = \begin{cases} x^2 & \text{if} & x \neq 0 \\ 1 & \text{if} & x = 0 \end{cases}$$

at $x = 0$.

First, the value of the function at $x = 0$ is

$$f(0) = 1$$

Also,

$$\lim_{x \to 0^-} f(x) = \lim_{x \to 0^-} x^2 = 0, \qquad \lim_{x \to 0^+} f(x) = \lim_{x \to 0^+} x^2 = 0$$

Then,

$$\lim_{x \to 0} f(x) = 0 \qquad f(0) = 1$$

Thus, condition (3) is not obeyed, so the function is discontinuous at $x = 0$. However, for $x \neq 0$, it is continuous. See Figure 7.16.

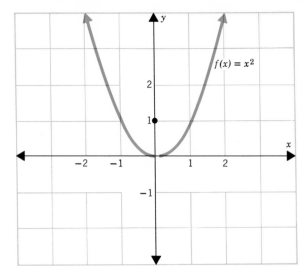

**Figure 7.16**

In the above example, the function is discontinuous because of its value when $x = 0$. If it is possible to redefine $f(0)$ as 0, then it would be continuous for all $x$ in its domain.

If

$$f(x) = \begin{cases} 6x & \text{if} & 0 \leqq x < 2 \\ 10 & \text{if} & x = 2 \\ 3x + 6 & \text{if} & 2 < x \leqq 3 \end{cases}$$

is $f$ continuous at $x = 2$?

First, $x = 2$ is in the domain of $f$ and $f(2) = 10$. Next,

$$\lim_{x \to 2^-} f(x) = \lim_{x \to 2^-} 6x = (6)(2) = 12$$

$$\lim_{x \to 2^+} f(x) = \lim_{x \to 2^+} (3x + 6) = 6 + 6 = 12$$

Thus,

$$\lim_{x \to 2} f(x) = 12, \qquad f(2) = 10$$

Hence the function is discontinuous at $x = 2$. See Figure 7.17.

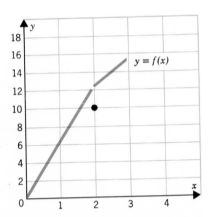

**Figure 7.17**

Notice that if $f(2)$ is redefined to be 12, then the function will be continuous on the closed interval $[0, 3]$.[1]

4.5
Example

The 1971 United States postage rates for air mail packages under 9 ounces are listed below. Graph the function describing this rate structure and determine points of discontinuity, if any.

| Number of ounces | 0-1 | 1-2 | 2-3 | 3-4 | 4-5 | 5-6 | 6-7 | 7-8 | 8-9 |
|---|---|---|---|---|---|---|---|---|---|
| Air mail cost in cents | 11 | 22 | 33 | 44 | 55 | 66 | 77 | 88 | 99 |

For air mail packages weighing less than 1 ounce, the charge is 11 cents. For packages weighing 1 or more ounces, but less than 2 ounces, the charge is 22 cents. This pattern continues up to packages weighing less than 8 ounces. For all packages 8 ounces or more, but less than 9 ounces the postage is $0.99.

A graph illustrating this is given in Figure 7.18.
Notice that the domain of this function is $0 < x < 16$, and the range is $\{0.11, 0.22, 0.33, \ldots, 0.99\}$. The function given in Figure 7.18 is usually

[1] See Appendix.

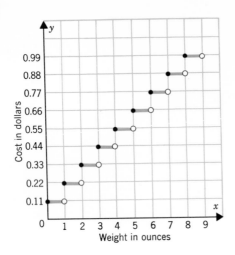

**Figure 7.18**

called a *step function* and is discontinuous at the points 1, 2, 3, 4, 5, 6, 7, and 8, and is continuous elsewhere.

Of course, just as with the evaluation of limits, the determination of continuity does not rely on graphical techniques. In fact, the definition of continuity makes no mention of the graph of the function. We determine continuity solely based on the expression defining the function.

Many of the functions we have already studied are continuous functions. For example,

**1. The linear function**

$$f(x) = mx + b$$

**is continuous for all** $x$.

**2. The quadratic function**

$$f(x) = ax^2 + bx + c, \qquad a \neq 0$$

**is continuous for all** $x$.

The following results enable us to construct new functions that are continuous by using functions we know are continuous.

**(I) If $f$ and $g$ are continuous at $x = a$, so is their sum $f + g$, their difference $f - g$, and their product $f \cdot g$.**
**(II) If $f$ and $g$ are continuous at $x = a$, and if $g(a) \neq 0$, then the function $f/g$ is also continuous at $x = a$.**

For example, since $f(x) = x^2$ and $g(x) = x^3 + 1$ are both continuous, the functions

$$x^2 + (x^3 + 1) \qquad \text{and} \qquad x^2 \cdot (x^3 + 1)$$

are each continuous. The function $f(x)/g(x) = x^2/(x^3 + 1)$ is continuous for all $x \neq -1$.

3. **The polynomial function**

$$f(x) = a_n \cdot x^n + a_{n-1} \cdot x^{n-1} + \cdots + a_1 \cdot x + a_0, \qquad a_n \neq 0$$

   **with $n \geq 0$ an integer is a continuous function.**
   This property is easily verified by noting that the function $a_k x^k$, $k \geq 0$, is continuous and a polynomial function is merely the sum of such functions.

4. **A rational function is the ratio of two polynomials. If $a$ is in the domain of a rational function (that is, the denominator polynomial is not equal to zero at $x = a$), then the rational function is continuous at $x = a$.**

We summarize by pointing out one of the features of a continuous function.

If a function is known to be continuous at $x = a$, then its limit at $x = a$ is easy to find—it is $f(a)$. Since many of the functions we shall encounter are continuous, the problem of finding their limit at a point will not be difficult.

1. For the function

$$f(x) = \begin{cases} 3x - 1 & \text{if} & -3 \leq x \leq 1 \\ 2x + 1 & \text{if} & x > 1 \end{cases}$$

   (a) Determine if the function is continuous at $x = 0$.
   (b) Determine if it is continuous at $x = 1$.
   (c) Graph the function.

2. For the function

$$f(x) = \begin{cases} 3x^2 & \text{if} & x < 0 \\ 1 & \text{if} & x = 0 \\ 2\lambda & \text{if} & x > 0 \end{cases}$$

   (a) Determine if the function is continuous at $x = 0$. (If not, can the function be redefined so that it is continuous at $x = 0$?)
   (b) Graph the function.

3. For the function

$$f(x) = \begin{cases} 2x + 1 & \text{if} & x \leq 0 \\ x^2 + 1 & \text{if} & x > 0 \end{cases}$$

   (a) Determine if the function is continuous at $x = 0$.
   (b) Graph the function.

4. For the function

$$f(x) = \begin{cases} \dfrac{1}{x} & \text{if} & -3 \leq x < 0 \\ -1 & \text{if} & x = 0 \\ x - 1 & \text{if} & 0 < x < 1 \\ x^2 - 1 & \text{if} & 1 \leq x \leq 2 \end{cases}$$

(a) Determine where the function is continuous.

(b) Graph the function.

5. Give a reason why the following functions are not continuous at $x = 1$.

(a) $f(x) = \dfrac{x^2 + 2x + 2}{x^2 - 1}$  (b) $f(x) = \dfrac{(x - 3)(x - 1)}{x - 1}$

6. Find two functions whose domain is $[0, 2]$ so that
   (a) the first is continuous on $[0, 2]$.
   (b) the second is continuous on $[0, 2]$ except at $x = 1$.

7. The owner of a grocery store can buy canned goods from a particular distributor in case lots according to the following price schedule:

   $3.00 per case for 5 cases or less
   2.50 per case for more than 5 cases but less than 10 cases
   2.25 per case for 10 or more cases but less than 20 cases
   2.00 per case for 20 or more cases

   (a) Find a cost function $C(x)$, where $C(x)$ represents the cost of buying $x$ cases.
   (b) Graph the cost function.
   (c) Find those values of $x$ where it is discontinuous.

8. An oil refinery has four distillation towers and operates them as they are needed to process available raw materials. Each tower has a fixed overhead operating cost of $500 per week; the raw material cost is fixed at $0.50 per gallon of refined oil; finally, each tower can process at most 10,000 gallons of refined oil each week.
   (a) Find the cost function $C(x)$; $x = $ number of gallons of refined oil for the refinery.
   (b) Find the domain of this function and graph it.
   (c) Find any points of discontinuity of the function.

9. The 1971 United States postage rates for first class mail and third class mail are given in the table below. Graph the functions describing the cost and determine points of discontinuity.

| Ounces | 0-1 | 1-2 | 2-3 | 3-4 | 4-5 | 5-6 | 6-7 | 7-8 | 8-9 | 9-10 | 10-11 | 11-12 | 12-13 |
|---|---|---|---|---|---|---|---|---|---|---|---|---|---|
| First class (cents) | 8 | 16 | 24 | 32 | 40 | 48 | 56 | 64 | 72 | 80 | 88 | 96 | 100 |
| Third class (cents) | 8 | 8 | 10 | 13 | 16 | 18 | 21 | 24 | 26 | 29 | 32 | 34 | 37 |

CHAPTER
REVIEW

Important
Terms

**limit**
**right-hand limit**
**left-hand limit**
**plus infinity** $+\infty$

**minus infinity** $-\infty$
**continuous at a point**
**step function**
**discontinuous**

1. Use a graphical approach to calculate the following limits.

(a) $\lim\limits_{x \to 3} (3x - 4)$

(d) $\lim\limits_{x \to 1} 5$

(b) $\lim\limits_{x \to 0^-} x^2$

(e) $\lim\limits_{x \to +\infty} \dfrac{1}{x}$

(c) $\lim\limits_{x \to -2} (3 - 2x)$

(f) $\lim\limits_{x \to -\infty} 2x$

2. Use a numerical approach to find the following limits.

(a) $\lim\limits_{x \to 3} 2x$

(d) $\lim\limits_{x \to 1} \dfrac{1}{(x - 1)^2}$

(b) $\lim\limits_{x \to -2} (x + 1)$

(e) $\lim\limits_{x \to +\infty} x^2$

(c) $\lim\limits_{x \to 4} \dfrac{x^2 - 16}{x - 4}$

(f) $\lim\limits_{x \to 0^+} \dfrac{1}{x^2}$

3. Use algebraic techniques to find the following limits.

(a) $\lim\limits_{x \to -2} \dfrac{x^2 + 4x + 4}{x^2 - 4}$

(d) $\lim\limits_{x \to -1} \dfrac{x^3 - 3x}{3x^3 - 1}$

(b) $\lim\limits_{x \to 3} (x^3 - 3x^2 + 1)$

(e) $\lim\limits_{x \to 0} \dfrac{1}{x^2 - 2x + 1}$

(c) $\lim\limits_{x \to 1} \dfrac{x^3 - 1}{x - 1}$

(f) $\lim\limits_{x \to 3} \dfrac{3x}{x^2 + 1}$

4. For the function

$$f(x) = \dfrac{x^2 + 2x + 1}{x^2 - 1}$$

find

(a) $\lim\limits_{x \to 1} f(x)$

(d) $\lim\limits_{x \to -\infty} f(x)$

(b) $\lim\limits_{x \to -1} f(x)$

(e) $\lim\limits_{x \to 0} f(x)$

(c) $\lim\limits_{x \to +\infty} f(x)$

(f) $\lim\limits_{x \to 4} f(x)$

5. Determine whether the following functions are continuous at the values indicated. Graph each function.

(a) $f(x) = \begin{cases} \dfrac{x^3 - 1}{x - 1} & \text{if} \quad x < 1 \\ 3x & \text{if} \quad x \geq 1 \end{cases}$  $a = 1$

(b) $f(x) = \begin{cases} \dfrac{|x|}{x} & \text{if} \quad x \neq 0 \\ 0 & \text{if} \quad x = 0 \end{cases}$  $a = 0$

(c) $f(x) = \begin{cases} \dfrac{1}{(x - 1)^2} & \text{if} \quad x \neq 1 \\ 3 & \text{if} \quad x = 1 \end{cases}$  $a = 1$

6. Compute

$$\lim_{x \to 4} \frac{f(x) - f(4)}{x - 4}$$

for the functions

(a) $f(x) = 4x$  (c) $f(x) = x^3$

(b) $f(x) = x^2$  (d) $f(x) = \sqrt{x}$

## Bibliography

*Mathematics*

Leithold, Louis, *Calculus and Analytic Geometry,* Second Edition, Harper and Row, New York, 1972. Chapter 2.

Salas, Saturnino and Einar Hille, *Calculus: One and Several Variables,* Second Edition, Xerox, Lexington, Mass., 1974. Chapter 2.

Thomas, George, *Calculus and Analytic Geometry,* Fourth Edition, Addison-Wesley, Reading, Mass., 1968. Chapter 2.

# 8

# THE DERIVATIVE

In order to appreciate the derivative as a tool in solving applied problems (Chapter 9), it is necessary to have an understanding of what it means to differentiate a function. To gain this insight, we shall proceed slowly in defining the derivative.

The first part of this chapter deals with the notion of an average rate of change and with applications to geometry, physics, and business. We follow with the meaning of an instantaneous rate of change and how it is interpreted relative to these same three areas. The latter part of the chapter gives formulas that make differentiation of many functions a relatively straightforward procedure.

On a Saturday in October, the following chart, prepared by the U.S. Weather Bureau, listed the hourly temperatures in Chicago from 3 a.m. to midnight.

**Table 8.1**

| Temperature °F | 44 | 44 | 44 | 45 | 44 | 44 | 44 | 44 | 45 | 45 | 46 |
|---|---|---|---|---|---|---|---|---|---|---|---|
| Time | 3 A.M. | 4 A.M. | 5 A.M. | 6 A.M. | 7 A.M. | 8 A.M. | 9 A.M. | 10 A.M. | 11 A.M. | Noon | 1 P.M. |
| | 47 | 47 | 46 | 47 | 47 | 47 | 50 | 50 | 49 | 47 | 46 |
| | 2 P.M. | 3 P.M. | 4 P.M. | 5 P.M. | 6 P.M. | 7 P.M. | 8 P.M. | 9 P.M. | 10 P.M. | 11 P.M. | 12 |

Most would agree that the change in temperature from 3 a.m. to 8 p.m. is 6 degrees F. But what is the general formula for computing change?

The change of 6 degrees F is obtained by taking the reading at 3 a.m. (44) and subtracting it from the reading at 8 p.m. (50). That is,

change from 3 a.m. to 8 p.m. = temperature at 8 p.m.

$$- \text{ temperature at 3 a.m.}$$
$$= \text{final reading} - \text{initial reading}$$
$$= 50 - 44 = 6$$

The graph of this data, using the x-axis for time and the y-axis for temperature, is given in Figure 8.1. In Figure 8.1, we use 13, 14, 15, etc. to stand for 1 p.m., 2 p.m., 3 p.m., etc. Also, to aid in visualizing this situation, we have connected each point by lines.

2.1
Example

What is the change in temperature from 11 a.m. to 8 p.m.? What is the corresponding change in time?

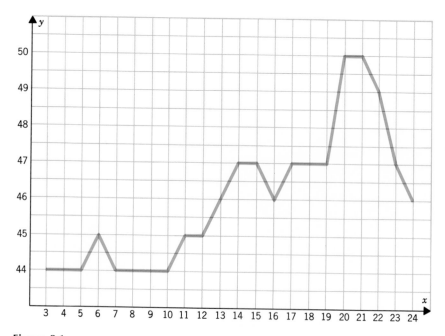

**Figure 8.1**

To compute the change in temperature, we note that the temperature at 11 a.m. is 45 and at 8 p.m. is 50. Thus, change in temperature from 11 a.m. to 8 p.m. $= 50 - 45 = 5$. The change in time is from 11 a.m. to 8 p.m., or 9 hours.

We use the mathematical symbol $\Delta x$, read as "delta x," to denote a change in x, and the mathematical symbol $\Delta y$ to denote a change in y. Thus, in the example above, the change in time from 11 a.m. to 8 p.m. (which we have decided to measure along the x-axis) is

$$\Delta x = 20 - 11 = 9$$

where 20 is the designation for 8 p.m. The change in temperature is

$$\Delta y = 50 - 45 = 5$$

The next example illustrates how to determine $\Delta x$ and $\Delta y$ when the function is given.

For the function

$$y = f(x) = 3x - 2$$

find $\Delta x$ and $\Delta y$, if x changes from 0 to 4.
    If the change in x is from 0 to 4, then

$$\Delta x = 4 - 0 = 4$$

To find the change in y, we need to find the value of y at 0 and at 4. At $x = 0$, the value of y is $f(0) = -2$ and at $x = 4$, the value of y is $f(4) = 10$. The change in y is

$$\Delta y = f(4) - f(0) = 10 - (-2) = 12$$

Figure 8.2, on the following page, illustrates the geometric significance of the changes $\Delta x$ and $\Delta y$ for the function given in Example 2.2.
    The value of $\Delta y$ can also be zero or negative, as the next example illustrates.

For the hourly temperature readings given in Table 8.1, find the change in temperature from 8 p.m. to midnight. What is the change from 1 p.m. to midnight?
    The change in temperature from 8 p.m. to midnight is

$$\Delta y = 46 - 50 = -4$$

The change from 1 p.m. to midnight is

$$\Delta y = 46 - 46 = 0$$

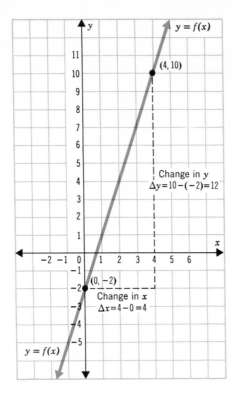

**Figure 8.2**

Each of the above examples deals with computing change, but none of them gives us information about the average rate at which the change is taking place. There is a significant difference between a change in temperature of 5 degrees over 10 hours and a change of 5 degrees over 1 hour. To measure this information we divide the change in temperature by the change in time. This ratio is called the *average rate of change* (of temperature with respect to time).

2.4
Example

For the hourly temperature readings given in Table 8.1, find the average rate of change of temperature with respect to time from 5 a.m. to noon.

We begin by computing the change in temperature from 5 a.m. to noon, namely,

$$\Delta y = 45 - 44 = 1$$

The corresponding change in time is

$$\Delta x = 12 - 5 = 7$$

The average rate of change is

$$\frac{\Delta y}{\Delta x} = \frac{1}{7} = 0.143$$

We interpret the value 0.143 to mean that the change in temperature from 5 a.m. to noon, *on the average,* amounts to an increase in temperature of 0.143 degrees each hour from 5 a.m. to noon. Of course, in reality the temperature has sometimes remained unchanged and sometimes increased by more than 0.143 over each hour of this period. However, the *average* change each hour is 0.143 degrees.

**For a function $y = f(x)$, the** *average rate of change* **is the ratio of the change in $y$ to the change in $x$. That is, average rate of change $= \Delta y / \Delta x$.**

Definition
of Average Rate
of Change

Thus, if the change in $x$ is from $x_1$ to $x_2$, then

$$\text{average rate of change} = \frac{\Delta y}{\Delta x} = \frac{f(x_2) - f(x_1)}{x_2 - x_1}$$

For the function $y = f(x) = x^2$, find the average rate of change as $x$ changes from 0 to 3.

2.5
Example

We begin by computing the change in $x$:

$$\Delta x = 3 - 0 = 3$$

The corresponding change in $y$ is the difference between the values of $f(x) = x^2$ at $x = 3$ and $x = 0$. Thus,

$$\Delta y = f(3) - f(0) = 3^2 - 0^2 = 9 - 0 = 9$$

The average rate of change is

$$\frac{\Delta y}{\Delta x} = \frac{9}{3} = 3$$

For an interpretation of the average rate of change, we look at the graph of $f(x) = x^2$. See Figure 8.3. The line connecting the two points $(0, 0)$ and $(3, 9)$ is called a *secant line,* and its slope is

Secant Line

$$m = \frac{9 - 0}{3 - 0} = 3$$

But this is the same as the average rate of change from 0 to 3.

**The geometric interpretation of average rate of change is that it measures the slope of the secant line joining two points on a curve.**

In general, consider a function $y = f(x)$ and locate two points on this curve. See Figure 8.4 on the following page. The slope of the secant line is the average rate of change, namely,

$$\frac{\Delta y}{\Delta x} = \frac{f(x_2) - f(x_1)}{x_2 - x_1}$$

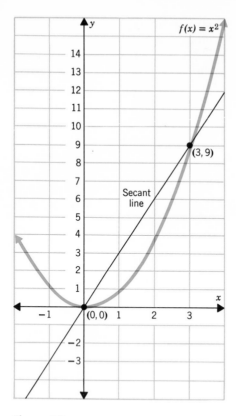

**Figure 8.3**

This quantity is significant for studying the derivative and is called a

Difference
Quotient

*difference quotient.*

The notion of an average rate of change can also be given a physical interpretation.

2.6
Example

Mr. Doody and his family leave on a car trip Saturday morning at 5 a.m. and arrive at their destination at 11 a.m. When he began the trip, the car's odometer read 26,700 miles and, when he arrived, it read 27,000 miles. What was his average speed for the trip?

Most of us know that average speed is computed by dividing the distance traveled by the elapsed time. The distance in this case is $27,000 - 26,700 = 300$ miles and the elapsed time is $11 - 5 = 6$ hours. Thus the average speed is

$$\text{average speed} = \frac{300}{6} = 50 \text{ miles per hour}$$

In other words, the average speed is the ratio of the change in distance to the change in time. Thus, if $s$ denotes distance and $t$ denotes time,

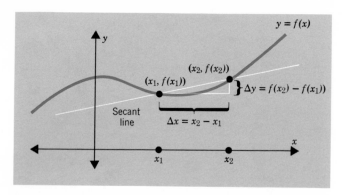

**Figure 8.4**

we have

$$\text{average speed} = \frac{\Delta s}{\Delta t}$$

Our final interpretation of average rate of change is to a business situation.

Suppose $C(x)$ is the total cost of producing and marketing $x$ units of a certain commodity. In this example, we assume the cost $C$ depends only on the number $x$ of units produced. Thus, the cost of producing $x_1$ units is $C(x_1)$. If we increase the number of units from $x_1$ to $x_2$, the cost will change from $C(x_1)$ to $C(x_2)$. The average rate of change in cost relative to units produced is the ratio of the change in cost to the change in units produced. That is,

$$\text{average rate of change in cost} = \frac{\Delta C}{\Delta x} = \frac{C(x_2) - C(x_1)}{x_2 - x_1}$$

The cost of producing and marketing a certain screwdriver is found to obey the formula

$$C(x) = \sqrt{x}, \qquad 0 \le x \le 100$$

where $x$ is measured in units of screwdrivers produced and $C(x)$ is measured in dollars. Find the average rate of change in cost from $x = 2$ to $x = 4$. What is the average rate of change in cost from $x = 2$ to $x = 8$?

We begin by computing the change in $x$ from $x = 2$ to $x = 4$:

$$\Delta x = 4 - 2 = 2$$

The change in cost from $x = 2$ to $x = 4$ is

$$\Delta C = \sqrt{4} - \sqrt{2} \approx 2 - 1.414 = 0.586$$

The average rate of change in cost from $x = 2$ to $x = 4$ is

$$\frac{\Delta C}{\Delta x} = \frac{0.586}{2} = 0.293$$

The change in x from $x = 2$ to $x = 8$ is

$$\Delta x = 8 - 2 = 6$$

The change in cost from $x = 2$ to $x = 8$ is

$$\Delta C = \sqrt{8} - \sqrt{2} = 2\sqrt{2} - \sqrt{2} \approx 1.414$$

The average rate of change in cost is

$$\frac{\Delta C}{\Delta x} = \frac{1.414}{6} = 0.236$$

How should these differences be interpreted? The first average rate of change in cost (from $x = 2$ to $x = 4$) says that the two extra units have an average cost of $0.293 each. The second average rate of change in cost (from $x = 2$ to $x = 8$) says the six extra units have an average cost of $0.236 each. In other words, after two units are produced, the average cost for the next two is $0.293 each and for the next six is $0.236 each.

As might be expected, the average rate of change in cost (from $x = 2$) is smaller when more units are produced. This is a reflection, of course, of assembly line procedures, and the like, which make mass-produced items relatively inexpensive.

To summarize, an average rate of change measures the ratio of one change to another change; that is, it measures the ratio of the change in y to the change in x. Geometrically the average rate of change is the slope of the secant line. Physically, an average rate of change can be used to find average speed, the ratio of the change in distance to the change in time. In business, the average rate of change of cost is the change in cost divided by the change in the number of items manufactured.

8.2
Exercise

1. For the function

$$f(x) = 5x - 2$$

(a) Find the change in y from $x = 0$ to $x = 4$.
(b) Find the change in y from $x = -3$ to $x = 2$.
(c) Find the average rate of change for (a).
(d) Find the average rate of change for (b).
(e) Compute the average rate of change from $x = a$ to $x = b$, where $a < b$. What do you conclude? Why? Look at the graph for a hint.

2. For the function

$$f(x) = x^2 - 1$$

(a) Find the change in y from $x = 1$ to $x = 3$.
(b) Find the change in y from $x = -1$ to $x = 1$.
(c) Find the average rate of change in (a).

(d) Find the average rate of change in (b).

(e) Find the slope of the secant line from $(0, f(0))$ to $(4, f(4))$.

3. For the function

$$f(x) = x^3$$

(a) Find the change in $y$ from $x = -1$ to $x = 1$.

(b) Find the change in $y$ from $x = 0$ to $x = 4$.

(c) Find the average rate of change in (a).

(d) Find the average rate of change in (b).

(e) Find the slope of the secant line from $(-2, f(-2))$ to $(2, f(2))$.

(f) Graph the function.

4. Find the slope of the secant line of

$$f(x) = x^2 - 2x + 1$$

(a) from $(0, f(0))$ to $(1, f(1))$

(b) from $(0, f(0))$ to $(3, f(3))$.

5. Consider the corn production data given in the table below.

| Investment $x$ (dollars) | Corn Output $y$ (bushels) |
|---|---|
| 700 | 12,700 |
| 1000 | 13,100 |
| 1200 | 14,700 |
| 1400 | 17,100 |
| 1600 | 19,000 |
| 2000 | 22,100 |
| 2200 | 21,700 |

Graph this data. Find the average rate of increase from $700 to $2200. What is the average rate of increase from $1000 to $1400. What is it from $1000 to $1200?

6. By adding fertilizer to the soil, increased crop yields can sometimes be obtained. The table below lists the corn yield obtained per acre by adding certain amounts of fertilizer.

| Fertilizer | Corn Yield/Acre |
|---|---|
| 0 pounds | 45 bushels |
| 10 pounds | 46.2 bushels |
| 20 pounds | 48 bushels |
| 30 pounds | 48.2 bushels |
| 40 pounds | 47.6 bushels |
| 50 pounds | 47.3 bushels |

Graph this data and use the amount of fertilizer added as the $x$-axis. What is the average rate of increase in yield from 0 to 50 pounds? What is the average rate of increase in yield from 10 to 40 pounds? From 10 to 30 pounds?

7. The distance a man can walk in time $t$ obeys the formula

$$s = \sqrt{t}$$

where s is measured in miles and t is measured in hours. What is his average speed from $t = 0$ to $t = 16$ hours? What is his average speed from $t = 1$ to $t = 4$ hours? From $t = 1$ to $t = 2$ hours?

*8. For each of the following functions, find the slope of the secant line from $(0, f(0))$ to an arbitrary point P. Use $(x, f(x))$ as the coordinates of P. Graph each function and the secant line.

(a) $f(x) = 3x - 2$      (d) $f(x) = x^3 + 8$

(b) $f(x) = x^2 + 4$      (e) $f(x) = \sqrt{x}$

(c) $f(x) = 2 - x^2$      (f) $f(x) = \dfrac{1}{x + 1}$

---

**8.3**
**INSTANTANEOUS RATE OF CHANGE; THE DERIVATIVE**

In Section 8.2 we define the meaning of average rate of change and give interpretations of this concept to geometry, physics, and business. The physics interpretation is one that we will now look at more closely.

Recall that in Example 2.6, page 226, Mr. Doody begins a trip at 5 a.m. and arrives at his destination at 11 a.m. the same day. The distance covered in that time is 300 miles, and we calculated his average speed to be $300/6 = 50$ miles per hour. This average speed of 50 mph accurately describes the speed over the entire journey, but gives no information at all about the actual speed at a certain specific time. Thus, average speed might reflect a journey in which for 3 hours the speed was 0 mph and for 3 hours the speed was 100 mph; or it might reflect an actual speed that remained fixed at 50 mph; or any one of a variety of speeds. How can we find out what the speed of the vehicle is at a particular instant in time?

The following example illustrates how this might be done when the relationship between distance and time is a known function.

**3.1**
**Example**

Let the function

$$s = f(t) = 6t(t + 1)$$

describe the distance s (in miles) a car travels after a time t (in hours), for $0 \leq t \leq 6$.

The average speed of the car over the entire journey is

$$\text{average speed} = \frac{\Delta s}{\Delta t} = \frac{f(6) - f(0)}{6 - 0} = 42 \text{ mph}$$

The average speed of the car from $t = 2$ to $t = 3$ hours is

$$\text{average speed} = \frac{\Delta s}{\Delta t} = \frac{f(3) - f(2)}{3 - 2} = 36 \text{ mph}$$

The average speed from $t = 2$ to $t = 2.5$ hours is

$$\text{average speed} = \frac{\Delta s}{\Delta t} = \frac{f(2.5) - f(2)}{2.5 - 2} = \frac{16.50}{0.5} = 33 \text{ mph}$$

The average speed from $t = 2$ to $t = 2.1$ hours is

$$\text{average speed} = \frac{\Delta s}{\Delta t} = \frac{f(2.1) - f(2)}{2.1 - 2} = \frac{3.06}{0.1} = 30.6 \text{ mph}$$

As time gets closer to $t = 2$, the average speed is approaching a value. This value is called the *instantaneous speed* at $t = 2$. To find the instantaneous speed, we need to use the limit concept and let the time $t$ get closer to 2. For our example, we have

$$\text{instantaneous speed at } t = 2 \text{ is } \lim_{t \to 2} \frac{f(t) - f(2)}{t - 2}$$

$$= \lim_{t \to 2} \frac{6t(t + 1) - 36}{t - 2}$$

$$= \lim_{t \to 2} \frac{6t^2 + 6t - 36}{t - 2}$$

$$= \lim_{t \to 2} \frac{6(t^2 + t - 6)}{t - 2}$$

$$= \lim_{t \to 2} 6(t + 3) = 30$$

Thus the actual speed of the car at $t = 2$ hours is 30 mph.

**The instantaneous speed at time $t$ is the limiting value (if it exists) of the average speed $\Delta s / \Delta t$ as the time change ($\Delta t$) approaches zero.**  Instantaneous Speed

In comparing the concepts of average rate of change and of instantaneous rate of change, we notice that average rates of change take place on an interval, whereas instantaneous rates are evaluated at a point.

Let us examine what this process means geometrically. Suppose we have a continuous function $y = f(x)$. The average rate of change $\Delta y / \Delta x$ measures the slope of the secant line joining two points on the curve. If we fix the initial point at $(a, f(a))$ and let the terminal point be $(x_1, f(x_1))$, the slope of this secant line is

$$\frac{\Delta y}{\Delta x} = \frac{f(x_1) - f(a)}{x_1 - a}$$

See Figure 8.5 on the following page.

Figure 8.6 illustrates what occurs as $x_1$ approaches $a$ along the $x$-axis. For example, as $x_1$ approaches $a$, it assumes all values from $a$ to $x_1$. Some of these values are the $x_2$ and $x_3$ of Figure 8.6. Let us see what happens to these secant lines as $x$ approaches $a$. It is apparent that the secant lines $L_1, L_2, L_3$ are becoming better and better approximations to what we would agree is the tangent line to $y = f(x)$ at $(a, f(a))$.

**Thus, the *tangent line* to a curve at a point $(a, f(a))$ is defined as the limiting position of the secant lines from $(a, f(a))$ to $(x, f(x))$ as $x$ approaches $a$.**  Definition of Tangent Line

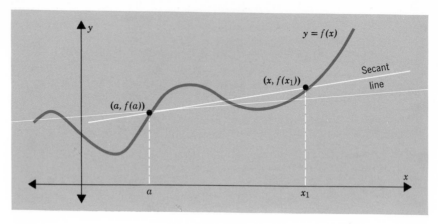

**Figure 8.5**

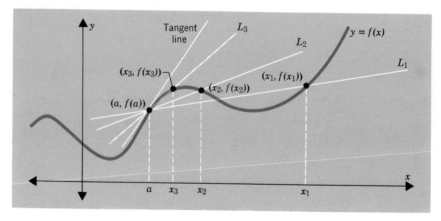

**Figure 8.6**

And what is the significance now of the average rate of change $\Delta y / \Delta x$? Recall that $\Delta y / \Delta x$ measures the slope of a secant line. Then it is clear that if the limiting position (as $\Delta x \to 0$) of the secant line is the tangent line, then the limiting value of $\Delta y / \Delta x$ is the slope of the tangent line.

Geometric
Interpretation

**For a function $y = f(x)$, the limiting value of the average rate of change $\Delta y / \Delta x$ as $\Delta x \to 0$ is the slope of the tangent line.**

To summarize, suppose we have a continuous function $y = f(x)$ and we locate a point $(a, f(a))$ on its graph. The slope of the tangent line to this curve at the point $(a, f(a))$ is given by the limit (if it exists) of the average rate of change from $(a, f(a))$ to an arbitrary point $(x, f(x))$ as $x$ approaches $a$. That is,

Slope of the
Tangent
Line

slope of tangent line of $y = f(x)$ at $(a, f(a))$ is $\lim\limits_{x \to a} \dfrac{f(x) - f(a)}{x - a}$

To find the equation of this tangent line, we proceed as follows. We know the slope and we know a point on the tangent line $(a, f(a))$. Hence the point-slope form of a straight line can be used to find the equation of the tangent line. That is, if

$$m = \lim_{x \to a} \frac{f(x) - f(a)}{x - a}$$

is the slope of the tangent line and if $(a, f(a))$ is a point on the tangent line, the equation of the tangent line is

$$y - f(a) = m(x - a)$$

Equation of
Tangent Line

Find the slope and equation of the tangent line to the curve

3.2
Example

$$y = f(x) = x^2$$

at the point $(2, 4)$. Graph the function and the tangent line.

First, we compute the average rate of change from $(2, 4)$ to an arbitrary point $(x, f(x))$

$$\frac{\Delta y}{\Delta x} = \frac{f(x) - f(2)}{x - 2} = \frac{x^2 - 4}{x - 2}$$

The slope of the tangent line to $f(x) = x^2$ at $(2, 4)$ is the limit of $\Delta y / \Delta x$ as $x$ approaches 2. Thus,

slope of tangent line at $(2, 4)$ is $\lim_{x \to 2} \frac{x^2 - 4}{x - 2} = \lim_{x \to 2} (x + 2) = 4$

The slope of the tangent line is 4, and a point on it is $(2, 4)$. Hence the equation of this tangent line is

$$y - 4 = 4(x - 2) \quad \text{or} \quad y = 4x - 4$$

Figure 8.7 illustrates the function and its tangent line at $(2, 4)$.

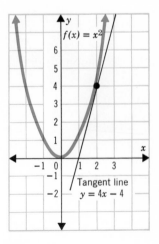

**Figure 8.7**

Thus far we have noted two interpretations of the limit of an average rate of change—one as an instantaneous speed at a point in time, and the other as the slope of a tangent line at a point on a curve. This quantity

$$\lim_{\Delta x \to 0} \frac{\Delta y}{\Delta x} \qquad \text{or} \qquad \lim_{x \to a} \frac{f(x) - f(a)}{x - a}$$

has many other interpretations in a variety of different areas. For this reason it is given a special name: *the derivative of* $y = f(x)$ *at* $x = a$.

**Definition of the Derivative**

**Let $y = f(x)$ be a function and let $a$ be in the domain of $f$. If the limit**

$$\lim_{x \to a} \frac{f(x) - f(a)}{x - a}$$

**exists, then the function $y = f(x)$ is said to be** *differentiable at* $x = a$. **In this case, the** *derivative of* $f(x)$ *at* $x = a$, **denoted by** $f'(a)$, **is**

$$f'(a) = \lim_{x \to a} \frac{f(x) - f(a)}{x - a}$$

The notation $f'(a)$ is read "f prime of a."

**3.3 Example**

Find the derivative of $f(x) = x^3$ at $x = 2$. Find the derivative of $f(x) = x^3$ at $x = a$.

First, we compute the average rate of change from $x = 2$ to an arbitrary $x$.

$$\frac{\Delta y}{\Delta x} = \frac{f(x) - f(2)}{x - 2} = \frac{x^3 - 8}{x - 2}$$

The derivative of $f(x) = x^3$ at $x = 2$ is the limit of $\Delta y / \Delta x$ as $x \to 2$. Thus,

$$f'(2) = \lim_{x \to 2} \frac{x^3 - 8}{x - 2} = \lim_{x \to 2} (x^2 + 2x + 4) = 12$$

For the second part, we proceed to find the average rate of change from $x = a$ to an arbitrary $x$.

$$\frac{\Delta y}{\Delta x} = \frac{f(x) - f(a)}{x - a} = \frac{x^3 - a^3}{x - a}$$

The derivative is

$$f'(a) = \lim_{x \to a} \frac{x^3 - a^3}{x - a} = \lim_{x \to a} (x^2 + xa + a^2) = 3a^2$$

Notice that for $a = 2$, the two results are in agreement.

The derivative of a function is the limit of a difference quotient, and, as we saw in Chapter 7, limits are sometimes infinite. However, since the derivative can be interpreted as the slope of a tangent line, when the limit of a difference quotient is $+\infty$ or $-\infty$, the tangent line is vertical (slope is undefined). The next example illustrates this situation.

Find the slope of the tangent line to $f(x) = \sqrt{x}$ at $(0, 0)$.
3.4
Here we are asking for the value of the limit
Example

$$\lim_{x \to 0^+} \frac{f(x) - f(0)}{x - 0}$$

The reason this limit is right-handed is that the domain of $f(x) = \sqrt{x}$ is $x \geq 0$.
Thus,

$$\lim_{x \to 0^+} \frac{f(x) - f(0)}{x - 0} = \lim_{x \to 0^+} \frac{\sqrt{x}}{x} = \lim_{x \to 0^+} \frac{1}{\sqrt{x}} = +\infty$$

Thus, the slope of the tangent line to $f(x) = \sqrt{x}$ at $(0, 0)$ is undefined. This means the function has a vertical tangent at $(0, 0)$. See Figure 8.8.

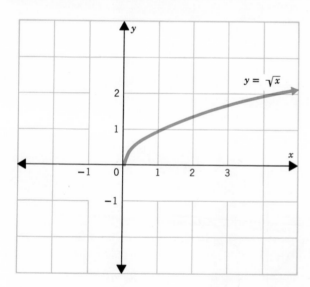

**Figure 8.8**

Observe that when the limit of a difference quotient is infinite, the function has a vertical tangent line. When the limit does not exist at a point, the function has no tangent line at that point. The next example illustrates a situation in which there is no tangent line at a particular point.

Consider the function $f(x) = |x|$. Does it have a tangent line at $(0, 0)$?

In order for $f(x) = |x|$ to have a tangent line at $(0, 0)$, it must have a derivative at $x = 0$. Thus, we need to examine the limit

$$\lim_{x \to 0} \frac{|x| - |0|}{x - 0} = \lim_{x \to 0} \frac{|x|}{x}$$

and determine whether it exists. If we refer to Figure 7.15, page 213, we see that

$$\lim_{x \to 0^-} \frac{|x|}{x} = -1, \qquad \lim_{x \to 0^+} \frac{|x|}{x} = 1$$

Thus, $\lim_{x \to 0} \frac{|x|}{x}$ does not exist, so that $f(x) = |x|$ has no derivative at $x = 0$. This means $f(x) = |x|$ has no tangent line at $(0, 0)$.

Figure 8.9 illustrates the way this function looks at the point where it has no derivative. Notice that there is a corner at $(0, 0)$, that is, the curve is not smooth at $(0, 0)$. For our purposes, at points where a curve has no derivative, one of three possibilities can occur: (1) the curve is either not smooth (has corners like $\vee$ or $\wedge$); or (2) the curve has vertical tangent lines; or (3) the curve is not continuous at the point in question.

For the function

$$f(x) = \begin{cases} x^2 & \text{if} & x \leq 0 \\ 2x & \text{if} & x > 0 \end{cases}$$

determine if $f'(0)$ exists.

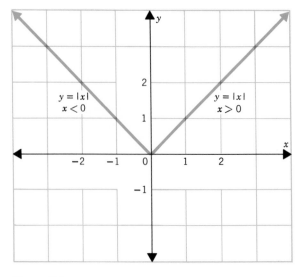

**Figure 8.9**

The derivative of the function at $x = 0$ is

$$f'(0) = \lim_{x \to 0} \frac{f(x) - f(0)}{x - 0} = \lim_{x \to 0} \frac{f(x)}{x}$$

The rule for $f(x)$ depends on whether $x < 0$ or $x > 0$. As a result, we must look at the two limits

$$\lim_{x \to 0^-} \frac{f(x)}{x} \quad \text{and} \quad \lim_{x \to 0^+} \frac{f(x)}{x}$$

The result is

$$\lim_{x \to 0^-} \frac{f(x)}{x} = \lim_{x \to 0^-} \frac{x^2}{x} = \lim_{x \to 0^-} x = 0$$

$$\lim_{x \to 0^+} \frac{f(x)}{x} = \lim_{x \to 0^+} \frac{2x}{x} = \lim_{x \to 0^+} 2 = 2$$

Since these two limits are not equal, $f'(0)$ does not exist. See Figure 8.10 for an illustration.

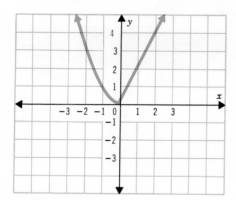

**Figure 8.10**

We turn now to an application of the derivative to economics.

To increase profits, a company may decide to increase its production. Associated with this increase are added costs, such as new capital investments, additional labor costs, increased storage facilities, added sales and advertising expenses, and so on. The question that concerns management is how will the cost be affected by an increase in production?

We need to measure the rate of change of cost as output changes. This measure, called the *marginal cost MC*, is frequently described by economists as the additional cost of producing an additional unit of output. If we know the cost function $C(x)$, the marginal cost function is the derivative of the cost function. That is,

$$MC = \lim_{x \to x_0} \frac{C(x) - C(x_0)}{x - x_0} = C'(x_0)$$

Discrete
Marginal Cost

If the cost function is not known or if output can only be varied by discrete increments, we introduce the *discrete marginal cost DMC*, which is defined by

$$DMC = \frac{C(x) - C(x_0)}{x - x_0} = \frac{\Delta C}{\Delta x}$$

If $x - x_0 = \Delta x = 1$, discrete marginal cost measures the additional cost of producing one additional unit of output.

In the calculus portion of this book, we assume that cost functions are differentiable. As a result, we give the following definition.

Marginal Cost

**The derivative of the cost function $C(x)$ is the** *marginal cost MC,* **that is, the incremental cost of producing one additional unit above $x$ units. Thus,**

$$MC = C'(x)$$

In Example 2.7 on page 227, we discussed a cost function

$$C(x) = \sqrt{x}, \qquad 0 \leqq x \leqq 100$$

in which $x$ represents the number of screwdrivers produced and $C(x)$ is the cost in dollars of production. If 64 units are produced, the cost associated with producing one additional unit is the marginal cost $MC$ and is given by

$$MC = C'(64) = \lim_{x \to 64} \frac{\sqrt{x} - 8}{x - 64}$$

$$= \lim_{x \to 64} \frac{(\sqrt{x} - 8)}{(\sqrt{x} - 8)(\sqrt{x} + 8)} = \frac{1}{\sqrt{64} + 8} = \frac{1}{16} = 0.06$$

In economics, *marginal analysis,* the study of changes in quantities, is important. In Section 9.6 of Chapter 9 we discuss some applications of marginal analysis.

8.3
Exercise

1. Find the equation of the tangent line to each of the following functions at the point given. Graph each function and its tangent line.
   (a) $f(x) = x^2$        at $(3, 9)$
   (b) $f(x) = x^2$        at $(-1, 1)$
   (c) $f(x) = x^2 + 2x + 1$    at $(-1, 0)$
   (d) $f(x) = x^3 + 1$        at $(1, 2)$
   (e) $f(x) = 1/x$        at $(1, 1)$
2. Find the derivative of each of the following functions.
   (a) $f(x) = 5$        at $x = 3$
   (b) $f(x) = 2x + 3$    at $x = 1$

(c) $f(x) = 3x - 5$     at $x = 2$
(d) $f(x) = \sqrt{x}$     at $x = 4$

(e) $f(x) = \dfrac{1}{x^2}$     at $x = 2$

3. Find the derivative of the function

$$f(x) = mx + b$$

at $x = a$. Explain your answer.
4. Find the derivative of the function

$$f(x) = x^2$$

at $x = a$.

5. For the function

$$f(x) = \begin{cases} x^3 & \text{if} & x \leq 0 \\ x^2 & \text{if} & x > 0 \end{cases}$$

determine
(a) if $f$ is continuous at $x = 0$;
(b) if $f'(0)$ exists.
Graph the function and give a geometric interpretation to the answers found in (a) and (b).
6. Repeat the directions of problem 5 for the function

$$f(x) = \begin{cases} 2x & \text{if} & x \leq 0 \\ x^2 & \text{if} & x > 0 \end{cases}$$

7. The total cost of producing $x$ units of a particular item is

$$C(x) = 2 + x^3$$

Find
(a) the average cost from 0 to 10 units;
(b) the marginal cost when $x = 10$;
(c) the average cost from 0 to $a$ units;
(d) the marginal cost when $x = a$ units.
8. Do problem 7 if the cost function is given by

$$C(x) = 10 + x^2$$

9. The shock waves from an atomic blast travel according to the function

$$s(t) = t^2 + 2t$$

where $s$ (measured in miles) is the distance from the explosion site and $t$ is the time (in seconds), where $0 \leq t \leq 30$. Find
(a) the average speed from $t = 0$ to $t = 30$;
(b) the instantaneous speed at $t = 10$, $t = 15$, $t = 25$;
(c) how long it takes the shock waves to travel 8 miles. What is its speed at this point?

10. A circle of radius $r$ has area $A = \pi r^2$ and circumference $C = 2\pi r$. If the radius changes from $r$ to $r + \Delta r$, find
   (a) the change in area;
   (b) the change in circumference;
   (c) the average rate of change of area with respect to the radius;
   (d) the average rate of change of circumference with respect to the radius;
   (e) the instantaneous rate of change of area with respect to the radius;
   (f) the instantaneous rate of change of circumference with respect to the radius.

**An Alternate
Definition of
the Derivative**

*11. An alternate way of computing the derivative of a function $y = f(x)$ at $x = a$ is to find

$$f'(a) = \lim_{h \to 0} \frac{f(a + h) - f(a)}{h}$$

Verify the validity of this formula by using the Definition of the Derivative, page 234, and setting $x = a + h$. (Note that $x \to a$ corresponds to $h \to 0$.)

**Differentiable
Functions are
Also Continuous**

*12. Example 3.5 on page 236 and problem 6 above illustrate that a function may be continuous at $x = a$ and yet not have a derivative at $x = a$. Prove that if a function is differentiable at $a$, then it must be continuous at $x = a$. Hint: To establish continuity for $y = f(x)$ at $x = a$, it must be shown that $\lim_{x \to a} f(x) = f(a)$ or that $\lim_{x \to a} [f(x) - f(a)] = 0$. Use the fact that

$$f(x) - f(a) = \left[ \frac{f(x) - f(a)}{x - a} \right] \cdot (x - a)$$

*13. Because of the result given in Problem 12, if a function is not continuous at $x = a$, it cannot have a derivative at $x = a$. Use this fact to show that the following functions have no derivative at the value given. Graph each function.

(a) $f(x) = \begin{cases} 2x & \text{if} & x < 0 \\ 3x - 2 & \text{if} & x \geq 0 \end{cases}$  at  $x = 0$

(b) $f(x) = \begin{cases} x^2 - 1 & \text{if} & x < 0 \\ \sqrt{x} & \text{if} & x \geq 0 \end{cases}$  at  $x = 0$

(c) $f(x) = \begin{cases} \dfrac{x^2 - 1}{x - 1} & \text{if} & x \neq 1 \\ 0 & \text{if} & x = 1 \end{cases}$  at  $x = 1$

(d) $f(x) = \dfrac{1}{x - 1}$  at  $x = 1$

The technique for computing the derivative of a function, as introduced in the last section, is a rather long, tedious process. It requires calculating the average rate of change $\Delta y/\Delta x$ of a function $y = f(x)$, and then finding the instantaneous rate of change by taking the limit of $\Delta y/\Delta x$ as $\Delta x \to 0$. Fortunately, for most of the functions we shall study, it is possible to obtain formulas for finding their derivatives. The purpose of this section is to derive formulas for the derivative of the function $f(x) = x^n$ (for $n$ any real value). In the next section, some other general formulas for differentiation are discussed.

We begin by considering the constant function

$$f(x) = c$$

where $c$ is a real number. Geometrically, this function is a horizontal line whose slope is zero. This means that the average rate of change of $y$ with respect to $x$ is always zero, so that the instantaneous rate of change, the derivative, is also zero.

Algebraically, the differentiation process is carried out as follows: Let $x_0$ be the value of $x$ at which we wish to compute the derivative. Then, the average rate of change of $y = f(x) = c$ from $x_0$ to $x$ is

$$\frac{\Delta y}{\Delta x} = \frac{f(x) - f(x_0)}{x - x_0} = \frac{c - c}{x - x_0} = \frac{0}{x - x_0} = 0$$

Clearly, the limit of $\Delta y/\Delta x$ as $\Delta x \to 0$ is 0, so that[1] $\frac{d}{dx} c = 0$ at any choice of $x_0$.

**Theorem 4.1**

**For the constant function $f(x) = c$, the derivative is $f'(x) = 0$. That is,**

Derivative of a
Constant Function

$$\frac{d}{dx} c = 0$$

**In other words, the derivative of a constant is zero.**

Find the derivative of $f(x) = 6$.

Since 6 is a constant, $\frac{d}{dx} 6 = 0$.

4.1
Example

---

[1] The notation $\frac{d}{dx} f(x)$ is sometimes used instead of $f'(x)$. The reader should feel comfortable using either of the two notations $\frac{d}{dx} f(x)$ or $f'(x)$, as each will be used extensively.

Let us now investigate the derivative of the function $f(x) = x^n$ at $x = x_0$ for some choices of $n$ to see if a pattern appears.

$n = 1$

$$\lim_{x \to x_0} \frac{f(x) - f(x_0)}{x - x_0} = \lim_{x \to x_0} \frac{x - x_0}{x - x_0} = \lim_{x \to x_0} 1 = 1$$

$n = 2$

$$\lim_{x \to x_0} \frac{f(x) - f(x_0)}{x - x_0} = \lim_{x \to x_0} \frac{x^2 - x_0^2}{x - x_0} = \lim_{x \to x_0} (x + x_0) = 2x_0$$

$n = 3$

$$\lim_{x \to x_0} \frac{f(x) - f(x_0)}{x - x_0} = \lim_{x \to x_0} \frac{x^3 - x_0^3}{x - x_0} = \lim_{x \to x_0} (x^2 + x_0 x + x_0^2) = 3x_0^2$$

If we drop the subscript 0 in $x_0$ from these answers, we have

$$\frac{d}{dx} x = 1, \qquad \frac{d}{dx} x^2 = 2x, \qquad \frac{d}{dx} x^3 = 3x^2$$

From this pattern we conjecture the following theorem.

**Theorem 4.2**

Derivative of $x^n$ **For the function $f(x) = x^n$, $n$ a positive integer, the derivative is $f'(x) = nx^{n-1}$. That is,**

$$\frac{d}{dx} x^n = nx^{n-1}$$

We can prove this result without too much trouble.

$$\lim_{x \to x_0} \frac{f(x) - f(x_0)}{x - x_0} = \lim_{x \to x_0} \frac{x^n - x_0^n}{x - x_0} = \lim_{x \to x_0} [x^{n-1} + x_0 x^{n-2} + \cdots + x_0^{n-1}]$$

$$= \underbrace{x_0^{n-1} + x_0^{n-1} + \cdots + x_0^{n-1}}_{n \text{ terms}} = nx_0^{n-1}$$

Dropping the subscript 0 in $x_0$ gives the result.

4.2
Example

Find the derivative of $f(x) = x^4$.

We can use either the Definition of a Derivative given on page 234 of the last section or else Theorem 4.2. The definition technique requires we find the limit of the average rate of change of $f(x) = x^4$:

$$\lim_{x \to x_0} \frac{x^4 - x_0^4}{x - x_0} = \lim_{x \to x_0} (x^3 + x_0 x^2 + x_0^2 x + x_0^3) = 4x_0^3$$

In other words, $\frac{d}{dx} x^4 = 4x^3$.

The result of this example illustrates that the derivative of a function at any value of $x$ is also a function.

The formula given in Theorem 4.2 when $n = 4$ gives the same result with much less effort. Although formulas for differentiation allow us to compute derivatives with ease, do not forget that a derivative is, in actuality, the limit of an average rate of change.

So far, the formula in Theorem 4.2 has only been shown to be valid when $n$ is a positive integer. However, this formula is true for *any* real value of $n$. That is,

$$\frac{d}{dx} x^n = nx^{n-1} \qquad \text{for any real value of } n \qquad (4.1)$$

In Problems 6 and 7 of Exercise 8.4, page 244, the reader is asked to verify this formula when $n \leq -1$ is a negative integer and for $n = 1/q$, where $q \geq 2$ is an integer.

Find $f'(4)$ if $f(x) = x^3$.

Here, using the formula (4.1), we find

$$f'(x_0) = 3x_0^{3-1} = 3x_0^2$$

Thus,

$$f'(4) = 3 \cdot 4^2 = 48$$

Find $f'(4)$ if $f(x) = x^{3/2}$.

Here,

$$f'(x_0) = \frac{3}{2} x_0^{\frac{3}{2}-1} = \frac{3}{2} x_0^{1/2} = \frac{3}{2} \sqrt{x_0}$$

$$f'(4) = \frac{3}{2} \sqrt{4} = \frac{3}{2} \cdot 2 = 3$$

1. Find the derivative of each of the following functions for the values indicated.

(a) $f(x) = x^4$    at    $x_0 = 2$

(b) $f(x) = x^2$    at    $x_0 = 1$

(c) $f(x) = x^{-1}$    at    $x_0 = 2$

(d) $f(x) = x^{2/3}$    at    $x_0 = 8$

(e) $f(x) = \dfrac{1}{x^2}$    at    $x_0 = 3$

(f) $f(x) = x^{-1/2}$    at    $x_0 = 3$

2. Use formula 4.1 to find the equation of the tangent line to each of the following functions at the point indicated. Graph your result.

(a) $f(x) = x^4$      at      $(1, 1)$

(b) $f(x) = \sqrt{x}$      at      $(4, 2)$

(c) $f(x) = x^4$      at      $(2, 16)$

(d) $f(x) = \dfrac{1}{x^2}$      at      $(3, \frac{1}{9})$

(e) $f(x) = \dfrac{1}{\sqrt[3]{x}}$      at      $(-8, -\frac{1}{2})$

(f) $f(x) = \sqrt[3]{x}$      at      $(-8, -2)$

3. Suppose

$$f(x) = \begin{cases} x & \text{if} & x < 0 \\ 0 & \text{if} & x = 0 \\ x^2 & \text{if} & x > 0 \end{cases}$$

(a) Is $f$ continuous at $x = 0$?

(b) Is $f$ differentiable at $x = 0$?

(c) What is $f'(-1)$?

(d) What is $f'(1)$?

4. If a ball is dropped from a building, it will fall according to the law

$$s = 16t^2$$

where $t$ is the time measured in seconds and $s$ is the distance in feet. (This is the law for freefall on the planet earth, if air resistance is neglected.) Find the instantaneous speed of the ball after 2 seconds. If the building is 144 feet high, with what speed will the ball strike the ground?

5. A young child travels $s$ feet down a slide in $t$ seconds, where $s = t^{3/2}$. What is the child's instantaneous speed after 1 second? If the slide is 8 feet long, with what speed does the child strike the ground?

*6. Prove that if $n \leq -1$ is a negative integer, the derivative of the function $f(x) = x^n$ at $x = x_0$ is

$$f'(x_0) = nx_0^{n-1}$$

*7. Prove that if $q \geq 2$ is a positive integer, the derivative of the function $f(x) = \sqrt[q]{x}$ at $x = x_0$ is

$$f'(x_0) = \frac{1}{q}x_0^{\frac{1}{q}-1}$$

Hint: Let $\alpha = \sqrt[q]{x}, \beta = \sqrt[q]{x_0}$,
    Then

$$\frac{\sqrt[q]{x} - \sqrt[q]{x_0}}{x - x_0} = \frac{\alpha - \beta}{\alpha^q - \beta^q} = \frac{1}{\alpha^{q-1} + \alpha^{q-2}\beta + \cdots + \alpha\beta^{q-2} + \beta^{q-1}}$$

*8. If $y = f(x)$ is a continuous function on an interval $[a, b]$ and is differentiable on $(a, b)$, there is at least one value $x_0$ in $(a, b)$ at which the slope of the tangent line equals the slope of the line joining $(a, f(a))$ and $(b, f(b))$. That is, there is a point $(x_0, f(x_0))$, $a < x_0 < b$, at which

$$f'(x_0) = \frac{f(b) - f(a)}{b - a}$$

This result is called the *Mean Value Theorem*. See Figure 8.11.

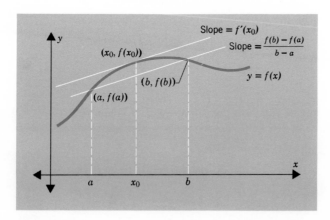

**Figure 8.11**

Verify the Mean Value Theorem by finding the point $(x_0, f(x_0))$ of each of the following functions on the interval indicated.

(a) $f(x) = x^2 + 2x + 1$     $[0, 3]$

(b) $f(x) = \dfrac{1}{x^2}$     $[1, 2]$

(c) $f(x) = x^{3/2}$     $[0, 1]$

In the last section, we obtained a formula for finding the derivative of $x^n$ (for any real value of $n$). However, many of the functions actually encountered in business consist not of the function $x^n$, but of various combinations of it. In this section we shall learn how to find the derivative of functions that are sums, products, and quotients of the function $x^n$.

For the purpose of this section, we assume that all functions mentioned actually have derivatives.

Our first result tells how to find the derivative of a constant times a function.

246

### Theorem 5.1

Derivative of a
Constant Times
a Function

**The derivative of a constant times a function equals the constant times the derivative of the function. That is, if C is a constant and f is a differentiable function**

$$\frac{d}{dx}[Cf(x)] = C\frac{d}{dx}f(x)$$

5.1
Example

If $f(x) = 10x^3$, find $f'(x)$.

Here the function is the product of 10 times $x^3$. Thus,

$$\frac{d}{dx}f(x) = \frac{d}{dx}(10x^3) = 10\frac{d}{dx}x^3 = 10 \cdot 3x^2 = 30x^2$$

Often a complicated-looking function is really just the sum or difference of two simple functions. Our next result is for such functions.

### Theorem 5.2

Derivative of
a Sum

**The derivative of the sum (or difference) of two differentiable functions equals the sum (or difference) of their derivatives. That is,**

$$\frac{d}{dx}[f(x) \pm g(x)] = \frac{d}{dx}f(x) \pm \frac{d}{dx}g(x) = f'(x) \pm g'(x)$$

**Proof**

To compute $\frac{d}{dx}[f(x) + g(x)]$, we need to find the limit of the average rate of change of $f(x) + g(x)$.

$$\lim_{x \to x_0} \frac{[f(x) + g(x)] - [f(x_0) + g(x_0)]}{x - x_0}$$

$$= \lim_{x \to x_0} \frac{[f(x) - f(x_0)] + [g(x) - g(x_0)]}{x - x_0}$$

$$= \lim_{x \to x_0} \left[\frac{f(x) - f(x_0)}{x - x_0} + \frac{g(x) - g(x_0)}{x - x_0}\right]$$

$$= \lim_{x \to x_0} \left[\frac{f(x) - f(x_0)}{x - x_0}\right] + \lim_{x \to x_0} \left[\frac{g(x) - g(x_0)}{x - x_0}\right] = f'(x_0) + g'(x_0)$$

The proof for the difference of two functions is similar, and is left as an exercise. See Problem 10, page 251.

5.2
Example

If $f(x) = x^2 + \sqrt{x}$, find $f'(x)$.

Here $f(x)$ is the sum of two functions. Thus,

$$\frac{d}{dx}f(x) = \frac{d}{dx}[x^2 + \sqrt{x}] = \frac{d}{dx}x^2 + \frac{d}{dx}\sqrt{x}$$

$$= 2x + \frac{1}{2\sqrt{x}}$$

The above example demonstrates how to find the derivative of a function that is the sum of two functions whose derivatives are known. The next result indicates how to find the derivative of a function that is the product of two functions whose derivatives are known.

### Theorem 5.3

**The derivative of the product of two differentiable functions equals the first function times the derivative of the second plus the second function times the derivative of the first; that is,**

Derivative of a Product

$$\frac{d}{dx}[f(x) \cdot g(x)] = f(x)\frac{d}{dx}g(x) + g(x)\frac{d}{dx}f(x)$$
$$= f(x)g'(x) + g(x)f'(x)$$

The proof of this result is given as Problem 12 in Exercise 8.5.

If $f(x) = \sqrt{x}(x + 1)$, find $f'(x)$.

5.3
Example

Here the function is the product of $\sqrt{x}$ times $x + 1$. Thus, using Theorem 5.3, we have

$$\frac{d}{dx}[\sqrt{x}(x + 1)] = \sqrt{x}\frac{d}{dx}(x + 1) + (x + 1)\frac{d}{dx}\sqrt{x}$$
$$= \sqrt{x} \cdot 1 + (x + 1) \cdot \frac{1}{2\sqrt{x}} = \frac{3x + 1}{2\sqrt{x}}$$

Note that $f(x) = \sqrt{x}(x + 1) = x^{3/2} + x^{1/2}$. Using the result of the last section, we have

$$f'(x) = \frac{3}{2}x^{1/2} + \frac{1}{2x^{1/2}} = \frac{3x + 1}{2x^{1/2}}$$

Our last result in this section deals with a formula for finding the derivative of a function that can be expressed as the radio of two functions whose derivatives are known.

### Theorem 5.4

**If $g \neq 0$, and $f$ are two differentiable functions, then**

Derivative of a Quotient

$$\frac{d}{dx}\left[\frac{f(x)}{g(x)}\right] = \frac{g(x)\frac{d}{dx}f(x) - f(x)\frac{d}{dx}g(x)}{[g(x)]^2} = \frac{g(x)f'(x) - f(x)g'(x)}{[g(x)]^2}$$

If $f(x) = (x^2 + 1)/(x - 3)$, find $f'(x)$.

Here the function is the ratio of $x^2 + 1$ to $x - 3$. Thus,

$$\frac{d}{dx}\left(\frac{x^2 + 1}{x - 3}\right) = \frac{(x - 3)\dfrac{d}{dx}(x^2 + 1) - (x^2 + 1)\dfrac{d}{dx}(x - 3)}{(x - 3)^2}$$

$$= \frac{(x - 3)(2x) - (x^2 + 1)(1)}{(x - 3)^2}$$

$$= \frac{2x^2 - 6x - x^2 - 1}{(x - 3)^2} = \frac{x^2 - 6x - 1}{(x - 3)^2}$$

The above theorems are all quite useful for finding the derivative of a function, which is really the sum, difference, product, or quotient of simple functions. Most of the functions that we will encounter can be correctly differentiated by using the previous results—provided one goes slowly and step-by-step in using these results.

We turn now to another concept involving marginal analysis.

To increase profits, a company may decide to increase its sales. The question that concerns management is how will revenue be affected by an increase in sales?

We need to measure the rate of change of revenue as output changes. This measure, called the *marginal revenue MR*, is frequently described by economists as the additional revenue from selling an additional unit of output. If we know the revenue function $R(x)$, the marginal revenue function is the derivative of the revenue function. That is,

$$MR = \lim_{x \to x_0} \frac{R(x) - R(x_0)}{x - x_0} = R'(x)$$

**Discrete Marginal Revenue**

If the revenue function is not known or if output can only be varied by discrete increments, we introduce the discrete marginal revenue *DMR*, which is defined by

$$DMR = \frac{R(x) - R(x_0)}{x - x_0} = \frac{\Delta R}{\Delta x}$$

If $x - x_0 = \Delta x = 1$, discrete marginal revenue measures the additional revenue from selling one additional unit of output. In the calculus portion of this book, we assume that revenue functions are differentiable. As a result we give the following definition.

**Marginal Revenue**

**The derivative of the revenue function $R(x)$ is the marginal revenue *MR*, the incremental revenue produced by one additional unit above $x$ units. Thus,**

$$MR = \frac{d}{dx}R(x)$$

After researching supply and demand factors, a manufacturer determines that in order to sell exactly x units of a particular commodity, he must charge a price of p dollars per unit. At a price p per unit, his total revenue R is the product of the price p per unit times the number x of units sold. That is, $R(x) = xp$.

Suppose the price (in dollars) that must be charged for each unit sold is found to be $50 so that

$$p = p(x) = 50$$

(a) Find the revenue function.
(b) Find the marginal revenue.

(a) We begin by finding the revenue function:

$$R(x) = xp(x) = 50x$$

(b) The marginal revenue MR is

$$MR = R'(x) = 50$$

The fact that marginal revenue is always $50 reflects a fixed price of $50 per unit.

Suppose that in the previous example the cost for x units is

$$C(x) = 1000 + 0.01x^2$$

The profit $P(x)$ is

$$P(x) = R(x) - C(x) = xp(x) - C(x) = 50x - 0.01x^2 - 1000$$

Find
(a) The profit when $x = 1000$.
(b) Those values of x for which $P'(x) = 0$.
(c) The profit for the solution found in (b).

(a) Here

$$P(1000) = 50(1000) - 0.01(1000)(1000) - 1000$$
$$= 40(1000) - 1000 = 39,000$$

(b) The derivative of $P(x)$ is

$$P'(x) = 50 - 0.02x$$

Solving the equation, $P'(x) = 0$, we find that

$$x = 2500$$

(c) The value of $P(x)$ at $x = 2500$ is

$$P(2500) = 50(2500) - 0.01(2500)(2500) - 1000$$
$$= 25(2500) - 1000 = 61,500$$

1. Find the derivative of each of the following functions.
   (a) $f(x) = 5x^3 - 2x$
   (b) $f(x) = \sqrt{x} - x$
   (c) $f(x) = \sqrt{x} + \sqrt[3]{x}$
   (d) $f(x) = 3x^2 + 9$
   (e) $f(x) = 3x + 1/x$
   (f) $f(x) = x^5 - 3x^2 + 2x - 1$
   (g) $f(x) = x^2 + 2\sqrt{x}$
   (h) $f(x) = x^3(\sqrt{x} + 1)$
   (i) $f(x) = \dfrac{x^{3/2} - 2}{x}$
   (j) $f(x) = \dfrac{x^2 + 2x + 1}{x - 1}$

2. Find the slope of the tangent line to each of the following functions at the point indicated.
   (a) $f(x) = x^3/(x + 1)$ at $(0, 0)$
   (b) $f(x) = \sqrt{x}(x^2 + 2)$ at $(1, 3)$
   (c) $f(x) = x^2/(x - 1)$ at $(2, 4)$
   (d) $f(x) = x^{3/2}/(x + 1)$ at $(1, \frac{1}{2})$
   (e) $f(x) = 5x^2 + 2x - 3$ at $(2, 21)$

3. For each of the functions below, find those values of $x$, if any, at which the function has a horizontal tangent line, that is, those values for which $f'(x) = 0$. Graph each function and its horizontal tangent lines.
   (a) $f(x) = 3x^2 - 12x + 4$
   (b) $f(x) = x^2 + 4x - 3$
   (c) $f(x) = x^3 - 3x + 2$

4. If the price function for each unit is $p(x) = 1000 - 0.005x$, find the following.
   (a) The revenue function.
   (b) The marginal revenue $MR$ when $x = 20$.

5. In Problem 4, if the cost function is $C(x) = 0.5x^2 + 3.13x + 500$, find the following.
   (a) The profit function $P(x)$.
   (b) The profit if 20 units are sold.
   (c) $P'(x)$.
   (d) The value of $x$ for which marginal cost equals marginal revenue.

6. The Royal Electric Company manufactures heavy duty electrical transformers. Through past experience, management finds that the relationship between the price $p$ (measured in dollars) it charges and the number $x$ of units sold is

$$p = 18,000 - 2000x$$

The cost to the company is fixed at 2000 per unit. Find the following:
   (a) The revenue function $R(x)$.
   (b) The cost function $C(x)$.
   (c) The profit function $P(x)$.
   (d) Marginal revenue.
   (e) Marginal cost.
   (f) The profit at the value of $x$ for which $MR = MC$.

(a) $R(x) = 18,000x - 2000x^2$

(b) $C(x) = 2000x$

(c) $P(x) = -2000x^2 + 16,000x$

(d) $MR \sim 18,000 - 4000x$

(e) $MC = 2000$

(f) $\quad 18,000 - 2000x = 2000$
$\quad\quad 16,000 = 4000x$
$\quad\quad\quad 8H = x$

7. The relationship[2] between satisfaction $S$ and total reward $r$ has been found to be

$$S(r) = \frac{ar}{g - r}$$

where $g \geqslant 0$ is the predetermined goal level and $a > 0$ is the perceived justice per unit of reward. Show that the instantaneous rate of change of satisfaction with respect to reward is inversely proportional to the square of the difference between the personal goal of the individual and the amount of reward received.

8. The relationship[3] between the amount $A(t)$ of work output and the elapsed time $t$, $t \geq 0$, was found through empirical means to be

$$A(t) = a_3 t^3 + a_2 t^2 + a_1 t + a_0$$

where $a_0, a_1, a_2, a_3$ are constants. Find the instantaneous rate of change of work output at time $t$.

*9. Prove that $\frac{d}{dx}[Cf(x)] = C\frac{d}{dx}f(x)$, where $C$ is a constant.

*10. Prove that $\frac{d}{dx}[f(x) - g(x)] = \frac{d}{dx}f(x) - \frac{d}{dx}g(x)$.

11. Find the derivative of $[f(x)]^2 = f(x) \cdot f(x)$.

*12. Prove Theorem 5.3.

Hint:

$$\frac{f(x)g(x) - f(x_0)g(x_0)}{x - x_0}$$

$$= \frac{f(x)g(x) - f(x_0)g(x) + f(x_0)g(x) - f(x_0)g(x_0)}{x - x_0}$$

$$= \frac{[f(x) - f(x_0)]g(x) + f(x_0)[g(x) - g(x_0)]}{x - x_0}$$

$$= g(x)\left[\frac{f(x) - f(x_0)}{x - x_0}\right] + f(x_0)\left[\frac{g(x) - g(x_0)}{x - x_0}\right]$$

Since $g(x)$ differentiable, it is continuous at $x_0$, so that $\lim_{x \to x_0} g(x) = g(x_0)$.

*13. Prove that if $f(x) \neq 0$ is differentiable, then

$$\frac{d}{dx}\frac{1}{f(x)} = -\frac{\frac{d}{dx}f(x)}{[f(x)]^2}$$

[2]R. Carzo and J. N. Yanouzas, *Formal Organization: A Systems Approach*, Irwin Press, Homewood, Ill., 1967.
[3]M. R. Neifeld and A. T. Poffenberger, "A Mathematical Analysis of Curves," *Journal of General Psychology 1*, (1928), 448–456.

Hint:

$$\frac{\frac{1}{f(x)} - \frac{1}{f(x_0)}}{x - x_0} = \frac{f(x_0) - f(x)}{x - x_0} \cdot \frac{1}{f(x)f(x_0)}$$

$$= \frac{-1}{f(x)f(x_0)} \left[ \frac{f(x) - f(x_0)}{x - x_0} \right]$$

*14. Verify the result of Problem 13 using the rule for differentiating the quotient of two functions.

8.6
COMPOSITE
FUNCTIONS; THE
POWER RULE

In the previous section, the rules for differentiating functions that could be represented as the sum, product, or quotient of the function $x^n$ are given. At this stage you may be tempted to think that you can find the derivative of any function made up of such functions. That this is not the case is easily seen by examining a function like $f(x) = \sqrt{2x + 3}$. We need a further rule or technique to handle this type of function. In this section, a rule is given for finding the derivative of a function that is the combination or *composite* of two other functions.

We begin with an example to illustrate the procedure.

6.1
Example

Consider the function

$$y = \sqrt{2x + 3}$$

Here, $y$ is a function of $x$, that can be written as a combination of two simpler functions—the square root function and a linear function. In particular, if we set

$$y = \sqrt{g(x)} \text{ and } g(x) = 2x + 3$$

then upon combining these two functions, we get the original function

$$y = \sqrt{2x + 3}$$

That is, the composite of the functions $y = \sqrt{g(x)}$ and $g(x) = 2x + 3$ is the function $y = \sqrt{2x + 3}$.

Other examples are

$y = (x^2 + 1)^{1/2}$      if    $y = [g(x)]^{1/2}$    and    $g(x) = x^2 + 1$
$y = (x^2 + 1)^{1/3}$      if    $y = [g(x)]^{1/3}$    and    $g(x) = x^2 + 1$
$y = (x^3 - x^2 + 1)^{-3/4}$   if   $y = [g(x)]^{-3/4}$   and    $g(x) = x^3 - x^2 + 1$

For composite functions that can be written in the form

$$[g(x)]^n$$

where $n$ is any real constant, the formula for $\dfrac{d}{dx}[g(x)]^n$ is given by the *Power Rule*, which we state without proof.

**Theorem 6.1**

**If $g$ is a differentiable function and $n$ is any real number,**

$$\frac{d}{dx}[g(x)]^n = n[g(x)]^{n-1} \cdot g'(x)$$

The student should notice the similarity between the Power Rule for differentiating a function raised to a power and the formula for differentiating $x$ raised to a power.

Find the derivative of the function

6.2
Example

$$f(x) = (x^2 + 1)^3$$

Here we could, of course, expand the right-hand side and proceed according to techniques already discussed. However, the significance of the power rule is that it enables us to find derivatives of functions like this without resorting to tedious (and sometimes impossible) computation.

The function $f(x) = (x^2 + 1)^3$ is the function $g(x) = x^2 + 1$ raised to the power 3. By the Power Rule,

$$\frac{d}{dx}f(x) = \frac{d}{dx}(x^2 + 1)^3 = 3 \cdot (x^2 + 1)^2 \cdot \frac{d}{dx}(x^2 + 1)$$
$$= 3(x^2 + 1)^2 \cdot 2x = 6x \cdot (x^2 + 1)^2$$

Additional examples of the derivative of composite functions are:

6.3
Example

(a) $f(x) = (3 - x^3)^{-5}$
   $f'(x) = -5 \cdot (3 - x^3)^{-6} \cdot (-3x^2) = 15x^2(3 - x^3)^{-6}$

(b) $f(x) = (2x + 3)^{3/2}$
   $f'(x) = \frac{3}{2} \cdot (2x + 3)^{1/2} \cdot 2 = 3(2x + 3)^{1/2}$

(c) $f(x) = \sqrt[3]{(x^3 - 3x^2 + 1)}$
   $f'(x) = \frac{1}{3} \cdot (x^3 - 3x^2 + 1)^{-2/3} \cdot (3x^2 - 6x) = (x^2 - 2x)(x^3 - 3x^2 + 1)^{-2/3}$

Find the derivative of

6.4
Example

$$f(x) = x\sqrt{x^2 + 1}$$

Here the function is the product of $x$ and $\sqrt{x^2 + 1}$. Thus we begin by using the rule for differentiating a product. That is,

$$f'(x) = x\frac{d}{dx}\sqrt{x^2 + 1} + \sqrt{x^2 + 1} \cdot (1)$$

We continue by using the Power Rule. Then

$$f'(x) = x \cdot \frac{1}{2} (x^2 + 1)^{-1/2} \cdot 2x + \sqrt{x^2 + 1}$$

$$= \frac{x^2}{\sqrt{x^2 + 1}} + \sqrt{x^2 + 1} = \frac{x^2 + x^2 + 1}{\sqrt{x^2 + 1}} = \frac{2x^2 + 1}{\sqrt{x^2 + 1}}$$

6.5
Example

A destroyer is traveling due north on a straight course at a constant speed of 15 miles per hour. At 2 p.m. the destroyer is 50 miles due south of a tanker that is moving west at 5 miles per hour. At what rate of speed are the ships approaching each other two hours later? At 6 p.m. are the ships approaching each other or receding from each other? When are the ships closest?

First we construct Figure 8.12 that shows the relative position of the destroyer and the steamer at an arbitrary time $t$ after 2 p.m.

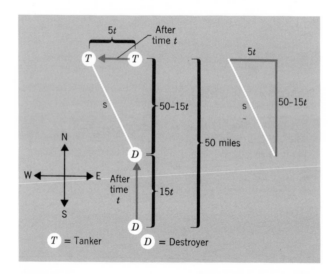

**Figure 8.12**

From the Pythagorean theorem, the distance $s$ separating the two ships at time $t$ is

$$s(t) = \sqrt{(5t)^2 + (50 - 15t)^2}$$
$$= \sqrt{250t^2 - 1500t + 2500}$$

Note that when $t = 0$, the ships are 50 miles apart as stipulated. The speed at which the ships are approaching two hours later is given by $s'(2)$. Using the Power Rule we have

$$s'(t) = \frac{1}{2} [250t^2 - 1500t + 2500]^{-1/2}(500t - 1500)$$

$$= \frac{250(t - 3)}{\sqrt{250t^2 - 1500t + 2500}} = \frac{50(t - 3)}{\sqrt{10t^2 - 60t + 100}}$$

When $t = 2$,

$$s'(2) = \frac{-50}{\sqrt{40 - 120 + 100}} = \frac{-50}{2\sqrt{5}} = -5\sqrt{5}$$

The fact that $s'(2) < 0$ means the ships are approaching at the rate of $5\sqrt{5}$ mph.

At 6 p.m. (when $t = 4$), we have

$$s'(4) = \frac{50}{\sqrt{160 - 240 + 100}} = \frac{50}{2\sqrt{5}} = 5\sqrt{5}$$

Thus the ships are moving apart at the rate of $5\sqrt{5}$ mph at 6 p.m.

Since for $t < 3$, $s'(t) < 0$ (the ships are approaching) and for $t > 3$, $s'(t) > 0$ (the ships are receding), it follows that at $t = 3$ the ships are closest.

8.6
Exercise

1. Use the Power Rule found on page 253 to find the derivative of each of the following functions
   (a) $y = (2x^2 + x + 1)^3$
   (b) $y = (3x + 5)^{3/2}$
   (c) $y = \sqrt{3x^2 + 1}$
   (d) $y = (5x^4 - 1)^6$

2. Find the equation of the tangent line to

$$y = 2\sqrt{x^2 - 1}$$

   at the point $(3, 4\sqrt{2})$.

3. If $f(x) = x\sqrt{1 - x^2}$, find the values of $x$ at which $f'(x) = 0$. Are there any values of $x$ for which $f'(x)$ does not exist?

4. If $y = (x^2 - 1)^{3/2}$, find those points on the curve at which the tangent line is horizontal.

5. At 6 p.m. one ship, traveling 8 mph in an easterly direction, is 52 miles due west of a second ship that is moving at a speed of 12 mph due north. At what rates are the ships approaching each other at 7 p.m.? Are they approaching or receding from each other at 10 p.m.? At what time are they closest?

6. A submarine, submerged at 200 feet, is moving along at the rate of 15 feet per second and passes under a stationary destroyer. How fast is the distance from the submarine to the destroyer changing after one minute?

7. The amount of pollution in a certain lake is found to be

$$A(t) = (t^{1/4} + 3)^3$$

   where $t$ is measured in years and $A(t)$ is measured in appropriate units. What is the instantaneous rate of change of the amount of pollution? At what rate is the amount of pollution changing after 16 years?

Earlier in this chapter we noticed that the derivative of a function $y = f(x)$ is also a function, called the *derivative function* $f'(x)$.

For example, if

$$f(x) = 6x^3 - 3x^2 + 2x - 5$$

then

$$f'(x) = 18x^2 - 6x + 2$$

Second
Derivative

The derivative of the derivative function $f'(x)$ is called the *second derivative of $f(x)$*, and is denoted by $f''(x)$, or by $d^2y/dx^2$. For the example above,

$$f''(x) = \frac{d^2y}{dx^2} = \frac{d}{dx} f'(x) = 36x - 6$$

Continuing in this fashion, we can find the *third derivative* $f'''(x) = d^3y/dx^3$, the *fourth derivative* $f^{iv}(x) = d^4y/dx^4$, and so on, provided these derivatives exist.

7.1
Example

Find the first, second, and third derivatives of the function

$$f(x) = x^4 + 3x^3 - 2x^2 + 5x - 6$$

Here,

$$f'(x) = 4x^3 + 9x^2 - 4x + 5$$

$$f''(x) = \frac{d}{dx} f'(x) = 12x^2 + 18x - 4$$

$$f'''(x) = \frac{d}{dx} f''(x) = 24x + 18$$

7.2
Example

For the function

$$f(x) = \sqrt{x^2 + 4}$$

find those values of $x$ at which $f'(x) = 0$ and $f''(x) = 0$.

Use the Power Rule with $y = \sqrt{g(x)}$ and $g(x) = x^2 + 4$. Then,

$$f'(x) = \frac{1}{2\sqrt{x^2 + 4}} (2x) = \frac{x}{\sqrt{x^2 + 4}}$$

Now $f'(x) = 0$ if

$$\frac{x}{\sqrt{x^2 + 4}} = 0 \qquad \text{or} \qquad x = 0$$

Next, using the rule for differentiating a quotient,

$$f''(x) = \frac{1 \cdot \sqrt{x^2 + 4} - x \cdot \dfrac{2x}{2\sqrt{x^2 + 4}}}{x^2 + 4} = \frac{x^2 + 4 - x^2}{(x^2 + 4)^{3/2}} = \frac{4}{(x^2 + 4)^{3/2}}$$

Notice that $f''(x)$ is never zero; in fact, $f''(x) > 0$ for all $x$.

In Chapter 9, the applications we study require that we be able to find all values of $x$ for which $f'(x) = 0$. It will also be necessary for us to compute the second derivative $f''(x)$ and to determine where it equals zero.

When the distance $s$ traveled by a particle is given as a function of the time $t$, namely as $s = f(t)$, the first derivative $ds/dt$ gives the instantaneous speed of the particle. If we use $v$ to denote the instantaneous speed, then

$$v = \frac{ds}{dt}$$

Speed

The *acceleration a* of this particle is defined as the instantaneous rate of change of speed with respect to time. Then,

$$a = \frac{dv}{dt}$$

Acceleration

In other words, acceleration is the second derivative of the function $s = f(t)$ with respect to time; that is,

$$a = \frac{d^2s}{dt^2}$$

Galileo (1564–1642), in the sixteenth century, found that all falling bodies obeyed the law that, when they are dropped, the distance they fall is proportional to the square of the time $t$. Of great importance is the fact that the constant of proportionality is the same for all bodies. Thus, Galileo's law states that the distance $s$ a body falls in time $t$ is given by

7.3
Example

$$s = -ct^2$$

where $t$ is the time and $c$ is the constant of proportionality. The minus sign means that the body is falling.

The instantaneous speed $v$ of a freely falling body is

$$v = \frac{ds}{dt} = -2ct$$

Its acceleration $a$ is

$$a = \frac{dv}{dt} = \frac{d^2s}{dt^2} = -2c$$

Thus the acceleration of a freely falling body is a constant. Usually, we denote this constant by $-g$ so that

$$a = -g$$

Here $g$ is called the *acceleration of gravity*. For the planet earth, $g$ is approximately

$$g = 32 \text{ feet/second/second} = 980 \text{ centimeters/second/second}$$

1. Find $f'(x)$ and $f''(x)$ for each of the following functions:
   (a) $f(x) = x^3 - 3x^2 + 1$
   (b) $f(x) = 1/x$
   (c) $f(x) = x^2 - 2x + 1$
   (d) $f(x) = \sqrt{x + 5}$
   (e) $f(x) = \sqrt{x^2 + 4}$
   (f) $f(x) = x/(x^2 + 1)$
   (g) $f(x) = (x^2 - 1)^{3/2}$

2. For the functions in Problem 1, find those values of $x$, if any, at which $f'(x) = 0$. For values of $x$ for which $f'(x) = 0$, find the corresponding value of $f''(x)$.

3. A ball is thrown straight up by a person six feet tall with an initial speed of 80 feet per second. The distance $s$ in feet from the ground the ball travels in $t$ seconds is

$$s = 6 + 80t - 16t^2$$

Find the instantaneous speed of the ball after 2 seconds. When will the ball reach its highest point? (Here $v = 0$.) What is the maximum height the ball reaches? What is the acceleration of the ball at any time $t$?

4. A bullet is fired horizontally into a bale of paper. The distance $s$ in meters the bullet travels in $t$ seconds is given by

$$s = 8 - (2 - t)^3 \qquad \text{for} \qquad 0 \leqq t \leqq 2$$

Find the instantaneous speed of the bullet after 1 second. Find the acceleration of the bullet at any time $t$. Interpret your answer.

change
average rate of change
secant line
slope of secant line
difference quotient
average speed
instantaneous rate of change
marginal revenue
marginal cost
discrete marginal revenue

discrete marginal cost
instantaneous speed
slope of tangent line
equation of tangent line
derivative of a function
composite function
power rule
second derivative
acceleration

For the functions in Problems 1–4, find
(a) The average rate of change from $x = 0$ to $x = 1$.
(b) The slope of the secant line from $(0, f(0))$ to $(3, f(3))$.
(c) The instantaneous rate of change at $x = 1$.
(d) The slope of the tangent line at $(3, f(3))$.
(e) The derivative at $x = 0$.
(f) The equation of the tangent line at $(1, f(1))$.
(g) The derivative.
(h) The second derivative.
(i) Values of $x$ at which $f'(x) = 0$ and $f''(x) = 0$.
Sketch the graph.
1. $y = f(x) = x^2 + 1$
2. $y = f(x) = \sqrt{x}$
3. $y = f(x) = x^3$
4. $y = f(x) = 1/(x + 1)$
For the functions in Problems 5–9, find (a) $f'(x)$; (b) $f''(x)$; (c) values of $x$ at which $f'(x) = 0$, if any; (d) the value of $f''(x)$ for the values found in (c).
5. $y = f(x) = 2x^3 + 3x^2 - 12x + 6$
6. $y = f(x) = x\sqrt{x + 1}$
7. $y = f(x) = x/\sqrt{x + 1}$
8. $y = f(x) = x^{3/2}$
9. $y = f(x) = \sqrt{x^2 + 9}$
10. Using only the Definition of a Derivative, find the derivative of

$$f(x) = 2x^2 - x + 4 \qquad \text{at} \qquad x = 0$$

11. At noon, a carrier is 10 miles due west of a destroyer. The carrier is traveling east at 2 mph and the destroyer is going south at 4 mph. When are the ships closest?

## Bibliography

*Mathematics*

Chover, Joshua, *The Green Book of Calculus*, W. A. Benjamin, Menlo Park, Calif., 1972.

Leithold, Louis, *Calculus and Analytic Geometry*, Second Edition, Harper and Row, New York, 1972. Chapter 3.

Salas, Saturnino and Einar Hille, *Calculus: One and Several Variables*, Second Edition, Xerox, Lexington, Mass., 1974. Chapter 3.

Thomas, George, *Calculus and Analytic Geometry*, Fourth Edition, Addison-Wesley, Reading, Mass., 1968. Chapter 3.

# 9

# APPLICATIONS OF THE DERIVATIVE

In this chapter we discuss applications of the derivative. The first application is the analysis of the behavior of a function and its graph. For this we must introduce some new concepts, such as the notions of an increasing function, a relative maximum, concavity of a function, all of which can be handled through the use of the derivative.

Additional applications concern models in business and economics that require optimizing certain functions. For example, when a government formulates fiscal policy, it may find that it is not always better to raise taxes to increase revenue. Sometimes higher taxes do not produce higher revenue as we shall see. Another example involves the question of when the best time might be to replace an appliance, taking into consideration depreciation, resale value, repair costs, and so on.

The use of the derivative is not restricted to these areas since just about every discipline is concerned with some aspect of the theory of optimization. The discussion given here will enable the reader to understand applications of the derivative when they are encountered in a particular area of interest.

9.2
RELATIVE
MAXIMA AND
RELATIVE
MINIMA

In observing the behavior of a continuous function, such as the one whose graph is in Figure 9.1, we notice, as we proceed from left to right, that a portion of the function is increasing and another part is decreasing. Some points on the graph are "higher" than the surrounding points, while others are "lower" that surrounding points. In this section we give a technique for determining when functions increase or decrease, and for finding these "high" and "low points." But first we need to introduce some terminology.

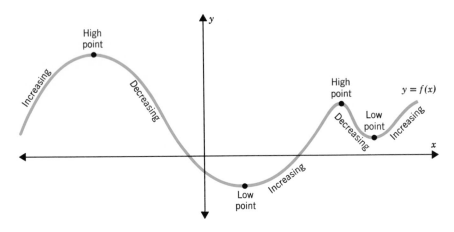

**Figure 9.1**

To arrive at a definition for an increasing function and a decreasing function, we examine the graphs given in Figures 9.2 and 9.3. Notice in Figure 9.2 when the function is increasing, its height at $x_1$ is smaller than it is at $x_2$, that is, $f(x_1) < f(x_2)$. Similarly, in Figure 9.3, where the function is decreasing, its height at $x_1$ is larger than it is at $x_2$, that is, $f(x_1) > f(x_2)$. This leads us to make the following definition.

Definition
of an Increasing
Function;
Decreasing
Function

**Let $y = f(x)$ be a function defined on an interval $I$ and let $(a, b)$, $(c, d)$ be subintervals contained in $I$.**

**(a) $y = f(x)$ is _increasing_ on $(a, b)$ means that for any choice of $x_1 < x_2$ in $(a, b)$, $f(x_1) < f(x_2)$.**

**(b) $y = f(x)$ is _decreasing_ on $(c, d)$ means that for any choice of $x_1 < x_2$ in $(c, d)$, $f(x_1) > f(x_2)$.**

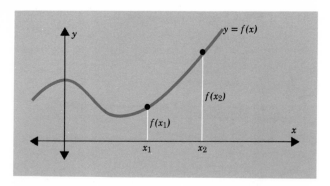

**Figure 9.2**

The Definition of an Increasing Function describes the behavior of the graph as one examines it from left to right. Also notice that we speak of a function as increasing *on an open interval* and that to test whether it is increasing requires testing *any* choice of values $x_1$, $x_2$ in that interval. Does this mean that every time we want to determine the behavior of a function, we have to go through the tedious process of selecting intervals and points in those intervals? The answer is no for differentiable functions, since the derivative provides us with a simple straightforward tool.

For the function of Figure 9.2, if we construct tangent lines where the function is increasing, we observe that each tangent line has something in common—its slope is positive. Since the first derivative of a function gives the slope of its tangent line at each point, we can use the first derivative to determine where a function is increasing by merely determining where, if at all, its derivative is positive.

**Thus, a differentiable function is increasing on $(a, b)$ if its first derivative is positive throughout $(a, b)$. Similarly, a function is decreasing on $(c, d)$ if its first derivative is negative throughout $(c, d)$. At values of $x$ for which $f'(x) = 0$, the tangent line to the function is horizontal.**

Test for
Increasing and
Decreasing
Function

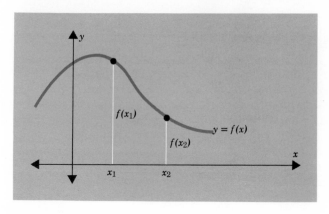

**Figure 9.3**

For the function $f(x) = x^2 + 1$, find those points, if any, at which the function has a horizontal tangent line. Determine for what values of $x$ the function is increasing or decreasing. Use this information to graph the function.

First, we compute $f'(x)$.

$$f'(x) = 2x$$

Now, $f'(x) = 0$ whenever $x = 0$. Thus, the function has a horizontal tangent line at the point $(0, 1)$. Also, $f'(x) = 2x$ is negative whenever $x < 0$. Thus, for $x < 0$, the function is decreasing. Similarly, when $x > 0$, the function is increasing. Figure 9.4 illustrates these results.

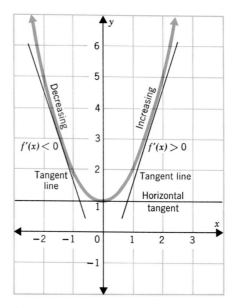

**Figure 9.4**

Thus, when the derivative of a function is negative, the graph of the function is falling while, when the derivative is positive, the graph is rising.

Consider the function

$$f(x) = 2x^3 - 9x^2 + 12x - 5$$

Find those points, if any, at which the function has a horizontal tangent line and determine where the function is increasing and where it is decreasing. Graph the function.

First, we find $f'(x)$.

$$f'(x) = 6x^2 - 18x + 12 = 6(x^2 - 3x + 2)$$

Factoring gives

$$f'(x) = 6(x - 2)(x - 1)$$

Now, $f'(x) = 0$ whenever $x = 2$ or $x = 1$.

Thus, the function has horizontal tangent lines at the points $(2, -1)$ and $(1, 0)$.

Also, whenever $x > 2$, the quantities $x - 2$ and $x - 1$ are both positive so that $f'(x) > 0$. Whenever $x < 1$, the quantities $x - 2$ and $x - 1$ are both negative so that $f'(x) > 0$. Thus, for $x > 2$ or $x < 1$ the function is increasing.

When $1 < x < 2$, we have $x - 1 > 0$ and $x - 2 < 0$, so that $f'(x) < 0$ and the function is decreasing.

To graph the function, we first plot those points at which it has a horizontal tangent line. See Figure 9.5.

For $x$ between 1 and 2, we know the function is decreasing and so we sketch this part of the graph showing $y$ decreasing as $x$ moves from 1 to 2. For $x > 2$, the function is increasing and for $x < 1$, it is increasing, so that as $x$ moves from left to right, the value of $f(x)$ gets larger.

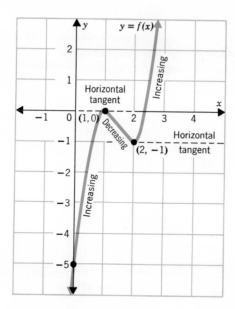

**Figure 9.5**

In Figure 9.5, we notice that for $x = 1$, the value of $f(x)$ is larger than it is for any other value of $x$ close to 1. In this case, we say the point $(1, 0)$ is a *relative maximum*. The reason we use the word "relative" is that it is only around $x = 1$ or in an interval containing $x = 1$ that the value $f(1)$ is larger than it is for other values of $x$. As is clear from the graph, the value of $f(x)$ does get larger than $f(1)$ for values of $x$ "far away" from $x = 1$.

Similarly, for values of $x$ in an interval containing $x = 2$, we see that the value of $f(x)$ is smallest at $x = 2$. That is, the point $(2, -1)$ is a *relative minimum*.

**Definition of Relative Maximum**

**A point $(x_0, f(x_0))$ is called a *relative maximum* of a function $y = f(x)$ if**

$$f(x_0) > f(x)$$

**for any choice of $x \neq x_0$ in an interval containing $x_0$. Here $f(x_0)$ is called a *relative maximum value* of the function.**

**Definition of Relative Minimum**

**A point $(x_0, f(x_0))$ is called a *relative minimum* of a function $y = f(x)$ if**

$$f(x_0) < f(x)$$

**for any choice of $x \neq x_0$ in an interval containing $x_0$. Here $f(x_0)$ is called a *relative minimum value* of the function.**

To find all the relative maxima and relative minima of a function $y = f(x)$ could be a difficult task. However, if the function is differentiable, a fairly straight forward test is available for locating relative maxima and relative minima. It is apparent that every relative maximum and relative minimum of a function $y = f(x)$ must occur at a point at which the tangent line is horizontal, that is, at a value of $x$ for which

**Critical Value**

**Critical Point**

$f'(x) = 0$. For this reason, such values of $x$ are called *critical values*. The corresponding point on the graph is called a *critical point*.

But there are critical points that are neither a relative maximum nor a relative minimum. If we examine the ways in which a horizontal tangent line can occur, we get a clue as to how we can ascertain whether the critical point is a relative maximum, relative minimum, or neither. See Figure 9.6.

This leads us to formulate the following test for relative maxima and relative minima.

**Theorem 2.1**

**First Derivative Test**

**Let $y = f(x)$ be a function that is differentiable on an open interval $I$. Suppose $(x_0, f(x_0))$ is a critical point of the function, so that $f'(x_0) = 0$.**

(a) **A critical point $(x_0, f(x_0))$ is a relative maximum if the function is increasing to the left of $x_0$ while it is decreasing to the right of $x_0$. Refer to Figure 9.6(a).**
(b) **A critical point $(x_0, f(x_0))$ is a relative minimum if the function is decreasing to the left of $x_0$ and increasing to the right of $x_0$. Refer to Figure 9.6(b).**

Figure 9.6(c) and 9.6(d) illustrate the situations where the critical point is neither a relative maximum nor a relative minimum.

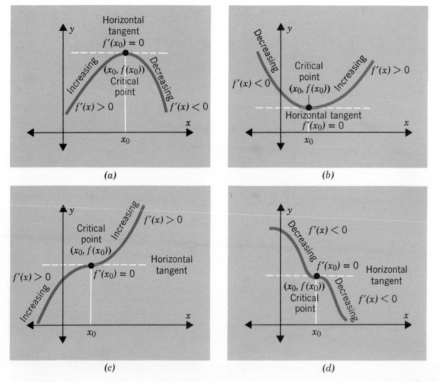

**Figure 9.6**

2.3
Example

Find all critical points of the function

$$f(x) = 3x^3 - 9x$$

Determine which, if any, are relative maxima or relative minima and graph the function.

First, we find $f'(x)$.

$$f'(x) = 9x^2 - 9 = 9(x^2 - 1) = 9(x - 1)(x + 1)$$

The critical values obey $f'(x) = 0$ and are found to be $x = -1$, $x = 1$. The corresponding critical points are $(-1, 6)$ and $(1, -6)$.

To see if $(-1, 6)$ is a relative maximum, a relative minimum, or neither, we must find the sign of $f'(x)$ around $x = -1$. Now for $x$ just less than $-1$, we have $f'(x) > 0$ and for $x$ just larger than $-1$ (but not larger than 1), we have $f'(x) < 0$. This means the function is increasing to the left of $x = -1$ and is decreasing to the right of $x = -1$. Hence, $(-1, 6)$ is a relative maximum.

For the critical point $(1, -6)$, we notice that for $x < 1$, $f'(x) < 0$ and for $x > 1$, $f'(x) > 0$. Hence, $(1, -6)$ is a relative minimum.

To graph the function, notice that for all $x < -1$, the first derivative is positive so that it is increasing; and for all $x > 1$, $f'(x)$ is also positive so that it is increasing.

The behavior of the function for $-1 < x < 1$ remains to be

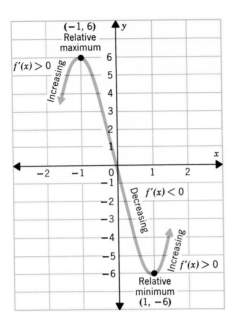

**Figure 9.7**

found. Clearly in the interval $-1 < x < 1$, the function cannot have a relative maximum or a relative minimum since, if it did, a horizontal tangent would occur there, and we know this only happens at $(-1, 6)$ and $(1, -6)$. Also since the function is continuous, and passes through $(0, 0)$, we can merely connect the graph as Figure 9.7 illustrates. This is a result of the fact that $f'(x) < 0$ for $-1 < x < 1$, which shows that the function is decreasing in that interval.

The student may find it useful to employ a table that summarizes the behavior of a function. For the function in the previous example, the table would consist of the following:

| Interval | Sign of $x + 1$ | Sign of $x - 1$ | Sign of $f'(x)$ | Behavior |
|---|---|---|---|---|
| $x < -1$ | Negative | Negative | Positive | Increasing |
| $-1 < x < 1$ | Positive | Negative | Negative | Decreasing |
| $x > 1$ | Positive | Positive | Positive | Increasing |

The First Derivative Test for locating the relative maxima and relative minima of a function requires that the function be differentiable. For functions that are not differentiable, the absence of a horizontal tangent does not imply that the function has no relative maxima or minima in an interval. For example, the function $f(x) = |x|$ on the interval $[-1, 1]$ has no horizontal tangent anywhere and yet $(0, 0)$ is an obvious relative minimum. Of course, the reason for this is that $f(x) = |x|$ has no derivative at $x = 0$. See Example 3.5 in Chapter 8, page 236.

The next example shows that not every critical point need be a relative maximum or a relative minimum.

Find all critical points of the function

2.4
Example

$$f(x) = x^3 + 1$$

Determine which, if any, are relative maxima or relative minima and graph the function.

First,

$$f'(x) = 3x^2$$

Clearly, the only critical value is $x = 0$. The critical point is $(0, 1)$.

Now for $x < 0$, we have $f'(x) > 0$, so that the function is increasing. For $x > 0$, we have $f'(x) > 0$, so that the function is increasing. Thus, the critical point $(0, 1)$ is neither a relative maximum nor a relative minimum. However, at the point $(0, 1)$, the function has a horizontal tangent. Also, since $f'(x) > 0$ for all $x \neq 0$, we conclude the function is increasing everywhere, except at $(0, 0)$. See Figure 9.8.

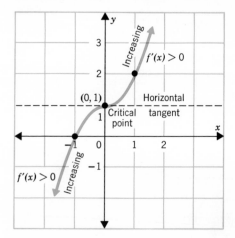

**Figure 9.8**

Thus far we have learned how to find relative maxima and relative minima for differentiable functions $y = f(x)$ by applying the First Derivative Test. To use this test we first find all critical points. Each critical point then becomes a candidate for being a relative maximum, a relative minimum, or neither. To decide what the critical point is, requires determining the sign of $f'(x)$ around the critical value. This is sometimes cumbersome. The next test, although it requires that the function has a second derivative, is sometimes easier to use.

Second Derivative
Test

**Theorem 2.2**

**Let $y = f(x)$ be a function that is differentiable on an open interval I and suppose that the second derivative $f''(x)$ exists on I. Let $(x_0, f(x_0))$ be a critical point of the function so that $f'(x_0) = 0$.**

**1. If $f''(x_0) < 0$, then $(x_0, f(x_0))$ is a relative maximum.**
**2. If $f''(x_0) > 0$, then $(x_0, f(x_0))$ is a relative minimum.**
**3. If $f''(x_0) = 0$, the test gives no results.**

If $f''(x_0) = 0$, or if the function has no second derivative, then the Second Derivative Test cannot be used; however, the First Derivative Test can still be used.

To see just how much faster the Second Derivative Test can be, we return to the function of Example 2.3, page 267. Here

$$f(x) = 3x^3 - 9x$$
$$f'(x) = 9x^2 - 9 = 9(x - 1)(x + 1)$$

The critical values are $x = 1$ and $x = -1$.

$$f''(x) = 18x$$
$$f''(1) = 18 > 0 \qquad f''(-1) = -18 < 0$$

Thus, the point $(1, -6)$ is a relative minimum and the point $(-1, 6)$ is a relative maximum.

2.5
Example

Find all relative maxima and relative minima of the function

$$f(x) = 2x^3 + 3x^2 - 12x + 1$$

First, we find the critical values. They obey

$$f'(x) = 6x^2 + 6x - 12 = 0$$
$$x^2 + x - 2 = 0$$
$$(x + 2)(x - 1) = 0$$
$$x = -2 \qquad x = 1$$

Thus the critical values are $-2$ and $1$.
The second derivative is

$$f''(x) = 12x + 6$$

We now test each critical value. Then

$$f''(-2) = 12(-2) + 6 = -18 < 0, \qquad f''(1) = 18 > 0$$

Thus, $(-2, 21)$ is a relative maximum, and $(1, -6)$ is a relative minimum.
Figure 9.9 gives a sketch of the graph.

Although the Second Derivative Test provides a relatively easy way to find relative maxima and relative minima for functions having second-order derivatives, it gives no result about relative extrema when

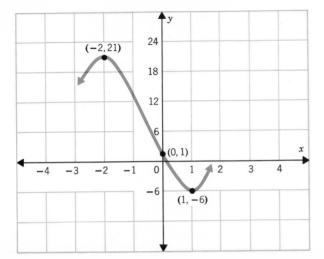

**Figure 9.9**

$f''(x_0) = 0$. However, as we shall see in a later section, this does provide additional information about the behavior of the function at such values of $x$.

1. Determine on what interval the function $y = f(x)$ is increasing if the derivative $f'(x)$ is
   (a) $f'(x) = (x - 1)^2(x + 2)$
   (b) $f'(x) = x(x - 1)$
   (c) $f'(x) = x^2(2x - 1)$
   What are the critical values of each function?
2. For each of the following functions, find all critical values. Using the First Derivative Test, tell whether each critical point is a relative maximum, a relative minimum, or neither. Sketch the graph.
   (a) $f(x) = x^3 - 3x^2$
   (b) $f(x) = x^2 - 5x + 6$
   (c) $f(x) = x^3 - 9x^2 + 27x - 27$
   (d) $f(x) = \dfrac{1}{x}$
   (e) $f(x) = x^4$
   (f) $f(x) = x^4 - 2x^2 + 1$
3. For the functions in Problem 2 above, use the Second Derivative Test to find relative maxima and relative minima. Sketch the graph.
4. Using either the First Derivative Test or the Second Derivative Test, locate all relative maxima and relative minima of each of the following functions.

(a) $f(x) = \frac{3}{4}x^{4/3} - x$    (d) $f(x) = x^2 + 16/x^2$

(b) $f(x) = x^2 + 16/x$    (e) $f(x) = x^{3/2}/\sqrt{x} - 18$

(c) $f(x) = \frac{1}{2}x^2 - 1/x$

5. At 10 a.m. a ship moving east at 6 mph is 30 miles due west of another ship moving north at 12 mph. Find the time at which the two ships are closest. What is the minimum distance?

*6. If $f(x) = 4x^2 - 3/x$, find the positive value of $x$ that makes $f(x + 1) - f(x)$ least.

7. A firm can sell as many units as it can produce at $30.00 per unit. The total cost to the firm of producing $x$ units is

$$C = \$25 + 2x + 0.01x^2$$

The profit function is given by $30x - C$. Find the number of units the firm should produce to obtain maximum profit. What is the maximum profit?

8. An airplane crosses the Atlantic Ocean (3000 miles) with an airspeed of 500 mph.

(a) Find the time saved with a 25 mph tailwind.

(b) Find the time lost with a 50 mph headwind.

(c) If the cost per person is

$$C(x) = 100 + \frac{x}{10} + \frac{36,000}{x}$$

where $x$ is the ground speed and $C(x)$ is the cost in dollars, what is the cost per passenger for quiescent conditions (no wind)?

(d) What is the cost with a tailwind of 25 mph?

(e) What is the cost with a headwind of 50 mph?

(f) What groundspeed minimizes the cost?

(g) What is the minimum cost per passenger?

Average Cost

9. The quantity $C(x)/x$ is called the *average cost* of producing $x$ units. Show that the average cost is a minimum when it equals the marginal cost.

Average Revenue

10. The quantity $R(x)/x$ is called the *average revenue* from selling $x$ units. Show that the average revenue is a maximum when it equals the marginal revenue.

11. For the function $f(x) = ax^2 + bx + c$, $a \neq 0$, show that $x = -b/2a$ is a critical value. Show that the corresponding critical point is a relative maximum, if $a < 0$, and a relative minimum, if $a > 0$.

*12. If a function $y = f(x)$ has the three properties:

Rolle's Theorem

1. It is continuous on the closed interval $[a, b]$

2. It is differentiable on the open interval $(a, b)$

3. $f(a) = f(b) = 0$

then there is at least one point $(x_0, f(x_0))$, $a < x_0 < b$, at which $f'(x_0) = 0$.

This result is called Rolle's Theorem.

Verify Rolle's Theorem by finding the point(s) $(x_0, f(x_0))$ of each of the following functions on the interval indicated.
(a) $f(x) = 2x(x - 1)$     $[0, 1]$    (b) $f(x) = x^4 - 1$     $[-1, 1]$
(c) $f(x) = x^4 - 2x^2 - 8$     $[-2, 2]$

In the definition of relative maximum (relative minimum), the use of the term "relative" refers to the fact that, at the critical value, the function has the largest (smallest) value in an interval containing the critical value. The relative maximum (minimum) value for a continuous function on a closed interval may not be the largest (smallest) value of the function on the interval. The largest and smallest values of a function, if they exist, are called the *absolute maximum* and the *absolute minimum* of the function.

**Let $y = f(x)$ be a continuous function whose domain is $D$. The largest value of $f(x)$ for $x \in D$, if it exists, is called the *absolute maximum* of the function. The smallest value of $f(x)$ for $x \in D$, if it exists, is the *absolute minimum* of the function.**

Figure 9.10 illustrates some of the many situations that can occur and will help us devise a way for finding the absolute maximum (minimum), when they exist.

In Figure 9.10(a), the largest value of $f(x)$ on $[a, b]$ is $f(x_0)$, and it occurs at the point $(x_0, f(x_0))$. This is also a relative maximum of the function. Thus the absolute maximum may be a relative maximum value.

The absolute minimum of the function in Figure 9.10(a) is $f(a)$, and it occurs at the end point $(a, f(a))$. Also, the absolute maximum of the function in Figure 9.10(b) occurs at the end point $(b, f(b))$. Thus, the absolute maximum (minimum) of a function may occur at an end point.

In Figure 9.10(b), we observe that the absolute minimum occurs at $(0, 0)$, a point at which the function has no tangent line. Thus the

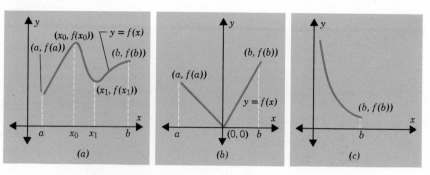

**Figure 9.10** (a) Domain of $f$ is $[a, b]$ the absolute maximum if $f(x_0)$ (this occurs at a relative maximum); the absolute minimum is $f(a)$ (this occurs at an endpoint. (b) Domain of $f$ is $a, b$; the absolute maximum is $f(a)$ (this occurs at an endpoint); the absolute minimum is $f(a)$ (at an endpoint). (c) Domain of $f$ is $[0, b]$; there is no absolute maximum; the absolute minimum is $f(b)$ (this occurs at an endpoint).

absolute maximum (minimum) of a function might occur at points where $f'(x)$ does not exist.

In Figure 9.10(c), the function has no absolute maximum since there is no largest value of $f(x)$ on $(0, b]$.

The following result is stated without proof and tells us that a certain type of function always has an absolute maximum and an absolute minimum.

**If a continuous function has as its domain a closed interval, the absolute maximum and absolute minimum exist.**

With this in mind, we state a procedure for finding the absolute maximum and absolute minimum of a continuous function.

Test for
Absolute
Maximum and
Absolute Minimum

**If a continuous function $y = f(x)$ has a closed interval $[a, b]$ as domain, we can find the absolute maximum (or minimum) by choosing the largest (or smallest) value from among**

**1. The value of $f(x)$ at critical points (points at which $f'(x) = 0$) in $(a, b)$.**
**2. $f(a)$**
**3. $f(b)$**
**4. The value of $f(x)$ at points at which $f'(x)$ does not exist in $(a, b)$.**

In the event critical values of $y = f(x)$ are found that are not in the interval $(a, b)$, these critical values should be ignored since we are concerned only with the function in the interval $[a, b]$.

3.1
Example

Consider the function $f(x) = x^3 - 3x$. If the domain of $f$ is $[0, 2]$, find the absolute maximum and absolute minimum.

The critical values obey

$$f'(x) = 3x^2 - 3 = 3(x^2 - 1) = 3(x - 1)(x + 1) = 0$$

The critical values are

$$x = -1 \qquad x = 1$$

We ignore the critical value $x = -1$ since it is not in the domain, $0 \leqq x \leqq 2$. For the critical value $x = 1$,

$$f(1) = -2$$

The values of $f(x)$ at the end points 0 and 2 are

$$f(0) = 0 \qquad f(2) = 2$$

There are no points at which $f'(x)$ does not exist. Thus, the absolute maximum of $f(x)$ on $[0, 2]$ is 2 and the absolute minimum is $-2$.

3.2
Example

Find the absolute maximum and absolute minimum of

$$f(x) = x^{2/3} \qquad \text{on} \qquad [-1, 8]$$

First, we locate the critical values, if any. Thus,

$$f'(x) = \frac{2}{3}x^{-1/3} = \frac{2}{3x^{1/3}}$$

Since $f'(x)$ is never zero, there are no critical values.

Next, we find the value of $f(x)$ at the end points. There

$$f(-1) = 1$$
$$f(8) = 4$$

Since $f'(x)$ does not exist at $x = 0$, we check the value of $f(x)$ at $x = 0$ according to rule 4 on page 274.

$$f(0) = 0$$

The absolute maximum of $f(x) = x^{2/3}$ on $[-1, 8]$ is 4 and the absolute minimum is 0. Figure 9.11 illustrates this situation.

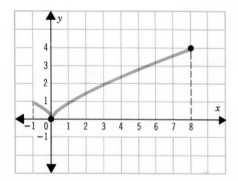

**Figure 9.11**

For the functions in Problems 1–7, find the absolute maximum and the absolute minimum on the domain indicated.

1. $f(x) = x^3 - 3x^2,$    $[-1, 4]$
2. $f(x) = x^2 - 5x + 6,$    $[-3, 3]$
3. $f(x) = x^3 - 9x^2 + 27x - 27,$    $[-2, 2]$

4. $f(x) = \dfrac{1}{x},\ [1, 3]$

5. $f(x) = x^4,$    $[-1, 4]$
6. $f(x) = x^4 - 2x^2 + 1,\ [-2, 3]$
7. $f(x) = x^{2/5},\ [-1, 32]$
8. Find the absolute maximum and absolute minimum of $f(x) = x\sqrt{1 - x^2}$ on its domain.
9. The relationship between profit $P$ of a firm and the selling price $x$ of its goods is

$$P = 1000x - 25x^2 \qquad 0 \leq x \leq 40$$

For what range of selling prices is profit increasing? For what selling price is profit maximized?
10. A truck has a top speed of 75 miles per hour and, when traveling at the rate of $x$ miles per hour, consumes gasoline

at the rate of $1/200(1600/x + x)$ gallons per mile. If the length of the trip is 200 miles and the price of gasoline is 60 cents per gallon, the cost is

$$C(x) = 0.60\left(\frac{1600}{x} + x\right)$$

where $C(x)$ is measured in dollars. What is the most economical speed for the truck? Use the interval $[10, 75]$.

11. If the driver of the truck in Problem 10 is paid $8.00 per hour, what is the most economical speed for the truck?

9.4
CONCAVITY

In the previous sections, we learned how to determine where a differentiable function is increasing and decreasing and where it has a relative maximum (minimum). What we are missing is the ability to determine whether the graph of the function opens up or opens down on a given interval; that is, we need to know the *concavity* of the function. For example, the parabola $y = f(x) = x^2 + 1$ obviously opens up, or to be more precise, is *concave up* on its domain. See Figure 9.4 on page 264. When tangent lines are drawn at every point of this parabola, we notice they are always below the curve itself. This leads us to formulate the following definition.

Definition
of Concave up

**A differentiable function is** *concave up* **on** $(a, b)$ **if the tangent line to the function at every point lies below its graph.**

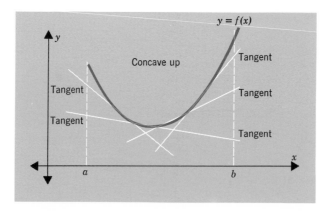

**Figure 9.12**

Figure 9.12 illustrates this concept.
Similarly the concept of concave down is defined as follows.

Definition
of Concave Down

**A differentiable function is** *concave down* **on** $(a, b)$ **if the tangent line to the function at every point lies above its graph.**

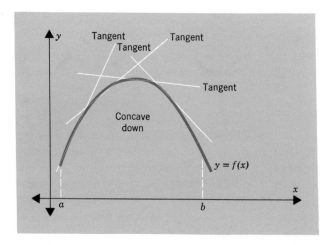

**Figure 9.13**

Figure 9.13 illustrates this concept.

Notice that a function may sometimes be concave up and sometimes concave down. See Figure 9.14.

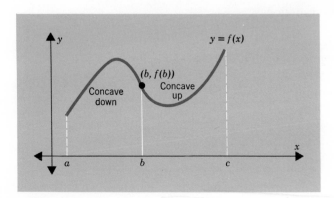

**Figure 9.14**

Here the function is concave down on $(a, b)$ and concave up on $(b, c)$. The point $(b, f(b))$ is particularly significant, since it is at this point that the curve changes from being concave down to being concave up. This point is called an *inflection point*.

Inflection Point

Observe that the slopes of the tangent lines (measured by $f'(x)$) in Figure 9.12 are increasing on $(a, b)$. If $f'(x)$ is an increasing function, its derivative $f''(x)$ is positive on $(a, b)$. Similarly, in Figure 9.13, the slopes of the tangent lines (measured by $f'(x)$) are decreasing on $(a, b)$. If $f'(x)$ is a decreasing function, its derivative $f''(x)$ is negative on $(a, b)$.

The second derivative of a function provides a test for determining where a function is concave up and where it is concave down.

Theorem 4.1

Let $y = f(x)$ be a function and let $f''(x)$ be its second derivative.

1. If $f''(x) > 0$ for all $x \in (a, b)$, then the function is concave up on $(a, b)$.
2. If $f''(x) < 0$ for all $x \in (a, b)$, then the function is concave down on $(a, b)$.

In this theorem, we are assuming that the second derivative of the function exists and is continuous at every point of the interval $(a, b)$.

Let us return to the notion of an inflection point and find a test for locating such points. At an inflection point $(x_0, f(x_0))$, the concavity of the function changes. This means the sign of $f''(x)$ must change as we pass from one side of the inflection point to the other side. It also means that at the inflection point $(x_0, f(x_0))$ we must have $f''(x_0) = 0$.

Thus, to find inflection points of a function,

1. **Find all points $(x, f(x))$ at which $f''(x) = 0$.**
2. **Determine the concavity on either side of these points.**
3. **If there is a change in concavity, the point is an inflection point; otherwise, it is not.**

Find where the function

$$f(x) = x^3 - 6x^2 + 9x + 30$$

is concave up and concave down. Find all inflection points and sketch the graph.

First, we compute $f'(x)$ and $f''(x)$.

$$f'(x) = 3x^2 - 12x + 9$$
$$f''(x) = 6x - 12 = 6(x - 2)$$

When $x > 2$, we see that $f''(x) > 0$. Thus, the function is concave up for $x > 2$. Similarly, it is concave down for $x < 2$.

To find the inflection points, set

$$f''(x) = 6(x - 2) = 0$$

The only candidate for an inflection point is $(2, 32)$. Since for $x < 2$, the function is concave down and for $x > 2$, it is concave up, the point $(2, 32)$ is an inflection point.

To graph the function, we use the information above plus whatever we can find out about the function from $f'(x)$. First, we find the critical values, if any

$$f'(x) = 3x^2 - 12x + 9 = 0$$
$$3(x^2 - 4x + 3) = 0$$
$$(x - 1)(x - 3) = 0$$

Thus, $x = 1$ and $x = 3$ are critical values and

$$f''(1) = 6(1 - 2) < 0, \qquad f''(3) = 6(3 - 2) > 0$$

That is, (1, 34) is a relative maximum and (3, 30) is a relative minimum. Figure 9.15 gives the graph.

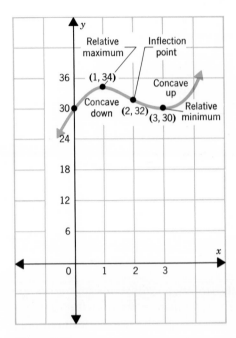

**Figure 9.15**

The next example illustrates that the concavity of a function can change without an inflection point occurring.

Discuss the behavior of the function $f(x) = 1/x$.

We begin by noting that the domain of $f$ is $\{x \mid x \neq 0\}$ and that the function is continuous, except at $x = 0$, where it is discontinuous. Next, we find $f'(x)$.

$$f'(x) = -\frac{1}{x^2}$$

We notice that the first derivative is always negative. This means there are no critical values and the function is decreasing on its domain.

The second derivative is

$$f''(x) = \frac{2}{x^3}$$

Clearly,

$$f''(x) < 0 \text{ for } x < 0, \qquad f''(x) > 0 \text{ for } x > 0$$

That is, the function is concave down for negative values of $x$ and is concave up for positive values of $x$.

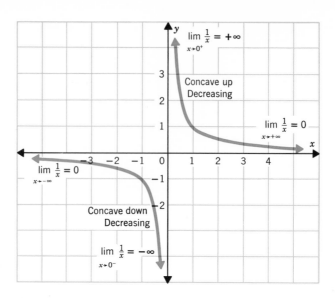

**Figure 9.16**

Since $f''(x)$ cannot equal zero, there are no inflection points. To aid in graphing $f(x) = 1/x$, let us also see how the function behaves as $x \to +\infty$ and as $x \to -\infty$. Of course, from Example 2.3, see page 200, we know that

$$\lim_{x \to +\infty} \frac{1}{x} = 0 \qquad \lim_{x \to -\infty} \frac{1}{x} = 0$$

See Figure 9.16 for the graph.

The preceding example illustrates a function that changes concavity without an inflection point occurring. It is also possible for a function to have an inflection point that cannot be detected by the Test for an Inflection Point. The reason for this is that the Test requires determining where the second derivative is zero. Thus points at which the second derivative does not exist may be inflection points.

To find inflection points for such a function, we must test the concavity on either sides of points for which the second derivative does not exist. The next example illustrates such a function.

4.3
Example

Find all inflection points of the function

$$f(x) = x^{5/3}$$

The derivatives are

$$f'(x) = \frac{5}{3} x^{2/3}$$

$$f''(x) = \frac{10}{9} x^{-1/3} = \frac{10}{9x^{1/3}}$$

Here $f''(x)$ is never zero.

We observe, though, that $f''(x)$ does not exist at $x = 0$. In addition, the function is concave down for $x < 0$ and concave up for $x > 0$. Thus, the point $(0,0)$ is an inflection point. See Figure 9.17.

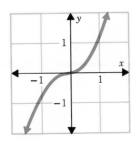

**Figure 9.17**

The following six points summarize the procedure for obtaining the graph of a function.

1. **Determine its domain.**
2. **Determine the behavior of the function at points of discontinuity, if there are any.**
3. **Determine the behavior of the function for very large values of $x$ by finding $\lim\limits_{x \to +\infty} f(x)$ and $\lim\limits_{x \to -\infty} f(x)$, if this is possible.**
4. **Find the critical values and where the function is increasing and decreasing.**
5. **Find inflection points and where the function is concave up and concave down.**
6. **Find relative maxima and relative minima.**

Sketch the graph of

4.4
Example

$$f(x) = \frac{x}{x^2 + 1}$$

1. The domain of $f$ is all real numbers.
2. The function is continuous for all $x$.
3. $\lim\limits_{x \to -\infty} \frac{x}{x^2 + 1} = 0 \qquad \lim\limits_{x \to +\infty} \frac{x}{x^2 + 1} = 0$
4. $f'(x) = \dfrac{d}{dx} \dfrac{x}{x^2 + 1} = \dfrac{(x^2 + 1) - x \cdot 2x}{(x^2 + 1)^2} = \dfrac{-x^2 + 1}{(x^2 + 1)^2}$

$$= \frac{-(x^2 - 1)}{(x^2 + 1)^2}$$

The critical values obey

$$x^2 - 1 = 0 \quad \text{or} \quad x = 1, x = -1$$

Also, for $x < -1$, $f'(x) < 0$, so the function is decreasing; for $-1 < x < 1$, $f'(x) > 0$, so the function is increasing; for $x > 1$, $f'(x) < 0$, so the function is decreasing.

5. $f''(x) = \dfrac{(x^2 + 1)^2(-2x) + (x^2 - 1) \cdot 4x(x^2 + 1)}{(x^2 + 1)^4}$

$$= \frac{(x^2 + 1)}{(x^2 + 1)^4}[-2x(x^2 + 1) + 4x(x^2 - 1)]$$

$$= \frac{2x^3 - 6x}{(x^2 + 1)^3} = \frac{2x(x^2 - 3)}{(x^2 + 1)^3}$$

For $f''(x)$ to equal zero, the numerator must equal zero. Candidates for inflection points are

$$(0, 0), \quad \left(\sqrt{3}, \frac{\sqrt{3}}{4}\right), \quad \left(-\sqrt{3}, \frac{-\sqrt{3}}{4}\right)$$

| | | Sign of $f''(x)$ | Conclusion | |
|---|---|---|---|---|
| $x = 0$ | $x < 0$ | Positive | Concave up | $(0, 0)$ is an inflection point |
| | $x > 0$ | Negative | Concave down | |
| $x = \sqrt{3}$ | $x < \sqrt{3}$ | Negative | Concave down | $\left(\sqrt{3}, \frac{\sqrt{3}}{4}\right)$ is an inflection point |
| | $x > \sqrt{3}$ | Positive | Concave up | |
| $x = -\sqrt{3}$ | $x < -\sqrt{3}$ | Negative | Concave down | $\left(-\sqrt{3}, -\frac{\sqrt{3}}{4}\right)$ is an inflection point |
| | $x > \sqrt{3}$ | Positive | Concave up | |

6. The relative maxima and relative minima are found by testing $f''(x)$ at the critical values.

$$f''(-1) = \frac{2(-1)(-2)}{8} = \frac{1}{2} > 0$$

$$f''(1) = \frac{2(-2)}{8} = -\frac{1}{2} < 0$$

Thus, $(-1, -1/2)$ is a relative minimum and $(1, 1/2)$ is a relative maximum.

A sketch is given in Figure 9.18.

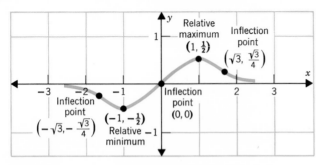

**Figure 9.18**

For the functions in Problems 1–10, find points of inflection.

1. $f(x) = x^3 - 9x^2 + 2$
2. $f(x) = x^5 - 1$
3. $f(x) = x^4 - 4x^3 + 10$
4. $f(x) = x^2(x + 1)$
5. $f(x) = (x + 1)^2(x - 3)$
6. $f(x) = x^4(x + 5)$
7. $f(x) = x(x - 3)(x - 4)$
8. $f(x) = x + 1/x$
9. $f(x) = \dfrac{4}{x^2 + 4}$
10. $f(x) = \dfrac{x}{x + 1}$

For the functions in Problems 11–15, locate the relative maxima, relative minima, and points of inflection. Graph each function.

11. $f(x) = x^3 - 9x^2 + 2$
12. $f(x) = x^4 - 4x^3 + 10$
13. $f(x) = x^5 - 5x$
14. $f(x) = x(x - 3)(x - 4)$
15. $f(x) = x^{2/3}(x - 2)^{1/3}$
16. The cost (in dollars) of producing $x$ units is given by the relationship

$$C = 0.001x^3 - 0.3x^2 + 30x + 42$$

Find where this cost function is concave up and where it is concave down and find the inflection point. Interpret the significance of your answer to a business situation.

In this section we briefly discuss how the techniques introduced in previous sections can be applied to solve certain problems. Even though many of the problems we solve here are oversimplified, their solutions provide insight into ways of approaching and eventually solving slightly more complex and realistic problems.

For example, a common problem we shall solve is to construct a box of fixed volume using the least amount of material. It is worthwhile for us to understand the source of this solution and, more important, to gain experience in setting up the mathematics of such problems.

In general, the type of problem we discuss requires that some quantity be minimized or maximized. We assume that the quantity we wish to optimize can be represented by a function. Once this function is determined, the problem can be reduced to the question of determining at what point the function assumes its absolute maximum or absolute minimum.

Even though each applied problem has its unique features, it is possible to outline in a rough way a procedure for obtaining a solution. This procedure is outlined below:

1. **Identify the quantity for which a maximum or a minimum value is to be found.**
2. **Assign symbols to represent all variables in the problem. If possible, use a figure to assist you.**
3. **Determine the relationships between these variables.**
4. **Express the quantity to be optimized as a function of one of these variables.**
5. **Apply the techniques of the previous sections to this function to determine the absolute maximum or absolute minimum.**

The following examples illustrate this procedure.

5.1
Example

From each corner of a square piece of sheet metal 18 inches on a side, remove a small square of side $x$ inches and turn up the edges to form an open box. What should be the dimensions of the box so as to maximize the volume?

The quantity to be maximized is the volume, so let us denote it by $V$ and denote the dimensions of the side of the small square by $x$ as shown in Figure 9.19. Although the area of sheet metal is fixed, the sides of the square can be changed so that they can be treated as variables. If $y$ denotes the portion left after cutting the $x$'s to make the square, we have

$$y = 18 - 2x$$

The height of the box is $x$, while the area of the base of the box is $y^2$. The volume $V$ is

$$V = x \cdot y^2$$

Since we have a function of two variables, we need to reduce it to one variable. We can do this by substituting for $y$ in the formula for the volume. This gives

$$V = x(18 - 2x)^2$$

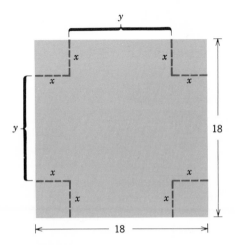

**Figure 9.19**

In this example, the function to be maximized, namely,

$$V = x(18 - 2x)^2$$

mathematically has as domain the set of real numbers. Physically, however, the only values for $x$ that make sense are those between 0 and 9. Thus, we want to find the absolute maximum of

$$V = x(18 - 2x)^2 \qquad 0 \leq x \leq 9.$$

To find the value of $x$ that maximizes $V$, we differentiate and find the critical values, if any.

$$\begin{aligned} V'(x) &= (18 - 2x)^2 + 2x(18 - 2x)(-2) \\ &= (18 - 2x)(18 - 6x) \end{aligned}$$

Set $V'(x) = 0$ and solve for $x$.

$$(18 - 2x)(18 - 6x) = 0$$

$$18 - 2x = 0 \qquad \text{or} \qquad 18 - 6x = 0$$

$$x = 9 \qquad \text{or} \qquad x = 3$$

At the end points, $x = 0$ and $x = 9$, the volume is zero and hence at $x = 3$, $V$ attains its absolute maximum.

The maximum volume is

$$V = 3(18 - 6)^2 = 432 \text{ cubic inches}$$

The dimensions of the box are 3, 12, and 12 inches.

A certain manufacturer makes a playpen whose flexible construction permits the linkage of its four sides (each side of length $c$ and normally square-shaped) to be attached at right angles

5.2
Example
Playpen Problem[1]

[1] Adapted from *Proceedings, Summer Conference for College Teachers on Applied Mathematics*, University of Missouri—Rolla, 1971.

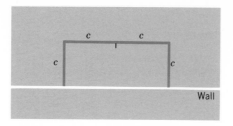

**Figure 9.20**

to a wall (the side of a house, for example). See Figure 9.20. When the playpen is placed as in Figure 9.20, the area enclosed is $2c^2$, which doubles the child's play area. Is there a configuration that will do better than double the child's play area?

Since the playpen must be attached at right angles to the wall, the possible configurations depend on the amount of wall that is used as a fifth side for the playpen. See Figure 9.21.

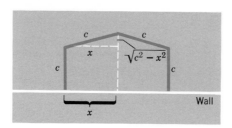

**Figure 9.21**

Let $x$ represent half the length of wall used as a fifth side. The area $A$ is a function of $x$ and is the sum of two rectangles (with sides $c$ and $x$) and two right triangles (hypotenuse $c$ and base $x$). Thus, the quantity to be maximized is

$$A(x) = 2cx + x\sqrt{c^2 - x^2}, \quad 0 \le x \le c$$

To compute the maximum area, we note that

$$A'(x) = 2c + \sqrt{c^2 - x^2} - \frac{x^2}{\sqrt{c^2 - x^2}}$$

The critical values obey

$$2c\sqrt{c^2 - x^2} + (c^2 - x^2) - x^2 = 0$$
$$2c\sqrt{c^2 - x^2} = 2x^2 - c^2$$
$$4c^2(c^2 - x^2) = 4x^4 - 4c^2x^2 + c^4$$
$$4x^4 = 3c^4$$
$$x = c\sqrt[4]{3/4} = .931c$$

We compute $A(x)$ at the endpoints $x = 0, x = c$ and at the critical value $x = c\sqrt[4]{3/4} = .931c$. The results are

$$A(0) = 0$$
$$A(c) = 2c^2$$
$$A(.931c) = 2.20c^2$$

Thus, a wall length of $1.862c$ will maximize the area.
If we take $c = 1$ (unit length), the area for $x_1 = .931$ is

$$A = 2x_1 + x_1 \sqrt{1 - x_1^2} = 2.20$$

Thus, a configuration like the one in Figure 9.21 increases the play area by about 10 percent (from 2 to 2.20).

A can company wishes to produce a cylindrical container with a capacity of 1000 cubic centimeters. The top and bottom of the container must be made of material that costs $0.05 per square centimeter, while the sides of the container can be made of material costing $0.03 per square centimeter. Find the dimensions that will minimize the total cost of the container.

Figure 9.22 shows a cylindrical container and the areas of its top, bottom, and lateral surface.
As indicated in the figure, if we let $h$ stand for the height of the can and $r$ the radius, then the total area of the bottom and the top is $2\pi r^2$ and the area of the lateral surface of the can is $2\pi rh$. The total cost $C$ of manufacturing the can is

$$C = (\$0.05)(2\pi r^2) + (\$0.03)(2\pi rh)$$

This is the function we wish to minimize.

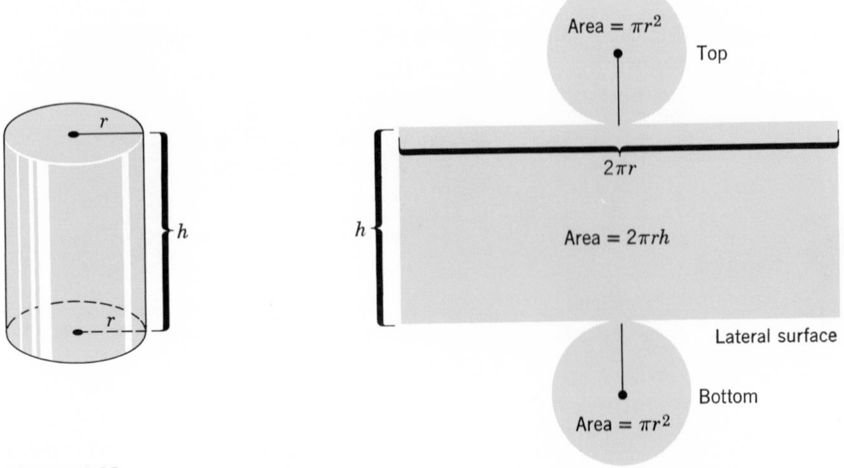

Area $= \pi r^2$    Top

$2\pi r$

Area $= 2\pi rh$

Lateral surface

Area $= \pi r^2$    Bottom

**Figure 9.22**

The cost function is a function of two variables $h$ and $r$, but there is a relationship between $h$ and $r$, since the volume of the cylinder is fixed at 1000 cubic centimeters. That is,

$$V = 1000 = \pi r^2 h$$

$$h = \frac{1000}{\pi r^2}$$

Substituting this value into the cost function $C$, we get

$$C = 0.1\pi r^2 + 0.06\pi r \cdot \frac{1000}{\pi r^2}$$

$$= 0.1\pi r^2 + \frac{60}{r}$$

To find the value of $r$ that gives minimum cost, we differentiate $C$ with respect to $r$. Thus

$$\frac{dC}{dr} = C'(r) = 0.2\pi r - \frac{60}{r^2}$$

$$= \frac{0.2\pi r^3 - 60}{r^2}$$

The critical values obey $C'(r) = 0$ or

$$0.2\pi r^3 - 60 = 0 \quad \text{or} \quad r^3 = \frac{300}{\pi} \quad \text{or} \quad r = \sqrt[3]{\frac{300}{\pi}} \approx 4.57$$

Using the Second Derivative Test,

$$C''(r) = 0.2\pi + \frac{120}{r^3}$$

and $$C''\left(\sqrt[3]{\frac{300}{\pi}}\right) = 0.2\pi + \frac{120\pi}{300} > 0$$

Thus, for $r = \sqrt[3]{300/\pi} = 4.57$ centimeters, the cost is a relative minimum.

Since the only physical constraint is that $r$ be positive, the relative minimum value is the absolute minimum. The corresponding height of this can is

$$h = \frac{1000}{\pi r^2} = \frac{1000}{20.89\pi} \approx 15.24 \text{ centimeters}$$

These are the dimensions that will minimize the cost of the material.

If the material cost of the top, bottom, and lateral surfaces of a cylindrical container is the same, then minimum cost is the same as minimum surface area. It can be shown (see Problem 14) that for any fixed volume, minimum surface area is obtained when the height equals twice the radius.

A company charges $200 for each set of tools on orders of 150 or less sets. The cost to the buyer on every set is reduced by $1 for each set in excess of 150. For what size order is revenue a maximum?

For an order of exactly 150 sets, the company's revenue is

$$\$200(150) = \$30,000$$

For an order of 160 sets (which is 10 in excess of 150), the per set charge is $200 - 10(1) = 190$ and the revenue is

$$\$190(160) = \$30,400$$

To solve the problem, let $x$ denote the number of sets sold. The revenue $R$ is

$$R = \text{(number of sets)(cost per set)}$$
$$= x(\text{cost per set})$$

The charge per set is

$$200 - 1 \text{ (number of sets in excess of 150)}$$
$$= 200 - 1(x - 150) = 350 - x$$

Hence, the revenue $R$ is

$$R = x(350 - x) = 350x - x^2$$

To find the number of sets leading to maximum revenue, we find the critical values of $R(x)$.

$$R'(x) = 350 - 2x$$
$$R'(x) = 0 \quad \text{when} \quad x = 175$$

Since $R''(x) = -2 < 0$ for all $x$, there is a relative maximum at $x = 175$. Thus, a purchase of 175 sets maximizes the company's revenue. The maximum revenue is

$$R = (350)(175) - (175)^2 = \$30,625$$

Of course, the company would set this figure as the most it would allow anyone to purchase on this plan, since revenue to the company starts to decrease for orders in excess of 175.

---

1. The total cost for ordering candy is approximately $C(x) = 0.005x + 4500(1/x)$. For what value of $x$ is the cost a minimum?
2. The sum of two positive numbers is 18. Find the numbers if their product is to be a maximum.
3. The sum of two positive numbers is 18. Find the numbers if the product of their squares is to be a maximum.
4. A cylindrical container is to be produced whose capacity is 10 cubic feet. The top and bottom of the container are to be made of a material that costs $2 per square foot,

while the side of the container is made of material costing $1.50 per square foot. Find the dimensions that will minimize the total cost of the container.

5. A box with a square base is to be made from a square piece of cardboard 12 inches on a side by cutting out a square from each corner and turning up the sides. Find the dimensions of the box that yield maximum volume.

6. A car rental agency has 200 cars (identical model). The owner finds that at a price of $180 per month, he can rent all the cars; however, for each $10 increase in rental, one of the cars is not rented. What should he charge so as to maximize his income?

7. A charter flight club charges its members $200 per year. For each applicant in excess of 60, the charge for each one (all of them) is reduced by $2. What number of members leads to a maximum revenue?

8. A box is to be made from a rectangular piece of sheet metal whose dimensions are 40 by 60 centimeters by cutting out a square from each corner and turning up the sides. Find the dimensions of the box that yield maximum volume.

9. Find the area of the largest rectangle that can be inscribed in a circle of radius 3.

10. Find the dimensions of the rectangle of largest area that can be enclosed by 200 feet of fencing.

11. A printer plans on having 50 square inches of printed matter per page and is required to allow for margins of 1 inch on each side and 2 inches on the top and bottom. What are the most economical dimensions for each page, if the cost per page depends on the area of the page?

12. A telephone company is asked to provide telephone service to a customer whose house is located 2 miles away from the road along which the telephone lines run. The nearest telephone box is located 5 miles down this road. If the cost to connect the telephone line is $50 per mile along the road and $60 per mile away from the road, where along the road from the box should the company connect the telephone line so as to minimize construction cost?

Hint: Let $x$ denote the distance from the box to the connection so that $5 - x$ is the distance from this point to the point on the road closest to the house.

*13. A truck has a top speed of 75 miles per hour and, when traveling at the rate of $x$ miles per hour, consumes gasoline at the rate of $1/200(1600/x + x)$ gallons per mile. This truck is to be taken on a 200-mile trip by a driver who is to be paid at the rate of $b$ dollars per hour plus a commission of $c$ dollars. Since the time required for this trip at $x$ miles per hour is $200/x$, the total cost, if gasoline costs $a$ dollars per gallon, is

$$C(x) = \left(\frac{1600}{x} + x\right) a + \left(\frac{200}{x}\right) b + c$$

Find the most economical possible speed under each of the following sets of conditions:

(a) $b = 0$, $c = 0$;
(b) $a = 0.50$, $b = 8.00$, $c = 500$;
(c) $a = 0.60$, $b = 10.00$, $c = 0$.

*14. Prove that a cylindrical container of fixed volume $V$ requires the least material (minimum surface area) when its height is twice its radius.

---

In this section, we examine how the derivative can be used in certain business models as a guide to decision making. We begin the discussion by developing a business model for profit, revenue, and cost.

The profit of most firms depends upon the revenue derived from the sale of a product and the cost of manufacturing, distributing, and selling this product. If $P$ is the profit, $R$ the revenue, and $C$ the cost, it is clear that

$$\begin{aligned} \text{Profit} &= \text{Revenue} - \text{Cost} \\ P &= R - C \end{aligned}$$

Revenue is the amount of money derived from the sale of a product and depends upon the price of the product and the quantity of the product that is actually sold. But the price and the quantity sold are not independent: one is a function of the other. This relationship between price and quantity is called the *demand function*. If $p$ represents price and $x$ represents quantity, we write the demand function as

Demand Function

$$p = p(x)$$

This relationship depends, of course, on the nature of the product and the competition from other products.

For example, the demand function for corn is usually a decreasing function so that, as the quantity $x$ of corn to be sold increases, the price of the corn will decline. See Figure 9.23.

In particular, however, if a quantity $x^*$ of corn is offered, it will bring a price $p^*$ on the open market. As a result, a farmer, who is not in a position to affect the supply of corn, can only expect a price $p^*$ for his corn crop, no matter how much he has to sell. This is an example of free competition. Thus, for the whole market, the demand function is decreasing while for a particular farmer the price is fixed at a maximum price $p^*$, no matter how much he has to sell.

In general, for the entire market, when the price is high, quantities demanded are low; and the price is low when quantities demanded are

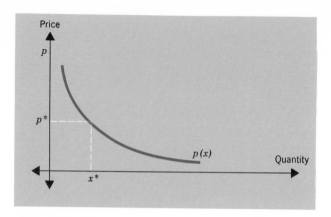

**Figure 9.23**

high. That is, demand functions are decreasing, so that, if the demand function is a straight line, its slope is negative.

The revenue $R$ of a firm is the product of the price of the product times the quantity of the product sold. That is,

$$R = x \cdot p$$

Thus, we can express revenue as a function of $x$ alone by using the demand function. That is,

$$R = xp(x)$$

In practice, a demand function is found through surveys, analysis of data, history, and other sources available to the economist. The next example illustrates how a linear demand function can be constructed. It is critical to observe that the fundamental assumption made here is the linear nature of the demand function.

**6.1
Example**

Dan's Toy Store has observed that each week 1000 electric trucks are sold at a price of \$5.00 per truck. When there is a special, the trucks sell for \$4.00 each and 1200 per week are sold. Assuming a linear demand function, construct the demand function and find the revenue function.

Let $p$ be the price of each truck and $x$ be the number sold. If the demand function $p = p(x)$ is linear, then we know that $(1000, 5)$ and $(1200, 4)$ are two points on the line $p = p(x)$. Thus, the demand function is

$$p - 4 = \frac{-1}{200}(x - 1200)$$

$$p = \frac{-1}{200}x + 10$$

The revenue function is

$$R = px = \frac{-x^2}{200} + 10x$$

The demand function obtained in the above example is not meant to reflect extreme situations. For example, we do not expect to sell $x = 0$ trucks nor do we expect to sell too many trucks in excess of 1500, since even during a special only 1200 are sold. The demand function does represent the relationship between price and quantity in a certain range, in this case, perhaps $500 < x < 1500$.

Our next example illustrates a constant demand function.

A farmer, no matter how much wheat he can grow, can expect to sell it at $2.00 per bushel. If he produces $x$ bushels, what is his revenue?

Since the price he receives per bushel is fixed at $2.00 maximum per bushel, the demand function is

$$p = \$2.00$$

The revenue is

$$R = px = 2x$$

We turn now to the cost $C$ to a firm. The cost $C$ is composed of two types of costs, fixed costs and variable costs. Fixed costs remain the same no matter how much is produced or manufactured. Examples of fixed costs are mortgage payments, interest, insurance, real estate taxes, and salaries of people who will be employed even through a time of zero production. Variable costs change as production changes. Examples are cost of raw material and salaries of people directly related to production.

It is clear that if $C$ is the cost, $VC$ is the variable cost, and $FC$ is the fixed cost, then

$$C = VC + FC$$

Also, we assume that $FC$ is a constant, that $VC$ is a function of the quantity produced, and that, when zero quantity is produced, the variable cost is zero.

Let us assume that the farmer in Example 6.2 can produce anywhere from 0 to 15,000 bushels of wheat. Suppose his cost function in dollars is

$$C = \frac{x^2}{10,000} + 500$$

where $x$ represents the number of bushels produced. We interpret this cost function as consisting of fixed costs of $500 and variable costs of $x^2/10,000$ dollars. Here the fixed cost of $500 is due to costs of land, equipment, and so on. The variable cost represents the cost of planting, fertilizing, and harvesting the crop. For example, the cost of producing 15,000 bushels is

$$C = \frac{(15,000)(15,000)}{10,000} + 500$$

$$= 22,500 + 500 = \$23,000$$

Of importance is the question of how the cost $C$ changes as the quantity $x$ produced changes. Of particular interest is the marginal cost. The marginal cost is

$$MC = \frac{dC}{dx} = \frac{x}{5000}$$

For $x = 5000$ bushels, the marginal cost is

$$MC = 1$$

and, for $x = 6000$ bushels, the marginal cost is

$$MC = 1.2$$

The difference in marginal cost is an indication that the cost is increasing from \$1 per bushel to \$1.20 per bushel. This increase is all right, provided it is not detrimental to the total profit picture. That is, the combination of cost *and* revenue is what is critical—not cost alone. Thus, we need to ask how the revenue function changes relative to the quantity produced. Comparing this to the marginal cost will provide valuable information to the farmer.

**6.4
Example**

If the wheat farmer obtains a price of \$2 per bushel, the revenue function is

$$R = 2x$$

The marginal revenue is

$$MR = \frac{dR}{dx} = 2$$

The marginal revenue is constant ($MR = 2$) since the demand function is constant. This means the marginal revenue for 5000 bushels of wheat is the same as for 6000 bushels of wheat. That is, the revenue is increasing at a constant rate.

Thus, we have here a situation where the marginal cost is increasing and the marginal revenue is fixed. This is all right until the marginal cost begins to exceed the marginal revenue, because this means that the cost of producing additional quantity exceeds the revenue coming from this additional quantity. Our problem then is to determine at what point to stop production so that profit is maximized. It is reasonable to conjecture that this point is where marginal revenue and marginal cost are equal.

This fact can be easily verified by using the tests for maxima and minima. The profit function is

$$P = R - C$$

To maximize this, we find the critical values, which obey

$$\frac{d}{dx}P = \frac{d}{dx}(R - C) = 0$$

or

$$\frac{d}{dx}R - \frac{d}{dx}C = 0$$

or

$$MR - MC = 0$$

Thus, the profit $P$ is maximized at that quantity $x$ for which marginal revenue equals marginal cost.

**The equality $MR = MC$ is the basis for the classical economic criterion for maximum profit—that marginal revenue and marginal cost be equal.**

We return to our wheat farmer. How much wheat should he produce to maximize profits?

His marginal revenue and marginal cost are

$$MR = 2 \qquad MC = \frac{x}{5000}$$

These are equal when

$$2 = \frac{x}{5000} \qquad x = 10,000$$

Thus, the farmer should produce 10,000 bushels of wheat to insure a maximum profit. The profit for 10,000 bushels is

$$P = 2(10,000) - \left[\frac{(10,000)^2}{10,000} + 500\right]$$

$$= 20,000 - 10,500 = \$9,500$$

Note that maximum profit occurs for production that is 5000 bushels under the maximum output of 15,000 bushels. For a 15,000 bushel production, the profit is

$$P = 2(15,000) - 23,000 = \$7000$$

Thus, maximum production may not insure maximum profit.

1. During a fixed period, a retail store can sell $x$ units of a product at a price of $p$ cents per unit where

$$p = 20 - 0.03x$$

The cost of making $x$ units is $C$ cents, where

$$C = 3 + 0.02x$$

What number of units will lead to maximum profits?

2. Let the cost function be $C(x) = 2x + 5$ and the revenue function be $R(x) = 8x - x^2$, where $x$ is the number of units produced (in thousands).
   (a) Find the marginal revenue.
   (b) Find the marginal revenue at $x = 3, x = 4$.
   (c) Find the marginal cost.
   (d) What is the fixed cost?
   (e) What is the variable cost at $x = 4$?
   (f) What is the break-even point, that is, $R(x) = C(x)$? Interpret your answer.
   (g) What is the profit function?
   (h) What is the most profitable output?
   (i) What is the maximum profit?
   (j) What is the marginal revenue at the most profitable output?
   (k) What is the revenue at the most profitable output?
   (l) What is the variable cost at the most profitable output?
   (m) Graph $MR$ and $MC$.
   (n) Graph $R(x)$ and $C(x)$.

3. Suppose the cost function is given by $C(x) = x^2 + 5$ and the demand function is $p = 12 - 2x$, where $p$ is the price in dollars and $x$ is the number of units produced (in thousands). Answer the questions asked in Problem 2.

4. A certain item can be produced at a unit cost of $10 for all possible outputs. The demand function for the product is $p = 90 - 0.02x$, where $p$ is the price in dollars and $x$ is the number of units.
   (a) How many units should be produced to maximize profits?
   (b) What is the price that gives maximum profit?
   (c) What is the maximum profit?

5. A coal company can produce $x$ tons of coal at a daily cost of $C$ dollars, where

$$C = 200 + 35x + 0.02x^2$$

The coal can be sold at a price of $39 per ton. How many tons should be produced each day so as to maximize profits?

6. A tractor company can manufacture at most 1000 heavy-duty tractors per year. Furthermore, from past demand data, the company knows that the number of heavy-duty tractors it can sell depends only on the price $p$ of each unit. The company also knows that the cost to produce the units is a function of the number $x$ of units sold.

Assume the demand function is $p = 19,000 - 2x$ and the cost function is $C = 1,000,000 + 10,000x + 3x^2$. How many units should be produced to maximize profits?

*7. Let $x$ be the total number of items produced per year and $p$ the price at which each is sold. If the cost for producing $x$ items is $C = ax^2 + bx + c$ and $p = r - sx$, what value of $x$ produces maximum profit? Here $a$, $b$, $c$, $r$, $s$ are constants.

## Optimization of Tax Revenue[2]

In determining the tax rate on excise tax, cars, telephones, etc., the government is always faced with the following problem: How large should the tax be so that the tax revenue will be as large as possible? Let us examine the situation more carefully. The moment the government places a tax on a product the price of this product for the consumer may increase and the quantity demanded decrease. A very large tax may cause the quantity demanded to diminish to zero, and the result is that no tax revenue is collected. On the other hand, if no tax is levied there will be no tax revenue at all. Thus the problem is to find the tax rate that optimizes tax revenue. (Tax revenue is the product of the tax per unit times the actual market quantity consumed.)

Let us assume that because of long time experience in levying taxes, the government is able to determine that the relation between the market quantity consumed of a certain product and the related tax is

$$t = \sqrt{27 - 3x^2}$$

where $t$ denotes the amount of tax per unit of a product and $x$ is the market quantity consumed (measured in appropriate units).

Notice that the relationship between tax rate and quantity consumed conforms to the restrictions discussed earlier. For example, when the tax rate $t = 0$, then the quantity consumed is $x = 3$; when the tax is at a maximum ($t = 5.2$ percent), the quantity consumed is zero. Figure 9.24 illustrates the graph of this relationship.

[2]Adapted from P. H. Davis and W. M. Whyburn, *Introduction to Mathematical Analysis with Applications to Problems of Economics*, Addison-Wesley, Reading, Mass., 1958.

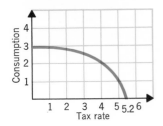

**Figure 9.24**

It must be pointed out that the relationship between tax rate and consumption is derived by government economists and is subject to both change and criticism.

The revenue $R$ due to the tax rate $t$ is the product of tax rate per unit by the market quantity consumed:

$$R = xt = x(27 - 3x^2)^{1/2}$$

where $R$ is measured in dollars. Since both $x$ and $t$ are assumed to be non-negative, the domain of $R$ is $0 \leq x \leq 3$. Also $R = 0$ at both $x = 0$ and $x = 3$, so that for some positive value of $x$ between 0 and 3, $R$ attains its absolute maximum.

To find the absolute maximum, we take the derivative of $R$ with respect to $x$ using the formula for the derivative of a product and the Power Rule. Thus,

$$R' = (27 - 3x^2)^{1/2} + \frac{1}{2}x(27 - 3x^2)^{-1/2} \cdot (-6x)$$

$$= \frac{27 - 3x^2 - 3x^2}{(27 - 3x^2)^{1/2}} = \frac{27 - 6x^2}{(27 - 3x^2)^{1/2}}$$

The critical values obey

$$27 - 6x^2 = 0 \text{ or } x^2 = 4.5$$

Thus, since $0 \leq x \leq 3$, the lone critical value is $x = \sqrt{4.5} = 2.12$.

To find the absolute maximum, we compare the value of $R$ at the end points $x = 0$, $x = 3$, with its value at $x = 2.12$. Then

$$\underset{\text{at } x = 0}{R} = 0, \qquad \underset{\text{at } x = \sqrt{4.5}}{R} = \sqrt{4.5}\sqrt{13.5} = (2.12)(3.67) = 7.79, \qquad \underset{\text{at } x = 3}{R} = 0$$

Thus, at $x = 2.12$ the revenue is maximized. The tax rate corresponding to maximum revenue is

$$t = \sqrt{27 - 3x^2} = \sqrt{13.5} = 3.67$$

This means that, for a tax rate of 3.67 percent, a maximum revenue $R = 7.79$ is generated.

### Optimal Trade-in Time[3]

Car owners are quite often faced with the following problem: When is the best time for the car to be traded in?

Two major considerations form the framework of determining optimal trade-in time. The first is the estimated cost of repairs needed to maintain the car; the second is the replacement cost of the car. We wish to express these costs as functions of time $t$ and then determine the value of $t$ that minimizes the total cost.

Let us first determine the relationship between time $t$ ($t$ measured in months) of ownership and the number of repairs of a car. Assuming the

[3] Adapted from H. Brems, *Quantitative Economic Theory*, Wiley, New York, 1968.

average cost per repair is $50, we can set $k$, the total number of repairs, equal to

$$k = \frac{1}{10} t^{3/2}$$

Notice that as the time $t$ increases, the total number $k$ of repairs also increases and that a new car ($t = 0$) is expected to have zero repairs. Thus, this relationship between $k$ and $t$ appears reasonable. The number of repairs per month is $k/t$, and, if the average cost per repair is $50, the repair cost per month is $50(k/t)$.

At the end of time $t$, suppose the car is replaced. Then the number of replacements per month is $1/t$. If the cost of replacement is $2800, the replacement cost per month is $2800(1/t)$.

If all capital costs are ignored, the function

$$C(t) = 50\frac{k}{t} + 2800\frac{1}{t} = 5t^{1/2} + 2800\frac{1}{t}$$

represents the repair and replacement costs per month.

Our problem is to determine that value of $t(t > 0)$ for which the cost $C(t)$ of repair and replacement is a minimum. Then

$$C'(t) = 5 \cdot \frac{1}{2} t^{-1/2} + 2800(-1)t^{-2}$$

$$= \frac{5}{2} t^{-1/2} - 2800t^{-2}$$

$$= \frac{5t^{3/2} - 5600}{2t^2}$$

The critical values obey

$$5t^{3/2} - 5600 = 0$$
$$t^{3/2} = 1120$$
$$t = 107.85 \text{ months}$$

The minimum cost of repair and replacement per month is

$$C(107.85) = 5(10.385) + \frac{2800}{107.85}$$

$$= 51.93 + 25.96$$
$$= \$77.89$$

## Minimizing Storage Cost

Tami's Famous Hamburger Palace requires 45,000 hamburger patties every quarter (three months) based on estimated daily sales of 475 hamburgers plus an additional 25 that are either burned or eaten by employees each day. These hamburgers are packed in boxes of ten patties each. The manager of the restaurant, for each order he places, incurs order charges of 45¢ due to handling and delivery. He is also aware that, if he places a large order, he must be prepared to store the patties in a freezer. He estimates the cost of storing each box of patties to be 2¢ per box. How many boxes of patties should be ordered and how many orders should be placed to minimize the cost of storage and of ordering?

To begin, let $x$ denote the number of boxes of patties ordered each time an order is placed. Then, the storage cost for $x$ boxes is

$$\text{storage cost} = \$0.02x$$

If $x$ boxes are ordered each time an order is placed, and if a total of 4500 boxes (45,000 ÷ 10) are required, then the number of orders necessary is

$$\frac{4500}{x}$$

(If $4500/x$ is not an integer, we approximate by using the closest integer to $4500/x$.) Each order carries an order charge of $0.45 so that the order cost is

$$\text{order cost} = \$0.45 \left( \frac{4500}{x} \right)$$

The cost function $C(x)$ to be minimized is

$$C(x) = \text{storage cost} + \text{order cost} = \$0.02x + \$0.45 \left( \frac{4500}{x} \right)$$

Of course the domain of $C(x)$ is $1 \leq x \leq 4500$. (At most 4500 boxes are required.)

To find the absolute minimum of $C(x)$, we first find the critical values. They obey

$$C'(x) = 0.02 - \frac{2025}{x^2} = 0$$

$$0.02x^2 = 2025$$

$$x^2 = \frac{2025}{0.02} = \frac{202,500}{2} = 101,250$$

$$x = 318.2$$

The cost at $x = 318.2$ is

$$C(318.2) = 6.36 + 6.36 = \$12.72$$

Testing the end points $x = 4500$ and $x = 1$, we find

$$C(4500) = 0.02(4500) + 0.45 = \$90.45$$
$$C(1) = \$2025.02$$

Thus, the minimum cost is achieved when $x = 318.2$ boxes are ordered and $4500/x = 14.14$ orders are placed.

1. The average cost per repair of a television is found to be $10 and the number of repairs $k$ is given by $k = t^{4/3}$, where $t$ is measured in years. The replacement cost is estimated to be $250. Ignoring capital costs, find the optimal time for trading the television in.

2. On a particular product, government economists determine that the relationship between tax rate $t$ and the quantity $x$ consumed is

$$t + 3x^2 = 18$$

Graph this relationship and explain how it could be justified. Find the optimal tax rate and the revenue generated by this tax rate. Graph the revenue function $R$.

| | |
|---|---|
| increasing function | concave up |
| decreasing function | concave down |
| relative maximum | inflection point |
| relative minimum | demand function |
| critical value | revenue function |
| critical point | cost function |
| First Derivative Test | profit function |
| Second Derivative Test | marginal revenue |
| absolute maximum | marginal cost |
| absolute minimum | |

1. For each of the following functions, find where the function is increasing and decreasing. Locate all relative maxima and all relative minima. Determine where the function is concave up and concave down. Find all inflection points. Sketch the graph.

(a) $f(x) = x^3 - 3x^2 + 3x - 1$

(b) $f(x) = \dfrac{x}{x + 2}$

(c) $f(x) = \sqrt{x - 2}$

(d) $f(x) = \dfrac{1}{x^2}$

(e) $f(x) = \dfrac{x^2 + 1}{x}$

(f) $f(x) = \dfrac{x^3}{x^2 + 1}$

(g) $f(x) = \dfrac{x^2 + 1}{x^2}$

(h) $f(x) = \sqrt{\dfrac{1}{x}}$

2. Find the absolute maximum and absolute minimum of each of the following functions on the domain indicated.

(a) $f(x) = x^3 - 3x^2 + 3x - 1 \qquad [-10, 10]$

(b) $f(x) = \dfrac{x}{x + 2} \qquad [-1, 2]$

(c) $f(x) = \sqrt[3]{x^2 + 4} \qquad [-2, \sqrt{23}]$

(d) $f(x) = x + \dfrac{1}{x} \qquad \left[\dfrac{1}{2}, 5\right]$

(e) $f(x) = 1 - x^{4/5} \qquad [-1, 1]$

3. A company's history shows that profits increase, as a result of advertising, according to

$$P(x) = 150 + 120x - 3x^2$$

where $x$ is the number of dollars spent on advertising (measured in thousands). How much should be spent on advertising to maximize profits?

4. A beer can is cylindrical and holds 500 cubic centimeters of beer. If the cost of the material used to make the sides, top, and bottom is the same, what dimensions should the can have to minimize cost?

5. The demand function of a certain mobile home producer is

$$p = 2402.50 - 0.5x^2$$

where $p$ is the price and $x$ is the number of units sold. The cost of production for $x$ units is

$$C = 1802.5x + 1500$$

How many units need to be sold to maximize profit?

6. A distributor of refrigerators has average monthly sales of 1500 refrigerators each selling for $300. A special month-long promotion, he has found, will enable him to sell 200 additional refrigerators for each $15 decrease in price. What should he charge for each refrigerator during the month of promotion in order to maximize his revenue?

Bibliography

*Mathematics*

Chover, Joshua, *The Green Book of Calculus*. W. A. Benjamin, Menlo Park, Calif., 1972.

Leithold, Louis, *Calculus and Analytic Geometry*, Second Edition, Harper and Row, New York, 1972. Chapter 4.

Salas, Saturnino and Einar Hille, *Calculus: One and Several Variables*, Second Edition, Xerox, Lexington, Mass. 1974. Chapter 3.

Thomas, George, *Calculus and Analytic Geometry*, Fourth Edition, Addison-Wesley, Reading, Mass., 1968. Chapter 4.

*Applied*

Batschelet, E., *Introduction to Mathematics for Life Sciences*, Springer-Verlag, New York, 1972.

Chiang, Alpha, *Fundamental Methods of Mathematical Economics*, Second Edition, McGraw-Hill, New York, 1974.

Ferguson, C. E., *Microeconomic Theory*, Third Edition, Irwin Press, Homewood, Illinois, 1972.

Grossman, Stanley and James Turner, *Mathematics for the Biological Sciences*, Macmillan, New York, 1974.

Springer, C. H., R. E. Herlihy, and R. I. Beggs, *Advanced Methods and Models*, Mathematics for Management Series, Volume 2, Irwin Press Homewood, Ill., 1965.

Thrall, Robert M., Ed., *Some Mathematical Models in Biology*, University of Michigan, Ann Arbor, 1967.

# 10

# THE EXPONENTIAL AND LOGARITHM FUNCTIONS

Until now, our study of the calculus has been concerned, for the most part, with polynomial functions and ratios of polynomial functions (the rational functions). Although these functions occur in many practical situations, there are other functions that are equally important and useful. Two of these functions are the *exponential function* and the *logarithm function.*

   The purpose of this chapter is to introduce these functions and to illustrate some of the many models that require their use. Our major concern is to define these functions, graph them, list some useful properties they possess, and obtain formulas for finding their derivatives. We shall discover that the exponential function is indispensable in many areas and can be used, for instance, to describe the growth of the gross national product and the relationship between price and demand of many commodities.

We begin with a brief review[1] of exponents. Recall that if $a$ is a real number and $n \geq 1$ is a positive integer, then $a^n$ means $a$ times itself $n$ times; thus, for example

$$2^3 = 2 \cdot 2 \cdot 2, \qquad 5^2 = 5 \cdot 5, \qquad \pi^4 = \pi \cdot \pi \cdot \pi \cdot \pi$$

In this definition $a$ is the *base* and $n$ is the *exponent*.

Two useful properties of exponents are

**Laws of
Exponents**

$$a^m \cdot a^n = a^{m+n}, \qquad (a^m)^n = a^{m \cdot n}$$

At this point we define raising $a$ to the zero power and to a negative power in such a way that the Laws of Exponents are preserved. Thus, if $a \neq 0$,

$$a^0 = 1, \qquad a^{-n} = \frac{1}{a^n}, \qquad n \geq 1 \text{ an integer}$$

For example,

$$5^0 = 1, \qquad 2^{-3} = \frac{1}{2^3} = \frac{1}{8}$$

With this meaning given to raising $a$ to a power $n$, where $n$ is *any* integer, we turn to the question of raising $a$ to a rational number exponent. Again we carefully define the meaning of $a^{p/q}$, so that the Laws of Exponents are retained. Thus,

$$a^{p/q} = (\sqrt[q]{a})^p, \qquad q \geq 2 \text{ is an integer and } p \text{ is any integer}$$

where $\sqrt[q]{a}$ denotes the qth root of $a$. Here we need to restrict the base $a$ somewhat, since even roots of negative numbers do not exist in the real number system. Thus, $a^{p/q}$ has meaning except where $a < 0$ and $q$ is even. (We assume that $p/q$ is in lowest terms.)

For example,

$$8^{2/3} = (\sqrt[3]{8})^2 = 2^2 = 4$$
$$(-27)^{2/3} = (\sqrt[3]{-27})^2 = (-3)^2 = 9$$

Expressions such as $(-4)^{1/2}$, $(-25)^{3/4}$, and the like, are assigned no meaning.

The next logical advancement is to speak of raising $a$ to any real-number exponent. When we do this, we obtain $a^x$, where $x$ is a real number. The restrictions on the base $a$ are that $a > 0$ and $a \neq 1$. Thus, for our purposes, no meaning is assigned to expressions like $(-3)^{\sqrt{2}}$.

**Definition
of an
Exponential
Function**

**An** *exponential function* **is one of the form**

$$y = f(x) = a^x$$

**where $a > 0$, $a \neq 1$ is a real constant.**

---

[1] The reader is encouraged to review these concepts in the Appendix, page 569.

The reason for the name given this particular function is that the independent variable $x$ appears as an exponent.

To gain insight into the nature of the graph of an exponential function, we study a few examples.

Graph the exponential function

$$f(x) = 2^x$$

We begin by looking at some of the points on the graph of

$$f(x) = 2^x$$

| $x$ | $-10$ | $-5$ | $-4$ | $-3$ | $-2$ | $-1$ | $-0.5$ |
|---|---|---|---|---|---|---|---|
| $f(x) = 2^x$ | $2^{-10} = 0.00098$ | $2^{-5} = 0.031$ | $2^{-4} = 0.0625$ | $2^{-3} = 0.125$ | $2^{-2} = 0.25$ | $2^{-1} = 0.5$ | $2^{-.5} = 0.707$ |

| $x$ | $0$ | $0.5$ | $1$ | $2$ | $\sqrt{7}$ | $3$ | $5$ | $10$ |
|---|---|---|---|---|---|---|---|---|
| $f(x) = 2^x$ | $2^0 = 1.0$ | $2^{0.5} = 1.414$ | $2^1 = 2.0$ | $2^2 = 4.0$ | $2^{\sqrt{7}} = 6.258$ | $2^3 = 8$ | $2^5 = 32$ | $2^{10} = 1024$ |

Notice that for increasingly negative values of $x$, the value of $2^x$ is very close to zero, but positive. For large positive values of $x$, the value of $2^x$ is very large and positive. From the values in the table above, we conclude that the domain of $f(x) = 2^x$ is the set of real numbers and the range is the set of positive real numbers. Figure 10.1 illustrates the graph.

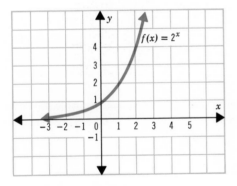

**Figure 10.1**

The graph of $f(x) = 2^x$ in Figure 10.1 is typical of all exponential functions whose base is larger than one. Such functions are positive everywhere and are increasing functions on their domain. Each of their graphs passes through the point $(0, 1)$ and thereafter rises rapidly as $x$ increases. Indeed, for the function $a^x$, $a > 1$, we have

$$\lim_{x \to +\infty} a^x = +\infty \qquad \lim_{x \to -\infty} a^x = 0$$

In addition, $f(x) = a^x$, $a > 1$, is a continuous function. See the graphs in Figure 10.2.

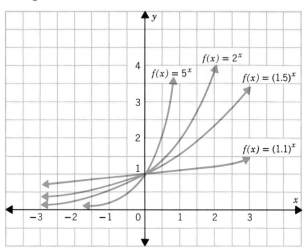

**Figure 10.2**

Exponential functions, like those in Figure 10.2, are often used as models for describing such phenomena as the growth of bacteria in a culture, population growth, and compound interest. We refer to such

Growth Curves curves as *growth curves*.

For example, if we observe the gross national product (GNP) in the United States over the last 60 years, we see that a good model of this situation is a growth curve whose base is larger than one. See Figure 10.3. The figure consists of the actual GNP (curve in color) and an

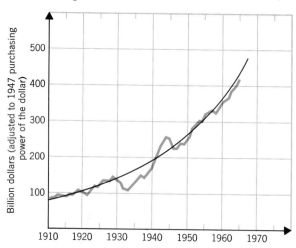

**Figure 10.3**

exponential function (black curve). The equation of the exponential function is determined by using the technique of curve fitting that is usually studied in statistics.

Graph the exponential function

$$f(x) = \left(\frac{1}{2}\right)^x$$

Again, we look at some points on the graph.

| x | $-10$ | $-5$ | $-2$ | $-1$ | 0 |
|---|---|---|---|---|---|
| $f(x) = \left(\frac{1}{2}\right)^x$ | $\left(\frac{1}{2}\right)^{-10} = 1024$ | $\left(\frac{1}{2}\right)^{-5} = 32$ | $\left(\frac{1}{2}\right)^{-2} = 4$ | $\left(\frac{1}{2}\right)^{-1} = 2$ | $\left(\frac{1}{2}\right)^{0} = 1$ |

| x | 1 | 2 | 5 | 10 |
|---|---|---|---|---|
| $f(x) = \left(\frac{1}{2}\right)^x$ | $\left(\frac{1}{2}\right)^{1} = 0.5$ | $\left(\frac{1}{2}\right)^{2} = 0.25$ | $\left(\frac{1}{2}\right)^{5} = 0.031$ | $\left(\frac{1}{2}\right)^{10} = 0.00098$ |

Thus, for increasingly negative values of x, the value of $(1/2)^x$ becomes large and positive; for large positive values of x, $(1/2)^x$ is close to zero and positive. Figure 10.4 illustrates the graph.

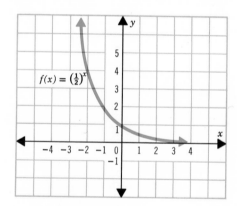

**Figure 10.4**

The graph of $f(x) = (1/2)^x$ in Figure 10.4 is typical of all exponential functions whose base is smaller than one. Such functions are positive everywhere and are decreasing on their domain. Each of their graphs passes through the point $(0, 1)$ and thereafter the graph decreases as x increases. Indeed, for the function $a^x$, $0 < a < 1$, we have

$$\lim_{x \to -\infty} a^x = +\infty \qquad \lim_{x \to +\infty} a^x = 0$$

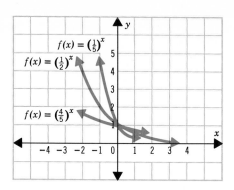

**Figure 10.5**

In addition, $f(x) = a^x$, $0 < a < 1$, is a continuous function. See the graphs in Figure 10.5.

Exponential functions like those in Figure 10.5 are often used as models for describing phenomena such as radioactive decay, depreciation, and price-demand curves. We refer to such curves as *decay curves*.

**Decay Curves**

For example, the price-demand curve for a particular commodity may be described by the graph in Figure 10.6. Here we measure price along the vertical axis and demand along the horizontal axis. The curve itself closely resembles an exponential function whose base is less than one.

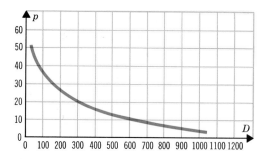

**Figure 10.6**

We conclude this section with an examination of some models that employ the exponential function. In our first example we compute compound interest.

**2.3**
**Example**

A man deposits $100 in a bank that pays 5 percent interest per annum compounded annually. How much is in his account after $x$ years? We assume the interest paid is left in the account.

We begin to build the model by looking at what happens to the balance in his account after one year. After one year, the initial balance $B_0$ of $100 increases by the amount

$(0.05)(\$100) = \$5$. That is, if $B_1$ is the new balance after one year, then

$$B_1 = \$100 + (0.05)\$100 = \$105 \qquad B_1 = B_0 + 0.05B_0 = (1 + 0.05)$$

After another year, the new balance $B_2$ is

$$B_2 = \$105 + (0.05)(\$105) = \$110.25$$
$$B_2 = B_1 + 0.05B_1 = (1 + 0.05)B_1$$
$$= (1 + 0.05)^2 B_0$$

After another year, the balance $B_3$ is

$$B_3 = \$110.25 + 0.05(\$110.25)$$
$$= \$115.76$$
$$B_3 = B_2 + 0.05B_2 = (1 + 0.05)B_2$$
$$= (1 + 0.05)^3 B_0$$

As the process continues, we see that the balance $B_x$ after $x$ years is

$$B_x = (1 + 0.05)^x B_0$$

Thus, the balance after $x$ years is given as an exponential function whose base is larger than one.

A \$4500 car depreciates in such a way that the car's value each year is 2/3 of its value a year earlier. What is the worth of the car after 18 months? What is it worth after 40 months? After $t$ months?

To solve the problem, we need to construct a model that will relate the worth $W$ of the car to the time $t$ of ownership. In other words, we seek a function

$$W = f(t)$$

where $W$ is the worth in dollars and $t$ is the time in months. We may assume that at time $t = 0$ the car is worth its original cost \$4500. Thus

$$4500 = f(0)$$

We further know that after 12 months ($t = 12$), the value is 2/3 of \$4500 or \$3000. That is,

$$3000 = f(12) \qquad \text{or} \qquad \frac{2}{3}(4500) = f(12)$$

After 12 more months, the new value is 2/3 of \$3000 or \$2000.

$$2000 = f(24) \qquad \text{or} \qquad \frac{2}{3} \times \frac{2}{3}(4500) = f(24)$$

After 12 more months

$$\left(\frac{2}{3}\right)^3 (4500) = f(36) = f(3 \cdot 12)$$

In general, we conclude that

$$\left(\frac{2}{3}\right)^{n}(4500) = f(n \cdot 12)$$

This formula is accurate for multiples of 12 months. But we want to know the value after 18 months. We solve the dilemma by making the assumption that depreciation behaves the same between multiples of 12 as it does for multiples of 12. This assumption is equivalent to setting $t = 12n$. Then

$$W = f(t) = \$4500\left(\frac{2}{3}\right)^{t/12}$$

Thus, for example,

$$W = f(18) = \$4500\,(2/3)^{3/2} = \$2449.49$$
18 months
$$W = f(40) = \$4500\,(2/3)^{10/3} = \$1164.77$$
40 months

In computing $(2/3)^{3/2}$ and $(2/3)^{10/3}$, we used a calculator. In the next section, we learn how to compute quantities like these without a calculator.

2.5
Example
Cost of a Car
Due to Depreciation

A new car costing $4500 depreciates in such a way that each year it is worth 2/3 of what it was worth a year earlier. What is the cost of the car due to depreciation after 18 months? After $t$ months?

We began by noting that

Cost due to depreciation = $4500 − worth of car

Thus, using the result of Example 2.4, we have

Cost due to depreciation = $4500 − $4500$(2/3)^{t/12}$
= $4500$[1 − (2/3)^{t/12}]$

The graph of this function is given in Figure 10.7.

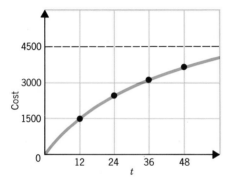

**Figure 10.7**

We observe that the cost due to depreciation starts by increasing rapidly and then levels off as it approaches $4500. The horizontal line at $4500 is called an *asymptote;* obviously the cost of depreciation never quite reaches this value.

Asymptote

10.2
Exercise

1. Graph the functions
   (a) $f(x) = 3^x$     (d) $f(x) = 100(1.08)^x$
   (b) $f(x) = (\frac{1}{10})^x$     (e) $f(x) = 100[1 - 1.05^x]$
   (c) $f(x) = 4^{0.5x}$     (f) $f(x) = 100 - 92 \cdot (\frac{1}{3})^{0.5x}$

2. A sum of $1000 is placed in an account that pays 7 percent interest compounded annually. What is the balance in the account after 5 years? Assume interest is left in the account.

3. The earnings of 3M Co. have been increasing at an annual rate of 10 percent. Find a function that expresses the relationship between time and earnings.

4. The proportion of batteries that still maintain a charge after $x$ miles of use is

$$f(x) = \left(\frac{1}{3}\right)^{0.00015x}$$

   Graph this function and estimate from the graph the value of $f(x)$ for $x = 10{,}000$, $20{,}000$ and $30{,}000$ miles.

5. The annual profit of a company due to a particular item is found to be

$$P(x) = \$10{,}000 + \$25{,}000(1/4)^{0.5x}$$

   where $x$ is the number of years the item has been on the market. Graph this function and estimate the profit for $x = 1$, 3, and 5 years.

6. The demand for a new product increases rapidly, at first, and then levels off. Suppose the percentage of actual buyers obeys

$$f(x) = 100 - 90(1/3)^x$$

   where $x$ is the number of months the product is on the market. Graph the function and determine to what proportion of the market the new product sells for $x = 2$, 3, and 5 months.

7. If $f(x) = a^x$, show that
   (a) $f(x + 1) = af(x)$
   (b) $f(x + 1) - f(x) = (a - 1)f(x)$
   (c) $f(x + h) = a^h f(x)$

We turn now to the logarithm function. Consider the relationship

$$x = a^y \qquad a > 0 \qquad a \neq 1$$

10.3
THE LOGARITHM
FUNCTION

between $x$ and $y$. Of course this is recognizable as an exponential relationship between $x$ and $y$.

Definition
of a Logarithm
Function
**If, in this relationship, we solve for $y$ in terms of $x$, we obtain the** *logarithm function,* **denoted by $y = \log_a x$ and read as "$y$ is the log to the base $a$ of $x$."**

Thus, $y = \log_a x$ means $a^y = x$.

For example,

$$
\begin{array}{lllll}
y = \log_2 1 & \text{means} & 2^y = 1 & \text{or} & y = 0 \\
y = \log_3 3 & \text{means} & 3^y = 3 & \text{or} & y = 1 \\
y = \log_a x & \text{means} & a^y = x &
\end{array}
$$

In particular,

$$\log_a 1 = 0 \qquad \log_a a = 1$$

The logarithm function, $y = f(x) = \log_a x$, is a name for $a^y = x$, so that the domain of the logarithm function is the set of positive real numbers $x$, while the range is the set of all real numbers $y$. The graphs of some logarithm functions are given in Figure 10.8.

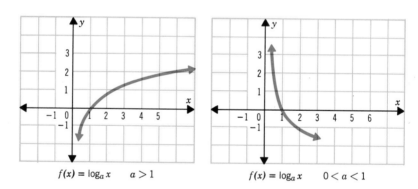

$f(x) = \log_a x \qquad a > 1$    $f(x) = \log_a x \qquad 0 < a < 1$

**Figure 10.8**

Note that $f(x) = \log_a x$, $a > 1$, is increasing, while $f(x) = \log_a x$, $0 < a < 1$, is decreasing. Each function is continuous on its domain, namely, $x > 0$, and passes through the point $(1, 0)$. Also, for $a > 1$,

$$\lim_{x \to 0^+} \log_a x = -\infty \qquad \lim_{x \to +\infty} \log_a x = +\infty$$

and for $0 < a < 1$,

$$\lim_{x \to 0^+} \log_a x = +\infty \qquad \lim_{x \to +\infty} \log_a x = -\infty$$

Logarithms obey certain properties that are easy to derive from their definition. These properties are often used to facilitate computation.

If $M$, $N$ represent positive real numbers and $r$ is any real number, then

1. $\log_a (MN) = \log_a M + \log_a N$

Properties of
Logarithms

2. $\log_a \dfrac{M}{N} = \log_a M - \log_a N$

3. $\log_a M^r = r \log_a M$

For example, from the Partial Table of Logarithms (see page 596), we find that

$$\log_{10} 2 = 0.3010 \qquad \log_{10} 3 = 0.4771$$

These values and the Properties of Logarithms enable us to compute

(a) $\log_{10} 6$    (b) $\log_{10} \dfrac{2}{3}$    (c) $\log_{10} 32$

Here

(a) $\log_{10} 6 = \log_{10} (3 \cdot 2) = \log_{10} 3 + \log_{10} 2 = 0.3010 + .4771 = 0.7781$
(b) $\log_{10} 2/3 = \log_{10} 2 - \log_{10} 3 = 0.3010 - 0.4771 = -0.1761$
(c) $\log_{10} 32 = \log_{10} 2^5 = 5 \log_{10} 2 = 5(0.3010) = 1.5050$

Another useful property of logarithms involves changing the base. The formula for expressing $\log_a M$, in terms of logarithms to the base $b$, is

$$\log_a M = \frac{\log_b M}{\log_b a}$$

Change of Base
Formula

One use of the Change of Base Formula is that it enables us to compute quantities like $\log_2 5$ and $\log_{1.2} 3$ by having a knowledge of only common logarithm tables (values of $\log_{10} M$).

To illustrate this, suppose we wish to compute

(a) $\log_2 5$    (b) $\log_{1.2} 3$

(a) We accomplish this by changing the base from 2 to 10 as follows:

$$\log_2 5 = \frac{\log_{10} 5}{\log_{10} 2}$$

From the Partial Table of Logarithms, page 596, we find that

$$\log_2 5 = \frac{0.6990}{0.3010} = 2.32$$

(b) To compute $\log_{1.2} 3$, we change the base to 10 as follows:

$$\log_{1.2} 3 = \frac{\log_{10} 3}{\log_{10} 1.2}$$

From the Partial Table of Logarithms, page 596, we find that

$$\log_{1.2} 3 = \frac{0.4771}{0.0792} = 6.02$$

The next example illustrates how logarithms can be used to solve a problem that occurs in finance.

At 8 percent interest compounded quarterly, how long will it take for a principal to double in value?

In this problem, let $P$ denote the principal or initial balance. The final balance is to be $2P$ and the quarterly rate of interest is 0.02. Let $x$ denote the number of quarters. We wish to determine the value of $x$ in the equation

$$2P = P(1 + 0.02)^x$$
$$2 = 1.02^x$$

To find $x$, we take logarithms of both sides and obtain

$$\log_{10} 2 = \log_{10} 1.02^x = x \log_{10} 1.02$$

Solve for $x$. Then, using the Table of Common Logarithms,

$$x = \frac{\log_{10} 2}{\log_{10} 1.02} = \frac{0.3010}{0.0086} = 35 \text{ quarters}$$

Thus, since interest is compounded quarterly, a principal invested at 8 percent compounded quarterly will double in $35/4 = 8.75$ years.

In early studies of logarithms, *common logarithms,* or logarithms employing the base 10, are used because they facilitate computation in a decimal system. For our purposes, however, we shall find *natural logarithms,* or logarithms to the base e, more appropriate. The *number e,* as we shall see in a later section, is an irrational number whose decimal expansion to five places is

$$e = 2.71828\ldots$$

The reason for the adjective "natural" is that many interesting applications require the use of this natural base e.

When the base e is used for the logarithm function, namely, $f(x) = \log_e x$, this is called the *natural logarithm* and is usually written without the base e as ln $x$.

When the natural base e is used in the exponential function, we obtain

$$f(x) = e^x$$

Since $e > 1$, this function is an increasing function.

A Partial Table of Values for $e^x$ is found on page 619.

The proportion of people responding to the advertisement of a new product after it has been on the market $t$ days is

$$1 - e^{-0.2t}$$

The marketing area contains 10,000,000 potential customers, and each response to the advertisement results in profit to the company of $0.70 (on the average). This profit is exclusive of advertising cost. The fixed cost of producing the advertising is $30,000 and the variable cost is $5000 for each day the advertisement runs.

(a) Find $\lim\limits_{t \to +\infty} (1 - e^{-0.2t})$ and interpret the answer.

(b) What percentage of customers respond after 10 days of advertising?

(c) What is the cost function $C(t)$?

(d) After 28 days of advertising, what is the net profit?

(a) Here

$$\lim_{t \to +\infty} (1 - e^{-0.2t}) = 1$$

The interpretation is that eventually everyone will respond to the advertisement.

(b) The proportion of customers that respond after 10 days is found by substituting $t = 10$ into the response function $1 - e^{-0.2t}$. Thus, for $t = 10$, we consult a Partial Table of Values for $e^x$, page 619, and find that

$$1 - e^{-2} = 1 - 0.135 = 0.865$$

Thus, 86.5 percent of the potential customers have responded after 10 days of advertising.

(c) The cost function is

$$C(t) = \$30{,}000 + \$5000t$$

(d) The net profit function is the profit from sales less advertising cost. The profit from sales is

$$R(t) = 10{,}000{,}000(1 - e^{-0.2t})(.70) = 7{,}000{,}000(1 - e^{-0.2t}).$$

Thus the net profit is

$$P(t) = R(t) - C(t) = \\ \$7{,}000{,}000(1 - e^{-0.2t}) - \$30{,}000 - \$5000t$$

For $t = 28$,

$$\begin{aligned} P(28) &= \$7{,}000{,}000(1 - e^{-5.6}) - \$30{,}000 - \$140{,}000 \\ &= \$7{,}000{,}000(0.9963) - \$170{,}000 \\ &= \$6{,}974{,}100 - \$170{,}000 \\ &= \$6{,}804{,}100 \end{aligned}$$

1. Graph these functions:

(a) $f(x) = \log_3 x$    (c) $f(x) = 5 + \ln x$

(b) $f(x) = \log_{1/3} x$    (d) $f(x) = \ln (x - 1)$

2. Find

(a) $\log_2 2$          (d) $\log_3 15 - \log_3 5$
(b) $\log_{10} 1$       (e) $\log_2 32$
(c) $\log_{10} 10^4$    (f) $\log_{1/2} 32$

3. Given that $\log_{10} 2 = 0.3010$, $\log_{10} 3 = 0.4771$, $\log_{10} 5 = 0.6990$, compute the quantities

(a) $\log_{10} 12$      (e) $\log_{10} 250$
(b) $\log_{10} 7.5$     (f) $\log_{10} 12.5$
(c) $\log_{10} 36$      (g) $\log_{10} 30$
(d) $\log_{10} (1/8)$   (h) $\log_{10} (1/2)$

4. How long will it take a principal to double at 16 percent compounded quarterly?

5. How long does it take for an investment to double at 12 percent compounded quarterly? How long will it take to triple at this rate?

6. If, in Example 3.2, page 316, the response function is

$$1 - e^{-0.1t}$$

and the other information remains the same, answer the questions (b) and (d).

7. If, in Example 3.2, page 316, the response function is

$$1 - e^{-0.05t}$$

the profit per response is $0.10, and all other data is the same, answer questions (b) and (d).

*8. If $f(x) = \log_a x$, show that

$$f(x + h) - f(x) = \log_a \left(1 + \frac{h}{x}\right)$$

---

10.4
THE DERIVATIVE
OF THE
EXPONENTIAL
AND LOGARITHM
FUNCTIONS

In the course of finding the derivative of the exponential and logarithm functions, the reader may find it necessary to refer to Chapter 8, where the derivative is first introduced. This review will, of course, serve to reinforce the important ideas of the calculus.

We begin by considering the exponential function

$$f(x) = a^x \qquad a > 0 \qquad a \neq 1$$

To find the derivative of $f(x) = a^x$, we use the alternate form for finding derivatives, introduced in Problem 11, Exercise 8.3, page 240.

$$f'(x) = \lim_{h \to 0} \frac{f(x + h) - f(x)}{h}$$

Thus for $f(x) = a^x$, we have

$$f'(x) = \frac{d}{dx} a^x = \lim_{h \to 0} \frac{a^{x+h} - a^x}{h} = \lim_{h \to 0} a^x \left[\frac{a^h - 1}{h}\right]$$

$$f'(x) = a^x \lim_{h \to 0} \frac{a^h - 1}{h}$$

**319**
10.4
THE DERIVATIVE
OF THE
EXPONENTIAL AND
LOGARITHM
FUNCTIONS

In particular, the derivative of $a^x$ at $x = 0$ is

$$f'(0) = \lim_{h \to 0} \frac{a^h - 1}{h}$$

since $a^0 = 1$.

The limit above is the slope of the tangent line of $f(x) = a^x$ at the point $(0, 1)$ and the value of this limit depends upon the choice of $a$. We observe in Figure 10.9 that the slope of the tangent line to $f(x) = 2^x$ at $(0, 1)$ is less than 1, and that the slope of the tangent line to $f(x) = 3^x$ at $(0, 1)$ is greater than 1. From this, we conjecture that there should be a value of $a$, $2 < a < 3$, for which the slope of the tangent line at $(0, 1)$ is exactly 1. This particular value of $a$ is the number $e = 2.71828 \ldots$, referred to earlier. Thus,

$$\lim_{h \to 0} \frac{e^h - 1}{h} = 1$$

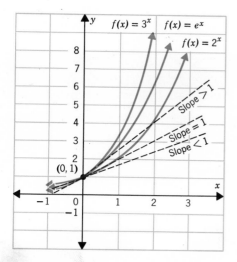

**Figure 10.9**

Using this result, we find that

$$\frac{d}{dx} e^x = \lim_{h \to 0} \frac{e^{x+h} - e^x}{h} = \lim_{h \to 0} \frac{e^x(e^h - 1)}{h} = e^x \lim_{h \to 0} \frac{e^h - 1}{h} = e^x \cdot 1 = e^x$$

Hence,

$$\frac{d}{dx} e^x = e^x$$

**The derivative of the exponential function $e^x$ is itself.**

Find the derivative of

$$f(x) = xe^x$$

Here we use the formula for the derivative of a product. Then

$$f'(x) = \frac{d}{dx} xe^x = x\frac{d}{dx} e^x + e^x \frac{d}{dx} x = xe^x + e^x \cdot 1 = e^x(x + 1)$$

In Section 8.6 of Chapter 8 (pp. 252–255), the notion of a composite function is introduced and the Power Rule is used to find the derivative of certain composite functions. We now take up the question of forming composite functions using the exponential function $e^x$ and the natural logarithm function $\ln x$.

For example, the composite function $y = e^{x^2+1}$ is composed of the two functions $y = e^{g(x)}$, $g(x) = x^2 + 1$. Other examples follow.

$$y = e^{x^3} \qquad \text{if} \quad y = e^{g(x)} \quad \text{and} \quad g(x) = x^3$$
$$y = \ln(x^2 + 2) \quad \text{if} \quad y = \ln g(x) \quad \text{and} \quad g(x) = x^2 + 2$$

**The formula for finding the derivative of a composite function** $y = e^{g(x)}$, **where** $g(x)$ **is a differentiable function, is**

$$\frac{d}{dx} e^{g(x)} = e^{g(x)}g'(x) \qquad\qquad (4.1)$$

Find the derivative of

$$f(x) = e^{x^2+1}$$

Using (4.1), where $g(x) = x^2 + 1$, we find

$$f'(x) = \frac{d}{dx} e^{x^2+1} = e^{x^2+1} \cdot 2x$$

For the situation described in Example 3.2, page 233, how many days should the advertisement run to maximize profits?

Profit is a maximum when marginal revenue equals marginal cost. From (c) and (d),

$$MR = \$7{,}000{,}000(0.2)e^{-0.2t}$$
$$MC = \$5000$$

Setting $MR = MC$, we have

$$\$5000 = \$1{,}400{,}000e^{-0.2t}$$
$$e^{0.2t} = 280$$

From the Partial Table of Values of $e^x$, page 619, we find that $e^{5.63} \approx 280$. Thus,

$$0.2t = 5.63$$

$$t = \frac{56.3}{2} = 28.2$$

**321**
10.4
THE DERIVATIVE
OF THE
EXPONENTIAL AND
LOGARITHM
FUNCTIONS

Thus, the company should advertise the product for approximately 28 days to maximize profit.

To find the derivative of ln $x$, we observe that, if $y = \ln x$, then $e^y = x$. That is,

$$e^{\ln x} = x$$

If we differentiate both sides with respect to $x$, we obtain from (4.1)

$$e^{\ln x} \frac{d}{dx} \ln x = 1$$

$$\frac{d}{dx} \ln x = \frac{1}{e^{\ln x}}$$

But $e^{\ln x} = x$. Thus,

$$\boxed{\frac{d}{dx} \ln x = \frac{1}{x}} \qquad (4.2)$$

Find the slope of the tangent line to $f(x) = \ln x$ at $(1,0)$. What is the equation of this tangent line? Sketch the graph.

4.4
Example

Using formula (4.2), the slope of the tangent line is

$$f'(1) = \frac{1}{1} = 1$$

Since $(1,0)$ is a point on this tangent line, its equation is

$$y - 0 = 1 \cdot (x - 1) \qquad \text{or} \qquad y = x - 1$$

See Figure 10.10.

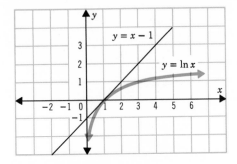

**Figure 10.10**

**4.5 Example**

Find the derivative of

$$f(x) = x \ln x$$

Here

$$f'(x) = \frac{d}{dx} x \ln x = x \frac{d}{dx} \ln x + \ln x \frac{d}{dx} x$$

$$= x \cdot \frac{1}{x} + \ln x \cdot 1 = \ln x + 1$$

The problem of determining the derivative of the logarithm function $\log_a x$ for any base $a$ is solved by using the Change of Base Formula. First, if $f(x) = \log_a x$, we change over to the natural base e. Then

$$f(x) = \log_a x = \frac{\log_e x}{\log_e a} = \frac{\ln x}{\ln a}$$

Since $\ln a$ is a constant, we have

$$f'(x) = \frac{d}{dx} \log_a x = \frac{1}{\ln a} \frac{d}{dx} \ln x = \frac{1}{\ln a} \frac{1}{x}$$

Thus,

$$\frac{d}{dx} \log_a x = \frac{1}{(\ln a) x} \qquad (4.3)$$

**4.6 Example**

Find the derivative of

$$f(x) = \log_2 x$$

Using (4.3) we have

$$f'(x) = \frac{d}{dx} \log_2 x = \frac{1}{(\ln 2) x}$$

Sometimes it becomes necessary to differentiate the natural logarithm of a composite function, such as $\ln g(x)$.

**The rule for finding the derivative of composite functions such as $f(x) = \ln g(x)$, where $g(x)$ is a differentiable function, is**

$$\frac{d}{dx} \ln g(x) = \frac{g'(x)}{g(x)} \qquad (4.4)$$

**4.7 Example**

Find the derivative of

$$f(x) = \ln (x^2 + 1)$$

Here $g(x) = x^2 + 1$ and

$$f'(x) = \frac{d}{dx} \ln (x^2 + 1) = \frac{1}{x^2 + 1} \frac{d}{dx} (x^2 + 1) = \frac{2x}{x^2 + 1}$$

**323**
10.4
THE DERIVATIVE
OF THE
EXPONENTIAL AND
LOGARITHM
FUNCTIONS

Finally, we have yet to find the derivative of $f(x) = a^x$, where $a > 0$, $a \neq 1$, is any real constant.

To solve this problem we use (4.4) and the Definition of a Logarithm. Then,

$$y = a^x$$

$$x = \log_a y = \frac{\ln y}{\ln a} = \frac{\ln a^x}{\ln a}$$

Differentiate with respect to $x$ and use (4.4), where $g(x) = a^x$. Then,

$$1 = \frac{1}{\ln a} \frac{d}{dx} \ln a^x = \frac{1}{\ln a} \cdot \frac{1}{a^x} \frac{d}{dx} a^x$$

Thus,

$$\frac{d}{dx} a^x = (\ln a) a^x \qquad (4.5)$$

Find the derivative of

$$f(x) = 2^x$$

4.8
Example

Here, using (4.5),

$$f'(x) = \frac{d}{dx} 2^x = (\ln 2) 2^x$$

Graph the function

$$f(x) = xe^{-x}$$

4.9
Example

The domain of this function is all real numbers and it is continuous on its domain.

Since $e^{-x}$ is always positive, the function is negative when $x < 0$ and is positive when $x > 0$. Also, $f(0) = 0$.

The first derivative is

$$f'(x) = x(-e^{-x}) + (1)e^{-x} = (1 - x)e^{-x}$$

Again, since $e^{-x}$ is always positive, $f'(x)$ has the same sign as $1 - x$. Hence we conclude that the function is decreasing for $x > 1$ and increasing for $x < 1$. Also, $x = 1$ is a critical value.

The second derivative is

$$f''(x) = \frac{d}{dx} f'(x) = (1 - x)(-e^{-x}) + (-1)(e^{-x})$$

$$= (x - 2)e^{-x}$$

This is clearly positive for $x > 2$ and negative for $x < 2$. Hence we conclude that the graph is concave up for $x > 2$ and concave down for $x < 2$. Since $f''(2) = 0$, the point $(2, .27)$ is an inflection point.

To locate the relative maxima and relative minima, we use the Second Derivative Test. Thus, at the critical value $x = 1$, the sign of the second derivative is negative so that the point $(1, f(1))$ is a relative maximum. The value of the function at $x = 1$ is $f(1) = e^{-1} = 0.368$.

Put all this information together and draw the graph. See Figure 10.11.

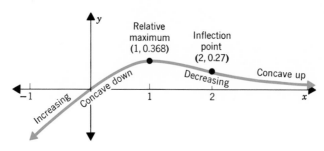

**Figure 10.11**

10.4
Exercise

1. Find the derivative of each of the following functions:

   (a) $f(x) = e^{x^2}$                    (e) $f(x) = \left(\dfrac{1}{3}\right)^x$

   (b) $f(x) = \ln x^2$                    (f) $f(x) = 2^{-x}$
   (c) $f(x) = e^{-x}$                     (g) $f(x) = \log_3 x$
   (d) $f(x) = e^x + \ln x$                (h) $f(x) = \log_{1/2} x$

2. Find the equation of the tangent line to each of the following functions at the point indicated:

   (a) $f(x) = x^3 e^x$ at $(0, 0)$      (c) $f(x) = \dfrac{1}{1 + e^x}$ at $(0, 1/2)$

   (b) $f(x) = x \ln x$ at $(1, 0)$      (d) $f(x) = \dfrac{x}{\ln x}$ at $(2, 2/\ln 2)$

3. Find the derivative of each of the following functions:
   (a) $f(x) = e^{x^4}$                   (d) $f(x) = \ln (2x^2 + 2x + 1)$
   (b) $f(x) = e^{\sqrt{x}}$              (e) $f(x) = e^{1/x}$
   (c) $f(x) = \ln (\ln x)$

4. Find the first, second and third derivatives of each of the following functions:
   (a) $f(x) = x^2 e^x$                   (c) $f(x) = e^{ax}$, a constant
   (b) $f(x) = \ln x$                     (d) $f(x) = x \ln x$

5. The cost (in dollars) of producing $x$ units (measured in thousands) of a certain product is found to be

$$C(x) = \$20 + \ln (x + 1)$$

Find the marginal cost.

6. The revenue (in dollars) derived from the sale of $x$ units (measured in thousands) of the product in Problem 5 is

$$R(x) = 0.1x$$

Find the number of units that will maximize profit.

7. Find the absolute maximum and the absolute minimum of the following functions.

(a) $f(x) = e^x$ $[-10, 10]$      (c) $f(x) = \dfrac{\ln x}{x}$ $[1, 3]$

(b) $f(x) = e^{-x}$ $[-10, 10]$      (d) $f(x) = xe^x$ $[0, 4]$

*8. Find the derivative of order $n$ of
(a) $f(x) = e^{ax}$, a constant
(b) $f(x) = \ln x$

*9. If $y = f(x) \cdot g(x)$, $\ln y = \ln f(x) + \ln g(x)$, then

$$\frac{1}{y}\frac{dy}{dx} = \frac{1}{f(x)}\frac{df(x)}{dx} + \frac{1}{g(x)}\frac{dg(x)}{dx}.$$

This is called *logarithmic differentiation*. Using this technique, find the derivative of each of the following functions.

Logarithmic Differentiation

(a) $y = (x^2 + 1)\sqrt{x + 2}$      (c) $y = \dfrac{\sqrt{x - 1}\, e^x}{x^2 + 1}$

(b) $y = (x^3 + 1)(x - 1)(x^4 + 1)$

*10. The function

$$f(x) = \frac{1}{\sqrt{2\pi}}\, e^{-x^2/2}$$

is often encountered in probability theory and is called the *normal density function*. Determine where this function is increasing and decreasing, find all relative maxima and relative minima, find all inflection points, and determine intervals of concavity. Graph the function.

Normal Density Function

11. Find the value of $x$ that maximizes the function

$$E(x) = 75{,}000\,(1 - 0.15^x) - 500x$$

We have seen that many models in business and economics require the use of an exponential function. Such curves we have termed *growth curves* or *decay curves* depending on whether they are increasing or decreasing functions.

For example, we used a growth curve to measure the increase in gross national product per unit time. We also observed that often the relationship between price and demand is a decay curve.

Such curves can be used to reflect accurately situations in which the values of the function increase without bound (or decrease to zero). Curves of this type, however, cannot be used if the growth (or decay), after a fast start, begins to level off, approaching a maximum value. For example, the value of a car depreciates very fast initially, but then levels off and, of course, can never depreciate more than its original cost. The demand for a new product, such as novelty toys (hula-hoops, big wheels, etc.) starts high, increases rapidly, and then levels off. See Example 2.5 on page 312. Curves of this kind are called *modified growth curves* and

**Modified Growth Curve**

their general equation is

$$f(x) = C(1 - b^{-ax})$$

where $a$ and $C$ are positive real numbers and $b > 1$ is a real number. Figure 10.12 illustrates a modified growth curve. Notice that the line $y = C$ is an asymptote and that it is approached but never reached.

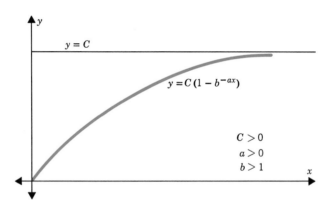

**Figure 10.12**

The modified growth curve, if used as a model for the growth in sales of a new product, may not accurately reflect the real situation. Sometimes the initial rate of growth is slow, and, as time progresses, the rate increases to a maximum value and then begins to decline. In other words, the modified growth curve may only be a good model for what happens at the end of the sales cycle. Curves that describe a situation in which the *rate* of growth is slow at first, increases to a maximum rate, and then

**Logistic Curve**

decreases are called *logistic curves* or *saturation curves*. These curves are best characterized by their "S" shape. Figure 10.13 illustrates a typical logistic curve.

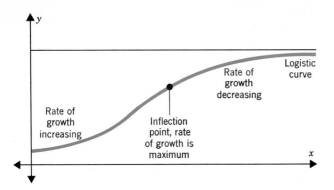

**Figure 10.13**

5.1
Example

The sales of a new line of color televisions over a period of time is expected to follow the relationship

$$f(x) = \frac{10{,}000}{1 + 100e^{-x}}$$

where $x$ is measured in years. Analyze the graph of this function, determine the year in which a maximum sales rate is achieved, and find the upper limit to sales in any year.

First, the domain of this function is $\{x \,|\, x \geq 0\}$ and the function is continuous on its domain. The $y$-intercept is

$$y = f(0) = \frac{10{,}000}{1 + 100} = 99.01$$

This represents the predicted number of sets sold when production commences.

Next, we investigate the behavior of the value of $f(x)$ as $x \to +\infty$.

$$\lim_{x \to +\infty} \frac{10{,}000}{1 + 100e^{-x}} = \frac{10{,}000}{1 + 100 \cdot 0} = 10{,}000$$

This number represents an upper estimate for sales.

The derivative of the function is

$$f'(x) = \frac{10{,}000}{(1 + 100e^{-x})^2} \, 100e^{-x} = \frac{1{,}000{,}000e^{-x}}{(1 + 100e^{-x})^2}$$

Clearly, $f'(x) > 0$ for $x \geq 0$. Thus the function is increasing, which means that sales are increasing each year.

The second derivative is

$$f''(x) = 1{,}000{,}000 \frac{d}{dx}[e^{-x}(1 + 100e^{-x})^{-2}]$$

$$= 1{,}000{,}000\,[-e^{-x}(1 + 100e^{-x})^{-2} + 2e^{-x}100e^{-x}(1 + 100e^{-x})^{-3}]$$

$$= 1{,}000{,}000\left[\frac{-e^{-x}(1 + 100e^{-x}) + 200e^{-2x}}{(1 + 100e^{-x})^3}\right]$$

$$= 1{,}000{,}000e^{-x}\left[\frac{100e^{-x} - 1}{(1 + 100e^{-x})^3}\right]$$

The inflection points, if there are any, obey

$$100e^{-x} - 1 = 0$$
$$e^x = 100$$
$$x = 4.6 \text{ (approximately)}$$

There is an inflection point at this value of $x$. Moreover, at $x = 4.6$, the first derivative $f'(x)$ achieves its maximum value. Thus, at 4.6 years, the rate of sales achieves its maximum. The graph is given in Figure 10.14. Observe that 10,000 sales is the most that can be achieved.

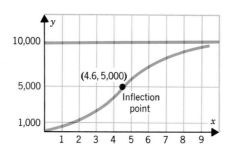

**Figure 10.14**

---

10.5
Exercise

1. Analyze and graph each of the following functions:

   (a) $f(x) = \dfrac{5000}{1 + 5e^{-x}}$

   (b) $f(x) = \dfrac{20,000}{1 + 50e^{-x}}$

2. In a town of 50,000 people, the number of people at time $t$ who have influenza is

$$N(t) = \frac{10,000}{1 + 9999e^{-t}}$$

   where $t$ is measured in days. Note that the flu is spread by the one person who has it at $t = 0$. At what time $t$ is the rate of spreading of flu the greatest? Graph the function.

*3. In general, a logistic curve is of the form

$$f(x) = \frac{M}{1 + ae^{-bx}}$$

   where $a > 0, M > 0, b > 0$ are real numbers. At what value of $x$ is the derivative $f'(x)$ a maximum?

1. Graph the functions:

   (a) $f(x) = \left(\dfrac{1}{3}\right)^x$

   (b) $f(x) = 100(1 - 1.03^x)$
2. How long will it take \$10,000 to double if it can be invested at 12 percent compounded monthly?
3. Find the derivative of each of the following functions:
   
   (a) $f(x) = e^{x^3}$        (d) $f(x) = x^2 \ln x$
   
   (b) $f(x) = 1/e^{-x}$       (e) $f(x) = \ln(x^3 - 3x + 4)$
   
   (c) $f(x) = \ln(1/x)$       (f) $f(x) = e^{x+2}$
4. Analyze and graph the function $f(x) = 2000/(1 + 4e^{-x})$
5. In a city of 50,000 people, the number of people at time $t$ who have heard a certain rumor obeys $N(t) = 50{,}000/(1 + 49{,}999e^{-t})$. At what time $t$ is the rate of spreading of the rumor greatest? Graph the function $N(t)$.
6. An advertising company conducts a special campaign to promote sales of a certain product. They estimate that the benefits of the campaign will result in extra sales and, when the campaign is over, the extra sales will obey a decay curve of the form

$$S = 4000e^{-0.3t}$$

where $S$ is the amount of extra sales and $t$ is the time in days after the advertising campaign is over. How many extra sales are obtained 10 days after the close of the advertising campaign? What is the rate of extra sales at $t = 10$? Graph the function and interpret it.

Bibliography

*Mathematics*

Chover, Joshua, *The Green Book of Calculus*, W. A. Benjamin, Menlo Park, Calif., 1972.

Leithold, Louis, *Calculus and Analytic Geometry*, Second Edition, Harper and Row, New York, 1972. Chapter 8.

Salas, Saturnino and Einar Hille, *Calculus: One and Several Variables*, Second Edition, Xerox, Lexington, Mass., 1974. Chapter 5.

*Applied*

Batschelet, E., *Introduction to Mathematics for Life Sciences,* Springer-Verlag, New York, 1972.

Chiang, Alpha, *Fundamental Methods of Mathematical Economics,* Second Edition, McGraw-Hill, New York, 1974.

Furguson, C. E., *Microeconomic Theory,* Third Edition, Irwin Press, Homewood, Ill., 1972.

Grossman, Stanley and James Turner, *Mathematics for the Biological Sciences,* Macmillan, New York, 1974.

Springer, C. H., R. E. Herlihy, and R. I. Beggs, *Advanced Methods and Models,* Mathematics for Management Series, Volume 2, Irwin Press, Homewood, Ill., 1965.

Thrall, Robert M., Ed., *Some Mathematical Models in Biology,* University of Michigan, Ann Arbor, 1967.

# 11

# THE INVERSE OF DIFFERENTIATION

With this chapter we begin our study of the integral calculus. The integral calculus may itself be subdivided into two parts: the *indefinite integral,* which is concerned with the inverse process of differentiation, (usually referred to as finding the antiderivative of a function); and the *definite integral,* which plays a major role in applications to geometry (finding area under a curve), to business and economics (marginal analysis, consumers' surplus, maximizing profit over time) and to probability.

In this chapter we concentrate on the techniques for finding anti-derivatives of functions and defining the indefinite integral. In Chapter 12 we define the definite integral and discuss various applications in geometry and business and economics. Applications of the definite integral to probability is deferred to Chapter 16.

We have already learned that to each differentiable function $f(x)$ there corresponds a derivative function $f'(x)$. It is also natural to ask the following question: If a function $f(x)$ is given, can we find a function $F(x)$ whose derivative is $f(x)$? That is, is it possible to find a function $F(x)$ so that $F'(x) = dF/dx = f(x)$? If such a function $F(x)$ can be found, it is called *an antiderivative* of $f(x)$.

For example, an antiderivative of $2x$ is $x^2$ since $\dfrac{d}{dx} x^2 = 2x$. Another function whose derivative is $2x$ is $x^2 + 3$ since $\dfrac{d}{dx}(x^2 + 3) = 2x$. This leads us to suspect that the function $f(x) = 2x$ has an unlimited number of antiderivatives. Indeed any of the functions

$$x^2, \quad x^2 + \frac{1}{2}, \quad x^2 + 2, \quad x^2 + \sqrt{5}, \quad x^2 - \pi, \quad x^2 - 1, \ldots, x^2 + K$$

where $K$ is any constant, has the property that its derivative is $2x$. We conjecture that all the antiderivatives of $2x$ are given by $x^2 + K$, where $K$ is any constant. This is plausible since we can think of no others. In fact, this conjecture is true, and we will accept it without proof.

Let

$$f(x) = x^5$$

Find all functions $F(x)$ such that

$$F'(x) = f(x) = x^5$$

That is, find all antiderivatives of $x^5$.

Clearly, all the functions whose derivative is $x^5$ are of the form

$$F(x) = \frac{x^6}{6} + K$$

where $K$ is any constant. This is so since

$$F'(x) = \frac{d}{dx}\left(\frac{x^6}{6} + K\right) = x^5.$$

**Definition
of
Antiderivative**

**A function $F(x)$ is called an *antiderivative* of the function $f(x)$ on the interval $I$ if and only if $F(x)$ is differentiable on $I$ and $F'(x) = f(x)$ for all $x \in I$. The interval $I$ may be open or closed or half-open.**

**In general, once an antiderivative $F(x)$ of $f(x)$ is found, all the antiderivatives of $f(x)$ are of the form**

$$F(x) + K$$

**where $K$ is a constant.**

See Problem 6 in Exercise 11.2, page 337, for an outline of the proof of this result.

If

$$f(x) = x^{1/2}$$

find all its antiderivatives.

Recall that the derivative of the function $\frac{2}{3}x^{3/2}$ is

$$\frac{2}{3} \cdot \frac{3}{2} x^{1/2} = x^{1/2}$$

Hence, all the antiderivatives of $f(x) = x^{1/2}$ are

$$F(x) = \frac{2}{3} x^{3/2} + K$$

where $K$ is any constant.

In the above example, you may ask how did we know to choose the function $\frac{2}{3}x^{3/2}$. The answer is in two parts. First, we know that

$$\frac{d}{dx} x^n = nx^{n-1}$$

That is, differentiation reduces the exponent by one. Antidifferentiation is the inverse process, so it should increase the exponent by one. This is how we obtained the $x^{3/2}$ part of $\frac{2}{3}x^{3/2}$. Second, the $\frac{2}{3}$ factor is needed so that when we differentiate $x^{3/2}$ we get $x^{1/2}$ and not $\frac{3}{2}x^{1/2}$.

Thus, because

$$\frac{d}{dx} x^{n+1} = (n + 1)x^n$$

for any real number $n$, it follows that

All the antiderivatives of $x^n$ are $\dfrac{x^{n+1}}{n + 1} + K$

for $n \neq -1$ and $K$ any constant. The case for which $n = -1$ is treated in Section 11.5.

If

$$f(x) = x^5 + x^{1/2}$$

find all its antiderivatives.

Since the derivative of a sum is the sum of its derivatives, we can find an antiderivative of $f(x)$ by first finding antiderivatives of $x^5$ and $x^{1/2}$, and then adding them. Thus from Examples 2.1 and 2.2, we see that

$$F(x) = \frac{x^6}{6} + \frac{2}{3}x^{3/2}$$

is an antiderivative of $f(x) = x^5 + x^{1/2}$. If we add a constant $K$ to $F(x)$, we get all the antiderivatives of $f(x)$; that is,

$$F(x) = \frac{x^6}{6} + \frac{2}{3}x^{3/2} + K$$

It should be noted that the presence of a constant $K$ in the antiderivative of a function offers us a great deal of flexibility, since the undetermined constant $K$ can assume any value that a particular practical situation demands.

For example, since the derivative of the cost of production is the marginal cost, the antiderivative of a marginal cost function gives the cost.

**2.4
Example**

By experimenting with various production techniques, a manufacturer finds that the marginal cost of production is given by the function

$$MC = 2x + 6$$

where $x$ is the number of units produced and $MC$ is the marginal cost in dollars. The fixed cost of production is known to be $9. Find the cost of production.

Here the derivative $\frac{d}{dx} C(x)$ of the cost of production is the marginal cost of production $MC$. That is,

$$\frac{d}{dx} C(x) = MC = 2x + 6$$

Thus,

$$C(x) = x^2 + 6x + K$$

where $K$ is a constant. We can find the value of the constant $K$ by observing that of all the cost functions whose derivative is $2x + 6$, only *one* has a fixed cost of production of $9. See Figure 11.1. This means that when $x = 0$ items are produced, the fixed cost will be $9. That is,

$$C(0) = (0)^2 + 6(0) + K = 9 \qquad \text{or} \qquad K = 9$$

Thus, the cost function is

$$C(x) = x^2 + 6x + 9$$

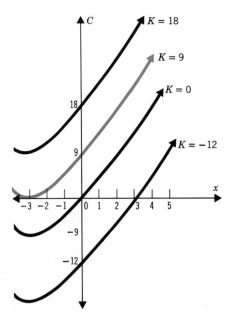

**Figure 11.1**

2.5
Example

Suppose the manufacturer in the previous example receives a per unit price of $60. This means the instantaneous rate of change of revenue with respect to quantity is the constant 60, that is,

$$MR = 60$$

(a) Find the revenue function $R(x)$.
(b) Find the profit function $P(x)$.
(c) Find the sales volume that yields maximum profit.
(d) What is the profit at this sales volume?

(a) First, recall that the derivative of the revenue function $R(x)$ equals marginal revenue. Thus,

$$\frac{d}{dx} R(x) = MR = 60$$

Hence,

$$R(x) = 60x + K$$

Now of all these revenue functions, only one fits the data: the one for which sales equal zero for $x = 0$ units sold. See Figure 11.2. Thus,

$$0 = 60(0) + K \text{ or } K = 0$$

This means the revenue function is

$$R(x) = 60x$$

(b) The profit function $P(x)$ is the difference between revenue and cost.

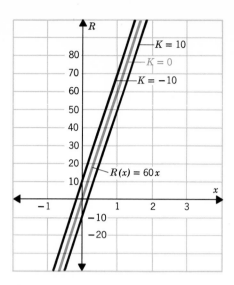

**Figure 11.2**

That is,

$$P(x) = R(x) - C(x)$$
$$= 60x - (x^2 + 6x + 9)$$
$$= -x^2 + 54x - 9$$

(c) The maximum profit is obtained when marginal revenue equals marginal cost.

$$MR = MC$$
$$60 = 2x + 6$$
$$2x = 54$$
$$x = 27$$

Thus, when sales total 27 units, a maximum profit is obtained.
(d) The profit for sales of 27 units is

$$P(27) = -27(27) + 54(27) - 9 = 720$$

The profit of $720 for sales totaling 27 units can also be found by differentiating the profit function $P(x)$ and finding those $x$ for which $P'(x) = 0$. To verify this,

$$P'(x) = -2x + 54 = 0$$
$$x = 27$$

---

**11.2
Exercise**

1. Find all antiderivatives of each of the following functions.
   (a) $4x^5$    (d) $5x^{3/2}$    (g) $2x^{-2}$
   (b) $x^{4/3}$    (e) $x^{5/2}$    (h) $3x^{-3}$
   (c) $\sqrt{x}$    (f) $1/\sqrt{x}$

2. Find all antiderivatives of each of the following functions.
   (a) $f(x) = 4x^3 - 3x^2 + 1$     (e) $f(x) = 0$
   (b) $f(x) = x^2 - \sqrt{x}$     (f) $f(x) = 2 - 3x + 4x^2$
   (c) $f(x) = 4x^{3/2} - 1$     (g) $f(x) = x^{28} + 1$
   (d) $f(x) = 3x - 1/x^2$
3. Find all the antiderivatives of $f(x) = 2x - 1$. Graph them for $K = -1$, $K = 0$, $K = 1$, $K = 5$.
4. The marginal cost of production is found to be

$$MC = 1000 - 20x + x^2$$

where $x$ is the number of units produced. The fixed cost of production is $9000. Find the cost function.
5. In Problem 4, the manufacturer fixes the price per unit at $3400.
   (a) Find the revenue function.
   (b) Find the profit function.
   (c) Find the sales volume that yields maximum profit.
   (d) What is the profit at this sales volume?
*6. If $F(x)$ is an antiderivative of $f(x)$, then any other antiderivative $G(x)$ of $f(x)$ is given by

$$G(x) = F(x) + K, \; K \text{ constant}$$

An outline of a proof follows: Since $F(x)$ and $G(x)$ are each an antiderivative of $f(x)$,

$$F'(x) = f(x) \quad \text{and} \quad G'(x) = f(x)$$

Thus,

$$G'(x) - F'(x) = 0 \quad \text{or} \quad \frac{d}{dx}[G(x) - F(x)] = 0$$

In Chapter 8, two notations are used to represent the derivative of a function $y = f(x)$: $f'(x)$ and $\frac{d}{dx} f(x)$. In this section, we introduce a symbol to represent all the antiderivatives of a function. In addition, we give some important properties of this concept.

**Let $F(x)$ be an antiderivative of the function $f(x)$. The** *indefinite integral* **of $f(x)$, denoted by $\int f(x)\, dx$, is**

**Indefinite Integral**

$$\int f(x)\, dx = F(x) + K$$

**where $K$ is an arbitrary constant.**
Thus, the indefinite integral of $f(x)$ is a symbol for all the antiderivatives of $f(x)$.

In the expression, $\int f(x)\, dx$, the symbol $\int$ is called an *integral sign* and indicates that the operation of antidifferentiation is to be performed on the function $f(x)$; the $dx$ reinforces the fact that the operation is to be performed with respect to the variable $x$. The function $f(x)$ is called the *integrand*.

**Integrand**

To summarize, the indefinite integral $\int f(x)\,dx$ is an instruction to find all the antiderivatives of the function $f(x)$, just as $\dfrac{d}{dx}\,f(x)$ is an instruction to differentiate $f(x)$ with respect to $x$.

Thus, for example,

$$\int x^2\,dx = \frac{x^3}{3} + K \qquad \int x^5\,dx = \frac{x^6}{6} + K$$

Based on the intimate relationship that exists between the process of differentiation and that of indefinite integration or antidifferentiation, we can construct a table of formulas or laws that gives the antiderivatives of several well-known functions. The letters $c$ and $n$ below will denote real constants.

| Function | Indefinite Integral |
|----------|---------------------|
| $f(x)$ | $\int f(x)\,dx$ |
| $c$ | $\int c\,dx = cx + K$ |
| $x^n$ | $\int x^n\,dx = \dfrac{x^{n+1}}{n+1} + K, \qquad n \neq -1$ |

In addition to the above formulas, the following properties of the indefinite integral are useful. These properties follow immediately from the differentiation formulas we studied previously.

**Theorem 3.1**
**Let $f(x)$ be a function that has an antiderivative. The indefinite integral of a constant $k$ times $f(x)$ equals $k$ times the indefinite integral of $f(x)$. In other words,**

$$\int kf(x)\,dx = k\int f(x)\,dx$$

Proof
Let $F(x)$ be an antiderivative of $f(x)$. Then,

$$\frac{d}{dx}\,[kF(x)] = k\frac{d}{dx}\,F(x) = kF'(x) = kf(x)$$

Hence $kF(x)$ is an antiderivative of $kf(x)$. Thus we may write

$$\int kf(x)\,dx = k\int f(x)\,dx$$

$$\int 3x^4 \, dx = 3 \int x^4 \, dx = 3 \cdot \frac{x^5}{5} + K = \frac{3x^5}{5} + K$$

**Theorem 3.2**
**Let $f(x)$ and $g(x)$ be functions that have antiderivatives. Then, the indefinite integral of their sum (or difference) equals the sum (or difference) of their indefinite integrals.**

$$\int [f(x) \pm g(x)] \, dx = \int f(x) \, dx \pm \int g(x) \, dx$$

Proof
Let $F(x)$ and $G(x)$ be antiderivatives of $f(x)$ and $g(x)$, respectively. Then,

$$\frac{d}{dx} [(F(x) \pm G(x)] = \frac{d}{dx} F(x) \pm \frac{d}{dx} G(x) = f(x) \pm g(x)$$

Hence,

$$\int [f(x) \, dx \pm g(x)] \, dx = \int f(x) \, dx \pm \int g(x) \, dx$$

Just as with derivatives of sums involving more than two functions, the above result can be extended to sums of three or more functions. The next example illustrates this.

Evaluate

$$\int \left( 7x^5 + \frac{1}{2} x^2 - x^{1/2} \right) dx$$

Using an extension of Theorem 3.2, we write

$$\int \left( 7x^5 + \frac{1}{2} x^2 - x^{1/2} \right) dx = \int 7x^5 \, dx + \int \frac{1}{2} x^2 \, dx - \int x^{1/2} \, dx$$

$$= 7 \int x^5 \, dx + \frac{1}{2} \int x^2 \, dx - \int x^{1/2} \, dx$$

$$= \frac{7x^6}{6} + \frac{1}{2} \frac{x^3}{3} - \frac{x^{3/2}}{3/2} + K$$

$$= \frac{7}{6} x^6 + \frac{1}{6} x^3 - \frac{2}{3} x^{3/2} + K$$

Evaluate

$$\int \frac{15 \, dx}{x^5}$$

The integral above can be written as

$$\int 15x^{-5}\, dx$$

Using a formula from Table 10.1 and Theorem 3.1 on page 338, we have

$$\int 15x^{-5}\, dx = 15 \int x^{-5}\, dx = \frac{15x^{-4}}{-4} + K = \frac{-15}{4x^4} + K$$

The above example illustrates that to find the indefinite integral often requires an algebraic manipulation that transforms the integrand to conform with established formulas.

---

**11.3
Exercise**

Evaluate the following indefinite integrals.

1. $\int 6\, dx$

2. $\int 3x\, dx$

3. $\int x^{-4}\, dx$

4. $\int (x^2 + 2)\, dx$

5. $\int (4x^3 + 3x^2 - 4)\, dx$

6. $\int (x^7 + 1)\, dx$

7. $\int (3\sqrt{x} + x)\, dx$

8. $\int \left( x - \frac{1}{x^2} \right) dx$

9. $\int (4x^{3/2} + x^{1/2})\, dx$

10. $\int x(x - 1)\, dx$

11. $\int \frac{3x^5 + 1}{x^2}\, dx$

12. $\int \frac{x^2 + 2x + 1}{x^4}\, dx$

13. $\int \frac{x^3 - 8}{x - 2}\, dx$

14. $\int \frac{x^2 - 4}{x + 2}\, dx$

15. Verify that

(a) $\int (x \cdot \sqrt{x})\, dx \neq \int x\, dx \cdot \int \sqrt{x}\, dx$

(b) $\int x(x^2 + 1)\, dx \neq x \int (x^2 + 1)\, dx$

(c) $\int \frac{x^2 - 1}{x - 1}\, dx \neq \dfrac{\int (x^2 - 1)\, dx}{\int (x - 1)\, dx}$

16. Given the marginal revenue function $MR = 50x - x^2$, where $x$ is the number of unit sales (in thousands), determine the revenue function and draw its graph. Find the maximum revenue.

17. Suppose that the marginal cost of a product is given by $x^3 - 4x^2 + 8x$ and the fixed cost is known to be 4. Find the cost function.

18. Find the cost function $C(x)$ and draw its graph if the marginal cost function is $MC = 14x - 280$, where $x$ is the number of units produced. Assume the cost is 4300 when the number of units produced is zero. Find the minimum cost.

19. Given $MR = 2 + 7x$, where $MR$ denotes marginal revenue, find the revenue function.

The Power Rule introduced in Chapter 8 is a strong tool for finding the derivative of some composite functions. For example, to find the derivative of $f(x) = (x^4 + 1)^8$, we use the Power Rule and obtain

$$f'(x) = 8 \cdot 4x^3(x^4 + 1)^7 \qquad (4.1)$$

The Power Rule is also advantageous for determining certain kinds of indefinite integrals. Compare the result found above with the problem of evaluating

$$\int (x^4 + 1)^7 \cdot 4x^3 \, dx$$

Integrating both sides of (4.1) we find that

$$\int f'(x) \, dx = \int 8 \cdot 4x^3(x^4 + 1)^7 \, dx = 8 \cdot \int (x^4 + 1)^7 \cdot 4x^3 \, dx$$

In other words, since $f(x) = (x^4 + 1)^8$ is an antiderivative of $f'(x)$,

$$\frac{(x^4 + 1)^8}{8} + K = \int (x^4 + 1)^7 \cdot 4x^3 \, dx$$

Evaluate

$$\int (x^4 + 1)^{700} 4x^3 \, dx$$

Once again, by the use of the Power Rule, we have

$$(x^4 + 1)^{700} 4x^3 = \frac{d}{dx} \frac{(x^4 + 1)^{701}}{701}$$

Thus, integrating both sides we get

$$\int (x^4 + 1)^{700} 4x^3 \, dx = \frac{(x^4 + 1)^{701}}{701} + K$$

A question many ask at this point is, where did the $4x^3$ go? The only answer is a reminder that integration is the inverse of differentiation and that

$$\frac{d}{dx} \frac{(x^4 + 1)^{701}}{701} = (x^4 + 1)^{700} 4x^3$$

Since $4x^3$ appears in the differentiation process, it must disappear in the integration process—wherever it comes from when we differentiate is where it must go when we integrate.

Let us investigate more carefully the procedure used above to evaluate the indefinite integral.

We notice that the integrand in Example 4.1 is of the form

$$[g(x)]^n g'(x)$$

where $g(x) = x^4 + 1$ and $n = 700$. But this integrand is the derivative of

$$\frac{[g(x)]^{n+1}}{n + 1}$$

since by the Power Rule

$$\frac{d}{dx} \frac{[g(x)]^{n+1}}{n + 1} = [g(x)]^n g'(x)$$

Hence, whenever the integrand consists of both a function $g(x)$ raised to any real number $n$ and its derivative $g'(x)$, we have

$$\int [g(x)]^n g'(x) \, dx = \frac{[g(x)]^{n+1}}{n + 1} + K, \quad n \neq -1 \qquad (4.2)$$

where $K$ is a constant.

Sometimes the above formula requires slight modification in order to be used. The next example illustrates this.

**4.2 Example**     Evaluate

$$\int (x^3 + 1)^4 x^2 \, dx$$

Here, if $g(x) = x^3 + 1$, then $g'(x) = 3x^2$. Thus, except for a multiple of three, the above formula applies. To remedy this, we use Theorem 3.1, page 338, and we write the problem as

$$\int (x^3 + 1)^4 x^2 \, dx = \frac{1}{3} \int (x^3 + 1)^4 \, 3x^2 \, dx$$

Now with $g(x) = x^3 + 1$ and $n = 4$, we have

$$\int (x^3 + 1)^4 x^2 \, dx = \frac{1}{3} \cdot \frac{(x^3 + 1)^5}{5} + K$$

The technique of integration by the Power Rule is summarized as follows:

**Determine whether the integrand is of the form $[g(x)]^n g'(x)$, except possibly for a constant factor. (There is no substitute for experience in making this determination.) If the answer is no, a technique other than the one described here must be used. If the answer is yes, apply (4.2).**

The next example illustrates a possible approach when the integrand is not of the required form.

Evaluate

$$\int (x^3 + 1)^2 \, dx$$

If we let $g(x) = x^3 + 1$, then $g'(x) = 3x^2$. But no $x^2$ term appears. Thus, the technique above cannot be used. Instead, we expand the integrand by actually squaring $x^3 + 1$. Then

$$\int (x^3 + 1)^2 \, dx = \int (x^6 + 2x^3 + 1) \, dx$$

$$= \int x^6 \, dx + \int 2x^3 \, dx + \int dx$$

$$= \frac{x^7}{7} + \frac{x^4}{2} + x + K$$

Evaluate

$$\int (x^3 + 1)^{-5/2} x^2 \, dx$$

Here $g(x) = x^3 + 1$, $g'(x) = 3x^2$. This is just like Example 4.2, page 342. Thus,

$$\int (x^3 + 1)^{-5/2} x^2 \, dx = \frac{1}{3} \int (x^3 + 1)^{-5/2} 3x^2 \, dx$$

$$= \frac{1}{3} \frac{(x^3 + 1)^{-3/2}}{-3/2} + K$$

$$= \frac{-2}{9} (x^3 + 1)^{-3/2} + K$$

1. Evaluate the following integrals.

(a) $\int (3x - 1)^3 \, dx$

(f) $\int \frac{(\sqrt{x} + 1)^5}{\sqrt{x}} \, dx$

(b) $\int (3x - 1)^{-3} \, dx$

(g) $\int \frac{(x^{1/3} - 1)^6}{x^{2/3}} \, dx$

(c) $\int (x^2 + 2)^6 4x \, dx$

(h) $\int (x^3 - x)(3x^2 - 1) \, dx$

(d) $\int (3x + 1)^{70} \, dx$

(i) $\int \frac{(x + 1) \, dx}{(x^2 + 2x + 3)^{1/4}}$

(e) $\int \frac{dx}{(3 + 5x)^2}$

2. Find a function $f(x)$ satisfying the conditions

$$f'(x) = 1/\sqrt{x + 1} \text{ with } f(0) = 1$$

3. Find a function $f(x)$ satisfying the conditions

$$f'(x) = x/\sqrt{3x^2 - 1}, \text{ with } f(1) = 1 + \sqrt{2/3}$$

4. If the marginal cost is known to be $x\sqrt{3x^2 + 1}$, find the cost function $C(x)$, if it is known that $C(0) = 20$.

5. The rate of increase of pollution in a certain lake is found to obey

$$A'(t) = \frac{3}{4} \frac{(t^{1/4} + 3)^2}{t^{3/4}}$$

where $t$ is measured in years and the amount $A(t)$ is measured in appropriate units of pollutant. If, at time $t = 0$, the amount of pollutant is 27 units, find the amount of pollutant after 16 years.

6. Use the Power Rule to verify the formula

$$\int (ax + b)^n \, dx = \frac{(ax + b)^{n+1}}{a(n + 1)} + K, \qquad a \neq 0, \qquad n \neq -1$$

**11.5**
**THE INDEFINITE**
**INTEGRAL OF**
**$e^x$ AND $1/x$**

Earlier, when we found the indefinite integral of the function $f(x) = x^n$, it was necessary to exclude the case where $n = -1$. (See page 338.) The purpose of this section is to determine $\int \frac{1}{x} \, dx$ and, in addition, to introduce the indefinite integral of $e^x$.

The first two results are an immediate consequence of the facts that

$$\frac{d}{dx} e^x = e^x \text{ and } \frac{d}{dx} \ln x = 1/x.$$

Then,

$$\int e^x \, dx = e^x + K$$

(5.1)

$$\int \frac{1}{x} \, dx = \ln |x| + K$$

where $K$ is a constant. We use $\ln |x|$ because the domain of the logarithm function is the set of positive real numbers.

The above two indefinite integrals can be used to find indefinite integrals such as

$$\int e^{2x+1} \, dx, \qquad \int e^{x^2} x \, dx, \qquad \int e^{-x} \, dx$$

$$\int \frac{x}{x^2 + 5} \, dx, \qquad \int \frac{dx}{3x + 1}$$

Although none of these are in the form (5.1), they can be reduced to this form.

First, we recall [see (4.1) on page 320] that, if $g(x)$ is a differentiable function,

$$\frac{d}{dx} e^{g(x)} = e^{g(x)}g'(x)$$

Hence, it follows that

$$\int e^{g(x)}g'(x)\, dx = e^{g(x)} + K \qquad (5.2)$$

where $K$ is a constant.

5.1
Example

Evaluate the indefinite integral

$$\int e^{2x+1}\, dx$$

Here $g(x) = 2x + 1$ and $g'(x) = .2$. As noted in Example 4.2 on page 342, we can insert a 2 in the integrand as follows:

$$\int e^{2x+1}\, dx = \frac{1}{2} \int e^{2x+1} \cdot 2\, dx$$

This is now of the form (5.2), so that

$$\int e^{2x+1}\, dx = \frac{1}{2} e^{2x+1} + K$$

The formula [see (4.4) on page 322] for the derivative of $\ln g(x)$, where $g(x)$ is a differentiable function, provides an additional method for computing certain indefinite integrals. Because

$$\frac{d}{dx} \ln g(x) = \frac{g'(x)}{g(x)}$$

it follows, by taking the antiderivative of both sides, that

$$\int \frac{d}{dx} \ln g(x)\, dx = \int \frac{g'(x)}{g(x)}\, dx$$

or

$$\int \frac{g'(x)}{g(x)}\, dx = \ln |g(x)| + K$$

**Thus, whenever an integrand is a ratio in which the numerator is the derivative of the denominator, the antiderivative is the natural logarithm of the absolute value of the denominator.**

Evaluate

$$\int \frac{x\,dx}{x^2 + 5}$$

We recognize that, except for a factor of two, the numerator is the derivative of the denominator. Thus

$$\int \frac{x\,dx}{x^2 + 5} = \frac{1}{2}\int \frac{2x\,dx}{x^2 + 5} = \frac{1}{2}\ln|x^2 + 5| + K$$

Evaluate

$$\int \left( xe^{x^2} + \frac{1}{3x + 1} \right) dx$$

Here

$$\int \left( xe^{x^2} + \frac{1}{3x + 1} \right) dx = \int xe^{x^2}\,dx + \int \frac{dx}{3x + 1}$$

$$= \frac{1}{2}\int 2xe^{x^2}\,dx + \frac{1}{3}\int \frac{3\,dx}{3x + 1}$$

$$= \frac{1}{2} e^{x^2} + \frac{1}{3}\ln|3x + 1| + K$$

Evaluate each of the following indefinite integrals.

1. $\displaystyle\int \frac{dx}{x + 1}$

2. $\displaystyle\int \frac{dx}{3x - 5}$

3. $\displaystyle\int \frac{x + 1}{x^2 + 2x + 2}\,dx$

4. $\displaystyle\int \frac{x\,dx}{x^2 + 4}$

5. $\displaystyle\int e^{-x}\,dx$

6. $\displaystyle\int x^2 e^{x^3 + 1}\,dx$

7. $\displaystyle\int \frac{e^x}{e^x + 1}\,dx$

8. $\displaystyle\int (e^x + e^{-x})\,dx$

9. $\displaystyle\int \frac{1}{e^x}\,dx$

10. $\displaystyle\int \frac{1}{x\ln x}\,dx$

11. $\displaystyle\int \frac{e^{\sqrt{x}}}{\sqrt{x}}\,dx$

In this section, we discuss another technique for evaluating indefinite integrals, so that we can handle problems like

$$\int xe^x\,dx, \qquad \int \ln x\,dx, \qquad \int x\ln x\,dx$$

This method, referred to as *integration by parts,* is based on the Product Rule for differentiation and is an effective and versatile technique for integration.

Recall that if $u$ and $v$ are differentiable functions of $x$, then

$$\frac{d}{dx}(u \cdot v) = \frac{du}{dx} \cdot v + u \cdot \frac{dv}{dx}$$

Integrating both sides we get

$$u \cdot v = \int v \cdot \frac{du}{dx} \cdot dx + \int u \frac{dv}{dx} \cdot dx$$

Or

$$\int u \cdot \frac{dv}{dx} \cdot dx = uv - \int v \frac{du}{dx} dx$$

In abbreviated notation this is

$$\int u\, dv = u \cdot v - \int v\, du$$

Integration by
Parts
Formula

Let us see how to use this formula with some specific integrals.

Evaluate

6.1
Example

$$\int xe^x\, dx$$

Let

$$u = x \quad \text{and} \quad dv = e^x\, dx$$

Then

$$du = dx \quad \text{and} \quad v = e^x$$

so

$$\int u\, dv = u \cdot v - \int v\, du = xe^x - \int e^x\, dx$$
$$= xe^x - e^x + K$$

Had we made the choice of

$$u = e^x \quad \text{and} \quad dv = x\, dx$$

we would find that

$$du = e^x\, dx \quad \text{and} \quad v = \frac{x^2}{2}$$

Then

$$\int xe^x\, dx = \frac{x^2}{2} e^x - \int \frac{x^2 e^x}{2}\, dx$$

Thus, instead of simplifying the integral, we obtain a more complicated one.

How then does one know which factor to call $u$ and which $dv$? It is largely done by trial and error, but the following guide will be helpful in most cases: **Let $dv$ be the most complicated part of the expression that can be easily integrated.**

Evaluate

$$\int x \ln x \, dx$$

Here $\ln x$ is the more "complicated" of the two factors, but it is *not* easily integrated. Since $x$ is the next complicated part that can be integrated easily, let

$$u = \ln x \qquad dv = x \, dx$$

$$du = \frac{1}{x} dx \qquad v = \frac{x^2}{2}$$

Then

$$\int x \ln x \, dx = \frac{x^2}{2} \ln x - \int \frac{x^2}{2} \cdot \frac{1}{x} \, dx$$

$$= \frac{x^2}{2} \ln x - \frac{x^2}{4} + K$$

$$= \frac{x^2}{2} \left[ \ln x - \frac{1}{2} \right] + K$$

Sometimes it is necessary to integrate by parts more than once to solve a particular problem. The next example is a case in point.

Evaluate

$$\int x^2 e^x \, dx$$

Let

$$u = x^2 \qquad \text{and} \qquad dv = e^x \, dx$$

Then

$$du = 2x \, dx \qquad \text{and} \qquad v = e^x$$

and

$$\int x^2 e^x \, dx = x^2 e^x - \int 2x e^x \, dx$$

We must still evaluate $\int x e^x \, dx$. In Example 6.1, page 347, we found (by using the integration by parts technique) that

$$\int x e^x \, dx = x e^x - e^x + K$$

Thus,

$$\int x^2 e^x \, dx = x^2 e^x - 2[x e^x - e^x] + K = x^2 e^x - 2x e^x + 2e^x + K$$

Find all the antiderivatives of ln x.

To find all the antiderivatives of ln $x$, we use the by-parts formula. Taking $u = \ln x$, $dv = dx$, we find

$$\int \ln x \, dx = x \ln x - \int x \cdot \frac{1}{x} \, dx = x \ln x - x + K$$

or

$$\int \ln x \, dx = x(\ln x - 1) + K$$

The integration by parts formula is useful for the evaluation of indefinite integrals whose integrand is composed of $e^x$ times a polynomial function of x or ln x times a polynomial function of x. It can also be used for other types of indefinite integrals, which we shall not require for subsequent applications and so shall not discuss.

With the method of integration by parts, we end our discussion of techniques for evaluating indefinite integrals. Although many other techniques exist, to introduce them here would require a much more lengthy discussion than space permits. See the Bibliography for textbooks containing such topics.

At this point the student may well be under the impression that it is possible to find an antiderivative of *any* function. This is not true. In fact, there are many functions, such as $e^{x^2}$, that possess no antiderivative.

In Problems 1–6, evaluate the following integrals by using the integration by parts formula.

1. $\int xe^{2x} \, dx$

2. $\int \sqrt{x} \ln x \, dx$

3. $\int (\ln x)^2 \, dx$

4. $\int xe^{-3x} \, dx$

5. $\int x(\ln x)^2 \, dx$

6. $\int x^2 e^{-x} \, dx$

7. Find the function $f(x)$ satisfying the conditions $f'(x) = xe^{-x}$, with $f(0) = 6$.

8. If the marginal revenue is $x^2 \ln x$, find the revenue function $R(x)$, if it is known that $R(1) = 6$.

antiderivative
indefinite integral
integrand

integration by the Power Rule
integration by parts

1. Find all antiderivatives of each of the following functions.

(a) $f(x) = x^{1/3} - \sqrt{x}$    (d) $f(x) = x^2 + 1/x$

(b) $f(x) = 3 + e^{-x}$    (e) $f(x) = x\sqrt{x^2 - 1}$

(c) $f(x) = \dfrac{1}{(1 + x)^{1/2}}$    (f) $f(x) = \dfrac{2x^2}{\sqrt{x^3 - 2}}$

2. Find all the antiderivatives of $f(x) = 4x + 1$. Graph them for $K = -2, K = 0, K = 4$.

3. Evaluate

(a) $\displaystyle\int x^2(x - 1)\, dx$    (d) $\displaystyle\int (x^2 + 2x - 3)\, dx$

(b) $\displaystyle\int \sqrt{3x - 2}\, dx$    (e) $\displaystyle\int (x + 1)^3\, dx$

(c) $\displaystyle\int (x^4 + 1)^{-3/2} x^3\, dx$    (f) $\displaystyle\int (x^2 - 1)^{3/2} x\, dx$

4. Find a function $f(x)$ satisfying the conditions $f'(x) = 1/\sqrt{x}$ with $f(1) = 1$.

5. The marginal revenue of a company is found to be

$$MR = 64x - x^2$$

where $x$ is the number (in thousands) of units sold. Find the revenue function and determine the number of sales that maximizes revenue.

6. Evaluate each of the following integrals

(a) $\displaystyle\int \dfrac{dx}{3x + 2}$    (d) $\displaystyle\int e^{-\frac{1}{2}x}\, dx$

(b) $\displaystyle\int x^3 e^{3x^4}\, dx$    (e) $\displaystyle\int \dfrac{x^{3/2}\, dx}{x^{5/2} + 2}$

(c) $\displaystyle\int xe^{-\frac{1}{2}x}\, dx$    (f) $\displaystyle\int x^2 \ln x\, dx$

## Bibliography

*Mathematics*

Leithold, Louis, *Calculus and Analytic Geometry*, Second Edition, Harper and Row, New York, 1972. Chapter 5.

Salas, Saturnino and Einar Hille, *Calculus: One and Several Variables*, Second Edition, Xerox, Lexington, Mass., 1974. Chapter 4.

# 12

# THE DEFINITE INTEGRAL AND APPLICATIONS

In this chapter we define the definite integral and apply it to two fields: one in geometry and the other in business. The geometric application is to find the area under a curve $y = f(x)$; the business applications are the learning curve, consumer's surplus, and maximizing profit over time.

We now come to the second fundamental notion of the integral calculus: *the definite integral*. The purpose of this section is to give an intuitive approach to this concept[1].

[1] Another approach to the definite integral, Riemann sums, is presented in Appendix II, page 581.

**Let $f(x)$ be a continuous function defined on an interval $I$ and let $F(x)$ be an antiderivative of $f(x)$. For $a, b \in I$ the value**

$$F(b) - F(a)$$

**is called the** *definite integral from $a$ to $b$ of $f(x)$.*

For example the definite integral from 2 to 3 of $f(x) = x^2$ is computed by first finding an antiderivative of $f(x)$. One such antiderivative is $F(x) = x^3/3$. Thus,

definite integral from 2 to 3 of $x^2$ is $F(3) - F(2) = 27/3 - 8/3 = 19/3$.

We will use the notation

$$\int_a^b f(x)\, dx$$

to represent the definite integral from $a$ to $b$ of $f(x)$. In the example above,

$$\int_2^3 x^2\, dx = \frac{19}{3}$$

In $\int_a^b f(x)\, dx$ the numbers $a$ and $b$ are termed the *lower* and *upper*

*limits of integration,* respectively. Also, if $F(x)$ is an antiderivative of $f(x)$, we sometimes write

$$\int_a^b f(x)\, dx = F(x)\, \Big|_a^b = F(b) - F(a)$$

In computing $\int_a^b f(x)\, dx$, we find that the choice of an antiderivative of $f(x)$ does not matter. Indeed, if $F(x)$ is an antiderivative of $f(x)$ and $G(x)$ is any other antiderivative, then by Problem 6 of Exercise 11.2, (page 337),

$$G(x) = F(x) + K$$

where $K$ is a constant. Hence,

$$\int_a^b f(x)\, dx = F(b) - F(a) = [F(b) + K] - [F(a) + K]$$

$$= G(b) - G(a)$$

**Thus, any antiderivative of $f(x)$ can be used to evaluate $\int_a^b f(x)\, dx$.**

Evaluate

$$\int_1^2 x^3 \, dx$$

Since $x^4/4$ is an antiderivative of $x^3$, we get

$$\int_1^2 x^3 \, dx = \frac{x^4}{4} \bigg|_1^2 = \frac{(2)^4}{4} - \frac{(1)^4}{4}$$

$$= 4 - \frac{1}{4} = \frac{15}{4}$$

It is important to distinguish between the indefinite integral and the definite integral. The indefinite integral is a symbol for all the antiderivatives of a function; each antiderivative is, of course, a function. The definite integral, on the other hand, is a number.

Evaluate

$$\int_1^4 \sqrt{x} \, dx$$

Since $2/3x^{3/2}$ is an antiderivative of $\sqrt{x}$, we get

$$\int_1^4 \sqrt{x} \, dx = \frac{2}{3} x^{3/2} \bigg|_1^4 = \frac{2}{3} (4)^{3/2} - \frac{2}{3} (1)^{3/2}$$

$$= \frac{16}{3} - \frac{2}{3} = \frac{14}{3}$$

We list below some properties of definite integrals.

(I) If $f(x)$ is continuous on the interval $[a, b]$ and has an antiderivative on $[a, b]$, then

$$(a) \int_a^b f(x) \, dx = -\int_b^a f(x) \, dx$$

$$(b) \int_a^a f(x) \, dx = 0$$

For example,

$$\int_4^1 \sqrt{x} \, dx = -\int_1^4 \sqrt{x} \, dx = -\frac{14}{3} \qquad \text{and} \qquad \int_1^1 x \, dx = 0$$

The results cited above in (I) are an immediate consequence of the Fundamental Property of Integral Calculus. Specifically, if $F(x)$

is an antiderivative of $f(x)$, then

(a) $\displaystyle\int_a^b f(x)\, dx = F(b) - F(a) = -[F(a) - F(b)] = -\int_b^a f(x)\, dx$

(b) $\displaystyle\int_a^a f(x)\, dx = F(a) - F(a) = 0$

(II) If $f(x)$ is continuous and has an antiderivative on the interval $[a, b]$, and if $c$ is between $a$ and $b$, then

$$\int_a^b f(x)\, dx = \int_a^c f(x)\, dx + \int_c^b f(x)\, dx$$

A use of property II will be discussed later in the chapter.

(III) If $f(x)$ is continuous and has an antiderivative on the interval $[a, b]$ and $k$ is a constant, then

$$\int_a^b kf(x)\, dx = k\int_a^b f(x)\, dx$$

For example,

$$\int_1^2 16x^2\, dx = 16\int_1^2 x^2\, dx = 16\left[\frac{x^3}{3}\,\Big|_1^2\right] = 16\left[\frac{8}{3} - \frac{1}{3}\right] = 16\cdot\frac{7}{3} = \frac{112}{3}$$

(IV) If $f(x)$ and $g(x)$ are continuous and have antiderivatives on the interval $[a, b]$, then

$$\int_a^b [f(x) \pm g(x)]\, dx = \int_a^b f(x)\, dx \pm \int_a^b g(x)\, dx$$

For example,

$$\int_1^2 (x^2 + \sqrt{x})\, dx = \int_1^2 x^2\, dx + \int_1^2 \sqrt{x}\, dx = \frac{x^3}{3}\,\Big|_1^2 + \frac{2}{3}x^{3/2}\,\Big|_1^2$$

$$= \frac{7}{3} + \frac{2}{3}(2\sqrt{2} - 1) = \frac{4\sqrt{2}}{3} + \frac{5}{3}$$

2.3
Example

Evaluate

$$\int_1^2 3x(x^2 - 1)\, dx$$

Here

$$\int_1^2 3x(x^2 - 1)\, dx = \int_1^2 (3x^3 - 3x)\, dx = \int_1^2 3x^3\, dx - \int_1^2 3x\, dx$$

$$= 3\int_1^2 x^3\, dx - 3\int_1^2 x\, dx = 3\left[\frac{x^4}{4}\Big|_1^2\right] - 3\left[\frac{x^2}{2}\Big|_1^2\right]$$

$$= 3\left[4 - \frac{1}{4}\right] - 3\left[2 - \frac{1}{2}\right] = 3\left(\frac{15}{4}\right) - 3\left(\frac{3}{2}\right) = \frac{27}{4}$$

Of importance in business is the determination of the variable cost of producing a consecutive number of units. The cost can be computed once the marginal cost *MC* is known as a function *MC(x)* of the quantity *x* of units produced. In this case the *variable cost of producing the ath unit through the bth unit* is given by the formula

Variable
Cost

$$VC = \int_{a-1}^b MC(x)\, dx$$

The next example illustrates a use of this formula.

The marginal cost for a certain commodity is

2.4
Example

$$MC(x) = 2x^2 - 3x + 2$$

Determine the variable cost of producing 12 through 16 units.
   Here $a - 1 = 12 - 1 = 11$, $b = 16$, and

$$VC = \int_{11}^{16} (2x^2 - 3x + 2)\, dx = \left[2\frac{x^3}{3} - \frac{3x^2}{2} + 2x\right]\Big|_{11}^{16}$$

$$= [2730.67 - 384 + 32] - [887.33 - 181.5 + 22] = \$1650.84$$

Thus, the variable cost of producing twelve through sixteen units is $1650.84.

1. Evaluate the following definite integrals.

12.2
Exercise

(a) $\int_0^3 x^2\, dx$      (e) $\int_{-1}^3 (x^3 - 2)\, dx$

(b) $\int_{-1}^{-1} 2x^2\, dx$      (f) $\int_1^5 5\, dx$

(c) $\int_1^3 4t^3\, dt$      (g) $\int_2^3 (2x^2 - x + 1)\, dx$

(d) $\int_3^2 (x + 1)\, dx$      (h) $\int_2^3 \frac{dx}{x^2}$

2. Evaluate each of the following definite integrals

(a) $\int_0^1 e^{-x}\, dx$    (d) $\int_0^1 x^2 e^{x^3}\, dx$

(b) $\int_1^3 \dfrac{dx}{x+1}$    (e) $\int_{-2}^2 e^{\frac{-7}{2}x}\, dx$

(c) $\int_0^1 \dfrac{\sqrt{x}}{x^{3/2}+1}\, dx$    (f) $\int_2^3 \dfrac{dx}{x \ln x}$

3. Evaluate the following definite integrals.

(a) $\int_1^3 x e^{2x}\, dx$    (d) $\int_0^4 (1 + xe^{-x})\, dx$

(b) $\int_1^2 x e^{-3x}\, dx$    (e) $\int_1^3 x^2 \ln x\, dx$

(c) $\int_1^5 \ln x\, dx$    (f) $\int_1^2 x \ln x\, dx$

4. The marginal cost for a certain commodity is

$$MC(x) = 3x^2 - 2x + 4$$

Determine the variable cost of producing 5 to 10 units.

Even
Function

5. A continuous function $f(x)$ is said to be an *even function* if $f(-x) = f(x)$. It can be shown that, if $f(x)$ is an even function, then

$$\int_{-a}^a f(x)\, dx = 2 \int_0^a f(x)\, dx, \qquad a > 0$$

Verify the above formula by evaluating the following definite integrals.

(a) $\int_{-1}^1 x^2\, dx$    (b) $\int_{-1}^1 (x^4 + x^2)\, dx$

Odd
Function

6. A continuous function $f(x)$ is said to be an *odd function* if $f(-x) = -f(x)$. It can be shown that, if $f(x)$ is an odd function, then

$$\int_{-a}^a f(x)\, dx = 0, \qquad a > 0$$

Verify the above formula by evaluating the following definite integrals.

(a) $\int_{-1}^1 x\, dx$    (b) $\int_{-1}^1 x^3\, dx$

In this section, we illustrate how the antiderivative, definite integral, and area under a curve are related to each other. What is area? In plane geometry, we learn how to find the area of certain geometric figures, such as squares, rectangles, and circles. For example, the area of a square with a side of length 3 feet is 9 square feet. The reason is that the square can be subdivided into 9 smaller squares, each having side length one.

We also learn that the area of a rectangle, with length $a$ units and with width $b$ units, is $a \cdot b$ square units.

All area problems (whether it is of finding the area of a square, or rectangle, or circle, or trapezoid) have certain features in common. For example, whenever the area of an object is computed, it is expressed as a number of square units; this number is never negative. *Thus one property of area is that it is non-negative.*

Consider the trapezoid given in Figure 12.1. This trapezoid has been decomposed into two nonoverlapping geometric figures, a triangle (whose area is $A_1$) and a rectangle (whose area is $A_2$). Clearly the area of the trapezoid is the sum $A_1 + A_2$ of the two component areas. Thus, as long as two regions do not overlap (except perhaps for a common boundary), the total area can be found by adding the component areas. We sometimes call this the *additive property of area.*

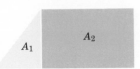

**Figure 12.1**

**Thus, to summarize, two properties of area are:**

**(I)** Area $\geq 0$.
**(II) If $A$ and $B$ are two nonoverlapping regions whose areas are known, then**

**total area of $A$ and $B$** = Area of $A$ + Area of $B$

The above two properties enable us to compute the area of polygons and, in fact, any region bounded by straight lines. However, we still are not able to calculate the area of a region bounded by an arbitrary curve. For example, the problem of determining the area "under the curve" $f(x) = x^2$ from $x = 0$ to $x = 1$, that is, the area of the region bounded by $f(x) = x^2$, the $x$-axis and the vertical line $x = 1$, cannot be solved using the methods of plane geometry. See Figure 12.2.

The next result gives a technique for evaluating areas like the one in Figure 12.2.

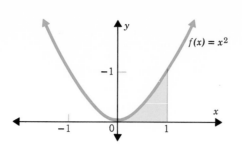

**Figure 12.2**

### Theorem 3.1

**Suppose** $y = f(x)$ **is a continuous function defined on an open interval** $I$ **and** $f(x) \geq 0$ **for all points** $x$ **in** $I$**. Then for** $a, b \in I$**, the definite integral**

$$\int_a^b f(x)\, dx$$

**is the area under the graph of** $y = f(x)$ **and above the** $x$**-axis between the lines** $x = a$ **and** $x = b$**.**

Figure 12.3 illustrates the statement of Theorem 3.1.

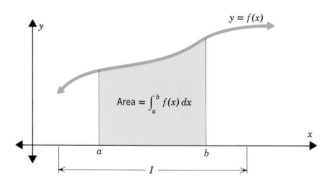

**Figure 12.3**

A plausible argument for Theorem 3.1 is given below; it relies heavily on geometric intuition.

Choose a point $x_0 \in I$ so that $x_0 < a$. Suppose $x \in I$ is an arbitrary point for which $x > x_0$. Let $A(x)$ denote the area bounded by $y = f(x)$ and the $x$-axis from $x_0$ to $x$. See Figure 12.4. We want to show that $A'(x) = f(x)$ for all $x \in I$, $x > x_0$.

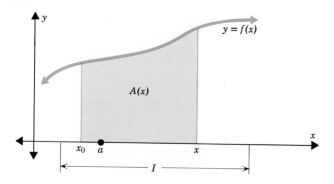

**Figure 12.4**

Choose $h > 0$ so that $x + h \in I$. Then $A(x + h)$ is the area bounded by $y = f(x)$ and the $x$-axis from $x_0$ to $x + h$. See Figure 12.5.

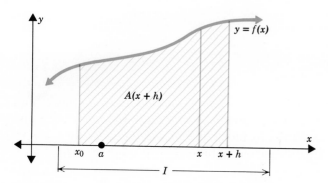

**Figure 12.5**

The difference $A(x + h) - A(x)$ is just the area bounded by $y = f(x)$ and the $x$-axis from $x$ to $x + h$. See Figure 12.6.

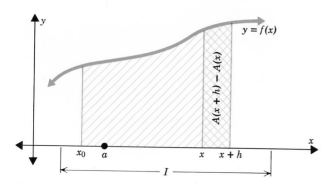

**Figure 12.6**

Construct a rectangle with base equal to $h$ and area equal to $A(x + h) - A(x)$. The height of the rectangle is then

$$\frac{A(x + h) - A(x)}{h}$$

since the above represents the area of the rectangle divided by its base $h$.

Next, superimpose this rectangle on Figure 12.6 to obtain Figure 12.7.

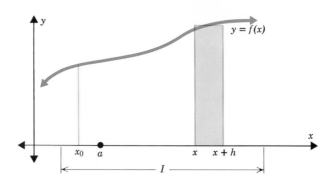

**Figure 12.7**

Since $y = f(x)$ is assumed to be a continuous function, and since both the rectangle and the shaded area have the same base and the same area, the upper edge of the rectangle must cross the graph of $y = f(x)$.

As we let $h \to 0^+$, the height of the rectangle tends to $f(x)$; that is,

$$\frac{A(x + h) - A(x)}{h} \to f(x) \quad \text{as} \quad h \to 0^+$$

A similar argument applies if we choose $h < 0$. Thus,

$$\lim_{h \to 0} \frac{A(x + h) - A(x)}{h} = f(x)$$

or

$$A'(x) = f(x)$$

Since the choice of $x$ is arbitrary (except for the condition that $x > x_0$), it follows that

$$A'(x) = f(x) \quad \text{for all } x \in I, x > x_0$$

In other words, we have shown that the area $A(x)$ is an antiderivative of $f(x)$ on $I$. Hence,

$$\int_a^b f(x) \, dx = A(x) \Big|_a^b = A(b) - A(a)$$

But the area we seek to find is the one bounded by $y = f(x)$ and the $x$-axis from $a$ to $b$. Since $a$ and $b$ are in $I$, this is merely the quantity $A(b) - A(a)$. See Figure 12.8.

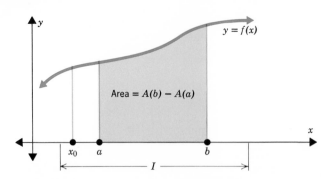

**Figure 12.8**

Hence,

Area bounded by $y = f(x)$ and x-axis from a to b $= \int_a^b f(x)\, dx$

The significance of this result is that it enables us to find the area under a curve $y = f(x)$, provided three conditions are met: $f$ must be continuous; $f$ must be non-negative; and $f$ must have an antiderivative on $[a, b]$. If all three conditions hold, then

area bounded by $y = f(x)$, the x-axis, $x = a$, $x = b$ is $\int_a^b f(x)\, dx$

$$(2.1)$$

We return now to solve the area problem, cited on page 357.

Find the area of the region bounded by $f(x) = x^2$, the x-axis, $x = 0$, and $x = 1$.

**3.1 Example**

Since the conditions of (2.1) are met, the area is given by the definite integral:

$$\int_0^1 x^2\, dx = \frac{x^3}{3}\bigg|_0^1 = \frac{1}{3}$$

Thus the area illustrated in Figure 12.2, page 358, is 1/3 square units.

A drawback to this result is the condition that the function must be non-negative on $I$. Suppose a function is continuous on the interval $I$: $a \leq x \leq b$ and has an antiderivative on $I$, but is negative for $a \leq x \leq c$ and is positive for $c \leq x \leq b$. How, in this situation, do we compute the area bounded by $y = f(x)$, the x-axis, $x = a$ and $x = b$? See Figure 12.9.

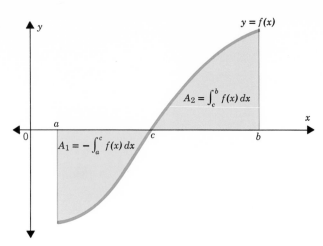

**Figure 12.9**

We notice in Figure 12.9, that the area $A$ in question is composed of two nonoverlapping areas $A_1$ and $A_2$, so that, by the additive property of area,

$$A = A_1 + A_2$$

We further know that on the interval $[c, b]$, the function is nonnegative so that

$$A_2 = \int_c^b f(x)\, dx$$

To find the area $A_1$, we note that, since $f(x) \leq 0$ on $a \leq x \leq c$, then $-f(x) \geq 0$, and, by symmetry, the area $A_1$ equals

$$A_1 = \int_a^c [-f(x)]\, dx = -\int_a^c f(x)\, dx$$

The next example illustrates this procedure for calculating area.

**3.2**
**Example**

Find the area bounded by the curve $f(x) = x^3$, the $x$-axis, $x = -1$, and $x = 1/2$.

The desired area is given by the shaded region in Figure 12.10. Notice that it is composed of two regions: $A_1$, in which $f(x) < 0$ over the interval $[-1, 0)$; and $A_2$, in which $f(x) > 0$ over the interval $(0, \frac{1}{2}]$. Thus, to attack the problem we use the additive property of area. Since $f(x) < 0$ for $-1 \leq x < 0$,

$$A_1 = -\int_{-1}^0 x^3\, dx = -\frac{x^4}{4}\Big|_{-1}^0 = \frac{1}{4}$$

For the area $A_2$, we have

$$A_2 = \int_0^{1/2} x^3\, dx = \frac{x^4}{4}\Big|_0^{1/2} = \frac{1}{64}$$

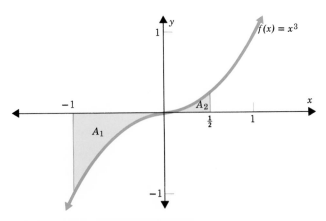

**Figure 12.10**

The total area $A$ (since the regions do not overlap) is

$$A = A_1 + A_2 = \frac{1}{4} + \frac{1}{64} = \frac{17}{64}$$

The previous example illustrates the necessity of graphing the function before any attempt is made to compute area.

Find the area bounded by $f(x) = x^2 - 4$ and the $x$-axis from $x = 0$ to $x = 4$.

On the interval $[0, 4]$, the curve crosses the $x$-axis at $x = 2$ since $f(2) = 0$. Also, $f(x) < 0$ from $x = 0$ to $x = 2$, and $f(x) > 0$ from $x = 2$ to $x = 4$. The areas $A_1$ and $A_2$ as depicted in Figure 12.11 are

3.3
Example

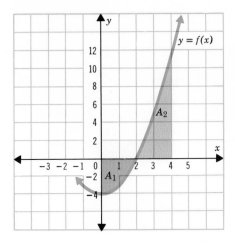

**Figure 12.11**

$$A_1 = -\int_0^2 (x^2 - 4)\, dx = -\left(\frac{x^3}{3} - 4x\right)\Big|_0^2 = -\left(\frac{8}{3} - 8\right) = \frac{16}{3}$$

$$A_2 = \int_2^4 (x^2 - 4)\, dx = \left(\frac{x^3}{3} - 4x\right)\Big|_2^4 = \left(\frac{64}{3} - 16\right) - \left(\frac{8}{3} - 8\right)$$

$$= \frac{56}{3} - 8$$

The total area is

$$A = A_1 + A_2 = \frac{16}{3} + \frac{56}{3} - 8 = \frac{72}{3} - 8 = 16$$

**3.4
Example**

Find the area of the region bounded by the graphs of the equations

$$f(x) = 2x^2 \qquad g(x) = 2x + 4$$

First, we graph each of the functions.

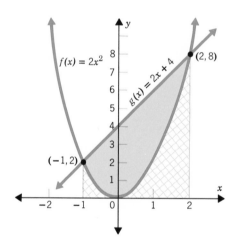

**Figure 12.12**

The area to be calculated (shaded portion of Figure 12.12) lies under the line $g(x) = 2x + 4$ and above the curve $f(x) = 2x^2$. To find this area, we first need to find the values of $x$ at which the curves meet, that is, all values of $x$ for which $2x^2 = 2x + 4$. The solutions of this equation are

$$x = -1 \qquad x = 2$$

It is clear from Figure 12.12 that, if we subtract the area under $f(x) = 2x^2$, between $x = -1$ to $x = 2$, from the area under $g(x) = 2x + 4$, between $x = -1$ to $x = 2$, we will have the area in question. Thus the area we seek is

$$A = \int_{-1}^{2} g(x)\,dx - \int_{-1}^{2} f(x)\,dx = \int_{-1}^{2} [g(x) - f(x)]\,dx$$

$$= \int_{-1}^{2} [(2x + 4) - 2x^2]\,dx = \left(x^2 + 4x - \frac{2x^3}{3}\right)\Big|_{-1}^{2}$$

$$= \left(4 + 8 - \frac{16}{3}\right) - \left(1 - 4 + \frac{2}{3}\right) = 9$$

The technique used in Example 2.3 can be used whenever we are asked to determine the area of a region bounded by the graphs of two continuous non-negative functions $f(x)$ and $g(x)$ from $x = a$ to $x = b$.

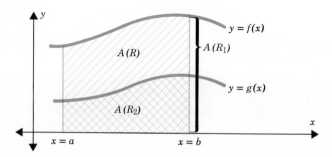

**Figure 12.13**

Suppose, as depicted in Figure 12.13, $f(x) \geq g(x) \geq 0$ for $x \in [a, b]$, and we wish to determine the area between $f(x)$ and $g(x)$, $x = a$ and $x = b$. If we denote this area by $A(R)$, the area under $f(x)$ by $A(R_1)$, and the area under $g(x)$ by $A(R_2)$, then

$$A(R) = A(R_1) - A(R_2)$$

$$= \int_{a}^{b} f(x)\,dx - \int_{a}^{b} g(x)\,dx = \int_{a}^{b} [f(x) - g(x)]\,dx$$

The next example illustrates this technique.

Find the area of the region bounded by the graphs of the equations

3.5
Example

$$f(x) = 10x - x^2$$
$$g(x) = 30 - 3x$$

Let us first find the points of intersection of the two graphs, that is, find all values of $x$ for which

$$f(x) = g(x)$$

Then,

$$30 - 3x = 10x - x^2$$
$$x^2 - 13x + 30 = 0$$
$$(x - 3)(x - 10) = 0$$

Thus the points where the two curves meet are $(3, 21)$ and $(10, 0)$. We also see that for $3 \leqq x \leqq 10$,

$$f(x) \geqq g(x) \geqq 0$$

Thus, the required area, given by the shaded area in Figure 12.14, is

$$\int_3^{10} [(10x - x^2) - (30 - 3x)]\, dx = \int_3^{10} [-x^2 + 13x - 30]\, dx$$

$$= \left( \frac{-x^3}{3} + \frac{13x^2}{2} - 30x \right) \Big|_3^{10} = \frac{343}{6}$$

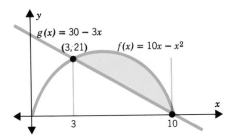

**Figure 12.14**

The technique just discussed depends for its validity on the fact that $f(x) \geqq g(x)$ on $I$. In the event this is not true, the area must be computed by employing the additive property of area.

The rate of sales of a new product is given by

$$f(x) = 100 - 90e^{-x}$$

where $x$ is the number of days the product is on the market. The total sales during the first 4 days is the area under the curve from $x = 0$ to $x = 4$. See Figure 12.15. Find the total sales.
Here we must evaluate

$$\int_0^4 f(x)\, dx = \int_0^4 (100 - 90e^{-x})\, dx = (100x + 90e^{-x}) \Big|_0^4$$

$$= 400 + 90e^{-4} - 90 = 310 + 90e^{-4}$$
$$= 310 + 90(0.018) = 311.62$$

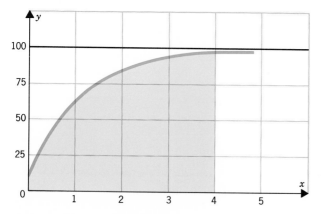

**Figure 12.15**

3.7
Example

A company has current sales of $1,000,000 per month and profit to the company averages 10 percent of sales. The company's past experience with a certain advertising strategy is that sales will increase by 2 percent per month over the length of the advertising campaign (12 months). The company now needs to decide whether to embark on a similar campaign whose total cost will be $130,000. The decision will be yes provided the increase in sales due to the campaign results in profits that exceed $13,000. (This is a 10 percent return on the advertising investment.)

The monthly rate of sales during the advertising campaign obeys a growth curve of the form

$$\$1,000,000e^{0.02t}$$

where $t$ is measured in months. The total sales after 12 months (the length of the campaign) is

$$\text{Total sales} = \int_0^{12} 1,000,000e^{0.02t}\,dt$$

$$= \frac{1,000,000e^{0.02t}}{0.02}\Big|_0^{12}$$

$$= 50,000,000[e^{0.24} - 1]$$

$$= 50,000,000(0.271)$$

$$= \$13,550,000 \text{ (approximately)}$$

The profit to the company is 10 percent of sales so that the profit due to the increase in sales is

$$0.10(13,550,000 - 12,000,000) = \$155,000$$

This $155,000 profit was achieved through the expenditure of $130,000 in advertising. Thus, the advertising yielded a true profit of

$$\$155,000 - \$130,000 = \$25,000$$

Since this represents more than a 10 percent return on cost of the advertising, the company should proceed with the advertising campaign.

In Problems 1–10, set up definite integrals that represent the area described and find the area:

1. Bounded by the line $f(x) = 3x + 2$ and the x-axis from $x = 2$ to $x = 6$. Check your result by using the formula for finding the area of a trapezoid.
2. Bounded by $f(x) = x$ and the x-axis from $x = 0$ to $x = 4$.
3. Bounded by $f(x) = 1/x^2$ and the axis from $x = 1$ to $x = 4$.
4. Bounded by $f(x) = \sqrt{x}$ and the x-axis from $x = 1$ to $x = 2$.
5. Bounded by $f(x) = xe^{-x}$ and the x-axis from $x = 0$ to $x = 1$.
6. Bounded by $f(x) = 1/(x + 1)$ and the x-axis from $x = 1$ to $x = 3$.
7. Bounded by $f(x) = e^{3x}$ and the x-axis from $x = 0$ to $x = 2$.
8. Bounded by the curves $f(x) = 4 - x^2$ and $g(x) = x + 2$.
9. Bounded by the curves $f(x) = 16 - x^2$ and $g(x) = x^2$
   (a) from $x = 0$ to $x = 1$
   (b) the total area between the two curves
10. Bounded by the curves $f(x) = 2 + x - x^2$ and $g(x) = -x - 1$.
11. Find the area of the triangle with sides $f(x) = -x/2 + 7/2$, $g(x) = x - 4$, and $h(x) = -5x + 8$.
12. If the rate of sales of a certain product obeys

$$f(x) = 1340 - 850e^{-x}$$

find the total sales during the first 5 years.
13. A company whose annual sales are currently $10,000,000 has reason to believe that sales will experience an increase of 8 percent per year for the next 5 years. What will the total sales be in 5 years?

\*14. If $y = f(x)$ is continuous on an interval $I: a \leq x \leq b$, then there is a value of $c$, $a < c < b$, so that

$$\int_a^b f(x)\, dx = f(c)(b - a)$$

The interpretation of this result is that there is a rectangle with base $(b - a)$ and height $f(c)$, whose area is numerically equal to the area $\int_a^b f(x)\, dx$. See the illustration. Verify this result by finding $c$ for the functions given below. Graph each function.
(a) $f(x) = x^2$, $a = 0$, $b = 1$
(b) $f(x) = 1/x^2$, $a = 1$, $b = 4$

**369**
12.4
BUSINESS
APPLICATIONS OF
THE DEFINITE
INTEGRAL

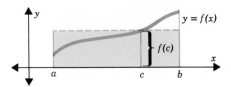

*15. If $y = f(x)$ is continuous on the interval $I$ and if it has an antiderivative on $I$, then for some $a$ in $I$

$$\frac{d}{dx} \int_a^x f(t)\, dt = f(x) \qquad \text{for} \qquad x > a \text{ in } I$$

This result gives us a technique for finding the derivative of a definite integral in which the lower limit is fixed and the upper limit is variable. Use this result to find

(a) $\dfrac{d}{dx} \displaystyle\int_1^x t^2 \, dt$

(b) $\dfrac{d}{dx} \displaystyle\int_2^x \sqrt{t^2 - 2} \, dt$

(c) $\dfrac{d}{dx} \displaystyle\int_5^x \sqrt{t^2 + 2t} \, dt$

In this section we discuss three applications of the definite integral to business and economic situations.

12.4
BUSINESS
APPLICATIONS
OF THE
DEFINITE
INTEGRAL

### The Learning Curve

Quite often the managerial planning and control component of a production industry is faced with the problem of predicting labor time requirements and cost per unit of product. The tool used to achieve such predictions is the so-called *learning curve*. The basic assumption made here is that, in certain production industries such as assembling of televisions and cars, the worker learns from experience. As a result, the more often he repeats an operation, the more efficient he becomes and, hence, his direct labor input per unit of product declines. If the *rate* of improvement is regular enough, the learning curve can be used to predict future reductions in labor requirements.

The general form of the function describing such a situation is

$$f(x) = cx^k$$

where $f(x)$ is the number of hours of direct labor required to produce the $x$th unit, $-1 \leq k < 0$ and $c > 0$. The choice of $x^k$, with $-1 \leq k < 0$, guarantees that, as the number $x$ of units produced increases, the direct labor input decreases. See Figure 12.16.

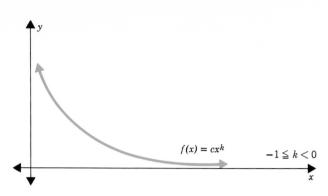

**Figure 12.16**

The function $f(x) = cx^k$, describes a rate of learning per unit produced. This rate is measured in terms of labor hours per unit; thus the function $f(x)$ shows that the number of direct labor hours declines as more items are produced.

Once a learning curve has been determined for a gross production process, it can be used as a predictor to determine the number of production hours for future work. **If a learning curve is known, the total number of labor hours required to produce units numbered** $a$ **through** $b$ **is**

$$N = \int_a^b f(x)\,dx = \int_a^b cx^k\,dx$$

4.1
Example Caryl's Air Conditioning Company manufactures air conditioners on an assembly line. From experience it was determined the first 100 air conditioners required 1272 labor hours. For each subsequent 100 air conditioners (1 unit), less labor hours were required according to the learning curve

$$f(x) = 1272x^{-0.25}$$

where $f(x)$ is the rate of labor hours required to assemble the xth unit (each unit being 100 air conditioners). This curve was determined after 30 units had been manufactured.

The company is in the process of bidding for a large contract involving 5000 additional air conditioners or 50 additional units. The company can estimate the labor hours required to assemble these units by evaluating

$$N = \int_{30}^{80} 1272x^{-0.25}\,dx$$
$$= \frac{1272x^{0.75}}{0.75}\Big|_{30}^{80}$$
$$= 1696[80^{0.75} - 30^{0.75}]$$
$$= 1696[26.75 - 12.82]$$
$$= 1696[13.93] = 23{,}625.28$$

**371**
12.4
BUSINESS
APPLICATIONS OF
THE DEFINITE
INTEGRAL

Thus the company can bid estimating the total labor hours needed as 23,625.28.

1. After producing 35 units, a company determines that its production facility is following a learning curve of the form

$$f(x) = 1000x^{-0.5}$$

where $f(x)$ is the rate of labor hours required to assemble the $x$th unit. How many total labor hours should they estimate are required to produce an additional 25 units.

2. Danny's Auto Shop has found that, after tuning up 50 cars, a learning curve of the form

$$f(x) = 1000x^{-1}$$

is being followed. How many total labor hours should they estimate are required to tune up an additional 50 cars?

*3. In the construction of a learning curve, how would you interpret the situation in which $k \to 0^-$.

## Consumer's Surplus

Suppose the price $p$, a consumer is willing to pay for a quantity $x$, of a particular commodity is governed by the demand curve

$$p = D(x)$$

In general the function $D(x)$ is a decreasing function, indicating that, as the price of the commodity increases, the quantity the consumer is willing to buy declines.

Suppose the price $p$ that a producer is willing to charge for a quantity $x$ of a particular commodity is governed by the supply curve

$$p = S(x)$$

In general, the function $S(x)$ is an increasing function since, as the price $p$ of a commodity increases, the more the producer is willing to supply the commodity.

The point of intersection of the demand curve and the supply curve is called the *equilibrium point E*. If the coordinates of $E$ are $(x^*, p^*)$, then $p^*$, the *market price*, is the price a consumer is willing to pay for, and a producer is willing to sell for, a quantity $x^*$, the *demand level*, of the commodity. See Figure 12.17.

The total revenue of the producer at a market price $p^*$, and a demand level $x^*$, is $p^*x^*$ (the price per unit times the number of units). This revenue can be interpreted geometrically as the area of the rectangle $0p^*Ex^*$ in Figure 12.17.

Equilibrium
Point

Market
Price

Demand
Level

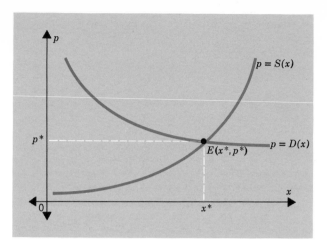

**Figure 12.17**

In a free market economy, there are times when some consumers would be willing to pay more for a commodity than the market price $p^*$ that they actually do pay. The benefit of this to consumers is called *consumer's surplus* (CS) and is determined by the formula

Consumer's
Surplus

$$CS = \int_0^{x^*} D(x) \, dx - p^*x^* \tag{4.1}$$

Of course, $\int_0^{x^*} D(x) \, dx$ is merely the area under the demand curve $D(x)$ from $x = 0$ to $x = x^*$, and represents the total revenue that would have been generated by the willingness of some consumers to pay more. By subtracting $p^*x^*$ (the revenue actually achieved), the result is a surplus CS to the consumer. See Figure 12.18.

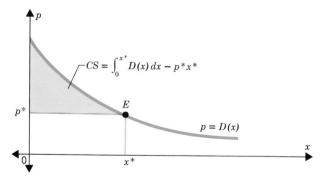

**Figure 12.18**

In a free market economy, there are also times when some producers would be willing to sell at a price below the market price $p^*$ that the consumer actually pays. The benefit of this to the producer is called *producer's surplus* (PS) and is calculated by the formula

$$PS = p^*x^* - \int_0^{x^*} S(x)\, dx \qquad (4.2)$$

Producer's Surplus

Of course, $\int_0^{x^*} S(x)\, dx$ is merely the area under the supply curve $S(x)$ from $x = 0$ to $x = x^*$, and represents the total revenue that would have been generated by some producer's willingness to sell at a lower price. By subtracting this amount from $p^*x^*$ (the revenue actually achieved), the result is a surplus to the producer, PS. See Figure 12.19.

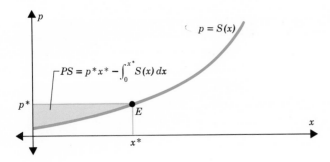

**Figure 12.19**

Example 4.2 illustrates a situation in which both the supply and demand curves are linear.

Find the CS and PS defined by the demand curve $D(x) = 18 - 3x$ and the supply curve $S(x) = 3x + 6$, where $p^* = D(x^*) = S(x^*)$.

4.2 Example

    Let us first determine the equilibrium point $E$, by solving the equation

$$D(x) = S(x)$$
$$18 - 3x = 3x + 6$$
$$6x = 12$$
$$x^* = 2$$

To find $p^*$, we compute $D(x^*)$. Then

$$p^* = D(x^*) = D(2) = 18 - 6 = 12$$

To find $CS$ and $PS$, we use formulas (4.1) and (4.2). Then

$$CS = \int_0^2 (18 - 3x)\, dx - (2)(12)$$

$$= \left(18x - \frac{3x^2}{2}\right)\Big|_0^2 - 24$$

$$= 36 - 6 - 24 = 6$$

and

$$PS = (2)(12) - \int_0^2 (3x + 6)\, dx$$

$$= 24 - \left(\frac{3x^2}{2} + 6x\right)\Big|_0^2$$

$$= 24 - (6 + 12) = 6$$

Thus, in this example, the consumer's surplus and producers surplus each equal \$6.

**12.4.2
Exercise**

1. Find $CS$ and $PS$ defined by the demand curve

$$D(x) = 20 - 5x$$

and supply curve

$$S(x) = 4x + 8$$

Sketch the appropriate graphs.
2. Follow the same directions as in Problem 1 if

$$D(x) = -0.4x + 15, \qquad S(x) = 0.8x + 0.5$$

3. Find the consumer's surplus if the demand curve is

$$D(x) = 50 - 0.025x^2$$

and it is known that the market quantity is 20 units.

## Maximizing Profit over Time

The model introduced here is concerned with business operations of a special character. In oil drilling, mining, and other depletion operations, the initial revenue rate is generally higher than the revenue rate after a period of time has passed. That is, revenue rate, as a function of time, is a decreasing function (this is because depletion is occurring).

The cost rate of such operations generally increases with time because of inflation and other reasons. That is, cost rate, as a function of time, is an increasing function. The problem that management faces is to determine the time $t^*$ that maximizes the profit function $P(t)$.

To construct a model, we denote the cost and the revenue function by $C(t)$ and $R(t)$, respectively, where $t$ denotes time. This representation

**375**
12.4
BUSINESS
APPLICATIONS OF
THE DEFINITE
INTEGRAL

of cost and revenue deviates from the usual economic definitions of cost per unit times number of units, and price per unit times number of units. The derivatives $C'(t)$ and $R'(t)$, taken with respect to time, represent cost and revenue as time rates. Furthermore, we make the natural assumption that the revenue rate, say dollars per week, is greater than cost rate at the beginning of the business operation under consideration. Also, as time goes on, we assume the cost rate increases to the revenue rate, and thereafter exceeds it. The optimum time at which the business operation should terminate is that point in time where the rates are equal. That is, the optimum time $t^*$ obeys

$$C'(t^*) = R'(t^*)$$

The profit rate $P'(t)$ is the difference between the revenue rate and the cost rate. That is,

$$P'(t) = R'(t) - C'(t)$$

Hence,

$$P(t) = \int_0^t [R'(t) - C'(t)]\, dt$$

The maximum profit is obtained when $t = t^*$, since $P'(t^*) = R'(t^*) - C'(t^*) = 0$. Thus, the maximum profit is $P(t^*)$. Geometrically, the maximum profit $P(t^*)$ is the area bounded by the curves $C'(t)$ and $R'(t)$ from $t = 0$ to $t = t^*$. See Figure 12.20.

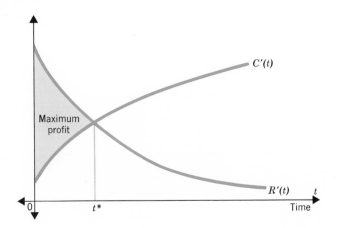

**Figure 12.20**

Notice that in Figure 12.20 the revenue rate function obeys the assumptions made in constructing the model: it is decreasing and it is very high initially. Also, the cost rate function is increasing and is concave down, indicating the cost rate eventually levels off.

The G-B Oil Company's revenue rate, in millions of dollars per year, at time $t$ years is

$$R'(t) = 9 - t^{1/3}$$

and the corresponding cost rate function, also in millions of dollars, is

$$C'(t) = 1 + 3t^{1/3}$$

We wish to determine how long the oil company should continue to operate and what total profit will be at the end of the operation.

Recall that the time $t^*$ of optimal termination is found when

$$\begin{aligned}
C'(t) &= R'(t) \\
9 - t^{1/3} &= 1 + 3t^{1/3} \\
8 &= 4t^{1/3} \\
2 &= t^{1/3} \\
t^* &= 8 \text{ years}
\end{aligned}$$

The revenue and cost rate functions are given in Figure 12.21.

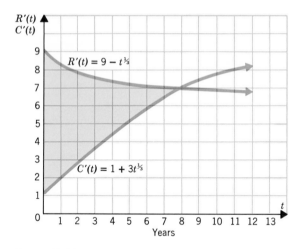

**Figure 12.21**

At $t^* = 8$ both revenue and cost rates are 7 million dollars per year. The profit $P(t^*)$ is

$$\begin{aligned}
P(t^*) &= \int_0^8 [R'(t) - C'(t)] \, dt \\
&= \int_0^8 [(9 - t^{1/3}) - (1 + 3t^{1/3})] \, dt \\
&= (8t - 3t^{4/3})\Big|_0^8 = 16 \text{ (millions of dollars)}
\end{aligned}$$

In the above example we were forced to overlook the *fixed* cost for the cost function at time $t = 0$. This is because, if $C(t)$ contains a constant (the fixed cost), then it becomes zero when we take the derivative $C'(t)$. Thus, in the final analysis of the problem, total profit should be reduced by the amount corresponding to the fixed cost.

1. The revenue and the cost rate of Gold Star mining operation are, respectively,

$$R'(t) = 19 - t^{1/2}$$

and

$$C'(t) = 3 + 3t^{1/2}$$

where $t$ is measured in years and $R$, $C$ are measured in millions of dollars. Determine how long the operation should continue and the profit that can be generated during this period.

12.4.3
Exercise

**definite integral**
**lower limit of integration**
**upper limit of integration**
**fundamental property of**
**   integral calculus**
**variable cost**
**additive property of area**

**learning curve**
**equilibrium point**
**market price**
**demand level**
**consumer's surplus**
**producer's surplus**

CHAPTER
REVIEW

Important
Terms

1. Find the area bounded by $f(x) = 2x - 5$ and the x-axis
   (a) from $x = 3$ to $x = 6$
   (b) from $x = 0$ to $x = 1$
   (c) from $x = 2$ to $x = 4$
2. Find the area between the curves $f(x) = x^2$ and $g(x) = x^3$.
3. Find the area bounded by $f(x) = x^3 - x$ and the x-axis from $x = -1$ to $x = 2$.
4. Find the area between $f(x) = 2x/(x^2 + 1)$ and the x-axis from $x = 0$ to $x = 2$.
5. Find the area between $f(x) = xe^{3x^2}$ and the x-axis from $x = 0$ to $x = 1$.
6. Find the area between the curves $2x + 3y = 6$ and $y = 1/x$.
7. Find the area between $f(x) = x^2$ and $g(x) = \sqrt{x}$.
8. Find the area between the curves $f(x) = -x^2 + 2x + 2$ and $g(x) = x^2 - 4x + 2$.

Review
Exercises

*Mathematics*

Leithold, Louis, *Calculus and Analytic Geometry,* Second Edition, Harper and Row, New York, 1972. Chapter 6.

Salas, Saturnino and Einar Hille, *Calculus: One and Several Variables,* Second Edition, Xerox, Lexington, Mass., 1974. Chapter 9.

Thomas, George, *Calculus and Analytic Geometry,* Fourth Edition, Addison-Wesley, Reading, Mass., 1968. Chapters 5 and 6.

*Applied*

Batschelet, E., *Introduction to Mathematics for Life Sciences,* Springer-Verlag, New York, 1972.

Chiang, Alpha, *Fundamental Methods of Mathematical Economics,* Second Edition, McGraw-Hill, New York, 1974.

Furguson, C. E., *Microeconomic Theory,* Third Edition, Irwin Press, Homewood, Ill., 1972.

Grossman, Stanley and James Turner, *Mathematics for the Biological Sciences,* Macmillan, New York, 1974.

Springer, C. H., R. E. Herlihy, and R. I. Baggs, *Advanced Methods and Models,* Mathematics for Management Series, Volume 2, Irwin Press, Homewood, Ill., 1965.

Thrall, Robert M., (Ed.), *Some Mathematical Models in Biology,* University of Michigan, Ann Arbor, 1967.

# 13

# INTRODUCTION TO THE THEORY OF SETS; COUNTING TECHNIQUES

With this chapter, we begin the third portion of the text—the study of situations that lead to probabilistic models. In particular, this chapter serves to acquaint the reader with the notation of set theory (first discussed in Chapter 1) and some of its applications. The remainder of the chapter deals with the solution of counting problems.

The reader is encouraged to review Section 1.1 of Chapter 1 before proceeding further.

When we see two people, we can usually relate them in many ways. We say that they have the same color eyes, or that one is taller than the other, or that one is heavier than the other.

We shall discuss *four* ways of relating two sets. If we look at the sets

$$A = \{1, 2\}, \qquad B = \{1, 2, 3\}$$

we notice that the elements of the set $A$ are also elements of the set $B$. This is one way of comparing two sets.

Consider the following two sets.

$$A = \{1, 2\}, \qquad B = \{4, 5\}$$

If we look at these two sets, we notice that each of these sets possesses the same number of elements. This is easily seen by "matching" or "corresponding" elements of these sets. If we use a double arrow "$\leftrightarrow$" to denote this "match," then

$$1 \leftrightarrow 4, \qquad 2 \leftrightarrow 5 \qquad \text{or} \qquad 1 \leftrightarrow 5, \qquad 2 \leftrightarrow 4$$

Here we would say that the sets $A$ and $B$ are *equivalent*.

These, and other, *relations between sets* are defined more carefully below.

**Definition of Equality**

**Let $A$ and $B$ be two nonempty sets. We say that $A$ *is equal to* $B$, written as**

$$A = B$$

**if and only if $A$ and $B$ have the same elements.**

If two sets $A$ and $B$ are *not* equal, we write

$$A \neq B$$

One result of the Definition of Equality is that the order in which elements of set are listed is immaterial. Thus, $\{2, 3, 4\}$ and $\{4, 3, 2\}$ are equal sets.

**Definition of Equivalence**

**Let $A$ and $B$ be two nonempty sets. We say that $A$ *is equivalent to* $B$, written as**

$$A \sim B$$

**if and only if there can be found a one-to-one correspondence between the elements of $A$ and $B$. By one-to-one correspondence we mean that for each element in $A$, there can be matched one element in $B$; and each element in $B$ can be matched to exactly one element in $A$.**

If two sets $A$ and $B$ are *not* equivalent, we write

$$A \nsim B$$

There is a relationship between the concept of equality and that of equivalence.

If two sets $A$ and $B$ are equal, so that they have the *same* elements, it is easy to see that $A$ and $B$ must also be equivalent.

The necessary one-to-one correspondence is found merely by associating or matching each element in $A$ with the identical element of $B$. Since the elements of $A$ and $B$ are the same, the elements of the two sets $A$ and $B$ are in one-to-one correspondence, and hence the sets are equivalent.

Suppose we consider the converse. That is, suppose two sets $A$ and $B$ are equivalent. Are they then equal? Or can two sets be equivalent without being equal? The following example gives us the answer.

2.1
Example

Let two sets $A$ and $B$ be given by

$$A = \{1, 2, 3\}, \qquad B = \{7, 8, 9\}$$

Clearly, $A$ is not equal to $B$. However, since we can match the elements of $A$ and $B$ by

$$1 \leftrightarrow 7, \qquad 2 \leftrightarrow 8, \qquad 3 \leftrightarrow 9$$

it is seen that $A$ is equivalent to $B$.

The following result has thus been established.

If two sets $A$ and $B$ are equal, then $A$ and $B$ are equivalent. The converse is *not* true. Thus, two sets $A$ and $B$ may be equivalent, and yet be unequal.

**Let $A$ and $B$ be two nonempty sets. We shall say that** $A$ *is a subset of* **$B$ or that** $A$ *is contained in* $B$**, written as**

Definition
of Subset

$$A \subseteq B$$

**if and only if every element of $A$ is also an element of $B$.**

If a set $A$ is not a subset of a set $B$, we write

$$A \nsubseteq B$$

The definition that $A$ is a subset of $B$ could have been given equivalently as "there are no elements in set $A$ that are not also elements in set $B$." Of course, $A \subseteq B$ if and only if whenever $x \in A$, then $x \in B$ for all $x$. This latter way of interpreting the meaning of $A \subseteq B$ is useful for obtaining various laws that sets obey.

**Definition of Proper Subset**  **Let $A$ and $B$ be two nonempty sets. We shall say that** $A$ *is a proper subset of $B$ or that $A$ is properly contained in $B$,* **written as**

$$A \subset B$$

**if and only if every element of the set $A$ is also an element of set $B$, but there is at least one element in set $B$ that is *not* in set $A$.**

✳  The student should notice that $A$ is a proper subset of $B$ means that there are *no* elements of $A$ that are not also elements of $B$, but there is at least one element of $B$ which is not in $A$.

If a set $A$ is *not* a proper subset of a set $B$, we write

$$A \not\subset B$$

The following example illustrates some uses of the four relations $=$, $\sim$, $\subseteq$, and $\subset$ just defined.

**2.2 Example**  Consider three sets $A$, $B$, and $C$ given by

$$A = \{1, 2, 3\}, \qquad B = \{1, 2, 3, 4, 5\}, \qquad C = \{1, 2, 3\}$$

Below are some of the relations between pairs of these sets:
(a) $A = C$
(b) $A \sim C$
(c) $A \subseteq B$
(d) $A \subset B$
(e) $A \subseteq C$
(f) $C \subseteq A$

In comparing the two definitions given above of "subset" and "proper subset," the student should notice that if a set $A$ is a subset of a set $B$, then either $A$ is a proper subset of $B$, or else $A$ equals $B$. That is,

$$A \subseteq B \text{ if and only if either } A \subset B \text{ or } A = B.$$

✳ Also, if $A$ is a proper subset of $B$, we can infer that $A$ is a subset of $B$, but $A$ does not equal $B$. That is,

$$A \subset B \text{ if and only if } A \subseteq B \text{ and } A \neq B$$

The distinction that is made between "subset" and "proper subset" is rather subtle and is quite important. Let us try to describe this distinction further by using some familiar everyday examples.

We often hear "I *do not* weigh more than 200 pounds." What this means is the weight in question equals 200 pounds or is less than 200 pounds. If $A$ is a subset of $B$, then $A$ equals $B$ or $A$ is a proper subset of $B$. If one's weight is less than 200 pounds, then his weight does not exceed 200 pounds and does not equal 200 pounds. If $A$ is a proper subset of $B$, we know that $A$ is a subset of $B$, but $A \neq B$.

We can think of the relation $\subset$ as a refinement of the relation $\subseteq$. On the other hand, the relation $\subseteq$ is an extension of $\subset$, in the sense that $\subseteq$ may include equality whereas, with $\subset$, equality cannot be included.

Because of the way the relation $\subseteq$ (is a subset of) has been defined, it is easy to see that for any set $A$

$$\varnothing \subseteq A$$

The reason for this is that there is no element of the set $\varnothing$ which is not also in $A$, since the empty set $\varnothing$ has no elements.

Also, if $A$ is any nonempty set, that is, any set having at least one element, then

$$\varnothing \subset A$$

Thus far we have talked about comparing pairs of sets by means of the relations $\subset$ and $\subseteq$. We have said $A$ is a subset of $B$, or $A$ equals $B$, or $B$ is a subset of $A$. For some pairs of sets, none of these relations can be used. This situation is illustrated by the following example.

Consider two sets $A$ and $B$ whose elements are

$$A = \{1, 2, 3\} \qquad B = \{3, 4\}$$

2.3
Example

Notice that not every element in $A$ is in $B$. Thus

$$A \nsubseteq B$$

Also, notice that not every element in $B$ is in $A$. Then

$$B \nsubseteq A$$

Finally, $A$ and $B$ are *not* equal. They have different elements. Thus

$$A \neq B$$

That is, the sets $A$ and $B$ given in Example 2.3 are *not comparable*.

Thus, at times, we cannot say about any two sets $C$ and $D$ that either (1) $C$ is a subset of $D$, or (2) $C$ is equal to $D$, or (3) $D$ is a subset of $C$. When we can say one of the above three about two sets $C$ and $D$, then $C$ and $D$ are said to be *comparable*.

Comparable
Sets

In a meaningful situation the elements that may be considered are usually limited to some specific, all-encompassing set. For example, in discussing students eligible to graduate from Midwestern University, the discussion would be limited to students enrolled at the University. Thus the following definition is given.

**The *universal set* U is defined as that set consisting of all elements under consideration.**

Definition of
the Universal
Set

Thus, if $A$ is any set and if $U$ is the universal set, then every element in $A$ must be in $U$ (since $U$ consists of all elements under consideration).

Hence

$$A \subseteq U$$

for *any* set A.

Replace the asterisk by those relations $=$, $\sim$, $\subset$, $\subseteq$, that give a true statement, or by *none of these,* if none of these relations holds.

1. $\{1, 3, 7\} * \{1, 3\}$
2. $\{4, 9\} * \{9, 10, 4\}$
3. $\{5, 7\} * \{5, 8\}$
4. $\{0, 1, 4\} * \{0, 5, 8, 9\}$
5. $\varnothing * \{1, 3\}$
6. $\{0\} * \{1, 3\}$
7. $\{5, 8, 9, 15\} * \{9\}$
8. $\{2, 3\} * \{2, 3, 6, 8, 0\}$
9. $\{2, 3\} * \{2, 3\}$
10. If $A \subseteq B$ and $B \subseteq C$, what do you conclude? Why?
11. Give an example of two sets that are not comparable.
12. Write down all possible subsets of (a) the set $\{a, b, c, d\}$ and (b) the set $\{a, b, c\}$.
13. If the universal set is the set of people, let A denote the subset of fat people, let B denote the subset of bald people, and let C denote the subset of bald and fat people. Write down several correct relations involving A, B, and C.

In the last section, we discussed relations between sets. In this section, we introduce operations that are performed on sets. The student is already familiar with many operations that are performed on numbers. For example, we speak of "taking the square root of a number", or "squaring a number." These are examples of *unary operations,* since they are operations performed on only *one* number. Also, we speak of "adding two numbers", or "multiplying two numbers." These are examples of *binary* operations, since they involve *two* numbers.

**Let A and B be any two sets. The** *union of A with B,* **written as**

$$A \cup B$$

**is defined to be that set consisting of those elements either in** A **or in** B **or in both** A **and** B**. That is, in set-builder notation,**

$$A \cup B = \{x \mid x \in A \text{ or } x \in B\}$$

Let *A* and *B* be any two sets. The *intersection of A with B,* **written as**

$$A \cap B$$

**is defined as the set consisting of those elements that are** *both* **in** *A* **and in** *B.* **Thus**

$$A \cap B = \{x \mid x \in A \text{ and } x \in B\}$$

The student should recognize that to find the intersection of two sets *A* and *B* means to find the elements *common* to *A* and *B.*

**If two sets** *A* **and** *B* **have no elements in common, that is, if**

$$A \cap B = \varnothing$$

**then** *A* **and** *B* **are called** *disjoint sets.*

A *Venn diagram* is a pictoral representation of relationships involving sets. Usually, sets are represented by interlocking circles, which are enclosed in a rectangle that represents the universal set *U.*

Use a Venn diagram to illustrate (a) $A \cap B$ and (b) $A \cup B$. Since $A \cap B$ consists of those elements both in *A* and in *B,* it is seen that the shaded region of Figure 13.1(a) is $A \cap B$. Since $A \cup B$ consists of elements either in *A* or in *B,* the shaded region of Figure 13.1(b) represents $A \cup B$.

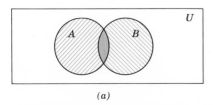

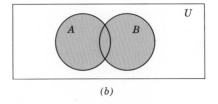

(a)                              (b)

**Figure 13.1**

Venn diagrams are very useful for illustrating and motivating properties of sets. However, they are not intended to be a substitute for logical proofs.

Consider the three sets

$$A = \{1, 3, 5\}, \quad B = \{3, 4, 5, 6\}, \quad C = \{6, 7\}$$

Then

$$A \cup B = \{1, 3, 5\} \cup \{3, 4, 5, 6\} = \{1, 3, 4, 5, 6\}$$
$$A \cap B = \{1, 3, 5\} \cap \{3, 4, 5, 6\} = \{3, 5\}$$
$$A \cap C = \{1, 3, 5\} \cap \{6, 7\} = \varnothing$$

Here $A$ and $C$ are disjoint sets.

The next result states a relationship between the operations of union and intersection. This theorem says that the intersection of two sets is always a subset of the union of the two sets. That is, every element of the intersection is also an element of the union. Figure 13.1 serves as motivation for this result.

**For any two sets $A$ and $B$, we have**

$$A \cap B \subseteq A \cup B$$

The following result states that the intersection of a set $A$ with any other set is a subset of the set $A$. It further says that a set $A$ is always a subset of the union of $A$ with any set. Thus, every element both in a set $A$, and in some other set, is also in $A$. Finally, every element in a set $A$ is also in either $A$ or any other set. A careful look at Figure 13.1 should convince the reader that these statements are valid.

**Let $A$ and $B$ be two sets. Then**

$$A \cap B \subseteq A, \qquad A \subseteq A \cup B$$

Thus far, two operations involving sets have been introduced. These two operations (union $\cup$ and intersection $\cap$) are examples of binary operations.

We are now ready to introduce an operation on sets involving one set—that is, a *unary* operation.

**Definition of Complement** **Let $A$ be any set. The *complement of $A$*, written as**

$$\overline{A} \text{ (or } A', \text{ or } -A)$$

**is defined as the set consisting of elements in the universe $U$ which are not in $A$. Thus**

$$\overline{A} = \{x \,|\, x \notin A\}$$

The shaded region in Figure 13.2 illustrates the complement $\overline{A}$.

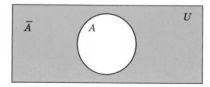

**Figure 13.2**

If $U$ = universal set = $\{0, 1, 2, 3, 4\}$ and if $A = \{0, 1, 2\}$, then

$$\bar{A} = \{3, 4\}$$

Use a Venn diagram to illustrate that

$$\bar{A} \cap \bar{B} = \overline{A \cup B}$$

First, we draw two diagrams. See Figure 13.3.

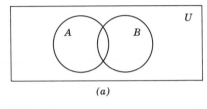
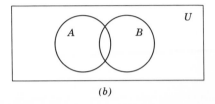

(a)           (b)

**Figure 13.3**

The diagram on the left we use for $\bar{A} \cap \bar{B}$; the one on the right is for $\overline{A \cup B}$.

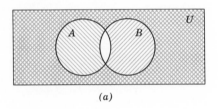
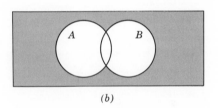

(a)           (b)

**Figure 13.4**

Thus, in Figure 13.4 (a) $\bar{A} \cap \bar{B}$ is represented by the cross-hatched region; and in Figure 13.4(b) $\overline{A \cup B}$ is represented by the shaded region. Since these regions correspond, this illustrates that the two sets $\bar{A} \cap \bar{B}$ and $\overline{A \cup B}$ are equal.

Use a Venn diagram to illustrate

$$A \cup B = (A \cap \bar{B}) \cup (A \cap B) \cup (\bar{A} \cap B)$$

First, we construct Figure 13.5.

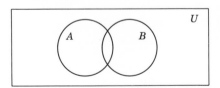

**Figure 13.5**

Now, shade the regions $A \cap \bar{B}$, $A \cap B$, and $\bar{A} \cap B$. See Figure 13.6.

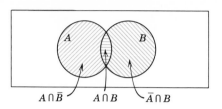

$A \cap \bar{B}$    $A \cap B$    $\bar{A} \cap B$

**Figure 13.6**

Clearly, the region shaded above is the set $A \cup B$.

**3.6 Example**

Use a Venn diagram to illustrate

$$(A \cup B) \cap C$$

First we construct Figure 13.7(a). Then we shade $A \cup B$ and $C$ as in (b). The cross-hatched region is the set $(A \cup B) \cap C$.

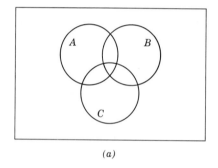 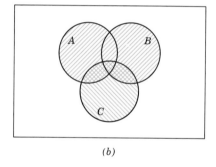

(a)                          (b)

**Figure 13.7**

**3.7 Example**

Find the most general conditions on two sets $A$ and $B$ so that

$$A \cup B = B$$

Here it is known that the elements of $A \cup B$ and those of $B$ are the same. But the elements of $A \cup B$ consist of all elements either in $A$ or in $B$. Now, if we demand that elements either in $A$ or $B$ are the same as those in $B$, we must have every element in $A$ also in $B$. For, if $A$ had elements not found in $B$, then $A \cup B$ would contain elements not found in $B$, and hence $A \cup B$ and $B$ would not be equal. Thus, if $A \cup B = B$, then $A \subseteq B$.

**3.8 Example**

If $U$ = universal set = $\{1, 2, 3, 4\}$ and if $A$ and $B$ are two non-empty sets, find all possibilities for $A$ if

$$A \cap B = \{3\} \quad \text{and} \quad B = \{2, 3\}$$

Here, because $A \cap B \subseteq A$, we know that the element 3 must be in set $A$. Since $B = \{2, 3\}$, if 2 were an element of $A$, we would have 2 in their intersection. Since $2 \notin A \cap B$, then $2 \notin A$. Thus, the only possible elements for $A$ are

$$A = \{3\}, \qquad A = \{1, 3\}, \qquad A = \{3, 4\}, \qquad A = \{1, 3, 4\}$$

1. If $A$ is any set and $U$ is the universal set, evaluate the following:
   (a) $A \cup \varnothing$          (c) $A \cup U$
   (b) $A \cap \varnothing$          (d) $A \cap U$
2. If $U =$ universal set $= \{x \mid x$ is a digit$\}$ and if $A = \{0, 1, 5, 7\}$, $B = \{2, 3, 5, 8\}$, $C = \{5, 6, 9\}$, find
   (a) $A \cup B$                    (e) $\bar{A} \cap \bar{B}$
   (b) $B \cap C$                    (f) $A \cup (B \cap A)$
   (c) $\overline{A \cap B}$          (g) $(C \cup A) \cap (\bar{A})$
   (d) $\bar{A} \cap \bar{B}$          (h) $(A \cup B) \cup (B \cap C)$
3. If $U =$ universal set $= \{1, 2, 3, 4, 5\}$ and if $A = \{3, 5\}$, $B = \{1, 2, 3\}$, $C = \{2, 3, 4\}$, find
   (a) $\bar{A} \cup \bar{C}$          (e) $\overline{A \cap C}$
   (b) $(A \cup B) \cap C$            (f) $\overline{A \cup B}$
   (c) $A \cup (B \cap C)$            (g) $\bar{A} \cap \bar{B}$
   (d) $(A \cup B) \cap (A \cup C)$
4. Consider the sets
   $A = \{x \mid x$ is a customer of IBM$\}$
   $B = \{x \mid x$ is a secretary employed by IBM$\}$
   $C = \{x \mid x$ is a computer operator at IBM$\}$
   $D = \{x \mid x$ is a stockholder of IBM$\}$
   $E = \{x \mid x$ is a member of Board of Directors of IBM$\}$
   Describe the sets
   (a) $A \cap E$                    (c) $B \cap D$
   (b) $A \cup D$                    (d) $C \cap E$
5. Use Venn diagrams to illustrate the following.
   (a) $\bar{A} \cap B$              (e) $(A \cup B) \cap (A \cup C)$
   (b) $(\bar{A} \cap \bar{B}) \cup C$   (f) $A \cup (B \cap C)$
   (c) $A \cap (A \cup B)$            (g) $A = (A \cap B) \cup (A \cap \bar{B})$
   (d) $A \cup (A \cap B)$            (h) $B = (A \cap B) \cup (\bar{A} \cap B)$
6. Use Venn diagrams to illustrate the following.
   (a) $A \cap (B \cup C) = (A \cap B) \cup (A \cap C)$     (distributive law)
   (b) $A \cap (A \cup B) = A$     (absorption law)
   (c) $\overline{A \cap B} = \bar{A} \cup \bar{B}$     (De Morgan's law)
   (d) $A \cup A = A$     (idempotent law)
   (e) $(A \cup B) \cup C = A \cup (B \cup C)$     (associative law)
7. If $A = \{1, 2, 3\}$, $B = \{3, 4, 5, 6\}$, $C = \{3, 5, 7\}$, find
   (a) $A \cup B$                    (e) $A \cap C$
   (b) $A \cup C$                    (f) $B \cap C$
   (c) $(A \cup B) \cap C$            (g) $(A \cap B) \cap C$
   (d) $A \cap B$                    (h) $(A \cap B) \cup C$

8. If $A = \{1, 3, 5, 7\}$, $B = \{2, 4\}$, $C = \{1, 2, 3\}$, $U =$ universal
set $= \{1, 2, 3, 4, 5, 7\}$, find
(a) $\overline{A} \cup \overline{B}$                (e) $\overline{U \cap B}$
(b) $\overline{A} \cap \overline{B}$                (f) $\overline{C \cup B}$
(c) $\overline{A} \cap \overline{B}$                (g) $\overline{C \cap A}$
(d) $\overline{A \cup B}$

*9. Find the most general condition on the sets $A$ and $B$ so
that
(a) $A \cap B = A \cup B$          (b) $A \cap B = A$

*10. If $U =$ universal set $= \{1, 2, 3, 4, 5, 6\}$, $C = \{1, 3\}$, and $A$
and $B$ are nonempty, find all possibilities for $A$ in each
of the following.
(a) $A \cup B = U$     and     $A \cap B = \{3\}$     and
$B = \{2, 3, 4\}$
(b) $A \cap B = \emptyset$     and     $A \cup B = \{1, 2, 3, 4, 5\}$     and
$B \cup C = \{1, 2, 3\}$

---

**13.4
COUNTING**

The idea of counting is really one of comparison. That is, when counting
one generally takes the objects to be counted and matches each of these
objects exactly once to the counting numbers 1, 2, 3, and so on, until
*no* objects remain.

Even before numbers had names and symbols assigned to them, this
method of counting was used. Early cavemen determined how many
of their herd of cattle did not return from pasture by using rocks. As
each cow left, a rock was placed aside. As each cow returned, a rock
was removed from the pile. If rocks remained after all the cows returned,
it was then known that some cows were missing.

It is rather important to realize that cavemen were able to do this
without developing a language or symbolism for numbers. We have a
highly developed language and symbolism for numbers. For example,
there is no question of understanding what is meant by the symbol 2316,
two thousand three hundred sixteen.

---

**4.1
Example**

Consider the set $L$ of letters in the alphabet

$$L = \{a, b, c, d, e, f, \ldots, x, y, z\}$$

Also, consider the set

$$\{1, 2, 3, 4, 5, \ldots, 24, 25, 26\}$$

Clearly, these two sets are equivalent, that is, we can match up
their elements in a one-to-one correspondence. Because of this,
we say that the set $L$ has 26 elements or that the *cardinal number*
of the set $L$ is 26 and we write $c(L) = 26$.

The empty set ∅ **has no elements and its** *cardinal number* **is defined to be zero so that**

Definition of Cardinal Number

$$c(\emptyset) = 0$$

**A set** $A$ **is said to have** $n$ **members or have** *cardinal number* $n$ **provided**

$$A \sim \{1, 2, 3, \ldots, n\}$$

**and we write**

$$c(A) = n$$

**where** $n \geqq 1$ **is a positive integer.**

Sets obeying the conditions above are called *finite sets*.

Finite Sets

A survey of a group of people indicated there were 25 with brown eyes and 15 with black hair. If 10 people had both brown eyes and black hair and 23 people had neither, how many people were interviewed?

4.2 Example

If we let $A$ denote the set of persons with brown eyes, and $B$ the set of persons with black hair, then the data given tells us

$$c(A) = 25, \qquad c(B) = 15, \qquad c(A \cap B) = 10$$

Now, the number of persons with either brown eyes or black hair cannot be $c(A) + c(B)$, since those with both would be counted twice. The correct procedure then would be to subtract off those with both. That is,

$$c(A \cup B) = c(A) + c(B) - c(A \cap B) = 25 + 15 - 10 = 30$$

Clearly, the sum of those people found either in $A$ or in $B$ and those found neither in $A$ nor in $B$ is the total interviewed. Thus, the number of people interviewed is

$$30 + 23 = 53$$

See Figure 13.8.

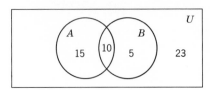

**Figure 13.8**

This example leads us to formulate the following result.

Theorem 4.1

**Let $A$ and $B$ be two finite sets. Then**

$$c(A \cup B) = c(A) + c(B) - c(A \cap B)$$

The next section will give us a way of handling problems in which more than two sets are needed.

1. What is the cardinal number of the following sets?
   (a) Set $D$ of digits $= \{0, 1, 2, 3, 4, 5, 6, 7, 8, 9\}$
   (b) $A = \{1, 3, 5, 7\}$
   (c) $A = \{0, 1, 2\}$
2. For the two sets $A = \{1, 2, 3, 5\}$ and $B = \{4, 6, 8\}$, find the cardinal number of
   (a) $A$  (c) $A \cap B$
   (b) $B$  (d) $A \cup B$
3. For the sets $A = \{1, 3, 6, 8\}$, $B = \{8\}$, and $C = \{8, 10\}$, find the cardinal number of the following.
   (a) $A \cup (B \cap C)$  (c) $A \cup (B \cup C)$
   (b) $A \cap (B \cap C)$  (d) $(A \cap B) \cup C$
4. If $c(A) = m$ and $c(B) = n$ and $c(A \cup B) = m + n$, what is $c(A \cap B)$?
5. If $c(A) = m$, $c(B) = n$, and $c(A \cup B) = r$, where $r$ is less than $m + n$, explain how to determine the cardinal number of $A \cap B$.
6. If $c(A) = 10$, $c(A \cup B) = 29$, and $c(A \cap B) = 5$, what is $c(B)$?
7. If $c(A) = c(B)$, $c(A \cup B) = 16$, and $c(A \cap B) = 6$, find $c(B)$.
8. Motors Incorporated in one day manufactured 325 cars with automatic transmissions, 216 with power steering, and 89 with both these options. How many cars were manufactured, if every car had at least one option?
9. In 1948, according to a study made by Berelsa, Lazarfeld, and McPhee, the influence of religion and age on voting in Elmira, New York was given by the following table.

| | Age | | |
|---|---|---|---|
| | Below 35 | 35–54 | Over 54 |
| Protestant voting Republican | 82 | 152 | 111 |
| Protestant voting Democratic | 42 | 33 | 15 |
| Catholic voting Republican | 27 | 33 | 7 |
| Catholic voting Democratic | 44 | 47 | 33 |

Find
(a) The number of voters who are Catholic or Republican or both.

**393**
13.5
APPLICATION OF
THE TECHNIQUES
OF COUNTING TO
SURVEY ANALYSIS

(b) The number of voters who are Catholic or over 54 or both.

(c) The number of Democratic voters below 35 or over 54.

Venn diagrams are very useful for depicting certain practical results. The following examples illustrate how Venn diagrams can be used to solve some practical problems in survey analysis.

13.5
APPLICATION OF
THE TECHNIQUES
OF COUNTING
TO SURVEY
ANALYSIS

In a survey of 75 consumers, 12 indicated they would be buying a new car, 18 said they would buy a new refrigerator, and 24 said they would buy a new stove. Of these, 6 were buying both a car and a refrigerator, 4 were buying a car and a stove, and 10 were buying a stove and refrigerator. One person indicated he would buy all three items.

5.1
Example

(a) How many are buying none of these items?
(b) How many are buying only a car?
(c) How many are buying only a stove?
(d) How many are buying only a refrigerator?

Denote the set of people buying cars, refrigerators, and stoves by $C$, $R$, and $S$, respectively. Then we know from the data given that

$$c(C) = 12, \quad c(R) = 18, \quad c(S) = 24$$
$$c(C \cap R) = 6, \quad c(C \cap S) = 4, \quad c(S \cap R) = 10$$
$$c(C \cap R \cap S) = 1$$

We use the information given above in the reverse order. Thus, beginning with the fact that $c(C \cap R \cap S) = 1$, we place a 1 in that set. See Figure 13.9(a). Now $c(C \cap R) = 6$, $c(C \cap S) = 4$, and $c(S \cap R) = 10$. Thus, we place $6 - 1 = 5$ in the proper region

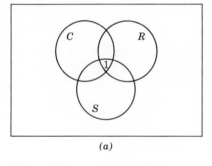

(a)

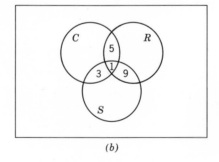

(b)

**Figure 13.9**

(giving a total of 6 in the set $C \cap R$). Similarly, we place 3 and 9 in the proper regions for the sets $C \cap S$ and $S \cap R$. See Figure 13.9(b). Now, $c(C) = 12$ and 9 of these 12 are already accounted for. Also, $c(R) = 18$, with 15 accounted for, and $c(S) = 24$, with 13 accounted for. See Figure 13.9(c). Finally, the number in $\overline{C \cup R \cup S}$ is the total of 75 less those accounted for in $C$, $R$, and $S$, namely, $3 + 5 + 1 + 3 + 3 + 9 + 11 = 35$. Thus

$$c(\overline{C \cup R \cup S}) = 75 - 35 = 40$$

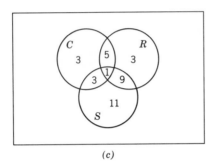 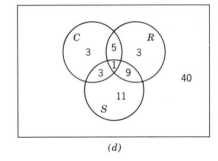

(c)                                    (d)

**Figure 13.9 (Con't)**

See Figure 13.9(d). From this figure, it is easy to see that 40 are buying none of the items, 3 are only buying cars, 3 are only buying refrigerators, and 11 are only buying stoves.

**5.2**
**Example**

In a survey of 10,281 people, restricted to ones who were either black or married or male, the following data was obtained:

Black: 3490
Male: 5822
Married: 4722
Black males: 1745
Married males: 859
Married blacks: 1341
Black married males: 239

The data is not valid. Why?
Just as in the previous example, denote the set of people who were black by $B$, married by $H$, and male by $M$. Then we know that

$$c(B) = 3490, \quad c(M) = 5822, \quad c(H) = 4722$$
$$c(B \cap M) = 1745, \quad c(H \cap M) = 859$$
$$c(H \cap B) = 1341, \quad c(H \cap M \cap B) = 239$$

Since $H \cap M \cap B \neq \emptyset$, we use the situation depicted in Figure 13.10. This means that

$$239 + 1102 + 620 + 1506 + 3457 + 643 + 2761 = 10{,}328$$

people were interviewed. However, it is given that only 10,281 were interviewed. This means the data is not valid.

**395**
13.5
APPLICATION OF
THE TECHNIQUES
OF COUNTING TO
SURVEY ANALYSIS

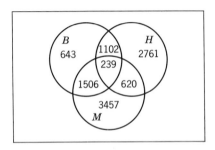

**Figure 13.10**

1. Blood is classified as being either Rh positive or Rh negative, and according to type. If blood contains an A antigen, it is type A; if it has a B antigen, it is type B; if it has both an A and B antigen, it is type AB; and if it has neither antigen, it is type O. Use a Venn diagram to illustrate these possibilities. How many different possibilities are there?

2. In a survey of 75 college students, it was found that, of the three weekly news magazines "Time," "Newsweek," and "U.S. News and World Report,"
   (a) 23 read "Time."
   (b) 18 read "Newsweek."
   (c) 14 read "U.S. News and World Report."
   (d) 10 read "Time and Newsweek."
   (e) 9 read "Time" and "U.S. News and World Report."
   (f) 8 read "Newsweek" and "U.S. News and World Report."
   (g) 5 read all three.
       (i) How many read none of these three magazines?
       (ii) How many read Time alone?
       (iii) How many read Newsweek alone?
       (iv) How many read U.S. News and World Report alone?
       (v) How many read neither Time nor Newsweek?
       (vi) How many read Time or Newsweek or both?

3. A staff member at a large engineering school was presenting data to show that the students there received a liberal education as well as a scientific one. "Look at our record," he said. "Out of one senior class of 500 students, 281 are taking English, 196 are taking English and History, 87 are taking History and a foreign language, 143 are taking a foreign language and English, and 36 are taking all of these." He was fired. Why?

4. Of the cars sold during the month of July, 90 had air conditioning, 100 had automatic transmissions, and 75 had power steering. Five cars had all three of these extras. Twenty cars had none of these extras. Twenty cars had only air conditioning; 60 cars had only automatic transmissions;

and 30 had only power steering. Ten cars had both automatic transmission and power steering.

(a) How many cars had both power steering and air conditioning?

(b) How many had both automatic transmission and air
conditioning?

(c) How many had neither power steering nor automatic
transmission?

(d) How many cars were sold in July?

(e) How many had automatic transmission or air conditioning or both?

*5. A survey of 52 families from a suburb of Chicago indicated
that there was a total of 241 children below the age of 18.
Of these, 109 were male, 132 were below the age of 11,
143 had police records, and 69 males were of age under
11. If 45 females under 11 had police records and 30 males
under 11 had police records, how many children over 11
and under 18 had police records?

## 13.6 PERMUTATIONS

In Section 13.4 the concepts of a finite set and the number of elements
in a set are discussed. Although it may appear at first glance that counting
the elements of a set is easy, many counting problems are complicated
and difficult.

In the final two sections of this chapter we discuss two general types
of counting problems that can be solved by employing formulas. These
two types of problems are called permutation problems (Section 13.6)
and combination problems (Section 13.7).

Before discussing the nature of a permutation and a combination, we
introduce a useful shorthand notation—the *factorial symbol.*

**Definition
of Factorial**

**The symbol $n!$, read as "$n$ factorial," means**

$$0! = 1, \qquad 1! = 1, \qquad n! = n(n-1)(n-2) \cdots (3)(2)(1), \qquad n \geqq 1$$

Thus, to compute $n!$, we find the product of all consecutive integers
from 1 to $n$ inclusive. For example,

$$4! = (4)(3)(2)(1) = 24 \qquad 3! = (3)(2)(1) = 6$$

A justification that $0! = 1$ may be found in Problem 3 of Exercise 13.7.
A formula we shall find useful is

$$(n+1)! = (n+1) \cdot n!$$

For example, since $5! = 5 \cdot 4!$,

$$\frac{5!}{4!} = \frac{5 \cdot 4!}{4!} = 5$$

We begin the study of permutations by considering the following problem.

In traveling from New York to Los Angeles, Mr. Doody wishes to stop over in Chicago. If he has 5 different routes to choose from in going from New York to Chicago and has 3 routes to choose from in going from Chicago to Los Angeles, in how many ways can Mr. Doody travel from New York to Los Angeles?

To solve this problem, we notice that corresponding to each of the 5 routes from New York to Chicago, there are 3 routes from Chicago to Los Angeles. Thus, in all, there are $5 \cdot 3 = 15$ different routes (see Figure 13.11). These 15 different routes can be enumerated as

$$1A, 1B, 1C \qquad 2A, 2B, 2C \qquad 3A, 3B, 3C \qquad 4A, 4B, 4C \qquad 5A, 5B, 5C$$

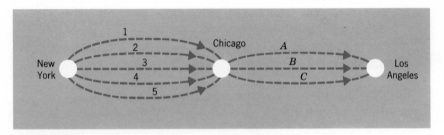

**Figure 13.11**

This same problem can also be interpreted by using a *tree diagram* (see Figure 13.12).

Tree Diagram

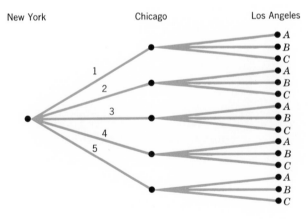

**Figure 13.12**

Of course it is easy to see that there is a total of 15 different routes.

In general, we are led to the principle in Theorem 6.1.

**Theorem 6.1 Fundamental Principle of Counting**

**If we can perform a first task in $p$ different ways, a second task in $q$ different ways, a third task in $r$ different ways, ..., then the total act of performing the first task, followed by performing the second task, and so on, can be done in $p \cdot q \cdot r \ldots$ ways.**

6.1
Example

In a city election, there are 4 candidates for mayor, 3 candidates for vice-mayor, 6 candidates for treasurer, and 2 for secretary. In how many ways can these 4 offices be filled?

Again, we reason as follows. Corresponding to each of the 4 possible mayors, there are 3 vice-mayors. These 2 offices can be filled in $4 \cdot 3 = 12$ different ways. Also, corresponding to each of these 12 possibilities, we have 6 different choices for treasurer—giving $12 \cdot 6 = 72$ different possibilities. Finally, to each of these 72 possibilities there can correspond 2 choices for secretary. Thus, all told, these offices can be filled in $4 \cdot 3 \cdot 6 \cdot 2 = 144$ different ways. A partial illustration is given by the tree diagram in Figure 13.13.

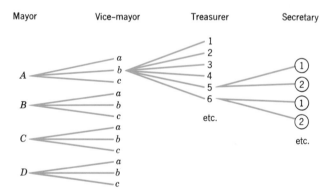

**Figure 13.13**

In Problem 12, Exercise 13.2, page 384, the student was asked to list all the subsets of the set $\{a, b, c, d\}$. With the aid of the Fundamental Theorem of Counting, we can determine a general formula for how many subsets a finite set has.

6.2
Example

Consider a set $A$ that has $n$ elements. How many subsets does $A$ have? (Remember that $A$ and $\emptyset$ are both subsets of $A$.)

If $n$ is very small, it is easy enough to list all the subsets and proceed to count them. However, this will not do if $n$ is large, nor does it give us a formula to use to calculate this quantity. Thus, we attack the problem by considering an arbitrary subset $X$ of $A$.

Any element of the set $A$ is either in $X$ or not in $X$—that is, there are two choices for each element. Since there are $n$ such elements, each giving rise to two choices, we have altogether

$$2 \cdot 2 \cdot 2 \cdots 2 = 2^n$$

possible subsets of $A$.

Thus, the set $S = \{a, b, c, d\}$ has $2^4 = 2 \cdot 2 \cdot 2 \cdot 2 = 16$ subsets. These are

$\varnothing, \{a\}, \{b\}, \{c\}, \{d\}, \{a, b\}, \{a, c\}, \{a, d\}, \{b, c\}, \{b, d\}, \{c, d\}, \{a, b, c\}, \{a, b, d\}, \{b, c, d\}, \{a, c, d\}, \{a, b, c, d\}.$

From how many different batting orders must the manager of a baseball team (nine men) select? If he adheres to the rule that the pitcher always bats last and his star home run hitter is always clean-up (fourth), then from how many possibilities must he select?

6.3
Example

In the first slot, any of the nine players can be chosen. In the second slot, any one of the remaining eight can be chosen; and so on, so that there are

$$9 \cdot 8 \cdot 7 \cdot 6 \cdot 5 \cdot 4 \cdot 3 \cdot 2 \cdot 1 = 9! = 362{,}880$$

possible batting orders.

For the second problem, the first position can be filled in any one of seven ways, the second in any six ways, the third in any of five ways, the fourth has been designated, the fifth in any of four ways, ..., so that here there are

$$7 \cdot 6 \cdot 5 \cdot 4 \cdot 3 \cdot 2 \cdot 1 = 7! = 5040$$

different batting orders of nine men after two have been designated.

Suppose we are setting up a code of three letter words and have six different letters $a$, $b$, $c$, $d$, $e$, and $f$, from which to choose. If the code must not repeat any letter more than once, and if such words as $abc$ and $bac$ are considered different, how many different words can be formed?

6.4
Example

We solve the problem by using the Fundamental Principle of Counting. Thus, in selecting a first letter, we have six choices. Since whatever letter is chosen cannot be repeated, we have five choices available for the second letter and four for the last letter. In all, then, there are $6 \cdot 5 \cdot 4 = 120$ three letter words that can be formed. See Figure 13.14 for a partial tree diagram illustration of this solution.

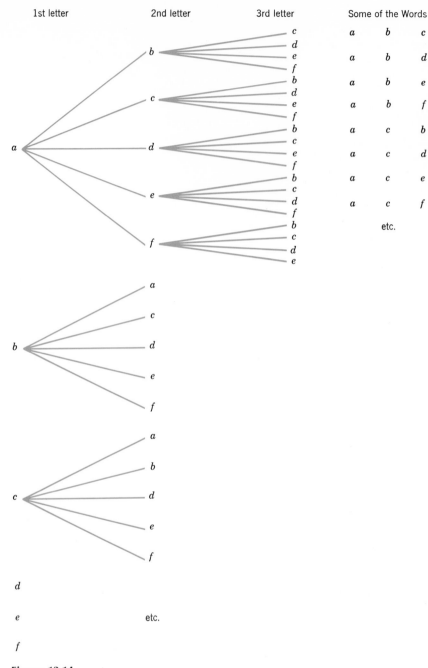

**Figure 13.14**

We observe two important features of the previous two examples. First, no item was repeated (that is, replacements were not allowed); second, order was important (for example *abc* and *bac* are different words). When these two characteristics appear in a counting problem, it is called a *permutation*.

**The number of** *permutations of n different things taken r at a time,*
**denoted by** $P(n, r)$**, means the number of all possible different arrange-**
**ments of** *r* **things chosen from** *n* **different things, in which order is**
**important.**

Let us obtain a general formula for $P(n, r)$. We wish to find the number
of possible different arrangements of $r$ quantities that are chosen from
$n$ different quantities in which no item is repeated and order is important.
The first entry can be filled by any one of the $n$ possibilities, the second
by any one of the remaining $(n - 1)$, the third by any one of the now
remaining $(n - 2)$, and so on. Since there are $r$ positions to be filled,
the number of possibilities is

$$P(n, r) = \underbrace{n(n - 1)(n - 2) \ldots}_{r \text{ factors}}$$

For example, if $n = 6$ and $r = 2$,

$$P(6, 2) = \underbrace{6 \cdot 5}_{2 \text{ factors}} = 30$$

Also,

$$P(7, 3) = \underbrace{7 \cdot 6 \cdot 5}_{3 \text{ factors}} = 210; \qquad P(5, 5) = \underbrace{5 \cdot 4 \cdot 3 \cdot 2 \cdot 1}_{5 \text{ factors}} = 5! = 120$$

To obtain the last factor in the expression for $P(n, r)$, we observe the
following pattern:

first factor is $n$
second factor is $n - 1$
third factor is $n - 2$
$\vdots$
rth factor is $\quad n - (r - 1) = n - r + 1$

**Thus, the number of different arrangements of** *r* **objects chosen from**
*n* **objects in which**

**1. The** *n* **objects are all different.**
**2. No object is repeated more than once in an arrangement.**
**3. Order is important.**

**is given by the formula**

$$P(n, r) = n(n - 1) \cdots (n - r + 1)$$

Using factorial notation, the formula for $P(n, r)$ becomes

$$P(n, r) = \frac{n!}{(n - r)!}$$

The student is asked to verify this formula in Problem 3, Exercise 13.6.

A station wagon has nine seats in it. In how many different ways can five people be seated?

The first person can choose any one of the nine seats. The second person can then choose from any of the eight seats left. The third from seven seats, the fourth from six, and the fifth person from five seats. Thus, in all, there are

$$9 \cdot 8 \cdot 7 \cdot 6 \cdot 5 = 15{,}120$$

different seating arrangements.

In Example 6.5, we observe that the properties of a permutation are satisfied: the nine seats are all different, no seat is taken more than once, and order is important. We conclude that Example 6.5 is asking for the number of permutations of 9 people taken 5 at a time. That is,

$$P(9, 5) = 9 \cdot 8 \cdot 7 \cdot 6 \cdot 5 = 15{,}120$$

Suppose, in the above example, there were nine people to be seated in the nine passenger station wagon. In this case, the number of possible arrangements is

$$P(9, 9) = 9 \cdot 8 \cdot 7 \cdot 6 \cdot 5 \cdot 4 \cdot 3 \cdot 2 \cdot 1 = 9! = 362{,}880$$

In general, the number of permutations of $n$ different objects taken $n$ at a time is

$$P(n, n) = n!$$

We conclude this section with counting problems that are a variation of the type just studied. Recall that a permutation problem requires that the objects be distinct. Many problems, however, contain duplications of an object. The next example illustrates how such problems can be solved.

How many different three letter words (real or imaginary) can be formed from the letters in the word
(a) $M \, A \, D$     (b) $D \, A \, D$

(a) The word $M \, A \, D$ contains three different letters, order is important, and no letter can be repeated. The number of different words is a permutation of 3 things taken 3 at a time or

$$P(3, 3) = 3! = 6$$

The six different words are

$$M \, A \, D, \quad M \, D \, A, \quad A \, M \, D$$
$$D \, A \, M, \quad D \, M \, A, \quad A \, D \, M$$

(b) The word $D \, A \, D$ contains three letters, and, if all were different [as in (a)], the answer would be $P(3, 3) = 3!$ different words. However, there are two $D$'s that we cannot distinguish so that 3! must be too large. [For example, if in (a) we set $M = D$, then $M \, A \, D$ and $D \, A \, M$ are the same.] If $N$ is the number of different arrangements of $D \, A \, D$, and we think of the $D$'s as different letters, say $D_1$ and $D_2$, the number of different arrangements of $D_1 \, A \, D_2$ is $2!N$. But we have treated all letters as distinct so that

$$2!N = 3!$$

$$N = \frac{3!}{2!} = 3$$

The three different arrangements are $D \, A \, D, D \, D \, A,$ and $A \, D \, D$.

6.7
Example

How many different words (real or imaginary) can be formed from the word

### SEVEN

The word contains five letters and, if none were the same, the answer would be $P(5, 5) = 5!$ different words. However, there are two $E$'s, which we cannot distinguish, and so, 5! must be too large. Let $N$ denote the number of different words that can be formed from the word *SEVEN*. If we think of the $E$'s as different letters, then the number of different words that can be formed from *SEVEN* is $2!N$. But in this case we have treated all the letters as distinct so that there would be 5! different words. Thus,

$$2!N = 5!$$

$$N = \frac{5!}{2!} = 5 \cdot 4 \cdot 3 = 60$$

different words that can be formed from the word *SEVEN*.

As another example, how many different words (real or imaginary) can be formed from the word

### MISSISSIPPI

The word contains 11 letters and, if none were the same, the answer would be $P(11, 11) = 11!$ different words. However, the fact that there are four $I$'s, four $S$'s, and two $P$'s tells us that 11! must be too large—since we cannot distinguish one $I$ from another, and so on. Suppose N denotes the number of different rearrangements of MISSISSIPPI, where we cannot recognize the difference between the four $I$'s or between the four $S$'s or between the two $P$'s. Now if suddenly we *can* recognize the difference between the four $I$'s, but we still cannot recognize the difference between the $S$'s or between the $P$'s, then there will be 4! times as many different rearrangements of MISSISSIPPI (because there are 4! ways to rearrange the $I$'s in their same four places). That is, there are now 4!N different rearrangements of MISSISSIPPI. If we think of the $S$'s as distinct also, there will be 4!(4!N) rearrangements of MISSISSIPPI with the $P$'s treated alike. Finally, treating the P's as different letters, there are $2!4!4!N$ rearrangements of MISSISSIPPI, in which now we have treated every letter as distinct. But, with every letter treated as distinct, MISSISSIPPI has $11!$ rearrangements. Thus,

$$2!4!4!N = 11!$$

or

$$N = \frac{11!}{2!4!4!} = \frac{39,916,800}{1,152} = 34,650$$

6.8
Example

How many different vertical arrangements are possible for ten flags if two are white, three are red, and five are blue.

Here we want the different arrangements of ten objects, not all different. Thus, following the argument above, we have

$$\frac{10!}{2!3!5!} = \frac{10 \cdot 9 \cdot 8 \cdot 7 \cdot 6 \cdot 5!}{2 \cdot 3 \cdot 2 \cdot 5!} = 2520$$

different arrangements.

13.6
Exercise

1. Find the value of
   (a) $P(6, 4)$           (d) $P(5, 4)$
   (b) $P(7, 2)$           (e) $P(8, 7)$
   (c) $P(5, 1)$           (f) $P(6, 6)$
2. Find $x$ if
   (a) $P(x, 3) = 60$      (b) $P(6, x) = 30$
3. Show that

$$P(n, r) = \frac{n!}{(n - r)!}$$

4. A woman has four blouses and five skirts. How many different outfits can she wear?
5. XYZ Company wants to build a complex consisting of a factory, office building, and warehouse. If the building contractor has three different kinds of factories, two different office buildings, and four different warehouses, how many models must he build to show all possibilities to XYZ Company.
6. Cars Incorporated has three different car models and six color schemes. If you are one of the dealers, how many cars must you display to show each possibility.
7. How many different words (real or imaginary) can be formed from the word *economic*?
8. On a mathematics test there are 10 multiple-choice questions, with 4 possible answers, and 15 true-false questions. In how many possible ways can the 25 questions be answered?

9. A person has 3 pairs of shoes, 8 pairs of socks, 4 pairs of slacks, and 9 sweaters. How many outfits are possible?
10. There are 14 teachers in a math department. A student is asked to indicate his favorite and his least favorite teacher. In how many ways is this possible?
11. A house has 3 doors and 12 windows. In how many ways can a burglar rob the house, if he enters through a window and exits through a door?
12. An automobile manufacturer produces 3 different models. *A* and *B* can come in any of 3 body styles; *C* can come in only 2. Each car can come either in black or in green. How many distinguishable car types are possible? (Hint: Use a tree diagram.)

Up to this point, we have been concerned with the order in which *n* distinct objects can be rearranged without repeating. However, in many cases, order is not important. For example, in a draw poker hand, the order in which one receives his cards is not important at all—rather it is what cards are received that is important. That is, with poker hands, we are concerned with the *combination* of the cards—not the particular order of the cards.

To further emphasize the role that order plays in a counting problem, suppose we have four letters *a, b, c, d* and wish to choose two of them without repeating any letter more than once.

If order is important, then we have $P(4, 2) = 4 \cdot 3 = 12$ possible arrangements, namely,

$$ab, ac, ad \qquad bc, bd, cd \qquad ba, ca, da \qquad cb, db, dc$$

If order is not a consideration, we have 6 selections, namely,

$$ab, ac, ad, bc, bd, cd$$

The latter counting problem is typical of combination problem.

**The number of** *combinations of n different things taken r at a time,* **denoted by** $C(n, r)$**, is defined to be the number of all possible selections of r objects chosen from n objects, neglecting the order of selection.**  Definition of a Combination

We proceed to obtain a formula for $C(n, r)$.

There are $C(n, r)$ combinations of *n* different things taken *r* at a time. Since each of these has *r* objects, each can be permuted in *r!* different ways. Thus, by the Fundamental Principle of Counting, there are

$$r! \cdot C(n, r)$$

different arrangements of *n* things taken *r* at a time. But this is just the number of permutations of $n$ things taken $r$ at a time. Hence,

$$r!C(n, r) = P(n, r)$$

$$C(n, r) = \frac{P(n, r)}{r!}$$

For example,

$$C(4, 2) = \frac{P(4, 2)}{2!} = \frac{12}{2} = 6$$

Using the result of Problem 3 in Exercise 13.6, page 404, it is easy to verify that

$$C(n, r) = \frac{n!}{r!(n - r)!}$$

**Thus, the number of different arrangements of $r$ objects chosen from $n$ objects in which**

**1. The $n$ objects are all different.**
**2. No object is repeated more than once.**
**3. Order is not important.**

**is given by the formula**

$$C(n, r) = \frac{n!}{(n - r)!r!}$$

7.1
Example

From a deck of 52 cards, a hand of 5 cards is dealt. How many different hands are possible?

If the order of reception of the cards is considered, there are

$$52 \cdot 51 \cdot 50 \cdot 49 \cdot 48$$

different hands. But order is not important. Thus, since corresponding to each hand of five cards there are 5! different arrangements, we see that the number of different hands, without regard to order, is

$$\frac{52 \cdot 51 \cdot 50 \cdot 49 \cdot 48}{5!} = 2{,}598{,}960$$

Of course, we can also arrive at this result by recognizing that the number of different hands is $C(52, 5)$. That is,

$$C(52, 5) = \frac{52!}{5!47!} = \frac{52 \cdot 51 \cdot 50 \cdot 49 \cdot 48}{5 \cdot 4 \cdot 3 \cdot 2 \cdot 1}$$

$$= 2{,}598{,}960$$

A sociologist needs a sample of 12 welfare recipients located in a large metropolitan area. He divides the city into 4 areas—northwest, northeast, southwest, southeast. Each section contains 25 welfare recipients. He may select the 12 recipients in any way he wants—all from the same area, 2 from the southwest area and 10 from the northwest area, and so on. How many different groups of 12 recipients are there?

7.2
Example

Since order of selection is not important, and since the selection is of 12 things from a possible $4 \cdot 25 = 100$ things, there are $C(100, 12)$ different groups. That is

$$C(100, 12) = \frac{100!}{12!88!}$$

Sometimes the notation $\binom{n}{r}$, read as "$n$ things taken $r$ at a time", is used in place of $C(n, r)$. Here, $\binom{n}{r}$ is called a *binomial coefficient*. A display of $\binom{n}{r}$ for $n = 0$ to $n = 6$ is given in Figure 13.15. This display is called a *Pascal triangle*.

Binomial Coefficient

Pascal Triangle

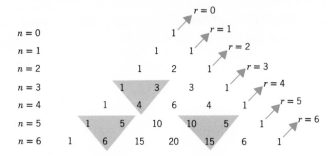

**Figure 13.15**

For example, $\binom{5}{2} = 10$, is in the row marked $n = 5$ and on the diagonal marked $r = 2$.

Notice that successive entries can be obtained by adding the two nearest entries in the row above it. The shaded triangles in Figure 13.15 illustrate this. For example, $10 + 5 = 15$, etc.

A fraternity house has three bedrooms and ten students. One bedroom has three beds, the second has two beds, and the third has five beds. In how many different ways can the students be assigned beds?

7.3
Example

First of all, there are ten beds. There are $\binom{10}{3}$ ways of assigning the beds in the first bedroom. For the seven remaining students, we can assign the beds in the second bedroom in $\binom{7}{2}$ ways. Finally, the remaining five students can be assigned the five remaining beds in $\binom{5}{5}$ ways. In all, by the Fundamental Principle of Counting, there are

$$\binom{10}{3} \cdot \binom{7}{2} \cdot \binom{5}{5} = \frac{10!}{3!7!} \cdot \frac{7!}{2!5!} \cdot \frac{5!}{0!5!} = \frac{10!}{2!3!5!} = 2520$$

different ways.

Notice that in the above example, the number of different ways the 10 beds can be assigned is $10!/2!3!5!$, in which the bedrooms have 2 beds, 3 beds, and 5 beds respectively. Sometimes $10!/2!3!5!$ is written using the notation $\binom{10}{2, 3, 5}$. Of course, the number of total beds must be the same as the number of students in order to use this result.

7.4
Example
Voting
Paradox

This example, from the field of political science, is sometimes referred to as the "voting paradox." Suppose three voters are to vote on three proposals (or candidates) A, B, and C, and they are to list their order of preference. Then there are six possible orderings.

$$ABC, ACB, BAC, BCA, CAB, CBA$$

In how many different ways can the three voters select their choices of ordering?

To answer the question, we consider three possibilities:

(a) All three voters select the same ordering.
(b) Two of the voters choose the same ordering and the other one selects one of the other five remaining orderings.
(c) Each of the three voters selects a different ordering.

For (a), it is clear that there are 6 ways in which all three voters select the same orderings. For (b), we see that there are 6 choices for a given pair of voters to agree on, leaving 5 choices for the third voter to choose or $6 \cdot 5 = 30$ ways for a given pair of voters to agree and the third disagree. However, there are 3 possible pairs of voters. Thus, there are

$$3 \cdot 6 \cdot 5 = 90$$

ways for a pair of voters to agree on an ordering, while the third disagrees. Finally, for (c), if all three are to choose a different ordering, there are 6 orderings for the first voter to choose from, leaving only 5 for the second, and 4 for the third. Thus for (3) there are

$$6 \cdot 5 \cdot 4 = 120$$

ways for each of the three voters to choose a different ordering.

If either (a) or (b) is the result of the vote, these $90 + 6 = 96$ possibilities clearly indicate a majority opinion as to which order is preferred. In (c), 30 of the 120 possible no-majority outcomes result in a paradox. For example, suppose the voting resulted in

$$ABC, BCA, CAB$$

Notice that two voters prefer $A$ to $B$, and two voters prefer $B$ to $C$, but two voters also prefer $C$ to $A$. This is called the "voters paradox," since some of the results are indecisive.

We close this section with an example that further illustrates a difference between a permutation and a combination.

Consider a set of five students {Mike, Katy, Danny, Tammie, Jack}. In how many ways can two students be chosen from this set?

7.5
Example

As stated, the solution will depend on how the question is interpreted. For example, is the selection (Mike, Katy) different from (Katy, Mike)? Also, is it possible to select Danny twice as in (Danny, Danny)? Usually, the setting of the problem and the practical considerations of the problem will answer these questions and lead us to the correct answers.

The table on page 410 lists three cases and the assumptions of each case.

---

1. Find the value of
   (a) $C(6, 4)$    (d) $C(5, 4)$
   (b) $C(7, 2)$    (e) $C(8, 7)$
   (c) $C(5, 1)$    (f) $C(8, 8)$
2. Find $x$ if
   (a) $C(x, 2) = 10$    (b) $C(7, x) = 35$
3. Interpret the meaning of $C(n, 0)$ and $C(n, n)$. Can you now justify our definition of 0!
4. Show that

$$C(n, r) = \frac{n!}{(n - r)!r!}$$

5. Write down entries in the Pascal triangle for $n = 7, 8, 9, 10$.

13.7
Exercise

| Assumption | Case 1<br>Without replacement and with regard to order | Case 2<br>Without replacement and without regard to order | Case 3<br>With replacement and with regard to order |
|---|---|---|---|
| Selections by name | (Mike, Katy), (Mike, Danny), (Mike, Tammie), (Mike, Jack)<br><br>(Katy, Mike), (Katy, Danny), (Katy, Tammie), (Katy, Jack)<br><br>(Danny, Mike), (Danny, Katy), (Danny, Tammie), (Danny, Jack)<br><br>(Tammie, Mike), (Tammie, Katy), (Tammie, Danny), (Tammie, Jack)<br><br>(Jack, Mike), (Jack, Katy), (Jack, Danny), (Jack, Tammie) | (Mike, Katy), (Mike, Danny), (Mike, Tammie), (Mike, Jack)<br><br>(Katy, Danny), (Katy, Tammie), (Katy, Jack)<br><br>(Danny, Tammie), (Danny, Jack)<br><br>(Tammie, Jack) | (Mike, Mike), (Mike, Katy), (Mike, Danny), (Mike, Tammie), (Mike, Jack)<br><br>(Katy, Mike), (Katy, Katy), (Katy, Danny), (Katy, Tammie), (Katy, Jack)<br><br>(Danny, Mike), (Danny, Katy), (Danny, Danny), (Danny, Tammie), (Danny, Jack)<br><br>(Tammie, Mike), (Tammie, Katy), (Tammie, Danny), (Tammie, Tammie), (Tammie, Jack)<br><br>(Jack, Mike), (Jack, Katy), (Jack, Danny), (Jack, Tammie), (Jack, Jack) |
| Number of selections | 20 | 10 | 25 |
| Rule | Permutation<br>$P(5,2) = 5 \cdot 4 = 20$ | Combination<br>$C(5,2) = \dfrac{5 \cdot 4}{2} = 10$ | Fundamental Principle of Counting<br>$5 \cdot 5 = 25$ |

6. Show that

$$C(n, r) = C(n, n - r)$$

This fact should be checked by referring to the Pascal triangle.

7. A basketball team has six men who play at guard (two of five starting positions). How many different teams are possible? The remaining three positions are assumed filled. Further assume that it is not possible to distinguish a left guard from a right guard.

8. On a basketball team of twelve men, two play only at center, three play only at guard, and the rest play at forward (5 men on a team: 2 forwards, 2 guards and 1 center). How many different teams are possible? Assume it is not possible to distinguish left and right guards and left and right forwards.

9. The Student Affairs Committee has three faculty, two administrators, and five students on it. In how many ways can a subcommittee of one faculty, one administrator, and two students be formed?

10. Of 1352 stocks traded one day on the New York Stock Exchange, 641 advanced, 234 declined, and the remainder were unchanged. In how many ways can this happen?

11. A mathematics department is allowed to tenure 4 of 17 eligible teachers. In how many ways can the selection for tenure be made?

12. How many different hands are possible in a bridge game? A bridge hand consists of 13 cards dealt from a deck of 52 cards.

13. The United States Senate has 100 members. Suppose it is desired to place each senator on exactly 1 of 7 possible committees. The first committee has 22 members, the second 13, the third 10, the fourth 5, the fifth 16, the sixth and seventh 17 apiece. In how many ways can these committees be formed?

14. In how many ways can ten children be placed on three teams of 3, 3, and 4 members?

15. A person has a penny, nickel, dime, quarter, half dollar, silver dollar. If he chooses 3 coins at random, how many sums are possible?

| | | |
|---|---|---|
| empty set (∅) | intersection (∩) | CHAPTER |
| null set (∅) | disjoint sets | REVIEW |
| element | complement | |
| set-builder notation | cardinal number | Important |
| equivalent sets | finite sets | Terms |
| equal sets | Venn diagram | |

one-to-one correspondence
subset ($\subseteq$)
proper subset ($\subset$)
comparable sets
universal set($U$)
operation
union ($\cup$)

factorial
tree diagram
fundamental principle of counting
permutation
combination
Pascal triangle

Exercises Part A

Circle each correct answer or answers. Some questions have more than one correct answer. Replace the asterisk * by all correct symbols.

| a. | b. | c. | d. | e. | f. | g. |
|----|----|----|----|----|----|----|
| $\in$ | $\notin$ | $\subset$ | $\subseteq$ | $\sim$ | $=$ | none of these |

1. a  b  c  d  e  f  g    1. $0 * \emptyset$
2. a  b  c  d  e  f  g    2. $\{0\} * \{1, 0, 3\}$
3. a  b  c  d  e  f  g    3. $\{5, 6\} \cap \{2, 6\} * \{8\}$
4. a  b  c  d  e  f  g    4. $\{2, 3\} \cup \{3, 4\} * \{3\}$
5. a  b  c  d  e  f  g    5. $\{8, 9\} * \{9, 10, 11\}$
6. a  b  c  d  e  f  g    6. $1 * \{1, 3, 5\} \cap \{3, 4\}$
7. a  b  c  d  e  f  g    7. $5 * \{0, 5\}$
8. a  b  c  d  e  f  g    8. $\emptyset * \{1, 2, 3\}$
9. a  b  c  d  e  f  g    9. $\emptyset * \{1, 2\} \cap \{3, 4, 5\}$
10. a  b  c  d  e  f  g    10. $\{2, 3\} * \{3, 4\}$
11. a  b  c  d  e  f  g    11. $\{1, 2\} * \{1\} \cup \{3\}$
12. a  b  c  d  e  f  g    12. $5 * \{1\} \cup \{2, 3\}$
13. a  b  c  d  e  f  g    13. $\{4, 5\} \cup \{5, 6\} * \{4, 5\}$
14. a  b  c  d  e  f  g    14. $\{6, 8\} * \{8, 9, 10\}$
15. a  b  c  d  e  f  g    15. $\{6, 7, 8\} \cap \{8\} * \{6\}$
16. a  b  c  d  e  f  g    16. $4 * \{6, 8\} \cap \{4, 8\}$

Part B

1. For the sets

$$A = \{1, 3, 5, 6, 8\}, \quad B = \{2, 3, 6, 7\}, \quad C = \{6, 8, 9\}$$

find
(a) $(A \cap B) \cup C$
(b) $(A \cup B) \cap C$
(c) $(A \cup B) \cap B$

2. For the sets, $U =$ universal set $= \{1, 2, 3, 4, 5, 6, 7\}$,

$$A = \{1, 3, 5, 6\}, \quad B = \{2, 3, 6, 7\}, \quad C = \{4, 6, 7\}$$

find
(a) $A \cup B$
(b) $(B \cap C) \cap A$
(c) $\bar{B} \cup \bar{A}$

3. If $U$ = universal set = $\{1, 2, 3, 4, 5\}$, find all sets $A$ for which $A \cap B = \{1\}$, $B = \{1, 4, 5\}$.

4. If $U$ = universal set = $\{1, 2, 3, 4, 5, 6\}$ and if $A = \{1, 3, 4\}$, $B = \{2, 4, 6\}$, $C = \{3, 4, 5\}$, find
   (a) $(A \cap B) \cup C$
   (b) $A \cap \bar{B}$
   (c) $(A \cup C) \cap B$
   (d) $(A \cap B) \cap \bar{C}$

5. If $A$ and $B$ are sets and if $c(A) = 24$, $c(A \cup B) = 33$, $c(B) = 12$, find $c(A \cap B)$.

6. During June, Colleen's Motors sold 75 cars with air conditioning, 95 with power steering, and 100 with automatic transmission. Twenty cars had all 3 options, 10 cars had none of these options, and 10 cars were sold that had only air conditioning. In addition, 50 cars had both automatic transmission and power steering and 60 cars had both automatic transmission and air conditioning.
   (a) How many cars were sold in June?
   (b) How many cars had only power steering?

7. In a survey of 125 college students, it was found that of three newspapers, the Wall Street Journal, N.Y. Times, and Chicago Tribune

   > 60 read the Tribune,
   > 40 read the Times,
   > 15 read the Journal,
   > 25 read the Tribune and Times,
   > 8 read the Times and Journal,
   > 3 read the Tribune and Journal,
   > 1 read all three.

   (a) How many read none of these papers?
   (b) How many read only the Tribune?
   (c) How many read neither the Tribune nor the Times?
   *(d) How many read the Tribune if and only if they read the Journal?

8. You are to set up a code of two digit words using the digits 1, 2, 3, 4 without using any digit more than once. What is the maximum number of words in such a language? If the words 12 and 21, for example, designate the same word, how many words are possible?

9. A person has 4 history, 5 English and 6 math books. How many ways can they be arranged on a shelf if books of the same subject must be together?

10. A small town consists of a north side and a south side. The north side has 16 houses and the south side has 10 houses. A poll taker is asked to visit 4 houses on the north side and 3 on the south side. In how many ways can this be done?

11. A ceremony is to include 7 speeches and 6 musical selections.
    (a) How many programs are possible?
    (b) How many programs are possible if speeches and musical selections are to be alternated?

12. There are 7 boys and 6 girls willing to serve on a committee. How many 7 member committees are possible if a committee is to contain
    (a) Three boys and 4 girls?
    (b) At least one member of both sexes?

13. Colleen's Ice Cream Parlor offers 31 different flavors to choose from, and specializes in double dip cones. How many different cones are there to choose from, if you may select the same flavor for each dip? How many different cones are there to choose from, if you cannot repeat any flavor. Assume that a cone with vanilla on top of chocolate is different than a cone with chocolate on top of vanilla. How many are there if you consider any cone having chocolate on top and vanilla on the bottom the same as having vanilla on top and chocolate on the bottom?

14. You are to set up a code of three-digit words using the digits 1, 2, 3, 4, 5, 6 without using any digit more than once in the same word. What is the maximum number of words in such a language? If the words 124, 142, etc. designate the same word, how many different words are possible?

15. Five people are to line up for a group photograph. If two of them cannot stand each other and refuse to stand next to each other, in how many ways can the photograph be taken?

16. The figure below indicates a route between two houses A and B of a city in which the lines are streets. A person at A wishes to reach B and he can only travel in two directions, to the right and up. How many different paths are there from A to B?

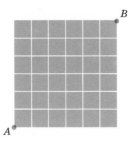

17. A cab driver picks up a passenger at point A (see the figure on page 415) whose destination is point B. After completing the trip, the driver is to proceed to his garage at point C. If he must travel to the right or up, how many different routes are there from A to C?

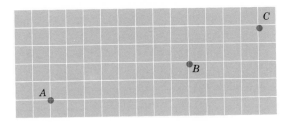

Below are six problems concerning counting; worked-out solutions are found in the Answers.

Part C

1. In how many ways can we choose 3 words, one each from 5 three-letter words, 6 four-letter words, and 8 five-letter words?
2. A newborn child can be given 1, 2, or 3 names. In how many ways can a child be named if we can choose from 100 names?
3. In how many ways can 5 girls and 3 boys be divided into 2 teams of 4, if each team is to include at least 1 boy?
4. A meeting is to be addressed by 5 speakers, A, B, C, D, E. In how many ways can the speakers be ordered, if B must not precede A?
5. What is the answer to the preceding problem, if B is to speak immediately after A?
6. An automobile license number contains 1 or 2 letters followed by a 4-digit number. Compute the maximum number of different licenses.

**Bibliography**

*Applied*

Arrow, Kenneth, J., *Social Choice and Individual Values,* Wiley, New York; 1951.

Benson, Oliver, "The Use of Mathematics in the Study of Political Science," paper presented to a symposium sponsored by The American Academy on Political and Social Science, Philadelphia, June 1963.

Black, Duncan, *The Theory of Committees and Elections,* Cambridge University Press, Cambridge, 1958.

Riker, William H., "Voting and the Summations of Preferences," *American Political Science Review, 55* (1961), pp. 900–911.

Slapley, L. S., and M. Shubik, "A Method for Evaluating the Distribution of Power in a Committee System," *The American Political Science Review, 48* (1954), pp. 787ff.

# 14

# INTRODUCTION TO PROBABILITY

Probability theory is a part of mathematics which is useful for discovering and investigating the *regular* features of *random events*. Although it is not really possible to give a precise and simple definition of what is meant by the words "random" and "regular," our hope is that the explanation and the examples given below will make the understanding of these concepts easier.

**14.1 INTRODUCTION**

It is convenient to regard certain phenomena in the real world as *chance phenomena*. By this we mean phenomena that do not always produce the same observed outcome, and for which the outcome of any given observation of the phenomena may not be predictable, but which has a certain "long-range" behavior known as *statistical regularity*.

Chance Phenomena

In some cases, we know the phenomenon under investigation sufficiently well to feel justified in making *exact* predictions with respect to the result of each individual observation. Thus, if one wants to know the time and place of a solar eclipse, we do not hesitate to predict, based on astronomical data, the exact answer to such a question.

However, in many cases our knowledge is not precise enough to allow exact predictions in particular situations. Some examples of such cases, called *random events,* are:

(a) Tossing a fair coin gives a result that is either a head or a tail. For any one throw, we cannot predict the result, although it is obvious that it is determined by definite causes (such as the initial velocity of the coin, the initial angle of throw, the surface on which the coin rests). Even though some of these causes can be controlled, we cannot predetermine the result of any particular toss. Thus, the result of tossing a coin is a *random event.*

(b) In a series of throws with an ordinary die, each throw yields, as its result, one of the numbers 1, 2, 3, 4, 5, or 6. Thus, the result of throwing a die is a *random event.*

(c) The sex of a newborn baby is either male or female. However, the sex of a newborn baby cannot be predicted in any particular case. This, too, is an example of a *random event.*

(d) Suppose that a box contains several objects (some of which are of perfect quality and some are defective). Select an object. Since it is not possible to know ahead of time whether the object is perfect or defective, the result of selecting an object in this manner is a *random event.*

The above examples demonstrate that in studying a sequence of random experiments, it is not possible to forecast individual results. These are subject to irregular, random fluctuations which cannot be exactly predicted. However, if the number of observations is large, that is, if we deal with a *mass phenomenon,* some regularity appears.

In example (a), we cannot predict the result of any particular toss. However, if we perform a long sequence of tosses, we notice that the number of times heads occurs is approximately equal to the number of times tails appears. That is, it seems *reasonable* to say that in any toss of this fair coin, a head or a tail is *equally likely* to occur. As a result, we might *assign a probability* of 1/2 for obtaining a head (or tail) on a particular toss.

The student should test this result for himself by flipping a coin 25 times, 50 times, and 100 times, noting the results. Of interest is the fact that K. Pearson, in tossing a coin 24,000 times, obtained heads 12,012 times.

For example (b), the appearance of any particular face is a random event. If, however, we perform a long series of tosses, any face is as *equally likely* to occur as any other, provided the die is fair. Here, we might *assign a probability* of 1/6 for obtaining a particular face.

For example (c), our intuition tells us that a boy baby and a girl baby are equally likely to occur. If we follow this reasoning, we might *assign a probability* of 1/2 to having a boy baby. However, were we to consult the data found in Figure 14.1 we would see that it might be more accurate to *assign a probability* of .512 to having a boy baby.

| Year of Birth | Number of Births | | Total Number of Births $b + g$ | Ratio of Births | |
|---|---|---|---|---|---|
| | Boys $b$ | Girls $g$ | | $\dfrac{b}{b+g}$ | $\dfrac{g}{b+g}$ |
| 1950 | 1,863,000 | 1,768,000 | 3,631,000 | .513 | .487 |
| 1951 | 1,960,000 | 1,863,000 | 3,823,000 | .513 | .487 |
| 1952 | 2,005,000 | 1,908,000 | 3,913,000 | .512 | .488 |
| 1953 | 2,034,000 | 1,931,000 | 3,965,000 | .513 | .487 |
| 1954 | 2,090,000 | 1,988,000 | 4,078,000 | .512 | .488 |
| 1955 | 2,103,000 | 2,001,000 | 4,104,000 | .512 | .488 |
| 1956 | 2,162,000 | 2,056,000 | 4,218,000 | .513 | .487 |
| 1957 | 2,207,000 | 2,101,000 | 4,308,000 | .512 | .488 |
| 1958 | 2,179,000 | 2,076,000 | 4,255,000 | .512 | .488 |
| 1959 | 2,174,000 | 2,071,000 | 4,245,000 | .512 | .488 |
| 1960 | 2,180,000 | 2,078,000 | 4,258,000 | .512 | .488 |
| Total | 22,957,000 | 21,841,000 | 44,798,000 | .512 | .488 |

**Figure 14.1** *Births of boys and girls (United States Census 1950–1960)*

The examples below illustrate some of the kinds of problems we shall encounter and solve in this chapter.

A fair die with six faces is thrown. With what probability will the face five occur?

1.1
Example

A fair coin is tossed. If it comes up heads (H), a fair die is rolled and the experiment is finished. If the coin comes up tails (T), the coin is tossed again and the experiment is finished. With what probability will the situation heads first, five second, occur?

1.2
Example

A room contains 50 people. With what probability will at least two of them have the same birthday?

1.3
Example

A factory produces light bulbs of which 80 percent are not defective. A sample of six bulbs is taken. With what probability will three or more of them be defective?

1.4
Example

Two dice, each with six faces, are rolled. With what probability will their total be 11, if they are fair? If one is "loaded" in a certain way, what is the probability of an 11?

1.5
Example

A group of 1200 people contains 50 who qualify for an executive position and 500 females. Furthermore, suppose 35 females qualify. With what probability will a person chosen at random be both qualified and female?

1.6
Example

Other questions that can be answered by using probability theory are given below as illustrations of the power of probability theory. The interested reader should continue on to Chapters 15 and 16 for a deeper study of probability.

Consider a telephone exchange with a finite number of lines. Suppose that the exchange is constructed in such a way that an incoming call that finds all the lines busy does not wait, but is lost. This is called an exchange without waiting lines. The most important problem to be solved, *before* the exchange is constructed, is to determine, for any time *t*, the probability of finding all the lines busy at time *t*.

People arrive at random times at a ticket counter to be served by an attendant, lining up on queue if others are waiting. Given information about the rate of arrival and the length of time an attendant requires to serve each customer, how much of the time is the attendant idle? How much of the time is the line more than 15 persons long? What would be the effect of adding another attendant? If the people are not allowed to wait in line, but must go elsewhere, what percentage of arrivals go unanswered? The same questions can be asked about gas stations, booths in toll roads, hospital beds, and so on.

The following problem occurs quite often in physics and biology and was formulated by Galton in 1874 in his study of the disappearance of family lines. Given that a man of a known family has a probability of

$$p_0, p_1, p_2, \ldots$$

of producing zero, one, two male offsprings, what is the probability that the family will eventually die out?

Suppose that an infectious disease is spread by contact, that a susceptible person has a chance of catching it with each contact with an infected person, but that one becomes immune after having had the disease and can no longer transmit it. Some of the questions we would like answered are: How many susceptibles will be left when the number of infected is zero? How long will the epidemic last? For a given community, what is the probability that the disease will die out?

1. Consult the United States census from 1960–1970 and construct a table similar to Figure 14.1. What probability would you assign to the birth of a boy baby based on this data?

2. Pick a page at random in your telephone directory and list the last digit of every number. Are all digits used equally often?

3. Toss a die six times and record the face shown. Denote this number by $x$ ($x$ can take the values 1, 2, 3, 4, 5, 6). Repeat the experiment 20 more times and tabulate the results. Do you observe any regularity?

4. Suppose a needle is dropped at random onto a floor that is marked with parallel lines 6 inches apart. Suppose the needle is 4 inches long. With what probability does the needle fall between the two lines? Perform the experiment 20 times and record the number of times the needle rests completely within the two lines. This is a version of the Buffon needle problem. An illustration is provided in Figure 14.2, and a solution may be found in *Mathematics in the Modern World*.[1]

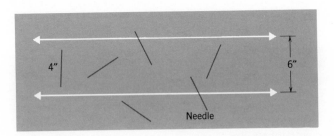

**Figure 14.2**

5. Conduct the following experiment with your classmates. Assume that you have $90 and your classmate has $10. Flip a fair coin. If you lose, you give him a dollar and, if you win, he gives you a dollar. The play ends when one of the players loses all his money. Can you guess how *long* the game will last? Can you guess who has the better chance of winning?

6. Conduct the following experiment in your classes. Find out how many students would bet that no two students had the same birthday. List the birthdays of each student and verify whether any two have the same birthday. Would you have won or lost the bet? See Section 14.3 for a table that provides a rationale for betting one way or the other.

7. (Chevalier de Mere's problem) Which of the following random events do you think is more likely to occur (a) to obtain at least one ace (face is one) in a simultaneous throw of four fair dice or (b) to obtain at least one double ace in a series of 24 throws of a pair of fair dice. See Problem 15 in Exercise 14.6.

[1] *Mathematics in the Modern World*, readings from *Scientific American*, W. H. Freeman, San Francisco, 1968, pp. 169ff.

8. Pick an editorial from your daily newspaper which contains at least 1000 words. List the number of times each letter of the alphabet is used. Based on this, what probability might you assign to the occurrence of a letter in an editorial?

14.2
SAMPLE
SPACES AND
ASSIGNMENT OF
PROBABILITIES

In studying probability we are concerned with experiments, real or conceptual, and their outcomes. In this study we try to formulate in a precise manner a mathematical theory that closely resembles the experiment in question. The first stage of development of a mathematical theory is the building of what is termed a *mathematical model*. This model is then used as a predictor of outcomes of the experiment. The purpose of this section is to learn how a probabilistic model can be constructed.

We begin by writing down the associated *sample space* of an experiment; that is, we write down all outcomes that can occur as a result of the experiment.

For example, if the experiment consists of flipping a coin, we would ordinarily agree that the only possible outcomes are "heads" and "tails." If we denote these outcomes by $H$ and $T$, respectively, a sample space for the experiment is the set $\{H, T\}$.

2.1
Example

Consider an experiment in which, for the sake of simplicity, one die is green and the other is red. When the two dice are rolled, the set of outcomes consists of all the different ways that the dice may come to rest. This is referred to as a set of all *logical possibilities*. This experiment can be displayed in two different ways. One way is to use a tree diagram. See Figure 14.3.

Another way is to let $g$ and $r$ denote, respectively, the number that comes up on the green die and the red die. Then an *outcome* can be represented by an ordered pair $(g, r)$, where both $g$ and $r$ can assume all values of a set $S$ whose members are 1, 2, 3, 4, 5, 6. Thus, a sample space $S$ of this experiment is the set

$$S = \{(g, r) \mid 1 \leqq g \leqq 6, 1 \leqq r \leqq 6\}$$

Also, notice that the number of elements in $S$ is 36, which is found by applying the Fundamental Principle of Counting, namely, $6 \cdot 6 = 36$. Figure 14.4 illustrates a graphical representation for $S$.

In the above example, we touched on some fundamental concepts, which we now introduce as definitions.

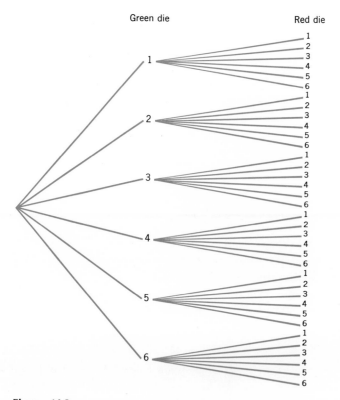

Green die          Red die

**Figure 14.3**

A *sample space S*, associated with a real or conceptual experiment, is
the set of all logical possibilities that can occur as a result of the experiment. Each element of a sample space $S$ is called an *outcome*.

Definition
of a Sample
Space; Outcome

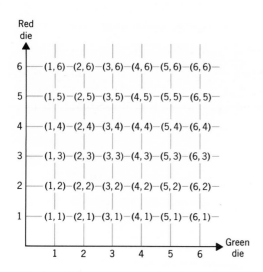

**Figure 14.4**

The theory of probability begins as soon as a sample space has been specified. The sample space of an experiment plays the same role as the universal set in set theory for all questions concerning the experiment.

In this chapter, we confine our attention to those cases for which the sample space is finite, that is, to those situations in which it is possible to have only a finite number of outcomes.

The reader should notice that in our definition we say *a* sample space, rather than *the* sample space, since an experiment can be described in many different ways. In general, it is a safe guide to include as much detail as possible in the description of the outcomes of the experiment in order to answer all pertinent questions concerning the result of the experiment.

**2.2**
**Example**

Consider the set of all families with three children. Describe the sample space for the experiment of drawing one family from the set of all possible three-child families.

One way of describing the sample space is by denoting the number of girls in the family. The only possibilities are members of the set

$$\{0, 1, 2, 3\}$$

That is, a three-child family can have 0 girls, 1 girl, 2 girls, or 3 girls.

This sample space has four outcomes. A disadvantage of describing the experiment using this sample space is that a question such as "Was the second child a girl" cannot be answered. Thus, this method of classifying the outcomes may be too coarse, since it may not provide enough wanted information.

Another way is by first defining $B$ and $G$ as "Boy" and "Girl," respectively. Then the sample space might be given as

$$\{BBB, BBG, BGB, BGG, GBB, GBG, GGB, GGG\} \qquad (2.1)$$

where $BBB$ means first born is a boy, second born is a boy, third born is a boy, and so on. This can be depicted by the use of the tree diagram in Figure 14.5. Notice that the experiment has 8 possible outcomes.

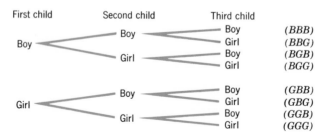

| First child | Second child | Third child | |
|---|---|---|---|
| | | Boy | (*BBB*) |
| | Boy | Girl | (*BBG*) |
| Boy | | Boy | (*BGB*) |
| | Girl | Girl | (*BGG*) |
| | | Boy | (*GBB*) |
| | Boy | Girl | (*GBG*) |
| Girl | | Boy | (*GGB*) |
| | Girl | Girl | (*GGG*) |

**Figure 14.5**

The advantage of this classification of the sample space is that each outcome of the experiment corresponds to exactly one element in the sample space.

**An *event* is a subset of a sample space. If an event has exactly one element, that is, consists of only one outcome, it is called a *simple event*.** Definition of Event, Simple Event

Every event can be written as the union of simple events. For example, a sample space of Example 2.2 is given in (2.1). The event $E$ that the family consists of exactly two boys is

$$E = \{BBG, BGB, GBB\}$$

The event $E$ is the union of the three simple events $\{BBG\}$, $\{BGB\}$, $\{GBB\}$. That is

$$E = \{BBG\} \cup \{BGB\} \cup \{GBB\}$$

Since a sample space $S$ is also an event, we can express a sample space $S$ as the union of simple events. Thus, if the sample space $S$ consists of $n$ outcomes,

$$S = \{e_1, e_2, \ldots, e_n\}$$

then

$$S = \{e_1\} \cup \{e_2\} \cup \ldots \cup \{e_n\}$$

In the two-dice experiment of Example 2.1, page 422, involving a green and red die, let $A$ be the event that the green die registers less than or equal to 3 and the red die is 5, and let $B$ be the event that the green die is 2 and the red die is 5 or 6. Describe the event $A$ or $B$. 2.3 Example

Here

$$A = \{(g, r) \,|\, g \leqq 3, r = 5\}, \qquad B = \{(g, r) \,|\, g = 2, r = 5, 6\}$$
$$= \{(1, 5), (2, 5), (3, 5)\} \qquad\qquad = \{(2, 5), (2, 6)\}$$

Clearly, $A$ has three members and $B$ has two members. The event $A$ *or* $B$ is merely the union of $A$ with $B$. Thus

$$A \cup B = \{(1, 5), (2, 5), (3, 5), (2, 6)\}$$

That is, the event $A$ *or* $B$ has four members. Of course, the event $A$ *and* $B$, namely, $A \cap B$, has one member, $(2, 5)$.

We are now in a position to formulate a definition for the probability of a simple event of a sample space.

**Let $S$ denote a sample space. To each simple event $\{e\}$ of $S$, we assign a real number, $P(\{e\})$, called the *probability of the simple event $\{e\}$*, which has the two properties:** Definition 14.1 Probability of a Simple Event

**(I)** $P(\{e\}) \geq 0$, **for all simple events** $\{e\}$ **in** $S$;

**(II) The sum of the probabilities of all the simple events of** $S$ **equals one.**

If the sample space $S$ is given by

$$S = \{e_1, e_2, \ldots e_n\}$$

then

(I) $P(\{e_1\}) \geq 0, \quad P(\{e_2\}) \geq 0, \ldots, P(\{e_n\}) \geq 0$

(II) $P(\{e_1\}) + P(\{e_2\}) + \cdots + P(\{e_n\}) = 1$

The real number assigned to the simple event $\{e\}$ is *completely arbitrary* within the framework of the above restrictions. For example, let a die be thrown. A sample space $S$ is then

$$S = \{1, 2, 3, 4, 5, 6\}$$

There are six simple events in $S$: $\{1\}, \{2\}, \{3\}, \{4\}, \{5\}, \{6\}$. Either of the following two assignments of probabilities are acceptable.

(I)

$$P(\{1\}) = \frac{1}{6}, \quad P(\{2\}) = \frac{1}{6}, \quad P(\{3\}) = \frac{1}{6}$$

$$P(\{4\}) = \frac{1}{6}, \quad P(\{5\}) = \frac{1}{6}, \quad P(\{6\}) = \frac{1}{6}$$

This choice is in agreement with the above definition, since the probability of each simple event is nonnegative and their sum is one. This is an example of a "fair" die in which each simple event is equally likely to occur.

(II)

$$P(\{1\}) = 0, \quad P(\{2\}) = 0, \quad P(\{3\}) = \frac{1}{3}$$

$$P(\{4\}) = \frac{2}{3}, \quad P(\{5\}) = 0, \quad P(\{6\}) = 0$$

This choice is in agreement with the above definition, since the proba- is the existence of a "loaded" die in which only a 3 or a 4 appears and a four is twice as likely to occur as a 3.

**2.4
Example**

A coin is weighted so that heads $\{H\}$ is five times more likely to occur than tails $\{T\}$. What probability should we assign to heads? to tails?

Let $x$ denote the probability that tails occurs.
Then $P(\{T\}) = x$ and

$$P(\{H\}) = 5x$$

From Definition 14.1, we must have

$$P(\{H\}) + P(\{T\}) = 5x + x = 1$$

Then

$$x = \frac{1}{6}$$

Thus, we would assign

$$P(\{H\}) = \frac{5}{6}, \qquad P(\{T\}) = \frac{1}{6}$$

Suppose probabilities have been assigned to each simple event of $S$. We now raise the question: What is the probability of an event? Let $S$ be a sample space and let $E$ be any event of $S$. It is clear that either $E = \emptyset$ or $E$ is a simple event or $E$ is the union of two or more simple events.

**If $E = \emptyset$, we define the** probability of $\emptyset$ **to be**

$$P(\emptyset) = 0$$

**In this case, the event $E = \emptyset$ is said to be** impossible.
  **If $E$ is simple, Definition 14.1 is applicable.**
  **If $E$ is the union of $r$ simple events $\{e_{i_1}\}, \{e_{i_2}\}, \ldots, \{e_{i_r}\}$, we define the** probability of $E$ **to be**

$$P(E) = P(\{e_{i_1}\}) + P(\{e_{i_2}\}) + \cdots + P(\{e_{i_r}\})$$

Definition 14.2
Probability of
an Event

In particular, if the sample space $S$ is given by

$$S = \{e_1, e_2, \ldots, e_n\}$$

we see from Definitions 14.1 and 14.2 that

$$P(S) = P(\{e_1\}) + \cdots + P(\{e_n\}) = 1$$

Thus, the probability of $S$, the sample space, is one.

Let two coins be tossed. A sample space $S$ is

$$S = \{HH, TH, HT, TT\}$$

2.5
Example

This can be depicted in two ways. See Figure 14.6.
  Let $E$ be the event that they are both heads or both tails. Compute the probability for event $E$ with the following two assignments of probabilities:

(a) $P(\{HH\}) = P(\{TT\}) = P(\{HT\}) = P(\{TH\}) = \frac{1}{4}$

(b) $P(\{HH\}) = \frac{1}{9}, P(\{TT\}) = \frac{4}{9}, P(\{TH\}) = \frac{2}{9}, P(\{HT\}) = \frac{2}{9}$

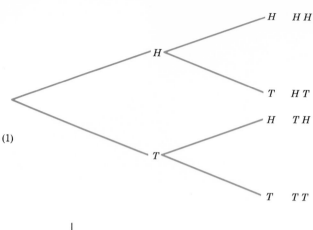

(1)

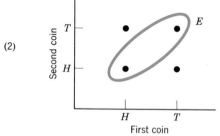

(2)

$E$ = same result on both tosses = $\{HH, TT\}$

**Figure 14.6**

Here the event $E$ is $\{HH, TT\}$; and from Definition 14.2, we have

(a) $P(E) = P(\{HH\}) + P(\{TT\}) = \dfrac{1}{4} + \dfrac{1}{4} = \dfrac{1}{2}$

(b) $P(E) = P(\{HH\}) + P(\{TT\}) = \dfrac{1}{9} + \dfrac{4}{9} = \dfrac{5}{9}$

The fact that we have obtained different probabilities for the same event is not unexpected, since it stems from our original assignment of probabilities to the simple events of the experiment. Any assignment that conforms to the restrictions given in Definition 14.1 is mathematically correct. The question of which assignment should be made is not a mathematical question, but is one that depends on the real world situation to which the theory is applied. In this example the coins were fair in case (a) and were loaded in case (b).

Now that we have introduced the concepts of sample space, event, and probability of events, we introduce the idea of a probabilistic model.

**To construct a probabilistic model we need to do the following:**

**(a) List all possible outcomes of the experiment under investigation, that is, give a sample space; or, if this is not easy to do, determine the number of simple events in the sample space.**

**(b)** **Assign to each simple event a probability $P(\{e\})$ such that Definition 14.1 is satisfied.**

Consider the following experiment.

2.6
Example

A fair coin is tossed. If it comes up heads $H$, a fair die is rolled and the experiment is finished; if it comes up tails $T$, the coin is tossed again. Describe a probabilistic model for this experiment.

First, all the possible outcomes of this experiment are

$$S: H1, H2, H3, H4, H5, H6, TT, \text{ and } TH$$

where $H1$ indicates head for the coin and a 1 for die, and so on. See Figure 14.7.

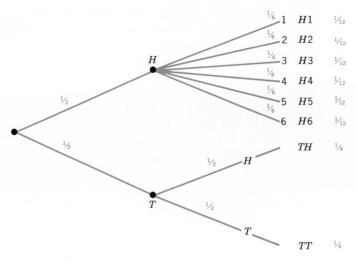

**Figure 14.7**

To each of these eight possible outcomes we assign the probability to be, respectively,

$$P: \frac{1}{12}, \frac{1}{12}, \frac{1}{12}, \frac{1}{12}, \frac{1}{12}, \frac{1}{12}, \frac{1}{4}, \frac{1}{4}$$

The above discussion constitutes a model, called a *probabilistic* or *stochastic model*, for the experiment.

For this model, let $E$ be the event

$$E = \{H2, H4, TH\}$$

The probability of the event $E$, by Definition 14.2, is

$$P(E) = P(\{H2\}) + P(\{H4\}) + P(\{TH\})$$
$$= \frac{1}{12} + \frac{1}{12} + \frac{1}{4} = \frac{5}{12}$$

1. Below are described certain experiments. List the elements in each sample space and find the number of simple events in each sample space associated with the experiment.
   (a) Tossing a coin 5 times.
   (b) Tossing a coin until a head appears. (This is an example of an infinite sample space.)
   (c) Five coins tossed once. (Compare your answer to the answer found in 1(a)).
   (d) A box contains five balls numbered 1, 2, 3, 4, 5. A ball is drawn at random.
   (e) The same as in (d), except the ball is then replaced and a second drawing is made.
   (f) Tossing two dice and then a coin.
   (g) Tossing a die and two coins.
   (h) The vote of a single voter for three offices (President, senator, congressman) if two people, a Democrat and a Republican, are candidates for each office.

2. Below are described certain experiments. Find the number of simple events in each sample space associated with the experiment.
   (a) A poker hand (five cards) is dealt from an ordinary deck of cards (52 cards).
   (b) A committee of five people is chosen at random from a group of six men and five women.
   (c) Three coins are tossed once.
   (d) Three dice are tossed once.

3. Construct probabilistic models for the experiments in problems 1(a), 1(c), 1(d), 1(e), 1(f), 1(g), 1(h), 2(a), 2(b), 2(c), and 2(d). You may assign any valid probabilities.

4. A study reveals two major rival companies $G$ and $H$, and four minor firms, $a, b, c, d$, who always ally themselves with one of the two major companies on prices. Free competition results if each major company is backed by two smaller ones. Construct the sample space and the events that maintain free competition.

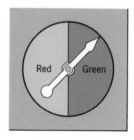
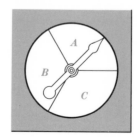
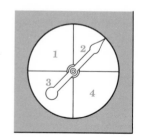

5. Three spinners are pictured above. If the experiment is to spin a spinner, the set of outcomes is:

Spinner 1: {red, green}
Spinner 2: {A, B, C}
Spinner 3: {1, 2, 3, 4}

Draw tree diagrams to find the number of possible outcomes when the experiment is
(a) First spinner 1 is spun and then spinner 2.
(b) Spinners 3, 2, and 1 are spun in this order.
(c) Spinner 1 is spun two times and the spinners 3 and 2 each one time in this order.

6. An accountant applies for a job to Midwest Steel and Western Steel. Let the event of his acceptance by Midwest be denoted by $A$, and that of his acceptance by Western be denoted by $B$. Using set notation, write expressions for the following events:
(a) that he will be rejected by Midwest
(b) that he will be rejected by Western
(c) that he will be rejected by both
(d) that he will be rejected by at least one
(e) that he will be rejected by exactly one
(f) that he will be accepted by both
(g) that he will be accepted by at least one
(h) that he will be accepted by exactly one

7. If the events $E$ and $F$ are

$E$: common stocks are a good buy
$F$: corporate bonds are a good buy

state in words the meaning of
(a) $P(E \cup F)$     (d) $P(E \cup \bar{F})$
(b) $P(\bar{E})$         (e) $P(\bar{E} \cup F)$
(c) $P(\bar{E} \cap \bar{F})$    (f) $P(\bar{E} \cap F)$

8. In Example 2.5, page 427, if the events $E$, $F$, $G$ are
(a) $E$: at least one head
(b) $F$: exactly one tail
(c) $G$: tails on both tosses
find $P(E)$, $P(F)$, $P(G)$, for the two given assignments of probabilities.

9. A red die and green die are tossed. If $r$ denotes the result on the red die and $g$ the result on the green die, give verbal descriptions of the following algebraically described events:
(a) $r = 3g$       (d) $r + g = 8$
(b) $r - g = 1$    (e) $g = r^2$
(c) $r \leqq g$       (f) $r = g$
Graph each of these events using Figure 14.4 as a backdrop.

10. In a T-maze an animal may turn either to the right (R) or to the left (L). His behavior in making such "choices" is studied. Suppose a rat runs a T-maze three times. List the set of all possible outcomes and assign valid probabilities

to each simple event. Find the probability of each of the events:

(a) $E$: run to the right two consecutive times.
(b) $F$: never run to the right.
(c) $G$: run to the left on the first trial.
(d) $H$: run to the right on the second trial.

11. Let $S = \{e_1, e_2, e_3, e_4, e_5, e_6, e_7\}$ be a given sample space. Let the probabilities assigned to the simple events be given as follows:

$$P(\{e_1\}) = P(\{e_2\}) = P(\{e_6\})$$
$$P(\{e_3\}) = 2P(\{e_4\}) = \tfrac{1}{2}P(\{e_1\})$$
$$P(\{e_5\}) = \tfrac{1}{2}P(\{e_7\}) = \tfrac{1}{4}P(\{e_1\})$$

(a) Find $P(\{e_1\})$, $P(\{e_2\})$, $P(\{e_3\})$, $P(\{e_4\})$, $P(\{e_5\})$, $P(\{e_6\})$, $P(\{e_7\})$.

(b) If $A = \{e_1, e_2\}$, $B = \{e_2, e_3, e_4\}$, $C = \{e_5, e_6, e_7\}$, $D = \{e_1, e_5, e_6\}$, find $P(A), P(B), P(C), P(D), P(A \cup B)$, $P(A \cap D), P(D \cap B), P(A \cap \bar{B})$.

12. Three cars, $C_1$, $C_2$, $C_3$, are in a race. If the probability of $C_1$ winning is $p$, that is, $P(C_1) = p$ and $P(C_1) = \tfrac{1}{2}P(C_2)$ and $P(C_3) = \tfrac{1}{2}P(C_2)$, find $P(C_1)$, $P(C_2)$, and $P(C_3)$. Find $P(C_1 \cup C_2)$, $P(C_1 \cup C_3)$. Assume a tie is impossible.

13. Consider an experiment with a loaded die such that the probability of any of the faces appearing in a toss is equal to that face times the probability that a one will occur. That is, $P(\{6\}) = 6 \cdot P(\{1\})$, $P(\{5\}) = 5 \cdot P(\{1\})$, and so on.

(a) Describe the sample space.
(b) If $P(\{1\})$ is the probability for face one to show, find $P(\{1\}), P(\{2\}), P(\{3\}), P(\{4\}), P(\{5\})$, and $P(\{6\})$.
(c) Let $A$ be the event "even numbered face,"
    $B$ be the event "odd numbered face,"
    $C$ be the event "prime number as face" (2, 3, 5 are prime).
    Find $P(A), P(B), P(C), P(A \cup B), P(A \cup \bar{C})$.

---

**14.3**
**PROPERTIES OF**
**THE PROBABILITY**
**OF AN EVENT**

In this section, we state and prove results involving the probability of an event after the probabilistic model has been determined. The main tool we employ is that of set theory.

**Definition**
**of Mutually**
**Exclusive Events**

**Two or more events of a sample space $S$ are said to be** *mutually exclusive* **if and only if they have no simple events in common.**

That is, if we treat the events as sets, they are disjoint.

The following result gives us a way of computing probabilities for mutually exclusive events.

**Theorem 3.1**

**Let $E$ and $F$ be two events of a sample space $S$. If $E$ and $F$ are mutually exclusive, that is, if $E \cap F = \varnothing$, then the probability of the event "$E$ or $F$" is the sum of their probabilities, namely,**

$$P(E \cup F) = P(E) + P(F)$$

Since $E$ and $F$ can be written as a union of simple events in which no simple event of $E$ appears in $F$, and no simple event of $F$ appears in $E$, the result follows.

In the experiment of tossing two fair dice, what is the probability of obtaining either a sum of 7 or a sum of 11?

Let $E$ and $F$ be the events

$$E: \text{sum is } 7, \qquad F: \text{sum is } 11$$

Since the dice are fair,

$$P(E) = \frac{6}{36}, \qquad P(F) = \frac{2}{36}$$

The two events $E$ and $F$ are mutually exclusive. Thus the probability that the sum is 7 or 11 is

$$P(E \cup F) = P(E) + P(F) = \frac{6}{36} + \frac{2}{36} = \frac{8}{36} = \frac{2}{9}$$

The probability of any simple event of a sample space $S$ is nonnegative. Furthermore, since any event $E$ of $S$ is the union of simple events in $S$, and since $P(S) = 1$, it is easy to see that

$$0 \leq P(E) \leq 1$$

To summarize, the probability of an event $E$ of a sample space $S$ has three properties:

I: *Positiveness:* $0 \leq P(E) \leq 1$ for every event $E$ of $S$
II: *Certainty:* $P(S) = 1$
III: *Union:* $P(E \cup F) = P(E) + P(F)$ for any two events $E$ and $F$ of $S$ for which $E \cap F = \varnothing$.

Let $E$ be an event of a sample space. The complement of $E$ is then the event "not $E$" in $S$. The next theorem gives a relationship between their probabilities.

**Theorem 3.2**

**Let $E$ be an event of a sample space $S$. Then,**

$$P(\bar{E}) = 1 - P(E)$$

**where $\bar{E}$ is the complement of $E$.**

Proof
We know that

$$S = E \cup \bar{E}, \qquad E \cap \bar{E} = \emptyset$$
$$P(S) = P(E) + P(\bar{E})$$

Now, apply Property II, setting $P(S) = 1$. Then

$$P(\bar{E}) = 1 - P(E)$$

This theorem gives us a tool for finding the probability that an event does not occur, if we know the probability that it does occur. Thus, the probability $P(\bar{E})$, that $E$ does not occur, is obtained by subtracting from 1 the probability $P(E)$ that $E$ does occur.

**3.2**
**Example**

In a study of people over 40 with an MBA degree, it is reasonable to assign a probability of .756 that such a person will have annual earnings in excess of $15,000. The probability that such a person will not have earnings in excess of $15,000, is

$$1 - .756 = .244$$

**3.3**
**Example**

In an experiment using two fair dice find

(a) The probability that the sum of the faces is less than or equal to 7.
(b) The probability that the sum of the faces is greater than 7.

The number of simple events in the event $E$ described in (a) is 21. The number of simple events of the sample space $S$ is 36. Thus, because the dice are fair,

$$P(E) = \frac{21}{36} = \frac{7}{12}$$

For (b), we need to find $P(\bar{E})$. Clearly,

$$P(\bar{E}) = 1 - P(E) = 1 - \frac{7}{12} = \frac{5}{12}$$

That is, the probability that the sum of the faces is greater than 7 is 5/12.

**3.4**
**Example**
**Birthday**
**Problem**

An interesting problem, in which Theorem 3.2 is used, is the so-called *birthday problem*. In general, the problem is to find the probability that, in a group with $r$ people, there are at least two people having the same birthday (the same month and day of the year).

To solve the problem, let us first determine the number of simple events in the sample space. There are 365 possibilities for each person's birthday. Since there are *r* people in the group, there are 365$^r$ possibilities for the birthdays. For, if there is one person in the group, there are 365 days on which his birthday can fall. For 2 people there are $(365)(365) = 365^2$ days. In general, using the Fundamental Principle of Counting, for *r* people there are 365$^r$ possibilities.

Next, we assume a person is no more likely to be born on one day than another, so that we assign the probability 1/365$^r$ to each simple event.

We wish to find the probability that at least two people have the same birthday. To count the elements in this set is difficult; it is much easier to count the elements of the event

$E$: no two people have the same birthday

Notice that the event $\overline{E}$ is that at least two people have the same birthday. To find the probability of $E$, we proceed as follows. Choose one person at random. There are 365 possibilities for his birthday. Choose a second person. There are 364 possibilities for his birthday, if no two people are to have the same birthday. Choose a third person. There are 363 possibilities left for his birthday. Finally, we arrive at the *r*th person. There are $365 - (r - 1)$ possibilities left for his birthday. By the Fundamental Principle of Counting, the total number of possibilities is $365 \cdot 364 \cdot 363 \cdots (365 - r + 1)$.

Hence, the probability of event $E$ is

$$P(E) = \frac{365 \cdot 364 \cdot 363 \cdots (365 - r + 1)}{365^r}$$

The probability of two or more people having the same birthday is then $P(\overline{E}) = 1 - P(E)$.

Figure 14.8 gives the probability for two or more people having the same birthday for some values of *r*. Notice that the probability is better than 1/2 for any group of people whose number exceeds 22.

The next result provides a technique for finding the probability of the union of two events when they are not disjoint. The student should compare this result with that of Theorem 4.1 on page 392 of Chapter 13.

| | Number of People | | | | | | | | | | | | | | |
|---|---|---|---|---|---|---|---|---|---|---|---|---|---|---|---|
| | 5 | 10 | 15 | 20 | 21 | 22 | 23 | 24 | 25 | 30 | 40 | 50 | 60 | 70 | 80 | 90 |
| Probability that two or more have same birthday | .027 | .117 | .253 | .411 | .444 | .476 | .507 | .538 | .569 | .706 | .891 | .970 | .994 | .99916 | .99991 | .99999 |

**Figure 14.8**

Theorem 3.3

**For any two events $E$ and $F$ of a sample space $S$**

$$P(E \cup F) = P(E) + P(F) - P(E \cap F)$$

Proof

From Example 3.5 of Chapter 13, page 387, we have

$$E \cup F = (E \cap \bar{F}) \cup (E \cap F) \cup (\bar{E} \cap F)$$

Since $E \cap \bar{F}$, $E \cap F$, and $\bar{E} \cap F$ are pair-wise disjoint, we can use an extension of Property III to write

$$P(E \cup F) = P(E \cap \bar{F}) + P(E \cap F) + P(\bar{E} \cap F) \qquad (3.1)$$

From Exercise 13.3, Problems 5(g), 5(h), page 389, we have

$$E = (E \cap F) \cup (E \cap \bar{F})$$
$$F = (E \cap F) \cup (\bar{E} \cap F)$$

Since $E \cap F$ and $E \cap \bar{F}$ are disjoint and $E \cap F$ and $\bar{E} \cap F$ are disjoint, we have

$$P(E) = P(E \cap F) + P(E \cap \bar{F})$$
$$P(F) = P(E \cap F) + P(\bar{E} \cap F) \qquad (3.2)$$

From (3.1) and (3.2), we obtain

$$P(E \cup F) = P(E) + P(F) - P(E \cap F)$$

3.5
Example

Consider the two events

$E$: A shopper spends at least \$40 for food
$F$: A shopper spends at least \$15 for meat

From experience, we assign

$$P(E) = .56 \qquad P(F) = .63$$

The probability that a shopper spends at least \$40 for food and \$15 for meat is .33. What is the probability that a shopper spends at least \$40 for food or at least \$15 for meat?

Here we are looking for the probability of $E \cup F$. From Theorem 3.3, we know

$$P(E \cup F) = P(E) + P(F) - P(E \cap F)$$
$$= .56 + .63 - .33 = .86$$

3.6
Example

In an experiment with two fair dice, consider the events

$E$: the sum of the faces is 8
$F$: doubles are thrown

What is the probability of obtaining either $E$ or $F$?

Here

$$E = \{(2,6), (3,5), (4,4), (5,3), (6,2)\}$$
$$F = \{(1,1), (2,2), (3,3), (4,4), (5,5), (6,6)\}$$
$$E \cap F = \{(4,4)\}$$

Also

$$P(E) = \frac{5}{36}, \qquad P(F) = \frac{6}{36}, \qquad P(E \cap F) = \frac{1}{36}$$

Thus, the probability of E or F is

$$P(E \cup F) = \frac{5}{36} + \frac{6}{36} - \frac{1}{36} = \frac{10}{36} = \frac{5}{18}$$

We conclude this section with a brief discussion of the relation between the probability of an event and the "odds" of this event occurring.

**Let E be an event of a sample space S. We say that** odds *for E are a to b* **if and only if**

Definition
of Odds

$$P(E) = \frac{a}{a + b}$$

Using this condition the odds for E are $P(E)$ to $P(\overline{E})$.

Let E be the event "Cubs win the pennant," and let us say that the odds for E are 12 to 5. Then

3.7
Example

$$P(E) = \frac{12}{12 + 5} = \frac{12}{17}$$

If, on the other hand, we are given the probability of an event, the odds for or against this particular event can be determined from the given probability. The odds for E are merely the ratio of $P(E)$ to $P(\overline{E})$.

Let E be the event "White Sox win the pennant," and let

3.8
Example

$$P(E) = .05$$

Thus, since $P(\overline{E}) = .95$, the odds for E are .05 to .95 or 1 to 19. A fair bet would be $19 for one who thinks they cannot win and $1 for anyone who thinks the Sox can win.

When one hears odds on horse races or other sporting events, the numbers given usually reflect the odds *against* an event. For example, when a Las Vegas gambler says the odds are 2:1, he means the odds against the event occurring are 2:1, in which case the odds *for* the event are 1:2.

1. A die is rolled. Let $E$ be the event "die shows 4," and $F$ be the event "die shows even number." Are events $E$ and $F$ mutually exclusive?

2. The Chicago Black Hawks hockey team has a probability for winning of .6 and a probability for losing of .25. What is the probability for a tie?

3. An experiment contains exactly four mutually exclusive events $A, B, C,$ and $D$. State, for each of the following, why it is not permissible to assign the following probabilities.
   (a) $P(A) = .7$    $P(B) = .0$    $P(C) = .4$    $P(D) = .0$
   (b) $P(A) = .3$    $P(B) = .4$    $P(C) = .1$    $P(D) = .1$
   (c) $P(A \cup B) = .5$    $P(A) = .3$    $P(B) = .4$
   (d) $P(A) = -.5$    $P(B) = .5$    $P(C) = .2$    $P(D) = .8$

4. Use Figure 14.8 to find the approximate probability that two or more United States Senators have the same birthday. What is the probability that two or more members of the House of Representatives have the same birthday?

5. Suppose $E$ is the event "at least two people have birthdays in the same month" (disregarding the day and year). Find the probability of event $E$ for a group of two people; for a group of three people; for a group of four people.

6. At a Milex tune-up, brake repair shop, Mike, the manager, has found that a car will require a tune-up with probability .6, a brake job with probability .1, and both with probability .02.
   (a) What is the probability a car requires either a tune-up or a brake job?
   (b) What is the probability a car requires a tune-up, but not a brake job?
   (c) What is the probability a car requires neither repair?

7. Through observation it has been determined that the probability for a given number of people waiting in line at a particular checkout register of a supermarket is:

| Number waiting in line | 0 | 1 | 2 | 3 | 4 or more |
|---|---|---|---|---|---|
| Probability | .10 | .15 | .20 | .24 | .31 |

Find the probability of
(a) At most two people in line.
(b) At least two people in line.
(c) At least one person in line.

8. A student needs to pass both mathematics and English in order to graduate. He estimates his probability of passing Mathematics at .4 and English at .6, and he estimates his probability of passing at least one of them at .8. What is his probability of passing both courses?

9. After mid-term exams, the student in Problem 8 reassesses his probability of passing Mathematics to .7. He feels his probability of passing at least one of these courses is still .8, but he has only a probability of .1 of passing both courses. If his probability of passing English is less than .4, he will drop English. Should he drop English? Why?

10. If two fair dice are thrown, what are the odds of obtaining a 7? An 11? A 7 or 11?

11. If the odds for event $A$ are 1 to 5 and for event $B$ are 1 to 3, what are the odds for the event $A$ or $B$ if the event $A$ and $B$ is impossible?

12. Using the Definition of Odds show that the odds for the event $E$ are $P(E)$ to $P(\bar{E})$.

13. In a track contest, the odds that $A$ will win are 1 to 2 and the odds that $B$ will win are 2 to 3. Find the probability and the odds that $A$ or $B$ wins the race, assuming a tie is impossible.

14. It has been estimated that in 70 percent of the fatal accidents involving two cars, at least one of the drivers is drunk. If you hear of a two-car fatal accident, what odds should you give a friend that at least one of the drivers is drunk?

15. If $A$ and $B$ represent two mutually exclusive events, such that $P(A) = .35$, $P(B) = .50$, find each of the following:
   (a) $P(A \cup B)$    (d) $P(\bar{A})$
   (b) $P(\overline{A \cup B})$    (e) $P(A \cap B)$
   (c) $P(\bar{B})$

16. Let $A$ and $B$ be events of a sample space $S$ and let $P(A) = .5$, $P(B) = .3$, and $P(A \cap B) = .1$. Find the probabilities for each of the following events:
   (a) $A$ or $B$          (c) $B$ but not $A$
   (b) $A$ but not $B$     (d) neither $A$ nor $B$

*17. If $A \subseteq B$, show that $P(A) \leq P(B)$. Hint: Decompose $B$ into two parts, those that are in $A$ and those that are only in $B$, but not in $A$; that is $B = A \cup (B \cap \bar{A})$.

*18. Generalize Theorem 3.3 by showing that the probability of the occurrence of at least one among three events $A$, $B$, $C$ is given by

$$P(A \cup B \cup C) = P(A) + P(B) + P(C)$$
$$- P(A \cap B) - P(A \cap C) - P(B \cap C)$$
$$+ P(A \cap B \cap C)$$

*19. If in Problem 18, the events $A$, $B$, $C$ are mutually exclusive events, that is, $A \cap B = \emptyset$, $B \cap C = \emptyset$, $A \cap C = \emptyset$, then the probability of A or B or C is

$$P(A \cup B \cup C) = P(A) + P(B) + P(C)$$

For example, the probability that XYZ Company has earnings of between $2.00 and $2.25 per share is .25; the probability of earnings per share between $2.26 and $2.50 is .20; and the probability of earnings per share over $2.51 is .10. What is the probability that earnings per share will exceed $2.00?

14.4
PROBABILITY
FOR EQUALLY
LIKELY EVENTS

Thus far we have seen that, in some cases, it is reasonable to assign the same probability to each simple event of the sample space. Such events are termed *equally likely events*.

Equally Likely
Events

Equally likely events occur when items are selected randomly. For example, in randomly selecting one person from a group of 10, the probability of selecting a particular individual is 1/10. If a card is chosen randomly from a deck of 52 cards, the probability of drawing a particular card is 1/52. In general, if a sample space S has n equally likely simple events, the probability assigned to each simple event is $1/n$.

Theorem 4.1

**Let a sample space S be given by**

$$S = \{e_1, e_2, \ldots, e_n\}$$

**Suppose each of the simple events $\{e_1\}, \ldots, \{e_n\}$ are equally likely to occur. If E is the union of m of these n simple events, then**

$$P(E) = m/n$$

Proof
Since the simple events $\{e_1\}, \ldots, \{e_n\}$ are equally likely, we know that

$$P(\{e_1\}) = \cdots = P(\{e_n\}) \tag{4.1}$$

Since

$$S = \{e_1\} \cup \cdots \cup \{e_n\}$$

we have

$$P(S) = P(\{e_1\}) + \cdots + P(\{e_n\}) = 1 \tag{4.2}$$

To satisfy both (4.1) and (4.2) we must have

$$P(\{e_1\}) = P(\{e_2\}) = \cdots = P(\{e_n\}) = 1/n$$

Now, for the event E of S, in which the m events have been reordered for convenience, we have

$$E = \{e_1\} \cup \cdots \cup \{e_m\}$$

Thus

$$P(E) = P(\{e_1\}) + \cdots + P(\{e_m\}) = \underbrace{1/n + \cdots + 1/n}_{m \text{ times}} = m/n$$

Theorem 4.1 is sometimes stated in the following way.

**If an experiment has $n$ equally likely outcomes, among which the event $E$ occurs $m$ times, then the probability of event $E$, written as $P(E)$, is $m/n$. That is**

$$P(E) = \frac{\textbf{number of possible ways that the event } E \textbf{ can take place}}{\textbf{number of all logical possibilities}} = \frac{m}{n}$$

**If the fact that the event $E$ has occurred is termed a** *success,* **then**

$$P(E) = \frac{\textbf{number of successes}}{\textbf{number of all logical possibilities}} = \frac{m}{n} \qquad (4.3)$$

**Event $E$ not occurring is referred to as a** *failure.*

Thus to compute the probability of an event $E$, in which the outcomes are equally likely, count the number of simple events in $E$, $c(E)$, and divide by the total number of simple events in the sample space, $c(S)$. Then

$$P(E) = \frac{c(E)}{c(S)}$$

Often Theorem 4.1 is used to define *probability*. Had we decided to define the probability of an event by using Theorem 4.1, the properties I, II, and III previously stated would still be valid.

For, suppose an experiment resulted in no successes at all. By Theorem 4.1, we have

$$P(\text{success}) = \frac{0}{n} = 0 \qquad (4.4)$$

If the experiment resulted in all events in the sample space being successes, then $m = n$, and

$$P(\text{success}) = m/n = n/n = 1$$

From this result and (4.4) we see that

$$0 \leqq P(\text{success}) \leqq 1$$

Suppose $E$ is an event with $m$ successes in a sample space $S$ of $n$ elements. Then

$$P(E) = m/n$$

Now $\bar{E}$ contains $n - m$ elements. Hence

$$\begin{aligned} P(\bar{E}) &= (n - m)/n \\ &= n/n - m/n \\ &= 1 - m/n \\ &= 1 - P(E) \end{aligned}$$

In a two-dice experiment, we present the following in terms of events:

(a) The sum of the faces is 3.
(b) The sum of the faces is 7.
(c) The sum of the faces is 7 or 3.
(d) The sum of the faces is 7 and 3.

Find the probability of these events assuming the dice are fair.

Now

(a) The sum of the faces is 3 if and only if the outcome is the event $A = \{(1, 2), (2, 1)\}$. The probability of the simple event $\{(1, 2)\}$ is $1/36$ and the probability of the simple event $\{(2, 1)\}$ is $1/36$. Thus

$$P(A) = \frac{2}{36} = \frac{1}{18}$$

(b) The sum of the faces is 7 if and only if the outcome is a member of the event $B = \{(1, 6), (2, 5), (3, 4), (4, 3), (5, 2), (6, 1)\}$. Again

$$P(B) = \frac{6}{36} = \frac{1}{6}$$

(c) The sum of the faces is 7 or 3 if and only if the outcome is a member of $A \cup B$.

$$A \cup B = \{(2, 1), (1, 2), (1, 6), (2, 5), (3, 4), (4, 3), (5, 2), (6, 1)\}$$

Thus

$$P(A \cup B) = \frac{8}{36} = \frac{2}{9}$$

(d) The sum of the faces is 3 and 7 if and only if the outcome is a member of $A \cap B$. Since $A \cap B = \emptyset$, the event is impossible. That is, $P(A \cap B) = 0$.

A box contains 41 light bulbs, of which 5 are defective. All bulbs look alike and have equal probability of being chosen. Three light bulbs are picked at random. What is the probability that all 3 are nondefective? What is the probability that all 3 are defective? What is the probability that at least 2 are defective?

Let $A$ be the event "3 light bulbs selected are nondefective." The number of elements in the event $A$ is the number of combinations of 36 nondefective light bulbs taken 3 at a time. That is

$$\binom{36}{3} = \frac{36!}{3!(36 - 3)!} = \frac{36!}{3!33!}$$

The number of elements in the sample space $S$ is equal to the number of combinations of 41 light bulbs taken 3 at a time, namely,

$$\binom{41}{3} = \frac{41!}{3!38!}$$

Using (4.3), the probability $P(A)$ is then

$$P(A) = \frac{\binom{36}{3}}{\binom{41}{3}} = \frac{\frac{36!}{3!33!}}{\frac{41!}{3!38!}} = .6698$$

Define $B$ as the event "3 bulbs are defective." Then $B$ can occur in $\binom{5}{3}$ ways, that is, the number of ways in which 3 defective bulbs can be chosen from 5 defective ones. The probability $P(B)$ is

$$P(B) = \frac{\binom{5}{3}}{\binom{41}{3}} = \frac{\frac{5!}{3!2!}}{\frac{41!}{38!3!}} = .000938$$

What is the probability of the event $C$ "at least 2 are defective"?

The event $C$ is equivalent to asking for the probability of selecting either two or three defective bulbs. Thus

$$P(C) = \frac{\binom{5}{2}\binom{36}{1}}{\binom{41}{3}} + P(B) = .0338 + .000938 = .0347$$

4.3
Example

Find the probability of obtaining (a) a straight and (b) a flush in a poker hand. (A poker hand is a set of 5 cards chosen at random from a deck of 52 cards.)

(a) A straight consists of five consecutive cards not all of the same suit. The sample space contains $\binom{52}{5}$ simple events, each equally likely to occur. Now, for the straight $4, 5, 6, 7, 8$, the 4 can be drawn in 4 different ways, as can the 5, the 6, the 7, and the 8 for a total of $4^5$ ways. There are a total of 10 different kinds of straights $(A, 2, 3, 4, 5), (2, 3, 4, 5, 6), \ldots, (9, 10, J, Q, K)$, and $(10, J, Q, K, A)$. Thus, all told there are $10 \cdot 4^5$ straights. However, among these are the straight flushes (36), and the four royal flushes, which, as stronger hands, should not be included in the straight category. Thus, there are

$$10 \cdot 4^5 - 36 - 4 = 10{,}240 - 40 = 10{,}200$$

straights. The probability of drawing a straight is then

$$\frac{10,200}{\binom{52}{5}} = .0039$$

(b) A flush consists of five cards in a single suit, excluding a straight flush or royal flush. The number of ways of obtaining a flush in a given suit is $\binom{13}{5} = 1287$. Since there are four different suits, there is a total of $4(1287) = 5148$ flushes. However, straight flushes (36) and the four royal flushes, each being stronger than a regular flush, should not be included in the flush category. Thus, there are

$$5148 - 36 - 4 = 5108$$

flushes. The probability for a flush is then

$$\frac{5108}{\binom{52}{5}} = .0020$$

14.4
Exercise

1. In a throw of two fair dice, what is the probability that the numbers on their upper faces add up to 3? To 4? To 11?

2. If a fair die is thrown, what is the probability that the upper face shows more than 3? Less than 3? An even number? An odd number?

3. When two fair coins are tossed, what is the probability that both show heads? That they show one head and one tail?

4. In a throw of two fair dice what is the probability that the number on one die is double the number on the other?

5. In a throw of two fair dice what is the probability that one die gives a 5 and the other die a number less than 5?

6. From a sales force of 150 men, one will be chosen to attend a special sales meeting. If 52 are single, 72 are college graduates, and three-fourths of the 52 single men are college graduates, what is the probability that a salesman selected at random will be neither single nor a college graduate.

7. Two fair dice are thrown. Let $A$ be the event that the sum of the faces is odd and $B$ be the event that at least one ace appears. Describe the events $A \cap B, A \cup B$, and $A \cap \bar{B}$ and find their probability.

8. Through a mix-up on the production line, 6 defective refrigerators were shipped out with 44 good ones. If 5 are

selected at random, what is the probability that all 5 are defective? What is the probability that at least 2 of them are defective?

9. In an election two amendments are proposed. The results indicated that of 1000 people eligible to cast a ballot, 480 voted in favor of Amendment I, 390 approved of Amendment II, 120 voted for both, and 100 approved of neither. If an eligible voter is selected at random (that is, any one is as likely to be chosen as another), compute the following probabilities:
   (a) The voter will be in favor of I, but not II.
   (b) The voter will be in favor of II, but not I.
   (c) The voter voted no for both.
   (d) The voter did not vote at all.

10. In a game of bridge, find the probability that a hand of 13 cards consists of 5 spades, 4 hearts, 3 diamonds, and 1 club.

11. Find the probability of obtaining each of the following poker hands.
   (a) Royal flush (ten, jack, queen, king, ace in a single suit).
   (b) Straight flush (five in a sequence in a single suit, but not a royal flush).
   *(c) Four of a kind (four cards of the same face value).
   *(d) Full house (one pair and one triple of the same face values).
   *(e) Straight or better.

*12.[1] An elevator starts with 5 passengers and stops at 8 floors. Find the probability that no 2 passengers leave at the same floor. Assume that all arrangements of discharging the passengers have the same probability.

---

The student will recall that in Chapter 13 we introduced the concept of complement for sets. By complement we mean the complement of a set A *relative to the universal set U*. By relative complement we mean the complement of a set A *relative to another set B*, that is, the elements in A and not in B.

In a similar way we would like to introduce a concept known as *conditional probability*. Recall that, whenever we compute the probability of an event, we do it relative to the entire sample space in question. Thus, when we ask for the probability $P(E)$ of the event $E$, this probability $P(E)$ represents an appraisal of the likelihood that a chance experiment will produce an outcome in the set $E$ relative to a sample space $S$.

However, sometimes we would like to compute the probability of an event $E$ of a sample space relative to another event $F$ of the same sample

[1] William Feller, *An Introduction to Probability Theory And its Applications,* Third edition, Wiley, New York, 1968.

space. That is, if we have *prior* information that the outcome must be in a set *F*, this information should be used to reappraise the likelihood that the outcome will also be in *E*. This reappraised probability is denoted by $P(E|F)$, and is read as the *conditional probability of E given F*.

Let us discuss some examples to illustrate the above, and then state a formal definition.

5.1
Example

Consider the experiment of flipping two fair coins. As we have previously seen, the sample space *S* is

$$S = \{HH, HT, TH, TT\}$$

Figure 14.9 illustrates the sample space and, for convenience, the probability of each event.

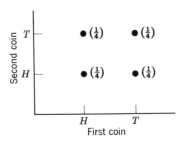

**Figure 14.9**

Suppose the experiment is performed by another person and we have no knowledge of the result, but we are informed that at least one tail was tossed. This information means the outcome *HH* could not have occurred. But the remaining outcomes *HT*, *TH*, *TT* are still possible. How does this alter the probabilities of the remaining outcomes?

For instance, we might be interested in calculating the probability of the event $\{TT\}$. The three simple events $\{TH\}$, $\{HT\}$, $\{TT\}$ were each assigned the probability (1/4) *before* we knew the information that at least one tail occurred, so it is not reasonable to assign them this same probability now. Since only three outcomes are now possible, we assign to each of them the probability 1/3. See Figure 14.10.

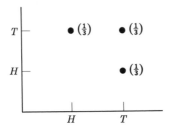

**Figure 14.10**

Consider the experiment of drawing a single card from a deck of 52 playing cards. We are interested in the event $E$ consisting of the outcome, a black ace is drawn. Since we may assume that there are 52 equally likely possible outcomes, we have

$$P(E) = \frac{2}{52}$$

However, suppose a card is drawn and we are informed that it is a spade. How should this information be used to *reappraise* the likelihood of the event $E$?

Clearly, since the event $F$ "a spade has been drawn" has occurred, the event "not spade" is no longer possible. Hence, the sample space has changed from 52 playing cards to 13 spade cards. Therefore, we must compute the probability of event $E$ relative to the new sample space $F$. This probability is denoted by $P(E|F)$ and has the value

$$P(E|F) = \frac{1}{13}$$

Let us analyze this situation more carefully. The event $E$ is "a black ace is drawn." We have computed the probability of event $E$ knowing event $F$ has occurred. This means we are computing a probability relative to a *new* sample space $F$. That is, $F$ is treated as the universal set. Thus, we can only consider that part of $E$ that is included in $F$; that is, we consider $E \cap F$. See Figure 14.11. Thus, the probability of $E$ given $F$ is the ratio of the number of entries in $E \cap F$ to the number of entries in $F$. Since $P(E \cap F) = 1/52$ and $P(F) = 13/52$, then

$$P(E|F) = \frac{1/52}{13/52} = \frac{1}{13}$$

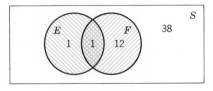

**Figure 14.11**

**Let $E$, $F$ be events of a sample space $S$ and suppose $P(F) > 0$. The** *conditional probability of event $E$ assuming the event $F$,* **denoted by** $P(E|F)$, **is defined as**

$$P(E|F) = \frac{P(E \cap F)}{P(F)}$$

Suppose a population of 1000 people includes 70 accountants and 520 females. Let $E$ be the event "a person is an accountant." Let $F$ be the event "a person is female." Then

$$P(E) = \frac{70}{1000} = .07, \qquad P(F) = \frac{520}{1000} = .52$$

Instead of studying the entire population, we may want to investigate the female subpopulation and ask for the probability that a female chosen at random also be an accountant. If there are 40 females who are accountants, the ratio 40/520 represents the conditional probability of the event $E$ (accountant) assuming the event $F$ (the person chosen is female). In symbols, we would write

$$P(E|F) = \frac{40}{520} = \frac{1}{13}$$

Figure 14.12 illustrates that in computing $P(E|F)$, we form the ratio of the number of entries in $E$ and in $F$ with the number that is in $F$.

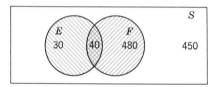

**Figure 14.12**

Alternately, using the Definition of Conditional Probability, we see that

$$P(E \cap F) = \frac{40}{1000}, \qquad P(F) = \frac{520}{1000}$$

$$P(E|F) = \frac{40/1000}{520/1000} = \frac{40}{520} = \frac{1}{13}$$

In the Definition of Conditional Probability, if we replace $F$ by $S$, the sample space, we get

$$P(E|S) = \frac{P(E \cap S)}{P(S)}$$

But $E \cap S = E$ and $P(S) = 1$. This reduces to

$$P(E|S) = P(E)$$

as expected.

In Example 2.2, page 424, we considered a three-child family. The sample space $S$ is

$$S = \{BBB, BBG, BGG, BGB, GGG, GGB, GBB, GBG\}$$

We assume each simple event is equally likely, so that each is assigned a probability of 1/8. Let $E$ be the event "the family has three boys" and let $F$ be the event "the first child is a boy." What is the probability that the family has three boys, given that the first born is a boy?

Here we want to find $P(E|F)$. The events $E$ and $F$ are

$$E = \{BBB\}, \qquad F = \{BBB, BBG, BGB, BGG\}$$

Clearly, $E \cap F = \{BBB\}$ and

$$P(E \cap F) = \frac{1}{8}, \qquad P(F) = \frac{1}{2}$$

Thus

$$P(E|F) = \frac{P(E \cap F)}{P(F)} = \frac{1/8}{1/2} = \frac{1}{4}$$

Thus, in three-child families, in which the first born is a boy, the family will consist of three boys with probability 1/4.

Motors Incorporated has two plants to manufacture cars. Plant I manufactures 80 percent of the cars and Plant II manufactures 20 percent. At plant I, 85 out of every 100 cars are rated standard quality or better. At plant II only 65 out of every 100 cars are rated standard quality or better. We would like to find the answer to the following questions.

(1) What is the probability that a customer obtains a standard quality car, if he buys a car from Motors Inc.?

(2) What is the probability that the car came from Plant I, if it is known that the car is of standard quality?

Let

$A$: "The car purchased is of standard quality."
$B$: "The car is of standard quality and came from Plant I."
$C$: "The car is of standard quality and came from Plant II."
$D$: "The car came from plant I."

As a preliminary step, we make the following computations.

The percentage of cars manufactured in Plant I that are of standard quality is just 85 percent of 80 percent, which is equal to 68 percent. Similarly the percentage of cars manufactured in Plant II that are of standard quality is just 65 percent of 20 percent, which is equal to 13 percent.

To answer (1), we then have

$$P(B) = .68, \qquad P(C) = .13$$

Since $B \cap C = \emptyset$,

$$P(A) = P(B \cup C) = P(B) + P(C) = .68 + .13 = .81$$

Thus, a total of 81 percent of the cars are of standard quality.

To answer (2), we need to compute $P(D|A)$. Since $D \cap A = B$, we have

$$P(D|A) = \frac{P(D \cap A)}{P(A)} = \frac{P(B)}{P(A)} = \frac{.68}{.81} = .8395$$

1. If $E, F$ are events with $P(E) = .4, P(F) = .2$, and $P(E \cap F) = .1$, find the probability of $E$ given $F$. Find $P(F|E)$.

2. If $E, F$ are events with $P(E \cap F) = .1$ and $P(E|F) = .2$, find $P(F)$.

3. Let $E$ be the event "a person is an executive" and let $F$ be the event "a person earns over \$25,000 per year." State in words what is expressed by each of the following probabilities:

   (a) $P(E|F)$   (c) $P(\bar{E}|\bar{F})$

   (b) $P(F|E)$   (d) $P(\bar{E}|F)$

4. A recent poll of residents in a certain community revealed the following information about voting preferences:

   |        | Democrat | Republican | Independent |
   |--------|----------|------------|-------------|
   | Male   | 50       | 40         | 20          |
   | Female | 60       | 30         | 25          |

   Define events to be
   - $M$: resident is male
   - $F$: resident is female
   - $D$: resident is a Democrat
   - $R$: resident is a Republican
   - $I$: resident is an Independent

   Find

   (a) $P(F|I)$   (d) $P(D|M)$

   (b) $P(R|F)$   (e) $P(M|R \cup I)$

   (c) $P(M|D)$   (f) $P(I|M)$

5. For a 3-child family, find the probability of exactly 2 girls, given that the first born is a girl.

6. A fair coin is tossed 4 successive times. Find the probability of obtaining 4 heads. Does the probability change if we are told that the second throw resulted in a head?

7. In a rural area in the north, registered Republicans outnumber registered Democrats by 3 to 1. In a recent election, all Democrats voted for the Democratic candidate and enough Republicans also voted for the Democratic candidate so that he won by a ratio of 5 to 4. If a voter

is selected at random, what is the probability he is Republican? What is the probability he is Republican, if it is known he voted for the Democratic candidate?

8. A pair of fair dice is thrown, and we are told that at least one of them shows a 2. Knowing this, what is the probability that the total is seven?

9. In a small town, it is known that 25 percent of the families have no children, 25 percent have 1 child, 18 percent have 2 children, 16 percent have 3 children, 8 percent have 4 children, and 8 percent have 5 or more children. Find the probability that a family has more than 2 children, if it is known that it has at least 1 child.

10. If $E$ and $F$ are two events with $P(E) > 0$, $P(F) > 0$, show that

$$P(F) \cdot P(E|F) = P(E) \cdot P(F|E)$$

*11. In a sample of people it is found that 35 percent of the men and 70 percent of the women are under 160 pounds. Assume that 50 percent of the sample are men. If a person is selected at random and this person is under 160 pounds, what is the probability that this person is a woman?

*12. If the probability that a married man will vote in a given election is .50, the probability that a married woman will vote in the election is .60, and the probability that a woman will vote in the election given that her husband votes is .90, find
   (a) The probability that a husband and wife will both vote in the elections.
   (b) The probability that a married man will vote in the election given that at least one member of the married couple will vote.

*13. Of the freshmen in a certain college, it is known that 40 percent attended private secondary schools and 60 percent attended public schools. The registrar reports that 30 percent of all students who attended private schools maintain an A average in their freshman year and that 24 percent of the freshmen had an A average. At the end of the year, one student is chosen at random from the freshman class and he has an A average. What is the conditional probability that the student attended private schools? Hint: use a Venn diagram.

One of the more important concepts in probability is that of independence. In this section we define what is meant by two events being *independent*. First, however, we try to develop an intuitive idea of the meaning of independent events.

452

6.1
Example

Consider a group of 36 students. Suppose that $E$ and $F$ are two properties that each student either has or does not have. For example, the events $E$ and $F$ might be

$E$: "student has blue eyes"
$F$: "student is a male"

With regard to these two properties, suppose it is found that the 36 students are distributed as follows:

| | Blue Eyes $E$ | Not Blue Eyes $\bar{E}$ | Total |
|---|---|---|---|
| Male $F$ | 6 | 6 | 12 |
| Female $\bar{F}$ | 12 | 12 | 24 |
| Total | 18 | 18 | 36 |

If we choose a student at random, the probabilities corresponding to the events $E$ and $F$ are

$$P(E) = \frac{18}{36} = \frac{1}{2}$$

$$P(F) = \frac{12}{36} = \frac{1}{3}$$

$$P(E \cap F) = \frac{6}{36} = \frac{1}{6}$$

$$P(E|F) = \frac{P(E \cap F)}{P(F)} = \frac{1/6}{1/3} = \frac{1}{2} = P(E)$$

In this example, the probability of $E$ given $F$ equals the probability of $E$. This situation can be described by saying that the information that the event $F$ has occurred does not affect a change in the probability of the event $E$. If this is the case, we say that $E$ is independent of $F$.

Definition
of Independent
Events

**Let $E$ and $F$ be two events of a sample space $S$ with $P(F) > 0$. The** event $E$ is independent of the event $F$ **if and only if**

$$P(E|F) = P(E)$$

In Exercise 14.5, Problem 10, page 451, it was shown that

$$P(F)P(E|F) = P(E)P(F|E) \tag{6.1}$$

provided $P(E) > 0$ and $P(F) > 0$. If $E$ is independent of $F$, then we know that $P(E|F) = P(E)$. Substituting this into (6.1), we find that

$$P(F|E) = P(F)$$

That is, the event $F$ is independent of $E$.

Thus, if two events $E$ and $F$ have positive probabilities and if the event $E$ is independent of $F$, then $F$ is also independent of $E$. In this case, $E$ and $F$ are called *independent events.*

This leads us to the following theorem on independent events.

Independent
Events

**Theorem 6.1**
**Two events $E$ and $F$ of a sample space $S$ are independent events if and only if**

$$P(E \cap F) = P(E) \cdot P(F)$$

**That is, the probability of $E$ and $F$ is equal to the product of the probability of $E$ and the probability of $F$.**

Proof
If $E, F$ are independent, then

$$P(E|F) = \frac{P(E \cap F)}{P(F)} \text{ and } P(E|F) = P(E)$$

Thus

$$P(E \cap F) = P(E) \cdot P(F)$$

Conversely, if $P(E \cap F) = P(E) \cdot P(F)$, then

$$P(E|F) = \frac{P(E \cap F)}{P(F)} = \frac{P(E) \cdot P(F)}{P(F)} = P(E)$$

That is, $E$ and $F$ are independent events.

Theorem 6.1 is used to verify whether two events are independent. On the other hand, if it is known that two events are independent, the formula of the theorem provides a way to compute the probability of both events occurring.

Suppose a red die and a green die are thrown. Let event $E$ be "throw a 5 with the red die" and event $F$ be "throw a 6 with the green die."

In this experiment, the events $E$ and $F$ are

$$E = \{(5, 1), (5, 2), (5, 3), (5, 4), (5, 5), (5, 6)\}$$
$$F = \{(1, 6), (2, 6), (3, 6), (4, 6), (5, 6), (6, 6)\}$$

Thus

$$P(E) = \frac{1}{6}$$

$$P(F) = \frac{1}{6}$$

6.2
Example

Also, the event $E$ and $F$ is

$$E \cap F = \{(5,6)\}$$

Then

$$P(E \cap F) = \frac{1}{36}$$

Thus, $E$ and $F$ are independent events since $P(E \cap F) = P(E) \cdot P(F)$.

<table>
<tr><td>6.3<br>Example</td><td>

In Exercise 14.2, Problem 10, show that the events $E$ and $G$ are not independent, but that the events $G$ and $H$ are independent.
The events $E$ and $G$ are

</td></tr>
</table>

$$E = \{RRL, LRR, RRR\}$$
$$G = \{LLL, LLR, LRL, LRR\}$$

The sample space $S$ has eight elements so that

$$P(E) = \frac{3}{8}, \qquad P(G) = \frac{1}{2}$$

Also, the event $E$ and $G$ is

$$E \cap G = \{LRR\}$$

and

$$P(E \cap G) = \frac{1}{8}$$

Since $P(E \cap G) \neq P(E) \cdot P(G)$, the events $E$ and $G$ of Problem 10, Exercise 14.2, are not independent. Thus running to the right two consecutive times and running to the left on the first trial are dependent.
    Next, the event $H$ is

$$H = \{RRL, RRR, LRL, LRR\}$$

and

$$P(H) = \frac{1}{2}$$

The event $G$ and $H$ and its probability are

$$G \cap H = \{LRL, LRR\}, \qquad P(G \cap H) = \frac{1}{4}$$

Since $P(G \cap H) = P(G) \cdot P(H)$, the events $G$ and $H$ are independent. Thus running to the left on the first trial and running to the right on the second trial are independent events.

    The above example illustrates that the question of whether two events are independent can be answered by simply showing that Theorem 6.1 is or is not satisfied. Although we may often suspect two events $E$ and $F$ to be independent, our intuition must be checked by computing $P(E)$, $P(F)$, and $P(E \cap F)$ and determining whether $P(E \cap F) = P(E) \cdot P(F)$.

However, sometimes in constructing a probabilistic model for an experiment, an *assumption* of independence is made. The following example illustrates such a situation.

In a group of seeds, 1/4 of which should produce white plants, the best germination that can be obtained is 75 percent. If one seed is planted, what is the probability that it will grow into a white plant?

Let G and W be the events

G: the plant will grow
W: the seed will produce a white plant

Assume that W does not depend on G and vice versa, so that W and G are independent events.

Then, the probability that the plant grows and is white, namely, $P(W \cap G)$ is

$$P(W \cap G) = P(W) \cdot P(G) = \frac{1}{4} \cdot \frac{3}{4} = \frac{3}{16}$$

Thus, 3 out of 16 times, a white plant will grow.

There is a danger that mutually exclusive events and independent events may be confused. A source of this confusion is the common expression "have nothing to do with each other." This expression provides a description of independence when applied to everyday events; but when it is applied to sets, it suggests nonoverlapping. Nonoverlapping sets are mutually exclusive, but are not necessarily independent. See Problem 6 in Exercise 14.6.

1. If $A$ and $B$ are independent events, $P(A) = .6$, and $P(A \cap B) = .3$, find $P(B)$.
2. If $A$ and $B$ are independent events, find $P(B)$ if $P(A) = .2$ and $P(A \cup B) = .3$.
3. In Problem 10, Exercise 14.2, are the two events $E$ and $F$ independent?
4. For a three-child family, let $E$ be the event "the family has at most one boy" and $F$ be the event "the family has children of both sexes." Are $E$ and $F$ independent events?
5. For a two-child family, are the events $E$ and $F$, as defined in Problem 4, independent?
6. Give an example of two events that are
   (a) independent, but not mutually exclusive (disjoint)
   (b) not independent, but mutually exclusive (disjoint)
   (c) not independent and not mutually exclusive (disjoint)
7. Show that whenever two events are both independent and mutually exclusive, then at least one of them is impossible.

8. A die is loaded so that

$$P\{1\} = P\{2\} = P\{3\} = \frac{1}{4}$$

$$P\{4\} = P\{5\} = P\{6\} = \frac{1}{12}$$

If $A = \{1, 2\}$, $B = \{2, 3\}$, $C = \{1, 3\}$, show that any pair of these events is independent.

9. Consider the experiment of three throws of a fair coin. Define the events $E$ and $F$ to be

$E$: a head turns up on the first throw
$F$: a tail turns up on the second throw

Show that $E$ and $F$ are independent events.

10. In a survey of 100 people, categorized as drinkers or nondrinkers, with or without a liver ailment, the following data was obtained

|  | $F$<br>Liver<br>Ailment | $\bar{F}$<br>No Liver<br>Ailment |
|---|---|---|
| Drinkers $E$ | 52 | 18 |
| Nondrinkers $\bar{E}$ | 8 | 22 |

(a) Are the events $E$ and $F$ independent?
(b) Are the events $\bar{E}$ and $\bar{F}$ independent?
(c) Are the events $E$ and $\bar{F}$ independent?

11. Let $E$ be any event. If $F$ is an impossible event, show that $E$ and $F$ are independent.

*12. Show that if $E$ and $F$ are independent events so are $\bar{E}$ and $\bar{F}$. (Hint: use the result of Problem 6(c) on page 389).

*13. Show that if $E$ and $F$ are independent events and if $P(E) \neq 0$, $P(F) \neq 0$, then $E$ and $F$ are not mutually exclusive.

*14. Three events $E$, $F$, $G$ are *independent* if any two of them are independent and

$$P(E \cap F \cap G) = P(E) \cdot P(F) \cdot P(G)$$

Use this definition to determine whether the events

$E$: "the first die shows a six"
$F$: "the second die shows a three"
$G$: "the sum on the two dice is seven"

for the experiment of tossing two fair dice are independent.

*15. Solve Problem 7 in Exercise 14.1, page 421. Hint:
(a) $P(\text{no ones are obtained}) = 5^4/6^4 = 625/1296 = .4823$

(b) The probability of not obtaining a double ace on any given toss is 35/36. Thus

$$P(\text{no double aces are obtained}) = (35/36)^{24} = .509$$

*16.2 A man has 10 keys of which only 1 fits his door. He tries them successively (without replacement). Find the probability that a key fits with exactly 5 tries.

In this section we consider experiments whose sample space can be divided or partitioned into two (or more) mutually exclusive events. This study involves a further application of conditional probabilities and leads us to the famous formula of Thomas Bayes, which was first published in 1763.

We begin by considering the following example.

Given two urns, I and II, suppose Urn I contains 4 black and 7 white balls. Urn II contains 3 black, 1 white, and 4 yellow balls. We select an urn at random and then draw a ball. What is the probability that we obtain a black ball?

Let $U_I$ and $U_{II}$ stand for the events "Urn I is chosen" and "Urn II is chosen," respectively. Similarly, let $B, W, Y$ stand for the event that a black, white, or yellow ball is chosen, respectively.

$$P(U_I) = P(U_{II}) = \frac{1}{2}$$

$$P(B|U_I) = \frac{4}{11}, \qquad P(B|U_{II}) = \frac{3}{8}$$

But using the result of Problem 5(g) in Exercise 13.3, page 389, the event $B$ can be written as

$$B = (B \cap U_I) \cup (B \cap U_{II})$$

Since $B \cap U_I$ and $B \cap U_{II}$ are disjoint, we add their probabilities. Then

$$P(B) = P(B \cap U_I) + P(B \cap U_{II})$$

Using the Definition of Conditional Probability, we have

$$P(B|U_I) = \frac{P(B \cap U_I)}{P(U_I)}, \qquad P(B|U_{II}) = \frac{P(B \cap U_{II})}{P(U_{II})}$$

Thus

$$P(B) = P(U_I) \cdot P(B|U_I) + P(U_{II}) \cdot P(B|U_{II})$$
$$= \frac{1}{2} \cdot \frac{4}{11} + \frac{1}{2} \cdot \frac{3}{8} = \frac{65}{176} = .369$$

---

[2] *Op. cit.*, Feller.

A solution to Example 7.1 can be depicted using a tree diagram. See Figure 14.13.

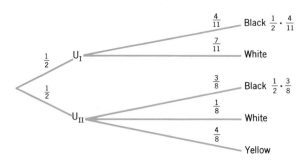

**Figure 14.13**

Suppose $A_1$ and $A_2$ are two nonempty, mutually exclusive events of a sample space $S$ and suppose $A_1 \cup A_2 = S$; that is,

$$A_1 \neq \varnothing, \qquad A_2 \neq \varnothing, \qquad A_1 \cap A_2 = \varnothing, \qquad S = A_1 \cup A_2$$

Partition    Here we say $A_1$ and $A_2$ form a *partition* of $S$. See Figure 14.14.

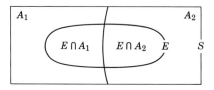

**Figure 14.14**

Let $E$ be any event in $S$. Using the result of Problem 5(g) in Exercise 13.3, page 389, we have

$$E = (E \cap A_1) \cup (E \cap A_2)$$

Now, $E \cap A_1$ and $E \cap A_2$ are disjoint. For,

$$(E \cap A_1) \cap (E \cap A_2) = (E \cap E) \cap (A_1 \cap A_2) = E \cap \varnothing = \varnothing$$

since $A_1$ and $A_2$ are disjoint. Using the Definition of Conditional Probability, the probability for $E$ is then

$$\begin{aligned} P(E) &= P(E \cap A_1) + P(E \cap A_2) \\ &= P(A_1) \cdot P(E|A_1) + P(A_2) \cdot P(E|A_2) \end{aligned} \tag{7.1}$$

The above formula is used to find the probability of an event $E$ of a sample space when the sample space is partitioned into two sets $A_1$ and $A_2$.

Of the applicants to a business school, it is felt that 80 percent are eligible to enter and 20 percent are not. To aid in the selection process, an admission test is administered which is designed so that an eligible candidate will pass 90 percent of the time, while an ineligible candidate will pass 30 percent of the time. What is the probability that an applicant for admission will pass the admissions test?

Here the sample space $S$ consists of the applicants for admission and $S$ can be partitioned into the two events

$A_1$: eligible applicant     $A_2$: ineligible applicant

which are disjoint and whose union is $S$. The event $E$ is

$E$: applicant passes admissions test

Now

$$P(A_1) = .8 \qquad P(A_2) = .2$$
$$P(E|A_1) = .9 \qquad P(E|A_2) = .3$$

Using the formula (7.1), we have

$$P(E) = P(A_1) \cdot P(E|A_1) + P(A_2) \cdot P(E|A_2) = (.9)(.8) + (.3)(.2)$$
$$= .72 + .06 = .78$$

Thus the probability that an applicant passes the admissions test is .78.

If we partition a sample space $S$ into three sets $A_1$, $A_2$, $A_3$ so that

$$S = A_1 \cup A_2 \cup A_3, \qquad A_1 \cap A_2 = \emptyset, \qquad A_2 \cap A_3 = \emptyset$$
$$A_1 \cap A_3 = \emptyset, \qquad A_1 \neq \emptyset, \qquad A_2 \neq \emptyset, \qquad A_3 \neq \emptyset$$

then by an extension of Problem 5(g), Exercise 13.3, page 389, any event $E$ in $S$ can be expressed by

$$E = (E \cap A_1) \cup (E \cap A_2) \cup (E \cap A_3)$$

The probability of event $E$ is

$$P(E) = P(E \cap A_1) + P(E \cap A_2) + P(E \cap A_3)$$
$$= P(A_1) \cdot P(E|A_1) + P(A_2) \cdot P(E|A_2) + P(A_3) \cdot P(E|A_3) \qquad (7.2)$$

since $E \cap A_1$, $E \cap A_2$, and $E \cap A_3$ are disjoint. See Figure 14.15.

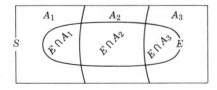

**Figure 14.15**

This formula is useful for finding the probability of an event $E$ of a sample space when the sample space is partitioned into three sets $A_1$, $A_2$, and $A_3$.

**7.3**
**Example**

Three machines I, II, and III manufacture, respectively, .4, .5, and .1 of the total production. The percentage of defective items produced by I, II, and III is 2, 4, and 1 percent, respectively. For an item chosen at random, what is the probability it is defective?

In this example, the sample space $S$ is partitioned into three events $A_1$, $A_2$, and $A_3$, defined by

$A_1$: item produced by machine I
$A_2$: item produced by machine II
$A_3$: item produced by machine III

Clearly the events $A_1$, $A_2$, $A_3$ are mutually exclusive and their union is $S$. Define the event $E$ in $S$ to be

$E$: item is defective

Now

$$P(A_1) = .4, \quad P(A_2) = .5, \quad P(A_3) = .1$$
$$P(E|A_1) = .02, \quad P(E|A_2) = .04, \quad P(E|A_3) = .01$$

Thus, using formula (7.2), we see that

$$P(E) = (.4)(.02) + (.5)(.04) + (.1)(.01)$$
$$= .008 + .020 + .001 = .029$$

Figure 14.16 gives a tree diagram solution to this problem.

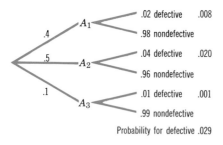

Probability for defective .029

**Figure 14.16**

To generalize formulas (7.1) and (7.2) to a sample space $S$ partitioned into $n$ sets, we proceed as follows.

**Definition of a Partition**

A sample space $S$ is *partitioned into* $n$ sets $A_1, A_2, \ldots, A_n$ provided

**(a) The intersection of any two of the sets is empty.**
**(b) Each set is nonempty.**
**(c)** $A_1 \cup A_2 \cup \cdots \cup A_n = S.$

Let $S$ be a sample space and let $A_1, A_2, A_3, \ldots, A_n$ be $n$ events that form a partition of the set $S$. If $E$ is any event in $S$, then

$$E = (E \cap A_1) \cup (E \cap A_2) \cup \cdots \cup (E \cap A_n)$$

Clearly, $E \cap A_1$, $E \cap A_2, \ldots$, $E \cap A_n$ are mutually exclusive events. Hence

$$P(E) = P(E \cap A_1) + P(E \cap A_2) + \cdots + P(E \cap A_n) \qquad (7.3)$$

In (7.3) replace $P(E \cap A_1)$, $P(E \cap A_2), \ldots, P(E \cap A_n)$, using the Definition of Conditional Probability. Then we obtain the formula

$$P(E) = P(A_1) \cdot P(E|A_1) + P(A_2) \cdot P(E|A_2) + \cdots + P(A_n) \cdot P(E|A_n)$$

$$(7.4)$$

In Example 7.2, page 459, suppose an applicant passes the admissions test. What is the probability that he was among those eligible; that is, what is the probability $P(A_1|E)$?

Here, by the Definition of Conditional Probability

$$P(A_1|E) = \frac{P(A_1 \cap E)}{P(E)} = \frac{P(A_1 \cdot P(E|A_1)}{P(E)}$$

But $P(E)$ is given by (7.4) when $n = 2$ or by (7.1). Thus

$$P(A_1|E) = \frac{P(A_1) \cdot P(E|A_1)}{P(A_1) \cdot P(E|A_1) + P(A_2) \cdot P(E|A_2)} \qquad (7.5)$$

Using the information supplied in Example 7.2, page 459, we find

$$P(A_1|E) = \frac{(.8)(.9)}{.78} = \frac{.72}{.78} = .923$$

Thus, the admissions test is a reasonably effective device. Less than 8 percent of the students passing the test are ineligible.

Equation (7.5) is known as *Bayes' formula* for the special case when the sample space is partitioned into two sets $A_1$ and $A_2$. The general formula is given in Theorem 7.1.

**Theorem 7.1 Bayes' Formula**

**Let $S$ be a sample space partitioned into $n$ events $A_1, \ldots, A_n$. Let $E$ be any event of $S$ for which $P(E) > 0$. The probability for the event $A_j$, $(j = 1, 2, \ldots, n)$, given the event $E$, is**

$$P(A_j|E) = \frac{P(A_j) \cdot P(E|A_j)}{P(A_1) \cdot P(E|A_1) + P(A_2) \cdot P(E|A_2) + \cdots + P(A_n) \cdot P(E|A_n)}$$

$$(7.6)$$

The proof is left as an exercise.

The following example will illustrate a use for Bayes' formula when the sample space $S$ is partitioned into three events.

Motors Incorporated has three plants, I, II, and III. Plant I produces 35 percent of the car output, plant II produces 20 percent, and plant III produces the remaining 45 percent. One percent of the output of plant I is defective, as is 1.8 percent of II, and 2 percent of III. The annual total output of Motors Incorporated is 1,000,000 cars. A car is chosen at random from the annual output and it is found to be defective. What is the probability that it came from plant I? II? III?

To answer these questions let us define the following events.

> $E$: car is defective
> $A_1$: car produced by plant I
> $A_2$: car produced by plant II
> $A_3$: car produced by plant III

Also, $P(A_1|E)$ indicates the probability that a car is produced by plant I, given that it was defective. $P(A_2|E)$ and $P(A_3|E)$ are similarly defined. To find these, we proceed as follows.

From the data given in the problem, we can determine the following.

$$P(A_1) = .35 \qquad P(E|A_1) = .010$$
$$P(A_2) = .20 \qquad P(E|A_2) = .018 \qquad (7.7)$$
$$P(A_3) = .45 \qquad P(E|A_3) = .020$$

Now

> $A_1 \cap E$ is the event "produced by plant I and is defective"
> $A_2 \cap E$ is the event "produced by plant II and is defective"
> $A_3 \cap E$ is the event "produced by plant III and is defective"

From the Definition of Conditional Probability, we find

$$P(A_1 \cap E) = P(A_1) \cdot P(E|A_1) = (.35) \cdot (.010) = .0035$$
$$P(A_2 \cap E) = P(A_2) \cdot P(E|A_2) = (.20) \cdot (.018) = .0036$$
$$P(A_3 \cap E) = P(A_3) \cdot P(E|A_3) = (.45) \cdot (.020) = .0090$$

Since $E = (A_1 \cap E) \cup (A_2 \cap E) \cup (A_3 \cap E)$, we have

$$P(E) = P(A_1 \cap E) + P(A_2 \cap E) + P(A_3 \cap E)$$
$$= .0035 + .0036 + .0090$$
$$= .0161$$

Thus, the probability that a defective car is chosen is .0161.

Given that the car chosen is defective, the probability that it came from Plant I is $P(A_1|E)$. To compute $P(A_1|E)$, $P(A_2|E)$, $P(A_3|E)$, we use Bayes' formula.

$$P(A_1|E) = \frac{P(A_1) \cdot P(E|A_1)}{P(A_1) \cdot P(E|A_1) + P(A_2) \cdot P(E|A_2) + P(A_3) \cdot P(E|A_3)}$$

$$= \frac{P(A_1) \cdot P(E|A_1)}{P(E)} = \frac{(.35)(.01)}{.0161} = .217$$

$$P(A_2|E) = \frac{P(A_2) \cdot P(E|A_2)}{P(E)} = \frac{.0036}{.0161} = \frac{36}{161} = .224 \qquad (7.8)$$

$$P(A_3|E) = \frac{P(A_3) \cdot P(E|A_3)}{P(E)} = \frac{.0090}{.0161} = \frac{90}{161} = .559$$

Compare the probabilities found in (7.7) with those in (7.8). The probabilities $P(E|A_1)$, $P(E|A_2)$, and $P(E|A_3)$ are probabilities of a defective car being produced by one of the plants *before* it is chosen and examined. This is what we refer to as a *priori probability,* that is, "before the fact" probability. The probabilities $P(A_1|E)$, $P(A_2|E)$, $P(A_3|E)$ are probabilities of a defective car being produced by one of the plants *after* we have examined and found it to be defective. This is referred as a *posteriori probability* or "after the fact" probability. Thus, Bayes' formula gives us a technique for computing a *posteriori probabilities.*

A Priori
Probability

A Posteriori
Probability

For example, before a car is chosen, the probability of choosing a defective car assuming it was from plant I is .01. After it is known that a defective car was chosen, the probability that it came from plant I is .217.

The residents of a community are examined for cancer. The examination results are classified as positive $(+)$, if a malignancy is suspected, and as negative $(-)$, if there are no indications of a malignancy. If a person has cancer, the probability of a suspected malignancy is .98; and the probability of reporting cancer where none existed is .15. If 5 percent of the community has cancer, what is the probability of a person not having cancer, if the examination is positive?

7.6
Example

Let us define the following events.

$A_1$: person has cancer
$A_2$: person does not have cancer
$E$: examination is positive

We want to know the probability of a person not having cancer, if it is known that the examination is positive; that is, we wish to find $P(A_2|E)$. Now

$$P(A_1) = .05, \qquad P(A_2) = .95$$
$$P(E|A_1) = .98 \qquad P(E|A_2) = .15$$

Using Bayes' formula we get

$$P(A_2|E) = \frac{P(A_2)P(E|A_2)}{P(A_1)P(E|A_1) + P(A_2)P(E|A_2)}$$

$$= \frac{(.95)(.15)}{(.05)(.98) + (.95)(.15)} = .744$$

Thus, even if the examination is positive, the person examined is more likely not to have cancer than to have cancer. The reason is that it is better for a healthy person to be examined more thoroughly, than for someone with cancer to go undetected.

7.7
Example

The manager of a Milex car repair shop knows from past experience that, when called by a person whose car will not start, the probabilities for various troubles (assuming no two troubles can occur simultaneously) are as follows:

| Event | Trouble | Probability |
|-------|---------|-------------|
| $A_1$: | Flooded | .3 |
| $A_2$: | Battery cable loose | .2 |
| $A_3$: | Points bad | .1 |
| $A_4$: | Out of gas | .3 |
| $A_5$: | Something else | .1 |

He also knows that if the person will hold the gas pedal down and try to start the car for 30 seconds, the probability that it will start $(E)$ is

$$P(E|A_1) = .9 \qquad P(E|A_2) = 0 \qquad P(E|A_3) = .2$$
$$P(E|A_4) = 0 \qquad P(E|A_5) = .2$$

(a) If a person has called and is instructed to "hold the pedal . . . ," what is the probability that his car will start?
(b) If his car does start when he "holds the pedal . . . ," what is the probability that his car was flooded?

To answer (a), we need to compute $P(E)$. Using (7.4) for $n = 5$, (the sample space is partitioned into five disjoint sets), we have

$$P(E) = P(A_1)P(E|A_1) + P(A_2)P(E|A_2) + P(A_3)P(E|A_3)$$
$$+ P(A_4)P(E|A_4) + P(A_5)P(E|A_5)$$
$$= (.3)(.9) + (.2)(0) + (.1)(.2) + (.3)(0) + (.1)(.2)$$
$$= .27 + .02 + .02 = .31$$

For (b), we use Bayes' theorem to compute the *a posteriori* probability $P(A_1|E)$.

$$P(A_1|E) = \frac{P(A_1) \cdot P(E|A_1)}{P(E)} = \frac{(.3)(.9)}{.31} = \frac{.27}{.31} = .87$$

Thus, the probability that the car is flooded, after it is known that holding down the pedal started the car, is .87.

A particular case of Bayes' formula, when the probability of each event of the partition is equally likely, is given below. If

$$P(A_1) = P(A_2) = \cdots = P(A_n)$$

we obtain

$$P(A_j|E) = \frac{P(E|A_j)}{P(E|A_1) + P(E|A_2) + \cdots + P(E|A_n)} \qquad (7.9)$$

In Example 7.5 let us assume that $P(A_1) = P(A_2) = P(A_3)$, so that the three plants' share of the total production is the same. In this case, we can use equation (7.9) to obtain the probability that a car is produced at Plant I, given that it was defective. Thus

$$P(A_1|E) = \frac{P(E|A_1)}{P(E|A_1) + P(E|A_2) + P(E|A_3)}$$

$$= \frac{.010}{.010 + .018 + .020}$$

$$= \frac{.010}{.048} = \frac{5}{24} = .208$$

1. In Example 7.2, find $P(A_2|E)$.
2. In Example 7.3, suppose it is known that a defective item was produced. Find the probability it came from machine I; from machine II; from machine III.
3. In Example 7.5, suppose $P(A_1) = P(A_2) = P(A_3) = 1/3$. Find $P(A_2|E)$ and $P(A_3|E)$.
4. In Example 7.7, compute the a *posteriori* probabilities $P(A_2|E)$, $P(A_3|E)$, $P(A_4|E)$, and $P(A_5|E)$.
5. In Example 7.6, compute $P(A_1|E)$.
6. Three urns contain colored balls as follows:

| Urn | Red (R) | White (W) | Blue (B) |
|-----|---------|-----------|----------|
| I   | 5       | 6         | 3        |
| II  | 3       | 4         | 5        |
| III | 7       | 5         | 4        |

One urn is chosen at random and a ball is withdrawn. The ball is red. What is the probability that it came from Urn I? from Urn II? from Urn III? Hint: Define the following events.

$E$: Ball selected is red
$U_I$: Urn I selected
$U_{II}$: Urn II selected
$U_{III}$: Urn III selected

Notice that $P(U_I) = P(U_{II}) = P(U_{III}) = 1/3$.

Also, the conditional probabilities are

$$P(E|U_{\mathrm{I}}) = \frac{5}{14}, \qquad P(E|U_{\mathrm{II}}) = \frac{3}{12} = \frac{1}{4}, \qquad P(E|U_{\mathrm{III}}) = \frac{7}{16}$$

Determine $P(U_{\mathrm{I}}|E)$, $P(U_{\mathrm{II}}|E)$, $P(U_{\mathrm{III}}|E)$, by using Bayes' formula.

7. Suppose that if a person with tuberculosis is given a TB screening, the probability that his condition will be detected is .90. If a person without tuberculosis is given a TB screening, the probability that he will be diagnosed incorrectly as having tuberculosis is .3. Suppose, further, that 11 percent of the adult residents of a certain city have tuberculosis. If one of these persons is diagnosed as having tuberculosis based on the screening, what is the probability that he actually has tuberculosis? Interpret your result.

8. Cars are being produced by two factories I and II, but I produces twice as many cars as II in a given time. Factory I is known to produce 2 percent defective and II produces 1 percent defective. A car is examined and found to be defective. What are the *a priori* and *a posteriori* probabilities that the car was produced by I?

9. An absent-minded nurse is supposed to give Mr. Brown a pill each day. The probability that she will forget to give the pill is 2/3. If he receives the pill, the probability that Brown will die is 1/3. If he does not get his pill, the probability that he will die is 3/4. Mr. Brown died. What is the probability that the nurse forgot to give Brown the pill?

10. An oil well is to be drilled in a certain location. The soil there is either rock (probability .53), clay (probability .21), or sand. If it is rock, a geological test gives a positive result with 35 percent accuracy; if it is clay, this test gives a positive result with 48 percent accuracy; and if it is sand, the test gives a positive result with 75 percent accuracy. Given that the test is positive, what is the probability the soil is rock? What is the probability the soil is clay? What is the probability the soil is sand?

*11. Prove Theorem 7.1.

In this section we study practical situations that can be interpreted by using a simple probabilistic model, called the *binomial probability model*. The model was first studied by J. Bernoulli about 1700 and, for this reason, the model is sometimes referred to as a *Bernoulli trial*.

The binomial probability model is a sequence of trials, each of which consists of repetition of a single experiment. We assume the outcome of one experiment does not affect the outcome of any other one; that is, we assume the trials to be independent. Furthermore, we assume that there are only two possible outcomes for each trial, and label them "S" for *success* and "*F*" for *failure*. This is a rather simple experiment and it may be classified completely in terms of a single number $p$, the probability for success,

$$p = P(S)$$

The probability for success is the same for each repetition of the experiment. Since the probability of success is $p$, then the probability of failure is $1 - p$; and we write

$$q = 1 - p = P(F)$$

Any random phenomenon for which the binomial probability model is appropriate is called a *Bernoulli trial*.

**Repeated trials of a random experiment are called** *Bernoulli trials* **if**

**(a) There are only two possible outcomes** $S$ **and** $F$ **in each trial.**
**(b) The probabilities of the outcomes** $S$ **and** $F$ **do not change from trial to trial.**
**(c) The trials are independent.**

Definition
of a Bernoulli
Trial

Many real-world situations have the characteristics of the binomial probability model. For example, in repeatedly running a subject through a T-maze, we may label a turn to the right by $S$ and a turn to the left by $F$. The assumption of independence of each trial is equivalent to presuming the subject has no memory.

In opinion polls, one individual's response is independent of any other person's response, and we may designate the answer "yes" by an $S$ and any other answer ("no," "don't know") by an $F$.

In testing T.V.'s, we have a sequence of independent trials (each test of a particular T.V. is a trial) and we label a nondefective T.V. with an $S$ and a defective one with an $F$.

When a sequence of experiments has more than two outcomes in each trial, we can convert it to a Bernoulli trial by considering the occurrence of an event $E$ as a success and that of the event $\bar{E}$ as a failure. In this case

$$p = P(S) = P(E) \text{ and } q = P(F) = P(\bar{E}).$$

Consider a Bernoulli trial that consists of six stages or six trials. One path or one particular outcome might appear as *FSSSFS*. Since we are assuming that the trials are independent, we get the probability for this particular outcome to be,

$$q \cdot p \cdot p \cdot p \cdot q \cdot p = q^2 \cdot p^4$$

The probability for a different outcome like *SFSFSS* is also equal to $q^2 p^4$. The same is true for any outcome that has *exactly* the same number of $S$'s and $F$'s regardless of their order. To analyze these trials in a systematic way, let us consider tree diagrams for the cases of 2 and 3 trials. See Figure 14.17.

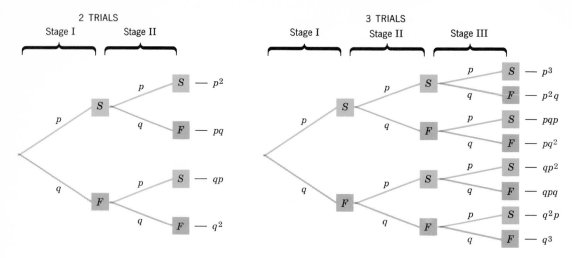

**Figure 14.17**

Several observations should be made with regard to the above two tree diagrams. First, notice that, if we sum the probabilities at the conclusion of the last trial of each experiment, we find that

$$p^2 + pq + qp + q^2 = p^2 + 2pq + q^2 = (p + q)^2$$
$$p^3 + p^2q + pqp + pq^2 + qp^2 + qpq + q^2p + q^3$$
$$= p^3 + 3p^2q + 3pq^2 + q^3 = (p + q)^3$$

In general with an experiment involving $n$ trials, the sum of the probabilities after the $n$th trial is $(p + q)^n$.

Second, notice that in a sequence of $n$ independent trials with two outcomes, any sequence that contains $k$ successes and $n - k$ failures has probability $p^k q^{n-k}$. To find the probability of obtaining exactly $k$ successes in $n$ trials, we must find the number of sequences having $k$ successes. This number is obtained by noting that the $k$ successes can appear in any $k$ of the $n$ trials; thus, the number of such sequences must be equal to the number of combinations of $k$ objects that can be taken from a set of $n$ objects, or $\binom{n}{k}$. If we multiply this number by the probability for obtaining this sequence, we obtain the result in Theorem 8.1.

### Theorem 8.1

**In a Bernoulli trial the probability of exactly $k$ successes in $n$ trials is given by**

$$b(n, k; p) = \binom{n}{k} p^k \cdot q^{n-k} = \frac{n!}{k!(n - k)!} p^k \cdot q^{n-k}$$

**in which** $q = 1 - p$.

The symbol $b(n, k; p)$, which represents the probability of exactly $k$ successes in $n$ trials, is called a *binomial probability*.

A common model for the above result is a coin-flipping experiment:

(a) There are exactly two possible mutually exclusive outcomes on each trial or toss (heads or tails).
(b) The outcome on any trial (toss) is independent of the outcome on any other trial (toss).
(c) The probability of a particular outcome (say $H$) remains constant from trial to trial (toss to toss); for example, on any toss the probability of $H$ is always $1/2$.

We would like to compute the probability of obtaining exactly one tail in six tosses of a fair coin.

Let $S$ denote the simple event "tail shows."
Let $F$ denote the simple event "head shows."

Using Theorem 8.1, in which $k = 1$, $n = 6$, and $p = 1/2 = P(S)$, we obtain

$$P(\text{exactly one success}) = b\left(6, 1; \frac{1}{2}\right) = \binom{6}{1}\left(\frac{1}{2}\right)^1\left(\frac{1}{2}\right)^{6-1}$$

$$= \frac{6}{64} = .09375$$

It is not always necessary to compute binomial probabilities. Table 9 (page 613) lists the values of the binomial probability $b(n, k; p)$ for $n = 2, 3, \ldots, 20$ and $p = .05, .10, .15, .20, .25, .30, .35, .40, .45,$ and $.50$. If a situation requires some other choice of $p$, more extensive tables should be used, or the computation should be done using Theorem 8.1. For large $n$, a different model should be used.

The reader will notice in Table 9 that there are no probabilities listed for $p > .50$. The reason for this (see Problem 16, Exercise 14.8) is that

$$b(n, k; p) = b(n, n - k; 1 - p)$$

For example, if $n = 6$, $k = 2$, and $p = .7$, then

$$b(6, 2; .7) = b(6, 4; .3) = .0595.$$

A machine produces light bulbs to meet certain specifications and 80 percent of the bulbs produced meet these specifications. A sample of 6 bulbs is taken from the machine's production. What is the probability that 3 or more of them fail to meet the specifications?

In this example, as in many other applications, it is necessary to compute the probability, not of exactly $k$ successes, but of at *least* or at *most* k successes. To obtain such probabilities we have to compute all the individual probabilities and add them.

In this example we are looking for the probability of the event A "at least three fail to meet specifications." But this event is just the union of the mutually exclusive events "exactly 3 failures," "exactly 4 failures," "exactly 5 failures," and "exactly 6 failures." Hence we use Theorem 8.1 for $n = 6$ and $k = 3, 4, 5$, and 6. Since the probability of failure is .20, we have

$$P(\text{exactly 3 failures}) = b(6, 3; .20) = .0819$$
$$P(\text{exactly 4 failures}) = b(6, 4; .20) = .0154$$
$$P(\text{exactly 5 failures}) = b(6, 5; .20) = .0015$$
$$P(\text{exactly 6 failures}) = b(6, 6; .20) = .0001$$

Therefore

$$P(\text{at least 3 failures}) = P(A) = .0819 + .0154 + .0015 + .0001 = .0989$$

Let us define the event E to be "less than 3 failures." Then,

$$P(E) = P(\text{exactly 2 failures}) + P(\text{exactly 1 failure}) + P(\text{exactly 0 failures})$$
$$= b(6, 2; .20) + b(6, 1; .20) + b(6, 0; .20)$$
$$= .2458 + .3932 + .2621 = .9011$$

Notice that since $\bar{E} = A$,

$$1 - P(E) = P(A).$$

Suppose that the normal rate of infection of a certain disease in cattle is 25 percent. To test a newly discovered serum, healthy animals are injected with it. How are we to evaluate the result of the experiment?

For an absolutely worthless serum, the probability that exactly k of n test animals remain free from infection may be equated to $b(n, k; 0.75)$. For $k = n = 10$ this probability is about 0.056. Thus, if, out of 10 test animals, none catches infection, this may be taken as an indication that the serum has had an effect, although it is not conclusive proof. Notice that, without serum, the probability that out of 17 animals at most 1 catches infection is about 0.0501, $[b(17, 0; .25) + b(17, 1; .25)]$. Therefore there is *stronger evidence* in favor of the serum if, out of 17 test animals, at most 1 gets infected, than, if out of 10, all remain healthy. For $n = 23$ the probability of at most 2 animals catching infection is about 0.0492, and thus at most 2 failures out of 23 is again better evidence for the serum than at most 1 out of 17, or 0 out of 10.

[3] P. V. Sukhatme and V. G. Panse, "Size of experiments for testing sera or vaccines," *Indiana Journal of Veterinary Science and Animal Husbandry, 13* (1943), pp. 75–82.

A man claims to be able to distinguish between two kinds of wines with 90 percent accuracy and presents his claim to an agency interested in promoting the consumption of one of the two kinds of wines. To check his claim, the following experiment is conducted: The man is to taste the two types of wines and distinguish between them. This is to be done 9 times with a 3-minute break after each taste. It is agreed that if the man is correct at least 6 out of the 9 times he is to be hired.

The main questions to be asked, on the one hand, is whether the above procedure gives sufficient protection to the hiring agency against a person guessing and, on the other hand, whether the man is given sufficient chance to be hired if he is really a wine connoisseur.

To answer the first question, let us assume that the man is guessing. Then in each trial he has a probability of 1/2 of identifying the wine correctly. Let $k$ be the number of correct identifications. Let us compute the binomial probability for $k = 6, 7, 8, 9$, to study the likelihood of the man being hired while guessing. Now

$$b\left(9, 6; \frac{1}{2}\right) + b\left(9, 7; \frac{1}{2}\right) + b\left(9, 8; \frac{1}{2}\right) + b\left(9, 9; \frac{1}{2}\right)$$

$$= .1641 + .0703 + .0176 + .0020 = .2540$$

Thus there is a likelihood of .254 that he will pass if he guesses.

To answer the second question in the case where the claim is true, we would like to find the sum of the probabilities $b(n, k; .90)$ for $k = 6, 7, 8, 9$. Then

$$b(9, 6; .90) + b(9, 7; .90) + b(9, 8; .90) + b(9, 9; .90)$$
$$= b(9, 3; .10) + b(9, 2; .10) + b(9, 1; .10) + b(9, 0; .10)$$
$$= .0446 + .1722 + .3874 + .3874 = .9916$$

We notice that the test is fair to the man, since it practically assures him the position. Furthermore, the company should like the test, because it assures them that they are picking the right person.

The student should administer a similar test in such a way that the answer to the first question is approximately .002 and the answer to the second part is approximately .500 and give interpretations to such a test.

1. Use Table 9 (page 613) to compute the following binomial probabilities.
   (a) $b(7, 5; .30)$  (d) $b(15, 8; .70)$
   (b) $b(8, 6; .40)$  (e) $b(8, 5; .60)$
   (c) $b(15, 10; \frac{1}{2})$  (f) $b(12, 6; .90)$
2. Use Theorem 8.1 to compute the following binomial probabilities
   (a) $b(6, 1; \frac{1}{3})$  (c) $b(8, 0; \frac{1}{6})$

(b) $b(3, 2; \frac{2}{3})$      (d) $b(8, 7; \frac{5}{6})$

3. What is the probability of obtaining exactly two sevens in five rolls of two fair dice?

4. An experiment is performed four times with two possible outcomes, $F$ (failure) and $S$ (success), with probabilities $1/4$ and $3/4$, respectively.
   (a) Draw the tree diagram describing the experiment.
   (b) Calculate the probability of exactly two successes and two failures by using (a).
   (c) Verify (b) by using Theorem 8.1 and Table 9.

5. Assuming all sex distributions to be equally probable, what is the probability that a family with exactly six children will have three boys and three girls?

6. A fair coin is tossed six times (or six coins are tossed simultaneously).
   (a) What is the probability of obtaining exactly two heads?
   (b) What is the probability of obtaining exactly two heads, if it is known that at least one head appeared?

7. What is the probability that in a family of seven children
   (a) four will be girls?
   (b) at least two are girls?
   (c) at least two and not more than four are girls?

8. For a baseball player with a .250 batting average, what is the probability he will have at least two hits in four times at bat? Of at least one hit in four times at bat.

9. If the probability of hitting a target is $1/5$, and 10 shots are fired independently, what is the probability of the target being hit at least twice?

10. Opinion polls based on small samples often yield misleading results. Suppose 65 percent of the people in a city are opposed to a bond issue and the others favor it. If 7 people are asked for their opinion, what is the probability that a majority of them will favor the bond issue?

11. A supposed coffee connoisseur claims he can distinguish between a cup of instant coffee and a cup of percolator coffee 75 percent of the time. You give him 6 cups of coffee and tell him that you will grant his claim if he correctly identifies at least 5 of the 6 cups.
    (a) What are his chances of having his claim granted, if he is in fact only guessing?
    (b) What are his chances of having his claim rejected, when in fact he really does have the ability he claims?

*12. How many times should a fair coin be flipped in order to have the probability of at least 1 head appearing be greater than .98?

*13. What is the probability that the birthdays of 6 people fall in 2 calendar months leaving exactly 10 months free? (Assume independence and equal probabilities for all months.)

*14. A book of 500 pages contains 500 misprints. Estimate the chance that a given page contains at least 3 misprints.

*15. In $n$ Bernoulli trials with $p = 1/3$, for what least value of $n$ does the probability of exactly 2 successes have its only maximum value?

*16. Prove the identity

$$b(n, k; p) = b(n, n - k; 1 - p)$$

probabilistic model
logical possibilities
outcome
sample space
event
simple event
mutually exclusive
odds
equally likely
success

failure
conditional probability
independent events
Bayes' formula
partition
binomial probability
Bernoulli trial
a priori
a posteriori

1. A survey of families with two children is made and the sexes of the children are recorded. Describe the sample space and draw a tree diagram of this random experiment.

2. A fair coin is tossed three times.
   (a) Construct a probabilistic model corresponding to this experiment.
   (b) Find the probabilities of the following events:
   (i) the first toss is $T$
   (ii) the first toss is $H$
   (iii) either the first toss is $T$ or the third toss is $H$
   (iv) at least one of the tosses is $H$
   (v) there are at least two $T$'s
   (vi) no tosses are $H$

3. Below is a set of 20 chips labeled by ordered pairs of numbers.

$$(1, 1)(1, 2)(1, 3)(1, 4)(1, 5)$$
$$(2, 1)(2, 2)(2, 3)(2, 4)(2, 5)$$
$$(3, 1)(3, 2)(3, 3)(3, 4)(3, 5)$$
$$(4, 1)(4, 2)(4, 3)(4, 4)(4, 5)$$

Let "$a$" denote the first component and "$b$" the second component of an ordered pair. One chip is drawn at random. Find the probability that it belongs to the subset described by:

(a) $a = 4$       (e) $a \neq 2$ and $b \neq 4$

(b) $a < 4$       (f) $a + b = 4$

(c) $a = 2$ and $b = 4$     (g) $a + b < 4$

(d) $a = 2$ or $b = 4$     (h) $a = b$

4. Jones lives at $O$. (See figure below.) He has 5 gas stations located 4 blocks away (dots). Each afternoon he checks on one of his gas stations. He starts at $O$. At each intersection he flips a fair coin. If it shows heads he will head North ($N$); otherwise he will head towards the East ($E$). What is the probability that he will end up at gas station $G$ before coming to one of the other stations?

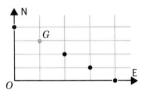

5. Consider the experiment of spinning the spinner in the figure below three times. (Assume the spinner cannot fall on a line.)

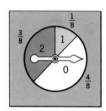

(a) Are all outcomes equally likely?

(b) If not, which of the outcomes has the highest probability?

(c) Let $F$ be the event "each digit will occur exactly once." Find $P(F)$.

6. If $E$ and $F$ are events with $P(E \cup F) = 5/8$, $P(E \cap F) = 1/3$, $P(E) = 1/2$ find:

(a) $P(\bar{E})$

(b) $P(F)$

(c) $P(\bar{F})$

7. If $E$ and $F$ represent mutually exclusive events, $P(E) = 0.30$, and $P(F) = 0.45$, find each of the following probabilities:

(a) $P(\bar{E})$        (e) $P(\overline{E \cap F})$

(b) $P(\bar{F})$        (f) $P(\overline{E \cup F})$

(c) $P(E \cap F)$    (g) $P(\bar{E} \cup \bar{F})$

(d) $P(E \cup F)$    (h) $P(\bar{E} \cap \bar{F})$

8. Three envelopes are addressed for three secret letters written in invisible ink. A secretary randomly places each of the letters in an envelope and mails them. What is the probability that at least one person receives the correct letter?

9. What are the odds in favor of a five, when a fair die is thrown?

10. A man is willing to give $7:6$ odds that the Bears will win the NFL title. What is the probability of the Bears winning?

*11. Show that if $E$ and $F$ are independent events then:

   (a) $E$ and $\bar{F}$ are independent

   (b) $\bar{E}$ and $F$ are independent

12. A biased coin is such that the probability of heads (H) is $1/4$ and the probability of tails (T) is $3/4$. Show that in flipping this coin twice the events,
   $E$: A head turns up in the first throw
   $F$: A tail turns up in the second throw
   are independent.

13. The records of the Dean of Students of Midwestern University show that 38 percent of the students failed mathematics, 27 percent of the students failed economics, and 9 percent of the students failed mathematics and economics. A student is selected at random.

   (a) If he failed economics, what is the probability that he failed mathematics?

   (b) If he failed mathematics, what is the probability that he failed economics?

   (c) What is the probability that he failed mathematics or economics?

14. The table below indicates a survey conducted by a deodorant producer.

| | Like the deodorant | Did not like the deodorant | No opinion |
|---|---|---|---|
| Group I | 180 | 60 | 20 |
| Group II | 110 | 85 | 12 |
| Group III | 55 | 65 | 7 |

   Let $E$ be the event—customer likes the deodorant.
   Let $F$ be the event—customer does not like the deodorant.
   Let $G$ be the event—customer is from Group I.
   Let $H$ be the event—customer is from Group II.
   Let $K$ be the event—customer is from Group III.

   Find: (a) $P(E|G)$   (e) $P(F|G)$
        (b) $P(G|E)$   (f) $P(G|F)$
        (c) $P(H|E)$   (g) $P(H|F)$
        (d) $P(K|E)$   (h) $P(K|F)$

15. In a factory, three machines $A_1$, $A_2$, $A_3$ produce, respectively, 55, 30, and 15 percent of total production. The percentages of defective output of these machines are 1, 2, and 3 percent, respectively. An item is chosen at random and it is defective. What is the probability it came from machine $A_1$? $A_2$? $A_3$?

16. A lung cancer test has been found to have the following

reliability. The test can detect 85 percent of the people who have cancer and does not detect 15 percent of these people. Among the noncancerous group it detects 92 percent of not having cancer, whereas 8 percent of this group are detected erroneously as having lung cancer. Statistics show that about 1.8 percent of the population have cancer. Suppose an individual is given the test for lung cancer and it shows that he has the disease. What is the probability that he actually has cancer?

17. Find the probability of throwing an 11 at least 3 times in 5 throws of a fair pair of dice.

18. Management believes that 1 out of 6 people watching a television advertisement about their new product will purchase the product. Five persons who watched the advertisement are picked at random. What is the probability that 0, 1, 2, 3, 4, or 5 persons will purchase the product?

19. Suppose that the probability of a player hitting a home run is 1/20. In 5 tries what is the probability that he hits at least 1 home run?

20. In a 12-item true-false examination,
    (a) What is the probability that a student will obtain all correct answers by chance if he is guessing?
    (b) If 7 correct answers constitute a passing grade, what is the probability that he will pass?
    (c) What are the odds in favor of passing?

## Bibliography

*Mathematics*

Feller, W., *An Introduction to Probability Theory and its Applications,* Wiley, New York, 1968.

Goldberg, S., *Probability: An Introduction,* Prentice-Hall, Englewood Cliffs, N.J., 1960.

*Applied*

Bush, R. R. and W. K. Estes, *Studies in Mathematical Learning Theory,* Stanford University Press, 1959.

"Mathematics in the Modern World", readings from *Scientific American,* W. H. Freeman, San Francisco, 1968.

Mosteller, F. and D. L. Wallace, *Inference and Disputed Authorship: The Federalist,* Addison-Wesley, Reading, Mass., 1964.

Schlafer, R., *Probability and Statistics for Business Decisions,* McGraw-Hill, New York, 1959.

Weaver, Warren, *Lady Luck,* Anchor Books, New York, 1963.

# 15

# EXPECTATION AND DECISION MAKING

An important concept, which had its origin in gambling and to which probability can be applied, is *expected value*. Gamblers, for instance, are quite concerned with the *expectation*, or *expected value* of a game. Suppose, for example, 1000 tickets are sold for $1 each to raffle off a television set worth $300. Out of the 1000 tickets, one ticket is worth

$300 and the remaining 999 are worth $0. Thus the *expected* (*average*) *value* of a ticket is

$$E = \frac{\$300 + \$0 + \cdots + \$0}{1000}$$

$$= \$300 \cdot \frac{1}{1000} + \$0 \cdot \frac{1}{1000} + \cdots + \$0 \cdot \frac{1}{1000} = \frac{\$300}{1000} = \$.30$$

Thus, if the raffle is to be nonprofit to all participants, the charge for each ticket should have been $0.30.

As another example of expectation, suppose that you are to receive $3.00 each time you obtain two heads on a single toss of two fair coins and $0 otherwise. Then the *expected value*, which we will denote by $E$, is

$$E = \$3.00 \cdot \frac{1}{4} + \$0 \cdot \frac{3}{4} = \$0.75$$

This means that you should be willing to pay $0.75 each time you toss the coins, if the game is to be a fair one. We arrive at the expected value $E$ by multiplying the amount earned for a given result of the toss, times the probability for that toss to occur, and adding all possibilities.

Another example is a game consisting of flipping a coin in which, if a head shows, the player loses $1, but, if a tail shows, he wins $2. Thus half of the time he loses a dollar, and the other half he will win two dollars. The expected value $E$ of the game is

$$E = 2 \cdot \frac{1}{2} + (-1) \cdot \frac{1}{2} = \frac{1}{2} = .50$$

Thus the player is expected to win $0.50 each time he plays.

In each of the above examples, we have assigned a payoff to each outcome in the sample space. For example, in the raffle problem a payoff of $300 is assigned to the outcome of winning (probability 1/1000) and $0 is assigned to the outcome of losing (probability 999/1000).

In the second example, the outcome $HH$ is assigned a payoff of $3.00 and the outcomes $HT$, $TH$, and $FF$ are assigned $0.

Finally, in the last example, the outcome $H$ is assigned a payoff of $-\$1$ and the outcome $T$ a payoff of $2.

Thus, in each experiment, we not only assign a probability to each outcome, but we also assign a payoff or number to each outcome.

The examples mentioned thus far lead us to the following definition.

**Definition of Expected Value** **If an experiment has $n$ outcomes that are assigned the payoffs $m_1, m_2, \ldots, m_n$, occurring with probabilities $p_1, p_2, \ldots, p_n$, respectively, then the *expected value* is given by**

$$E = m_1 \cdot p_1 + m_2 \cdot p_2 + \cdots + m_n \cdot p_n$$

Suppose the probabilistic model of an experiment consists of a sample space $S = \{e_1, e_2, \ldots, e_n\}$, corresponding probabilities $p_1, p_2, \ldots, p_n$, and corresponding payoffs $m_1, m_2, \ldots, m_n$. Then it is sometimes convenient to summarize the data of the experiment by listing the outcomes, probabilities, and payoffs in tabular form:

| Outcome | $e_1$ | $e_2$ | $e_3$ | $\ldots$ | $e_n$ |
|---|---|---|---|---|---|
| Probability | $p_1$ | $p_2$ | $p_3$ | $\ldots$ | $p_n$ |
| Payoff | $m_1$ | $m_2$ | $m_3$ | $\ldots$ | $m_n$ |

The expected value $E$ is

$$E = m_1 \cdot p_1 + m_2 \cdot p_2 + \cdots + m_n \cdot p_n$$

The term expected value is not to be interpreted as the value that will necessarily occur on a single trial. It is the average gain per game in a long series of games, and it is always a number.

In gambling, for instance, $E$ is interpreted as the average winning expected for the player in the long run. If $E$ is positive, we say that the game is favorable to the player; if $E = 0$, we say the game is fair; and if $E$ is negative, we say the game is unfavorable to the player.

When the payoff assigned to an outcome of an experiment is positive, it can be interpreted as profit, winnings, or gain. When it is negative, it represents losses, penalties, or deficits.

Consider the experiment of rolling a fair die. The player recovers an amount of dollars equal to the number of dots on the face that turns up, except when face 5 or 6 turns up, in which case he will lose $5 or $6, respectively. What is the expected value of the game?

1.1
Example

Since all faces are equally likely to occur, we assign a probability of 1/6 to each of them.

The payoffs for the outcomes 1, 2, 3, 4, 5, 6 are respectively, $1, $2, $3, $4, $−5, $−6. In tabular form we have

| Outcome | 1 | 2 | 3 | 4 | 5 | 6 |
|---|---|---|---|---|---|---|
| Probability | 1/6 | 1/6 | 1/6 | 1/6 | 1/6 | 1/6 |
| Payoff | 1 | 2 | 3 | 4 | −5 | −6 |

The expected value of the game is

$$E = \$1 \cdot \frac{1}{6} + \$2 \cdot \frac{1}{6} + \$3 \cdot \frac{1}{6} + \$4 \cdot \frac{1}{6} + (\$-5) \cdot \frac{1}{6} + (\$-6) \cdot \frac{1}{6}$$

$$= \$ - 1/6 = \$ - .16\tfrac{2}{3}$$

The player would expect to lose $.17 on each throw. This means that if the player began with $100, and played 10 times, he would expect to lose $10 \cdot 1/6 = \$1.67$, leaving him with $98.33. Actually, the player could have anywhere from $40 to $140 after 10 throws, since he could throw 10 consecutive 6's, and lose $60, or 10 consecutive 4's, and win $40. But he would *expect* to lose $1.67 after 10 throws.

1.2
Example

An oil company may bid for only one of two contracts for oil drilling in two different areas, I and II. It is estimated that a profit of $300,000 would be realized from the first field and $400,000 from the second field. Legal and other costs of bidding for the first oil field is $2500 and for the second, $5000. The probability of discovering oil in the first field is .60 and in the second, .70. The question is, which oil field should the company bid for; that is, for which oil field is the expectation larger?

In the first field, the company expects to discover oil .6 of the time at a gain of $300,000 and thus not to discover oil .4 of the time at a loss of $2500. The expectation $E_1$ is

$$E_1 = (\$300,000)(.6) + (-\$2,500)(.4) = \$179,000$$

Similarly, for the second field, the expectation $E_2$ is

$$E_2 = (\$400,000)(.7) + (-\$5,000)(.3) = \$278,500$$

Since the expected value for the second field exceeds that for the first, the oil company should bid on the second field.

1.3
Example

A laboratory contains 10 electronic microscopes, of which 2 are defective. If all microscopes are equally likely to be chosen and if 4 are chosen, what is the expected number of defective microscopes?

The sample of 4 microscopes can contain 0, 1, or 2 defective microscopes. The probability $p_0$ that none in the sample is defective, is

$$p_0 = \frac{\binom{2}{0}\binom{8}{4}}{\binom{10}{4}} = \frac{1}{3}$$

Similarly, the probabilities $p_1$ and $p_2$ for 1 or 2 defective microscopes is

$$p_1 = \frac{\binom{2}{1}\binom{8}{3}}{\binom{10}{4}} = \frac{8}{15} \quad , \quad p_2 = \frac{\binom{2}{2}\binom{8}{2}}{\binom{10}{4}} = \frac{2}{15}$$

Since we are interested in determining the expected number of defective microscopes, we assign a payoff of 0 to the outcome

"0 defectives are selected," a payoff of 1 to the outcome "1 defective is chosen," and a payoff of 2 to the outcome "2 defectives are chosen". The expected value $E$ is

$$E = 0 \cdot p_0 + 1 \cdot p_1 + 2 \cdot p_2 = \frac{8}{15} + \frac{4}{15} = \frac{4}{5}$$

Of course, we cannot have 4/5 of a defective microscope. However, we can interpret this to mean that, in the long run, such a sample will average just under one defective microscope.

If an event is a success in a Bernoulli trial, the expected value of the event is easy to compute.

If there are $n$ trials and $p$ is the probability for success, then for any single trial, the expected value $E$ is

$$E = 1 \cdot p + 0 \cdot (1 - p) = p$$

For $n$ such trials, the expected value is

$$E = n \cdot p$$

Thus, we have the following theorem.

**Theorem 1.1**

**In a Bernoulli process with $n$ trials, the expected value $E$ for a success is**

$$E = np$$

**where $p$ is the probability for success.**

To illustrate the usefulness of this result, we compute the expected value for obtaining tails by flipping a coin 5 times without using Theorem 1.1.

1.4
Example

In the case of a flip of a single fair coin 5 times, there are 6 possible outcomes: 0 tails, 1 tail, 2 tails, 3 tails, 4 tails, or 5 tails, each with the respective probabilities

$$\binom{5}{0}\left(\frac{1}{2}\right)^5, \binom{5}{1}\left(\frac{1}{2}\right)^5, \binom{5}{2}\left(\frac{1}{2}\right)^5, \binom{5}{3}\left(\frac{1}{2}\right)^5, \binom{5}{4}\left(\frac{1}{2}\right)^5, \binom{5}{5}\left(\frac{1}{2}\right)^5$$

Thus, the expected number of tails is

$$E = 0 \cdot \binom{5}{0}\left(\frac{1}{2}\right)^5 + 1 \cdot \binom{5}{1}\left(\frac{1}{2}\right)^5 + 2 \cdot \binom{5}{2}\left(\frac{1}{2}\right)^5$$

$$+ 3 \cdot \binom{5}{3}\left(\frac{1}{2}\right)^5 + 4 \cdot \binom{5}{4}\left(\frac{1}{2}\right)^5 + 5 \cdot \binom{5}{5}\left(\frac{1}{2}\right)^5 = \frac{5}{2}$$

Clearly, using Theorem 1.1 is much easier, since for $n = 5$ and $p = 1/2$, we obtain $E = 5 \cdot 1/2 = 5/2$.

15.1
Exercise

1. For the data given below, compute the expected value

(a)

| Outcome | $e_1$ | $e_2$ | $e_3$ | $e_4$ |
|---------|-------|-------|-------|-------|
| Probability | .4 | .2 | .1 | .3 |
| Payoff | 2 | 3 | $-2$ | 0 |

(b)

| Outcome | $e_1$ | $e_2$ | $e_3$ | $e_4$ |
|---------|-------|-------|-------|-------|
| Probability | 1/3 | 1/6 | 1/4 | 1/4 |
| Payoff | 1 | 0 | 4 | $-2$ |

2. A player rolls a fair die and receives a number of dollars equal to the number of dots appearing on the face of the die. What is the most the player should be willing to pay in order to play the game?

3. In the toss of a fair coin 3 times, a player wins $3, if 3 tails occur, $2 if 2 tails occur, and he loses $3 if no tails occur. If one tail occurs, no one wins.
   (a) What is the expected value of the game?
   (b) Is the game fair?
   (c) If the answer to (b) is no, how much should the player win or lose for a toss of exactly one tail to make the game fair?

4. A department store wishes to get rid of 11 purses that cost them $41 each, and 32 purses that cost them $9 each. If all purses are wrapped in 43 identical boxes and if each customer picks a box randomly, find:
   (a) Each customer's expectation.
   (b) The department store's expected profit if it charges $13 for each box.

5. Attendance at a football game in a certain city results in the following pattern. If it is extremely cold, the attendance will be 35,000; if it is cold, it will be 40,000; if it is moderate, 48,000; and if it is warm, 60,000. If the probabilities for extremely cold, cold, moderate, and warm are respectively .08, .42, .42, .08, how many fans are expected to attend each game?

6. The following data (source: 1970 census of the United States) gives information about family size in the United States for a household in which the wife resides and the

male head of household is in the age bracket 30–34. A family is chosen at random. Find the expected number of children in the family.

| Number of children | 0 | 1 | 2 | 3 |
|---|---|---|---|---|
| Proportion of families | 10.2% | 15.9% | 31.8% | 42.1% |

7. Assume that the odds for a certain race horse to win are 7 to 5. If a man receives $5 when the horse wins, how much should he pay when the horse loses to make the game fair?

8. In roulette, there are 38 equally likely possibilities: the numbers 1 to 36, 0, and 00 (double zero). What is the expected value for a gambler who bets $1.00 on number 15? In roulette, he wins $35 each time the number 15 turns up and loses $1 if any other number turns up. If he plays the number 15 for 200 consecutive times, what is his total expected gain?

9. A company operating a chain of supermarkets plans to open a new store in one of two locations. They conducted a survey of the two locations and estimated that the first location will show an annual profit of $15,000, if it is successful, and a $3000 loss otherwise. For the second location, the estimated annual profit, if successful, is $20,000; a $6000 loss results otherwise. The probability of success at each location is 1/2. What location should the management decide on in order to maximize its profit?

10. For Problem 9 assume probability of success at the first location is 2/3 and at the second location is 1/3. What location should be chosen?

11. A true-false test of 30 questions is scored according to the number of correct answers minus the number wrong. Find the expected number of correct answers of a student who just guesses on each question. What will his score be?

12. Find the number of times the face 5 is expected to occur in a sequence of 2000 throws of a pair of fair dice.

13. What is the expected number of tails that will turn up if a fair coin is tossed 582 times?

*14. A coin, weighted so that $P(H) = 1/4$ and $P(T) = 3/4$, is tossed until a head or 4 tails occur. Find the expected number of tosses of the coin.

*15. A box contains 3 defective bulbs and 9 good bulbs. If 5 bulbs are drawn from the box without replacement, what is the expected number of defective bulbs.

*16. Prove that if the payoff assigned to each outcome of an experiment with expected value $E$ is multiplied by a constant $c$, then the expected value of the new experiment is $c \cdot E$. Similarly, if to the payoff for each outcome, we add the same constant $k$, the expected value of the new game is $E + k$.

The field of operations research, the science of making optimal or best decisions, has experienced remarkable growth and development since the 1940s. The purpose of this section is to introduce the reader to some examples from operations research that utilize expectation.

2.1
Example

A national car rental agency rents cars for $16 per day (gasoline and mileage is an expense of the customer). The daily cost per car (for example, lease costs and overhead) is $6 per day. The daily profit to the company is $10 per car, if the car is rented, and the company incurs a loss each day of $6 per car, if the car is not rented. The daily profit depends on two factors: the demand for cars and the number of cars the company has to rent. The daily demand because of previous rental records is known to be

| Number of Customers | 8 | 9 | 10 | 11 | 12 |
|---|---|---|---|---|---|
| Probability | | .10 | .10 | .30 | .30 | .20 |

Find the expected number of customers. Determine the optimal number of cars the company should have available for rental. (This is the number that yields the largest expected profit.)
The expected number of customers is

$$8(.1) + 9(.1) + 10(.3) + 11(.3) + 12(.2) = 10.4$$

If 10.4 customers are expected, how many cars should be on hand? Surely the number should not exceed 11, since fewer than 11 customers are expected. However, the number may not be the integer closest to 10.4, since costs play a major role in the determination of profit. Thus, we need to compute the expected profit for each possible number of cars. The largest expected profit will tell us how many cars to have on hand.
For example, if there are 10 cars available, the expected profit for 8, 9, or 10 customers is

$$68(.1) + 84(.1) + 100(.8) = \$95.20$$

We obtain the entry 84(.1) by noting that the 10 cars cost the company $60, and 9 cars rented with probability .10 bring in $144, for a profit of $84. The entry 100(.8) is obtained since for 10 or more customers, (probability $.3 + .3 + .2 = .8$) the profit is $10 \times \$16 - \$60 = \$100$.

Table 15.1 lists the expected profit for 8 up to 12 cars. Clearly, the optimal stock size is 11 cars, since this number of cars maximizes expected profit.

**Table 15.1**

| Number of Cars | 8 | 9 | 10 | 11 | 12 |
|---|---|---|---|---|---|
| Expected Profit | $80.00 | $88.40 | $95.20 | $97.20 | $69.40 |

A factory produces electronic components, and each component must be tested. If the component is good, it will allow the passage of current; if the component is defective, it will block the passage of current. Let $p$ denote the probability a component is good. See Figure 15.1.

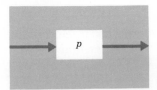

**Figure 15.1**

With this system of testing, a large number of components requires an equal number of tests. This increases the production cost of the electronic components since it requires one test per component. To reduce the number of tests, a quality control engineer proposes instead a new testing procedure: Connect the components pairwise in series.

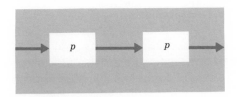

**Figure 15.2**

For two components in series, if the current passes, both components are good and only one test was required (Figure 15.2). The probability that two components are good is $p^2$. If the current does not pass, they must be sent individually to the quality control department where each component is tested separately. In this case, three tests are required. The probability that three tests are needed is $1 - p^2$. (One minus probability of success $p^2$). The expected number of tests for a pair of components is

$$E = 1 \cdot p^2 + 3(1 - p^2) = p^2 + 3 - 3p^2 = 3 - 2p^2$$

The number of tests saved for a pair is

$$2 - (3 - 2p^2) = 2p^2 - 1$$

The tests saved per component are

$$\frac{2p^2 - 1}{2} = p^2 - \frac{1}{2} \text{ tests}$$

The greater $p$, the greater the saving.

For example, if $p$ is almost 1, we have a saving of almost $1 - 1/2$ or $1/2$, which is 50% of the original number of tests needed. Of course if $p$ is small, say less than .7, we do not save anything since $(.7)^2 - 1/2$ is less than zero and we are wasting tests.

If the reliability of the components is very high, it might even be advisable to make larger groups. Suppose three components are connected in series (Figure 15.3). For individual testing,

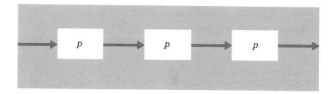

**Figure 15.3**

we need three tests. For group testing, we have

1 test needed with probability $p^3$
4 tests needed with probability $1 - p^3$

The expected number of tests is

$$E = 1 \cdot p^3 + 4(1 - p^3) = 4 - 3p^3 \text{ tests.}$$

The tests saved per component are

$$\frac{3p^3 - 1}{3} = p^3 - \frac{1}{3} \text{ tests}$$

In a similar way we can show that if the components are arranged in groups of four connected in series, then the tests saved per component are

$$p^4 - \frac{1}{4} \text{ tests}$$

In general for groups of $n$, the tests saved per component are

$$p^n - \frac{1}{n} \text{ tests}$$

Notice from the above formula that as $n$, the group size, gets very large, the tests saved per component gets very, very small; in fact

$$\lim_{n \to \infty} \left( p^n - \frac{1}{n} \right) = 0$$

To determine the optimal group size for $p = .9$, we use a table:

| Group size | Expected Tests Saved Per Component | Percent Saving |
|---|---|---|
| 2 | $p^2 - \frac{1}{2} = 0.81 - 0.50 = 0.31$ | 31 |
| 3 | $p^3 - \frac{1}{3} = 0.729 - 0.333 = 0.396$ | 39.6 |
| 4 | $p^4 - \frac{1}{4} = 0.6561 - 0.25 = 0.4061$ | 40.61 |
| 5 | $p^5 - \frac{1}{5} = 0.59049 - 0.2 = 0.39049$ | 39.05 |
| 6 | $p^6 - \frac{1}{6} = 0.531 - 0.167 = 0.364$ | 36.4 |
| 7 | $p^7 - \frac{1}{7} = 0.478 - 0.143 = 0.335$ | 33.5 |
| 8 | $p^8 - \frac{1}{8} = 0.430 - 0.125 = 0.305$ | 30.5 |

Thus, for $p = .9$, the optimal group size is 4, resulting in a substantial saving of approximately 41 percent.

We also note, as indicated, that larger group sizes do not increase savings.

**2.3 Example**

A $75,000 oil detector is lowered under the sea to detect oil fields and becomes detached from the ship. If the instrument is not found within 24 hours, it will crack under the pressure of the sea. It is assumed a skin diver will find it with probability .85, but it costs $500 to hire him. How many skin divers should be hired?

Let us assume that $x$ skin divers are hired. The probability that they will fail to discover the instrument is $(.15)^x$. Thus, the instrument will be found with probability $1 - (.15)^x$.

The expected gain from hiring the skin divers is

$$\$75{,}000(1 - (.15)^x) = \$75{,}000 - \$75{,}000(.15)^x$$

while the cost for hiring them is

$$\$500 \cdot x$$

Thus, the expected net gain denoted by $E(x)$ is

$$E(x) = \$75{,}000 - \$75{,}000(.15)^x - \$500x$$

The problem is then to choose $x$ so that $E(x)$ is maximum. We begin by evaluating $E(x)$ for various values of $x$.

$$E(1) = \$75{,}000 - \$75{,}000(.15)^1 - \$500(1) = \$63{,}250.00$$
$$E(2) = \$75{,}000 - \$75{,}000(.15)^2 - \$500(2) = \$72{,}312.50$$
$$E(3) = \$75{,}000 - \$75{,}000(.15)^3 - \$500(3) = \$73{,}246.88$$
$$E(4) = \$75{,}000 - \$75{,}000(.15)^4 - \$500(4) = \$72{,}962.03$$
$$E(5) = \$75{,}000 - \$75{,}000(.15)^5 - \$500(5) = \$72{,}494.31$$
$$E(6) = \$75{,}000 - \$75{,}000(.15)^6 - \$500(6) = \$71{,}999.15$$

Thus, the expected net gain is optimal when 3 divers are hired. Notice that hiring additional skin divers does not necessarily increase expected net gain. In fact, the expected net gain declines if more than 3 divers are hired.

The reader should refer to Problem 11 in Chapter 10, page 325, in which the extrema of the function

$$E(x) = 75000(1 - .15^x) - 500x$$

are found. Notice that the absolute maximum of $E(x)$ occurs at $x = 3.06$, which, when rounded off, agrees with the optimal solution found in the above example. The difference, of course, lies in the fact that only integer solutions are of importance in the practical solution. There is often more than one mathematical model that is applicable in a given situation.

1. A car agency has fixed costs of $8 per car per day and the revenue for each car rented is $14 per day. The daily demand is

| Number of customers | 7 | 8 | 9 | 10 | 11 |
|---|---|---|---|---|---|
| Probability | .10 | .20 | .40 | .20 | .10 |

Find the expected number of customers. Determine the optimal number of cars the company should have on hand each day. What is the expected profit in this case?

2. In Example 2.2, page 485, suppose $p = .8$. Show that the optimal group size is 3.

3. In Example 2.2, page 485, suppose $p = .95$. Show that the optimal group size is 5.
4. In Example 2.2, page 485, suppose $p = .99$. Compute savings for group sizes 10, 11, 12 and thus show that 11 is the optimal group size. Determine the percent saving.
5. In Example 2.3, page 487, suppose the probability of the skin divers discovering the instrument is .95. Find (a) an equation expressing the net expected gain; (b) the number $x$ of skin divers that maximizes the net gain.

## Introduction

Game theory, as a branch of mathematics, is a relatively new field concerned with the analysis of human behavior in conflicts of interest. In other words, game theory gives mathematical expression to the strategies of opposing players and offers techniques for choosing the best possible strategy. In most parlor games, it is relatively easy to define winning and losing and, on this basis, to quantify the best strategy for each player. However, game theory is not merely a tool for the gambler, so that he can take advantage of the odds, nor is it merely a method for winning games like ticktacktoe, matching pennies, or the Italian game called *mora*.

Gottfried Leibniz (1646–1716) is generally recognized as being the first to see the relationship between games of strategy and the theory of social behavior. For example, when union and management sit down at the bargaining table to discuss contracts, each has definite strategies open to him. Each will bluff, persuade, and try to discover the other's strategy, while at the same time trying to prevent the discovery of his own. If enough information is known, results from the theory of games can determine what is the best possible rational behavior or the best possible strategy for each player. Another application of game theory can be made to politics. If two people are vying for the same political office, each has open to him various campaign strategies. If it is possible to determine the impact of alternate strategies on the voters, the theory of games can be used to find the best strategy (usually the one that gains the most votes, while losing the least votes). Thus, game theory can be used in certain situations of conflict to indicate how people should behave to achieve certain goals. Of course, game theory does not tell us how people behave. Game theory is the study, then, of rational behavior in conflict situations.

**Any conflict or competition between** *two* **people is called a** *two-person game.*

Definition of a Two-Person Game

Let us consider some examples of two-person games.

In a game similar to "matching pennies," Player I picks heads or tails and Player II attempts to guess the choice. Player I will pay Player II $3 if both choose heads; Player I will pay Player II $2 if both choose tails. If Player II guesses incorrectly, he will pay Player I $5.

We use this example to illustrate some terminology. First, since two players are involved, this is a two-person game. Next, notice that no matter what outcome occurs ($HH,HT,TH,TT$), whatever is lost (or gained) by Player I is gained (or lost) by Player II. Such games are called *two-person zero-sum games*.

If we denote the gains of Player I by positive entries and his losses by negative entries, we can display this game in a $2 \times 2$ matrix as

$$\begin{array}{cc} & H \quad T \\ \begin{array}{c} H \\ T \end{array} & \begin{pmatrix} -3 & 5 \\ 5 & -2 \end{pmatrix} \end{array}$$

Each entry $a_{ij}$ of a matrix game is termed a *payoff* and the matrix is called the *game matrix* or the *payoff matrix*.

Conversely, any $m \times n$ matrix $A = (a_{ij})$ can be regarded as the game matrix for a two-person zero-sum game in which Player I chooses any one of the $m$ rows of $A$ and simultaneously Player II chooses any one of the $n$ columns of $A$. The entry in the row and column chosen is the payoff.

We will assume that the game is played repeatedly, and that the problem facing each player is what choice he should make so that he gains the most benefit. Thus, Player I wishes to maximize his winnings and Player II wishes to minimize his losses. By a strategy of Player I for a given matrix game $A$, we mean the decision by player I to select rows of $A$ in some manner.

Consider a two-person zero-sum game given by the matrix

$$\begin{pmatrix} 3 & 6 \\ -2 & -3 \end{pmatrix}$$

in which the entries denote the winnings of Player I. The game consists of Player I choosing a row and Player II simultaneously choosing a column, with the intersection of row and column giving the payoff for this play in the game. For example, if Player I chooses row one and Player II chooses column two, then Player I wins $6; if Player I chooses row two and Player II chooses column one, then Player I loses $2.

It is immediately evident from the matrix that this particular game is biased in favor of Player I. For, Player I will always choose row 1 since he cannot lose by doing so. Similarly, Player II, recognizing that Player I will choose row 1 will always choose column 1, since his losses are then minimized.

Thus, the *best strategy* for Player I is row 1 and the *best strategy* for Player II is column 1. When both players employ their best strategy, the result is that Player I wins $3. This amount is called the *value* of the game. Notice that the payoff $3 is the minimum of the entries in its row and is the maximum of the entries in its column.

**A game defined by a matrix is said to be** *strictly determined* **if and only if there is an entry of the matrix that is the smallest element in its row and is also the largest element in its column. This entry is then called a** *saddle point* **and is the** *value* **of the game.**

If a game has a positive value, the game favors Player I. If a game has a negative value, the game favors Player II. Any game whose value is zero is a *fair game*.

If a matrix game has a saddle point, it can be shown that the row containing the saddle point is the best strategy for Player I and the column containing the saddle point is the best strategy for Player II. This is why such games are called strictly determined games. Such games are also called games of *pure strategy*.

Of course, a matrix may have more than one saddle point, in which case each player has available to him more than one best strategy. However, the value of the game is always the same no matter how many saddle points the matrix may have. See Problem 4(i) in Exercise 15.3.1, page 493.

Determine whether the game defined by the matrix

$$\begin{pmatrix} 3 & 0 & -2 & -1 \\ 2 & -3 & 0 & -1 \\ 4 & 2 & 1 & 0 \end{pmatrix}$$

is strictly determined.

First, we look at each row and find the smallest entry in each row. These are:

row one: $-2$; row two: $-3$; row three: $0$

Next, we check to see if any of the above elements are also the largest in their column. The element $-2$ in row one is not the largest entry in column three; the element $-3$ in row two is not the largest entry in column two; however, the element $0$ in row three is the largest entry in its column. Thus, this game is strictly determined. Its value is $0$ so the game is fair.

The game of Example 3.3 is represented by a $3 \times 4$ matrix. This means that Player I has 3 strategies open to him, while Player II can choose from 4 strategies.

Two franchising firms Alpha Products and Omega Industries are each planning to add an outlet in a certain city. It is possible for the site to be located either in the center of the city or in a large suburb of the city. If both firms decide to build in the center of the city, Alpha Products will show an annual profit of $1000 more than the profit of Omega Industries. If both firms decide to locate their outlet in the suburb, then it is determined that Alpha Products' profit will be $2000 less than the profit of Omega Industries. If Alpha locates in the suburb and Omega in the city, then Alpha shows a profit of $4000 more than does Omega. Finally if Alpha locates in the city and Omega in the suburb, then Alpha has a profit of $3000 less than Omega's. Is there a best site for each firm to locate its franchise? The best site is the one that produces the most competition against the other firm instead of the one that produces the highest gross sales. Of course, the term "best" is very relative here and someone else may well have a different interpretation of what constitutes the best site.

If we assign rows as Alpha strategies and columns as Omega strategies and if we use positive entries to denote the gain of Alpha over that of Omega and negative entries for the gain of Omega over Alpha, then the matrix game for this situation is

$$\text{Alpha} \begin{array}{c} \text{City} \\ \text{Suburb} \end{array} \overset{\begin{array}{cc} \text{City} & \text{Suburb} \end{array}}{\begin{pmatrix} 1 & -3 \\ 4 & -2 \end{pmatrix}}$$

Omega

where the entries are in thousands of dollars.

This game is strictly determined and the saddle point is $-2$, which is the value of the game. Thus, if both firms locate in the suburb, this results in the best competition. This is so since Omega will always choose to locate in the suburb, guaranteeing a larger profit than Alpha. This being the case, Alpha, in order to minimize this larger profit of Omega, must always choose the suburb. Of course, the game is not fair since it is favorable to Omega.

Write the matrix game that corresponds to each of the following two-person conflict situations.
1. Tami and Laura simultaneously each show one or two fingers. If they show the same number of fingers, Tami pays Laura one dime. If they show a different number of fingers, Laura pays Tami one dime.
2. Tami and Laura simultaneously each show one or two fingers. If the total number of fingers shown is even, Tami pays Laura that number of dimes. If the total number of fingers shown is odd, Laura pays Tami that number of dimes.

3. Tami and Laura simultaneously and independently each write down one of the numbers 1, 4, or 7. If the sum of the numbers is even, Tami pays Laura that number of dimes. If the sum of the numbers is odd, Laura pays Tami that number of dimes.

4. Determine which of the following two-person, zero-sum games are strictly determined. For those that are, find the value of the game. All entries are the winnings of Player I, who plays rows.

(a) $\begin{pmatrix} -1 & 2 \\ -3 & 6 \end{pmatrix}$

(b) $\begin{pmatrix} 4 & 2 \\ 3 & 1 \end{pmatrix}$

(c) $\begin{pmatrix} 2 & 0 & -1 \\ 3 & 6 & 0 \\ 1 & 3 & 7 \end{pmatrix}$

(d) $\begin{pmatrix} 1 & 0 & 3 \\ -1 & 2 & 1 \end{pmatrix}$

(e) $\begin{pmatrix} 6 & 4 & -2 & 0 \\ -1 & 7 & 5 & 2 \\ 1 & 0 & 4 & 4 \end{pmatrix}$

(f) $\begin{pmatrix} 4 & 0 \\ 0 & -1 \end{pmatrix}$

(g) $\begin{pmatrix} -6 & -1 \\ 0 & 0 \end{pmatrix}$

(h) $\begin{pmatrix} 2 & 3 & -2 \\ -2 & 0 & 4 \\ 0 & -3 & -2 \end{pmatrix}$

(i) $\begin{pmatrix} 1 & -3 & -2 \\ 2 & 5 & 4 \\ 2 & 3 & 2 \end{pmatrix}$

5. For what values of a is the matrix

$$\begin{pmatrix} a & 8 & 3 \\ 0 & a & -9 \\ -5 & 5 & a \end{pmatrix} \quad < -9$$

$> 8$

strictly determined.

6. Show that the matrix

$$\begin{pmatrix} a & a \\ b & c \end{pmatrix}$$

is strictly determined for any choice of a, b, or c.

*7. Find necessary and sufficient conditions for the matrix

$$\begin{pmatrix} a & 0 \\ 0 & b \end{pmatrix}$$

to be strictly determined.

## Mixed Strategies

Consider a two-person zero-sum game given by the matrix

$$\begin{pmatrix} 6 & 0 \\ -2 & 3 \end{pmatrix}$$

3.5
Example

in which the entries denote the winnings of Player I. Is this game strictly determined? If so, find its value.

Again, we find that the smallest entry in each row is

$$\text{row one: } 0; \text{ row two: } -2$$

Now the entry 0 in row one is not the largest element in its column; similarly, the entry $-2$ in row two is not the largest element in its column. Thus, this game is not strictly determined.

At this stage, we would like to stress the point that a matrix game is not usually played just once. With this in mind, Player I might decide to always play row one since he may win $6 at best and win $0 at worst. Does this mean he should always employ this strategy? If he does, Player II would catch on and begin to choose column two since this strategy limits his losses to $0. However, after awhile, Player I would probably start choosing row two to obtain a payoff of $3. Thus, in a nonstrictly determined game, it would be advisable for the players to *mix* their strategies rather than to use the same one all the time. That is, a random selection is desirable. Indeed, to make certain that the other player does not discover the pattern of moves, it may be best not to have any pattern at all. For instance Player I may elect to play row one 40 percent of the time (that is, with probability .4) while Player II elects to play column two 80 percent of the time (that is, with probability .8). This idea of mixing strategies is important and useful in game theory. Games in which each player's strategies are *mixed* are termed *mixed-strategy games*.

Mixed-Strategy
Games

Suppose we know the probability for each player to choose a certain strategy. What meaning can be given to the term "payoff of a game" if mixed strategies are used? Since the payoff has been defined for a pair of pure strategies and in a mixed strategy situation we do not know which strategy is being used, it is not possible to define a payoff for a single game. However, in the long-run we do know how often each strategy is being used, and we can use this information to compute the *expected payoff* of the game.

Expected Payoff

For Example 3.5, if Player I chooses row one 50 percent of the time and row two 50 percent of the time and if Player II chooses column one 30 percent of the time and column two 70 percent of the time, the expected payoff of the game can be computed. For example, the strategy of row one, column one is chosen $(.5)(.3) = .15$ of the time. This strategy has a payoff of $6, so that the expected payoff will be $(\$6)(.15) = \$.90$. Figure 15.4 summarizes the entire process. Thus, the expected payoff $E$ of this game, when the given strategies are employed, is $1.65, which makes the game favorable to Player I.

If we look very carefully at the above derivation, we get a clue as to how the expected payoff of a game that is not strictly determined should be defined.

Let us consider a game defined by the $2 \times 2$ matrix

$$A = \begin{pmatrix} a_{11} & a_{12} \\ a_{21} & a_{22} \end{pmatrix}$$

| Strategy | Payoff | Probability | Expected Payoff |
|---|---|---|---|
| row one — column one | 6 | .15 | $.90 |
| row two — column one | −2 | .15 | −0.30 |
| row one — column two | 0 | .35 | .00 |
| row two — column two | 3 | .35 | 1.05 |
| | Total | 1.00 | $1.65 |

**Figure 15.4**

Let the strategy for Player I, who plays rows, be denoted by the row vector $P = (p_1 \quad p_2)$ and the strategy for Player II, who plays columns, be denoted by the column vector $Q = \begin{pmatrix} q_1 \\ q_2 \end{pmatrix}$. Now the probability that Player I wins the amount $a_{11}$ is $p_1 q_1$. Similarly, the probabilities that he wins $a_{12}$, $a_{21}$, and $a_{22}$ are $p_1 q_2$, $p_2 q_1$, and $p_2 q_2$ respectively. If we denote by $E(P, Q)$ the expectation of Player I, that is, the expected value of the amount I wins when Player I uses strategy $P$ and Player II uses strategy $Q$, then

$$E(P, Q) = p_1 q_1 a_{11} + p_1 q_2 a_{12} + p_2 q_1 a_{21} + p_2 q_2 a_{22}$$

Using matrix notation, the above can be expressed as

$$E(P, Q) = PAQ$$

In general, if $A$ is an $m \times n$ matrix game, we are led to the following definition.

Definition
of Expected
Payoff

**The** *expected payoff E* **of a two-person zero-sum game, defined by the matrix** *A,* **in which the row vector** *P* **and column vector** *Q* **define the respective strategy probabilities of Player I and Player II, is**

$$E = PAQ$$

If a matrix game $A = (a_{ij})$ of dimension $m \times n$ is strictly determined, then one of the entries is a saddle point. This saddle point can always be placed in the first row and first column by simply rearranging and renumbering the rows and columns of $A$. The value of the game is then $a_{11}$, and $P$ and $Q$ are vectors of the form

$$P = (1 \quad 0 \quad 0 \quad 0 \quad 0 \quad \cdots \quad 0)$$

and

$$Q = \begin{pmatrix} 1 \\ 0 \\ \vdots \\ 0 \end{pmatrix}$$

where $P$ is of dimension $1 \times m$ and $Q$ is of dimension $n \times 1$.

Find the expected payoff of the matrix game

$$\begin{pmatrix} 3 & -1 \\ -2 & 1 \\ 1 & 0 \end{pmatrix}$$

if Player I and Player II decide on the strategies

$$P = \begin{pmatrix} \frac{1}{3} & \frac{1}{3} & \frac{1}{3} \end{pmatrix}, \qquad Q = \begin{pmatrix} \frac{1}{3} \\ \frac{2}{3} \end{pmatrix}$$

The expected payoff $E$ of this game is

$$E = P \cdot \begin{pmatrix} 3 & -1 \\ -2 & 1 \\ 1 & 0 \end{pmatrix} \cdot Q = \begin{pmatrix} \frac{1}{3} & \frac{1}{3} & \frac{1}{3} \end{pmatrix} \begin{pmatrix} 3 & -1 \\ -2 & 1 \\ 1 & 0 \end{pmatrix} \begin{pmatrix} \frac{1}{3} \\ \frac{2}{3} \end{pmatrix}$$

$$= \begin{pmatrix} \frac{2}{3} & 0 \end{pmatrix} \begin{pmatrix} \frac{1}{3} \\ \frac{2}{3} \end{pmatrix} = \frac{2}{9}$$

Thus, the game is biased in favor of Player I and has an expected payoff of 2/9.

Most games are not strictly determined. That is, most games do not give rise to best pure strategies for each player. Examples of not strictly determined games are matching pennies (see Example 3.1, page 490), bridge, poker, and so on. In the next two sections, we discuss techniques for finding optimal strategies for games that are not strictly determined.

1. For the game of Example 3.5, find the expected payoff $E$ if Player I chooses row one 30 percent of the time and Player II chooses column one 40 percent of the time.
2. Find the expected payoff of the game

$$\begin{pmatrix} 4 & 0 \\ 2 & 3 \end{pmatrix}$$

for the strategies

(a) $P = \begin{pmatrix} \frac{1}{2} & \frac{1}{2} \end{pmatrix}$ $\quad Q = \begin{pmatrix} \frac{1}{2} \\ \frac{1}{2} \end{pmatrix}$

(b) $P = \begin{pmatrix} \frac{1}{2} & \frac{1}{2} \end{pmatrix}$  $Q = \begin{pmatrix} \frac{3}{4} \\ \frac{1}{4} \end{pmatrix}$

(c) $P = \begin{pmatrix} \frac{1}{4} & \frac{3}{4} \end{pmatrix}$  $Q = \begin{pmatrix} \frac{1}{2} \\ \frac{1}{2} \end{pmatrix}$

(d) $P = (0 \quad 1)$  $Q = \begin{pmatrix} 0 \\ 1 \end{pmatrix}$

3. Find the expected payoff of each of the following games for the strategies given

(a) $\begin{pmatrix} 4 & 0 \\ -3 & 6 \end{pmatrix}$  $P = \begin{pmatrix} \frac{2}{3} & \frac{1}{3} \end{pmatrix}$  $Q = \begin{pmatrix} \frac{1}{3} \\ \frac{2}{3} \end{pmatrix}$

(b) $\begin{pmatrix} 1 & 0 & 0 \\ 0 & 1 & 0 \\ 0 & 0 & 1 \end{pmatrix}$  $P = \begin{pmatrix} \frac{1}{3} & \frac{1}{3} & \frac{1}{3} \end{pmatrix}$  $Q = \begin{pmatrix} \frac{1}{3} \\ \frac{1}{3} \\ \frac{1}{3} \\ \frac{1}{3} \end{pmatrix}$

(c) $\begin{pmatrix} 4 & -1 & 0 \\ 2 & 3 & 1 \end{pmatrix}$  $P = \begin{pmatrix} \frac{1}{3} & \frac{2}{3} \end{pmatrix}$  $Q = \begin{pmatrix} \frac{2}{3} \\ \frac{1}{6} \\ \frac{1}{6} \end{pmatrix}$

*4. Show that in a 2 × 2 game

$$\begin{pmatrix} a_{11} & a_{12} \\ a_{21} & a_{22} \end{pmatrix}$$

the only not strictly determined games are those for which either

(a) $a_{11} > a_{12}, a_{11} > a_{21}, a_{21} < a_{22}, a_{12} < a_{22}$

or

(b) $a_{11} < a_{12}, a_{11} < a_{21}, a_{21} > a_{22}, a_{12} > a_{22}$

and all others are strictly determined.

## Optimal Strategy in Two-Person Zero-Sum Games with $2 \times 2$ Matrices

We have already seen that the best strategy for two-person zero-sum games that are strictly determined is found in the row and column containing the saddle point. Suppose the game is not strictly determined so that the conditions given in Problem 4, Exercise 15.3.2 are satisfied.

In 1927, John von Neumann, along with E. Borel, initiated research in the theory of games and proved that, even in non-strictly determined games, there is a single course of action that represents the best strategy. In practice, this means that a player in a game, in order to avoid always using a single strategy, may instead choose it randomly according to a fixed probability. This has the effect of making it impossible for his opponent to know what the player will do, since even he will not know until the final moment. That is, by selecting a strategy randomly according to the laws of probability, the actual strategy chosen at any one time cannot even be known to the one choosing it.

For example, in the Italian game of *mora* each player shows one, two, or three fingers and simultaneously calls out his guess as to what the sum of his and his opponent's fingers is. It can be shown that if he guesses four fingers each time and varies his own moves so that every 12 times he shows one finger five times, two fingers four times, and three fingers three times, he will, at worst, break even (in the long run).

Consider now a two-person zero-sum game given by the $2 \times 2$ matrix

$$A = \begin{pmatrix} a_{11} & a_{12} \\ a_{21} & a_{22} \end{pmatrix}$$

in which Player I chooses row strategies and Player II chooses column strategies.

It can be shown that the optimal strategy for Player I is given by $P = (p_1 \quad p_2)$, where

$$p_1 = \frac{a_{22} - a_{21}}{a_{11} + a_{22} - a_{12} - a_{21}}, \qquad p_2 = \frac{a_{11} - a_{12}}{a_{11} + a_{22} - a_{12} - a_{21}} \qquad (3.1)$$

with $a_{11} + a_{22} - a_{12} - a_{21} \neq 0$. Notice that $p_1 + p_2 = 1$, as must be the case. Similarly, the optimal strategy for Player II is given by $Q = \begin{pmatrix} q_1 \\ q_2 \end{pmatrix}$; where

$$q_1 = \frac{a_{22} - a_{12}}{a_{11} + a_{22} - a_{12} - a_{21}}, \qquad q_2 = \frac{a_{11} - a_{21}}{a_{11} + a_{22} - a_{12} - a_{21}} \qquad (3.2)$$

with $a_{11} + a_{22} - a_{12} - a_{21} \neq 0$. Again, $q_1 + q_2 = 1$. The expected payoff

$E$ of the game corresponding to these optimal strategies is

$$E = PAQ = \frac{a_{11} \cdot a_{22} - a_{12} \cdot a_{21}}{a_{11} + a_{22} - a_{12} - a_{21}}$$

When optimal strategies are used, the expected payoff $E$ of the game
is called the *value V* of the game.

For the matrix

$$\begin{pmatrix} -3 & 5 \\ 5 & -2 \end{pmatrix}$$

determine the optimal strategies and the value of the game.
Here, using the above formulas,

$$p_1 = \frac{-2 - 5}{-3 + (-2) - 5 - 5} = \frac{7}{15},$$

$$p_2 = \frac{-3 - 5}{-3 + (-2) - 5 - 5} = \frac{8}{15}$$

Thus, Player I's optimal strategy is to select row one with probability 7/15 and row two with probability 8/15. Also

$$q_1 = \frac{-2 - 5}{-3 + (-2) - 5 - 5} = \frac{7}{15},$$

$$q_2 = \frac{-3 - 5}{-3 + (-2) - 5 - 5} = \frac{8}{15}$$

Player II's optimal strategy is to select column one with probability 7/15 and column two with probability 8/15. The value $V$
of the game is

$$V = \frac{(-3)(-2) - (5)(5)}{-15} = \frac{-19}{-15} = \frac{19}{15}$$

Thus, in the long run, the game is favorable to Player I.

Find optimal strategies and the value of the game given in
Example 3.5, page 493. The matrix $A$ is

$$A = \begin{pmatrix} 6 & 0 \\ -2 & 3 \end{pmatrix}$$

Player I's optimal strategy is

$$p_1 = \frac{3 - (-2)}{6 + 3 - (-2) - 0} = \frac{5}{11}, \qquad p_2 = \frac{6 - 0}{11} = \frac{6}{11}$$

Player II's optimal strategy is

$$q_1 = \frac{3 - 0}{11} = \frac{3}{11}, \qquad q_2 = \frac{6 - (-2)}{11} = \frac{8}{11}$$

The value $V$ of the game is

$$V = \frac{(6)(3) - (-2)(0)}{11} = \frac{18}{11} = \$1.64$$

Thus, the game favors Player I whose optimal strategy is (5/11  6/11).

3.9
Example

In a presidential campaign, there are two candidates, a democrat ($D$) and a republican ($R$) and two issues, domestic issues and foreign issues. The units assigned to each candidate's strategy are given in Figure 15.5. We assume that positive entries indicate a strength for the democratic candidate, while negative entries indicate a weakness. We also assume that a strength of one candidate equals a weakness of the other so that the game is zero-sum. The question is what is the best strategy for each candidate? What is the value of the game?

|  |  | Republican | |
|---|---|---|---|
|  |  | Domestic | Foreign |
| Democrat | Domestic | 4 | −2 |
|  | Foreign | −1 | 3 |

**Figure 15.5**

Notice first that this game is not strictly determined. If $D$ chooses to always play his strongest hand (foreign issues), then $R$ will counter with domestic issues, in which case $D$ would also talk about domestic issues, in which case, etc., etc. There is no *single* strategy either can use.

Using the formulas given previously, we compute that the optimal strategy for the democrat is

$$p_1 = \frac{3 - (-1)}{4 + 3 - (-1) - (-2)} = \frac{4}{10} = .4, \qquad p_2 = \frac{4 - (-2)}{10} = .6$$

The optimal strategy for the republican is

$$q_1 = \frac{3 - (-2)}{10} = .5, \qquad q_2 = \frac{4 - (-1)}{10} = .5$$

Thus the best strategy for the democrat is to spend 40 percent of his time on domestic issues and 60 percent on foreign issues, while the republican should divide his time evenly between the two issues.

The value of the game is

$$V = \frac{3 \cdot 4 - (-1)(-2)}{10} = \frac{10}{10} = 1.0$$

Thus, no matter what the republican does, the democrat gains at least 1.0 units by employing his best strategy.

In a naval battle, attacking bomber planes are trying to sink ships in a fleet protected by an aircraft carrier with fighter planes. The bombers can attack either "high" or "low," with a low attack giving more accurate results. Similarly, the aircraft carrier can send its fighters at high altitudes or low altitudes to search for the bombers. If the bombers avoid the fighters, credit the bombers with 8 points; if the bombers and fighters meet, credit the bombers with $-2$ points. Also, credit the bombers with 3 additional points for flying low (since this results in more accurate bombing). Find optimal strategies for the bombers and the fighters. What is the value of the game?

First, we must set up the game matrix. Designate the bombers as playing rows and the fighters as playing columns. Also, each entry of the matrix will denote winnings of the bombers. Then the game matrix is

$$\begin{array}{cc} & \text{Fighters} \\ & \text{Low} \quad \text{High} \end{array}$$

$$\text{Bombers} \begin{array}{c} \text{Low} \\ \text{High} \end{array} \begin{pmatrix} 1 & 11 \\ 8 & -2 \end{pmatrix}$$

The reason for a 1 in row one, column one, is that $-2$ points are credited for the planes meeting, but 3 additional points are credited to the bombers for a low flight.

Next, using the formulas (3.1) and (3.2), the optimal strategies for the bombers ($p_1$ $p_2$) and for the fighters ($q_1$ $q_2$) are

$$p_1 = \frac{-10}{-20} = \frac{1}{2}, \qquad p_2 = \frac{-10}{-20} = \frac{1}{2}$$

$$q_1 = \frac{-13}{-20} = \frac{13}{20}, \qquad q_2 = \frac{-7}{-20} = \frac{7}{20}$$

The value $V$ of the game is

$$V = \frac{-2 - 88}{-20} = \frac{-90}{-20} = 4.5$$

Thus, the game is favorable to the bombers, if both players employ their optimal strategies.

The bombers can decide whether to fly high or low by flipping a fair coin and flying high whenever heads appears. The fighters can decide whether to fly high or low by using an urn with 13 black balls and 7 white balls. Each day, a ball should be selected at random and then replaced. If the ball is black, they will go low; if it is white, they go high.

1. Find the optimal strategies for each player and find the value of the following 2 × 2 games.

   (a) $\begin{pmatrix} 1 & 2 \\ 4 & 1 \end{pmatrix}$       (d) $\begin{pmatrix} 2 & 4 \\ 3 & -2 \end{pmatrix}$

   (b) $\begin{pmatrix} -3 & 2 \\ 1 & 0 \end{pmatrix}$       (e) $\begin{pmatrix} 3 & -2 \\ -1 & 2 \end{pmatrix}$

   (c) $\begin{pmatrix} 2 & -1 \\ -1 & 4 \end{pmatrix}$       (f) $\begin{pmatrix} 5 & 4 \\ -3 & 7 \end{pmatrix}$

2. In Example 3.9, page 500, suppose the candidates are assigned the following weights for each issue:

|  |  | Republican | |
|---|---|---|---|
|  |  | Domestic | Foreign |
| Democrat | Domestic | 4 | −1 |
|  | Foreign | 0 | 3 |

   What is each candidate's best strategy? What is the value of the game and whom does it favor?

3. For the situation described in Example 3.10, page 501, credit the bomber with 4 points for avoiding the fighters and with −6 points for meeting the fighters. Also, grant the bombers two additional points for flying low. What are the optimal strategies and the value of the game? Give instructions to the fighters and bombers as to how they decide whether to fly high or low.

4. A spy can leave an airport through two exits, one a relatively deserted exit and the other an exit heavily used by the public. His opponent, having been notified of the spy's presence in the airport, must guess which exit he will use. If the spy and opponent meet at the deserted exit, the spy will be killed; if the two meet at the heavily used exit, the spy will be arrested. Assign a payoff of 30 points to the spy if he avoids his opponent by using the deserted exit and of 10 points to the spy if he avoids his opponent by using the busy exit. Assign a payoff of −100 points to the spy if he is killed and −2 points if he is arrested. What are the optimal strategies and the value of the game?

*5. In a matrix game, $\begin{pmatrix} a_{11} & a_{12} \\ a_{21} & a_{22} \end{pmatrix}$, what can be said if

$$a_{11} + a_{22} - a_{12} - a_{21} = 0?$$

## Optimal Strategy in Other Two-Person Zero-Sum Games Using Geometric Methods

Thus far we have only discussed how to find optimal strategies for two-person zero-sum games which can be represented by a $2 \times 2$ matrix. In the remainder of this section, we shall give techniques for finding optimal strategies when the matrix is not $2 \times 2$.

We begin with the following definition.

If a matrix $A$ contains a row $r^*$ whose entries are all less than or equal to the corresponding entries in some other row $r$, then row $r$ is said to *dominate* row $r^*$ and $r^*$ is said to be *recessive*.

Definition
of Dominant Row
and Recessive
Row

In the matrix

3.11
Example

$$A = \begin{pmatrix} -6 & -3 & 2 & 2 \\ -2 & 0 & 3 & 2 \\ 5 & -2 & 4 & 0 \end{pmatrix}$$

row one is dominated by row two, since each entry in row one is less than or equal to its corresponding entry in row two; that is

$$-6 < -2, \quad -3 < 0, \quad 2 < 3, \quad 2 = 2$$

If the matrix $A$ of Example 3.11 were a game in which the entries represent winnings for Player I and if Player I chooses rows, it is clear that Player I would always choose row two over row one, since the values in row two always give greater benefit to him than those in row one. Thus, as far as the matrix representation of this game is concerned, we could represent it by the *reduced matrix*

Reduced Matrix

$$\begin{pmatrix} -2 & 0 & 3 & 2 \\ 5 & -2 & 4 & 0 \end{pmatrix}$$

in which row one of matrix $A$ is eliminated since it would never have been chosen.

If a matrix $A$ contains a column $c^*$ whose entries are all greater than or equal to the corresponding entries in some other column $c$, then column $c$ is said to *dominate* column $c^*$ and $c^*$ is said to be *recessive*.

Definition
of Dominant
Column and
Recessive Column

In the matrix

$$A = \begin{pmatrix} -6 & 2 & 4 \\ 4 & 4 & 2 \\ 1 & 3 & -1 \end{pmatrix}$$

column one dominates column two, since each entry in column two is greater than or equal to its corresponding entry in column one; that is

$$2 > -6, \qquad 4 = 4, \qquad 3 > 1$$

If the matrix $A$ in Example 3.12 is a matrix game in which the entries denote winnings for Player I and if Player II chooses columns, it is clear that Player II would always prefer column one over column two since the smaller entries indicate lower losses to Player II. For this reason, column two can be eliminated from the matrix $A$ and instead the reduced matrix

$$\begin{pmatrix} -6 & 4 \\ 4 & 2 \\ 1 & -1 \end{pmatrix}$$

will be used.

It is important to remember that when reducing a game matrix, *recessive rows* have entries *smaller* than those in another row and *recessive columns* have entries *larger* than those in another column.

By eliminating recessive rows and columns, find the reduced form of the matrix

$$A = \begin{pmatrix} -6 & -4 & 2 \\ 2 & -1 & 2 \\ -3 & 4 & 4 \end{pmatrix}$$

First we look at the rows of the matrix $A$. Notice that each entry in row three is greater than or equal to each entry in row one. Thus, row one is recessive and can be eliminated. The new matrix is

$$\begin{pmatrix} 2 & -1 & 2 \\ -3 & 4 & 4 \end{pmatrix}$$

Neither row one nor row two in the new matrix is recessive so we consider the columns. Notice that the entries of column three are greater than or equal to the corresponding entries in either column one or column two. Thus, column three is recessive. The reduced matrix is

$$\begin{pmatrix} 2 & -1 \\ -3 & 4 \end{pmatrix}$$

The above example shows how a $3 \times 3$ matrix game can sometimes be reduced to a $2 \times 2$ matrix by eliminating recessive rows and recessive columns.

Find optimal strategies for each player and find the value of the two-person, zero-sum game

$$\begin{pmatrix} -6 & -4 & 2 \\ 2 & -1 & 2 \\ -3 & 4 & 4 \end{pmatrix}$$

in which the entries denote the winnings of Player I, who chooses rows, and in which each player has three possible strategies.

By eliminating recessive rows and columns, this matrix reduces to

$$\begin{pmatrix} 2 & -1 \\ -3 & 4 \end{pmatrix}$$

Using the formulas (3.1) and (3.2), we find that the optimal strategy for Player I is

$$p_1 = \frac{7}{10}, \qquad p_2 = \frac{3}{10}$$

and the optimal strategy for Player II is

$$q_1 = \frac{5}{10}, \qquad q_2 = \frac{5}{10}$$

The value of the game is

$$V = \frac{5}{10}$$

Thus the game given in Example 3.14 is favorable to Player I and his best strategy is to choose row two 70 percent of the time and row three 30 percent of the time (row one is recessive).

Suppose we now consider two-person zero-sum games whose matrix representations are $2 \times m$ or $m \times 2$ $(m > 2)$ matrices that are not strictly determined and that contain no recessive rows or columns. For a $2 \times m$ matrix game, Player I has two strategies and Player II has $m$ strategies; for an $m \times 2$ matrix game, Player I has $m$ strategies and Player II has 2 strategies.

We begin with the following example to illustrate how to find optimal strategies.

Find the optimal strategy for each player in the $2 \times 3$ game

$$\begin{pmatrix} 4 & -1 & 0 \\ -1 & 4 & 2 \end{pmatrix}$$

in which entries denote winnings for Player I. What is the value of this game?

In the above game, Player I has two strategies and Player II has three strategies. Suppose $p$ is the probability that Player I plays row one. Then $1 - p$ is the probability that row two is played. Now let us compute the expected earnings of Player I in terms of $p$.

If Player II elects to play column one, then the expected earnings $E_1$ of Player I are equal to $4p - 1 \cdot (1 - p)$ or

$$\text{①} E_1 = 5p - 1$$

Similarly, if Player II selects column two and column three, the expected earnings for Player I are, respectively,

$$\text{②} E_1 = 4 - 5p, \qquad \text{③} E_1 = 2 - 2p$$

Next, we graph each of these three straight lines measuring $E_1$ along the $y$-axis and $p$ along the $x$-axis, and we look at the situation from Player II's point of view. He wishes to make Player I's earnings as small as possible, since then he maximizes his own earnings. Thus, Player II will always choose the strategy (line) whose height is least, since the height of each line measures winnings of Player I. In other words, Player II's best strategy lies along the darkened line in Figure 15.6.

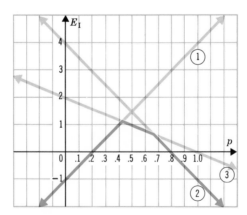

**Figure 15.6**

Player I, realizing this, will choose that value of $p$ that yields the most earnings for him. This value occurs at the intersection of the lines

$$\text{①} E_1 = 5p - 1, \qquad \text{③} E_1 = 2 - 2p$$

Their intersection is the point

$$p = \frac{3}{7}, \qquad E_1 = \frac{8}{7}$$

Thus, the optimal strategy for Player I is to choose row one 3/7 of the time and row two 4/7 of the time. The value of this game in this case is 8/7.

To find the optimal strategy for Player II, notice that Player I's optimal strategy comes from earnings calculated by using columns one and three of the matrix game. The matrix which results by eliminating column two from the matrix in Example 3.15 is

$$\begin{pmatrix} 4 & 0 \\ -1 & 2 \end{pmatrix}$$

The optimal strategy for Player II can now be found by the formula (3.2). It is

$$q_1 = \frac{2}{7}, \qquad q_2 = 0, \qquad q_3 = \frac{5}{7}$$

Thus, Player II's strategy is to play column one 2/7 of the time, column two 0 times (this is the column eliminated), and column three 5/7 of the time.

Find the optimal strategy for each player in the $5 \times 2$ matrix game

3.16
Example

$$\begin{pmatrix} -2 & 2 \\ -1 & 1 \\ 2 & 0 \\ 3 & -1 \\ 4 & -2 \end{pmatrix}$$

in which the entries denote winnings for Player I. What is the value of this game?

Here Player II has two strategies. Let $q$ be the probability that he chooses column one so that $1 - q$ is the probability that column two is chosen. Player I's earnings $E_1$ are then, respectively,

① $E_1 = -2q + 2(1 - q)$, ② $E_1 = -q + (1 - q)$, ③ $E_1 = 2q$,

④ $E_1 = 3q - (1 - q)$, ⑤ $E_1 = 4q - 2(1 - q)$

① $E_1 = -4q + 2$, ② $E_1 = -2q + 1$, ③ $E_1 = 2q$,

④ $E_1 = 4q - 1$, ⑤ $E_1 = 6q - 2$

Again we graph these five linear equations. See Figure 15.7.

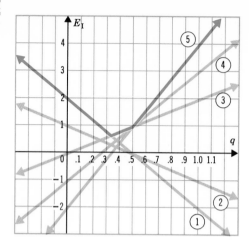

**Figure 15.7**

Player I may select any of the five strategies represented by the lines in Figure 15.7. Since the height of each line represents his earnings, he will employ strategies that carry him along the darkened line in Figure 15.7.

But Player II wants the earnings of Player I to be as small as possible. This occurs at the intersection of ① and ③. This point is $q = 1/3$, $E_1 = 2/3$. Thus, the optimal strategy for Player II is to choose column one 1/3 of the time and column two 2/3 of the time. The value of the game is 2/3 and it is favorable to Player I.

Now, to find Player I's optimal strategy, we notice that Player II's optimal strategy comes from lines ① and ③. If we eliminate rows two, four, five, and six from the matrix in Example 3.16, we obtain the matrix

$$\begin{pmatrix} -2 & 2 \\ 2 & 0 \end{pmatrix}$$

Applying formula (3.1), Player I's optimal strategy is

$$p_1 = \frac{-2}{-6} = \frac{1}{3}, \qquad p_3 = \frac{-4}{-6} = \frac{2}{3}$$

3.17
Example
Cultural
Anthropology

In 1960, Davenport[1] published an analysis of the behavior of Jamaican fishermen. Each fishing crew is confronted with a three-choice decision of fishing in the inside banks, the outside banks, or a combination of inside-outside banks. Fairly reliable estimates can be made of the quantity and quality of fish caught in these three areas under the two conditions that current is present, or not present.

[1] E. Davenport, "Jamaican Fishing: A Game Theory Analysis in Papers on Caribbean Anthropology," Yale University Publication in Anthropology, Nos. 57–64, 1960.

If we take the village as a whole as one player and the environment as another player, we have the components for a two-person zero-sum game, in which the village has three strategies (inside, inside-outside, outside) and the environment has two strategies (current, no current). Davenport computed an estimate of income claimed by the fisherman using each of the alternatives. This estimate is given in matrix form by

$$
\begin{array}{cc}
 & \text{Environment} \\
 & \text{current} \quad \text{no current}
\end{array}
$$

$$
\text{Village}
\begin{array}{c}
\text{Inside} \\
\text{Inside-outside} \\
\text{Outside}
\end{array}
\begin{pmatrix}
17.3 & 11.5 \\
5.2 & 17.0 \\
-4.4 & 20.6
\end{pmatrix}
$$

Here, the environment has two strategies. Let $q$ be the probability of current, so that $1 - q$ is the probability of no current. If $E_1$ represents the villagers' expected earnings, then

① $E_1 = 17.3q + 11.5(1 - q)$, ② $E_1 = 5.2q + 17(1 - q)$,

③ $E_1 = -4.4q + 20.6(1 - q)$

① $E_1 = 5.8q + 11.5$, ② $E_1 = -11.8q + 17$,

③ $E_1 = -25q + 20.6$

Figure 15.8 shows that the optimal strategy of the environment comes from the intersection of lines ① and ②.

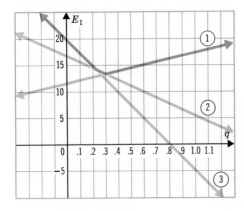

**Figure 15.8**

Computing this intersection we obtain

$$q = .31 \qquad 1 - q = .69$$

To obtain the optimal strategy of the village we note that the optimal strategy of the environment comes from lines ① and

②. If we eliminate row three from the matrix in Example 3.17 we find

$$\begin{pmatrix} 17.3 & 11.5 \\ 5.2 & 17.0 \end{pmatrix}$$

Applying previous formulas, the villager's optimal strategy is

$$p_1 = \frac{17.0 - 5.2}{34.3 - 16.7} = \frac{11.8}{17.6} = .67 \qquad p_2 = \frac{5.8}{17.6} = .33$$

Figure 15.9 compares the observed frequency of strategy usage as compared with the optimal usage as predicted by the game.

| | Observed | Predicted |
|---|---|---|
| Outside | 0 | 0 |
| Inside | .69 | .67 |
| Inside-outside | .31 | .33 |
| Current | .25 | .31 |
| No current | .75 | .69 |

**Figure 15.9**

3.18
Example
Simplified
Investment
Problem

The following is an example from a paper by J. D. Williams.[2] An investor plans to invest $10,000 during a period of international uncertainty as to whether there will be peace, a continuation of the cold war, or an actual war. His investment can be made in government bonds, armament stocks, or industrial stocks. The game is a struggle between the investor and nature. The matrix below gives the rates of interest for each player's strategy.

|  |  | Hot War | Cold War | Peace |
|---|---|---|---|---|
|  | Government bonds | 2 | 3 | 3.2 |
| Investor | Armament stocks | 18 | 6 | −2 |
|  | Industrial stocks | 2 | 7 | 12 |

Calculate the investor's optimal strategy.

First we look at the matrix to see if there is any row dominance or column dominance. Notice that row three dominates row one so that the reduced matrix for this game is

|  | Hot War | Cold War | Peace |
|---|---|---|---|
| Armament stock | 18 | 6 | −2 |
| Industrial stock | 2 | 7 | 12 |

[2] J. D. Williams, *La Strategie dans les actions humaines*, Dunod, Paris, 1956.

This is a 2 × 3 matrix that can be solved by the graphing method. The optimal strategy for the investor is

$$p_1 = 0, \qquad p_2 = \frac{5}{17}, \qquad p_3 = \frac{12}{17}$$

The value of the game is

$$V = 6.7$$

Thus the investor is assured of a return of at least 6.7 percent when he invests $5/17 = 0.29$ percent in armament stocks and $12/17 = 0.71$ percent in industrial stocks. In the event of a hot war the return is

$$18\left(\frac{5}{17}\right) + 2\left(\frac{12}{17}\right) = 6.7 \text{ percent}$$

In the event of a cold war the return is

$$6\left(\frac{5}{17}\right) + 7\left(\frac{12}{17}\right) = 6.7 \text{ percent}$$

In the event of peace the return is

$$(-2)\left(\frac{5}{17}\right) + 12\left(\frac{12}{17}\right) = 7.9 \text{ percent}$$

General White's army and the enemy are each trying to occupy three hills. General White has three regiments and the enemy has two regiments. A hill is occupied when one force has more regiments present than the other force; if both try to occupy a hill with the same number of regiments, a draw results. How should the troops be deployed to gain maximum advantage?

3.19
Example

We denote the three strategies available to General White as follows:

3: All three regiments used together to attack one hill.
2,1: Two regiments used together and one used by itself to attack two hills.
1,1,1: All three regiments used separately to attack three hills.

White's opponent has two strategies available, namely:

2: The two regiments used together to defend one hill.
1,1: The two regiments used separately to defend two of the hills.

Furthermore, White will play rows and the entries will denote White's expected winnings based on the rule that when White takes a hill, he earns one point; when a draw results, he earns zero points; and when he is defeated, he loses one point. Also, for each division that is overpowered, one point is earned.

|     | 200 | 020 | 002 | 110 | 101 | 011 |
|-----|-----|-----|-----|-----|-----|-----|
| 300 | 3   | 0   | 0   | 1   | 1   | −1  |
| 030 | 0   | 3   | 0   | 1   | −1  | 1   |
| 003 | 0   | 0   | 3   | −1  | 1   | 1   |
| 210 | 1   | −1  | 1   | 2   | 2   | 0   |
| 201 | 1   | 1   | −1  | 2   | 2   | 0   |
| 120 | −1  | 1   | 1   | 2   | 0   | 2   |
| 021 | 1   | 1   | −1  | 2   | 0   | 2   |
| 102 | −1  | 1   | 1   | 0   | 2   | 2   |
| 012 | 1   | −1  | 1   | 0   | 2   | 2   |
| 111 | 0   | 0   | 0   | 1   | 1   | 1   |

**Figure 15.10**

Figure 15.10 shows the points won (or lost) by General White for all possible deployments of his regiments. Notice that the order of deployment is quite important.

For example, if White deploys his regiments as 3,0,0 and his opponent uses the deployment 2,0,0, then White captures hill I, winning one point, and overpowers two regiments, winning two points, for a total score of three points. If White uses 0,2,1 and his opponent uses 0,1,1, then hill I is a standoff, White wins hill II and overpowers one regiment, and hill III is a draw. Here White has a total score of two points.

To determine the game matrix, we proceed as follows: If White uses a 3 deployment and his enemy uses a 2 deployment, then White expects to score 3 points $1/3$ of the time and score 0 points $2/3$ of the time. We assign an expected payoff to White of $3 \cdot 1/3 + 0 \cdot 2/3 = 1$ point in this case. If White uses a 2,1 deployment and his enemy uses a 1,1 deployment, then White expects to gain 2 points $2/3$ of the time and 0 points $1/3$ of the time for an expected payoff of $4/3$ points. The game matrix can be written as

$$
\begin{array}{cc}
 & \text{Enemy} \\
 & 2 \quad 1{,}1
\end{array}
$$

$$
\text{White} \quad
\begin{array}{c}
3 \\
2{,}1 \\
1{,}1{,}1
\end{array}
\begin{pmatrix}
1 & \dfrac{1}{3} \\
\dfrac{1}{3} & \dfrac{4}{3} \\
0 & 1
\end{pmatrix}
$$

Notice that the matrix above can be reduced, since row 2

dominates row 3. The reduced matrix is

$$\begin{array}{cc} & \text{Enemy} \\ & 2 \quad 1,1 \end{array}$$

$$\text{White} \quad \begin{array}{c} 3 \\ \\ 2,1 \end{array} \begin{pmatrix} 1 & \dfrac{1}{3} \\ \dfrac{1}{3} & \dfrac{4}{3} \end{pmatrix}$$

This matrix is not strictly determined. The optimal (mixed) strategy for General White is

$$p_1 = \frac{1}{\dfrac{7}{3} - \dfrac{2}{3}} = .6 \qquad p_2 = \frac{\dfrac{2}{3}}{\dfrac{5}{3}} = .4 \qquad p_3 = 0$$

The optimal strategy for the enemy is

$$q_1 = \frac{1}{\dfrac{5}{3}} = .6 \qquad q_2 = \frac{\dfrac{2}{3}}{\dfrac{5}{3}} = .4$$

The value of the game is

$$V = \frac{\dfrac{4}{3} - \dfrac{1}{9}}{\dfrac{5}{3}} = \frac{\dfrac{11}{9}}{\dfrac{5}{3}} = \frac{11}{15}$$

The game is favorable to General White who should deploy his troops in a 3 strategy 60 percent of the time and in a 2,1 strategy 40 percent of the time. Since no one hill is more likely to be chosen for attack than any other, it follows that each hill should be attacked by all three regiments 20 percent of the time. Furthermore, for the 2,1 deployment, each possible selection of the hills to receive 0,1, or 2 regiments (6 in all) will be used $40/6 = 6.67$ percent of the time.

---

1. Find the optimal strategies for each player in the following games in which Player I plays rows and entries denote winnings of Player I. What is the value of each game?

(a) $\begin{pmatrix} 8 & 3 & 8 \\ 6 & 5 & 4 \\ -2 & 4 & 1 \end{pmatrix}$

(b) $\begin{pmatrix} 2 & 1 & 0 & 6 \\ 3 & -2 & 1 & 2 \end{pmatrix}$

(d) $\begin{pmatrix} 4 & -5 & 5 \\ -6 & 3 & 3 \\ 2 & -6 & 3 \end{pmatrix}$

(e) $\begin{pmatrix} 1 & 3 & 0 \\ 0 & -3 & 1 \\ 0 & 4 & 1 \\ -2 & 1 & 1 \end{pmatrix}$

15.3.4
Exercise

(c) $\begin{pmatrix} 6 & -4 & 2 & -3 \\ -4 & 6 & -5 & 7 \end{pmatrix}$  (f) $\begin{pmatrix} 4 & 3 & -1 \\ 1 & 1 & 4 \\ 1 & 0 & 2 \end{pmatrix}$

2. Find optimal strategies for both players in each of the following games. What is the value of each game? Player I plays rows and the entries denote his winnings.

(a) $\begin{pmatrix} 3 & -1 & 0 \\ -2 & 1 & -1 \end{pmatrix}$   (d) $\begin{pmatrix} -5 & -4 & -3 & 2 & 3 \\ 3 & 2 & 1 & -2 & -4 \end{pmatrix}$

(b) $\begin{pmatrix} -1 & 1 \\ 5 & -3 \\ 1 & -2 \\ -2 & 5 \end{pmatrix}$   (e) $\begin{pmatrix} 6 & -4 \\ 4 & -3 \\ 1 & 0 \\ -3 & 2 \\ -5 & 4 \end{pmatrix}$

(c) $\begin{pmatrix} 3 & -2 & 2 \\ -1 & 1 & 0 \end{pmatrix}$

3. In a department store one area ($A$) is usually very crowded and the other area ($B$) is usually relatively empty. The store employs two detectives and has closed-circuit television ($T$) to control pilferage. The television covers $A$ and $B$ and the detectives can be in either area ($A$) or ($B$) or watching the television ($T$). The matrix below gives an estimate of the probability for the detectives to find and arrest a thief.

|  | | Thief | |
|---|---|---|---|
|  | | A | B |
| Detectives | TT | .51 | .75 |
|  | AA | .64 | .36 |
|  | BB | .19 | .91 |
|  | TA | .58 | .60 |
|  | TB | .37 | .85 |
|  | AB | .46 | .76 |

Here $TT$ means both detectives are at the television, $TA$ means the first detective is at the television and the second is in area $A$, and so on. Find the optimal strategy for the thief and the detectives. What is the value of the game?

4. This problem is from J. D. Williams.[3] Three antibiotics $A_1$, $A_2$, and $A_3$, and five types of bacilli $M_1$, $M_2$, $M_3$, $M_4$, and $M_5$ are involved in a study of the effectiveness of antibiotics on bacilli, with $A_1$ having a probability .3 of destroying $M_2$, and so on as given on page 515. Without knowing the proportion in which these germs are distributed during an epidemic, in what ratio should the antibiotics be mixed to have the greatest probability of being effective?

[3] J. D. Williams, *La Strategie dans les actions humaines*, Dunod, Paris, 1956.

Bacilli

$$\text{Antibiotics } \begin{array}{c} A_1 \\ A_2 \\ A_3 \end{array} \begin{pmatrix} .3 & .4 & .5 & 1 & 0 \\ .2 & .3 & .6 & 0 & 1 \\ .1 & .5 & .3 & .1 & 0 \end{pmatrix}$$

with column headers $M_1\ M_2\ M_3\ M_4\ M_5$

CHAPTER
REVIEW

Important
Terms

Review
Exercises

1. The figure below shows a spinning game for which a person pays $0.30 to purchase an opportunity to spin the dial. Each number on the table indicates the amount of payoff and its corresponding probability. Find the expected value of this game. Is the game fair?

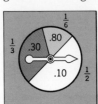

2. Consider the three urns in the figure below. The game is played in two stages. The first stage is to choose a ball from urn A. If, for example, the result is a ball marked I, then we go to urn I, and we select a ball from there. The number drawn on the second stage is the gain. Find the expected value of this game.

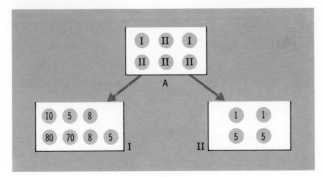

3. Determine which of the following two-person zero-sum games are strictly determined. For those that are, find the value of the game.

(a) $\begin{pmatrix} 5 & 3 \\ 2 & 2 \end{pmatrix}$ 　　　 (b) $\begin{pmatrix} 29 & 15 \\ 79 & 3 \end{pmatrix}$

(c) $\begin{pmatrix} 50 & 75 \\ 30 & 15 \end{pmatrix}$ 　　 (d) $\begin{pmatrix} 7 & 14 \\ 9 & 13 \end{pmatrix}$

(e) $\begin{pmatrix} 0 & 2 & 4 \\ 4 & 6 & 10 \\ 16 & 14 & 12 \end{pmatrix}$

4. Find the expected payoff of the game

$$\begin{pmatrix} -1 & 1 \\ 1 & -1 \end{pmatrix}$$

for the strategies:

(a) $P = \begin{pmatrix} \dfrac{1}{3} & \dfrac{2}{3} \end{pmatrix}$ 　 $Q = \begin{pmatrix} 1 \\ 0 \end{pmatrix}$

(b) $P = (0 \quad 1)$ 　 $Q = \begin{pmatrix} \dfrac{1}{2} \\ \dfrac{1}{2} \end{pmatrix}$

(c) $P = \begin{pmatrix} \dfrac{1}{2} & \dfrac{1}{2} \end{pmatrix}$ 　 $Q = \begin{pmatrix} \dfrac{1}{2} \\ \dfrac{1}{2} \end{pmatrix}$

5. Show that if a 2 × 2 or 2 × 3 matrix game has a saddle point, then either one row dominates the other or one column dominates another column.

6. Give an example to show that the result of Problem 5 is not true for 3 × 3 matrix games.

7. Find optimal strategies for each player in the following games. Assume Player I plays rows and entries denote winnings of Player I. What is the value of each game?

(a) $\begin{pmatrix} 4 & 6 & 3 \\ 1 & 2 & 5 \end{pmatrix}$ 　　 (b) $\begin{pmatrix} 1 & 6 \\ 5 & 2 \\ 7 & 4 \end{pmatrix}$

(c) $\begin{pmatrix} 2 & 1 \\ 4 & 0 \\ 3 & 4 \end{pmatrix}$ 　　 (d) $\begin{pmatrix} 0 & 3 & 2 \\ 4 & 2 & 3 \end{pmatrix}$

8. Consider a neighborhood in which there are only two competitive stores handling two different, but similar, brands of spark plugs. In ordinary circumstances each retailer pays $0.60 for each plug and sells it for $1.00. However, the

manufacturers from time to time have incentive plans in which they sell the plugs to the retailers for $0.40, provided the retailer will sell it for $0.70. Each month the retailers must decide, independently of one another, what the selling price for the spark plugs should be. From previous sales patterns, each retailer observes the following pattern: At the usual price, each sells 1000 plugs per month; if one retailer discounts the price and the other does not, the discount store will sell 2000 plugs each month and the other will sell only 300 plugs; if both stores discount the price, they will each sell 1300 plugs per month. Set up the game matrix for this problem. In your opinion, how should each store manager proceed?

9. *The blood testing problem.*[4] A group of 1000 people are subject to a blood test which can be administered in two ways: (i) each person can be tested separately (in this case 1000 tests are required) or (ii) the blood samples of 30 people can be pooled and analyzed together. If we use the second way and the test is negative, then one test suffices for 30 people. If the test is positive, each of the 30 persons can then be tested separately, and, in all, 30 + 1 tests are required for the 30 people.

   Assume the probability $p$, that the test is positive, is the same for all people and that the people to be tested are independent.

   (a) What is the probability that the test for a pooled sample of 30 people will be positive?
   (b) What is the expected number of tests necessary under plan (ii)?

## Bibliography

*Mathematics*

Maki, Daniel P. and Maynard Thompson, *Mathematical Models and Applications,* Englewood Cliffs, New Jersey, Prentice-Hall, 1973.

*Applied*

Alker, Hayward R., Jr., *Mathematics and Politics,* New York, Macmillan, 1965.
Buchler, Ira, and Hugo Nutini, *Game Theory in the Behavioral Sciences,* University of Pittsburgh Press, 1969.

[4]William Feller, *An Introduction to Probability Theory and its Applications,* Third Edition, Wiley, New York, 1968, pp. 239–240.

Kaplan, Martin and Nicholas Katzenbach, *The Political Foundations of International Law,* New York, Wiley, 1961.

Luce, R. Duncan and Howard Raiffa, *Games and Decisions,* New York, Wiley, 1957.

*Mathematics in the Modern World,* readings from *Scientific American,* San Francisco, W. H. Freeman, 1968, pp. 300–312.

Rapoport, A., *Strategy and Conscience,* New York, Harper and Row, 1964.

Shiebik, Martin, (Ed.), *Game Theory and Related Approaches to Social Behavior,* New York, Wiley, 1964.

Shiebik, Martin, *Strategy and Market Structure,* New York, Wiley, 1959.

# 16

# PROBABILITY AND CALCULUS

In this chapter we extend the concept of a sample space first introduced in Chapter 13. There we limited our discussion to probabilistic models that resulted in *finite* sample spaces, and we evolved a theory for handling several types of probability applications.

In this chapter we shall not only look again at finite sample spaces, but we shall also study sample spaces that are infinite. We shall find that infinite sample spaces fall into two categories: *discrete* sample spaces and *continuous* sample spaces.

The remainder of this chapter investigates the use of certain probability distributions that have wide-ranging applications. Two of the distributions selected for insertion in this chapter are the Poisson distribution and the normal distribution.

16.1
INTRODUCTION

This section introduces language that will be necessary for subsequent sections. The concepts of importance are <u>random variable</u>, discrete sample space, and continuous sample space.

Intuitively, a random variable is a quantity that is measured in connection with a random experiment. For example, if the random experiment involves weighing individuals, then the weight of each individual would be a random variable. As another example, if the random experiment is to determine the time between arrivals of customers in a gas station, then time between arrivals of customers at the gas station would be a random variable.

Let us consider some examples that demonstrate how to obtain random variables from random experiments.

When we perform a simple experiment, we are often interested not in a particular outcome, but rather in some number associated with that outcome. For example, in tossing a coin three times, we may be interested in the number of heads obtained, regardless of the particular sequence in which the heads appear. Similarly, the gambler throwing a pair of dice is interested in the sum of the faces rather than the particular number on each face.

Table 16.1 summarizes the results of the simple experiment of flipping a fair coin three times. The first column in the table gives a sample space of this experiment. The second column shows the number of heads for each simple event, and the third column shows the probabilities associated with each simple event.

**Table 16.1**

| | Number of Heads | Probability |
|---|---|---|
| HHH | 3 | 1/8 |
| HHT | 2 | 1/8 |
| HTH | 2 | 1/8 |
| THH | 2 | 1/8 |
| HTT | 1 | 1/8 |
| THT | 1 | 1/8 |
| TTH | 1 | 1/8 |
| TTT | 0 | 1/8 |

Suppose in this experiment we are interested only in the total number of "heads." This information is given in Table 16.2.

**Table 16.2**

| Number of Heads Obtained in Three Flips of a Coin | Probability |
|---|---|
| 0 | 1/8 |
| 1 | 3/8 |
| 2 | 3/8 |
| 3 | 1/8 |

The role of the random variable is to transform the original sample space {*HHH, HHT, HTH, HTT, THH, THT, TTH, TTT*} into a new sample space that consists of the number of heads that occur: {0, 1, 2, 3}. If *X* denotes the random variable, then *X* may take on any of the values 0, 1, 2, or 3. Clearly, from Table 16.2, the probability that the random variable *X* assumes the value 2 is

$$\text{Probability } (X = 2) = \frac{3}{8}$$

Also,

$$\text{Probability } (X = 5) = 0$$

Thus we see that a random variable indicates the rule of correspondence between any member of a sample space and a number assigned to it.

**A *random variable* is a function that associates or transforms each event of a sample space into a real number.**

We shall use the upper case letter *X* to represent a random variable. In the coin-flipping example, the random variable *X* is

$$X(HHH) = 3, X(HHT) = 2, X(HTH) = 2, X(THH) = 2$$
$$X(HTT) = 1, X(THT) = 1, X(TTH) = 1, X(TTT) = 0$$

Thus the random variable *X* indicates a relationship between the first two columns of Table 16.1 and pairs each outcome of the experiment with the real numbers 0, 1, 2, or 3.

Random variables fall into two classes: those related to discrete sample spaces and those associated with continuous sample spaces.

**A sample space is *discrete* if it is finite or if its elements can be placed in one-to-one correspondence with the set $N$ of natural numbers. A random variable is said to be *discrete* if it is defined over a discrete sample space.**

For example, the random experiment of flipping a fair coin until a head appears is represented by an infinite sample space that is discrete.

The sample space associated with the random experiment of measuring the height of each United States citizen is, of course, finite. However, each person has a unique height. Because of the proximity of all these different heights, we usually allow the random variable to assume any real number so that the number of possible heights is infinite and the random variable is *continuous*. In such cases, we also say the sample space is *continuous*.

Any practical problem that *measures* such dimensions as height, weight, time, and age will utilize a continuous random variable. As a result, the sample space associated to such experiments is also taken as *continuous*.

To summarize, continuous random variables represent *measured* data, while discrete random variables represent *counted* data.

In Problems 1–4 list the values of the given random variable *X* together with the probabilities of occurrence.

1. A fair coin is tossed two times. The random variable *X* is the number of heads obtained.
2. A fair die is tossed once. The random variable *X* is the number showing on the top face.
3. The random variable *X* is the number of female children in a family with three children. (Assume the probability of a female birth is 1/2.)
4. A job applicant takes a three question true-false examination, and guesses on each question. Let *X* be the number right minus the number wrong.

Classify the following random variables as discrete or continuous. If they are discrete, state whether the sample spaces are infinite or finite.

5. *X* is the number of tosses of a coin in the experiment of tossing a fair coin repeatedly until a head occurs.
6. *X* is the number of defective items in a lot of 10,000 items.
7. *X* is the length of time a person must wait in line to check out at a checkout counter.
8. *X* denotes the time elapsed in minutes between the arrival of airplanes at an airport.

Let us turn our attention to Table 16.2 of Section 16.2 (page 520). This table contains two columns: the first lists the values the random variable *X* can take on and the second the corresponding probability. The relationship between probability and the random variable is called a *probability function* or a *probability distribution function*. Such functions tell us how the total probability is distributed among the various values of the random variable.

The distinction between a discrete probability function and a continuous probability function depends on whether the random variable *X* is discrete or continuous. In this section, we discuss discrete probability distributions and in Section 16.4 we discuss continuous probability distributions.

The binomial probability function that assigns probabilities to the number of successes in *n* trials is an example of a discrete probability distribution function. For this function, *X* is the random variable whose value for any outcome of the experiment is the number of successes obtained. For the binomial distribution, we may write

$$P(X = k) = b(n, k; p) = \binom{n}{k} p^k q^{n-k}$$

where $P(X = k)$ denotes the probability that the random variable equals $k$, that is, that exactly $k$ successes are obtained.

We have seen that such probability functions provide us with answers to questions such as the probability of getting 1 head and 2 tails in 3 throws of a fair coin. Furthermore, it provides us with a probability for each possible value of the *random variable* "the number of heads which we obtain in 3 throws of a fair coin." Thus if we let $X$ denote such a random variable and use $f(x)$ for the probability that the random variable $X$ assumes the value $x$, then for the experiment of flipping a fair coin three times, we may write:

$$f(0) = P(X = 0) = \frac{1}{8} \qquad f(1) = P(X = 1) = \frac{3}{8}$$

$$f(2) = P(X = 2) = \frac{3}{8} \qquad f(3) = P(X = 3) = \frac{1}{8}$$

In the experiment of one toss of two fair dice, compute the value of the probability function at $x = 7$.
Here

$$f(7) = P(X = 7) = P\{(1, 6)\ (2, 5)\ (3, 4)\ (4, 3)\ (5, 2)\ (6, 1)\} = \frac{6}{36}$$

3.1
Example

We can compute the probabilities $f(2), f(3), \ldots, f(12)$ in a similar way. These values are summarized in the following table:

| Values of | $X$ | 2 | 3 | 4 | 5 | 6 | 7 | 8 | 9 | 10 | 11 | 12 |
|---|---|---|---|---|---|---|---|---|---|---|---|---|
| Probability function of x | $f(x)$ | 1/36 | 2/36 | 3/36 | 4/36 | 5/36 | 6/36 | 5/36 | 4/36 | 3/36 | 2/36 | 1/36 |

Whenever possible, we try to express probability functions by means of formulas that enable us to calculate probabilities associated with the various values that the random variable assumes.

For example, in the experiment of tossing a fair coin 3 times, the probability function is

$$f(x) = \binom{3}{x}\left(\frac{1}{2}\right)^3 = \frac{3!}{(3-x)!x!}\frac{1}{8} = \frac{3}{4x!(3-x)!}, \qquad x = 0, 1, 2, 3$$

where $x$ denotes the number of heads obtained.

Consider the experiment of a player rolling a fair die. He wins $2, if the outcome is 1, 2 or 3, and he loses $2, if the outcome is 4, 5 or 6. The random variable $X$ is

$$X(1) = X(2) = X(3) = +2$$
$$X(4) = X(5) = X(6) = -2$$

What is the probability for the random variable to assume the value 2? In other words, what is $P(X = 2)$?

Since the random variable takes on the value 2 at the outcomes 1, 2, and 3, we have

$$f(2) = P(X = 2) = \frac{1}{2}$$

Similarly,

$$f(-2) = P(X = -2) = \frac{1}{2}$$

Quite often in solving problems we are interested in the probability that a random variable $X$ assumes values less than or equal to some real number $z$. To denote such a situation we use the notation,

$$F(z) = P(X \leq z)$$

Cumulative
Distribution
Function

Here $F(z)$ is called the *cumulative distribution function* of the random variable $X$.

Return to the experiment of flipping a fair coin three times. From Table 16.2, if $z$ represents the number of heads, the cumulative distribution function $F(z)$ for $z = -1, 0, 1/2, 1, 5/2, 3, 5$ is

$$F(-1) = P(X \leq -1) = 0$$

$$F(0) = P(X \leq 0) = \frac{1}{8}$$

$$F\left(\frac{1}{2}\right) = P\left(X \leq \frac{1}{2}\right) = \frac{1}{8}$$

$$F(1) = P(X \leq 1) = \frac{4}{8}$$

$$F\left(\frac{5}{2}\right) = P\left(X \leq \frac{5}{2}\right) = \frac{7}{8}$$

$$F(3) = P(X \leq 3) = 1$$

$$F(5) = P(X \leq 5) = 1$$

In general,

$$F(z) = P(X \leq z) = \begin{cases} 0 & z < 0 \\ \dfrac{1}{8} & 0 \leq z < 1 \\ \dfrac{4}{8} & 1 \leq z < 2 \\ \dfrac{7}{8} & 2 \leq z < 3 \\ 1 & 3 \leq z \end{cases}$$

The reader will recall that the Bernoulli distribution function studied in Chapter 13 handles experiments consisting of repeated trials that are independent. Although this distribution has many applications, some natural phenomena and everyday applications do not conform to it. For instance when $n$ (the number of trials) is very large and $p$, the probability of success is very small, say 0.05, another probability distribution function, the *Poisson distribution,* is easier to use. We conclude this section with a discussion of this well-known and widely applied distribution function.

Experience has shown that the Poisson distribution is an excellent model to use for computing probabilities associated with the following random experiments:

(a) The number of cars arriving at a toll gate during a fixed period of time.
(b) The number of phone calls occurring within a certain time interval.
(c) The study of bacteria distribution in a culture.
(d) The arrival of customers at the checkout counter of a supermarket in a given time interval.
(e) The number of defects in a manufactured product.
(f) The number of earthquakes in a period of time.
(g) The number of typing errors on a given printed page.

For everyday random phenomena, such as those mentioned above, we use the following result, which we state without proof:

**For a random variable assuming the values $0, 1, 2, \ldots$, the probability that exactly $x$ successes occur in a given interval is**

The Poisson
Distribution
Function

$$f(x) = \frac{(np)^x e^{-np}}{x!} \qquad x = 0, 1, 2, \ldots$$

**where $n$ is the number of trials and $p$ is the probability of success. The random variable is known as a *Poisson variable* and $f(x)$ is the *Poisson distribution.* (Here $np$ is the average number of successes occurring in the given time interval.)**

A department store has found that the daily demand for black-and-white televisions averages 3 in 100. On a given day 50 televisions are sold. What is the probability that more than 3 of the 50 sales are requests for black and white televisions?

3.3
Example

We assume the problem to be a Poisson model since the probability that a black-and-white television is requested is small (.03). The random variable here is the occurrence of customers wanting to buy black-and-white televisions. Also, $n$, the number of sets sold, is 50, so that $np = 50(.03) = 1.5$. If $X$ is a Poisson random variable, then the probability that more than 3 of the sales are for black-and-white televisions is

$$P(X > 3) = 1 - P(X \leq 3) = 1 - [f(0) + f(1) + f(2) + f(3)]$$

$$= 1 - \left[ \frac{(1.5)^0}{0!} e^{-1.5} + \frac{(1.5)^1}{1!} e^{-1.5} + \frac{(1.5)^2}{2!} e^{-1.5} + \frac{(1.5)^3}{3!} e^{-1.5} \right]$$

$$= 1 - [.223 + .335 + .251 + .126] = .065$$

3.4
Example
Weather records show that, of the 30 days in November, on the average 3 days are snowy. What is the probability that November of next year will have at most 4 snowy days?

Let $X$ be a Poisson random variable. From the information given,

$$n = 30, \qquad p = \frac{3}{30}, \qquad np = 30 \cdot \frac{3}{30} = 3$$

The probability that at most 4 days are snowy is

$$P(X \leq 4) = f(0) + f(1) + f(2) + f(3) + f(4)$$

$$= e^{-3} + 3e^{-3} + \frac{9e^{-3}}{2} + \frac{27e^{-3}}{6} + \frac{81e^{-3}}{24}$$

$$= .050 + .149 + .224 + .224 + .168 = .815$$

The Poisson distribution, although a limiting case of the Bernoulli distribution, has many applications to problems that are not directly related to the Bernoulli distribution. The next example illustrates this.

3.5
Example
During a certain period, persons arrive at a ticket counter at an average rate of one every two minutes. What is the probability that, during a given one minute period, no persons arrive at the ticket counter? What is the probability at least two persons arrive in this one-minute period?

Before solving the problem, we observe that no information is given about the probability that exactly one person will arrive in a one-minute interval. However, we do know that this probability is small, and we know that the average rate of arrival in a one minute period is 1/2, so that $np = 1/2$.

If we use a Poisson distribution to solve the problem, the probability that no person arrives in the one-minute interval is

$$f(0) = \frac{(1/2)^0 e^{-1/2}}{0!} = e^{-1/2} = .607$$

Thus there is a 61 percent probability that no persons will arrive in a one-minute interval.

To answer the second question, we need to compute $f(2) + f(3) + \cdots$. It is much easier to consider the complementary event: "at most one person arrives." To do this, we need to compute $f(0)$ and $f(1)$.

Now,

$$f(1) = \frac{(np)\,e^{-np}}{1!} = \left(\frac{1}{2}\right)e^{-1/2} = .304$$

Hence, the probability that at most one person arrives in the one-minute interval is

$$P(X \leq 1) = f(0) + f(1) = .607 + .304 = .911$$

Thus the probability that two or more persons arrive during a one-minute period is

$$1 - .911 = .089$$

1. Assume $X$ is a Poisson random variable with $np = 6$. Find
   (a) $P(X \leq 5)$     (c) $P(X > 5)$
   (b) $P(X = 5)$     (d) $P(1 < X < 4)$

2. At a supermarket, customers arrive at a checkout counter at the rate of 60 per hour. What is the probability that 8 or fewer will arrive in a period of 10 minutes?

3. An insurance company insures 5000 people against loss of both eyes in a car accident. Based on previous data, the rates were computed on the assumption that on the average 8 persons in 100,000 will have car accidents each year that result in this type of injury. What is the probability that more than 3 of the insured will collect on their policy in a given year?

4. A machine produces parts to meet certain specifications and the probability that a part is defective is .05. A sample of 50 parts is taken. What is the probability that it will have two or more defective parts? Compute this probability using both the Poisson and the binomial distribution.

5. From past data it has been shown that the number of tornadoes hitting the Midwest each year is a random variable whose probability distribution can be approximated by a Poisson distribution with $np = 7$. Find the following:
   (a) The probability that in a given year, fewer than 5 tornadoes will hit the Midwest.
   (b) The probability that in a given year, no more than 7 tornadoes will hit the area.

Thus far the random experiments that we have encountered gave rise to probability models whose sample spaces are either finite or discrete. Quite often, however, we deal with random experiments that are neither finite nor discrete. Such random experiments may occur physically as approximations to discrete spaces with a very large number of simple events.

For example, if the random experiment involves weighing individuals, the weight of each individual is treated as a continuous random variable. Likewise, in the random experiment of determining the time between arrival of customers at a gas station, the time between arrival is treated as a continuous random variable.

Suppose we wish to compute the probability that a person selected at random in the United States will be between 22 and 24 years old if the only known information about the distribution of the population by ages is given by data grouped in 10-year intervals. See Figure 16.1.

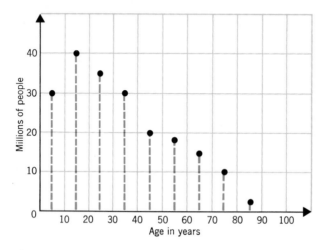

**Figure 16.1** *Age statistics*

In this illustration there are 30 million people in the age group 0–10, 40 million between the ages of 10 and 20, and so on. We also know that the total population is 200 million. From this, we can determine the probability that a person chosen at random falls into a given age group. For example, there are 40 million people in the age group 10–20 so that the probability a person is in the age group is 40/200 = .20. Figure 16.2 illustrates the distribution of probabilities for each age group.

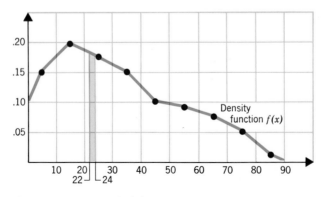

**Figure 16.2** *Age probabilities*

The function constructed by connecting the probability values by a smooth curve is called a *density function*. The area under the density curve from c to d represents the probability that a person is between the ages $x = c$ and $x = d$. That is,

$$P(c \leq x \leq d) = \int_c^d f(x)\, dx$$

Thus, the probability that a person is between 22 and 24 years of age is

$$\int_{22}^{24} f(x)\, dx$$

The density function in Figure 16.2 is called the *probability density* or, in this case, is the probability per unit age. Since a person's age must fall someplace on the diagram, the integral of the density function over all possible ages must equal 1. That is,

$$\int_0^{90} f(x)\, dx = 1$$

Also, the density function is greater than or equal to zero for any age. These comments lead us to construct the following definition for a density function.

**A function $y = f(x)$ is termed a *density function* if it has two properties:**

**(I)** $\int_a^b f(x)\, dx = 1$

Definition
of a Density
Function

**where $(a, b)$ is an interval containing all values that the random variable X can assume, and**

**(II)** $f(x) \geq 0$

An important and useful property of a density function is stated below.

**The probability that the outcome of an experiment results in a value of a random variable X between c and d is given by**

$$P(c \leq X \leq d) = \int_c^d f(x)\, dx \qquad \textbf{(4.1)}$$

Show that the function $f(x) = \frac{3}{56}(5x - x^2)$ is a density function over the interval $[0, 4]$.

If $f(x)$ is indeed a density function, it has to satisfy conditions

4.1
Example

I and II. Thus, for condition I, we evaluate

$$\int_0^4 \frac{3}{56}(5x - x^2)\, dx$$

$$= \frac{3}{56}\left(\frac{5x^2}{2} - \frac{x^3}{3}\right)\Big|_0^4$$

$$= \frac{3}{56}\left(\frac{(5)16}{2} - \frac{64}{3}\right)$$

$$= \frac{3}{56} \cdot \frac{56}{3} = 1$$

Hence, condition I is satisfied.
Condition II is also satisfied since

$$f(x) = \frac{3}{56}(5x - x^2) = \frac{3}{56} \cdot x \cdot (5 - x) \geqq 0$$

for all $x$ in the interval $[0, 4]$.
Thus, $f(x) = \frac{3}{56}(5x - x^2)$, for $x$ in $0 \leqq x \leqq 4$, is a density function.

**4.2
Example**

Compute the probability that the random variable $X$ with density function $\frac{3}{56}(5x - x^2)$ assumes values between 1 and 2.
To compute $P(1 \leqq X \leqq 2)$, we use (4.1). Thus

$$P(1 \leqq X \leqq 2) = \int_1^2 \frac{3}{56}(5x - x^2)\, dx = \frac{3}{56}\left[\frac{5x^2}{2} - \frac{x^3}{3}\right]\Big|_1^2$$

$$= \frac{3}{56}\left[\frac{(5)(4)}{2} - \frac{8}{3}\right] - \frac{3}{56}\left[\frac{5}{2} - \frac{1}{3}\right]$$

$$= \frac{3}{56}\left[\frac{22}{3} - \frac{13}{6}\right] = \frac{31}{112}$$

How does one obtain the density function $f(x)$? For individual random experiments, it is possible to construct them as we indicated in the example on age probabilities. However, the construction of a density function is usually a tedious and difficult task and often depends on the nature of the problem. Fortunately, several relatively simple density functions are available that can be used to fit most random experiments. As a result, in every example we discuss, the probability density function is given.

One such function is the *uniform density function* or the uniform distribution. This function is the simplest of probability functions and is one in which the random variable assumes all its values with equal probability. The density function for this random variable is

**Uniform Density
Function**

$$f(x) = \begin{cases} \dfrac{1}{b - a} & \text{if} \quad a \leqq x \leqq b \\ 0 & \text{if} \quad \text{other } x \end{cases}$$

The graph of this distribution is given in Figure 16.3.

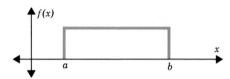

**Figure 16.3**

Notice that the function has the value zero outside the interval $a \leqq x \leqq b$.

4.3
Example

Verify that the uniform density function satisfies all the properties of a density function.

(1) The definite integral of $f(x)$ with limits of integration $a$ and $b$ is equal to 1. That is,

$$\int_a^b \frac{1}{b-a} \, dx = \frac{x}{b-a} \bigg|_a^b = \frac{b-a}{b-a} = 1$$

(II) Since $b > a$, $f(x) = 1/(b-a) > 0$, for $a < x < b$.

4.4
Example

Trains leave a terminal every 40 minutes. What is the probability that a passenger arriving at a random time to catch a train will have to wait more than 10 minutes?

Let $T$ (time) be a random variable and assume that $T$ is uniformly distributed for $0 \leq T \leq 40$. The probability that the passenger must wait at least 10 minutes is

$$P(T \geqq 10) = \int_{10}^{40} \frac{1}{40} \, dt = \frac{t}{40} \bigg|_{10}^{40} = \frac{40}{40} - \frac{10}{40} = \frac{3}{4}$$

The next density function we discuss is the exponential density function. It is a quite useful function and is used often in many applications.

**Let $X$ be a continuous random variable. Then $X$ is said to be** *exponentially distributed* **if $X$ has the density function**

Exponential
Density Function

$$f(x) = \begin{cases} \lambda e^{-\lambda x} & \text{if } x \geqq 0 \\ 0 & \text{if } x < 0 \end{cases}$$

**where $\lambda$ is a positive constant.**

The graph of the exponential density function is given in Figure 16.4.

Some situations that lead to the use of an exponential density function are listed below:

1. The life of an automobile tire where $X$ is the life expectancy in years.
2. The time between the arrival of customers at a service station where $X$ is this time.

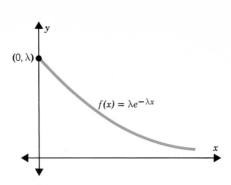

**Figure 16.4**

In general, any situation that deals with *waiting times* between successive events will lead to an exponential density function. In the exponential density function, the constant $\lambda$ plays the role of the average number of arrivals per unit time.

**4.5
Example**

Airplanes arriving at an airport follow a pattern similar to the exponential density distribution with an average of $\lambda = 15$ arrivals per hour. Determine the probability of an arrival within 0.1 hour (6 minutes).

The probability is

$$P(t \leq 0.1) = \int_0^{.1} 15e^{-15t}\, dt = -e^{-15t}\,\Big|_0^{.1} = -e^{-1.5} + 1$$

$$= 1 - .223 = .777$$

Thus, the probability of an arrival within 0.1 hour is .777.

The next example illustrates how the average $\lambda$ of an exponential density function can be calculated.

**4.6
Example**

From past data it is known that a certain machine normally produces one defective product in every 200. To detect defective products, an inspector tests a continuous stream of products and records the interval in which a defective product appears. Use an exponential density function to find the probability that after a defective product is found the next 200 are nondefective.

Let $X$ be the random variable that a product is defective starting from a defective one. The probability that the $(x + 1)^{st}$ product will be the next defective is

$$f(x) = \lambda e^{-\lambda x}$$

To determine $\lambda$ we note that when $x = 0$, $f(0) = \lambda e^{-\lambda \cdot 0} = 1/200$, since the probability that the first product selected is defective is 1/200. Thus, $\lambda = 1/200$ and the exponential density function is

$$f(x) = \frac{1}{200} e^{-x/200}$$

The probability that a defective product will be found within the first 200 items following a defective one is

$$\int_0^{200} \frac{1}{200} e^{-x/200} \, dx = -e^{-x/200} \Big|_0^{200} = -e^{-1} + 1 = .632$$

Thus, the probability that the next defective product will not be within the next 200 is $1 - .632 = .368$.

1. Show that the functions below are probability density functions over the indicated intervals.

   (a) $f(x) = \frac{4}{3} \cdot \frac{2}{(x+1)^2}$     $[0, 3]$

   (b) $f(x) = \frac{3}{250}(10x - x^2)$   $[0, 5]$
   (c) $f(x) = \frac{6}{27}(3x - x^2)$     $[0, 3]$

2. If $f(x) \geq 0$ is not a density function, we can find a constant $k$ such that $kf(x)$ satisfies the condition $\int_a^b kf(x) \, dx = 1$.

   For the functions below determine the constant $k$ that will make each one a density function over the interval indicated.
   (a) $(10x - x^2)$     $[0, 5]$
   (b) $(10x - x^2)$     $[0, 8]$

   (c) $\dfrac{1}{(x+1)^3}$     $[3, 7]$

3. The time between incoming telephone calls at a hotel switchboard has an exponential density distribution with $\lambda = 0.5$ minutes. What is the probability that there is an interval of at least 6 minutes between incoming calls?

4. The demand for an inventory item can be treated as a random variable with a density function given by

   $$f(x) = .02e^{-.02x}$$

   where $f(x)$ is the probability that $x$ items will be in demand over a one-week period. What is the probability that less than 5 items will be in demand? Less than 100? More than 10?

5. Let $T$ be the random variable that a subject in a psychological testing program will make a certain choice after $t$ seconds. If the probability density function is

   $$f(t) = .4e^{-.4t}$$

what is the probability that the subject will make the choice in less than 5 seconds?

6. Busses on a certain route run every 50 minutes. What is the probability that a person arriving at a random stop along the route will have to wait at least 30 minutes. Assume that the random variable $T$ is the time the person will have to wait and assume that $T$ is uniformly distributed.

7. A manufacturer of educational games for children finds through extensive psychological research that the average time it takes for a child in a certain age group to learn the rules of the game is predicted by a *beta probability density function,*

$$f(x) = \begin{cases} \dfrac{1}{4500}(30x - x^2) & 0 \leq x \leq 30 \\ 0 & \text{other } x \end{cases}$$

where $x$ is the time in minutes. What is the probability a child will learn how to play the game within 10 minutes? What is the probability a child will learn the game after 20 minutes? What is the probability the game is learned in at least 10 minutes, but no more than 20 minutes?

16.5
EXPECTATION,
VARIANCE, AND
STANDARD
DEVIATION

The concept of expectation, first introduced in Chapter 15, deals only with sample spaces having a finite number of outcomes. In this chapter we wish to generalize the concept of expectation using random variables defined over a continuous sample space. In addition, we introduce two measures of dispersion: the variance and the standard deviation, which are necessary for studying the normal distribution (Section 16.6).

We begin by referring to the Definition of Expectation for finite sample spaces as discussed in Chapter 15. There we defined expectation by associating both a probability and a payoff to each simple event of the sample space. These payoffs are nothing more than the values of a discrete random variable and the corresponding probability is the value of a probability function. **Thus, if $X$ is a discrete random variable with the probability distribution listed below,**

| $x$ | $x_1$ | $x_2$ | . . . | $x_n$ |
|-----|-------|-------|-------|-------|
| $P\,(X = x)$ | $f(x_1)$ | $f(x_2)$ | . . . | $f(x_n)$ |

Expected Value

**the** *expected value of X,* **or the** *mathematical expectation of X,* **is**

$$E(X) = x_1 f(x_1) + x_2 f(x_2) + \cdots + x_n f(x_n)$$

Find the expected number of men on a committee of 3 selected at random from 4 men and 3 women.

Let the random variable $X$ represent the number of men on the committee. The probability distribution of $X$ is given by

$$f(x) = \frac{\binom{4}{x}\binom{3}{3-x}}{\binom{7}{3}} \qquad x = 0, 1, 2, 3$$

Thus, for $x = 0, 1, 2, 3$, $f(x)$ assumes the following values respectively;

$$f(0) = \frac{1}{35}, \ f(1) = \frac{12}{35}, \ f(2) = \frac{18}{35}, \text{ and } f(3) = \frac{4}{35}$$

Therefore

$$E(X) = 0 \cdot \frac{1}{35} + 1 \cdot \frac{12}{35} + 2 \cdot \frac{18}{35} + 3 \cdot \frac{4}{35} = \frac{12}{7} = 1.7$$

Thus a committee with 3 members selected from 4 men and 3 women will contain on the average 1.7 men.

The expected value for a discrete random variable is the sum of the products of the random variable by the corresponding probabilities. We make the following definition when the random variable is continuous.[1]

Let $X$ be a continuous random variable with the density function $f(x)$, $a \leq x \leq b$. The *expected value of $X$* is

$$E(X) = \int_a^b x f(x)\, dx$$

Once again the expected value of the random variable $X$ is interpreted as the average value of the random variable. Thus, if $X$ is a random variable measuring heights, then $E(X)$ is the average height of the population.

In the next few examples we compute expected value using the density functions introduced earlier.

A passenger arrives at a train terminal where trains arrive every 40 minutes. Determine the expected waiting time using a uniform density function.

Let the random variable $T$ measure waiting time with uniform density function $f(t) = 1/40$, where $0 \leq T \leq 40$. The expected value $E(T)$ is

$$E(T) = \int_0^{40} t \frac{1}{40}\, dt = \frac{t^2}{80}\bigg|_0^{40} = \frac{1}{80}(40)^2 = \frac{1600}{80} = 20 \text{ minutes}$$

---

[1] The reader is referred to Appendix II, page 581, for a justification.

Show that the expected value of the random variable with a uniform density function $f(x) = 1/(b - a)$, $a \leqq x \leqq b$, is the midpoint of the interval $[a, b]$.

Let $X$ be a random variable with density function $f(x) = 1/(b - a)$, $a \leqq x \leqq b$. Then,

$$E(X) = \int_a^b x \frac{1}{b - a} \, dx = \frac{1}{2} \frac{x^2}{b - a} \Big|_a^b = \frac{1}{2} \cdot \frac{b^2 - a^2}{b - a}$$

$$= \frac{1}{2} \frac{(b - a)(b + a)}{b - a} = \frac{a + b}{2}$$

Thus, the expected value of $X$ is the midpoint of the interval $[a, b]$.

Although the expected value of a random variable $E(X)$ is a measure of the average, sometimes it does not provide us with enough information. For example, consider the two discrete random variables $X$ and $Y$ defined by Table 16.3.

**Table 16.3**

X:

| x | 4 | 6 | 8 | 10 | 12 | 14 | 16 |
|---|---|---|---|----|----|----|----|
| f(x) | 1/7 | 1/7 | 1/7 | 1/7 | 1/7 | 1/7 | 1/7 |

Y:

| y | 4 | 7 | 9 | 10 | 11 | 13 | 16 |
|---|---|---|---|----|----|----|----|
| f(y) | 1/7 | 1/7 | 1/7 | 1/7 | 1/7 | 1/7 | 1/7 |

Notice that $E(X) = E(Y) = 10$, yet the scores in each set are different; moreover, the scores for $X$ seem to be more closely clustered around 10 than those of $Y$.

Thus we need, in addition to the expected value of a random variable, another measure indicating the extent to which the scores are spread out. Such measures are called *measures of dispersion.*

The simplest measure of dispersion is the range. It is the difference between the highest value and the lowest value assumed by a random variable. For the data of Table 16.3 the range is $16 - 4 = 12$. We can see that the range is a poor measure of dispersion since it depends only on two measures and tells nothing about the rest of the scores.

Deviation from
the Mean

Another measure of dispersion is the *deviation from the mean:* the difference between the random variable $X$ and the expected value (the mean) of the random variable $E(X)$:

$$X - E(X)$$

The reason that this measure of dispersion is not widely used, however, is that, if we add all the deviations from the mean, the result is zero.

We need, therefore, a measure that will give us an idea of how much deviation is involved without having these deviations add up to zero. By squaring each deviation from the mean, adding them, and dividing by the number of scores, we obtain an average squared deviation, which is called the *variance* $\sigma^2$ of the set of scores. The formula for the variance is

$$\sigma^2 = \frac{[x_1 - E(X)]^2 + [x_2 - E(X)]^2 + \cdots + [x_n - E(X)]^2}{n}$$

where $E(X)$ is the mean (expected value) of the scores $x_1, x_2, \ldots, x_n$ and $n$ is the number of scores.

In order to apply this measure in practical situations (for instance, if our data represents dollars, we cannot talk about "squared dollars") we use the square root of the variance. This is called the *standard deviation* of $X$ and is denoted by $\sigma_x$. The formula is

$$\sigma_x = \sqrt{\frac{(x_1 - E(X))^2 + (x_2 - E(X))^2 + \cdots + (x_n - E(X))^2}{n}}$$

For the data of Table 16.3, we see that

$$\sigma_x = 4 \quad \text{and} \quad \sigma_y = 3.625$$

The fact that the standard deviation $\sigma_y$ is less than $\sigma_x$ is an indication that the values of the random variables $Y$ are more clustered around the mean than those of $X$.

We now begin to study the probability distribution of the continuous *normal* variable: the *normal distribution function*. This function is important in the field of probability and statistics, since it is an excellent model for many observed phenomenoma in nature. For example, heights of people, weights of people, test scores, coin tossing, all lead to data that have the same kind of probability distribution. This distribution is referred to as the normal distribution or the bell-shaped distribution. The bell-shaped normal distribution function evolved from the work of the famous mathematician, J. F. Carl Gauss (1777–1855) and is sometimes called a *Gaussian distribution*.

Consider an experiment in which a fair coin is tossed ten times. Find the probability distribution for tossing a head.

The probability for obtaining exactly $k$ heads is given by a binomial distribution $b(10, k; 1/2)$. Thus, from Table 9 (page 613), we obtain a distribution as given in Figure 16.5 on page 538.

If we plot these probabilities and connect the points by a smooth curve (see Figure 16.6), we obtain a density function, the normal curve.

This particular distribution for $n = 10$, and $p = 1/2$ is not a result of the choice of $n$ or $p$. As a matter of fact, the graph of any binomial probability $b(n, k; p)$ will give a normal curve. The student should verify this for the cases in which $n = 15$, $p = 1/3$; and $n = 8$, $p = 3/4$.

| No. Heads | Probability $b(10,k;1/2)$ |
|-----------|---------------------------|
| 0 | .0010 |
| 1 | .0098 |
| 2 | .0439 |
| 3 | .1172 |
| 4 | .2051 |
| 5 | .2461 |
| 6 | .2051 |
| 7 | .1172 |
| 8 | .0439 |
| 9 | .0098 |
| 10 | .0010 |

**Figure 16.5**

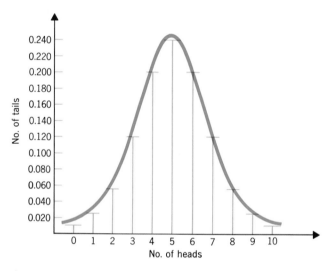

**Figure 16.6**

It can be shown that the function $f(x)$ whose graph appears in Figure 16.6 is given by

Normal
Density
Function

$$f(x) = \frac{1}{\sigma\sqrt{2\pi}}\, e^{-(x-m)^2/2\sigma^2}$$

Normal Curve

where $m$ and $\sigma > 0$ are constants. Here $f(x)$ is called a *normal density function* and its graph is called a *normal curve*.

Definition
of a Normal
Random Variable

**A random variable** $X$ **is a** *normal random variable* **if the probability assigned to the interval from** $a$ **to** $b$ **is the area from** $a$ **to** $b$ **between**

the $x$-axis and the normal density function $f(x)$. **That is,**

$$P(a \leqq X \leqq b) = \frac{1}{\sigma\sqrt{2\pi}} \int_a^b e^{-(x-m)^2/2\sigma^2} \, dx$$

where $m = E(X)$ **and** $\sigma$ **is the standard derivation** $\sigma_x$.

The standard deviation of a normal distribution plays a major role in describing the area under the normal curve. See Figure 16.7. For example, it can be shown that the area under the normal curve from $m - \sigma$ to $m + \sigma$ is approximately 68.27 percent of the total area under the curve. The area from $m - 2\sigma$ to $m + 2\sigma$ is approximately 95.45 percent of the total area under the curve. The area under the normal curve between $m - 3\sigma$ and $m + 3\sigma$ is approximately 99.73 percent of the total area.

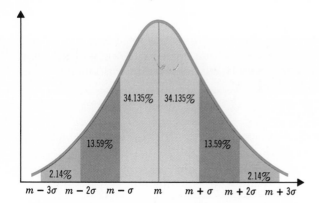

**Figure 16.7**

For example, suppose a set of normally distributed examination scores has expectation $m$ and standard deviation $\sigma$ as follows:

$$m = 100.5, \qquad \sigma = 10.31$$

Knowing this, we can infer that about 68 percent of the scores are between 90.19 and 110.81; about 95 percent have scores between 79.88 and 121.12; and about 99 percent have scores between 69.57 and 131.43.

The percent of items falling between the mean and a point determined by a fractional multiple of standard deviations can be ascertained by referring to a *normal curve table*. The use of such table will be introduced later in this chapter.

A normal curve is completely determined by $E(X)$ and $\sigma_x$. Hence, normal distributions of data with different means and different standard deviations give rise to different shapes of the normal curve. Figure 16.8 indicates how the normal curve will change if the standard deviation changes, while the mean is fixed. Notice that as the standard deviation increases, the normal curve flattens out.

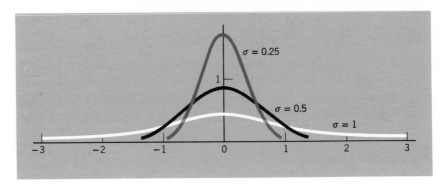

**Figure 16.8**

When a normal distribution has expected value $E(X) = 0$ and a standard deviation of $\sigma = 1$, its normal curve is called a *standard normal curve* and is denoted by $N(0, 1)$. Fortunately, every normal distribution can be changed to standard form. This is achieved by introducing a new random variable $Z$, defined as

where
$$Z = \frac{X - E(X)}{\sigma} \qquad (6.1)$$

$X =$ the "old" random variable
$E(X) =$ the expected value of the "old" $X$
$\sigma =$ the standard deviation of the "old" random variable

The new random variable $Z$ defined by (6.1) always has a zero mean and a unit standard deviation. Such random variables are said to be

Standard Score   expressed in *standard units* or *standard scores*. By expressing data in terms of standard units, it becomes possible to make a comparison of distributions. Furthermore, the total area under a standard normal curve is one.

The density function in this case reduces to

$$f(Z) = \frac{1}{\sqrt{2\pi}} e^{-(1/2)Z^2}$$

6.2
Example

A student receives a grade of 82 on a final examination in biology for which the mean is 73 and the standard deviation is 9. In his final examination in sociology, for which the mean grade is 81 and the standard deviation is 15, he receives an 89. In which examination is his relative standing higher?

In their present form, these distributions are not comparable, since they have different means and, more importantly, different

541
16.6
THE NORMAL
DISTRIBUTION

standard deviations. In order to compare the data, we transform the data to standard scores. For the biology data, the new score data for the student's examination score is

$$Z = \frac{82 - 73}{9} = \frac{9}{9} = 1$$

For the sociology data, the new score data for the students examination score is

$$Z = \frac{89 - 81}{15} = \frac{8}{15} = 0.533$$

This means the student's score in the biology exam is one standard unit above the mean, while his score in the sociology exam is 0.533 standard units above the mean. Hence, his relative standing is higher in biology.

The curve in Figure 16.8 with mean $\overline{X} = 0$ and standard deviation $\sigma = 1$ is the standard normal curve. For this curve, the areas between $Z = -1$ and 1, $Z = -2$ and 2, $Z = -3$ and 3 are equal, respectively, to 68.27 percent, 95.45 percent, and 99.73 percent of the total area under the curve, which is one. To find the areas cut off between other points, we proceed as in the following example.

Suppose, to begin with, we consider the standard normal curve illustrated in Figure 16.9. We wish to find the proportion of the area or the proportion of cases included between the two points 0.6 and 1.86 units from the mean.

6.3
Example

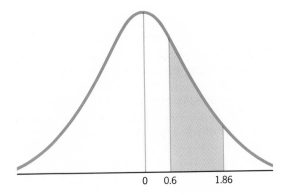

**Figure 16.9**

This problem is worked by using the normal curve table, given in Table 10 (page 618). We begin by checking the table to find the area of the curve cut off between the mean and a point equivalent to a standard score of 0.6 from the mean. This value appears in the second column of the table and is found to be

0.2257. Next we continue down the table in the lefthand column until we come to a standard score of 1.86. By looking in the column headed 0.06, we find that 0.4686 of the area is included between the mean and this point. Then the area of the curve between these two points is the difference between the two areas, 0.4686 − 0.2257, which is 0.2429. We can then state that approximately 24.29 percent of the cases fall between 0.6 and 1.86, *or that the probability* of a score falling between these two points is about 0.2429.

In the next illustration, we take two points that are on different sides of the mean. We wish to determine what proportion of the area of a normal curve falls between a standard score of −0.39 and one of 1.86 for the standard normal curve given in Figure 16.10.

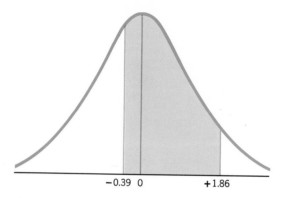

−0.39  0          +1.86

**Figure 16.10**

There are no values for negative standard scores in Table 10. As far as areas are concerned, because of the symmetry of normal curves, equal standard scores, whether positive or negative, give equal areas when taken from the mean. From the table we find that a standard score of −0.39 cuts off an area of 0.1517 between it and the mean. A standard score of 1.86 likewise includes 0.4686 of the area of the curve between it and the mean. The area included between both points is then equal to the sum of these two areas, 0.1517 + 0.4686, which is 0.6203. Thus, approximately 62.03 percent of the area is between −0.39 and 1.86. In other words, the probability of a score falling between these two points is about 0.6203.

16.6.1
Exercise

1. Draw the graph for the probability distribution of tossing a head in an experiment in which a biased coin is tossed 15 times and the probability that a head occurs is .3. *Hint:* Find $b(15, k; .3)$ for $k = 0, 1, \ldots, 15$, by using Table 9.
2. Follow the same directions as in Problem 1 for an experi-

ment in which a biased coin is tossed 8 times and the probability that heads appears is 3/4.

3. Given a normal distribution with a mean of 13.1 and a standard deviation of 9.3, find the Z score equivalent of the following scores:

$$7, 9, 13, 15, 29, 37, 41$$

4. Given the following standard scores or Z scores on a standard normal distribution, use Table 10 to find the area from the mean to each score.
   (a) 0.89      (e) −0.75
   (b) 1.10      (f) −2.31
   (c) 2.50      (g) 0.80
   (d) 3.00      (h) 3.03

5. An instructor assigns grades in an examination according to the following procedure:

      A if score exceeds $m + 1.6\sigma$
      B if score is between $m + 0.6\sigma$ and $m + 1.6\sigma$
      C if score is between $m - 0.3\sigma$ and $m + 0.6\sigma$
      D if score is between $m - 1.4\sigma$ and $m - 0.3\sigma$
      F if score is below $m - 1.4\sigma$

What percentage of each grade does this instructor give, assuming that the scores are normally distributed?

6. If the weight of 100 college students closely follows a normal distribution with a mean of 130 pounds and a standard deviation of 5.2 pounds,
   (a) How many of these students would you expect to be at least 142 pounds?
   (b) What range of weight would you expect to include the middle 70 percent of the students in this group?

7. If the average life of a certain make of clothing is 40 months with standard deviation of 7 months, what percentage of these clothes can be expected to last from 28 months to 42 months? Assume that clothing lifetime follows a normal distribution.

8. Records show that the average life expectancy of a pair of shoes is 2.2 years with a standard deviation of 1.7 years. A manufacturer guarantees that shoes lasting less than a year are replaced free. For every 1000 pairs he sells, how many pairs should he expect to replace free?

9. The attendance over a weekly period of time at a movie theater is normally distributed with a mean of 10,000 and a standard deviation of 1000 persons. Find
   (a) The range of attendance expected 75 percent of the time in the lowest 70 percent of the attendance figures.
   (b) The percentage of attendance figures that falls between 8500 and 11,000 persons.

(c) The percentage of the attendance figures that differ from the mean by 1500 persons or more.

10. Caryl, Mary, and Kathleen are vying for a position as secretary. Caryl, who is tested with group I gets a score of 76 on her test; Mary, who is tested with group II, gets a score of 89; and Kathleen, who is tested with Group III, gets a score of 21. If the average score for group I is 82, for group II is 93, and for group III is 24, and if the standard deviations for each group are 7, 2, and 9, respectively, which person has the highest relative standing?

11. In Mathematics 135, the average final grade is 75.0 and the standard deviation is 10.0. The professor's grade distribution shows that 15 students with grades from 68.0 to 82.0 received C's. Assuming the grades follow a normal distribution, how many students are in Mathematics 135?

In the remainder of this section, we consider some applications in which the distribution of the data we are dealing with is approximately a normal curve. In each of these applied problems the mean and the standard deviation are assumed to have been estimated by other techniques.

**6.4**
**Example**

Suppose that the number of customers entering a supermarket daily between 5 p.m. and 8 p.m., is a normal random variable with a mean of 276 and a standard deviation of 12. What is the probability that there will be less than 256 customers between 5 p.m. and 8 p.m.?

If $X$ is the normal random variable, we wish to find

$$P(X < 256)$$

with $m = 276$, $\sigma = 12$. Figure 16.11 illustrates the probability as an area.

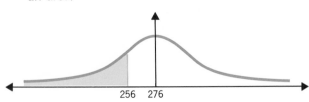

256   276

**Figure 16.11**

To compute the area, we need to transform $X$ into the standard curve. Since $m = 276$ and $\sigma = 24$, the standard score $Z$ at $X = 256$ is

$$Z = \frac{256 - 276}{24} = -\frac{20}{24} = -\frac{5}{6} = -.83$$

From Table 10, page 618, the probability that $Z$ is between 0 and .83 is .2967. The shaded area in Figure 16.11 is

$$.5000 - .2967 = .2033$$

We estimate the probability that less than 256 customers visit the supermarket is .2033. In terms of percentage, in the long run about 20% of the time, the store will have fewer customers than 256.

6.5
Example

The amount of Coke (in ounces) poured into cups by a vending machine is a normal random variable. A dial on the machine is set so that the mean is 7 ounces with standard deviation .13. What is the probability that the vending machine will pour between 6.8 and 7.3 ounces?

If $X$ is the random variable, we wish to find

$$P(6.8 \leq X \leq 7.3)$$

The standard scores at $X = 6.8$ and $X = 7.3$ are, respectively,

$$Z = \frac{6.8 - 7}{.13} = -1.54 \qquad Z = \frac{7.3 - 7}{.13} = 2.3$$

Consulting Table 10 page 618, we find that

$$P(6.8 \leq X \leq 7.3) = P(0 \leq Z \leq 1.54) + P(0 \leq Z \leq 2.3)$$
$$= .4382 + .4893 = .9275$$

Thus, the machine pours between 6.8 and 7.3 ounces of Coke about 93% of the time.

6.6
Example

Suppose the grade point average for students at a certain college is a normal random variable with mean 2.7 and standard deviation .30 and a student is placed on probation if his grade point is below 2.0. A student is selected at random. What is the probability that he is on probation?

To calculate $P(X < 2.0)$, we calculate the standard score at $X = 2.0$.

$$Z = \frac{2.00 - 2.7}{.30} = \frac{-.7}{.30} = -2.33$$

Using Table 10, the probability that a randomly selected student is on probation is .0099.

As mentioned earlier, the normal curve is a very good approximation to problems involving the use of the binomial distribution. The following example is an illustration of such a situation.

Suppose that a survey for introducing a new product is conducted and, in the course of the study, 1000 questionnaires are sent. We would like to know the probability of getting at least 210 replies, if it is assumed that the probability of a reply is .20.

The problem can be solved using the binomial distribution. We have 1000 trials and we are looking for the probability of at least 210 successes where the probability of success is .20. However, to compute this probability, we will have to find the sum of the probabilities corresponding to 210, 211, 212, ..., and 1000 successes. Evidently, this involves tremendous work. On the other hand, using the normal curve approximation, the problem is easier to solve.

Recall that the mean $m$ and standard deviation $\sigma$ of the binomial distribution are

$$m = n \cdot p = 1000 \cdot .20 = 200,$$
$$\sigma = \sqrt{npq} = \sqrt{1000 \cdot (.20)(.80)} = 12.65$$

The standard score at $X = 210$ is

$$Z = \frac{210 - 200}{12.65} = .79$$

The desired probability is

$$P(X > 210) = P(Z > .79) = .5000 - .2852 = .2148$$

This means that we expect to get at least 210 replies to 1000 questionnaires about 21 percent of the time, provided .20 is the correct estimated probability.

1. A machine produces bolts. The diameter of each bolt in inches is a random variable with mean 2.0 and standard deviation 0.011. What percentage of bolts will have diameters between 1.98 and 2.02?

2. In a small town, the monthly liquor expenditure of families with annual incomes between $8000 and $12,000 is (approximately) normally distributed with mean $35.50 and standard deviation of $4.05.
   (a) What proportion of these families have monthly liquor expenses less than $25?
   (b) Between $25 and $45?
   (c) Larger than $45?

3. The weekly salary of a worker in the car industry is considered to be a random variable with a mean of $176 and standard deviation of $22. In a large sample of workers, what percentage of workers earn between $150 and $250?

4. The scores of a math test are normally distributed with mean 65 and standard deviation 15.
   (a) What is the probability of obtaining a score between 60 and 75?

(b) Fifty students took the examination. What is the probability that at least 4 of them will score above 90?

(c) What score must a student obtain to be in the 75th percentile (25% score higher)?

5. If a spark plug has an average life of 3000 miles with standard deviation of 300 miles, what is the probability a plug will last no more than 2600 miles? What is the probability it will last over 3800 miles?

*6. An elevator is designed with a load limit of 3000 pounds and a capacity of 12 people. If the weights of all people using the elevator are normally distributed with a mean of 170 pounds and a standard deviation of 21 pounds, what is the probability that a group of 12 people will exceed the load limit?

*7. Suppose that the education level among adults in a certain state is normally distributed with mean 13.2 years and standard deviation 2.1. What is the probability that in a random survey of 100 adults you will find an average level of education between 10 and 11.5 years? More than 13 years?

*8. The annual rainfall is known to be a normal random variable with mean 24 inches and standard deviation 2 inches. For what annual rainfall in inches is the probability .15 that the mean will be exceeded?

9. According to Mendel, by cross-pollinating pure lime green peas with pure lime yellow peas, hybrid seeds are obtained. From these seeds, the resulting plants yielded 25 percent green seeds. How many hybrid seeds need to be planted so that there is a probability of 90 percent that at least 40 green seeds are obtained?

random variable
discrete random variable
continuous random variable
probability distribution function
cumulative distribution function
Poisson distribution function
density function
uniform density function

exponential density function
expected value
variance
standard deviation
normal distribution
normal density function
standard score
standard normal curve

1. Classify the following random variables as discrete or continuous. If they are discrete, state whether the sample space is infinite or finite.
   (a) X is the number of defective automobiles that come off an assembly line on a given day.
   (b) X is the age in years of voters in a local election.

2. A shipment of 1000 spark plugs from a certain manufacturer contains 3 percent that are defective or broken. Use a Poisson distribution to find the probability that at most 4 are defective or broken.

3. A fire department in a medium-sized city receives an average of 2.5 calls each minute. Use a Poisson distribution to find the probability that in a given minute no calls occur. What is the probability that exactly 4 calls will occur in a given minute?

4. Show that the function

$$f(x) = \frac{3}{688,000} (-x^2 + 200x - 5000)$$

is a probability density function over the interval $[20, 100]$.

5. A man, currently 20 years old, wishes to purchase life insurance. The company is interested in determining at what age $X$ (in years) he is likely to die. If the probability density function given in Problem 4 measures this likelihood, find the probability the man is likely to die on or before age 40. What is the probability he will die on or before age 60?

6. The average life expectancy of a dog is 14 years with a standard deviation of about 1.25 years. Assuming that the life spans of dogs are normally distributed, approximately how many dogs will die before reaching the age of 10 years, 4 months.

7. Assuming the height in inches of males over 21 years of age obeys a normal distribution, with mean 70 inches and standard deviation 3 inches, find
   (a) The probability a man selected at random is more than six feet tall.
   (b) The probability a man selected at random is between 5 feet 6 inches and 6 feet in height.

Bibliography

*Mathematics*

Dwass, Meyer, *First Steps in Probability*, McGraw-Hill, New York, 1967.
Freund, John E., *Mathematical Statistics*, Second Edition, Prentice Hall, Englewood Cliffs, N.J. 1971.
Hoel, Paul, *Introduction to Mathematical Statistics*, Third Edition, Wiley, New York, 1962.

# 17

# MATHEMATICS OF FINANCE

A knowledge of interest—whether on money borrowed or on money saved—is of ultimate importance today. The old adage "Neither a lender nor a borrower be" is not true in this age of charge accounts and golden passbook savings plans. This section gives a brief introduction into the mathematics behind the various kinds of interest on the market.

17.1
SIMPLE AND
COMPOUND
INTEREST

Very simply, *interest* is money paid for the use of money. The total amount of money borrowed (whether by an individual from a bank in the form of a loan, or by a bank from an individual in the form of a savings account) is called the *principal*. The *rate of interest* is the amount charged for the use of the principal for a given period of time (usually on a yearly or *per annum* basis). Rates of interest are generally expressed as a *percentage*.

Interest

Principal

Rate of Interest

By way of explanation, *r percent* means the ratio $r/100$. Thus,

$$5\% = \frac{5}{100} = 0.05, \qquad 10\% = \frac{10}{100} = 0.1, \qquad 100\% = \frac{100}{100} = 1$$

$$5\tfrac{3}{4}\% = \frac{5.75}{100} = \frac{575}{10,000} = 0.0575, \qquad 214\% = \frac{214}{100} = 2.14$$

**Definition of Simple Interest**  *Simple interest* **is interest computed on the principal for the entire period it is borrowed.**

**1.1 Example**  If $250 is borrowed for 9 months at a simple interest rate of 8 percent per annum, what will be the interest charged?

Here, the actual period the money is borrowed for is 9 months or 3/4 of a year. Thus, the interest charged will be the product of the principal ($250) times the annual rate of interest (0.08) times the period of time held in years (3/4). That is,

$$\text{interest charged} = \$(250)(0.08)\left(\frac{3}{4}\right) = \$15$$

In general, if a principal of $P$ dollars is borrowed at a simple interest rate $r$, expressed as a decimal expansion, for a period of $n$ years, the interest $I$ charged is

$$I = P \cdot n \cdot r$$

The amount $A$ owed at the end of a period of time is the sum of the principal and the interest. That is

$$A = P + I = P + P \cdot n \cdot r = P(1 + nr)$$

**1.2 Example**  Find the interest and amount if $500 is borrowed for 4 months at a simple interest rate of 10 percent per annum.

Here, the interest $I$ is

$$I = (\$500)\left(\frac{4}{12}\right)(0.10) = \$16.67$$

The amount $A$ due after the 4-month period is

$$A = P + I = \$500.00 + \$16.67 = \$516.67$$

**1.3 Example**  A man deposits $5000 in a bank that pays 5 percent per annum every six months. The man will withdraw $500 from his principal plus any interest accrued at each six-month period. How much total interest can he expect to receive?

Here the bank is borrowing $5000 at 5 percent interest and will pay off its debt in 10 equal installments of $500 each, every six months. The interest the bank will pay for the first six-month period is

$$I = \$5000\left(\frac{1}{2}\right)(0.05) = \$125$$

For the second six-month period, the principal is $4500. The interest is

$$I = (4500) \left(\frac{1}{2}\right) (0.05) = \$112.50$$

Continuing this way, we have

$$I = (4000) \left(\frac{1}{2}\right) (0.05) = \$100.00$$

$$. . . . . . . . . . . . . . . . . .$$

$$I = (1500) \left(\frac{1}{2}\right) (0.05) = \$37.50$$

$$I = (1000) \left(\frac{1}{2}\right) (0.05) = \$25.00$$

$$I = (500) \left(\frac{1}{2}\right) (0.05) = \$12.50$$

The total interest paid by the bank (received by the man) is

$$125.00 + 112.50 + 100.00 + \cdots + 37.50 + 25.00 + 12.50$$
$$= 12.50 + (12.50)(2) + (12.50)(3) + \cdots + (12.50)(10)$$
$$= (12.50)(1 + 2 + 3 + \cdots + 10)$$
$$= (12.50)\frac{(10)(11)}{2} = \$687.50$$

A result used in this example and worth knowing is that the sum of the first $n$ positive integers is $n(n + 1)/2$. That is,

$$1 + 2 + 3 + \cdots + n = \frac{n(n + 1)}{2}$$

If the interest due at the end of a unit payment period is added to the principal, so that the interest computed for this next unit payment period is based on this new principal amount (old principal plus interest), then the interest is said to have been *compounded*. That is, *compound interest* is simply interest paid on previously earned interest.

Quite often the term *effective rate of interest* is used. This is the equivalent annual rate of interest due to compounding. When interest is compounded annually, there is no difference between the per annum rate and the effective rate; however, when interest is compounded more than once a year, the effective rate always exceeds the per annum rate. The following example illustrates this distinction.

Compound Interest

Effective Rate
of Interest

A bank pays 5 percent per annum compounded quarterly. If $200 is placed in a savings account and the quarterly interest is left in the account, how much money is in the account after one year? What is the effective rate of interest?

1.4
Example

Here, at the first quarter (3 months), the interest earned is

$$I = (\$200)\left(\frac{1}{4}\right)(0.05) = \$2.50$$

The new principal is $P + I = 202.50$. The interest on this principal at the second quarter is

$$I = (202.50)\left(\frac{1}{4}\right)(0.05) = \$2.53$$

The interest at the third quarter on the principal of $205.03 ($202.50 + $2.53) is

$$I = (205.03)\left(\frac{1}{4}\right)(0.05) = \$2.56$$

The interest for the fourth quarter is

$$I = (207.59)\left(\frac{1}{4}\right)(0.05) = \$2.59$$

Thus, after one year, the total in the savings account is $210.18.

To find out what the effective rate of interest rate is, we use the formula $I = P \cdot n \cdot r$. The total interest paid for the one year period is $10.18 on a principal of $200. Thus

$$\$10.18 = (200)(1)(r)$$

Solving for $r$, we obtain

$$r = 0.0509$$

The effective rate of interest is thus 5.09 percent.

Let us develop a formula for computing the amount when interest is compounded. Suppose the principal is $P$, the rate of interest per payment period is $r$ (in decimal form), $n$ is the number of payment periods, and $A_n$ is the amount accrued after $n$ payment periods. Then, for the first payment period,

$$A_1 = P + Pr = P(1 + r)$$

For the second payment period, and subsequent ones,

$$A_2 = A_1 + A_1 r = A_1(1 + r) = P(1 + r)(1 + r) = P(1 + r)^2$$
$$A_3 = A_2 + A_2 r = A_2(1 + r) = P(1 + r)^3$$
$$\vdots$$
$$A_n = A_{n-1} + A_{n-1} r = A_{n-1}(1 + r) = P(1 + r)^n$$

**The amount $A_n$ accrued on a principal $P$ after $n$ payment periods at $r$ interest ($r$ in decimal form) per payment period is**

$$A_n = P(1 + r)^n \tag{1.1}$$

This formula is sometimes referred to as the *compound interest formula.*

Table 1 on page 588 gives values for $(1 + r)^n$ for typical rates of interest and number of payment periods.

In the compound interest formula (1.1), $n$ is the total number of payment periods, while $r = $ per annum rate $\div$ number of annual payments.

If \$300 is invested at 6 percent interest per annum paid (a) yearly (b) semiannually (c) quarterly (d) daily, what is the value after 4 years?

For this problem, $P = \$300$. The values of $n$ and $r$ vary depending on how often the interest is paid.

(a) Here $P = 300$, $n = 4$, $r = 0.06$. Now, we want to find $A_4$. Thus, using Table 1, we obtain

$$A_4 = \$300(1 + 0.06)^4 = (\$300)(1.262477) = 378.74$$

(b) Here, $P = \$300$, $n = 8$ (4 semi-annual payments), and $r = .03$ $(0.06 \div 2)$. We want to find $A_8$. Now

$$A_8 = \$300(1 + 0.03)^8 = (\$300)(1.26677) = \$380.03$$

(c) Here, $P = \$300$, $n = 16$ (4 quarterly payments), and $r = 0.015$ $(0.06 \div 4)$. We want to find $A_{16}$. Now

$$A_{16} = \$300(1 + 0.015)^{16} = (\$300)(1.268986) = \$380.70$$

(d) Here $P = \$300$, $n = (365)(4) = 1460$, and $r = 0.06/365 = 0.000165$.

For $A_{1460}$ we use a calculator and find

$$A_{1460} = \$300(1 + 0.000165)^{1460} = \$381.37$$

It is worth noting that although the difference between a bank's paying interest yearly and quarterly is fairly substantial, the difference between quarterly compounding and daily compounding is quite insignificant.

For computing the number of payment periods of a loan, we can use the *ordinary interest year* (based on a 360-day year) or the *exact interest year* (based on a 365-day year). In the former, each month has 30 days; in the latter, the exact number of days of the loan is used. In most problems, it will make no difference which measure of time is used; when there is an ambiguity, we shall stipulate what interest year should be used.

The compound interest formula for the amount $A_n$ accrued on a principal $P$ after $n$ payment periods at $r$ interest ($r$ in decimal form) is

$$A_n = P(1 + r)^n$$

If we solve for $P$ in the above formula, we obtain

$$P = A_n(1 + r)^{-n}$$

Present Value
In this formula, $P$ is called the *present value* of $A_n$ dollars due at the end of $n$ interest periods at a rate of $r$ per interest period. In other words, $P$ is the amount that must be invested for $n$ interest periods at a rate $r$ per interest period in order to accumulate $A_n$ dollars.

Table 2 on page 592 gives values for $(1 + r)^{-n}$ for typical rates of interest and number of payment periods.

The compound interest formula and the present value formula can be used to solve many different kinds of problems. The examples below illustrate some of these applications.

1.6
Example
How much money should be invested at 6 percent per annum so that after 4 years the amount will be $1000, when the interest is compounded (a) annually (b) quarterly (c) daily (use exact interest year for daily compounding)?

In this problem, we want to find the principal $P$ if we know the amount after 4 years, namely, $1000. Thus, we want the present value of $1000.

(a) Here, $n = 4$, $r = 0.06$, and $A_4 = \$1000$. Now, using Table 2, page 592, we have

$$P = \$1000(1.06)^{-4} = \$1000(0.792094) = \$792.09$$

(b) Here, $n = 16$, $r = 0.015$ $(0.06 \div 4)$, $A_{16} = \$1000$. Again

$$\$1000 = P(1 + 0.015)^{16}$$
$$P = \$1000(1.015)^{-16} = \$1000(0.788031) = \$788.03$$

(c) Here, $n = 365 \cdot 4 = 1460$, $r = 0.06/365 = 0.000165$ and $A_{1460} = \$1000$. Then

$$\$1000 = P(1 + 0.000165)^{1460}$$
$$P = \$1000(1.000165)^{-1460} = \$786.64$$

1.7
Example
What annual rate of interest compounded quarterly should one obtain if he wants to double his investment in five years?

Here, $P$ is the principal, $A = 2P$, and $n = 4 \cdot 5 = 20$. We want to find $r$ in the equation

$$2P = P(1 + r)^{20}$$
$$2 = (1 + r)^{20}$$
$$1 + r = \sqrt[20]{2}$$

Using Table 4 on page 596, we obtain

$$r = \sqrt[20]{2} - 1 = 1.035265 - 1 = 0.035265$$

The annual rate of interest needed to double principal in five years is $4r = 0.141060 = 14.1$ percent.

For the following two examples, a knowledge of logarithms is needed.

At 8 percent interest compounded quarterly, how long will it take for a principal to double in value?

In this problem, let $P$ denote the principal. The amount $A$ will then be $2P$. For $r = 0.08/4 = 0.02$, we need to find $n$ in the equation

$$2P = P(1 + 0.02)^n$$
$$2 = (1 + 0.02)^n$$

Using Table 3 on page 596 and the Change of Base Formula on page 315, we obtain

$$n = \log_{1.02} 2 = \frac{\log_{10} 2}{\log_{10} 1.02} = \frac{0.3010}{0.0086} = 35$$

Thus, since payments are made quarterly, principal invested at 8 percent compounded quarterly will double in $n/4 = 8.75$ years.

How long will it take a principal to double at 16 percent compounded quarterly?

Again, we want to find $n$ in the equation

$$2P = P(1 + 0.04)^n$$
$$2 = (1 + 0.04)^n$$
$$n = \frac{\log_{10} 2}{\log_{10} 1.04} = 17.7$$

Thus, principal will double in $17.7/4 = 4.425$ years if invested at 16 percent compounded quarterly.

Notice, from the results of the above two examples, that if the interest rate is doubled, the time necessary to double the principal is not halved.

1. Find the interest $I$ and amount $A$ for the following loans:
   (a) $420 for 3 months at 6 percent simple interest.
   (b) $6000 for 5 months at 7 percent simple interest.
   (c) $8000 for 18 months at 9 percent simple interest.
   (d) $400 for 10 years at 5 percent simple interest.
   (e) $60 for 2 years 3 months at 5 3/4 percent simple interest.
2. Find the principal $P$ for the following simple interest cases.

(a) The amount $A$ is $230 at 4 percent at the end of 6 months.

(b) The amount $A$ is $189.98 at 3 1/2 percent at the end of 18 months.

(c) The amount $A$ is $183.68 at 8 percent at the end of 2 years, 4 months.

3. Find the amount $A$ accrued for each of the following investments. What is the total interest earned on each investment?

    (a) $250 for 3 years at 6 percent per annum compounded

        (1) semi-annually     (2) quarterly

    (b) $3250 for 2 years 6 months at 6 percent per annum compounded

        (1) semi-annually     (2) quarterly

    (c) $4270 for 5 years 6 months at 8 percent per annum compounded

        (1) semi-annually     (2) quarterly

    (d) $60 for 18 months at 12 percent per annum compounded

        (1) semi-annually     (2) quarterly     (3) monthly

4. What is the effective rate of interest for a rate of 6 percent per annum compounded

    (1) semi-annually     (2) quarterly     (3) monthly?

5. Find the present value of the following:

    (a) The amount is $300 at the end of 3 years at 4 percent per annum compounded

        (1) annually     (2) semi-annually     (3) quarterly

    (b) The amount is $1000 at the end of 2 years at 6 percent per annum compounded

        (1) annually     (2) semi-annually     (3) quarterly

    (c) The amount is $150 at the end of 18 months at 18 percent per annum compounded

        (1) quarterly     (2) monthly

    (d) The amount is $300 at the end of 9 months at 18 percent per annum compounded

        (1) quarterly     (2) monthly

6. A man wants to borrow money for 3 months at 6 percent per annum interest payable in advance. How much should he borrow if he needs $250 immediately?

7. Easy Money Finance Company lends $500 to a man and requires him to repay in $27.50 per month installments of which $25 is for principal and $2.50 is for interest. What is the total amount of money paid to the finance company and what is the rate of interest?

8. Mr. Graff needs to borrow $300 for two years. Which of the following loans should he take: (a) 4.1 percent simple interest or (b) 4 percent per annum compounded semi-annually?

9. What rate of interest compounded semi-annually is needed to double an investment in 5 years?
10. If after two years, a $1000 investment is worth $2000, what is the annual rate of interest?
11. What rate of interest compounded quarterly is needed to double an investment in 4 years?
12. How long does it take for an investment to double at
    (a) 12 percent compounded quarterly?
    (b) 4 percent compounded quarterly?
13. Answer Problem 12 if the investment is to triple in value.

An *annuity* is a sequence of equal periodic payments. When the payments are made at the same time the interest is credited, the annuity is termed *ordinary*. We shall only concern ourselves with *ordinary annuities* in this section.

17.2
ANNUITY

Ordinary Annuity

One common example of an ordinary annuity is a life insurance policy—such as 20 payment life. In this example, 20 equal payments or premiums are paid on an annual basis, with a fixed interest paid on the anniversary date of the policy. Of course, the *payment period* could have been semi-annual, quarterly, or even monthly instead of yearly. The *term* of the annuity need not be 20 years, but could be any fixed length of time.

**The** *amount of an annuity* **is the sum of all payments made, plus all interest accumulated.**

Definition
of the Amount
of an Annuity

Find the amount of an annuity after 5 payments in which the payment is $100, paid on an annual basis at a rate of 5 percent per annum.

2.1
Example

After 5 payments, the first $100 payment will have accumulated interest compounded at 5 percent for 4 years. Its value $A_1$ after 4 years is

$$A_1 = \$100(1 + 0.05)^4 = \$100(1.215506) = \$121.55$$

The second payment of $100, made 1 year after the first payment, will accumulate interest compounded at 5 percent for 3 years. Its value $A_2$ at the end of the fifth payment is

$$A_2 = \$100(1 + 0.05)^3 = \$100(1.157625) = \$115.76$$

Similarly, the third, fourth, and fifth payments will have the values

$$A_3 = \$100(1 + 0.05)^2 = \$100(1.10250) = \$110.25$$
$$A_4 = \$100(1 + 0.05)^1 = \$100(1.05) = \$105.00$$
$$A_5 = \$100$$

The amount of the annuity after five payments is

$$A_1 + A_2 + A_3 + A_4 + A_5 = \$121.55 + \$115.76$$
$$+ \$110.25 + \$105.00 + \$100.00 = \$552.56$$

To develop a formula for the amount of an annuity, suppose \$1.00 is the payment for an annuity whose interest is $r$ percent per payment period (in decimal form) and whose term is $n$ payment periods. The first payment will accumulate the value $A_1$, compounded over $n - 1$ periods at $r$ percent per payment of an annuity whose interest is $r$ per payment period (in decimal form) and whose term is $n$ payment periods. The second payment will accumulate the value $A_2$ compounded over $n - 2$ periods at $r$ percent per payment period, and so on. Then

$$A_1 = \$1(1 + r)^{n-1}, \qquad A_2 = \$1(1 + r)^{n-2}, \ldots, A_n = \$1(1 + r)^0 = \$1$$

The total amount of the annuity, after $n$ payment periods, denoted by $s_{\overline{n}|r}$,[1] is

$$s_{\overline{n}|r} = A_1 + \cdots + A_n = (1 + r)^{n-1} + (1 + r)^{n-2} + \cdots + (1 + r) + 1$$
$$= [1 + (1 + r) + \cdots + (1 + r)^{n-1}]$$
$$= \frac{[1 + (1 + r) + \cdots + (1 + r)^{n-1}][1 - (1 + r)]}{1 - (1 + r)}$$
$$= \frac{[1 - (1 + r)^n]}{-r} = \frac{[(1 + r)^n - 1]}{r}$$

**Thus, if $P$ represents the payment in dollars made at each payment period for an annuity at $r$ percent interest per payment period, the amount $A$ of the annuity after $n$ payment periods is**

$$\boxed{A = \$P \cdot s_{\overline{n}|r}}$$

Some values for $s_{\overline{n}|r}$ are found in Table 5 on page 597.

Some values for $s_{\overline{n}|r}$ are found in Table 5 on page 597.

**2.2
Example**

Find the amount of an annuity of \$100 per year at 5 percent after 5 payments.

Here $P = \$100$ and $s_{\overline{5}|0.05} = 5.525631$. Thus, the amount $A$ is

$$A = P \cdot s_{\overline{5}|0.05} = \$100(5.525631) = \$552.56$$

**2.3
Example**

Mary decides to put aside \$100 every 3 months in a savings account that pays 5 percent quarterly. After making 7 deposits, how much money does Mary have?

This is an annuity problem in which $P = \$100$. To find the amount after 7 payments, we need to look up in Table 5 the

---

[1] $s_{\overline{n}|r}$ is sometimes read as "$s$ angle $n$ at $r$."

value of $s_{\overline{7}|0.0125}$. Now, $s_{\overline{7}|0.0125} = 7.268037$. Thus, the amount $A$ of money after seven deposits is

$$A = P \cdot s_{\overline{7}|0.0125} = \$100(7.268037) = \$726.80$$

To save for his son's college education, Mr. Graff decides to put aside every 6 months an amount of $50 in a time-deposit bank account paying 6 percent interest semi-annually. If he begins this savings program when his son is 6 months old, how much will he have saved by the time his son is 18 years old?

When his son is 18 years old, Mr. Graff will have made his 36th payment. The rate per payment period is 0.03. The principal $P$ is $50 and $s_{\overline{36}|0.03} = 63.275942$. The amount $A$ saved is

$$A = 50 \cdot s_{\overline{36}|0.03} = \$50(63.275942) = \$3163.80$$

Definition
of the Present
Value of an
Annuity

**The *present value* of an annuity is the sum of the present values of the payments.**

Thus the present value of an annuity is the amount of money needed now, so that, if it is invested at $r$ percent, $n$ equal payments can be withdrawn without any money left over.

Compute the present value of an annuity of $100 per year at 5 percent after 5 payments.

After the first payment, the present value $V_1$ is

$$V_1 = \$100(1 + 0.05)^{-1} = \$100(0.952381) = \$95.24$$

After the second payment, the present value $V_2$ for the second payment is

$$V_2 = \$100(1 + 0.05)^{-2} = \$100(0.907029) = \$90.70$$

Similarly

$$V_3 = \$100(1 + 0.05)^{-3} = \$100(0.863838) = \$86.38$$
$$V_4 = \$100(1 + 0.05)^{-4} = \$100(0.822702) = \$82.27$$
$$V_5 = \$100(1 + 0.05)^{-5} = \$100(0.783526) = \$78.35$$

The present value $V$ after 5 payments is

$$\begin{aligned} V &= V_1 + V_2 + V_3 + V_4 + V_5 \\ &= \$95.24 + \$90.70 + \$86.38 + \$82.27 + \$78.35 \\ &= \$432.94 \end{aligned}$$

Thus, a man needs $432.94 now, invested at 5 percent per annum, in order to withdraw $100 per year for the next 5 years.

| Payment | Present Value |
|---------|--------------|
| 1st | $100(1.05)^{-1} = \$95.24$ |
| 2nd | $100(1.05)^{-2} = \$90.70$ |
| 3rd | $100(1.05)^{-3} = \$86.38$ |
| 4th | $100(1.05)^{-4} = \$82.27$ |
| 5th | $100(1.05)^{-5} = \$78.35$ |
| Total | $432.94$ |

**Figure 17.1**

Figure 17.1 illustrates the results of Example 2.5.

To develop a formula for present values, suppose $1.00 is the payment for an annuity whose interest rate is $r$ percent per payment period (in decimal form) and whose term is $n$ payment periods. Then the present value $V_1$ of the first payment is

$$V_1 = (1 + r)^{-1}$$

The present value $V_2$ for the second payment is

$$V_2 = (1 + r)^{-2}$$

The present value $V_n$ for the $n$th payment is

$$V_n = (1 + r)^{-n}$$

The total present value $a_{\overline{n}|r}$[2] of the annuity is

$$a_{\overline{n}|r} = V_1 + \cdots + V_n = (1 + r)^{-1} + \cdots + (1 + r)^{-n}$$
$$= (1 + r)^{-n}[1 + (1 + r) + \cdots + (1 + r)^{n-1}]$$
$$= \frac{1 - (1 + r)^n}{1 - (1 + r)}(1 + r)^{-n} = \frac{(1 + r)^n - 1}{r(1 + r)^n}$$

**Thus, if $P$ represents the payment made in dollars, the present value $V$ of the annuity at a rate $r$ per payment period for $n$ payment periods is**

$$\boxed{V = \$P \cdot a_{\overline{n}|r}}$$

Some values for $a_{\overline{n}|r}$ are found in Table 6 on page 601.

**2.6
Example**

Find the present value of an annuity of $100 per year at 5 percent after 5 payments.

---

[2] $a_{\overline{n}|r}$ is sometimes read as "a angle $n$ at $r$."

Here, $P = \$100$ and $a_{\overline{5}|0.05} = 4.329477$. Then the present value $V$ is

$$V = \$100a_{\overline{5}|0.05} = \$100(4.329477) = \$432.95$$

A man agrees to pay $150 per month for 30 months to pay off a used car loan. If the interest of 18 percent per annum is charged monthly, how much did the car originally cost? How much interest was paid?

This is the same as asking for the present value $V$ of an annuity of $150 per month at 18 percent for 30 months. The original cost of the car is

$$V = \$150a_{\overline{30}|0.015} = \$150(24.015838)$$
$$= \$3602.38$$

The total payment is $(\$150)(30) = \$4500$. Thus the interest paid is

$$\$4500 - \$3602.38 = \$897.62$$

1. Find the amount and present value of the following annuities.
   (a) $1500 after 15 years at 6 percent compounded annually.
   (b) $600 after 10 years at 8 percent compounded semi-annually.
   (c) $9000 after 6 years at 12 percent compounded quarterly.
   (d) $10,000 after 8 years at 6 percent compounded quarterly.
   (e) $400 after 5 years at 12 percent compounded semi-annually.
2. Find the payment for the following annuities to obtain a present value of
   (a) $1000 after 5 years at 6 percent annually.
   (b) $2000 after 3 years at 12 percent semi-annually.
   (c) $6000 after 5 years at 10 percent semi-annually.
   (d) $1500 after 4 years at 12 percent quarterly.
   (e) $4000 after 12 years at 8 percent quarterly.
3. Mike each month deposits $10 in a special account paying 1/2 percent per month interest. How much is in Mike's account after 5 years?
4. A man at age 65 can expect to live for 15 years. If he can invest at 6 percent per annum compounded quarterly, how much does he need now to guarantee himself $250 every three months for the next 15 years?
5. A woman at age 65 can expect to live for 19 years. If she can invest at 6 percent per annum compounded quarterly, how much does she need now to guarantee herself $200 every three months for the next 19 years?

A loan with a fixed rate of interest is said to be *amortized,* if both principal and interest are paid by a sequence of equal payments made over equal periods of time.

When a loan of $V$ dollars is amortized at a particular rate $r$ of interest per payment period over $n$ payment periods, the question is what is the payment $P$? In other words, in amortization problems, we want to find the amount of payment $P$ which, after $n$ payment periods at $r$ percent interest per payment period, gives us a present value equal to the amount of the loan. Thus, we need to find $P$ in

$$V = P \cdot a_{\overline{n}|r}$$

Since we are interested in $P$, we can solve for $P$ obtaining

$$P = V \cdot \frac{1}{a_{\overline{n}|r}}$$

Table 7 on page 605 gives some values for $1/a_{\overline{n}|r}$.

3.1
Example

What monthly payment is necessary to pay off a loan of $800 at 18 percent per annum in two years? In three years?

For the two-year loan, $V = \$800$, $n = 24$, $r = 0.015$. Now, the monthly payment $P$ is

$$P = \$800\left(\frac{1}{a_{\overline{24}|0.015}}\right) = \$800(0.049924) = \$39.94$$

For the three-year loan, $V = \$800$, $n = 36$, $r = 0.015$ The monthly payment $P$ is

$$P = \$800\left(\frac{1}{a_{\overline{36}|0.015}}\right) = \$800(0.036152) = \$28.92$$

For the two-year loan, the total amount paid out is ($39.94)(24) = $958.56; for the three-year loan, the total amount paid out is ($26.92)(36) = $969.12. It should be clear that the longer the term of a debt, the more it costs the borrower to pay off the loan.

3.2
Example

Mr. and Mrs. Corey have just purchased a $35,000 house and have made a down payment of $10,000. They can amortize the balance ($25,000) at 9 percent for 7 years. What are the monthly payments? What is their total interest payment? After 3 years, what equity do they have in their house?

The monthly payment $P$ needed to pay off the loan of $25,000 at 9 percent for 7 years is

$$P = \$25,000\left(\frac{1}{a_{\overline{84}|0.0075}}\right)$$
$$= \$25,000(0.016089) = \$402.23$$

The total paid out for the loan is

$$(\$402.23)(84) = \$33,787.32$$

Thus, the interest on this loan amounted to $8,787.32.

After three years, (36 months), the present value of the loan is

$$(\$402.23) \cdot a_{\overline{48}|0.0075} = (\$402.23)(40.184780)$$
$$= \$16,163.52$$

Thus, the equity after three years is

$$\$25,000 - \$16,163.52 = \$8836.48$$

3.3
Example

When Mr. Nicholson died, he left an inheritance of $15,000 for his family to be paid to them over a ten-year period in equal amounts at the end of each year. If the $15,000 is invested at 6 percent, what is the annual payout to the family?

This example asks what annual payment is needed at 6 percent for 10 years to give a total of $15,000. That is, we can think of the $15,000 as a loan amortized at 6 percent for 10 years. The payment needed to pay off the loan is the yearly amount Mr. Nicholson's family will receive. Thus, the yearly payout $P$ is

$$P = (\$15,000)\left(\frac{1}{a_{\overline{10}|0.06}}\right) = (\$15,000)(0.135868)$$
$$= \$2038.02$$

Quite often, a person with a debt decides to accumulate sufficient funds to pay off his debt by agreeing to set aside enough money each month (or quarter or year) so that, when the debt becomes payable, the money set aside each month plus the interest earned equals the debt. The kind of fund created by such a plan is called a *sinking fund*. Com-  **Sinking Fund**
panies use sinking funds to accumulate capital for the purpose of purchasing new equipment.

We shall limit our discussion of sinking funds to those in which equal payments are made at equal time intervals. Usually, too, the debtor agrees to pay interest on his debt as a separate item, so that the amount necessary in a sinking fund need only equal the amount he originally borrows.

3.4
Example

A man borrows $3000 and agrees to pay interest quarterly at an annual rate of 8 percent. At the same time, he sets up a sinking fund in order to repay the loan at the end of 5 years. If the sinking fund earns interest at the rate of 6 percent compounded semi-annually, find the size of each semi-annual sinking fund deposit. Construct a table showing the growth of the sinking fund.

The quarterly interest payments due on the debt are

$$\$3000(0.02) = \$60$$

The size of the sinking deposit is calculated by using the formula

$$A = Ps_{\overline{n}|r}$$

in which $A$ represents the amount to be saved, and $P$ is the payment. Thus

$$P = \$3000\frac{1}{s_{\overline{n}|r}}$$

where $n = 10$ and $r = 0.03$. Values for $\dfrac{1}{s_{\overline{n}|r}}$ are found in Table 8 on page 609. Thus

$$P = \$3000\frac{1}{s_{\overline{10}|0.03}}$$
$$= \$3000(0.087231)$$
$$= \$261.69$$

Thus, semi-annual sinking fund payments of $261.69 are needed. The growth of the sinking fund is given in Figure 17.2.

| Payment | Interest | Sinking Fund Deposit | Total |
|---------|----------|----------------------|-------|
| 0 | — | — | — |
| 1 | —0— | 261.69 | 261.69 |
| 2 | 7.85 | 261.69 | 531.23 |
| 3 | 15.94 | 261.69 | 808.86 |
| 4 | 24.27 | 261.69 | 1094.82 |
| 5 | 32.84 | 261.69 | 1389.35 |
| 6 | 41.68 | 261.69 | 1692.72 |
| 7 | 50.78 | 261.69 | 2005.19 |
| 8 | 60.16 | 261.69 | 2327.04 |
| 9 | 69.81 | 261.69 | 2658.54 |
| 10 | 79.76 | 261.69 | 2999.99 |

**Figure 17.2**

**3.5**
**Example**

A gold mine is expected to yield an annual net return of $20,000 for the next 10 years, after which it will be worthless. An investor wants an annual return on his investment of 8 percent. If he can establish a sinking fund earning 5 percent annually, how much should he be willing to pay for the mine?

Let $A$ denote the purchase price. Then $0.08A$ represents an 8 percent return on investment. The quantity $A\,1/s_{\overline{10}|0.05}$ represents the annual payment into the sinking fund needed to obtain the amount $A$ in 10 years. The investor should be willing to pay an amount $A$ so that

$$0.08A + A\frac{1}{s_{\overline{10}|0.05}} = \$20,000$$

$$0.08A + 0.079505A = \$20,000$$

$$0.159505A = \$20,000$$

$$A = \$125,388 \text{ (rounded off to nearest dollar)}$$

1. What quarterly payment is needed to pay off a loan of $10,000 amortized after 10 years at 8 percent?
2. What monthly payment is needed to pay off a loan of $500 amortized at 1 1/2 percent per month for 2 years?
3. For the data of Example 3.2, what is Mr. and Mrs. Corey's equity after 4 years? After 6 years?
4. For Example 3.2, if Mr. and Mrs. Corey amortize their $25,000 loan at 6 percent for 8 years, what is their monthly payment?
5. In Example 3.3, if Mr. Nicholson left $15,000 to be paid over 20 years in equal yearly payments, and if this amount were invested at 8 percent, what would the annual payout be?
6. A man has a sum of $30,000 that he invests at 8 percent quarterly. What equal quarterly payments can he receive over a 10-year period? Over a 20-year period?
7. A company establishes a sinking fund to provide for the payment of $100,000 debt, maturing in 4 years. Contributions to the fund are to be made at the end of every 6 months. Find the amount of each semiannual deposit, if interest is at 8 percent compounded semi-annually. Construct a sinking fund schedule.
8. A state has $5,000,000 worth of tollway bonds that are due in 20 years. A sinking fund is established to pay off the debt. If the state can earn 5 percent annually on its money, what is the annual sinking fund deposit needed?
9. An investor wishes to know the amount he should pay for an oil well expected to yield an annual return of $30,000 for the next 30 years, after which the well will be dry. Find the amount he should pay to yield him a 10 percent annual return, if a sinking fund earns 6 percent annually.

**interest**
**simple interest**
**compound interest**
**principal**
**rate of interest**

**compound interest formula**
**annuity**
**ordinary annuity**
**payment period**
**amount of annuity**

per annum

present value of annuity

amount

amortization

effective annual rate of interest

equity

present value

sinking fund

1. Find the interest ($I$) and amount ($A$) if $400 is borrowed for 9 months at 12 percent simple interest.

2. Dan borrows $500 at 9 percent per annum simple interest for 1 year 2 months. What is the interest charged and what is the amount of the loan?

3. Find the amount of an investment of $100 after 2 years 3 months at 8 percent compounded quarterly.

4. Mike places $200 in a savings account that pays 5 percent per annum compounded quarterly. How much is in his account after 9 months?

5. Find the effective annual rate of interest for 8 percent compounded quarterly.

6. What rate of interest compounded annually should one obtain if he wants to double his investment in 10 years?

7. A car dealer offers Mike the choice of two loans:
   (a) $3000 for 3 years at 18 percent per annum simple interest;
   (b) $3000 for 3 years at 16 percent per annum compounded quarterly.
   Which loan costs Mike least?

8. (a) What annual rate of interest compounded quarterly is needed to double an investment in 5 years?
   (b) A bank pays 4 percent per annum compounded quarterly. How much should I invest now so that 2 years from now I will have $100.00 in the account?

9. Katy wants to buy a bicycle that costs $75 and will purchase it in 6 months. How much should she put in her savings account for this if she can get 6 percent per annum compounded monthly?

10. What annual rate of interest will double an investment in 6 years if the investment is placed in an account that receives interest compounded semiannually?

11. Mike decides he needs $500.00 6 years from now to buy a cheap car. If he can invest at 6 percent compounded quarterly, how much should he save every three months to buy the car?

12. Mr. and Mrs. Corey are newlyweds and want to purchase a home, but need a down payment of $10,000. If they want to buy their home in two years, how much should they save each month in their savings account that pays 6 percent per annum compounded monthly?

13. Mr. and Mrs. Corey have just purchased a $40,000 home

and made a 25 percent down payment. The balance can be amortized at 9 percent for 8 years and 4 months. What are the monthly payments? How much interest will be paid? What is their equity after 2 years?

14. Mike has just purchased a used car on time and will make equal payments of $50 per month for 18 months at 12 percent per annum charged monthly. How much did the car actually cost?

15. An inheritance of $25,000 is to be paid in equal amounts over a 5-year period at the end of each year. If the $25,000 can be invested at 8 percent per annum, what is the annual payment?

16. A mortgage of $25,000 is to be amortized at 9 percent per annum for 8 years. What are the monthly payments?

17. A state has $8,000,000 worth of construction bonds that are due in 25 years. What annual sinking fund deposit is needed if the state can earn 6 percent per annum on its money?

18. How much should Mr. Graff pay for a gold mine expected to yield an annual return of $20,000 that has a life expectancy of 20 years, if he wants to have a 15 percent annual return on his investment and he can set up a sinking fund that earns 7 percent a year?

19. Mr. Doody at age 70 is expected to live for 12 years, If he can invest at 8 percent per annum compounded quarterly, how much does he need now to guarantee himself $300 every three months for the next 12 years?

20. An oil well is expected to yield an annual net return of $25,000 for the next 15 years, after which it will run dry. An investor wants a return on his investment of 10 percent. He can establish a sinking fund earning 7 percent annually. How much should he pay for the oil well?

**Bibliography**

*Mathematics*

Kemeny, J., A. Schleifer, J. Snell, and G. Thompson, *Finite Mathematics with Business Applications*, Englewood, N.J., Prentice-Hall, 1962.

Mouzon, E., and P. Rees, *Mathematics of Finance*, Boston, Ginn, 1952.

Simpson, T., Z. Pirenian, and B. Crenshaw, *Mathematics of Finance*, Englewood, N.J., Prentice-Hall, 1951.

Tabor, O., *Mathematics of Finance*, Cambridge, Mass., Addison-Wesley, 1952.

# APPENDIX I: A Review of Algebra

A.1 Exponents
A.2 Factoring
A.3 Solving Equations
A.4 Complex Fractions
A.5 Absolute Value

In this Appendix we present a review of the basic techniques usually studied in intermediate algebra. As the student progresses through this book, he will find that the topics presented here are used extensively. This survey is meant to serve as a recollection of algebra already studied previously; it is not intended to substitute for the training of the usual algebra course.

The first topic we review is exponents. For $n$ any positive integer and $x$ any real number, we define

$$x^1 = x, \qquad x^2 = x \cdot x, \qquad x^n = \underbrace{x \cdot x \cdots x}_{n \text{ times}}$$

For $x \neq 0$ any real number,

$$x^0 = 1, \qquad x^{-1} = \frac{1}{x}, \qquad x^{-2} = \frac{1}{x^2}, \qquad x^{-n} = \frac{1}{x^n}$$

For example,

$$2^3 = 2 \cdot 2 \cdot 2 = 8 \qquad 3^{-2} = \frac{1}{3^2} = \frac{1}{9}$$

$$5x^{-2} = 5 \cdot \frac{1}{x^2} = \frac{5}{x^2} \qquad 8^0 = 1$$

$$\left(\frac{2}{3}\right)^{-2} = \frac{1}{\left(\frac{2}{3}\right)^2} = \frac{1}{\frac{4}{9}} = \frac{9}{4}$$

In the expression $x^n$, $x$ is termed the *base* and $n$ is the *exponent*.

**Laws of Exponents**

**The five Laws of Exponents are**

**I.** $x^n \cdot x^m = x^{n+m}$

**In words, when *multiplying* expressions with the *same* base, retain the base and *add* the exponents.**

**II.** $(x^n)^m = x^{n \cdot m}$

**In words, when an expression $x^n$ is raised to the power $m$, retain the base $x$ and multiply the exponents $n$ and $m$.**

**III.** $(ax)^n = a^n \cdot x^n$

**In words, if a product is raised to a power, this expression is equal to the product of each factor raised to the same power.**

**IV.** $\dfrac{x^n}{x^m} = x^{n-m}$

**In words, when *dividing* expressions with the same base, retain the base and *subtract* the exponents.**

**V.** $\left(\dfrac{x}{a}\right)^n = \dfrac{x^n}{a^n}$

As examples,

I. $x^2 \cdot x^4 = x^{2+4} = x^6, \qquad x^3 \cdot x^{-2} = x^{3+(-2)} = x^1 = x$

II. $(x^3)^4 = x^{3 \cdot 4} = x^{12}, \qquad (x^{-1})^4 = x^{-4} = \dfrac{1}{x^4}$

III. $(4x)^2 = 4^2 \cdot x^2 = 16x^2, \qquad 8x^3 = 2^3 \cdot x^3 = (2x)^3$

$\qquad (3x)^{-2} = 3^{-2} \cdot x^{-2} = \dfrac{1}{3^2} \cdot \dfrac{1}{x^2} = \dfrac{1}{9x^2}$

IV. $\dfrac{x^5}{x^3} = x^{5-3} = x^2, \qquad \dfrac{x^3}{x^5} = x^{3-5} = x^{-2} = \dfrac{1}{x^2} \qquad \dfrac{(x+1)^3}{x+1} = (x+1)^2$

V. $\left(\dfrac{x}{2}\right)^3 = \dfrac{x^3}{8}, \qquad \dfrac{x^2}{9} = \dfrac{x^2}{3^2} = \left(\dfrac{x}{3}\right)^2$

The Laws of Exponents as stated above are valid for integer exponents. By properly defining the meaning of $x^{p/q}$, $p$, $q \neq 0$ integers, they will also be valid for a rational number exponents. First, we introduce the notion of a *q*th root.

**Recall that the *q*th root of $x$, $\sqrt[q]{x}$, is a symbol for the number, which raised to the power $q$, equals $x$. If $x$ is positive, then $\sqrt[q]{x}$ is positive.**

For example,

$$\sqrt[3]{8} = 2 \quad \text{since} \quad 2^3 = 8; \quad \sqrt[2]{64} = 8 \quad \text{since} \quad 8^2 = 64$$

Here $\sqrt[3]{x}$ is the *cube root* of $x$ and $\sqrt[2]{x}$ is the *square root* of $x$. (Usually, we abbreviate square roots by $\sqrt{\phantom{x}}$, dropping the 2.)

Of course, no meaning is assigned to even roots of negative numbers since any real number raised to an even power is positive. For example, $\sqrt{4} = 2$, whereas $\sqrt{-4}$ has no meaning in the set of real numbers. Of course, $\sqrt[3]{27} = 3$ while $\sqrt[3]{-64} = -4$ since $(-4)^3 = -64$. Thus, meaning is given to odd roots of negative numbers. Finally, following the usual convention, even roots of positive numbers are *always* positive. Thus, even though $(2)^2 = 4$ and $(-2)^2 = 4$ in computing $\sqrt{4}$, we only take the positive root. That is, $\sqrt{4} = 2$.

Now we define $x^{p/q}$ as

$$x^{p/q} = (x^{1/q})^p = (\sqrt[q]{x})^p \quad \text{or} \quad x^{p/q} = (x^p)^{1/q} = \sqrt[q]{x^p}$$

With this definition, the Laws of Exponents are preserved for rational exponents.

As examples,

$$\sqrt[3]{x^2} = x^{2/3}$$
$$\sqrt{8} = \sqrt{4 \cdot 2} = \sqrt{4} \cdot \sqrt{2} = 2\sqrt{2}$$
$$\sqrt{x} \cdot \sqrt[3]{x} = x^{1/2} \cdot x^{1/3} = x^{1/2+1/3} = x^{5/6} = \sqrt[6]{x^5}$$
$$27^{1/3} = \sqrt[3]{27} = 3$$
$$(-32)^{1/5} = \sqrt[5]{-32} = -2$$
$$(\sqrt{x+2})^2 = [(x+2)^{1/2}]^2 = (x+2)^1 = x+2$$

Express each of the following as a single number.

1. $3^3$
2. $4^2$
3. $2^{-3}$
4. $4^{-2}$
5. $(\frac{1}{2})^3$
6. $(\frac{2}{3})^{-3}$
7. $(343)^{1/3}$
8. $(81)^{1/4}$
9. $(-243)^{1/5}$
10. $(-32)^{3/5}$
11. $2^{-1} + 4^{-1}$
12. $16^{1/2} + 8^{1/3}$
13. $(3^{-2})(3^4)$
14. $(9^{-3/2})(9^{1/2})$
15. $\dfrac{(2^{-2})(2^4)}{2^5}$
16. $\dfrac{(3^{-3/2})(3^{5/2})}{3^{1/2}}$
17. $(\sqrt{2})(\sqrt[4]{32})$
18. $(\sqrt[3]{3})(\sqrt{27})$
19. $\sqrt{\frac{81}{16}}$

Simplify each of the following expressions and write your answer using only positive exponents.

20. $x^4 \cdot x^2$

21. $\dfrac{(2^3)x^2}{x^5}$

22. $(ax^2)(3x^3)$

23. $\dfrac{(2x)^3}{(3x)^2}$

24. $(\sqrt{x} + 2)^4$

25. $\sqrt{x^3} \cdot \sqrt{x}$

26. $\sqrt[3]{(x+1)^2} \cdot \sqrt[3]{(x+1)^4}$

27. $\left(\dfrac{1}{\sqrt{x}}\right)^{-2}$

28. $x^{-1} + x^{-2}$

29. $4x^0 + x^{-1}$

## The Distributive Law

$$a \cdot (b + c) = ab + ac$$

plays a dual role in algebra. For example, to expand an expression such as $2(x + 5)$, we use the Distributive Law

$$2(x + 5) = 2x + 10$$

Also, to factor expressions such as $x^2 - x$ and $3x + 9$, we use the Distributive Law

$$x^2 - x = x(x - 1), \qquad 3x + 9 = 3(x + 3)$$

A further application of the Distributive Law enables us to find the following useful products:

(I)  $(x + a)^2 = x^2 + 2ax + a^2$
(II)  $(x + a)(x - a) = x^2 - a^2$
(III)  $(x + a)(x + b) = x^2 + (a + b)x + ab$

We arrive at these laws by using the Distributive Law. Thus, in (I), we have

$$(x + a)^2 = (x + a)(x + a) = x(x + a) + a(x + a)$$
$$= x \cdot x + x \cdot a + a \cdot x + a \cdot a$$
$$= x^2 + ax + ax + a^2 = x^2 + 2ax + a^2$$

It is well to note that the square of a sum has three terms, the middle term being $2ax$.

The derivation of (II) and (III) is left to the reader. See Problem 29 of Exercise A.2, page 574.

Examples of the above rules follow.

$$(x + 2)^2 = x^2 + 2(2x) + 2^2 = x^2 + 4x + 4$$
$$(x - 3)^2 = x^2 - 2(3x) + (-3)^2 = x^2 - 6x + 9$$
$$(x - 2)(x + 2) = x^2 - (2)^2 = x^2 - 4$$
$$(x + 1)(x + 3) = x^2 + x + 3x + 3 = x^2 + 4x + 3$$
$$(x - 2)(x - 3) = x^2 - 2x - 3x + 6 = x^2 - 5x + 6$$

If we read the laws (I), (II), and (III) from right to left, we have rules for factoring.

Factor

(a) $x^2 + 6x + 9$     (b) $x^2 - 9$     (c) $x^2 + 7x + 12$

(a) Here from (I)

$$x^2 + 6x + 9 = (x + 3)^2$$

(b) By (II)

$$x^2 - 9 = (x - 3)(x + 3)$$

The formula II is sometimes referred to as the *difference of two squares*.

(c) By (III)

$$x^2 + 7x + 12 = (x + 3)(x + 4)$$

We obtain these factors by trial and error, keeping in mind that we want to find a product that equals 12 (i.e., $4 \cdot 3$) whose sum is also 7 (i.e., $4 + 3$).

Some additional factoring principles are listed below.

(IV) $x^3 - a^3 = (x - a)(x^2 + ax + a^2)$
(V) $x^3 + a^3 = (x + a)(x^2 - ax + a^2)$
(VI) $(x + a)^3 = x^3 + 3ax^2 + 3a^2x + a^3$

For example,

$$x^3 - 8 = (x - 2)(x^2 + 2x + 4)$$
$$x^3 + 1 = (x + 1)(x^2 - x + 1)$$
$$(x + 2)^3 = x^3 + 6x^2 + 12x + 8$$

Find the following products.

1. $(x + 1)^2$
2. $(x + 4)(x - 4)$
3. $(x + 6)(x + 1)$
4. $(3x - 7)^2$
5. $(x + \sqrt{2})(x - \sqrt{2})$
6. $(2x + 5)(3x - 1)$
7. $(4x + 1)(x - 3)$
8. $(9x + 2)^2$
9. $(x + 1)^3$
10. $(x - 2)^3$
11. $(x - 1)(x^2 + x + 1)$
12. $(x + 2)(x^2 - 2x + 4)$
13. $(2x - 3)^3$

Factor the following expressions

14. $x^2 - 4$
15. $x^2 - 6x + 9$
16. $x^2 + 7x + 6$
17. $x^2 - 5$
18. $x^2 - 16$
19. $6x^2 + 13x - 5$
20. $x^2 - 7x + 12$
21. $9x^2 + 12x + 4$
22. $x^3 + 27$
23. $8x^3 - 1$
24. $4x^2 - 1$
25. $27x^3 + 1$
26. $x^3 + 3x^2 + 3x + 1$

27. Simplify

    (a) $(x + h)^2 - x^2$     (b) $(x + h)^3 - x^3$

28. Use $x = 9$, $a = 4$, and $b = 1$ to convince yourself of the following statements.

    (a) $\dfrac{x + a}{x} \neq a$            (b) $\dfrac{ax + b}{x} \neq a + b$

    (c) $(x + a)^2 \neq x^2 + a^2$    (d) $\sqrt{x + a} \neq \sqrt{x} + \sqrt{a}$

29. Verify laws (II) and (III) by repeated use of the Distributive Law on page 572.

---

**A.3
SOLVING
EQUATIONS**

To *solve an equation* means to find those values of the variable(s) that make a given statement true. The values, if any, are called *solutions* of the equation.

**Solution**

For example, the solution of the equation

$$x + 4 = 0$$

is $x = -4$, since $-4 + 4 = 0$. The solution of

$$2x - 6 = 0$$

is $x = 3$, since $(2)(3) - 6 = 0$.

**3.1
Example**

Solve the equation

$$2x - \frac{1}{4} = \frac{x}{3}$$

First we combine all like terms. Then,

$$2x - \frac{x}{3} - \frac{1}{4} = 0$$

$$\left(2 - \frac{1}{3}\right)x - \frac{1}{4} = 0$$

$$\frac{5}{3}x - \frac{1}{4} = 0$$

Next, we isolate the variable term on the left and the constant term on the right.

$$\frac{5}{3}x = \frac{1}{4}$$

Multiply by 3/5.

$$\frac{3}{5}\left(\frac{5}{3}x\right) = \left(\frac{3}{5}\right)\cdot\left(\frac{1}{4}\right) \qquad \text{or} \qquad x = \frac{3}{20}$$

When an expression can be factored, the Product Law is a useful tool.

**The Product Law states that whenever the product of two quantities is zero, at least one of the factors is zero. That is,**

$$\text{if } A \cdot B = 0, \quad \text{then } A = 0 \text{ or } B = 0 \text{ or both.}$$

Solve the equations

(a) $x^2 + 6x + 9 = 0$   (b) $x^2 - 9 = 0$   (c) $x^2 + 7x + 12 = 0$

(a) Here we factor the left side, obtaining

$$(x + 3)^2 = 0 \quad \text{or} \quad x + 3 = 0 \quad \text{or} \quad x = -3$$

Thus, $-3$ is the solution of the equation.

(b) We factor $x^2 - 9$ obtaining

$$(x - 3)(x + 3) = 0$$

By the Product Law

$$x - 3 = 0 \quad \text{or} \quad x + 3 = 0$$

$$x = 3 \quad \text{or} \quad x = -3$$

This equation has two solutions: 3 and $-3$.

(c) Factoring $x^2 + 7x + 12$, we find

$$(x + 3)(x + 4) = 0$$

By the Product Law

$$x + 3 = 0 \quad \text{or} \quad x + 4 = 0$$

The solutions are $-3$ and $-4$.

When the expression given in an equation cannot be factored, other techniques are required to find solutions. See, for example, the discussion in Chapter 2, page 54, where a formula is given for solving the quadratic equation.

Solve each of the following equations.

1. $2x + 8 = 0$
2. $2(2x - 3) = 5$
3. $3x - 7 = 2x$
4. $3x - \frac{1}{2} = x/2$
5. $x/2 + \frac{1}{3} = \frac{4}{3}$
6. $4 + x/3 = 1 - x$
7. $x/3 - x/6 = 1$
8. $2x^2 + x - 6 = 0$
9. $x^3 - 1 = 0$
10. $x^2 + 7x - 8 = 0$
11. $x^2 - 16 = 0$
12. $x^4 - 9x^2 = 0$
13. $(2x)^5 = 32$
14. $2x^5 = 64$
15. $x^2 - x - 12 = 0$
16. $x^3 - 6x^2 + 9x = 0$

In this section we review simplification of algebraic expressions. Of importance is the rule for adding two ratios; namely,

$$\frac{A}{B} + \frac{C}{D} = \frac{AD + BC}{BD}, \qquad B \neq 0, D \neq 0$$

For example,

$$\frac{x}{2} + \frac{3}{x} = \frac{x^2 + 6}{2x}$$

**4.1
Example**

Write the expression

$$\frac{3x}{x + 1} + \frac{2}{1 - x}, \qquad x \neq 1, x \neq -1$$

as a single ratio.
   Here,

$$\frac{3x}{x + 1} + \frac{2}{1 - x} = \frac{3x}{x + 1} + \frac{-2}{-(1 - x)} = \frac{3x}{x + 1} + \frac{-2}{x - 1}$$

$$= \frac{3x(x - 1) + (-2)(x + 1)}{(x + 1)(x - 1)} = \frac{3x^2 - 3x - 2x - 2}{(x + 1)(x - 1)}$$

$$= \frac{3x^2 - 5x - 2}{(x + 1)(x - 1)}$$

**4.2
Example**

Write

$$\frac{2}{x + h} - \frac{2}{x}, \qquad x \neq 0, h \neq 0$$

as a single ratio.
   Here

$$\frac{2}{x + h} - \frac{2}{x} = \frac{2x - 2(x + h)}{(x + h) \cdot x} = \frac{2x - 2x - 2h}{(x + h) \cdot x} = \frac{-2h}{(x + h) \cdot x}$$

**4.3
Example**

Write the expression

$$\frac{1}{\sqrt{x}} + \sqrt{x}$$

as a single ratio.

$$\frac{1}{\sqrt{x}} + \sqrt{x} = \frac{1}{x^{1/2}} + x^{1/2}$$

$$= \frac{1 + x^{1/2} \cdot x^{1/2}}{x^{1/2}} = \frac{1 + x}{x^{1/2}} = \frac{1 + x}{\sqrt{x}}$$

Rationalize the numerator

$$\frac{\sqrt{x + h} - \sqrt{x}}{h}$$

Here we rationalize the numerator by multiplying numerator and denominator by $\sqrt{x + h} + \sqrt{x}$. Then

$$\frac{\sqrt{x + h} - \sqrt{x}}{h} = \left[\frac{\sqrt{x + h} - \sqrt{x}}{h}\right]\frac{[\sqrt{x + h} + \sqrt{x}]}{[\sqrt{x + h} + \sqrt{x}]}$$

$$= \frac{x + h - x}{h[\sqrt{x + h} + \sqrt{x}]} = \frac{h}{h[\sqrt{x + h} + \sqrt{x}]}$$

$$= \frac{1}{\sqrt{x + h} + \sqrt{x}}$$

Solve the equation

$$\sqrt{x + 1} - \frac{1}{\sqrt{x + 1}} = 0$$

We write the left-hand side as a single ratio. Then,

$$\sqrt{x + 1} - \frac{1}{\sqrt{x + 1}} = \frac{x + 1 - 1}{\sqrt{x + 1}} = \frac{x}{\sqrt{x + 1}} = 0$$

The only solution is $x = 0$, since a ratio equals zero only when its numerator equals zero.

---

1. Write each of the following expressions as a single ratio.

   (a) $\dfrac{2}{3x - 3} + \dfrac{x + 1}{x^2}$    (b) $\dfrac{5}{3x} + \dfrac{1}{x + 1}$

   (c) $\dfrac{7}{x + h} - \dfrac{7}{x}$    (d) $\dfrac{x}{3} + \dfrac{2x - 5}{6}$

2. Rationalize the numerator of each of the following expressions.

   (a) $\dfrac{\sqrt{2x + 5} + \sqrt{2x}}{5}$    (b) $\dfrac{\sqrt{x + 4} - \sqrt{x}}{2}$

3. Write as a single ratio.

   (a) $x^{-1/4} + x^{1/4}$    (b) $\sqrt{2x + 3} - \dfrac{1}{\sqrt{2x + 3}}$

   (c) $\dfrac{1}{(x + h)^2} - \dfrac{1}{x^2}$

---

We now introduce the concept of *absolute value of a real number*. The absolute value of a number is the magnitude of that number, the non-negative value of that number. Thus, the absolute value of 5 is 5; the absolute value of $-6$ is 6. A definition of absolute value is given next.

**Definition of Absolute Value**

**The** *absolute value of a real number* x, **denoted by the** $|x|$, **is defined as**

$$x \text{ if } x \geq 0; \qquad -x \text{ if } x < 0$$

For example, since $-4 < 0$, then

$$|-4| = -(-4) = 4$$

Also,

$$|8| = 8, \qquad |0| = 0, \qquad |-15| = 15$$

**5.1 Example**

Find the set of all $x$ for which

$$|x + 4| = 13$$

Here there are two possibilities; either $x + 4 \geq 0$ or else $x + 4 < 0$. In the first instance, we have

$$|x + 4| = x + 4 = 13 \qquad \text{or} \qquad x = 9$$

In the second case, if $x + 4 < 0$, we have

$$|x + 4| = -(x + 4) = 13 \qquad \text{or} \qquad x = -17$$

Thus, the solutions are 9 and $-17$.

Some properties obeyed by absolute value are
(I) The absolute value of *any* real number is always non-negative; that is,

$$|x| \geq 0$$

(II) The absolute value of the product $|x \cdot y|$ of two real numbers equals the product of their absolute values $|x| \cdot |y|$; that is

$$|x \cdot y| = |x| \cdot |y|$$

(III) The absolute value of the sum $|x + y|$ of two real numbers never exceeds the sum of their absolute values $|x| + |y|$; that is,

$$|x + y| \leq |x| + |y|$$

(IV) The square of the absolute value of $x$ equals $x^2$; that is,

$$|x|^2 = x^2$$

The following example serves as an illustration of these four properties.

(I) $|-5| = 5 \geq 0, \qquad |0| = 0 \geq 0, \qquad |6| = 6 \geq 0$
(II) $|(-5)(-2)| = |10| = 10$ and $|-5| \cdot |-2| = 5 \cdot 2 = 10$
(III) $|-5 + 4| = |-1| = 1 \leq |-5| + |4| = 5 + 4 = 9$
(IV) $|-3|^2 = 3^2 = 9$ and $(-3)^2 = 9$

A geometric interpretation of the absolute value of a real number $x$ is that it measures the distance from the origin 0 to the point $x$. This means that the quantity $|x - a|$ measures the distance from $a$ to $x$.

For example, if $|x - 3| = 6$, then $x$ lies either 6 units to the right or 6 units to the left of 3. See Figure A.1.

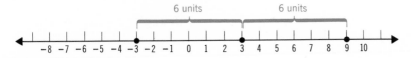

**Figure A.1**

That is, the solutions of $|x - 3| = 6$ are $-3$ and 9.

If we ask for all $x$ obeying $|x - 3| \leq 6$, we are asking for all points $x$ whose distance from 3 is less than or equal to 6. Clearly, from Figure A.1, the solution set is all $x$ from $-3$ to 9 inclusive. It is convenient to use the notation

$$-3 \leq x \leq 9$$

to symbolize the set of real numbers $x$ from $-3$ to 9 inclusive.

Find the solution set for

$$|x| < 7$$

Here we are asked to find all values of $x$, whose distance from the origin 0 is less than 7. From Figure A.1, it is clear that any $x$ between $-7$ and 7 satisfies the condition cited in Example 5.3. Then, the solution set is

$$\{x | -7 < x < 7\}$$

In general, if $|x| \leq a$, $a > 0$, then $x$ must obey

$$-a \leq x \leq a$$

and $\qquad$ if $|x| < a, \qquad a > 0$, then,

$$-a < x < a$$

Find all $x$ for which

$$|x + 3| < 6$$

Here think of $x + 3$ as a single unknown quantity so that by following the same pattern as in Example 5.3, we obtain

$$-6 < x + 3 < 6$$

If we add $-3$ to each term in the above inequality, we find

$$-6 + (-3) < (x + 3) + (-3) < 6 + (-3) \qquad \text{or} \qquad -9 < x < 3$$

The solution set is $\{x \mid -9 < x < 3\}$.

The terminology introduced next is important for the study of the calculus.

**Definition of Closed Interval; Open Interval**   **Let $a$ and $b$ be two real numbers with $a < b$. A** *closed interval* $[a, b]$ **is the set of all real numbers** $x$ **from $a$ to $b$,** *inclusive.* **That is,**

$$[a, b] = \{x \mid a \leq x \leq b\}$$

**An** *open interval* $(a, b)$ **consists of all real numbers** $x$ **between $a$ and $b$,** *exclusive of* **both $a$ and $b$. That is,**

$$(a, b) = \{x \mid a < x < b\}$$

**Finally, the** *half-open or half-closed or semi-open or semi-closed inter-vals* **are defined by**

$$[a, b) = \{x \mid a \leq x < b\}$$
$$(a, b] = \{x \mid a < x \leq b\}$$

See Figure A.2.

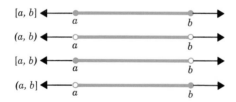

**Figure A.2**

We use an open circle ○ to mean that a point is not a member of the set while a darkened spot ● is used when a point is a member of the set.

Find the solution set for each of the following; and graph the solution

1. $|x| < 5$
2. $|x| \leq 3$
3. $|x - 3| < 4$
4. $|x| < 6$
5. $|x| \leq 4$
6. $|x + 2| \leq 6$
7. $|2x - 4| + 5 \leq 9$
8. $|3x - 7| \leq 10$

# APPENDIX II: The Riemann Integral

In this Appendix we provide a rationale for interpreting the definite integral $\int_a^b f(x)\,dx$ of a nonnegative function $y = f(x)$ as the area bounded by $y = f(x)$, the x-axis, $x = a$, $x = b$.

The area of a rectangle is given as the product of its base by its height. But what precisely is the area under a curve and how do we go about measuring it?

We begin by considering Figure A.3. Clearly, the area $A$ bounded by $y = f(x)$, the x-axis, $x = a$, $x = b$, lies between the area of the rectangle $r_1$, and the area of the rectangle $R_1$. That is,

$$\text{area } r_1 < A < \text{area } R_1$$

But these are not very good approximations to the area $A$. A better approximation can be obtained by selecting a value between $a$ and $b$, say $x_1$, and forming additional rectangular strips. See Figure A.4. Under these conditions we see that

$$\text{area } r_1 + \text{area } r_2 < A < \text{area } R_1 + \text{area } R_2$$

Suppose we select two values between $a$ and $b$, say $x_1$ and $x_2$, and form the corresponding rectangles. See Figure A.5.

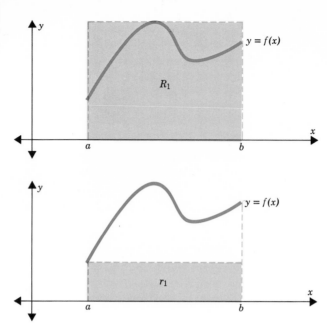

**Figure A.3**

Under these conditions, we have

$$\text{area } r_1 + \text{area } r_2 + \text{area } r_3 < A < \text{area } R_1 + \text{area } R_2 + \text{area } R_3$$

As we move from Figure A.3 to Figure A.5, we see that the more values we select between $a$ and $b$, the better is our approximation for $A$.

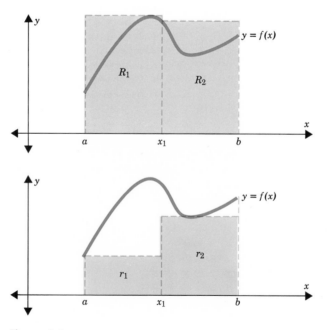

**Figure A.4**

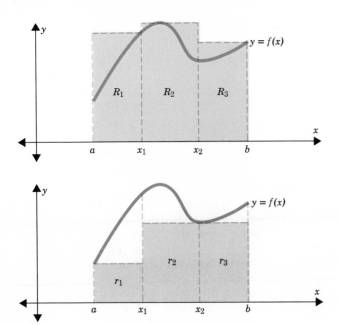

**Figure A.5**

Suppose we choose $n - 1$ values between $a$ and $b$, say $x_1, x_2, \ldots, x_{n-1}$ and form the corresponding rectangles. See Figure A.6.
Here

$$\text{area } r_1 + \text{area } r_2 + \cdots + \text{area } r_n < A < \text{area } R_1$$
$$+ \text{area } R_2 + \cdots + \text{area } R_n$$

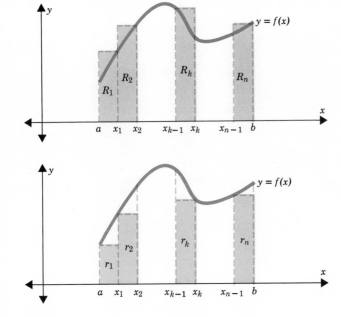

**Figure A.6**

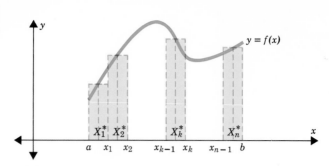

**Figure A.7**

The area of each rectangle is the product of its height by its base. Compare the areas $r_1$ and $R_1$. Their bases are the same $(x_1 - a)$ and the height of $R_1$ is larger than the height of $r_1$. The area between $y = f(x)$, the x-axis, $x = a$, and $x = x_1$, may be approximated by a rectangle with base $(x_1 - a)$ and height $f(X_1^*)$ where $X_1^*$ is some value between $a$ and $x_1$. Repeat this argument for each pair of rectangles $r_1$, $R_1$ and $r_2$, $R_2$ and $r_3$, $R_3$, etc. See Figure A.7.

The area $A$, then, is approximated by

$$A \approx f(X_1^*)(x_1 - a) + f(X_2^*)(x_2 - x_1) + \cdots + f(X_n^*)(b - x_{n-1})$$

To obtain the actual area $A$, we let the number of values chosen between $a$ and $b$ get arbitrary large; that is, we let $n \to +\infty$. Then

$$\text{area } A = \lim_{n \to +\infty} [f(X_1^*)(x_1 - a) + f(X_2^*)(x_2 - x_1) + \cdots + f(X_n^*)(b - x_{n-1})]$$

This limit, if it exists, is the area $A$ bounded by $y = f(x)$, the x-axis, $x = a$, $x = b$, and is called the *Riemann integral from a to b of* $f(x)$. We write

$$\int_a^b f(x)\, dx.$$

The general procedure for defining the Riemann integral $\int_a^b f(x)\, dx$ for a continuous function follows.

We begin by considering a continuous function $y = f(x)$ whose domain is $\{x \mid a \leq x \leq b\}$. See Figure A.8.

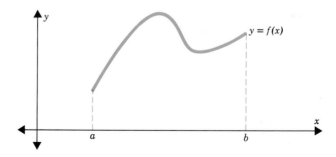

**Figure A.8**

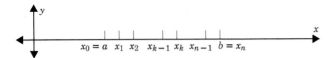

**Figure A.9**

Concentrate on the interval $[a, b]$. Suppose we partition or divide this interval into $n$ subintervals. Although there are no restrictions as to how this partition should be made, to make our notation as efficient as possible, we shall label each point of the subdivision by using a subscript. Thus, the point $a = x_0$ is the initial point, the first point of the subdivision is $x_1$, the second $x_2, \ldots$, and the $n$th point is $b = x_n$. See Figure A.9.

The original interval $[a, b]$ consists of $n$ subintervals and the length of each one is

$$\text{first,} \qquad \text{second,} \qquad \text{third,} \ldots,$$
$$\Delta x_1 = x_1 - x_0, \qquad \Delta x_2 = x_2 - x_1, \qquad \Delta x_3 = x_3 - x_2, \ldots,$$
$$\text{kth,} \ldots, \qquad\qquad \text{nth}$$
$$\Delta x_k = x_k - x_{k-1}, \ldots, \qquad \Delta x_n = x_n - x_{n-1}$$

We use the symbol $\Delta$, to denote the largest such length. (The value of $\Delta$, of course, depends on how the partition itself has been chosen.) We call $\Delta$ the *norm* of the partition.

Next, we concentrate on the function. Pick a value in each subinterval (you may select a value in the interval or either end point, if you wish) and evaluate the function at this value. To fix our ideas, let $X_k^*$ denote the value so chosen. The corresponding value of the function is $f(X_k^*)$. This represents the height of the function at $X_k^*$.

Multiply $f(X_1^*)$ times $\Delta x_1 = x_1 - x_0, f(X_2^*)$ times $\Delta x_2 = x_2 - x_1, \ldots, f(X_n^*)$ times $\Delta x_n = x_n - x_{n-1}$, and add up these products. The result is the sum

$$f(X_1^*) \Delta x_1 + f(X_2^*) \Delta x_2 + \ldots, + f(X_n^*) \Delta x_n$$

This is called a *Riemann sum* for the function $f$ on $[a, b]$.

Finally, we take the limit of this sum as the norm $\Delta \to 0$. If this limit exists, it is called the *Riemann integral of $f(x)$ from $a$ to $b$;* that is,

$$\int_a^b f(x)\, dx = \lim_{\Delta \to 0} [f(X_1^*) \Delta x_1 + f(X_2^*) \Delta x_2 + \cdots + f(X_n^*) \Delta x_n]$$

Compute, by using Riemann sums,         *Example*

$$\int_0^1 x\, dx$$

Choose a partition that divides the interval $[0, 1]$ in $n$ subintervals of equal length. This requires that each subinterval be of length $1/n$. The partition is

$$x_0 = 0, x_1 = \frac{1}{n}, \qquad x_2 = \frac{2}{n}, \ldots, x_k = \frac{k}{n}, \ldots, x_n = \frac{n}{n} = 1$$

**Figure A.10**

See Figure A.10.

The norm $\Delta$ of this partition is

$$\Delta = \frac{1}{n}$$

Next, we select a point $X_k^*$ in each subinterval. Suppose we agree to select the right end point of each subinterval. Then,

$$X_1^* = \frac{1}{n}, \qquad X_2^* = \frac{2}{n}, \ldots, X_n^* = 1$$

The Riemann sum for $f(x) = x$ is

$$f(X_1^*)\,\Delta x_1 + f(X_2^*)\,\Delta x_2 + \cdots + f(X_n^*)\,\Delta x_n$$

$$= \frac{1}{n} \cdot \frac{1}{n} + \frac{2}{n} \cdot \frac{1}{n} + \cdots + \frac{n}{n} \cdot \frac{1}{n}$$

$$= \frac{(1 + 2 + \cdots + n)}{n} \frac{1}{n}$$

But

$$1 + 2 + \cdots + n = \frac{n(n + 1)}{2}$$

Thus, the Riemann sum reduces to

$$\frac{n(n + 1)}{2n^2} = \frac{n^2 + n}{2n^2}$$

If we compute the limit of this quantity as $\Delta \to 0$, observing that since $\Delta = 1/n$, $\Delta \to 0$ and $n \to +\infty$ mean the same thing, we have

$$\int_0^1 x\,dx = \lim_{\Delta \to 0} [f(X_1^*)\,\Delta x_1 + f(X_2^*)\,\Delta x_2 + \cdots + f(X_n^*)\,\Delta x_n]$$

$$= \lim_{n \to +\infty} \frac{n^2 + n}{2n^2} = \lim_{n \to +\infty} \frac{1 + \dfrac{1}{n}}{2} = \frac{1}{2}$$

Since the evaluation of Riemann sums requires knowing some sums, we list common sums below. These should be used when the student does the problems in the exercises.

1. $1 + 2 + 3 + \cdots + n = \dfrac{n(n + 1)}{2}$

2. $1^2 + 2^2 + 3^2 + \cdots + n^2 = \dfrac{n(n + 1)(2n + 1)}{6}$

3. $1^3 + 2^3 + 3^3 + \cdots + n^3 = \dfrac{n^2(n + 1)^2}{4}$

The procedure outlined above for evaluating a Riemann integral by using the limit of a Riemann sum is long and tedious. The next result, the Fundamental Property of the Integral Calculus, provides a relatively straightforward technique for evaluating Riemann integrals.

**Theorem Fundamental Property of the Integral Calculus**
**If $y = f(x)$ is a continuous function on $[a, b]$ and if it has an antiderivative $F(x)$ on $[a, b]$, the Riemann integral of $f(x)$ from $a$ to $b$ is**

$$\int_a^b f(x)\, dx = F(b) - F(a)$$

Compute by the use of the Fundamental Property of Integral Calculus:

Example

$$\int_0^1 x\, dx$$

Here $F(x) = x^2/2$. Thus,

$$\int_0^1 x\, dx = F(1) - F(0) = \frac{1}{2} - \frac{0}{2} = \frac{1}{2}$$

Observe that this result is the same as the one obtained by using Riemann sums in the previous Example.

> In each of the following, evaluate the integral by the technique of Riemann sums, using a partition that divides the interval into $n$ equal parts and choosing the point $X^*$ as the right end point of each subinterval. Check your answer by using the Fundamental Property of the Integral Calculus.
>
> Exercise
>
> 1. $\displaystyle\int_0^1 3\, dx$   3. $\displaystyle\int_0^1 x^2\, dx$
>
> 2. $\displaystyle\int_0^2 x\, dx$   4. $\displaystyle\int_0^1 x^3\, dx$

# Tables

**Table 1**
$(1 + r)^n$
$r$ = rate of interest per payment period; $n$ = number of payment periods

| n | ¼% | ½% | ¾% | 1% | 1¼% |
|---|---|---|---|---|---|
| 1 | 1.002500 | 1.005000 | 1.007500 | 1.010000 | 1.012500 |
| 2 | 1.005006 | 1.010025 | 1.015056 | 1.020100 | 1.025156 |
| 3 | 1.007519 | 1.015075 | 1.022669 | 1.030301 | 1.037971 |
| 4 | 1.010038 | 1.020151 | 1.030339 | 1.040604 | 1.050945 |
| 5 | 1.012563 | 1.025251 | 1.038067 | 1.051010 | 1.064082 |
| 6 | 1.015094 | 1.030378 | 1.045852 | 1.061520 | 1.077383 |
| 7 | 1.017632 | 1.035529 | 1.053696 | 1.072135 | 1.090850 |
| 8 | 1.020176 | 1.040707 | 1.061599 | 1.082857 | 1.104486 |
| 9 | 1.022726 | 1.045911 | 1.069561 | 1.093685 | 1.118292 |
| 10 | 1.025283 | 1.051140 | 1.077583 | 1.104622 | 1.132271 |
| 11 | 1.027846 | 1.056396 | 1.085664 | 1.115668 | 1.146424 |
| 12 | 1.030416 | 1.061678 | 1.093807 | 1.126825 | 1.160755 |
| 13 | 1.032992 | 1.066986 | 1.102010 | 1.138093 | 1.175264 |
| 14 | 1.035574 | 1.072321 | 1.110276 | 1.149474 | 1.189955 |
| 15 | 1.038163 | 1.077683 | 1.118603 | 1.160969 | 1.204890 |
| 16 | 1.040759 | 1.083071 | 1.126992 | 1.172579 | 1.219890 |
| 17 | 1.043361 | 1.088487 | 1.135445 | 1.184304 | 1.235138 |
| 18 | 1.045969 | 1.093929 | 1.143960 | 1.196147 | 1.250577 |
| 19 | 1.048584 | 1.099399 | 1.152540 | 1.208109 | 1.266210 |
| 20 | 1.051205 | 1.104896 | 1.161134 | 1.220190 | 1.282037 |
| 21 | 1.053833 | 1.110420 | 1.169893 | 1.232392 | 1.298063 |
| 22 | 1.056468 | 1.115972 | 1.178667 | 1.244716 | 1.314288 |
| 23 | 1.059109 | 1.121552 | 1.187507 | 1.257163 | 1.330717 |
| 24 | 1.061757 | 1.127160 | 1.196414 | 1.269735 | 1.347351 |
| 25 | 1.064411 | 1.132796 | 1.205387 | 1.282432 | 1.364193 |
| 26 | 1.067072 | 1.138460 | 1.214427 | 1.295256 | 1.381245 |
| 27 | 1.069740 | 1.144152 | 1.223535 | 1.308209 | 1.398511 |
| 28 | 1.072414 | 1.149873 | 1.232712 | 1.321291 | 1.415992 |
| 29 | 1.075096 | 1.155622 | 1.241957 | 1.334504 | 1.433692 |
| 30 | 1.077783 | 1.161400 | 1.251272 | 1.347849 | 1.451613 |
| 31 | 1.080478 | 1.167207 | 1.260656 | 1.361327 | 1.469758 |
| 32 | 1.083179 | 1.173043 | 1.270111 | 1.374941 | 1.488130 |
| 33 | 1.085887 | 1.178908 | 1.279637 | 1.388690 | 1.506732 |
| 34 | 1.088602 | 1.184803 | 1.289234 | 1.402577 | 1.525566 |
| 35 | 1.091323 | 1.190727 | 1.298904 | 1.416603 | 1.544636 |
| 36 | 1.094051 | 1.196681 | 1.308645 | 1.430769 | 1.563944 |
| 37 | 1.096786 | 1.202664 | 1.318460 | 1.445076 | 1.583493 |
| 38 | 1.099528 | 1.208677 | 1.328349 | 1.459527 | 1.603287 |
| 39 | 1.102277 | 1.214721 | 1.338311 | 1.474122 | 1.623328 |
| 40 | 1.105033 | 1.220794 | 1.348349 | 1.488864 | 1.643619 |
| 41 | 1.107796 | 1.226898 | 1.358461 | 1.503752 | 1.664165 |
| 42 | 1.110565 | 1.233033 | 1.368650 | 1.518790 | 1.684967 |
| 43 | 1.113341 | 1.239198 | 1.378915 | 1.533978 | 1.706029 |
| 44 | 1.116125 | 1.245394 | 1.389256 | 1.549318 | 1.727354 |
| 45 | 1.118915 | 1.251621 | 1.399676 | 1.564811 | 1.748946 |
| 46 | 1.121712 | 1.257879 | 1.410173 | 1.580459 | 1.770808 |
| 47 | 1.124517 | 1.264168 | 1.420750 | 1.596263 | 1.792943 |
| 48 | 1.127328 | 1.270489 | 1.431405 | 1.612226 | 1.815355 |
| 49 | 1.130146 | 1.276842 | 1.442141 | 1.628348 | 1.838047 |
| 50 | 1.132972 | 1.283226 | 1.452957 | 1.644632 | 1.861022 |

| n | ¼% | ½% | ¾% | 1% | 1¼% |
|---|---|---|---|---|---|
| 51 | 1.135804 | 1.289642 | 1.463854 | 1.661078 | 1.884285 |
| 52 | 1.138644 | 1.296090 | 1.474833 | 1.677688 | 1.907839 |
| 53 | 1.141490 | 1.302571 | 1.485894 | 1.694466 | 1.931687 |
| 54 | 1.144344 | 1.309083 | 1.497038 | 1.711410 | 1.955833 |
| 55 | 1.147205 | 1.315629 | 1.508266 | 1.728525 | 1.980281 |
| 56 | 1.150073 | 1.322207 | 1.519578 | 1.745810 | 2.005034 |
| 57 | 1.152948 | 1.328818 | 1.530975 | 1.763268 | 2.030097 |
| 58 | 1.155830 | 1.335462 | 1.542457 | 1.780901 | 2.055473 |
| 59 | 1.158720 | 1.342139 | 1.554026 | 1.798770 | 2.081167 |
| 60 | 1.161617 | 1.348850 | 1.565681 | 1.816697 | 2.107181 |
| 61 | 1.164521 | 1.355594 | 1.577424 | 1.834864 | 2.133521 |
| 62 | 1.167432 | 1.362372 | 1.589254 | 1.853212 | 2.160190 |
| 63 | 1.170351 | 1.369184 | 1.601174 | 1.871744 | 2.187192 |
| 64 | 1.173277 | 1.376030 | 1.613182 | 1.890462 | 2.214532 |
| 65 | 1.176210 | 1.382910 | 1.625281 | 1.909366 | 2.242214 |
| 66 | 1.179150 | 1.389825 | 1.637471 | 1.928460 | 2.270242 |
| 67 | 1.182098 | 1.396774 | 1.649752 | 1.947745 | 2.298620 |
| 68 | 1.185053 | 1.403758 | 1.662125 | 1.967222 | 2.327352 |
| 69 | 1.188016 | 1.410777 | 1.674591 | 1.986894 | 2.356444 |
| 70 | 1.190986 | 1.417831 | 1.687151 | 2.006763 | 2.385900 |
| 71 | 1.193963 | 1.424920 | 1.699804 | 2.026831 | 2.415724 |
| 72 | 1.196948 | 1.432044 | 1.712553 | 2.047099 | 2.445920 |
| 73 | 1.199941 | 1.439205 | 1.725397 | 2.067570 | 2.476494 |
| 74 | 1.202941 | 1.446401 | 1.738337 | 2.088246 | 2.507450 |
| 75 | 1.205948 | 1.453633 | 1.751375 | 2.109128 | 2.538793 |
| 76 | 1.208963 | 1.460901 | 1.764510 | 2.130220 | 2.570528 |
| 77 | 1.211985 | 1.468205 | 1.777744 | 2.151522 | 2.602660 |
| 78 | 1.215015 | 1.475546 | 1.791077 | 2.173037 | 2.635193 |
| 79 | 1.218053 | 1.482924 | 1.804510 | 2.194767 | 2.668133 |
| 80 | 1.221098 | 1.490339 | 1.818044 | 2.216715 | 2.701485 |
| 81 | 1.224151 | 1.497790 | 1.831679 | 2.238882 | 2.735253 |
| 82 | 1.227211 | 1.505279 | 1.845417 | 2.261271 | 2.769444 |
| 83 | 1.230279 | 1.512806 | 1.859257 | 2.283884 | 2.804062 |
| 84 | 1.233355 | 1.520370 | 1.873202 | 2.306723 | 2.839113 |
| 85 | 1.236438 | 1.527972 | 1.887251 | 2.329790 | 2.874602 |
| 86 | 1.239529 | 1.535611 | 1.901405 | 2.353088 | 2.910534 |
| 87 | 1.242628 | 1.543289 | 1.915666 | 2.376619 | 2.946916 |
| 88 | 1.245735 | 1.551006 | 1.930033 | 2.400385 | 2.983752 |
| 89 | 1.248849 | 1.558761 | 1.944509 | 2.424389 | 3.021049 |
| 90 | 1.251971 | 1.566555 | 1.959092 | 2.448633 | 3.058812 |
| 91 | 1.255101 | 1.574387 | 1.973786 | 2.473119 | 3.097048 |
| 92 | 1.258239 | 1.582259 | 1.988589 | 2.497850 | 3.135761 |
| 93 | 1.261384 | 1.590171 | 2.003503 | 2.522829 | 3.174958 |
| 94 | 1.264538 | 1.598122 | 2.018530 | 2.548057 | 3.214645 |
| 95 | 1.267699 | 1.606112 | 2.033669 | 2.573537 | 3.254828 |
| 96 | 1.270868 | 1.614143 | 2.048921 | 2.599273 | 3.295513 |
| 97 | 1.274046 | 1.622213 | 2.064288 | 2.625266 | 3.336707 |
| 98 | 1.277231 | 1.630325 | 2.079770 | 2.651518 | 3.378416 |
| 99 | 1.280424 | 1.638476 | 2.095368 | 2.678033 | 3.420646 |
| 100 | 1.283625 | 1.646669 | 2.111084 | 2.704814 | 3.463404 |

# Table 1 (continued)

| n | 1½% | 1¾% | 2% | 2½% | 3% |
|---|---|---|---|---|---|
| 1 | 1.015000 | 1.017500 | 1.020000 | 1.025000 | 1.030000 |
| 2 | 1.030225 | 1.035306 | 1.040400 | 1.050625 | 1.060900 |
| 3 | 1.045678 | 1.053424 | 1.061208 | 1.076891 | 1.092727 |
| 4 | 1.061364 | 1.071859 | 1.082432 | 1.103813 | 1.125509 |
| 5 | 1.077284 | 1.090617 | 1.104081 | 1.131408 | 1.159274 |
| 6 | 1.093443 | 1.109702 | 1.126162 | 1.159693 | 1.194052 |
| 7 | 1.109845 | 1.129122 | 1.148686 | 1.188686 | 1.229874 |
| 8 | 1.126493 | 1.148882 | 1.171659 | 1.218403 | 1.266770 |
| 9 | 1.143390 | 1.168987 | 1.195093 | 1.248863 | 1.304773 |
| 10 | 1.160541 | 1.189444 | 1.218994 | 1.280085 | 1.343916 |
| 11 | 1.177949 | 1.210260 | 1.243374 | 1.312087 | 1.384234 |
| 12 | 1.195618 | 1.231439 | 1.268242 | 1.344889 | 1.425761 |
| 13 | 1.213552 | 1.252989 | 1.293607 | 1.378511 | 1.468534 |
| 14 | 1.231756 | 1.274917 | 1.319479 | 1.412974 | 1.512590 |
| 15 | 1.250232 | 1.297228 | 1.345868 | 1.448298 | 1.557967 |
| 16 | 1.268986 | 1.319929 | 1.372786 | 1.484506 | 1.604706 |
| 17 | 1.288020 | 1.343028 | 1.400241 | 1.521618 | 1.652848 |
| 18 | 1.307341 | 1.366531 | 1.428246 | 1.559659 | 1.702433 |
| 19 | 1.326951 | 1.390445 | 1.456811 | 1.598650 | 1.753506 |
| 20 | 1.346855 | 1.414778 | 1.485947 | 1.638616 | 1.806111 |
| 21 | 1.367058 | 1.439537 | 1.515666 | 1.679582 | 1.860295 |
| 22 | 1.387564 | 1.464729 | 1.545980 | 1.721571 | 1.916103 |
| 23 | 1.408377 | 1.490361 | 1.576899 | 1.764611 | 1.973586 |
| 24 | 1.429503 | 1.516443 | 1.608437 | 1.808726 | 2.032794 |
| 25 | 1.450945 | 1.542981 | 1.640606 | 1.853944 | 2.093778 |
| 26 | 1.472710 | 1.569983 | 1.673418 | 1.900293 | 2.156591 |
| 27 | 1.494800 | 1.597457 | 1.706886 | 1.947800 | 2.221289 |
| 28 | 1.517222 | 1.625413 | 1.741024 | 1.996495 | 2.287928 |
| 29 | 1.539981 | 1.653858 | 1.775845 | 2.046407 | 2.356565 |
| 30 | 1.563080 | 1.682800 | 1.811362 | 2.097568 | 2.427262 |
| 31 | 1.586526 | 1.712249 | 1.847589 | 2.150007 | 2.500080 |
| 32 | 1.610324 | 1.742213 | 1.884541 | 2.203757 | 2.575083 |
| 33 | 1.634479 | 1.772702 | 1.922231 | 2.258851 | 2.652335 |
| 34 | 1.658996 | 1.803724 | 1.960676 | 2.315322 | 2.731905 |
| 35 | 1.683881 | 1.835290 | 1.999889 | 2.373205 | 2.813862 |
| 36 | 1.709140 | 1.867407 | 2.039887 | 2.432535 | 2.898278 |
| 37 | 1.734778 | 1.900087 | 2.080685 | 2.493349 | 2.985227 |
| 38 | 1.760798 | 1.933338 | 2.122299 | 2.555682 | 3.074783 |
| 39 | 1.787210 | 1.967172 | 2.164745 | 2.619574 | 3.167027 |
| 40 | 1.814018 | 2.001597 | 2.208040 | 2.685064 | 3.262038 |
| 41 | 1.841229 | 2.036625 | 2.252200 | 2.752190 | 3.359899 |
| 42 | 1.868847 | 2.072266 | 2.297244 | 2.820995 | 3.460696 |
| 43 | 1.896880 | 2.108531 | 2.343189 | 2.891520 | 3.564517 |
| 44 | 1.925333 | 2.145430 | 2.390053 | 2.963808 | 3.671452 |
| 45 | 1.954213 | 2.182975 | 2.437854 | 3.037902 | 3.781596 |
| 46 | 1.983526 | 2.221177 | 2.486611 | 3.113851 | 3.895044 |
| 47 | 2.013279 | 2.260048 | 2.536343 | 3.191697 | 4.011895 |
| 48 | 2.043478 | 2.299599 | 2.587070 | 3.271489 | 4.132252 |
| 49 | 2.074130 | 2.339842 | 2.638812 | 3.353277 | 4.256219 |
| 50 | 2.105242 | 2.380789 | 2.691588 | 3.437109 | 4.381906 |

| n | 1½% | 1¾% | 2% | 2½% | 3% |
|---|---|---|---|---|---|
| 51 | 2.136821 | 2.422453 | 2.745420 | 3.523036 | 4.515423 |
| 52 | 2.168873 | 2.464846 | 2.800328 | 3.611112 | 4.650886 |
| 53 | 2.201406 | 2.507980 | 2.856335 | 3.701390 | 4.790412 |
| 54 | 2.234428 | 2.551870 | 2.913461 | 3.793925 | 4.934125 |
| 55 | 2.267944 | 2.596528 | 2.971731 | 3.888773 | 5.082148 |
| 56 | 2.301963 | 2.641967 | 3.031165 | 3.985992 | 5.234613 |
| 57 | 2.336493 | 2.688201 | 3.091788 | 4.085642 | 5.391651 |
| 58 | 2.371540 | 2.735245 | 3.153624 | 4.187783 | 5.553401 |
| 59 | 2.407113 | 2.783112 | 3.216697 | 4.292478 | 5.720003 |
| 60 | 2.443220 | 2.831816 | 3.281031 | 4.399790 | 5.891603 |
| 61 | 2.479868 | 2.881373 | 3.346651 | 4.509784 | 6.068351 |
| 62 | 2.517066 | 2.931797 | 3.413584 | 4.622529 | 6.250402 |
| 63 | 2.554822 | 2.983103 | 3.481856 | 4.738092 | 6.437914 |
| 64 | 2.593144 | 3.035308 | 3.551493 | 4.856544 | 6.631051 |
| 65 | 2.632042 | 3.088426 | 3.622523 | 4.977958 | 6.829982 |
| 66 | 2.671522 | 3.142473 | 3.694973 | 5.102407 | 7.034882 |
| 67 | 2.711595 | 3.197466 | 3.768873 | 5.229967 | 7.245928 |
| 68 | 2.752269 | 3.253422 | 3.844250 | 5.360716 | 7.463306 |
| 69 | 2.793553 | 3.310357 | 3.921135 | 5.494734 | 7.687205 |
| 70 | 2.835456 | 3.368288 | 3.999558 | 5.632103 | 7.917822 |
| 71 | 2.877988 | 3.427233 | 4.079549 | 5.772905 | 8.155356 |
| 72 | 2.921158 | 3.487210 | 4.161140 | 5.917228 | 8.400017 |
| 73 | 2.964975 | 3.548236 | 4.244363 | 6.065158 | 8.652017 |
| 74 | 3.009450 | 3.610330 | 4.329250 | 6.216787 | 8.911578 |
| 75 | 3.054592 | 3.673511 | 4.415835 | 6.372207 | 9.178925 |
| 76 | 3.100411 | 3.737797 | 4.504152 | 6.531512 | 9.454293 |
| 77 | 3.146917 | 3.803209 | 4.594235 | 6.694800 | 9.737922 |
| 78 | 3.194120 | 3.869765 | 4.686120 | 6.862170 | 10.030060 |
| 79 | 3.242032 | 3.937486 | 4.779842 | 7.033724 | 10.330961 |
| 80 | 3.290663 | 4.006392 | 4.875439 | 7.209567 | 10.640890 |
| 81 | 3.340023 | 4.076504 | 4.972948 | 7.389806 | 10.960117 |
| 82 | 3.390123 | 4.147842 | 5.072407 | 7.574552 | 11.288920 |
| 83 | 3.440975 | 4.220430 | 5.173855 | 7.763915 | 11.627588 |
| 84 | 3.492590 | 4.294287 | 5.277332 | 7.958013 | 11.976416 |
| 85 | 3.544978 | 4.369437 | 5.382878 | 8.156964 | 12.335708 |
| 86 | 3.598153 | 4.445902 | 5.490536 | 8.360888 | 12.705779 |
| 87 | 3.652125 | 4.523706 | 5.600347 | 8.569910 | 13.086953 |
| 88 | 3.706907 | 4.602870 | 5.712354 | 8.784158 | 13.479561 |
| 89 | 3.762511 | 4.683421 | 5.826601 | 9.003762 | 13.883948 |
| 90 | 3.818944 | 4.765380 | 5.943133 | 9.228856 | 14.300466 |
| 91 | 3.876233 | 4.848775 | 6.061995 | 9.459577 | 14.729480 |
| 92 | 3.934376 | 4.933628 | 6.183235 | 9.696066 | 15.171365 |
| 93 | 3.993392 | 5.019967 | 6.306900 | 9.938468 | 15.626506 |
| 94 | 4.053293 | 5.107816 | 6.433038 | 10.186930 | 16.095301 |
| 95 | 4.114092 | 5.197203 | 6.561699 | 10.441603 | 16.578160 |
| 96 | 4.175804 | 5.288154 | 6.692933 | 10.702643 | 17.075505 |
| 97 | 4.238441 | 5.380697 | 6.826791 | 10.970209 | 17.587770 |
| 98 | 4.302017 | 5.474859 | 6.963327 | 11.244464 | 18.115403 |
| 99 | 4.366547 | 5.570669 | 7.102594 | 11.525576 | 18.658865 |
| 100 | 4.432046 | 5.668156 | 7.244645 | 11.813715 | 19.218631 |

**Table 1 (continued)**

| n | 3½% | 4% | 4½% | 5% | 5½% |
|---|---|---|---|---|---|
| 1 | 1.035000 | 1.040000 | 1.045000 | 1.050000 | 1.055000 |
| 2 | 1.071225 | 1.081600 | 1.092025 | 1.102500 | 1.113025 |
| 3 | 1.108718 | 1.124864 | 1.141166 | 1.157625 | 1.174241 |
| 4 | 1.147523 | 1.169859 | 1.192519 | 1.215506 | 1.238825 |
| 5 | 1.187686 | 1.216653 | 1.246182 | 1.276282 | 1.306960 |
| 6 | 1.229255 | 1.265319 | 1.302260 | 1.340096 | 1.378843 |
| 7 | 1.272279 | 1.315932 | 1.360862 | 1.407100 | 1.454679 |
| 8 | 1.316809 | 1.368569 | 1.422101 | 1.477455 | 1.534687 |
| 9 | 1.362897 | 1.423321 | 1.486095 | 1.551328 | 1.619094 |
| 10 | 1.410599 | 1.480244 | 1.552969 | 1.628895 | 1.708144 |
| 11 | 1.459970 | 1.539454 | 1.622853 | 1.710339 | 1.802092 |
| 12 | 1.511069 | 1.601032 | 1.695881 | 1.795856 | 1.901207 |
| 13 | 1.563956 | 1.665073 | 1.772196 | 1.885649 | 2.005774 |
| 14 | 1.618695 | 1.731676 | 1.851945 | 1.979932 | 2.116091 |
| 15 | 1.675349 | 1.800943 | 1.935282 | 2.078928 | 2.232476 |
| 16 | 1.733986 | 1.872981 | 2.022370 | 2.182875 | 2.355263 |
| 17 | 1.794676 | 1.947900 | 2.113377 | 2.292018 | 2.484802 |
| 18 | 1.857489 | 2.025816 | 2.208479 | 2.406619 | 2.621466 |
| 19 | 1.922501 | 2.106849 | 2.307860 | 2.526950 | 2.765647 |
| 20 | 1.989789 | 2.191123 | 2.411714 | 2.653298 | 2.917757 |
| 21 | 2.059431 | 2.278768 | 2.520241 | 2.785963 | 3.078963 |
| 22 | 2.131512 | 2.369911 | 2.633652 | 2.925261 | 3.247537 |
| 23 | 2.206114 | 2.464715 | 2.752166 | 3.071524 | 3.426152 |
| 24 | 2.283328 | 2.563304 | 2.876014 | 3.225100 | 3.614590 |
| 25 | 2.363245 | 2.665836 | 3.005434 | 3.386355 | 3.813392 |
| 26 | 2.445959 | 2.772470 | 3.140679 | 3.555673 | 4.023125 |
| 27 | 2.531567 | 2.883368 | 3.282010 | 3.733456 | 4.244401 |
| 28 | 2.620172 | 2.998703 | 3.429700 | 3.920129 | 4.477843 |
| 29 | 2.711878 | 3.118651 | 3.584037 | 4.116136 | 4.724124 |
| 30 | 2.806794 | 3.243397 | 3.745318 | 4.321942 | 4.983951 |
| 31 | 2.905031 | 3.373133 | 3.913857 | 4.538039 | 5.258068 |
| 32 | 3.006708 | 3.508059 | 4.089981 | 4.764941 | 5.547262 |
| 33 | 3.111942 | 3.648381 | 4.274030 | 5.003188 | 5.852362 |
| 34 | 3.220860 | 3.794316 | 4.466362 | 5.253348 | 6.174242 |
| 35 | 3.333590 | 3.946089 | 4.667376 | 5.516015 | 6.513825 |
| 36 | 3.450266 | 4.103932 | 4.877376 | 5.791816 | 6.872085 |
| 37 | 3.571025 | 4.268090 | 5.096861 | 6.081407 | 7.250050 |
| 38 | 3.696011 | 4.438813 | 5.326219 | 6.385477 | 7.648803 |
| 39 | 3.825372 | 4.616366 | 5.565899 | 6.704751 | 8.069487 |
| 40 | 3.959260 | 4.801020 | 5.816365 | 7.039989 | 8.513309 |
| 41 | 4.097834 | 4.993061 | 6.078101 | 7.391988 | 8.981541 |
| 42 | 4.241258 | 5.192784 | 6.351616 | 7.761587 | 9.475525 |
| 43 | 4.389702 | 5.400495 | 6.637438 | 8.149667 | 9.996679 |
| 44 | 4.543341 | 5.616515 | 6.936123 | 8.557150 | 10.546496 |
| 45 | 4.702358 | 5.841175 | 7.248248 | 8.985008 | 11.126554 |
| 46 | 4.866941 | 6.074822 | 7.574420 | 9.434258 | 11.738514 |
| 47 | 5.037284 | 6.317815 | 7.915269 | 9.905971 | 12.384132 |
| 48 | 5.213589 | 6.570528 | 8.271456 | 10.401269 | 13.065260 |
| 49 | 5.396064 | 6.833349 | 8.643671 | 10.921333 | 13.783849 |
| 50 | 5.584927 | 7.106683 | 9.032636 | 11.467400 | 14.541961 |

| n | 3½% | 4% | 4½% | 5% | 5½% |
|---|---|---|---|---|---|
| 51 | 5.780399 | 7.390950 | 9.439105 | 12.040770 | 15.341768 |
| 52 | 5.982713 | 7.686588 | 9.863865 | 12.642808 | 16.185566 |
| 53 | 6.192108 | 7.994052 | 10.307739 | 13.274948 | 17.075772 |
| 54 | 6.408832 | 8.313814 | 10.771587 | 13.938696 | 18.014939 |
| 55 | 6.633141 | 8.646366 | 11.256308 | 14.635631 | 19.005761 |
| 56 | 6.865301 | 8.992221 | 11.762842 | 15.367412 | 20.051079 |
| 57 | 7.105586 | 9.351910 | 12.292170 | 16.135783 | 21.153887 |
| 58 | 7.354282 | 9.725986 | 12.845318 | 16.942572 | 22.317351 |
| 59 | 7.611682 | 10.115026 | 13.423357 | 17.789700 | 23.544805 |
| 60 | 7.878091 | 10.519627 | 14.027408 | 18.679185 | 24.839769 |
| 61 | 8.153824 | 10.940412 | 14.658641 | 19.613145 | 26.205957 |
| 62 | 8.439207 | 11.378028 | 15.318280 | 20.593802 | 27.647284 |
| 63 | 8.734580 | 11.833149 | 16.007603 | 21.623492 | 29.167885 |
| 64 | 9.040290 | 12.306475 | 16.727945 | 22.704667 | 30.772118 |
| 65 | 9.356700 | 12.798734 | 17.480703 | 23.839900 | 32.464585 |
| 66 | 9.684185 | 13.310684 | 18.267334 | 25.031895 | 34.250137 |
| 67 | 10.023131 | 13.843111 | 19.089364 | 26.283490 | 36.133895 |
| 68 | 10.373941 | 14.396835 | 19.948386 | 27.597664 | 38.121259 |
| 69 | 10.737029 | 14.972709 | 20.846063 | 28.977547 | 40.217928 |
| 70 | 11.112825 | 15.571617 | 21.784136 | 30.426425 | 42.429914 |
| 71 | 11.501773 | 16.194482 | 22.764422 | 31.947746 | 44.763559 |
| 72 | 11.904336 | 16.842261 | 23.788821 | 33.545133 | 47.225555 |
| 73 | 12.320987 | 17.515951 | 24.859318 | 35.222390 | 49.822961 |
| 74 | 12.752222 | 18.216589 | 25.977987 | 36.983509 | 52.563223 |
| 75 | 13.198550 | 18.945253 | 27.146997 | 38.832685 | 55.454201 |
| 76 | 13.660499 | 19.703063 | 28.368611 | 40.774319 | 58.504182 |
| 77 | 14.138116 | 20.491186 | 29.645199 | 42.813035 | 61.721911 |
| 78 | 14.633468 | 21.310833 | 30.979233 | 44.953687 | 65.116617 |
| 79 | 15.145639 | 22.163266 | 32.373298 | 47.201371 | 68.698030 |
| 80 | 15.675736 | 23.049797 | 33.830097 | 49.561440 | 72.476422 |
| 81 | 16.224387 | 23.971789 | 35.352451 | 52.039512 | 76.462625 |
| 82 | 16.792241 | 24.930660 | 36.943312 | 54.641487 | 80.668069 |
| 83 | 17.379969 | 25.927887 | 38.605761 | 57.373561 | 85.104813 |
| 84 | 17.988268 | 26.965002 | 40.343020 | 60.242239 | 89.785578 |
| 85 | 18.617857 | 28.043602 | 42.158456 | 63.254351 | 94.723785 |
| 86 | 19.269482 | 29.165346 | 44.055586 | 66.417069 | 99.933593 |
| 87 | 19.943914 | 30.331960 | 46.038086 | 69.737922 | 105.429940 |
| 88 | 20.641951 | 31.545238 | 48.109802 | 73.224818 | 111.228587 |
| 89 | 21.364420 | 32.807048 | 50.274743 | 76.886059 | 117.346159 |
| 90 | 22.112174 | 34.119330 | 52.537106 | 80.730362 | 123.800198 |
| 91 | 22.886100 | 35.484103 | 54.901276 | 84.766880 | 130.609209 |
| 92 | 23.687114 | 36.903467 | 57.371833 | 89.005224 | 137.792715 |
| 93 | 24.516163 | 38.379606 | 59.953566 | 92.455486 | 145.371314 |
| 94 | 25.374229 | 39.914790 | 62.651470 | 98.128260 | 153.366736 |
| 95 | 26.262327 | 41.511381 | 65.470793 | 103.034673 | 161.801907 |
| 96 | 27.181508 | 43.171836 | 68.416978 | 108.186406 | 170.701011 |
| 97 | 28.132861 | 44.898710 | 71.495742 | 113.595727 | 180.089567 |
| 98 | 29.117511 | 46.694658 | 74.713051 | 119.275513 | 189.994493 |
| 99 | 30.136624 | 48.562444 | 78.075138 | 125.239289 | 200.444190 |
| 100 | 31.191405 | 50.504942 | 81.588519 | 131.501253 | 211.468620 |

**Table 1 (continued)**

| n | 6% | 6½% | 7% | 7½% | 8% |
|---|---|---|---|---|---|
| 1 | 1.060000 | 1.065000 | 1.070000 | 1.075000 | 1.080000 |
| 2 | 1.123600 | 1.134225 | 1.144900 | 1.155625 | 1.166400 |
| 3 | 1.191016 | 1.207950 | 1.225043 | 1.242297 | 1.259712 |
| 4 | 1.262477 | 1.286466 | 1.310796 | 1.335469 | 1.360489 |
| 5 | 1.338226 | 1.370087 | 1.402552 | 1.435629 | 1.469328 |
| 6 | 1.418519 | 1.459142 | 1.500730 | 1.543302 | 1.586874 |
| 7 | 1.503630 | 1.553987 | 1.605781 | 1.659045 | 1.713824 |
| 8 | 1.593848 | 1.654996 | 1.718186 | 1.783478 | 1.850930 |
| 9 | 1.689479 | 1.762570 | 1.838459 | 1.917239 | 1.999005 |
| 10 | 1.790848 | 1.877137 | 1.967151 | 2.061032 | 2.158925 |
| 11 | 1.898299 | 1.999151 | 2.104852 | 2.215609 | 2.331639 |
| 12 | 2.012196 | 2.129096 | 2.252192 | 2.381780 | 2.518170 |
| 13 | 2.132928 | 2.267487 | 2.409845 | 2.560413 | 2.719624 |
| 14 | 2.260904 | 2.414874 | 2.578534 | 2.752444 | 2.937194 |
| 15 | 2.396558 | 2.571841 | 2.759032 | 2.958877 | 3.172169 |
| 16 | 2.540352 | 2.739011 | 2.952164 | 3.180793 | 3.425943 |
| 17 | 2.692773 | 2.917046 | 3.158815 | 3.419353 | 3.700018 |
| 18 | 2.854339 | 3.106654 | 3.379932 | 3.675804 | 3.996019 |
| 19 | 3.025599 | 3.308587 | 3.616527 | 3.951489 | 4.315701 |
| 20 | 3.207135 | 3.523645 | 3.869684 | 4.247851 | 4.660957 |
| 21 | 3.399564 | 3.752682 | 4.140562 | 4.566440 | 5.033834 |
| 22 | 3.603537 | 3.996606 | 4.430402 | 4.908923 | 5.436540 |
| 23 | 3.819750 | 4.256386 | 4.740750 | 5.277092 | 5.871464 |
| 24 | 4.048935 | 4.533051 | 5.072367 | 5.672874 | 6.341181 |
| 25 | 4.291871 | 4.827699 | 5.427433 | 6.098340 | 6.848475 |
| 26 | 4.549383 | 5.141500 | 5.807353 | 6.555715 | 7.396353 |
| 27 | 4.822346 | 5.475697 | 6.213867 | 7.047394 | 7.988061 |
| 28 | 5.111687 | 5.831617 | 6.648838 | 7.575948 | 8.627106 |
| 29 | 5.418388 | 6.210672 | 7.114257 | 8.144144 | 9.317275 |
| 30 | 5.743491 | 6.614366 | 7.612255 | 8.754955 | 10.062657 |
| 31 | 6.088101 | 7.044300 | 8.145113 | 9.411577 | 10.867669 |
| 32 | 6.453387 | 7.502179 | 8.715271 | 10.117445 | 11.737083 |
| 33 | 6.840590 | 7.989821 | 9.325340 | 10.876253 | 12.676049 |
| 34 | 7.251025 | 8.509160 | 9.978113 | 11.691972 | 13.690133 |
| 35 | 7.686087 | 9.062255 | 10.676581 | 12.568870 | 14.785344 |
| 36 | 8.147252 | 9.651301 | 11.423942 | 13.511535 | 15.968171 |
| 37 | 8.636087 | 10.278636 | 12.223618 | 14.524901 | 17.245625 |
| 38 | 9.154252 | 10.946747 | 13.079271 | 15.614268 | 18.625275 |
| 39 | 9.703507 | 11.658286 | 13.994820 | 16.785338 | 20.115297 |
| 40 | 10.285718 | 12.416075 | 14.974457 | 18.044239 | 21.724521 |
| 41 | 10.902861 | 13.223119 | 16.022669 | 19.397557 | 23.462483 |
| 42 | 11.557032 | 14.082622 | 17.144256 | 20.852373 | 25.339481 |
| 43 | 12.250454 | 14.997993 | 18.344354 | 22.416301 | 27.366640 |
| 44 | 12.985482 | 15.972862 | 19.628459 | 24.097524 | 29.555971 |
| 45 | 13.764610 | 17.011098 | 21.002451 | 25.904838 | 31.920449 |
| 46 | 14.590487 | 18.116820 | 22.472622 | 27.847701 | 34.474084 |
| 47 | 15.465916 | 19.294413 | 24.045706 | 29.936278 | 37.232011 |
| 48 | 16.393871 | 20.548550 | 25.728905 | 32.181498 | 40.210572 |
| 49 | 17.377504 | 21.884205 | 27.529929 | 34.595112 | 43.427418 |
| 50 | 18.420154 | 23.306679 | 29.457024 | 37.189745 | 46.901611 |

| n | 6% | 6½% | 7% | 7½% | 8% |
|---|---|---|---|---|---|
| 51 | 19.525363 | 24.821613 | 31.519016 | 39.978976 | 50.653740 |
| 52 | 20.696885 | 26.435018 | 33.725346 | 42.977399 | 54.706039 |
| 53 | 21.938698 | 28.153294 | 36.086121 | 46.200704 | 59.082522 |
| 54 | 23.255020 | 29.983258 | 38.612149 | 49.665757 | 63.809124 |
| 55 | 24.650321 | 31.932170 | 41.315000 | 53.390689 | 68.913854 |
| 56 | 26.129340 | 34.007761 | 44.207049 | 57.394990 | 74.426962 |
| 57 | 27.697100 | 36.218265 | 47.301543 | 61.699614 | 80.381119 |
| 58 | 29.358926 | 38.572452 | 50.612651 | 66.327086 | 86.811608 |
| 59 | 31.120462 | 41.079662 | 54.155536 | 71.301617 | 93.756537 |
| 60 | 32.987690 | 43.749840 | 57.946424 | 76.649238 | 101.257060 |
| 61 | 34.966951 | 46.593579 | 62.002673 | 82.397931 | 109.357625 |
| 62 | 37.064968 | 49.622162 | 66.342861 | 88.577776 | 118.106234 |
| 63 | 39.288865 | 52.847603 | 70.986861 | 95.221109 | 127.554733 |
| 64 | 41.646198 | 56.282697 | 75.955941 | 102.362692 | 137.759112 |
| 65 | 44.144970 | 59.941072 | 81.272857 | 110.039894 | 148.779841 |
| 66 | 46.793668 | 63.837242 | 86.961957 | 118.292886 | 160.682228 |
| 67 | 49.601288 | 67.986662 | 93.049294 | 127.164852 | 173.536806 |
| 68 | 52.577365 | 72.405796 | 99.562744 | 136.702216 | 187.415750 |
| 69 | 55.732007 | 77.112172 | 106.532136 | 146.954882 | 202.413330 |
| 70 | 59.075928 | 82.124464 | 113.989985 | 157.976498 | 218.606396 |
| 71 | 62.620483 | 87.462554 | 121.968642 | 169.824735 | 236.094908 |
| 72 | 66.377712 | 93.147620 | 130.506447 | 182.561591 | 254.982500 |
| 73 | 70.360375 | 99.202215 | 139.641898 | 196.253710 | 275.381101 |
| 74 | 74.581997 | 105.650359 | 149.416831 | 210.972738 | 297.411588 |
| 75 | 79.056917 | 112.517632 | 159.876009 | 226.795693 | 321.204515 |
| 76 | 83.800332 | 119.831279 | 171.067330 | 243.805370 | 346.900876 |
| 77 | 88.828352 | 127.620312 | 183.042042 | 262.090773 | 374.652946 |
| 78 | 94.158053 | 135.915632 | 195.854985 | 281.747581 | 404.625181 |
| 79 | 99.807536 | 144.750148 | 209.564834 | 302.878649 | 436.995196 |
| 80 | 105.795988 | 154.158908 | 224.234372 | 325.594547 | 471.954811 |
| 81 | 112.143748 | 164.179237 | 239.930778 | 350.014138 | 509.711196 |
| 82 | 118.872372 | 174.850887 | 256.725932 | 376.265199 | 550.488090 |
| 83 | 126.004715 | 186.216194 | 274.696748 | 404.485088 | 594.527138 |
| 84 | 133.564997 | 198.320247 | 293.925519 | 434.821470 | 642.089308 |
| 85 | 141.578897 | 211.211063 | 314.500305 | 467.433080 | 693.456453 |
| 86 | 150.073631 | 224.939782 | 336.515326 | 502.490560 | 748.932968 |
| 87 | 159.078049 | 239.560868 | 360.071399 | 540.177352 | 808.847606 |
| 88 | 168.622731 | 255.132325 | 385.276396 | 580.690654 | 873.555413 |
| 89 | 178.740095 | 271.715926 | 412.245744 | 624.242453 | 943.439846 |
| 90 | 189.464501 | 289.377461 | 441.102946 | 671.060636 | 1018.915031 |
| 91 | 200.832371 | 308.186996 | 471.980152 | 721.390183 | 1100.428236 |
| 92 | 212.882312 | 328.219151 | 505.018761 | 775.494447 | 1188.462491 |
| 93 | 225.655232 | 349.553396 | 540.370075 | 833.656529 | 1283.539492 |
| 94 | 239.194566 | 372.274366 | 578.195979 | 896.180769 | 1386.222649 |
| 95 | 253.546240 | 396.472200 | 618.669698 | 963.394325 | 1497.120463 |
| 96 | 258.759014 | 422.242893 | 661.976577 | 1035.648900 | 1616.890095 |
| 97 | 284.884555 | 449.688681 | 708.314935 | 1113.322566 | 1746.241303 |
| 98 | 301.977628 | 478.918445 | 757.896980 | 1196.821759 | 1885.940604 |
| 99 | 320.096286 | 510.048144 | 810.949769 | 1286.583390 | 2036.815854 |
| 100 | 329.302062 | 543.201275 | 867.716251 | 1383.077144 | 2199.761119 |

**Table 2**

$(1 + r)^{-n}$

$r$ = rate of interest per payment period; $n$ = number of payment periods

| $n$ | $\frac{1}{4}\%$ | $\frac{1}{2}\%$ | $\frac{3}{4}\%$ | $1\%$ | $1\frac{1}{4}\%$ |
|---|---|---|---|---|---|
| 1 | 0.997506 | 0.995025 | 0.992556 | 0.990099 | 0.987654 |
| 2 | 0.995019 | 0.990075 | 0.985167 | 0.980296 | 0.975461 |
| 3 | 0.992537 | 0.985149 | 0.977833 | 0.970590 | 0.963418 |
| 4 | 0.990062 | 0.980248 | 0.970554 | 0.960980 | 0.951524 |
| 5 | 0.987593 | 0.975371 | 0.963329 | 0.951466 | 0.939777 |
| 6 | 0.985130 | 0.970518 | 0.956158 | 0.942045 | 0.928175 |
| 7 | 0.982674 | 0.965690 | 0.949040 | 0.932718 | 0.916716 |
| 8 | 0.980223 | 0.960885 | 0.941975 | 0.923483 | 0.905398 |
| 9 | 0.977779 | 0.956105 | 0.934963 | 0.914340 | 0.894221 |
| 10 | 0.975340 | 0.951348 | 0.928003 | 0.905287 | 0.883181 |
| 11 | 0.972908 | 0.946615 | 0.921095 | 0.896324 | 0.872277 |
| 12 | 0.970482 | 0.941905 | 0.914238 | 0.887449 | 0.861509 |
| 13 | 0.968062 | 0.937219 | 0.907432 | 0.878663 | 0.850873 |
| 14 | 0.965648 | 0.932556 | 0.900677 | 0.869963 | 0.840368 |
| 15 | 0.963240 | 0.927917 | 0.893973 | 0.861349 | 0.829993 |
| 16 | 0.960837 | 0.923300 | 0.887318 | 0.852821 | 0.819746 |
| 17 | 0.958441 | 0.918707 | 0.880712 | 0.844377 | 0.809626 |
| 18 | 0.956051 | 0.914136 | 0.874156 | 0.836017 | 0.799631 |
| 19 | 0.953667 | 0.909588 | 0.867649 | 0.827740 | 0.789759 |
| 20 | 0.951289 | 0.905063 | 0.861190 | 0.819544 | 0.780009 |
| 21 | 0.948917 | 0.900560 | 0.854779 | 0.811430 | 0.770379 |
| 22 | 0.946550 | 0.896080 | 0.848416 | 0.803396 | 0.760868 |
| 23 | 0.944190 | 0.891622 | 0.842100 | 0.795442 | 0.751475 |
| 24 | 0.941835 | 0.887186 | 0.835831 | 0.787566 | 0.742197 |
| 25 | 0.939486 | 0.882772 | 0.829609 | 0.779768 | 0.733034 |
| 26 | 0.937144 | 0.878380 | 0.823434 | 0.772048 | 0.723984 |
| 27 | 0.934806 | 0.874010 | 0.817304 | 0.764404 | 0.715046 |
| 28 | 0.932475 | 0.869662 | 0.811220 | 0.756836 | 0.706219 |
| 29 | 0.930150 | 0.865335 | 0.805181 | 0.749342 | 0.697500 |
| 30 | 0.927830 | 0.861030 | 0.799187 | 0.741923 | 0.688889 |
| 31 | 0.925517 | 0.856746 | 0.793238 | 0.734577 | 0.680384 |
| 32 | 0.923209 | 0.852484 | 0.787333 | 0.727304 | 0.671984 |
| 33 | 0.920906 | 0.848242 | 0.781472 | 0.720103 | 0.663688 |
| 34 | 0.918610 | 0.844022 | 0.775654 | 0.712973 | 0.655494 |
| 35 | 0.916319 | 0.839823 | 0.769880 | 0.705914 | 0.647402 |
| 36 | 0.914034 | 0.835645 | 0.764149 | 0.698925 | 0.639409 |
| 37 | 0.911754 | 0.831487 | 0.758461 | 0.692005 | 0.631515 |
| 38 | 0.909481 | 0.827351 | 0.752814 | 0.685153 | 0.623719 |
| 39 | 0.907213 | 0.823235 | 0.747210 | 0.678370 | 0.616019 |
| 40 | 0.904950 | 0.819139 | 0.741648 | 0.671653 | 0.608413 |
| 41 | 0.902694 | 0.815064 | 0.736127 | 0.665003 | 0.600902 |
| 42 | 0.900443 | 0.811008 | 0.730647 | 0.658419 | 0.593484 |
| 43 | 0.898197 | 0.806974 | 0.725208 | 0.651900 | 0.586157 |
| 44 | 0.895957 | 0.802959 | 0.719810 | 0.645445 | 0.578920 |
| 45 | 0.893723 | 0.798964 | 0.714451 | 0.639055 | 0.571773 |
| 46 | 0.891494 | 0.794989 | 0.709133 | 0.632728 | 0.564714 |
| 47 | 0.889271 | 0.791034 | 0.703854 | 0.626463 | 0.557742 |
| 48 | 0.887053 | 0.787098 | 0.698614 | 0.620260 | 0.550857 |
| 49 | 0.884841 | 0.783182 | 0.693414 | 0.614119 | 0.544056 |
| 50 | 0.882635 | 0.779286 | 0.688252 | 0.608039 | 0.537339 |

| $n$ | $\frac{1}{4}\%$ | $\frac{1}{2}\%$ | $\frac{3}{4}\%$ | $1\%$ | $1\frac{1}{4}\%$ |
|---|---|---|---|---|---|
| 51 | 0.880434 | 0.775409 | 0.683128 | 0.602019 | 0.530705 |
| 52 | 0.878238 | 0.771551 | 0.678043 | 0.596058 | 0.524153 |
| 53 | 0.876048 | 0.767713 | 0.672995 | 0.590157 | 0.517682 |
| 54 | 0.873863 | 0.763893 | 0.667986 | 0.584313 | 0.511291 |
| 55 | 0.871684 | 0.760093 | 0.663013 | 0.578528 | 0.504979 |
| 56 | 0.869510 | 0.756311 | 0.658077 | 0.572800 | 0.498745 |
| 57 | 0.867342 | 0.752548 | 0.653179 | 0.567129 | 0.492587 |
| 58 | 0.865179 | 0.748804 | 0.648316 | 0.561514 | 0.486506 |
| 59 | 0.863021 | 0.745079 | 0.643490 | 0.555954 | 0.480500 |
| 60 | 0.860869 | 0.741372 | 0.638700 | 0.550450 | 0.474568 |
| 61 | 0.858722 | 0.737684 | 0.633945 | 0.545000 | 0.468709 |
| 62 | 0.856581 | 0.734014 | 0.629226 | 0.539604 | 0.462922 |
| 63 | 0.854445 | 0.730362 | 0.624542 | 0.534261 | 0.457207 |
| 64 | 0.852314 | 0.726728 | 0.619893 | 0.528971 | 0.451563 |
| 65 | 0.850189 | 0.723113 | 0.615278 | 0.523734 | 0.445988 |
| 66 | 0.848068 | 0.719515 | 0.610698 | 0.518548 | 0.440482 |
| 67 | 0.845953 | 0.715935 | 0.606152 | 0.513414 | 0.435044 |
| 68 | 0.843844 | 0.712374 | 0.601639 | 0.508331 | 0.429673 |
| 69 | 0.841740 | 0.708829 | 0.597161 | 0.503298 | 0.424368 |
| 70 | 0.839640 | 0.705303 | 0.592715 | 0.498315 | 0.419129 |
| 71 | 0.837547 | 0.701794 | 0.588303 | 0.493381 | 0.413955 |
| 72 | 0.835458 | 0.698302 | 0.583924 | 0.488496 | 0.408844 |
| 73 | 0.833374 | 0.694828 | 0.579577 | 0.483660 | 0.403797 |
| 74 | 0.831296 | 0.691371 | 0.575262 | 0.478871 | 0.398811 |
| 75 | 0.829233 | 0.687932 | 0.570980 | 0.474130 | 0.393888 |
| 76 | 0.827155 | 0.684509 | 0.566730 | 0.469435 | 0.389025 |
| 77 | 0.825093 | 0.681104 | 0.562511 | 0.464787 | 0.384222 |
| 78 | 0.823035 | 0.677715 | 0.558323 | 0.460185 | 0.379479 |
| 79 | 0.820983 | 0.674343 | 0.554167 | 0.455629 | 0.374794 |
| 80 | 0.818935 | 0.670988 | 0.550042 | 0.451118 | 0.370167 |
| 81 | 0.816893 | 0.667650 | 0.545947 | 0.446651 | 0.365597 |
| 82 | 0.814856 | 0.664329 | 0.541883 | 0.442229 | 0.361083 |
| 83 | 0.812824 | 0.661023 | 0.537849 | 0.437851 | 0.356625 |
| 84 | 0.810797 | 0.657735 | 0.533845 | 0.433515 | 0.352223 |
| 85 | 0.808775 | 0.654462 | 0.529871 | 0.429223 | 0.347874 |
| 86 | 0.806758 | 0.651206 | 0.525927 | 0.424974 | 0.343580 |
| 87 | 0.804746 | 0.647967 | 0.522012 | 0.420766 | 0.339338 |
| 88 | 0.802739 | 0.644743 | 0.518126 | 0.416600 | 0.335148 |
| 89 | 0.800737 | 0.641535 | 0.514269 | 0.412475 | 0.331011 |
| 90 | 0.798741 | 0.638343 | 0.510440 | 0.408391 | 0.326924 |
| 91 | 0.796749 | 0.635168 | 0.506641 | 0.404348 | 0.322888 |
| 92 | 0.794762 | 0.632008 | 0.502869 | 0.400344 | 0.318902 |
| 93 | 0.792780 | 0.628863 | 0.499126 | 0.396380 | 0.314965 |
| 94 | 0.790803 | 0.625735 | 0.495410 | 0.392456 | 0.311076 |
| 95 | 0.788831 | 0.622622 | 0.491722 | 0.388570 | 0.307236 |
| 96 | 0.786864 | 0.619524 | 0.488062 | 0.384723 | 0.303443 |
| 97 | 0.784901 | 0.616442 | 0.484429 | 0.380914 | 0.299697 |
| 98 | 0.782944 | 0.613375 | 0.480822 | 0.377142 | 0.295997 |
| 99 | 0.780991 | 0.610323 | 0.477243 | 0.373408 | 0.292342 |
| 100 | 0.779044 | 0.607287 | 0.473690 | 0.369711 | 0.288733 |

**Table 2 (continued)**

| n | 1½% | 1¾% | 2% | 2½% | 3% |
|---|---|---|---|---|---|
| 1 | 0.985222 | 0.982801 | 0.980392 | 0.975610 | 0.970874 |
| 2 | 0.970662 | 0.965898 | 0.961169 | 0.951814 | 0.942596 |
| 3 | 0.956317 | 0.949285 | 0.942322 | 0.928599 | 0.915142 |
| 4 | 0.942184 | 0.932959 | 0.923845 | 0.905951 | 0.888487 |
| 5 | 0.928260 | 0.916913 | 0.905731 | 0.883854 | 0.862609 |
| 6 | 0.914542 | 0.901143 | 0.887971 | 0.862297 | 0.837484 |
| 7 | 0.901027 | 0.885644 | 0.870560 | 0.841265 | 0.813092 |
| 8 | 0.887711 | 0.870412 | 0.853490 | 0.820747 | 0.789409 |
| 9 | 0.874592 | 0.855441 | 0.836755 | 0.800728 | 0.766417 |
| 10 | 0.861667 | 0.840729 | 0.820348 | 0.781198 | 0.744094 |
| 11 | 0.848933 | 0.826269 | 0.804263 | 0.762145 | 0.722421 |
| 12 | 0.836387 | 0.812058 | 0.788493 | 0.743556 | 0.701380 |
| 13 | 0.824027 | 0.798091 | 0.773033 | 0.725420 | 0.680951 |
| 14 | 0.811849 | 0.784365 | 0.757875 | 0.707727 | 0.661118 |
| 15 | 0.799852 | 0.770875 | 0.743015 | 0.690466 | 0.641862 |
| 16 | 0.788031 | 0.757616 | 0.728446 | 0.673625 | 0.623167 |
| 17 | 0.776385 | 0.744586 | 0.714163 | 0.657195 | 0.605016 |
| 18 | 0.764912 | 0.731780 | 0.700159 | 0.641166 | 0.587395 |
| 19 | 0.753607 | 0.719194 | 0.686431 | 0.625528 | 0.570286 |
| 20 | 0.742470 | 0.706825 | 0.672971 | 0.610271 | 0.553676 |
| 21 | 0.731498 | 0.694668 | 0.659776 | 0.595386 | 0.537549 |
| 22 | 0.720688 | 0.682720 | 0.646839 | 0.580865 | 0.521893 |
| 23 | 0.710037 | 0.670978 | 0.634156 | 0.566697 | 0.506692 |
| 24 | 0.699544 | 0.659438 | 0.621722 | 0.552875 | 0.491934 |
| 25 | 0.689206 | 0.648096 | 0.609531 | 0.539391 | 0.477606 |
| 26 | 0.679021 | 0.636950 | 0.597579 | 0.526235 | 0.463695 |
| 27 | 0.668986 | 0.625995 | 0.585862 | 0.513400 | 0.450189 |
| 28 | 0.659099 | 0.615228 | 0.574375 | 0.500878 | 0.437077 |
| 29 | 0.649359 | 0.604647 | 0.563112 | 0.488661 | 0.424346 |
| 30 | 0.639762 | 0.594248 | 0.552071 | 0.476743 | 0.411987 |
| 31 | 0.630308 | 0.584027 | 0.541246 | 0.465115 | 0.399987 |
| 32 | 0.620993 | 0.573982 | 0.530633 | 0.453771 | 0.388337 |
| 33 | 0.611816 | 0.564111 | 0.520229 | 0.442703 | 0.377026 |
| 34 | 0.602774 | 0.554408 | 0.510028 | 0.431905 | 0.366045 |
| 35 | 0.593866 | 0.544873 | 0.500028 | 0.421371 | 0.355383 |
| 36 | 0.585090 | 0.535502 | 0.490223 | 0.411094 | 0.345032 |
| 37 | 0.576443 | 0.526292 | 0.480611 | 0.401067 | 0.334983 |
| 38 | 0.567924 | 0.517240 | 0.471187 | 0.391285 | 0.325226 |
| 39 | 0.559531 | 0.508344 | 0.461948 | 0.381741 | 0.315754 |
| 40 | 0.551262 | 0.499601 | 0.452890 | 0.372431 | 0.306557 |
| 41 | 0.543116 | 0.491008 | 0.444010 | 0.363347 | 0.297628 |
| 42 | 0.535089 | 0.482563 | 0.435304 | 0.354485 | 0.288959 |
| 43 | 0.527182 | 0.474264 | 0.426769 | 0.345839 | 0.280543 |
| 44 | 0.519391 | 0.466107 | 0.418401 | 0.337404 | 0.272372 |
| 45 | 0.511715 | 0.458090 | 0.410197 | 0.329174 | 0.264439 |
| 46 | 0.504153 | 0.450212 | 0.402154 | 0.321146 | 0.256737 |
| 47 | 0.496702 | 0.442469 | 0.394268 | 0.313313 | 0.249259 |
| 48 | 0.489362 | 0.434858 | 0.386538 | 0.305671 | 0.241999 |
| 49 | 0.482130 | 0.427379 | 0.378958 | 0.298216 | 0.234950 |
| 50 | 0.475005 | 0.420029 | 0.371528 | 0.290942 | 0.228107 |

| n | 1½% | 1¾% | 2% | 2½% | 3% |
|---|---|---|---|---|---|
| 51 | 0.467985 | 0.412805 | 0.364243 | 0.283846 | 0.221463 |
| 52 | 0.461069 | 0.405705 | 0.357101 | 0.276923 | 0.215013 |
| 53 | 0.454255 | 0.398727 | 0.350099 | 0.270169 | 0.208750 |
| 54 | 0.447542 | 0.391869 | 0.343234 | 0.263579 | 0.202670 |
| 55 | 0.440928 | 0.385130 | 0.336504 | 0.257151 | 0.196767 |
| 56 | 0.434412 | 0.378506 | 0.329906 | 0.250879 | 0.191036 |
| 57 | 0.427992 | 0.371996 | 0.323437 | 0.244760 | 0.185472 |
| 58 | 0.421667 | 0.365598 | 0.317095 | 0.238790 | 0.180070 |
| 59 | 0.415435 | 0.359310 | 0.310878 | 0.232966 | 0.174825 |
| 60 | 0.409296 | 0.353130 | 0.304782 | 0.227284 | 0.169733 |
| 61 | 0.403247 | 0.347057 | 0.298806 | 0.221740 | 0.164789 |
| 62 | 0.397288 | 0.341088 | 0.292947 | 0.216332 | 0.159990 |
| 63 | 0.391417 | 0.335221 | 0.287203 | 0.211055 | 0.155330 |
| 64 | 0.385632 | 0.329456 | 0.281572 | 0.205908 | 0.150806 |
| 65 | 0.379933 | 0.323790 | 0.276051 | 0.200886 | 0.146413 |
| 66 | 0.374318 | 0.318221 | 0.270638 | 0.195986 | 0.142149 |
| 67 | 0.368787 | 0.312748 | 0.265331 | 0.191206 | 0.138009 |
| 68 | 0.363337 | 0.307369 | 0.260129 | 0.186542 | 0.133989 |
| 69 | 0.357967 | 0.302082 | 0.255028 | 0.181992 | 0.130086 |
| 70 | 0.352677 | 0.296887 | 0.250028 | 0.177554 | 0.126297 |
| 71 | 0.347465 | 0.291781 | 0.245125 | 0.173223 | 0.122619 |
| 72 | 0.342330 | 0.286762 | 0.240319 | 0.168998 | 0.119047 |
| 73 | 0.337271 | 0.281830 | 0.235607 | 0.164876 | 0.115580 |
| 74 | 0.332287 | 0.276983 | 0.230987 | 0.160855 | 0.112214 |
| 75 | 0.327376 | 0.272219 | 0.226458 | 0.156931 | 0.108945 |
| 76 | 0.322538 | 0.267537 | 0.222017 | 0.153104 | 0.105772 |
| 77 | 0.317771 | 0.262936 | 0.217664 | 0.149370 | 0.102691 |
| 78 | 0.313075 | 0.258414 | 0.213396 | 0.145726 | 0.099700 |
| 79 | 0.308449 | 0.253969 | 0.209212 | 0.142172 | 0.096796 |
| 80 | 0.303890 | 0.249601 | 0.205110 | 0.138705 | 0.093977 |
| 81 | 0.299399 | 0.245308 | 0.201088 | 0.135322 | 0.091240 |
| 82 | 0.294975 | 0.241089 | 0.197145 | 0.132021 | 0.088582 |
| 83 | 0.290615 | 0.236943 | 0.193279 | 0.128801 | 0.086000 |
| 84 | 0.286321 | 0.232868 | 0.189490 | 0.125660 | 0.083497 |
| 85 | 0.282089 | 0.228862 | 0.185774 | 0.122595 | 0.081065 |
| 86 | 0.277920 | 0.224926 | 0.182132 | 0.119605 | 0.078704 |
| 87 | 0.273813 | 0.221058 | 0.178560 | 0.116687 | 0.076412 |
| 88 | 0.269767 | 0.217256 | 0.175059 | 0.113841 | 0.074186 |
| 89 | 0.265780 | 0.213519 | 0.171627 | 0.111065 | 0.072026 |
| 90 | 0.261852 | 0.209847 | 0.168261 | 0.108356 | 0.069928 |
| 91 | 0.257982 | 0.206238 | 0.164962 | 0.105713 | 0.067891 |
| 92 | 0.254170 | 0.202691 | 0.161728 | 0.103135 | 0.065914 |
| 93 | 0.250414 | 0.199205 | 0.158557 | 0.100619 | 0.063994 |
| 94 | 0.246713 | 0.195778 | 0.155448 | 0.098165 | 0.062130 |
| 95 | 0.243067 | 0.192411 | 0.152400 | 0.095771 | 0.060320 |
| 96 | 0.239475 | 0.189102 | 0.149411 | 0.093435 | 0.058563 |
| 97 | 0.235936 | 0.185850 | 0.146482 | 0.091156 | 0.056858 |
| 98 | 0.232449 | 0.182653 | 0.143610 | 0.088933 | 0.055202 |
| 99 | 0.229014 | 0.179512 | 0.140794 | 0.086764 | 0.053594 |
| 100 | 0.225629 | 0.176424 | 0.138033 | 0.084647 | 0.052033 |

**Table 2 (continued)**

| n | 3½% | 4% | 4½% | 5% | 5½% |
|---|---|---|---|---|---|
| 1 | 0.966184 | 0.961538 | 0.956938 | 0.952381 | 0.947867 |
| 2 | 0.933511 | 0.924556 | 0.915730 | 0.907029 | 0.898452 |
| 3 | 0.901943 | 0.888996 | 0.876297 | 0.863838 | 0.851614 |
| 4 | 0.871442 | 0.854804 | 0.838561 | 0.822702 | 0.807217 |
| 5 | 0.841973 | 0.821927 | 0.802451 | 0.783526 | 0.765134 |
| 6 | 0.813501 | 0.790315 | 0.767896 | 0.746215 | 0.725246 |
| 7 | 0.785991 | 0.759918 | 0.734828 | 0.710681 | 0.687437 |
| 8 | 0.759412 | 0.730690 | 0.703185 | 0.676839 | 0.651599 |
| 9 | 0.733731 | 0.702587 | 0.672904 | 0.644609 | 0.617629 |
| 10 | 0.708919 | 0.675564 | 0.643928 | 0.613913 | 0.585431 |
| 11 | 0.684946 | 0.649581 | 0.616199 | 0.584679 | 0.554911 |
| 12 | 0.661783 | 0.624597 | 0.589664 | 0.556837 | 0.525982 |
| 13 | 0.639404 | 0.600574 | 0.564272 | 0.530321 | 0.498561 |
| 14 | 0.617782 | 0.577475 | 0.539973 | 0.505068 | 0.472569 |
| 15 | 0.596891 | 0.555265 | 0.516720 | 0.481017 | 0.447933 |
| 16 | 0.576706 | 0.533908 | 0.494469 | 0.458112 | 0.424581 |
| 17 | 0.557204 | 0.513373 | 0.473476 | 0.436297 | 0.402447 |
| 18 | 0.538361 | 0.493628 | 0.452800 | 0.415521 | 0.381466 |
| 19 | 0.520156 | 0.474642 | 0.433302 | 0.395734 | 0.361579 |
| 20 | 0.502566 | 0.456387 | 0.414643 | 0.376889 | 0.342729 |
| 21 | 0.485571 | 0.438834 | 0.396787 | 0.358942 | 0.324862 |
| 22 | 0.469151 | 0.421955 | 0.379701 | 0.341850 | 0.307926 |
| 23 | 0.453286 | 0.405726 | 0.363350 | 0.325571 | 0.291873 |
| 24 | 0.437957 | 0.390121 | 0.347703 | 0.310068 | 0.276657 |
| 25 | 0.423147 | 0.375117 | 0.332731 | 0.295303 | 0.262234 |
| 26 | 0.408838 | 0.360689 | 0.318402 | 0.281241 | 0.248563 |
| 27 | 0.395012 | 0.346817 | 0.304691 | 0.267848 | 0.235605 |
| 28 | 0.381654 | 0.333477 | 0.291571 | 0.255094 | 0.223322 |
| 29 | 0.368748 | 0.320651 | 0.279015 | 0.242946 | 0.211679 |
| 30 | 0.356278 | 0.308319 | 0.267000 | 0.231377 | 0.200644 |
| 31 | 0.344230 | 0.296460 | 0.255502 | 0.220359 | 0.190184 |
| 32 | 0.332590 | 0.285058 | 0.244500 | 0.209866 | 0.180269 |
| 33 | 0.321343 | 0.274094 | 0.233971 | 0.199873 | 0.170871 |
| 34 | 0.310476 | 0.263552 | 0.223896 | 0.190355 | 0.161963 |
| 35 | 0.299977 | 0.253415 | 0.214254 | 0.181290 | 0.153520 |
| 36 | 0.289833 | 0.243669 | 0.205028 | 0.172657 | 0.145516 |
| 37 | 0.280032 | 0.234297 | 0.196199 | 0.164436 | 0.137930 |
| 38 | 0.270562 | 0.225285 | 0.187750 | 0.156605 | 0.130739 |
| 39 | 0.261413 | 0.216621 | 0.179665 | 0.149148 | 0.123924 |
| 40 | 0.252572 | 0.208289 | 0.171929 | 0.142046 | 0.117463 |
| 41 | 0.244031 | 0.200278 | 0.164525 | 0.135282 | 0.111339 |
| 42 | 0.235779 | 0.192575 | 0.157440 | 0.128840 | 0.105535 |
| 43 | 0.227806 | 0.185168 | 0.150661 | 0.122704 | 0.100033 |
| 44 | 0.220102 | 0.178046 | 0.144173 | 0.116861 | 0.094818 |
| 45 | 0.212659 | 0.171198 | 0.137964 | 0.111297 | 0.089875 |
| 46 | 0.205468 | 0.164614 | 0.132023 | 0.105997 | 0.085190 |
| 47 | 0.198520 | 0.158283 | 0.126338 | 0.100949 | 0.080748 |
| 48 | 0.191806 | 0.152195 | 0.120898 | 0.096142 | 0.076539 |
| 49 | 0.185320 | 0.146341 | 0.115692 | 0.091564 | 0.072549 |
| 50 | 0.179053 | 0.140713 | 0.110710 | 0.087204 | 0.068767 |

| n | 3½% | 4% | 4½% | 5% | 5½% |
|---|---|---|---|---|---|
| 51 | 0.172998 | 0.135301 | 0.105942 | 0.083051 | 0.065182 |
| 52 | 0.167148 | 0.130097 | 0.101380 | 0.079096 | 0.061783 |
| 53 | 0.161496 | 0.125093 | 0.097014 | 0.075330 | 0.058563 |
| 54 | 0.156035 | 0.120282 | 0.092837 | 0.071743 | 0.055509 |
| 55 | 0.150758 | 0.115656 | 0.088839 | 0.068326 | 0.052616 |
| 56 | 0.145660 | 0.111207 | 0.085013 | 0.065073 | 0.049873 |
| 57 | 0.140734 | 0.106930 | 0.081353 | 0.061974 | 0.047273 |
| 58 | 0.135975 | 0.102817 | 0.077849 | 0.059023 | 0.044808 |
| 59 | 0.131377 | 0.098863 | 0.074497 | 0.056212 | 0.042472 |
| 60 | 0.126934 | 0.095060 | 0.071289 | 0.053536 | 0.040258 |
| 61 | 0.122642 | 0.091404 | 0.068219 | 0.050986 | 0.038159 |
| 62 | 0.118495 | 0.087889 | 0.065281 | 0.048558 | 0.036170 |
| 63 | 0.114487 | 0.084508 | 0.062470 | 0.046246 | 0.034284 |
| 64 | 0.110616 | 0.081258 | 0.059780 | 0.044044 | 0.032497 |
| 65 | 0.106875 | 0.078133 | 0.057206 | 0.041946 | 0.030803 |
| 66 | 0.103261 | 0.075128 | 0.054743 | 0.039949 | 0.029197 |
| 67 | 0.099769 | 0.072238 | 0.052385 | 0.038047 | 0.027675 |
| 68 | 0.096395 | 0.069460 | 0.050129 | 0.036235 | 0.026232 |
| 69 | 0.093136 | 0.066788 | 0.047971 | 0.034509 | 0.024865 |
| 70 | 0.089986 | 0.064219 | 0.045905 | 0.032866 | 0.023568 |
| 71 | 0.086943 | 0.061749 | 0.043928 | 0.031301 | 0.022340 |
| 72 | 0.084003 | 0.059374 | 0.042037 | 0.029811 | 0.021175 |
| 73 | 0.081162 | 0.057091 | 0.040226 | 0.028391 | 0.020071 |
| 74 | 0.078162 | 0.054895 | 0.038494 | 0.027039 | 0.019025 |
| 75 | 0.075766 | 0.052784 | 0.036836 | 0.025752 | 0.018033 |
| 76 | 0.073204 | 0.050754 | 0.035250 | 0.024525 | 0.017093 |
| 77 | 0.070728 | 0.048801 | 0.033732 | 0.023357 | 0.016202 |
| 78 | 0.068337 | 0.046924 | 0.032280 | 0.022245 | 0.015357 |
| 79 | 0.066026 | 0.045120 | 0.030890 | 0.021186 | 0.014556 |
| 80 | 0.063793 | 0.043384 | 0.029559 | 0.020177 | 0.013798 |
| 81 | 0.061636 | 0.041716 | 0.028287 | 0.019216 | 0.013078 |
| 82 | 0.059551 | 0.040111 | 0.027068 | 0.018301 | 0.012396 |
| 83 | 0.057538 | 0.038569 | 0.025903 | 0.017430 | 0.011750 |
| 84 | 0.055592 | 0.037085 | 0.024787 | 0.016600 | 0.011138 |
| 85 | 0.053712 | 0.035659 | 0.023720 | 0.015809 | 0.010557 |
| 86 | 0.051896 | 0.034287 | 0.022699 | 0.015056 | 0.010007 |
| 87 | 0.050141 | 0.032969 | 0.021721 | 0.014339 | 0.009485 |
| 88 | 0.048445 | 0.031701 | 0.020786 | 0.013657 | 0.008990 |
| 89 | 0.046807 | 0.030481 | 0.019891 | 0.013006 | 0.008522 |
| 90 | 0.045224 | 0.029309 | 0.019034 | 0.012387 | 0.008078 |
| 91 | 0.043695 | 0.028182 | 0.018215 | 0.011797 | 0.007656 |
| 92 | 0.042217 | 0.027098 | 0.017430 | 0.011235 | 0.007257 |
| 93 | 0.040789 | 0.026056 | 0.016680 | 0.010700 | 0.006879 |
| 94 | 0.039410 | 0.025053 | 0.015961 | 0.010191 | 0.006520 |
| 95 | 0.038077 | 0.024090 | 0.015274 | 0.009705 | 0.006180 |
| 96 | 0.036790 | 0.023163 | 0.014616 | 0.009243 | 0.005858 |
| 97 | 0.035546 | 0.022272 | 0.013987 | 0.008803 | 0.005553 |
| 98 | 0.034344 | 0.021416 | 0.013385 | 0.008384 | 0.005263 |
| 99 | 0.033182 | 0.020592 | 0.012808 | 0.007985 | 0.004989 |
| 100 | 0.032060 | 0.019800 | 0.012257 | 0.007604 | 0.004729 |

**Table 2 (continued)**

| n | 6% | 6½% | 7% | 7½% | 8% |
|---|----|-----|----|-----|----|
| 1 | 0.943396 | 0.938967 | 0.934579 | 0.930233 | 0.925926 |
| 2 | 0.889996 | 0.881659 | 0.873439 | 0.865333 | 0.857339 |
| 3 | 0.839619 | 0.827849 | 0.816298 | 0.804961 | 0.793832 |
| 4 | 0.792094 | 0.777323 | 0.762895 | 0.748801 | 0.735030 |
| 5 | 0.747258 | 0.729881 | 0.712986 | 0.696559 | 0.680583 |
| 6 | 0.704961 | 0.685334 | 0.666342 | 0.647962 | 0.630170 |
| 7 | 0.665057 | 0.643306 | 0.622750 | 0.602755 | 0.583490 |
| 8 | 0.627412 | 0.604231 | 0.582009 | 0.560702 | 0.540269 |
| 9 | 0.591898 | 0.567353 | 0.543934 | 0.521583 | 0.500249 |
| 10 | 0.558395 | 0.532726 | 0.508395 | 0.485194 | 0.463193 |
| 11 | 0.526788 | 0.500212 | 0.475093 | 0.451343 | 0.428883 |
| 12 | 0.496969 | 0.469683 | 0.444012 | 0.419854 | 0.397114 |
| 13 | 0.468839 | 0.441017 | 0.414964 | 0.390562 | 0.367698 |
| 14 | 0.442301 | 0.414100 | 0.387817 | 0.363313 | 0.340461 |
| 15 | 0.417265 | 0.388827 | 0.362446 | 0.337966 | 0.315242 |
| 16 | 0.393646 | 0.365095 | 0.338735 | 0.314387 | 0.291890 |
| 17 | 0.371364 | 0.342813 | 0.316574 | 0.292453 | 0.270269 |
| 18 | 0.350344 | 0.321890 | 0.295864 | 0.272049 | 0.250249 |
| 19 | 0.330513 | 0.302244 | 0.276508 | 0.253069 | 0.231712 |
| 20 | 0.311805 | 0.283797 | 0.258419 | 0.235413 | 0.214548 |
| 21 | 0.294155 | 0.266476 | 0.241513 | 0.218989 | 0.198656 |
| 22 | 0.277505 | 0.250212 | 0.225713 | 0.203711 | 0.183941 |
| 23 | 0.261797 | 0.234941 | 0.210947 | 0.189498 | 0.170315 |
| 24 | 0.246979 | 0.220602 | 0.197147 | 0.176277 | 0.157699 |
| 25 | 0.232999 | 0.207138 | 0.184249 | 0.163979 | 0.146018 |
| 26 | 0.219810 | 0.194496 | 0.172195 | 0.152539 | 0.135202 |
| 27 | 0.207368 | 0.182625 | 0.160930 | 0.141896 | 0.125187 |
| 28 | 0.195630 | 0.171479 | 0.150402 | 0.131997 | 0.115914 |
| 29 | 0.184557 | 0.161013 | 0.140563 | 0.122788 | 0.107328 |
| 30 | 0.174110 | 0.151186 | 0.131367 | 0.114221 | 0.099377 |
| 31 | 0.164255 | 0.141959 | 0.122773 | 0.106252 | 0.092016 |
| 32 | 0.154957 | 0.133295 | 0.114741 | 0.098839 | 0.085200 |
| 33 | 0.146186 | 0.125159 | 0.107235 | 0.091943 | 0.078889 |
| 34 | 0.137912 | 0.117520 | 0.100219 | 0.085529 | 0.073045 |
| 35 | 0.130105 | 0.110348 | 0.093663 | 0.079562 | 0.067635 |
| 36 | 0.122741 | 0.103613 | 0.087535 | 0.074011 | 0.062625 |
| 37 | 0.115793 | 0.097289 | 0.081809 | 0.068847 | 0.057986 |
| 38 | 0.109239 | 0.091351 | 0.076457 | 0.064044 | 0.053690 |
| 39 | 0.103056 | 0.085776 | 0.071455 | 0.059576 | 0.049713 |
| 40 | 0.097222 | 0.080541 | 0.066780 | 0.055419 | 0.046031 |
| 41 | 0.091719 | 0.075625 | 0.062412 | 0.051553 | 0.042621 |
| 42 | 0.086527 | 0.071010 | 0.058329 | 0.047956 | 0.039464 |
| 43 | 0.081630 | 0.066676 | 0.054513 | 0.044610 | 0.036541 |
| 44 | 0.077009 | 0.062606 | 0.050946 | 0.041498 | 0.033834 |
| 45 | 0.072650 | 0.058785 | 0.047613 | 0.038603 | 0.031328 |
| 46 | 0.068538 | 0.055197 | 0.044499 | 0.035910 | 0.029007 |
| 47 | 0.064658 | 0.051828 | 0.041587 | 0.033404 | 0.026859 |
| 48 | 0.060998 | 0.048665 | 0.038867 | 0.031074 | 0.024869 |
| 49 | 0.057546 | 0.045695 | 0.036324 | 0.028906 | 0.023027 |
| 50 | 0.054288 | 0.042906 | 0.033948 | 0.026889 | 0.021321 |
| 51 | 0.051215 | 0.040287 | 0.031727 | 0.025013 | 0.019742 |
| 52 | 0.048316 | 0.037829 | 0.029651 | 0.023268 | 0.018280 |
| 53 | 0.045582 | 0.035520 | 0.027711 | 0.021645 | 0.016925 |
| 54 | 0.043001 | 0.033352 | 0.025899 | 0.020135 | 0.015672 |
| 55 | 0.040567 | 0.031316 | 0.024204 | 0.018730 | 0.014511 |
| 56 | 0.038271 | 0.029405 | 0.022621 | 0.017423 | 0.013436 |
| 57 | 0.036105 | 0.027610 | 0.021141 | 0.016208 | 0.012441 |
| 58 | 0.034061 | 0.025925 | 0.019758 | 0.015077 | 0.011519 |
| 59 | 0.032133 | 0.024343 | 0.018465 | 0.014025 | 0.010666 |
| 60 | 0.030314 | 0.022857 | 0.017257 | 0.013046 | 0.009876 |
| 61 | 0.028598 | 0.021462 | 0.016128 | 0.012136 | 0.009144 |
| 62 | 0.026980 | 0.020152 | 0.015073 | 0.011290 | 0.008467 |
| 63 | 0.025453 | 0.018922 | 0.014087 | 0.010502 | 0.007840 |
| 64 | 0.024012 | 0.017767 | 0.013166 | 0.009769 | 0.007259 |
| 65 | 0.022653 | 0.016683 | 0.012304 | 0.009088 | 0.006721 |
| 66 | 0.021370 | 0.015665 | 0.011499 | 0.008454 | 0.006223 |
| 67 | 0.020161 | 0.014709 | 0.010747 | 0.007864 | 0.005762 |
| 68 | 0.019020 | 0.013811 | 0.010044 | 0.007315 | 0.005336 |
| 69 | 0.017943 | 0.012968 | 0.009387 | 0.006805 | 0.004940 |
| 70 | 0.016927 | 0.012177 | 0.008773 | 0.006330 | 0.004574 |
| 71 | 0.015969 | 0.011433 | 0.008199 | 0.005888 | 0.004236 |
| 72 | 0.015065 | 0.010736 | 0.007662 | 0.005478 | 0.003922 |
| 73 | 0.014213 | 0.010080 | 0.007161 | 0.005095 | 0.003631 |
| 74 | 0.013408 | 0.009465 | 0.006693 | 0.004740 | 0.003362 |
| 75 | 0.012649 | 0.008887 | 0.006255 | 0.004409 | 0.003113 |
| 76 | 0.011933 | 0.008345 | 0.005846 | 0.004102 | 0.002883 |
| 77 | 0.011258 | 0.007836 | 0.005463 | 0.003815 | 0.002669 |
| 78 | 0.010620 | 0.007358 | 0.005106 | 0.003549 | 0.002471 |
| 79 | 0.010019 | 0.006908 | 0.004772 | 0.003302 | 0.002288 |
| 80 | 0.009452 | 0.006487 | 0.004460 | 0.003071 | 0.002119 |
| 81 | 0.008917 | 0.006091 | 0.004168 | 0.002857 | 0.001962 |
| 82 | 0.008412 | 0.005719 | 0.003895 | 0.002658 | 0.001817 |
| 83 | 0.007936 | 0.005370 | 0.003640 | 0.002472 | 0.001682 |
| 84 | 0.007487 | 0.005042 | 0.003402 | 0.002300 | 0.001557 |
| 85 | 0.007063 | 0.004735 | 0.003180 | 0.002139 | 0.001442 |
| 86 | 0.006663 | 0.004446 | 0.002972 | 0.001990 | 0.001335 |
| 87 | 0.006286 | 0.004174 | 0.002777 | 0.001851 | 0.001236 |
| 88 | 0.005930 | 0.003920 | 0.002596 | 0.001722 | 0.001145 |
| 89 | 0.005595 | 0.003680 | 0.002426 | 0.001602 | 0.001060 |
| 90 | 0.005278 | 0.003456 | 0.002267 | 0.001490 | 0.000981 |
| 91 | 0.004979 | 0.003245 | 0.002119 | 0.001386 | 0.000909 |
| 92 | 0.004697 | 0.003047 | 0.001980 | 0.001289 | 0.000841 |
| 93 | 0.004432 | 0.002861 | 0.001851 | 0.001200 | 0.000779 |
| 94 | 0.004181 | 0.002686 | 0.001730 | 0.001116 | 0.000721 |
| 95 | 0.003944 | 0.002522 | 0.001616 | 0.001038 | 0.000668 |
| 96 | 0.003721 | 0.002368 | 0.001511 | 0.000966 | 0.000618 |
| 97 | 0.003510 | 0.002224 | 0.001412 | 0.000898 | 0.000573 |
| 98 | 0.003312 | 0.002088 | 0.001319 | 0.000836 | 0.000530 |
| 99 | 0.003124 | 0.001961 | 0.001233 | 0.000777 | 0.000491 |
| 100 | 0.002947 | 0.001841 | 0.001152 | 0.000723 | 0.000455 |

**Table 3**

Partial Table of Common Logarithms

$\log_{10} N$

| N | 0 | 1 | 2 | 3 | 4 | 5 | 6 | 7 | 8 | 9 |
|---|---|---|---|---|---|---|---|---|---|---|
| 1.0 | 0.0000 | 0043 | 0086 | 0128 | 0170 | 0212 | 0253 | 0294 | 0334 | 0374 |
| 1.1 | 0.0414 | 0453 | 0492 | 0531 | 0569 | 0607 | 0645 | 0682 | 0719 | 0755 |
| 1.2 | 0.0792 | 0828 | 0864 | 0899 | 0934 | 0969 | 1004 | 1038 | 1072 | 1106 |
| 1.3 | 0.1139 | 1173 | 1206 | 1239 | 1271 | 1303 | 1335 | 1367 | 1399 | 1430 |
| 1.4 | 0.1461 | 1492 | 1523 | 1553 | 1584 | 1614 | 1644 | 1673 | 1703 | 1732 |
| 1.5 | 0.1761 | 1790 | 1818 | 1847 | 1875 | 1903 | 1931 | 1959 | 1987 | 2014 |
| 1.6 | 0.2041 | 2068 | 2095 | 2122 | 2148 | 2175 | 2201 | 2227 | 2253 | 2279 |
| 1.7 | 0.2304 | 2330 | 2355 | 2380 | 2405 | 2430 | 2455 | 2480 | 2504 | 2529 |
| 1.8 | 0.2553 | 2577 | 2601 | 2625 | 2648 | 2672 | 2695 | 2718 | 2742 | 2765 |
| 1.9 | 0.2788 | 2810 | 2833 | 2856 | 2878 | 2900 | 2923 | 2945 | 2967 | 2989 |
| 2.0 | 0.3010 | | | | | | | | | |
| 3.0 | 0.4771 | | | | | | | | | |
| 4.0 | 0.6021 | | | | | | | | | |
| 5.0 | 0.6990 | | | | | | | | | |
| e | 0.4343 | | | | | | | | | |

**Table 4**

| n | $\sqrt[n]{2}$ |
|---|---|
| 2 | 1.414213 |
| 3 | 1.259921 |
| 4 | 1.189207 |
| 5 | 1.148698 |
| 6 | 1.122462 |
| 7 | 1.104090 |
| 8 | 1.090508 |
| 9 | 1.080060 |
| 10 | 1.071773 |
| 11 | 1.065041 |
| 12 | 1.059463 |
| 13 | 1.054766 |
| 14 | 1.050757 |
| 15 | 1.047294 |
| 16 | 1.044274 |
| 17 | 1.041616 |
| 18 | 1.039259 |
| 19 | 1.037155 |
| 20 | 1.035265 |

# Table 5

$s_{\overline{n}|r}$

$r$ = interest rate per payment period; $n$ = number of payment periods

| $n$ | $\frac{1}{4}\%$ | $\frac{1}{2}\%$ | $\frac{3}{4}\%$ | $1\%$ | $1\frac{1}{4}\%$ |
|---|---|---|---|---|---|
| 1 | 1.000000 | 1.000000 | 1.000000 | 1.000000 | 1.000000 |
| 2 | 2.002499 | 2.005000 | 2.007500 | 2.010000 | 2.012500 |
| 3 | 3.007505 | 3.015025 | 3.022556 | 3.030100 | 3.037656 |
| 4 | 4.015023 | 4.030100 | 4.045225 | 4.060401 | 4.075627 |
| 5 | 5.025060 | 5.050251 | 5.075564 | 5.101005 | 5.126572 |
| 6 | 6.037623 | 6.075502 | 6.113631 | 6.152015 | 6.190654 |
| 7 | 7.052717 | 7.105880 | 7.159483 | 7.213535 | 7.268037 |
| 8 | 8.070347 | 8.141409 | 8.213179 | 8.285670 | 8.358888 |
| 9 | 9.090523 | 9.182116 | 9.274778 | 9.368527 | 9.463374 |
| 10 | 10.113249 | 10.228027 | 10.344339 | 10.462212 | 10.581666 |
| 11 | 11.138532 | 11.279167 | 11.421921 | 11.566834 | 11.713936 |
| 12 | 12.166377 | 12.335563 | 12.507586 | 12.682502 | 12.860361 |
| 13 | 13.196793 | 13.397241 | 13.601393 | 13.809327 | 14.021115 |
| 14 | 14.229784 | 14.464227 | 14.703403 | 14.947421 | 15.196379 |
| 15 | 15.265359 | 15.536549 | 15.813679 | 16.096895 | 16.386334 |
| 16 | 16.303521 | 16.614231 | 16.932281 | 17.257864 | 17.591163 |
| 17 | 17.344280 | 17.697302 | 18.059273 | 18.430442 | 18.811052 |
| 18 | 18.387640 | 18.785789 | 19.194717 | 19.614747 | 20.046190 |
| 19 | 19.433609 | 19.879718 | 20.338678 | 20.810894 | 21.296277 |
| 20 | 20.482192 | 20.979116 | 21.491218 | 22.019003 | 22.562277 |
| 21 | 21.533398 | 22.084012 | 22.652402 | 23.239193 | 23.845014 |
| 22 | 22.587230 | 23.194432 | 23.822295 | 24.471585 | 25.143077 |
| 23 | 23.643699 | 24.310404 | 25.000962 | 25.716301 | 26.457365 |
| 24 | 24.702807 | 25.431957 | 26.188469 | 26.973463 | 27.788082 |
| 25 | 25.764564 | 26.559116 | 27.384883 | 28.243198 | 29.135433 |
| 26 | 26.828975 | 27.691912 | 28.590269 | 29.525630 | 30.499626 |
| 27 | 27.896046 | 28.830372 | 29.804696 | 30.820886 | 31.880871 |
| 28 | 28.965785 | 29.974524 | 31.028231 | 32.129095 | 33.279382 |
| 29 | 30.038200 | 31.124396 | 32.260943 | 33.450386 | 34.695374 |
| 30 | 31.113295 | 32.280018 | 33.502900 | 34.784890 | 36.129066 |
| 31 | 32.191078 | 33.441419 | 34.754172 | 36.132739 | 37.580679 |
| 32 | 33.271555 | 34.608626 | 36.014828 | 37.494066 | 39.050438 |
| 33 | 34.354734 | 35.781669 | 37.284939 | 38.869006 | 40.538568 |
| 34 | 35.440620 | 36.960577 | 38.564576 | 40.257696 | 42.045300 |
| 35 | 36.529221 | 38.145380 | 39.853810 | 41.660273 | 43.670866 |
| 36 | 37.620543 | 39.336107 | 41.152714 | 43.076876 | 45.115502 |
| 37 | 38.714594 | 40.532788 | 42.461359 | 44.507645 | 46.679446 |
| 38 | 39.811380 | 41.735452 | 43.779819 | 45.992721 | 48.262939 |
| 39 | 40.910909 | 42.944129 | 45.108168 | 47.412248 | 49.866225 |
| 40 | 42.013185 | 44.158850 | 46.446479 | 48.886371 | 51.489552 |
| 41 | 43.118218 | 45.379644 | 47.794828 | 50.375234 | 53.133172 |
| 42 | 44.226012 | 46.606543 | 49.153289 | 51.878987 | 54.797337 |
| 43 | 45.336577 | 47.839575 | 50.521938 | 53.397776 | 56.482304 |
| 44 | 46.449918 | 49.078773 | 51.900853 | 54.931754 | 58.188304 |
| 45 | 47.566043 | 50.324167 | 53.290109 | 56.481072 | 59.915686 |
| 46 | 48.684957 | 51.575788 | 54.689785 | 58.045882 | 61.664632 |
| 47 | 49.806669 | 52.833667 | 56.099958 | 59.626341 | 63.435440 |
| 48 | 50.931185 | 54.097835 | 57.520707 | 61.222604 | 65.228383 |
| 49 | 52.058514 | 55.368324 | 58.952113 | 62.834830 | 67.043738 |
| 50 | 53.188659 | 56.645166 | 60.384253 | 64.463178 | 68.881786 |

| $n$ | $\frac{1}{4}\%$ | $\frac{1}{2}\%$ | $\frac{3}{4}\%$ | $1\%$ | $1\frac{1}{4}\%$ |
|---|---|---|---|---|---|
| 51 | 54.321630 | 57.928392 | 61.847210 | 66.107810 | 70.742806 |
| 52 | 55.457433 | 59.218034 | 63.311064 | 67.768888 | 72.627092 |
| 53 | 56.596077 | 60.514125 | 64.785897 | 69.446577 | 74.534930 |
| 54 | 57.737566 | 61.816695 | 66.271791 | 71.141043 | 76.466616 |
| 55 | 58.881910 | 63.125778 | 67.768830 | 72.852453 | 78.422449 |
| 56 | 60.029113 | 64.441408 | 69.277096 | 74.580977 | 80.402730 |
| 57 | 61.179186 | 65.763614 | 70.796674 | 76.326787 | 82.407764 |
| 58 | 62.332134 | 67.092433 | 72.327649 | 78.090055 | 84.437861 |
| 59 | 63.487963 | 68.427895 | 73.870107 | 79.870956 | 86.493334 |
| 60 | 64.646682 | 69.770034 | 75.424132 | 81.669665 | 88.574500 |
| 61 | 65.808299 | 71.118885 | 76.989813 | 83.486361 | 90.681681 |
| 62 | 66.972818 | 72.474479 | 78.567236 | 85.321225 | 92.815202 |
| 63 | 68.140251 | 73.836852 | 80.156491 | 87.174437 | 94.975392 |
| 64 | 69.310600 | 75.206036 | 81.757665 | 89.046181 | 97.162584 |
| 65 | 70.483877 | 76.582066 | 83.370847 | 90.93643 | 99.377116 |
| 66 | 71.660086 | 77.964977 | 84.996128 | 92.846010 | 101.619330 |
| 67 | 72.839236 | 79.354802 | 86.633599 | 94.779970 | 103.889572 |
| 68 | 74.021333 | 80.751576 | 88.283351 | 96.722214 | 106.188191 |
| 69 | 75.206386 | 82.155334 | 89.945476 | 98.689436 | 108.515543 |
| 70 | 76.394402 | 83.566111 | 91.620067 | 100.676380 | 110.871988 |
| 71 | 77.585387 | 84.983941 | 93.307217 | 102.683094 | 113.257887 |
| 72 | 78.779350 | 86.408861 | 95.007022 | 104.709924 | 115.673611 |
| 73 | 79.976298 | 87.840905 | 96.719574 | 106.757024 | 118.119531 |
| 74 | 81.176238 | 89.280110 | 98.444971 | 100.824594 | 120.596025 |
| 75 | 82.379178 | 90.726511 | 100.183308 | 110.912840 | 123.103475 |
| 76 | 83.585124 | 92.180143 | 101.934683 | 113.021968 | 125.642268 |
| 77 | 84.794088 | 93.641044 | 103.699193 | 115.152188 | 128.212797 |
| 78 | 86.006071 | 95.109249 | 105.476936 | 117.303709 | 130.815456 |
| 79 | 87.221088 | 96.584796 | 107.268014 | 119.476747 | 133.450649 |
| 80 | 88.439139 | 98.067720 | 109.072523 | 121.671514 | 136.118782 |
| 81 | 89.660237 | 99.558058 | 110.890567 | 123.888229 | 138.820267 |
| 82 | 90.884387 | 101.055849 | 112.722246 | 126.127111 | 141.555520 |
| 83 | 92.111597 | 102.561128 | 114.567663 | 128.388382 | 144.324964 |
| 84 | 93.341875 | 104.073934 | 116.426920 | 130.672266 | 147.129026 |
| 85 | 94.575230 | 105.594304 | 118.300123 | 132.978988 | 149.968138 |
| 86 | 95.811667 | 107.122275 | 120.187373 | 135.308778 | 152.842740 |
| 87 | 97.051197 | 108.657887 | 122.088778 | 137.661866 | 155.753274 |
| 88 | 98.293823 | 110.201176 | 124.004444 | 140.038484 | 158.700190 |
| 89 | 99.539557 | 111.752182 | 125.934477 | 142.438869 | 161.683492 |
| 90 | 100.788406 | 113.310943 | 127.878986 | 144.863258 | 164.704991 |
| 91 | 102.040376 | 114.877498 | 129.838078 | 147.311890 | 167.763803 |
| 92 | 103.295475 | 116.451885 | 131.811864 | 149.785009 | 170.860850 |
| 93 | 104.553715 | 118.034145 | 133.800453 | 152.282859 | 173.996611 |
| 94 | 105.815098 | 119.624315 | 135.803956 | 154.805687 | 177.171568 |
| 95 | 107.079636 | 121.222438 | 137.822486 | 157.353744 | 180.386213 |
| 96 | 108.347334 | 122.828550 | 139.856154 | 159.927281 | 183.641040 |
| 97 | 109.618202 | 124.442693 | 141.905075 | 162.526554 | 186.936553 |
| 98 | 110.892247 | 126.064906 | 143.969368 | 165.151819 | 190.273260 |
| 99 | 112.172617 | 127.695231 | 146.049133 | 167.803338 | 193.651675 |
| 100 | 113.449899 | 129.333707 | 148.144501 | 170.481370 | 197.072322 |

**Table 5 (continued)**

| $n$ | $1\frac{1}{2}\%$ | $1\frac{3}{4}\%$ | $2\%$ | $2\frac{1}{2}\%$ | $3\%$ |
|---|---|---|---|---|---|
| 1 | 1.000000 | 1.000000 | 1.000000 | 1.000000 | 1.000000 |
| 2 | 2.015000 | 2.017500 | 2.020000 | 2.025000 | 2.030000 |
| 3 | 3.045225 | 3.052806 | 3.060400 | 3.075625 | 3.090900 |
| 4 | 4.090903 | 4.106230 | 4.121608 | 4.152515 | 4.183627 |
| 5 | 5.152267 | 5.178706 | 5.204040 | 5.256315 | 5.309136 |
| 6 | 6.229551 | 6.268706 | 6.308121 | 6.387737 | 6.468410 |
| 7 | 7.322994 | 7.378408 | 7.434283 | 7.547430 | 7.662462 |
| 8 | 8.432839 | 8.507530 | 8.582969 | 8.736116 | 8.892336 |
| 9 | 9.559332 | 9.656412 | 9.754628 | 9.954518 | 10.159106 |
| 10 | 10.702722 | 10.825399 | 10.949720 | 11.203381 | 11.463879 |
| 11 | 11.863262 | 12.014844 | 12.168715 | 12.483466 | 12.807795 |
| 12 | 13.041211 | 13.225103 | 13.412089 | 13.795552 | 14.192029 |
| 13 | 14.236830 | 14.456542 | 14.680331 | 15.140441 | 15.617790 |
| 14 | 15.450382 | 15.709532 | 15.973937 | 16.518952 | 17.086324 |
| 15 | 16.682138 | 16.984449 | 17.293416 | 17.931926 | 18.598913 |
| 16 | 17.932370 | 18.281676 | 18.639284 | 19.380224 | 20.156881 |
| 17 | 19.201355 | 19.601606 | 20.012070 | 20.864730 | 21.761587 |
| 18 | 20.489376 | 20.944634 | 21.412311 | 22.386348 | 23.414435 |
| 19 | 21.796716 | 22.311165 | 22.840558 | 23.946006 | 25.116868 |
| 20 | 23.123667 | 23.701610 | 24.297369 | 25.544656 | 26.870374 |
| 21 | 24.470522 | 25.116388 | 25.783316 | 27.183273 | 28.676485 |
| 22 | 25.837580 | 26.555925 | 27.298982 | 28.862855 | 30.536780 |
| 23 | 27.225143 | 28.020654 | 28.844962 | 30.584426 | 32.452883 |
| 24 | 28.633521 | 29.511015 | 30.421861 | 32.349036 | 34.426469 |
| 25 | 30.063024 | 31.027458 | 32.030298 | 34.157762 | 36.459263 |
| 26 | 31.513969 | 32.570438 | 33.670904 | 36.011706 | 38.553041 |
| 27 | 32.986678 | 34.140421 | 35.344322 | 37.911999 | 40.709632 |
| 28 | 34.481478 | 35.737878 | 37.051208 | 39.859799 | 42.930921 |
| 29 | 35.998701 | 37.363291 | 38.792232 | 41.856294 | 45.218849 |
| 30 | 37.538681 | 39.017148 | 40.568077 | 43.902701 | 47.575414 |
| 31 | 39.101761 | 40.699948 | 42.379438 | 46.000268 | 50.002677 |
| 32 | 40.688288 | 42.412197 | 44.227027 | 48.150275 | 52.502757 |
| 33 | 42.298612 | 44.154411 | 46.111568 | 50.354032 | 55.077840 |
| 34 | 43.933091 | 45.927113 | 48.033799 | 52.612883 | 57.730175 |
| 35 | 45.592088 | 47.730837 | 49.994475 | 54.928205 | 60.462080 |
| 36 | 47.275969 | 49.566127 | 51.994364 | 57.301409 | 63.275942 |
| 37 | 48.985109 | 51.433534 | 54.034251 | 59.733945 | 66.174221 |
| 38 | 50.719885 | 53.333621 | 56.114936 | 62.227293 | 69.159447 |
| 39 | 52.480683 | 55.266959 | 58.237235 | 64.782976 | 72.234231 |
| 40 | 54.267894 | 57.234131 | 60.401979 | 67.402550 | 75.401258 |
| 41 | 56.081912 | 59.235728 | 62.610019 | 70.087614 | 78.663295 |
| 42 | 57.923141 | 61.272353 | 64.862219 | 72.839804 | 82.023194 |
| 43 | 59.791988 | 63.344619 | 67.159464 | 75.660799 | 85.483890 |
| 44 | 61.688868 | 65.453150 | 69.502653 | 78.552318 | 89.048406 |
| 45 | 63.614201 | 67.598580 | 71.892706 | 81.516126 | 92.719858 |
| 46 | 65.568414 | 69.781555 | 74.330560 | 84.554030 | 96.501454 |
| 47 | 67.551940 | 72.002732 | 76.817171 | 87.667880 | 100.396498 |
| 48 | 69.565219 | 74.262760 | 79.353514 | 90.859577 | 104.408392 |
| 49 | 71.608698 | 76.562378 | 81.940584 | 94.131066 | 108.540644 |
| 50 | 73.682828 | 78.902220 | 84.579396 | 97.484343 | 112.796863 |

| $n$ | $1\frac{1}{2}\%$ | $1\frac{3}{4}\%$ | $2\%$ | $2\frac{1}{2}\%$ | $3\%$ |
|---|---|---|---|---|---|
| 51 | 75.788070 | 81.283009 | 87.270984 | 100.921451 | 117.180769 |
| 52 | 77.924891 | 83.705461 | 90.016403 | 104.444487 | 121.696192 |
| 53 | 80.093765 | 86.170307 | 92.816731 | 108.055599 | 126.347078 |
| 54 | 82.295171 | 88.678287 | 95.673065 | 111.756989 | 131.137490 |
| 55 | 84.529599 | 91.230157 | 98.586527 | 115.550914 | 136.071615 |
| 56 | 86.797543 | 93.826684 | 101.558257 | 119.439686 | 141.153763 |
| 57 | 89.099506 | 96.468651 | 104.589422 | 123.425679 | 146.388376 |
| 58 | 91.435998 | 99.156852 | 107.681210 | 127.511320 | 151.780027 |
| 59 | 93.807539 | 101.892097 | 110.834834 | 131.699103 | 157.333428 |
| 60 | 96.214651 | 104.675209 | 114.051531 | 135.991581 | 163.053431 |
| 61 | 98.657871 | 107.507025 | 117.332562 | 140.391370 | 168.945034 |
| 62 | 101.137739 | 110.388398 | 120.679212 | 144.901154 | 175.013384 |
| 63 | 103.654805 | 113.320195 | 124.092797 | 149.523683 | 181.263786 |
| 64 | 106.209628 | 116.303298 | 127.574652 | 154.261775 | 187.701699 |
| 65 | 108.802772 | 119.338605 | 131.126145 | 159.118319 | 194.332750 |
| 66 | 111.434813 | 122.427031 | 134.748668 | 164.096277 | 201.162733 |
| 67 | 114.106336 | 125.569504 | 138.443642 | 169.198684 | 208.197614 |
| 68 | 116.817931 | 128.766970 | 142.212514 | 174.428650 | 215.443543 |
| 69 | 119.570200 | 132.020392 | 146.056764 | 179.789366 | 222.906849 |
| 70 | 122.363753 | 135.330748 | 149.977899 | 185.284100 | 230.594054 |
| 71 | 125.199209 | 138.699037 | 153.977457 | 190.916203 | 238.511875 |
| 72 | 128.077197 | 142.126269 | 158.057006 | 196.689107 | 246.667232 |
| 73 | 130.998355 | 145.613479 | 162.218146 | 202.606335 | 255.067249 |
| 74 | 133.963330 | 149.161715 | 166.462508 | 208.671493 | 263.719266 |
| 75 | 136.972780 | 152.772045 | 170.791759 | 214.888280 | 272.630844 |
| 76 | 140.027372 | 156.445555 | 175.207593 | 221.260487 | 281.809769 |
| 77 | 143.127783 | 160.183352 | 179.711746 | 227.791999 | 291.264062 |
| 78 | 146.274699 | 163.986561 | 184.305980 | 234.486799 | 301.001983 |
| 79 | 149.468820 | 167.856326 | 188.992100 | 241.348968 | 311.032043 |
| 80 | 152.710852 | 171.793811 | 193.771941 | 248.382692 | 321.363004 |
| 81 | 156.001515 | 175.800202 | 198.647380 | 255.592259 | 332.003894 |
| 82 | 159.341538 | 179.876706 | 203.620327 | 262.982065 | 342.964010 |
| 83 | 162.731661 | 184.024548 | 208.692734 | 270.556617 | 354.252930 |
| 84 | 166.172636 | 188.244977 | 213.866588 | 278.320532 | 365.880518 |
| 85 | 169.665225 | 192.539264 | 219.143920 | 286.278545 | 377.856933 |
| 86 | 173.210204 | 196.908701 | 224.526798 | 294.435508 | 390.192641 |
| 87 | 176.808356 | 201.354604 | 230.017333 | 302.796396 | 402.898420 |
| 88 | 180.460482 | 205.878308 | 235.617680 | 311.366305 | 415.985373 |
| 89 | 184.167389 | 210.467389 | 241.330033 | 320.150463 | 429.464934 |
| 90 | 187.929900 | 215.164599 | 247.156633 | 329.154224 | 443.348881 |
| 91 | 191.748848 | 219.929980 | 253.099766 | 338.383079 | 457.649348 |
| 92 | 195.625081 | 224.778753 | 259.161761 | 347.842656 | 472.378828 |
| 93 | 199.559458 | 229.712382 | 265.344996 | 357.538722 | 487.550192 |
| 94 | 203.552850 | 234.732348 | 271.651895 | 367.477190 | 503.176698 |
| 95 | 207.606142 | 239.840165 | 278.084933 | 377.664119 | 519.271998 |
| 96 | 211.720234 | 245.037367 | 284.646631 | 388.105722 | 535.850158 |
| 97 | 215.896038 | 250.325521 | 291.339564 | 398.808365 | 552.925662 |
| 98 | 220.134278 | 255.706217 | 298.166354 | 409.778573 | 570.513433 |
| 99 | 224.436456 | 261.181070 | 305.129682 | 421.023038 | 588.628835 |
| 100 | 228.003043 | 266.751744 | 312.232215 | 432.548612 | 607.287700 |

**Table 5 (continued)**

| n | 3½% | 4% | 4½% | 5% | 5½% |
|---|---|---|---|---|---|
| 1 | 1.000000 | 1.000000 | 1.000000 | 1.000000 | 1.000000 |
| 2 | 2.035000 | 2.040000 | 2.045000 | 2.050000 | 2.055000 |
| 3 | 3.106225 | 3.121600 | 3.137025 | 3.152500 | 3.168025 |
| 4 | 4.214943 | 4.246464 | 4.278191 | 4.310125 | 4.342266 |
| 5 | 5.362466 | 5.416322 | 5.470710 | 5.525631 | 5.581091 |
| 6 | 6.550152 | 6.632975 | 6.716892 | 6.801913 | 6.888051 |
| 7 | 7.779407 | 7.898294 | 8.019152 | 8.142008 | 8.266894 |
| 8 | 9.051687 | 9.214226 | 9.380014 | 9.549109 | 9.721573 |
| 9 | 10.368496 | 10.582795 | 10.802114 | 11.026564 | 11.256259 |
| 10 | 11.731393 | 12.006107 | 12.288209 | 12.577892 | 12.875354 |
| 11 | 13.141992 | 13.486351 | 13.841179 | 14.206787 | 14.583498 |
| 12 | 14.601961 | 15.025805 | 15.464032 | 15.917126 | 16.385590 |
| 13 | 16.113030 | 16.626837 | 17.159913 | 17.712983 | 18.286798 |
| 14 | 17.676986 | 18.291911 | 18.932110 | 19.598632 | 20.292572 |
| 15 | 19.295680 | 20.023587 | 20.784054 | 21.578563 | 22.408663 |
| 16 | 20.971029 | 21.824530 | 22.719337 | 23.657492 | 24.641199 |
| 17 | 22.705015 | 23.697511 | 24.741707 | 25.840366 | 26.996402 |
| 18 | 24.499691 | 25.645412 | 26.855084 | 28.132384 | 29.481204 |
| 19 | 26.357180 | 27.671228 | 29.063563 | 30.539004 | 32.102670 |
| 20 | 28.279681 | 29.778077 | 31.371423 | 33.065954 | 34.868317 |
| 21 | 30.269470 | 31.969200 | 33.783137 | 35.719251 | 37.786075 |
| 22 | 32.328901 | 34.247968 | 36.303378 | 38.505214 | 40.864309 |
| 23 | 34.460413 | 36.617887 | 38.937030 | 41.430475 | 44.111846 |
| 24 | 36.666527 | 39.082602 | 41.689197 | 44.501998 | 47.537997 |
| 25 | 38.949855 | 41.645906 | 44.565210 | 47.727098 | 51.152587 |
| 26 | 41.313100 | 44.311742 | 47.570645 | 51.113453 | 54.965979 |
| 27 | 43.759059 | 47.084212 | 50.711324 | 54.669126 | 58.989108 |
| 28 | 46.290626 | 49.967580 | 53.993334 | 58.402582 | 63.233509 |
| 29 | 48.910798 | 52.966284 | 57.423034 | 62.322711 | 67.711302 |
| 30 | 51.622675 | 56.084955 | 61.007070 | 66.438846 | 72.435476 |
| 31 | 54.429469 | 59.328332 | 64.752388 | 70.760789 | 77.419427 |
| 32 | 57.334500 | 62.701465 | 68.666246 | 75.298828 | 82.677496 |
| 33 | 60.341208 | 66.209524 | 72.756227 | 80.063770 | 88.224758 |
| 34 | 63.453150 | 69.857905 | 77.030252 | 85.066958 | 94.077119 |
| 35 | 66.674010 | 73.652221 | 81.496619 | 90.320306 | 100.251361 |
| 36 | 70.007600 | 77.598309 | 86.163966 | 95.836321 | 106.765186 |
| 37 | 73.457866 | 81.702242 | 91.041345 | 101.628137 | 113.637271 |
| 38 | 77.028891 | 85.970331 | 96.138206 | 107.709544 | 120.887320 |
| 39 | 80.724903 | 90.409144 | 101.464425 | 114.095021 | 128.536123 |
| 40 | 84.550274 | 95.025510 | 107.030324 | 120.799772 | 136.605610 |
| 41 | 88.509534 | 99.826530 | 112.846689 | 127.839761 | 145.118918 |
| 42 | 92.607367 | 104.819591 | 118.924790 | 135.231749 | 154.100458 |
| 43 | 96.848625 | 110.012375 | 125.276405 | 142.993336 | 163.575984 |
| 44 | 101.238326 | 115.412870 | 131.913843 | 151.143003 | 173.572663 |
| 45 | 105.781668 | 121.029384 | 138.849966 | 159.700153 | 184.119159 |
| 46 | 110.484026 | 126.870560 | 146.098215 | 168.685160 | 195.245712 |
| 47 | 115.350967 | 132.945382 | 153.672635 | 178.119419 | 206.984226 |
| 48 | 120.388251 | 139.263206 | 161.587903 | 188.025389 | 219.368358 |
| 49 | 125.601839 | 145.833724 | 169.859359 | 198.426559 | 232.433618 |
| 50 | 130.997904 | 152.667073 | 178.503030 | 209.347992 | 246.217467 |
| 51 | 136.582830 | 159.773756 | 187.535667 | 220.815391 | 260.759427 |
| 52 | 142.363229 | 167.164706 | 196.974772 | 232.856160 | 276.101198 |
| 53 | 148.345942 | 174.851294 | 206.838636 | 245.498969 | 292.286761 |
| 54 | 154.538050 | 182.845345 | 217.146375 | 258.773917 | 309.362533 |
| 55 | 160.946882 | 191.159159 | 227.917962 | 272.712612 | 327.377472 |
| 56 | 167.580022 | 199.805525 | 239.174270 | 287.348243 | 346.383232 |
| 57 | 174.445322 | 208.797746 | 250.937112 | 302.715655 | 366.434311 |
| 58 | 181.550909 | 218.149655 | 263.229282 | 318.851437 | 387.588197 |
| 59 | 188.905191 | 227.875641 | 276.074601 | 335.794010 | 409.905548 |
| 60 | 196.516872 | 237.990667 | 289.497957 | 353.583710 | 433.450352 |
| 61 | 204.394962 | 248.510293 | 303.525365 | 372.262896 | 458.290121 |
| 62 | 212.548786 | 259.450704 | 318.184607 | 391.876039 | 484.496077 |
| 63 | 220.987993 | 270.828732 | 333.502287 | 412.469841 | 512.143361 |
| 64 | 229.722573 | 282.661881 | 349.509890 | 434.093334 | 541.311246 |
| 65 | 238.762862 | 294.968356 | 366.237835 | 456.798000 | 572.083364 |
| 66 | 248.119562 | 307.767089 | 383.718538 | 480.637899 | 604.547948 |
| 67 | 257.803747 | 321.077773 | 401.985872 | 505.669795 | 638.798088 |
| 68 | 267.826878 | 334.920883 | 421.075236 | 531.953284 | 674.931979 |
| 69 | 278.200818 | 349.317718 | 441.023622 | 559.550949 | 713.053237 |
| 70 | 288.937846 | 364.290426 | 461.869685 | 588.528495 | 753.271165 |
| 71 | 300.050671 | 379.862043 | 483.653821 | 618.954919 | 795.701079 |
| 72 | 311.552444 | 396.056524 | 506.418243 | 650.902666 | 840.464637 |
| 73 | 323.456779 | 412.898785 | 530.207064 | 684.447799 | 887.690192 |
| 74 | 335.777766 | 430.414735 | 555.066382 | 719.670188 | 937.513151 |
| 75 | 348.529988 | 448.631325 | 581.044370 | 756.653697 | 990.076374 |
| 76 | 361.728537 | 467.576577 | 608.191366 | 795.486382 | 1045.530574 |
| 77 | 375.389035 | 487.279640 | 636.559978 | 836.260701 | 1104.034758 |
| 78 | 389.527651 | 507.770825 | 666.205177 | 879.073734 | 1165.756665 |
| 79 | 404.161119 | 529.081656 | 697.184410 | 924.027421 | 1230.873281 |
| 80 | 419.306757 | 551.244922 | 729.557709 | 971.228793 | 1299.571310 |
| 81 | 434.982494 | 574.294718 | 763.387806 | 1020.790232 | 1372.047730 |
| 82 | 451.206880 | 598.266505 | 798.740257 | 1072.829742 | 1448.510354 |
| 83 | 467.999121 | 623.197166 | 835.683570 | 1127.471228 | 1529.178424 |
| 84 | 485.379090 | 649.125051 | 874.289330 | 1184.844790 | 1614.283236 |
| 85 | 503.367357 | 676.090053 | 914.632349 | 1245.087029 | 1704.068810 |
| 86 | 521.985214 | 704.133654 | 956.790805 | 1308.341380 | 1798.792593 |
| 87 | 541.254696 | 733.299000 | 1000.846391 | 1374.758448 | 1898.726187 |
| 88 | 561.198610 | 763.630957 | 1046.884479 | 1444.496370 | 2004.156123 |
| 89 | 581.840561 | 795.176195 | 1094.994280 | 1517.721189 | 2115.384712 |
| 90 | 603.204980 | 827.983241 | 1145.269024 | 1594.607245 | 2232.730868 |
| 91 | 625.317154 | 862.102572 | 1197.806130 | 1675.337609 | 2356.531064 |
| 92 | 648.203253 | 897.586673 | 1252.707404 | 1760.104489 | 2487.140272 |
| 93 | 671.890367 | 934.490139 | 1310.079238 | 1849.109716 | 2624.932984 |
| 94 | 696.406529 | 972.869744 | 1370.032805 | 1942.565195 | 2770.304297 |
| 95 | 721.780759 | 1012.784531 | 1432.684283 | 2040.693453 | 2923.671030 |
| 96 | 748.043082 | 1054.265909 | 1498.155074 | 2143.728127 | 3085.472935 |
| 97 | 775.224590 | 1097.467747 | 1566.572051 | 2251.914536 | 3256.173945 |
| 98 | 808.357450 | 1142.366453 | 1638.067795 | 2365.510255 | 3436.263509 |
| 99 | 832.474961 | 1189.061112 | 1712.780848 | 2484.785771 | 3626.257999 |
| 100 | 862.611582 | 1237.623554 | 1790.855984 | 2610.025058 | 3826.702184 |

## Table 5 (continued)

| n | 6% | 6½% | 7% | 7½% | 8% | n | 6% | 6½% | 7% | 7½% | 8% |
|---|---|---|---|---|---|---|---|---|---|---|---|
| 1 | 1.000000 | 1.000000 | 1.000000 | 1.000000 | 1.000000 | 51 | 308.756049 | 366.486352 | 435.985936 | 519.719680 | 620.671751 |
| 2 | 2.060000 | 2.065000 | 2.070000 | 2.075000 | 2.080000 | 52 | 328.281411 | 391.307965 | 467.504951 | 559.698656 | 671.325489 |
| 3 | 3.183600 | 3.199225 | 3.214900 | 3.230625 | 3.246400 | 53 | 348.978296 | 417.742982 | 501.230297 | 602.676055 | 726.031528 |
| 4 | 4.374616 | 4.407175 | 4.439943 | 4.472922 | 4.506112 | 54 | 370.916993 | 445.896276 | 537.316416 | 648.876758 | 785.114049 |
| 5 | 5.637093 | 5.693641 | 5.750739 | 5.808391 | 5.866601 | 55 | 394.172013 | 475.879534 | 575.928566 | 698.542515 | 848.923175 |
| 6 | 6.975318 | 7.063728 | 7.153291 | 7.244020 | 7.335929 | 56 | 418.822333 | 507.811705 | 617.243564 | 751.933203 | 917.837026 |
| 7 | 8.393838 | 8.522870 | 8.654021 | 8.787322 | 8.922803 | 57 | 444.951673 | 541.819465 | 661.450614 | 809.328194 | 992.263989 |
| 8 | 9.897468 | 10.076857 | 10.259802 | 10.446371 | 10.636628 | 58 | 472.648773 | 578.037730 | 708.752155 | 871.027808 | 1072.645104 |
| 9 | 11.491316 | 11.731852 | 11.977989 | 12.229849 | 12.487558 | 59 | 502.007700 | 616.610182 | 759.364807 | 937.354893 | 1159.456715 |
| 10 | 13.180795 | 13.494423 | 13.816448 | 14.147087 | 14.486562 | 60 | 533.128160 | 657.689845 | 813.520340 | 1008.656509 | 1253.213249 |
| 11 | 14.971642 | 15.371560 | 15.783599 | 16.208119 | 16.645487 | 61 | 566.115851 | 701.439684 | 871.466765 | 1085.305746 | 1354.470310 |
| 12 | 16.869941 | 17.370711 | 17.888451 | 18.423728 | 18.977126 | 62 | 601.082800 | 748.033264 | 933.469437 | 1167.703677 | 1463.827931 |
| 13 | 18.882137 | 19.499808 | 20.140643 | 20.805507 | 21.495296 | 63 | 638.147769 | 797.655426 | 999.812300 | 1256.281450 | 1581.934169 |
| 14 | 21.015066 | 21.767295 | 22.550487 | 23.365920 | 24.214920 | 64 | 677.436635 | 850.503029 | 1070.799156 | 1351.502560 | 1709.488897 |
| 15 | 23.275970 | 24.182169 | 25.129022 | 26.118364 | 27.152114 | 65 | 719.082832 | 906.785726 | 1146.755097 | 1453.865253 | 1847.248009 |
| 16 | 25.672528 | 26.754010 | 27.888053 | 29.077242 | 30.324283 | 66 | 763.227802 | 966.726798 | 1228.027951 | 1563.905145 | 1996.027847 |
| 17 | 28.212879 | 29.493021 | 30.840217 | 32.258035 | 33.750225 | 67 | 810.021470 | 1030.564038 | 1314.989908 | 1682.198029 | 2156.710075 |
| 18 | 30.905652 | 32.410067 | 33.999032 | 35.677387 | 37.450243 | 68 | 859.622755 | 1098.550703 | 1408.039199 | 1809.362883 | 2330.246878 |
| 19 | 33.759991 | 35.516722 | 37.378964 | 39.353191 | 41.446263 | 69 | 912.200122 | 1170.956497 | 1507.601942 | 1946.065099 | 2517.666628 |
| 20 | 36.785591 | 38.825309 | 40.995491 | 43.304681 | 45.761964 | 70 | 967.932127 | 1248.068670 | 1614.134075 | 2093.019979 | 2720.079956 |
| 21 | 39.992726 | 42.348954 | 44.865176 | 47.552532 | 50.422921 | 71 | 1027.008055 | 1330.193133 | 1728.123464 | 2250.996476 | 2938.686356 |
| 22 | 43.392289 | 46.101636 | 49.005738 | 52.118972 | 55.456754 | 72 | 1089.628537 | 1417.655689 | 1850.092102 | 2420.821210 | 3174.781254 |
| 23 | 46.995827 | 50.098242 | 53.436140 | 57.027894 | 60.893295 | 73 | 1156.006250 | 1510.803308 | 1980.598549 | 2603.382801 | 3429.763757 |
| 24 | 50.815576 | 54.354628 | 58.176669 | 62.304987 | 66.764758 | 74 | 1226.366622 | 1610.005523 | 2120.240443 | 2799.636508 | 3705.144851 |
| 25 | 54.864511 | 58.887679 | 63.249036 | 67.977861 | 73.105939 | 75 | 1300.948621 | 1715.655881 | 2269.657275 | 3010.609246 | 4002.556443 |
| 26 | 59.156381 | 63.715378 | 68.676469 | 74.076200 | 79.954414 | 76 | 1380.005534 | 1828.173516 | 2429.533280 | 3237.404937 | 4323.760948 |
| 27 | 63.705764 | 68.856877 | 74.483821 | 80.631915 | 87.350567 | 77 | 1463.805867 | 1948.004794 | 2600.600607 | 3481.210308 | 4670.661830 |
| 28 | 68.528110 | 74.332575 | 80.697689 | 87.679309 | 95.338828 | 78 | 1552.634216 | 2075.625104 | 2783.642642 | 3743.301081 | 5045.314764 |
| 29 | 73.639797 | 80.164192 | 87.346527 | 95.255257 | 103.965934 | 79 | 1646.792271 | 2211.540734 | 2979.497633 | 4025.048657 | 5449.939954 |
| 30 | 79.058184 | 86.374864 | 94.460783 | 103.399401 | 113.283209 | 80 | 1746.599804 | 2356.290888 | 3189.062458 | 4327.927299 | 5886.935134 |
| 31 | 84.801676 | 92.989230 | 102.073039 | 112.154356 | 123.345866 | 81 | 1852.395794 | 2510.449792 | 3413.296833 | 4653.521842 | 6358.889949 |
| 32 | 90.889776 | 100.033530 | 110.218151 | 121.565933 | 134.213535 | 82 | 1964.539537 | 2674.629030 | 3653.227602 | 5003.535984 | 6868.601137 |
| 33 | 97.343163 | 107.535710 | 118.933422 | 131.683377 | 145.950617 | 83 | 2083.411913 | 2849.479914 | 3909.953540 | 5379.801177 | 7419.089235 |
| 34 | 104.183752 | 115.525531 | 128.258761 | 142.559631 | 158.626667 | 84 | 2209.416623 | 3035.696113 | 4184.650276 | 5784.286270 | 8013.616357 |
| 35 | 111.434777 | 124.034691 | 138.236874 | 154.251603 | 172.316800 | 85 | 2342.981621 | 3234.016555 | 4478.575796 | 6219.107736 | 8655.705661 |
| 36 | 119.120864 | 133.096946 | 148.913455 | 166.820473 | 187.102144 | 86 | 2484.560511 | 3445.227421 | 4793.076093 | 6686.540805 | 9349.162105 |
| 37 | 127.268116 | 142.748247 | 160.337397 | 180.332008 | 203.070315 | 87 | 2634.634147 | 3670.167201 | 5129.591424 | 7189.031364 | 10098.095077 |
| 38 | 135.904202 | 153.026883 | 172.561014 | 194.856909 | 220.315940 | 88 | 2793.712188 | 3909.728077 | 5489.662807 | 7729.208723 | 10906.942661 |
| 39 | 145.058455 | 163.973630 | 185.640285 | 210.471177 | 238.941216 | 89 | 2962.334920 | 4164.860403 | 5874.939210 | 8309.899372 | 11780.498081 |
| 40 | 154.761961 | 175.631916 | 199.635105 | 227.256515 | 259.056512 | 90 | 3141.075010 | 4436.576330 | 6287.184940 | 8934.141819 | 12723.937900 |
| 41 | 165.047679 | 188.047991 | 214.609562 | 245.300754 | 280.300754 | 91 | 3330.539515 | 4725.953783 | 6728.287887 | 9605.202449 | 13742.852951 |
| 42 | 175.950540 | 201.271110 | 230.632231 | 264.698310 | 304.243515 | 92 | 3531.371874 | 5034.140785 | 7200.268024 | 10326.592628 | 14843.281143 |
| 43 | 187.507572 | 215.353732 | 247.776488 | 285.550683 | 329.582997 | 93 | 3744.254194 | 5362.359933 | 7705.286788 | 11102.087059 | 16031.743671 |
| 44 | 199.758026 | 230.351725 | 266.120841 | 307.966984 | 356.949636 | 94 | 3969.909436 | 5711.913330 | 8245.656841 | 11935.743587 | 17315.283134 |
| 45 | 212.743508 | 246.324588 | 285.749300 | 332.064508 | 386.505607 | 95 | 4209.104005 | 6084.187692 | 8823.852836 | 12831.924335 | 18701.505798 |
| 46 | 226.508118 | 263.335686 | 306.751749 | 357.969346 | 418.426055 | 96 | 4462.650238 | 6480.659896 | 9442.522521 | 13795.318672 | 20198.626205 |
| 47 | 241.098605 | 281.452505 | 329.224373 | 385.817046 | 452.900140 | 97 | 4731.409255 | 6902.902790 | 10104.499080 | 14830.967571 | 21815.516296 |
| 48 | 256.564521 | 300.746919 | 353.270078 | 415.753325 | 490.132150 | 98 | 5016.293804 | 7352.591470 | 10812.814002 | 15944.290138 | 23561.757575 |
| 49 | 272.958392 | 321.295468 | 378.998984 | 447.934824 | 530.342722 | 99 | 5318.271438 | 7831.509906 | 11570.710987 | 17141.111877 | 25447.698181 |
| 50 | 290.335895 | 343.179673 | 406.528912 | 482.529936 | 573.770138 | 100 | 5638.567708 | 8341.558067 | 12381.660732 | 18427.695266 | 27484.514007 |

# Table 6

$a_{\overline{n}|r}$

$r$ = interest rate per payment period; $n$ = number of payment periods

| $n$ | $\frac{1}{4}\%$ | $\frac{1}{2}\%$ | $\frac{3}{4}\%$ | $1\%$ | $1\frac{1}{4}\%$ |
|---|---|---|---|---|---|
| 1 | 0.997506 | 0.995025 | 0.992556 | 0.990099 | 0.987654 |
| 2 | 1.992524 | 1.985099 | 1.977723 | 1.970395 | 1.963115 |
| 3 | 2.985061 | 2.970248 | 2.955556 | 2.940985 | 2.926534 |
| 4 | 3.975123 | 3.950496 | 3.926110 | 3.901965 | 3.878058 |
| 5 | 4.962716 | 4.925867 | 4.889439 | 4.853431 | 4.817835 |
| 6 | 5.947846 | 5.896385 | 5.845597 | 5.795476 | 5.746010 |
| 7 | 6.930741 | 6.862074 | 6.794637 | 6.728194 | 6.662725 |
| 8 | 7.910741 | 7.822960 | 7.736613 | 7.651677 | 7.568124 |
| 9 | 8.888520 | 8.779064 | 8.671576 | 8.566017 | 8.462344 |
| 10 | 9.863860 | 9.730412 | 9.599579 | 9.471304 | 9.345525 |
| 11 | 10.836767 | 10.677027 | 10.520674 | 10.367628 | 10.217803 |
| 12 | 11.807249 | 11.618933 | 11.434912 | 11.255077 | 11.079311 |
| 13 | 12.775310 | 12.556152 | 12.342345 | 12.133740 | 11.930184 |
| 14 | 13.740957 | 13.488708 | 13.243022 | 13.003702 | 12.770552 |
| 15 | 14.704197 | 14.416626 | 14.136994 | 13.865052 | 13.600545 |
| 16 | 15.665033 | 15.339926 | 15.024312 | 14.717873 | 14.420291 |
| 17 | 16.623475 | 16.258633 | 15.905024 | 15.562251 | 15.229918 |
| 18 | 17.579525 | 17.172769 | 16.779180 | 16.398268 | 16.029548 |
| 19 | 18.533192 | 18.082357 | 17.646829 | 17.226008 | 16.819307 |
| 20 | 19.484480 | 18.987420 | 18.508019 | 18.045552 | 17.599315 |
| 21 | 20.433396 | 19.887980 | 19.362798 | 18.856982 | 18.369694 |
| 22 | 21.379946 | 20.784060 | 20.211214 | 19.660379 | 19.130562 |
| 23 | 22.324136 | 21.675682 | 21.053314 | 20.455820 | 19.882036 |
| 24 | 23.265970 | 22.562867 | 21.889145 | 21.243386 | 20.624233 |
| 25 | 24.205456 | 23.445639 | 22.718754 | 22.023155 | 21.357268 |
| 26 | 25.142599 | 24.324019 | 23.542188 | 22.795203 | 22.081252 |
| 27 | 26.077405 | 25.198029 | 24.359492 | 23.559607 | 22.796298 |
| 28 | 27.009879 | 26.067691 | 25.170711 | 24.316442 | 23.502517 |
| 29 | 27.940030 | 26.933025 | 25.975892 | 25.065784 | 24.200016 |
| 30 | 28.867859 | 27.794055 | 26.775079 | 25.807707 | 24.888905 |
| 31 | 29.793376 | 28.650802 | 27.568317 | 26.542284 | 25.569289 |
| 32 | 30.716584 | 29.503285 | 28.355649 | 27.269588 | 26.241273 |
| 33 | 31.637490 | 30.351527 | 29.137121 | 27.989691 | 26.904961 |
| 34 | 32.556099 | 31.195550 | 29.912775 | 28.702665 | 27.560455 |
| 35 | 33.472417 | 32.035373 | 30.682655 | 29.408579 | 28.207857 |
| 36 | 34.386451 | 32.871018 | 31.446804 | 30.107504 | 28.847266 |
| 37 | 35.298205 | 33.702505 | 32.205264 | 30.799509 | 29.478781 |
| 38 | 36.207685 | 34.529856 | 32.958079 | 31.484662 | 30.102500 |
| 39 | 37.114898 | 35.353091 | 33.705289 | 32.163032 | 30.718518 |
| 40 | 38.019848 | 36.172230 | 34.446937 | 32.834685 | 31.326932 |
| 41 | 38.922541 | 36.987293 | 35.183064 | 33.499688 | 31.927834 |
| 42 | 39.822983 | 37.798302 | 35.913711 | 34.158107 | 32.521317 |
| 43 | 40.721180 | 38.605275 | 36.638919 | 34.810007 | 33.107474 |
| 44 | 41.617136 | 39.408234 | 37.358729 | 35.455452 | 33.686394 |
| 45 | 42.510859 | 40.207198 | 38.073180 | 36.094507 | 34.258167 |
| 46 | 43.402353 | 41.002187 | 38.782312 | 36.727235 | 34.822881 |
| 47 | 44.291624 | 41.793221 | 39.486166 | 37.333698 | 35.380623 |
| 48 | 45.178676 | 42.580320 | 40.184780 | 37.973958 | 35.931479 |
| 49 | 46.063518 | 43.363502 | 40.878194 | 38.588077 | 36.475535 |
| 50 | 46.946152 | 44.142788 | 41.566445 | 39.196116 | 37.012874 |
| 51 | 47.826585 | 44.918198 | 42.249573 | 39.798135 | 37.543579 |
| 52 | 48.704822 | 45.689749 | 42.927616 | 40.394193 | 38.067733 |
| 53 | 49.580870 | 46.457462 | 43.600612 | 40.984349 | 38.585415 |
| 54 | 50.454732 | 47.221355 | 44.268597 | 41.568663 | 39.096706 |
| 55 | 51.326417 | 47.981447 | 44.931610 | 42.147191 | 39.601685 |
| 56 | 52.195926 | 48.737759 | 45.589687 | 42.719991 | 40.100430 |
| 57 | 53.063268 | 49.490307 | 46.242866 | 43.287120 | 40.593017 |
| 58 | 53.928446 | 50.239112 | 46.891182 | 43.848633 | 41.079523 |
| 59 | 54.791466 | 50.984191 | 47.534672 | 44.404587 | 41.560023 |
| 60 | 55.652335 | 51.725563 | 48.173372 | 44.955037 | 42.034590 |
| 61 | 56.511058 | 52.463247 | 48.807317 | 45.500037 | 42.503299 |
| 62 | 57.367637 | 53.197261 | 49.436542 | 46.039640 | 42.966221 |
| 63 | 58.222083 | 53.927623 | 50.061085 | 46.573901 | 43.423428 |
| 64 | 59.074396 | 54.654351 | 50.680977 | 47.102872 | 43.874991 |
| 65 | 59.924584 | 55.377464 | 51.296255 | 47.626606 | 44.320978 |
| 66 | 60.772652 | 56.096979 | 51.906953 | 48.145155 | 44.761460 |
| 67 | 61.618605 | 56.812914 | 52.513105 | 48.658569 | 45.196504 |
| 68 | 62.462449 | 57.525288 | 53.114744 | 49.166900 | 45.626177 |
| 69 | 63.304188 | 58.234117 | 53.711905 | 49.670198 | 46.050545 |
| 70 | 64.143828 | 58.939420 | 54.304620 | 50.168513 | 46.469674 |
| 71 | 64.981375 | 59.641214 | 54.892923 | 50.661894 | 46.883629 |
| 72 | 65.816832 | 60.339517 | 55.476847 | 51.150390 | 47.292473 |
| 73 | 66.650206 | 61.034345 | 56.056424 | 51.634049 | 47.696269 |
| 74 | 67.481502 | 61.725716 | 56.631686 | 52.112920 | 48.095081 |
| 75 | 68.310725 | 62.413648 | 57.202666 | 52.587050 | 48.488969 |
| 76 | 69.137879 | 63.098157 | 57.769395 | 53.056485 | 48.877994 |
| 77 | 69.962972 | 63.779261 | 58.331906 | 53.521272 | 49.262216 |
| 78 | 70.786006 | 64.456976 | 58.890229 | 53.981457 | 49.641695 |
| 79 | 71.606989 | 65.131320 | 59.444396 | 54.437087 | 50.016488 |
| 80 | 72.425923 | 65.802308 | 59.994438 | 54.888205 | 50.386655 |
| 81 | 73.242816 | 66.469958 | 60.540385 | 55.334856 | 50.752252 |
| 82 | 74.057672 | 67.134287 | 61.082268 | 55.777085 | 51.113335 |
| 83 | 74.870495 | 67.795311 | 61.620117 | 56.214936 | 51.469961 |
| 84 | 75.681291 | 68.453045 | 62.153962 | 56.648415 | 51.822184 |
| 85 | 76.490066 | 69.107508 | 62.683834 | 57.077674 | 52.170058 |
| 86 | 77.296823 | 69.758714 | 63.209760 | 57.502648 | 52.513637 |
| 87 | 78.101570 | 70.406681 | 63.731772 | 57.923414 | 52.852975 |
| 88 | 78.904308 | 71.051424 | 64.249898 | 58.340014 | 53.188124 |
| 89 | 79.705045 | 71.692959 | 64.764167 | 58.752489 | 53.519134 |
| 90 | 80.503785 | 72.331303 | 65.274607 | 59.160880 | 53.846059 |
| 91 | 81.300533 | 72.966470 | 65.781248 | 59.565228 | 54.168947 |
| 92 | 82.095294 | 73.598478 | 66.284117 | 59.965572 | 54.487849 |
| 93 | 82.888075 | 74.227341 | 66.783242 | 60.361952 | 54.802813 |
| 94 | 83.678877 | 74.853076 | 67.278652 | 60.754408 | 55.113890 |
| 95 | 84.467708 | 75.475697 | 67.770375 | 61.142978 | 55.421126 |
| 96 | 85.254571 | 76.095221 | 68.258436 | 61.527701 | 55.724569 |
| 97 | 86.039472 | 76.711663 | 68.742865 | 61.908615 | 56.024265 |
| 98 | 86.822415 | 77.325038 | 69.223687 | 62.285758 | 56.320262 |
| 99 | 87.603406 | 77.935361 | 69.700930 | 62.659166 | 56.612604 |
| 100 | 88.382449 | 78.542648 | 70.174620 | 63.028877 | 56.901338 |

**Table 6 (continued)**

| n | 1½% | 1¾% | 2% | 2½% | 3% |
|---|---|---|---|---|---|
| 1 | 0.985222 | 0.982801 | 0.980392 | 0.975610 | 0.970874 |
| 2 | 1.955883 | 1.948699 | 1.941561 | 1.927424 | 1.913470 |
| 3 | 2.912200 | 2.897984 | 2.883883 | 2.856024 | 2.828611 |
| 4 | 3.854385 | 3.830942 | 3.807729 | 3.761974 | 3.717098 |
| 5 | 4.782645 | 4.747855 | 4.713459 | 4.645828 | 4.579707 |
| 6 | 5.697187 | 5.648997 | 5.601431 | 5.508125 | 5.417191 |
| 7 | 6.598214 | 6.534641 | 6.471991 | 6.349390 | 6.230283 |
| 8 | 7.485925 | 7.405053 | 7.325481 | 7.170137 | 7.019692 |
| 9 | 8.360517 | 8.260494 | 8.162236 | 7.970865 | 7.786109 |
| 10 | 9.222184 | 9.101223 | 8.982585 | 8.752064 | 8.530203 |
| 11 | 10.071118 | 9.927492 | 9.786848 | 9.514208 | 9.252624 |
| 12 | 10.907505 | 10.739549 | 10.575341 | 10.257764 | 9.954004 |
| 13 | 11.731532 | 11.537641 | 11.348373 | 10.983185 | 10.634955 |
| 14 | 12.543361 | 12.322005 | 12.106248 | 11.690912 | 11.296073 |
| 15 | 13.343233 | 13.092880 | 12.849263 | 12.381377 | 11.937935 |
| 16 | 14.131264 | 13.850496 | 13.577709 | 13.055002 | 12.561102 |
| 17 | 14.907649 | 14.595082 | 14.291871 | 13.712197 | 13.166118 |
| 18 | 15.672561 | 15.326862 | 14.992031 | 14.353363 | 13.753513 |
| 19 | 16.426168 | 16.046056 | 15.678462 | 14.978891 | 14.323799 |
| 20 | 17.168639 | 16.752881 | 16.351433 | 15.589162 | 14.877475 |
| 21 | 17.900137 | 17.447549 | 17.011209 | 16.184548 | 15.415024 |
| 22 | 18.620824 | 18.130269 | 17.658048 | 16.765413 | 15.936916 |
| 23 | 19.330861 | 18.801247 | 18.292204 | 17.332110 | 16.443608 |
| 24 | 20.030405 | 19.460685 | 18.913925 | 17.884985 | 16.935542 |
| 25 | 20.719611 | 20.108781 | 19.523456 | 18.424376 | 17.413147 |
| 26 | 21.398632 | 20.745731 | 20.121035 | 18.950611 | 17.876842 |
| 27 | 22.067617 | 21.371726 | 20.706897 | 19.464010 | 18.327031 |
| 28 | 22.726717 | 21.986954 | 21.281272 | 19.964888 | 18.764108 |
| 29 | 23.376076 | 22.591601 | 21.844384 | 20.453549 | 19.188454 |
| 30 | 24.015838 | 23.185849 | 22.396455 | 20.930292 | 19.600441 |
| 31 | 24.646146 | 23.769876 | 22.937701 | 21.395407 | 20.000428 |
| 32 | 25.267139 | 24.343858 | 23.468334 | 21.849177 | 20.388765 |
| 33 | 25.878954 | 24.907969 | 23.988563 | 22.291880 | 20.765792 |
| 34 | 26.481728 | 25.462377 | 24.498591 | 22.723786 | 21.131836 |
| 35 | 27.075595 | 26.007250 | 24.998619 | 23.145157 | 21.487220 |
| 36 | 27.660684 | 26.542752 | 25.488842 | 23.556251 | 21.832252 |
| 37 | 28.237127 | 27.069044 | 25.969453 | 23.957318 | 22.167235 |
| 38 | 28.805052 | 27.586284 | 26.440640 | 24.348603 | 22.492461 |
| 39 | 29.364583 | 28.094628 | 26.902588 | 24.730344 | 22.808215 |
| 40 | 29.915845 | 28.594229 | 27.355478 | 25.102775 | 23.114772 |
| 41 | 30.458961 | 29.085237 | 27.799489 | 25.466121 | 23.412400 |
| 42 | 30.994050 | 29.567801 | 28.234793 | 25.820606 | 23.701359 |
| 43 | 31.521232 | 30.042064 | 28.661562 | 26.166445 | 23.981902 |
| 44 | 32.040622 | 30.508171 | 29.079962 | 26.503849 | 24.254274 |
| 45 | 32.552337 | 30.966262 | 29.490159 | 26.833023 | 24.518712 |
| 46 | 33.056490 | 31.416473 | 29.892313 | 27.154169 | 24.775449 |
| 47 | 33.553192 | 31.858942 | 30.286581 | 27.467482 | 25.024708 |
| 48 | 34.042554 | 32.293800 | 30.673119 | 27.773153 | 25.266706 |
| 49 | 34.524683 | 32.721180 | 31.052077 | 28.071369 | 25.501657 |
| 50 | 34.999688 | 33.141209 | 31.423605 | 28.362311 | 25.729764 |

| n | 1½% | 1¾% | 2% | 2½% | 3% |
|---|---|---|---|---|---|
| 51 | 35.467673 | 33.54013 | 31.787848 | 28.646157 | 25.951227 |
| 52 | 35.928742 | 33.959718 | 32.144949 | 28.923080 | 26.166240 |
| 53 | 36.382997 | 34.358445 | 32.495048 | 29.193249 | 26.374990 |
| 54 | 36.830539 | 34.750315 | 32.838282 | 29.456828 | 26.577660 |
| 55 | 37.271467 | 35.135445 | 33.174787 | 29.713979 | 26.774427 |
| 56 | 37.705879 | 35.513950 | 33.504693 | 29.964857 | 26.965464 |
| 57 | 38.133871 | 35.885946 | 33.828130 | 30.209617 | 27.150935 |
| 58 | 38.555537 | 36.251544 | 34.145226 | 30.448407 | 27.331005 |
| 59 | 38.970973 | 36.610854 | 34.456104 | 30.681372 | 27.505830 |
| 60 | 39.380269 | 36.963985 | 34.760886 | 30.908656 | 27.675564 |
| 61 | 39.783516 | 37.311041 | 35.059692 | 31.130396 | 27.840353 |
| 62 | 40.180804 | 37.652129 | 35.352639 | 31.346728 | 28.000343 |
| 63 | 40.572221 | 37.987351 | 35.639842 | 31.557783 | 28.155672 |
| 64 | 40.957755 | 38.316806 | 35.921414 | 31.763691 | 28.306478 |
| 65 | 41.337786 | 38.640596 | 36.197465 | 31.964577 | 28.452891 |
| 66 | 41.712105 | 38.958817 | 36.468103 | 32.160562 | 28.595040 |
| 67 | 42.080891 | 39.271564 | 36.733434 | 32.351768 | 28.733049 |
| 68 | 42.444228 | 39.578933 | 36.993563 | 32.538311 | 28.867038 |
| 69 | 42.802195 | 39.881015 | 37.248591 | 32.720303 | 28.997124 |
| 70 | 43.154872 | 40.177902 | 37.498619 | 32.897857 | 29.123421 |
| 71 | 43.502337 | 40.469682 | 37.743744 | 33.071080 | 29.246040 |
| 72 | 43.844667 | 40.756445 | 37.984062 | 33.240078 | 29.365087 |
| 73 | 44.181938 | 41.038275 | 38.219669 | 33.404954 | 29.480667 |
| 74 | 44.514224 | 41.315258 | 38.450656 | 33.565809 | 29.592881 |
| 75 | 44.841600 | 41.587477 | 38.677114 | 33.722740 | 29.701826 |
| 76 | 45.164138 | 41.855014 | 38.899131 | 33.875844 | 29.807598 |
| 77 | 45.481910 | 42.117950 | 39.116795 | 34.025214 | 29.910290 |
| 78 | 45.794985 | 42.376364 | 39.330191 | 34.170940 | 30.009990 |
| 79 | 46.103433 | 42.630333 | 39.539403 | 34.313112 | 30.106786 |
| 80 | 46.407323 | 42.879934 | 39.744513 | 34.451817 | 30.200763 |
| 81 | 46.706723 | 43.125242 | 39.945601 | 34.587138 | 30.292003 |
| 82 | 47.001697 | 43.366331 | 40.142746 | 34.719159 | 30.380586 |
| 83 | 47.292313 | 43.603274 | 40.336025 | 34.847960 | 30.466588 |
| 84 | 47.578633 | 43.836142 | 40.525515 | 34.973620 | 30.550085 |
| 85 | 47.860722 | 44.065004 | 40.711289 | 35.096214 | 30.631151 |
| 86 | 48.138643 | 44.289930 | 40.893421 | 35.215819 | 30.709855 |
| 87 | 48.412456 | 44.510988 | 41.071981 | 35.332506 | 30.786267 |
| 88 | 48.682222 | 44.728244 | 41.247040 | 35.446348 | 30.860454 |
| 89 | 48.948002 | 44.941763 | 41.418667 | 35.557412 | 30.932479 |
| 90 | 49.209854 | 45.151610 | 41.586929 | 35.665768 | 31.002407 |
| 91 | 49.467837 | 45.357847 | 41.751891 | 35.771481 | 31.070298 |
| 92 | 49.722007 | 45.560538 | 41.913618 | 35.874616 | 31.136621 |
| 93 | 49.972421 | 45.759742 | 42.072175 | 35.975235 | 31.200206 |
| 94 | 50.219134 | 45.955521 | 42.227622 | 36.073400 | 31.263336 |
| 95 | 50.462201 | 46.147932 | 42.380022 | 36.169171 | 31.322656 |
| 96 | 50.701675 | 46.337034 | 42.529433 | 36.262605 | 31.381219 |
| 97 | 50.937611 | 46.522883 | 42.675915 | 36.353761 | 31.438077 |
| 98 | 51.170060 | 46.705537 | 42.819524 | 36.442694 | 31.493279 |
| 99 | 51.399074 | 46.885048 | 42.960318 | 36.529458 | 31.546872 |
| 100 | 51.624704 | 47.061472 | 43.098351 | 36.614105 | 31.598905 |

**Table 6 (continued)**

| n | 3½% | 4% | 4½% | 5% | 5½% |
|---|---|---|---|---|---|
| 1 | 0.966184 | 0.961538 | 0.956938 | 0.952381 | 0.947867 |
| 2 | 1.899694 | 1.886095 | 1.872668 | 1.859410 | 1.846320 |
| 3 | 2.801637 | 2.775091 | 2.748964 | 2.723248 | 2.697933 |
| 4 | 3.673079 | 3.629895 | 3.587526 | 3.545950 | 3.505150 |
| 5 | 4.515052 | 4.451822 | 4.389977 | 4.329477 | 4.270284 |
| 6 | 5.328553 | 5.242137 | 5.157873 | 5.075692 | 4.995530 |
| 7 | 6.114544 | 6.002055 | 5.892701 | 5.786373 | 5.682967 |
| 8 | 6.873955 | 6.732745 | 6.595886 | 6.463213 | 6.334566 |
| 9 | 7.607686 | 7.435331 | 7.268791 | 7.107822 | 6.952195 |
| 10 | 8.316605 | 8.110896 | 7.912718 | 7.721735 | 7.537626 |
| 11 | 9.001551 | 8.760477 | 8.528917 | 8.306414 | 8.092536 |
| 12 | 9.663334 | 9.385074 | 9.118581 | 8.863252 | 8.618518 |
| 13 | 10.302738 | 9.985648 | 9.682852 | 9.393573 | 9.117078 |
| 14 | 10.920520 | 10.563123 | 10.222825 | 9.898641 | 9.589648 |
| 15 | 11.517411 | 11.118387 | 10.739546 | 10.379658 | 10.037581 |
| 16 | 12.094117 | 11.652295 | 11.234015 | 10.837770 | 10.462162 |
| 17 | 12.651320 | 12.165669 | 11.707191 | 11.274066 | 10.864608 |
| 18 | 13.189682 | 12.659297 | 12.159992 | 11.689587 | 11.246074 |
| 19 | 13.709837 | 13.133939 | 12.593294 | 12.085321 | 11.607653 |
| 20 | 14.212403 | 13.590326 | 13.007937 | 12.462210 | 11.950382 |
| 21 | 14.697974 | 14.029160 | 13.404724 | 12.821153 | 12.275244 |
| 22 | 15.167125 | 14.451115 | 13.784425 | 13.163003 | 12.583170 |
| 23 | 15.620410 | 14.856841 | 14.147775 | 13.488574 | 12.875042 |
| 24 | 16.058367 | 15.246963 | 14.495478 | 13.798642 | 13.151699 |
| 25 | 16.481514 | 15.622080 | 14.828209 | 14.093945 | 13.413933 |
| 26 | 16.890352 | 15.982769 | 15.146611 | 14.375185 | 13.662495 |
| 27 | 17.285364 | 16.329585 | 15.451303 | 14.643034 | 13.898100 |
| 28 | 17.667019 | 16.663063 | 15.742874 | 14.898127 | 14.121422 |
| 29 | 18.035767 | 16.983714 | 16.021889 | 15.141074 | 14.333101 |
| 30 | 18.392045 | 17.292033 | 16.288889 | 15.372451 | 14.533745 |
| 31 | 18.736276 | 17.588493 | 16.544391 | 15.592810 | 14.723929 |
| 32 | 19.068865 | 17.873551 | 16.788891 | 15.802677 | 14.904198 |
| 33 | 19.390208 | 18.147645 | 17.022862 | 16.002549 | 15.075069 |
| 34 | 19.700684 | 18.411197 | 17.246758 | 16.192904 | 15.237033 |
| 35 | 20.000661 | 18.664613 | 17.461012 | 16.374194 | 15.390552 |
| 36 | 20.290494 | 18.908282 | 17.666041 | 16.546852 | 15.536068 |
| 37 | 20.570525 | 19.142579 | 17.862240 | 16.711287 | 15.673098 |
| 38 | 20.841087 | 19.367864 | 18.049990 | 16.867893 | 15.804738 |
| 39 | 21.102500 | 19.584485 | 18.229656 | 17.017041 | 15.928662 |
| 40 | 21.355072 | 19.792774 | 18.401584 | 17.159086 | 16.046125 |
| 41 | 21.599103 | 19.993052 | 18.566110 | 17.294368 | 16.157464 |
| 42 | 21.834883 | 20.185627 | 18.723550 | 17.423208 | 16.262999 |
| 43 | 22.062688 | 20.370795 | 18.874210 | 17.545712 | 16.363032 |
| 44 | 22.28791 | 20.548841 | 19.018383 | 17.662773 | 16.457851 |
| 45 | 22.495450 | 20.720040 | 19.156347 | 17.774070 | 16.547726 |
| 46 | 22.700918 | 20.884653 | 19.288371 | 17.880066 | 16.632915 |
| 47 | 22.899438 | 21.042936 | 19.414709 | 17.981016 | 16.713664 |
| 48 | 23.091244 | 21.195131 | 19.535607 | 18.077158 | 16.790203 |
| 49 | 23.276564 | 21.341472 | 19.651298 | 18.168722 | 16.862751 |
| 50 | 23.455618 | 21.482184 | 19.762008 | 18.255925 | 16.931518 |

| n | 3½% | 4% | 4½% | 5% | 5½% |
|---|---|---|---|---|---|
| 51 | 23.628616 | 21.617485 | 19.867950 | 18.338977 | 16.996699 |
| 52 | 23.795764 | 21.747582 | 19.969330 | 18.418073 | 17.058483 |
| 53 | 23.957260 | 21.872675 | 20.066345 | 18.493403 | 17.117045 |
| 54 | 24.113295 | 21.992966 | 20.159182 | 18.565146 | 17.172555 |
| 55 | 24.264053 | 22.108612 | 20.248021 | 18.633472 | 17.225170 |
| 56 | 24.409713 | 22.219819 | 20.333034 | 18.698545 | 17.275043 |
| 57 | 24.550447 | 22.326749 | 20.414387 | 18.760519 | 17.322316 |
| 58 | 24.686423 | 22.429567 | 20.492236 | 18.819542 | 17.367124 |
| 59 | 24.817800 | 22.528429 | 20.566733 | 18.875754 | 17.409596 |
| 60 | 24.944734 | 22.623490 | 20.638022 | 18.929290 | 17.449854 |
| 61 | 25.067376 | 22.714894 | 20.706241 | 18.980276 | 17.488013 |
| 62 | 25.185870 | 22.802783 | 20.771523 | 19.028834 | 17.524183 |
| 63 | 25.300358 | 22.887291 | 20.833993 | 19.075080 | 17.558468 |
| 64 | 25.410974 | 22.968549 | 20.893773 | 19.119124 | 17.590965 |
| 65 | 25.517849 | 23.046682 | 20.950979 | 19.161070 | 17.621767 |
| 66 | 25.621110 | 23.121809 | 21.005722 | 19.201019 | 17.650964 |
| 67 | 25.720879 | 23.194048 | 21.058107 | 19.239066 | 17.678639 |
| 68 | 25.817275 | 23.263507 | 21.108236 | 19.275301 | 17.704871 |
| 69 | 25.910410 | 23.330295 | 21.156207 | 19.309810 | 17.729736 |
| 70 | 26.000397 | 23.394515 | 21.202112 | 19.342677 | 17.753304 |
| 71 | 26.087340 | 23.456264 | 21.246040 | 19.373987 | 17.775644 |
| 72 | 26.171343 | 23.515639 | 21.288077 | 19.403788 | 17.796819 |
| 73 | 26.252505 | 23.572730 | 21.328303 | 19.432179 | 17.816890 |
| 74 | 26.330923 | 23.627625 | 21.366797 | 19.459218 | 17.835914 |
| 75 | 26.406689 | 23.680408 | 21.403634 | 19.484970 | 17.853947 |
| 76 | 26.479892 | 23.731162 | 21.438884 | 19.509495 | 17.871040 |
| 77 | 26.550621 | 23.779963 | 21.472616 | 19.532853 | 17.887242 |
| 78 | 26.618957 | 23.826888 | 21.504896 | 19.555098 | 17.902599 |
| 79 | 26.684983 | 23.872007 | 21.535785 | 19.576283 | 17.917155 |
| 80 | 26.748776 | 23.915392 | 21.565345 | 19.596460 | 17.930953 |
| 81 | 26.810411 | 23.957107 | 21.593632 | 19.615677 | 17.944031 |
| 82 | 26.869962 | 23.997219 | 21.620700 | 19.633978 | 17.956428 |
| 83 | 26.927500 | 24.035787 | 21.646603 | 19.651407 | 17.968178 |
| 84 | 26.983092 | 24.072872 | 21.671390 | 19.668007 | 17.979316 |
| 85 | 27.036804 | 24.108531 | 21.695110 | 19.683816 | 17.989873 |
| 86 | 27.088699 | 24.142818 | 21.717809 | 19.698873 | 17.999879 |
| 87 | 27.138840 | 24.175787 | 21.739530 | 19.713212 | 18.009364 |
| 88 | 27.187285 | 24.207487 | 21.760316 | 19.726869 | 18.018355 |
| 89 | 27.234092 | 24.237969 | 21.780207 | 19.739875 | 18.026876 |
| 90 | 27.279316 | 24.267278 | 21.799241 | 19.752262 | 18.034954 |
| 91 | 27.323010 | 24.295459 | 21.817455 | 19.764059 | 18.042610 |
| 92 | 27.365227 | 24.322557 | 21.834885 | 19.775294 | 18.049868 |
| 93 | 27.406017 | 24.348612 | 21.851565 | 19.785994 | 18.056747 |
| 94 | 27.445427 | 24.373666 | 21.867526 | 19.796185 | 18.063267 |
| 95 | 27.483504 | 24.397756 | 21.882800 | 19.805891 | 18.069447 |
| 96 | 27.520294 | 24.420919 | 21.897417 | 19.815134 | 18.075306 |
| 97 | 27.555839 | 24.443191 | 21.911403 | 19.823937 | 18.080858 |
| 98 | 27.590183 | 24.464607 | 21.924788 | 19.832321 | 18.086122 |
| 99 | 27.623365 | 24.485199 | 21.937596 | 19.840306 | 18.091111 |
| 100 | 27.655525 | 24.504999 | 21.949853 | 19.847910 | 18.095839 |

**Table 6 (continued)**

| n | 6% | 6½% | 7% | 7½% | 8% |
|---|---|---|---|---|---|
| 1 | 0.943396 | 0.938967 | 0.934579 | 0.930233 | 0.925926 |
| 2 | 1.833393 | 1.820626 | 1.808018 | 1.795565 | 1.783265 |
| 3 | 2.673012 | 2.648475 | 2.624316 | 2.600526 | 2.577097 |
| 4 | 3.465106 | 3.425799 | 3.387211 | 3.349326 | 3.312127 |
| 5 | 4.212364 | 4.155679 | 4.100197 | 4.045885 | 3.992710 |
| 6 | 4.917324 | 4.841014 | 4.766540 | 4.693846 | 4.622880 |
| 7 | 5.582381 | 5.484520 | 5.389289 | 5.296601 | 5.206370 |
| 8 | 6.209794 | 6.088751 | 5.971298 | 5.857304 | 5.746639 |
| 9 | 6.801692 | 6.656104 | 6.515232 | 6.378887 | 6.246888 |
| 10 | 7.360087 | 7.188830 | 7.023581 | 6.864081 | 6.710081 |
| 11 | 7.886875 | 7.689042 | 7.498674 | 7.315424 | 7.138964 |
| 12 | 8.383844 | 8.158725 | 7.942686 | 7.735278 | 7.536078 |
| 13 | 8.852683 | 8.599742 | 8.357651 | 8.125840 | 7.903776 |
| 14 | 9.294984 | 9.013842 | 8.745468 | 8.489154 | 8.244237 |
| 15 | 9.712249 | 9.402669 | 9.107914 | 8.827120 | 8.559479 |
| 16 | 10.105895 | 9.767764 | 9.446649 | 9.141507 | 8.851369 |
| 17 | 10.477260 | 10.110577 | 9.763223 | 9.433960 | 9.121638 |
| 18 | 10.827603 | 10.432466 | 10.059087 | 9.706009 | 9.371887 |
| 19 | 11.158116 | 10.734710 | 10.335595 | 9.959078 | 9.603599 |
| 20 | 11.469921 | 11.018507 | 10.594014 | 10.194491 | 9.818147 |
| 21 | 11.764077 | 11.284983 | 10.835527 | 10.413480 | 10.016803 |
| 22 | 12.041582 | 11.535196 | 11.061240 | 10.617191 | 10.200744 |
| 23 | 12.303379 | 11.770137 | 11.272187 | 10.806689 | 10.371059 |
| 24 | 12.550357 | 11.990739 | 11.469334 | 10.982967 | 10.528758 |
| 25 | 12.783356 | 12.197877 | 11.653583 | 11.146946 | 10.674776 |
| 26 | 13.003166 | 12.392373 | 11.825779 | 11.299485 | 10.809978 |
| 27 | 13.210534 | 12.574998 | 11.986709 | 11.441381 | 10.935165 |
| 28 | 13.406164 | 12.746477 | 12.137111 | 11.573378 | 11.051078 |
| 29 | 13.590721 | 12.907490 | 12.277674 | 11.696165 | 11.158406 |
| 30 | 13.764831 | 13.058676 | 12.409041 | 11.810386 | 11.257783 |
| 31 | 13.929086 | 13.200635 | 12.531814 | 11.916638 | 11.349799 |
| 32 | 14.084043 | 13.333929 | 12.646555 | 12.015478 | 11.434999 |
| 33 | 14.230230 | 13.459089 | 12.753790 | 12.107421 | 11.513888 |
| 34 | 14.368141 | 13.576609 | 12.854009 | 12.192950 | 11.586934 |
| 35 | 14.498246 | 13.686957 | 12.947672 | 12.272511 | 11.654568 |
| 36 | 14.620987 | 13.790570 | 13.035208 | 12.346522 | 11.717193 |
| 37 | 14.736780 | 13.887859 | 13.117017 | 12.415370 | 11.775179 |
| 38 | 14.846019 | 13.979210 | 13.193473 | 12.479414 | 11.828869 |
| 39 | 14.949075 | 14.064986 | 13.264928 | 12.538989 | 11.878562 |
| 40 | 15.046297 | 14.145527 | 13.331709 | 12.594409 | 11.924613 |
| 41 | 15.138016 | 14.221152 | 13.394120 | 12.645962 | 11.967235 |
| 42 | 15.224543 | 14.292162 | 13.452449 | 12.693918 | 12.006699 |
| 43 | 15.306173 | 14.358837 | 13.506962 | 12.738528 | 12.043240 |
| 44 | 15.383182 | 14.421443 | 13.557908 | 12.780026 | 12.077074 |
| 45 | 15.455832 | 14.480228 | 13.605522 | 12.818629 | 12.108401 |
| 46 | 15.524370 | 14.535426 | 13.650020 | 12.854539 | 12.137409 |
| 47 | 15.589028 | 14.587254 | 13.691608 | 12.887943 | 12.164267 |
| 48 | 15.650027 | 14.635919 | 13.730474 | 12.919017 | 12.189137 |
| 49 | 15.707572 | 14.681615 | 13.766799 | 12.947922 | 12.212163 |
| 50 | 15.761861 | 14.724521 | 13.800746 | 12.974812 | 12.233485 |

| n | 6% | 6½% | 7% | 7½% | 8% |
|---|---|---|---|---|---|
| 51 | 15.813076 | 14.764808 | 13.832473 | 12.999525 | 12.253224 |
| 52 | 15.861393 | 14.802637 | 13.862124 | 13.023093 | 12.271506 |
| 53 | 15.906974 | 14.838157 | 13.889836 | 13.044737 | 12.288432 |
| 54 | 15.949976 | 14.871509 | 13.915735 | 13.064872 | 12.304103 |
| 55 | 15.990543 | 14.902825 | 13.939939 | 13.083602 | 12.318614 |
| 56 | 16.028814 | 14.932230 | 13.962560 | 13.101025 | 12.332050 |
| 57 | 16.064919 | 14.959840 | 13.983701 | 13.117233 | 12.344491 |
| 58 | 16.098980 | 14.985766 | 14.003459 | 13.132309 | 12.356010 |
| 59 | 16.131113 | 15.010109 | 14.021924 | 13.146334 | 12.366676 |
| 60 | 16.161428 | 15.032966 | 14.039181 | 13.159381 | 12.376552 |
| 61 | 16.190026 | 15.054428 | 14.055309 | 13.171517 | 12.385696 |
| 62 | 16.217006 | 15.074580 | 14.070383 | 13.182807 | 12.394163 |
| 63 | 16.242458 | 15.093503 | 14.084470 | 13.193308 | 12.402003 |
| 64 | 16.266470 | 15.111270 | 14.097635 | 13.203078 | 12.409262 |
| 65 | 16.289123 | 15.127953 | 14.109940 | 13.212165 | 12.415983 |
| 66 | 16.310493 | 15.143618 | 14.121439 | 13.220619 | 12.422207 |
| 67 | 16.330654 | 15.158327 | 14.132186 | 13.228483 | 12.427969 |
| 68 | 16.349673 | 15.172138 | 14.142230 | 13.235798 | 12.433305 |
| 69 | 16.367617 | 15.185106 | 14.151617 | 13.242603 | 12.438245 |
| 70 | 16.384544 | 15.197282 | 14.160389 | 13.248933 | 12.442820 |
| 71 | 16.400513 | 15.208716 | 14.168588 | 13.254821 | 12.447005 |
| 72 | 16.415578 | 15.219452 | 14.176251 | 13.260299 | 12.450977 |
| 73 | 16.429791 | 15.229532 | 14.183412 | 13.265394 | 12.454608 |
| 74 | 16.443199 | 15.238997 | 14.190105 | 13.270134 | 12.457971 |
| 75 | 16.455848 | 15.247885 | 14.196359 | 13.274543 | 12.461084 |
| 76 | 16.467781 | 15.256230 | 14.202205 | 13.278645 | 12.463967 |
| 77 | 16.479039 | 15.264065 | 14.207668 | 13.282460 | 12.466636 |
| 78 | 16.489659 | 15.271423 | 14.212774 | 13.286010 | 12.469107 |
| 79 | 16.499679 | 15.278331 | 14.217546 | 13.289311 | 12.471396 |
| 80 | 16.509131 | 15.284818 | 14.222005 | 13.292383 | 12.473514 |
| 81 | 16.518048 | 15.290909 | 14.226173 | 13.295240 | 12.475476 |
| 82 | 16.526460 | 15.296628 | 14.230069 | 13.297897 | 12.477293 |
| 83 | 16.534396 | 15.301998 | 14.233709 | 13.300370 | 12.478975 |
| 84 | 16.541883 | 15.307041 | 14.237111 | 13.302669 | 12.480532 |
| 85 | 16.548947 | 15.311775 | 14.240291 | 13.304809 | 12.481974 |
| 86 | 16.555610 | 15.316221 | 14.243262 | 13.306799 | 12.483310 |
| 87 | 16.561896 | 15.320395 | 14.246040 | 13.308650 | 12.484546 |
| 88 | 16.567827 | 15.324315 | 14.248635 | 13.310372 | 12.485691 |
| 89 | 16.573421 | 15.327995 | 14.251061 | 13.311974 | 12.486751 |
| 90 | 16.578699 | 15.331451 | 14.253328 | 13.313464 | 12.487732 |
| 91 | 16.583679 | 15.334696 | 14.255447 | 13.314851 | 12.488641 |
| 92 | 16.588376 | 15.337742 | 14.257427 | 13.316140 | 12.489482 |
| 93 | 16.592808 | 15.340603 | 14.259277 | 13.317340 | 12.490261 |
| 94 | 16.596988 | 15.343289 | 14.261007 | 13.318455 | 12.490983 |
| 95 | 16.600932 | 15.345812 | 14.262623 | 13.319493 | 12.491651 |
| 96 | 16.604653 | 15.348180 | 14.264134 | 13.320459 | 12.492269 |
| 97 | 16.608163 | 15.350404 | 14.265546 | 13.321357 | 12.492842 |
| 98 | 16.611475 | 15.352492 | 14.266865 | 13.322193 | 12.493372 |
| 99 | 16.614599 | 15.354452 | 14.268098 | 13.322970 | 12.493863 |
| 100 | 16.617546 | 15.356293 | 14.269251 | 13.323693 | 12.494318 |

**Table 7**

$$\frac{1}{a_{\overline{n}|r}}$$

$r$ = interest rate per payment period; $n$ = number of payment periods

| $n$ | $\frac{1}{4}\%$ | $\frac{1}{2}\%$ | $\frac{3}{4}\%$ | $1\%$ | $1\frac{1}{4}\%$ |
|---|---|---|---|---|---|
| 1 | 1.002500 | 1.005000 | 1.007500 | 1.010000 | 1.012500 |
| 2 | 0.501876 | 0.503753 | 0.505632 | 0.507512 | 0.509394 |
| 3 | 0.335002 | 0.336672 | 0.338346 | 0.340022 | 0.341701 |
| 4 | 0.251565 | 0.253133 | 0.254705 | 0.256281 | 0.257861 |
| 5 | 0.201503 | 0.203010 | 0.204522 | 0.206040 | 0.207562 |
| 6 | 0.168128 | 0.169595 | 0.171069 | 0.172548 | 0.174034 |
| 7 | 0.144289 | 0.145729 | 0.147175 | 0.148628 | 0.150089 |
| 8 | 0.126410 | 0.127829 | 0.129256 | 0.130690 | 0.132133 |
| 9 | 0.112505 | 0.113907 | 0.115319 | 0.116740 | 0.118171 |
| 10 | 0.101380 | 0.102771 | 0.104171 | 0.105582 | 0.107003 |
| 11 | 0.092278 | 0.093659 | 0.095051 | 0.096454 | 0.097868 |
| 12 | 0.084694 | 0.086066 | 0.087451 | 0.088849 | 0.090258 |
| 13 | 0.078276 | 0.079642 | 0.081022 | 0.082415 | 0.083821 |
| 14 | 0.072775 | 0.074136 | 0.075511 | 0.076901 | 0.078305 |
| 15 | 0.068008 | 0.069364 | 0.070736 | 0.072124 | 0.073526 |
| 16 | 0.063836 | 0.065189 | 0.066559 | 0.067945 | 0.069347 |
| 17 | 0.060156 | 0.061506 | 0.062873 | 0.064258 | 0.065660 |
| 18 | 0.056884 | 0.058232 | 0.059598 | 0.060982 | 0.062385 |
| 19 | 0.053957 | 0.055303 | 0.056667 | 0.058052 | 0.059455 |
| 20 | 0.051323 | 0.052666 | 0.054031 | 0.055415 | 0.056820 |
| 21 | 0.048939 | 0.050282 | 0.051645 | 0.053031 | 0.054437 |
| 22 | 0.046773 | 0.048114 | 0.049477 | 0.050864 | 0.052272 |
| 23 | 0.044795 | 0.046135 | 0.047498 | 0.048886 | 0.050297 |
| 24 | 0.042981 | 0.044321 | 0.045685 | 0.047073 | 0.048487 |
| 25 | 0.041313 | 0.042652 | 0.044016 | 0.045407 | 0.046822 |
| 26 | 0.039773 | 0.041112 | 0.042477 | 0.043869 | 0.045287 |
| 27 | 0.038347 | 0.039686 | 0.041052 | 0.042446 | 0.043867 |
| 28 | 0.037023 | 0.038362 | 0.039729 | 0.041124 | 0.042549 |
| 29 | 0.035791 | 0.037129 | 0.038497 | 0.039895 | 0.041322 |
| 30 | 0.034641 | 0.035979 | 0.037348 | 0.038748 | 0.040179 |
| 31 | 0.033565 | 0.034903 | 0.036274 | 0.037676 | 0.039109 |
| 32 | 0.032556 | 0.033895 | 0.035266 | 0.036671 | 0.038108 |
| 33 | 0.031608 | 0.032947 | 0.034320 | 0.035727 | 0.037168 |
| 34 | 0.030716 | 0.032056 | 0.033431 | 0.034840 | 0.036284 |
| 35 | 0.029875 | 0.031215 | 0.032592 | 0.034004 | 0.035451 |
| 36 | 0.029081 | 0.030422 | 0.031800 | 0.033214 | 0.034665 |
| 37 | 0.028330 | 0.029671 | 0.031051 | 0.032468 | 0.033923 |
| 38 | 0.027618 | 0.028960 | 0.030342 | 0.031761 | 0.033220 |
| 39 | 0.026943 | 0.028286 | 0.029669 | 0.031092 | 0.032554 |
| 40 | 0.026302 | 0.027646 | 0.029030 | 0.030456 | 0.031921 |
| 41 | 0.025692 | 0.027036 | 0.028423 | 0.029851 | 0.031321 |
| 42 | 0.025111 | 0.026456 | 0.027845 | 0.029276 | 0.030749 |
| 43 | 0.024557 | 0.025903 | 0.027293 | 0.028727 | 0.030205 |
| 44 | 0.024029 | 0.025375 | 0.026768 | 0.028204 | 0.029686 |
| 45 | 0.023523 | 0.024871 | 0.026265 | 0.027705 | 0.029190 |
| 46 | 0.023040 | 0.024389 | 0.025785 | 0.027228 | 0.028717 |
| 47 | 0.022578 | 0.023927 | 0.025325 | 0.126771 | 0.028264 |
| 48 | 0.022134 | 0.023485 | 0.024885 | 0.026334 | 0.027831 |
| 49 | 0.021709 | 0.023061 | 0.024463 | 0.025915 | 0.027416 |
| 50 | 0.021301 | 0.022654 | 0.024058 | 0.025513 | 0.027018 |

| $n$ | $\frac{1}{4}\%$ | $\frac{1}{2}\%$ | $\frac{3}{4}\%$ | $1\%$ | $1\frac{1}{4}\%$ |
|---|---|---|---|---|---|
| 51 | 0.020909 | 0.022263 | 0.023669 | 0.025127 | 0.026636 |
| 52 | 0.020532 | 0.021887 | 0.023295 | 0.024756 | 0.026269 |
| 53 | 0.020169 | 0.021525 | 0.022935 | 0.024400 | 0.025917 |
| 54 | 0.019820 | 0.021177 | 0.022589 | 0.024057 | 0.025578 |
| 55 | 0.019483 | 0.020841 | 0.022256 | 0.023726 | 0.025251 |
| 56 | 0.019159 | 0.020518 | 0.021935 | 0.023408 | 0.024937 |
| 57 | 0.018845 | 0.020206 | 0.021625 | 0.023102 | 0.024635 |
| 58 | 0.018543 | 0.019905 | 0.021326 | 0.022806 | 0.024343 |
| 59 | 0.018251 | 0.019614 | 0.021037 | 0.022520 | 0.024062 |
| 60 | 0.017969 | 0.019333 | 0.020758 | 0.022244 | 0.023790 |
| 61 | 0.017696 | 0.019061 | 0.020489 | 0.021978 | 0.023528 |
| 62 | 0.017431 | 0.018798 | 0.020228 | 0.021720 | 0.023274 |
| 63 | 0.017176 | 0.018543 | 0.019976 | 0.021471 | 0.023029 |
| 64 | 0.016928 | 0.018297 | 0.019731 | 0.021230 | 0.022792 |
| 65 | 0.016688 | 0.018058 | 0.019495 | 0.020997 | 0.022563 |
| 66 | 0.016455 | 0.017826 | 0.019265 | 0.020771 | 0.022341 |
| 67 | 0.016229 | 0.017602 | 0.019043 | 0.020551 | 0.022126 |
| 68 | 0.016010 | 0.017384 | 0.018827 | 0.020339 | 0.021917 |
| 69 | 0.015797 | 0.017172 | 0.018618 | 0.020133 | 0.021715 |
| 70 | 0.015590 | 0.016967 | 0.018415 | 0.019933 | 0.021519 |
| 71 | 0.015389 | 0.016767 | 0.018217 | 0.019739 | 0.021329 |
| 72 | 0.015194 | 0.016573 | 0.018026 | 0.019550 | 0.021145 |
| 73 | 0.015004 | 0.016384 | 0.017839 | 0.019367 | 0.020966 |
| 74 | 0.014819 | 0.016201 | 0.017658 | 0.019189 | 0.020792 |
| 75 | 0.014639 | 0.016022 | 0.017482 | 0.019016 | 0.020623 |
| 76 | 0.014464 | 0.015848 | 0.017310 | 0.018848 | 0.020459 |
| 77 | 0.014293 | 0.015679 | 0.017143 | 0.018684 | 0.020300 |
| 78 | 0.014127 | 0.015514 | 0.016981 | 0.018525 | 0.020144 |
| 79 | 0.013965 | 0.015354 | 0.016822 | 0.018370 | 0.019993 |
| 80 | 0.013807 | 0.015197 | 0.016668 | 0.018219 | 0.019847 |
| 81 | 0.013653 | 0.015044 | 0.016518 | 0.018072 | 0.019704 |
| 82 | 0.013503 | 0.014896 | 0.016371 | 0.017929 | 0.019564 |
| 83 | 0.013356 | 0.014750 | 0.016228 | 0.017789 | 0.019429 |
| 84 | 0.013213 | 0.014609 | 0.016089 | 0.017653 | 0.019297 |
| 85 | 0.013074 | 0.014470 | 0.015953 | 0.017520 | 0.019168 |
| 86 | 0.012937 | 0.014335 | 0.015820 | 0.017391 | 0.019043 |
| 87 | 0.012804 | 0.014203 | 0.015691 | 0.017264 | 0.018920 |
| 88 | 0.012674 | 0.014074 | 0.015564 | 0.017141 | 0.018801 |
| 89 | 0.012546 | 0.013948 | 0.015441 | 0.017021 | 0.018685 |
| 90 | 0.012422 | 0.013825 | 0.015320 | 0.016903 | 0.018571 |
| 91 | 0.012300 | 0.013705 | 0.015202 | 0.016788 | 0.018461 |
| 92 | 0.012181 | 0.013587 | 0.015087 | 0.016676 | 0.018353 |
| 93 | 0.012064 | 0.013472 | 0.014974 | 0.016567 | 0.018247 |
| 94 | 0.011950 | 0.013360 | 0.014864 | 0.016460 | 0.018144 |
| 95 | 0.011839 | 0.013249 | 0.014756 | 0.016355 | 0.018044 |
| 96 | 0.011730 | 0.013141 | 0.014650 | 0.016253 | 0.017945 |
| 97 | 0.011623 | 0.013036 | 0.014547 | 0.016153 | 0.017849 |
| 98 | 0.011518 | 0.012932 | 0.014446 | 0.016055 | 0.017756 |
| 99 | 0.011415 | 0.012832 | 0.014347 | 0.015959 | 0.017664 |
| 100 | 0.011314 | 0.012732 | 0.014250 | 0.015866 | 0.017574 |

**Table 7 (continued)**

| n | 1½% | 1¾% | 2% | 2½% | 3% |
|---|---|---|---|---|---|
| 1 | 1.015000 | 1.017500 | 1.020000 | 1.025000 | 1.030000 |
| 2 | 0.511278 | 0.513163 | 0.515050 | 0.518827 | 0.522611 |
| 3 | 0.343383 | 0.345067 | 0.346755 | 0.350137 | 0.353530 |
| 4 | 0.259445 | 0.261032 | 0.262624 | 0.265818 | 0.269027 |
| 5 | 0.209089 | 0.210621 | 0.212158 | 0.215247 | 0.218355 |
| 6 | 0.175525 | 0.177023 | 0.178526 | 0.181550 | 0.184598 |
| 7 | 0.151556 | 0.153031 | 0.154512 | 0.157495 | 0.160506 |
| 8 | 0.133584 | 0.135043 | 0.136510 | 0.139467 | 0.142456 |
| 9 | 0.119610 | 0.121058 | 0.122515 | 0.125457 | 0.128434 |
| 10 | 0.108434 | 0.109875 | 0.111327 | 0.114259 | 0.117231 |
| 11 | 0.099294 | 0.100730 | 0.102178 | 0.105106 | 0.108077 |
| 12 | 0.091680 | 0.093114 | 0.094560 | 0.097487 | 0.100462 |
| 13 | 0.085240 | 0.086673 | 0.088118 | 0.091048 | 0.094030 |
| 14 | 0.079723 | 0.081156 | 0.082602 | 0.085537 | 0.088526 |
| 15 | 0.074944 | 0.076377 | 0.077825 | 0.080766 | 0.083767 |
| 16 | 0.070765 | 0.072200 | 0.073650 | 0.076599 | 0.079611 |
| 17 | 0.067080 | 0.068516 | 0.069970 | 0.072928 | 0.075953 |
| 18 | 0.063806 | 0.065245 | 0.066702 | 0.069670 | 0.072709 |
| 19 | 0.060878 | 0.062321 | 0.063782 | 0.066761 | 0.069814 |
| 20 | 0.058246 | 0.059691 | 9.061157 | 0.064147 | 0.067216 |
| 21 | 0.055865 | 0.057315 | 0.058785 | 0.061787 | 0.064872 |
| 22 | 0.053703 | 0.055156 | 0.056631 | 0.059647 | 0.062747 |
| 23 | 0.051731 | 0.053188 | 0.054668 | 0.057696 | 0.060814 |
| 24 | 0.049924 | 0.051386 | 0.052871 | 0.055913 | 0.059047 |
| 25 | 0.048263 | 0.049730 | 0.051220 | 0.054276 | 0.057428 |
| 26 | 0.046732 | 0.048203 | 0.049699 | 0.052769 | 0.055938 |
| 27 | 0.045315 | 0.046791 | 0.048293 | 0.051377 | 0.054564 |
| 28 | 0.044001 | 0.045482 | 0.046990 | 0.050088 | 0.053293 |
| 29 | 0.042779 | 0.044264 | 0.045778 | 0.048891 | 0.052115 |
| 30 | 0.041639 | 0.043130 | 0.044650 | 0.047778 | 0.051019 |
| 31 | 0.040574 | 0.042070 | 0.043596 | 0.046739 | 0.049999 |
| 32 | 0.039577 | 0.041078 | 0.042611 | 0.045768 | 0.049047 |
| 33 | 0.038641 | 0.040148 | 0.041687 | 0.044859 | 0.048156 |
| 34 | 0.037762 | 0.039274 | 0.040819 | 0.044007 | 0.047322 |
| 35 | 0.036934 | 0.038451 | 0.040002 | 0.043206 | 0.046539 |
| 36 | 0.036152 | 0.037675 | 0.039233 | 0.042452 | 0.045804 |
| 37 | 0.035414 | 0.036943 | 0.038507 | 0.041741 | 0.045112 |
| 38 | 0.034716 | 0.036250 | 0.037821 | 0.041070 | 0.044459 |
| 39 | 0.034055 | 0.035594 | 0.037171 | 0.040436 | 0.043844 |
| 40 | 0.033427 | 0.034972 | 0.036556 | 0.039836 | 0.043262 |
| 41 | 0.032831 | 0.034382 | 0.035972 | 0.039268 | 0.042712 |
| 42 | 0.032264 | 0.033821 | 0.035417 | 0.038729 | 0.042192 |
| 43 | 0.031725 | 0.033287 | 0.034890 | 0.038217 | 0.041698 |
| 44 | 0.031210 | 0.032778 | 0.034388 | 0.037730 | 0.041230 |
| 45 | 0.030720 | 0.032293 | 0.033910 | 0.037268 | 0.040785 |
| 46 | 0.030251 | 0.031830 | 0.033453 | 0.036827 | 0.040363 |
| 47 | 0.029803 | 0.031388 | 0.033018 | 0.036407 | 0.039961 |
| 48 | 0.029375 | 0.030966 | 0.032602 | 0.036006 | 0.039578 |
| 49 | 0.028965 | 0.030561 | 0.032204 | 0.035623 | 0.039213 |
| 50 | 0.028572 | 0.030174 | 0.031823 | 0.035258 | 0.038865 |

| n | 1½% | 1¾% | 2% | 2½% | 3% |
|---|---|---|---|---|---|
| 51 | 0.028195 | 0.029803 | 0.031459 | 0.034909 | 0.038534 |
| 52 | 0.027833 | 0.029447 | 0.031109 | 0.034574 | 0.038217 |
| 53 | 0.027485 | 0.029105 | 0.030774 | 0.034254 | 0.037915 |
| 54 | 0.027151 | 0.028777 | 0.030452 | 0.033948 | 0.037626 |
| 55 | 0.026830 | 0.028461 | 0.030143 | 0.033654 | 0.037349 |
| 56 | 0.026521 | 0.028158 | 0.029847 | 0.033372 | 0.037084 |
| 57 | 0.026223 | 0.027866 | 0.029561 | 0.033102 | 0.036831 |
| 58 | 0.025937 | 0.027585 | 0.029287 | 0.032842 | 0.036588 |
| 59 | 0.025660 | 0.027314 | 0.029022 | 0.032593 | 0.036356 |
| 60 | 0.025393 | 0.027053 | 0.028768 | 0.032353 | 0.036133 |
| 61 | 0.025136 | 0.026802 | 0.028523 | 0.032123 | 0.035919 |
| 62 | 0.024888 | 0.026559 | 0.028286 | 0.031901 | 0.035714 |
| 63 | 0.024647 | 0.026325 | 0.028058 | 0.031688 | 0.035517 |
| 64 | 0.024415 | 0.026098 | 0.027839 | 0.031482 | 0.035328 |
| 65 | 0.024191 | 0.025880 | 0.027626 | 0.031285 | 0.035146 |
| 66 | 0.023974 | 0.025668 | 0.027421 | 0.031094 | 0.034971 |
| 67 | 0.023764 | 0.025464 | 0.027223 | 0.030910 | 0.034803 |
| 68 | 0.023560 | 0.025266 | 0.027032 | 0.030733 | 0.034642 |
| 69 | 0.023363 | 0.025075 | 0.026847 | 0.030562 | 0.034486 |
| 70 | 0.023172 | 0.024889 | 0.026668 | 0.030397 | 0.034337 |
| 71 | 0.022987 | 0.024710 | 0.026494 | 0.030238 | 0.034193 |
| 72 | 0.022808 | 0.024536 | 0.026327 | 0.030084 | 0.034054 |
| 73 | 0.022634 | 0.024367 | 0.026165 | 0.029936 | 0.033921 |
| 74 | 0.022465 | 0.024204 | 0.026007 | 0.029792 | 0.033792 |
| 75 | 0.022301 | 0.024046 | 0.025855 | 0.029654 | 0.033668 |
| 76 | 0.022141 | 0.023892 | 0.025708 | 0.029520 | 0.033548 |
| 77 | 0.021987 | 0.023743 | 0.025564 | 0.029390 | 0.033433 |
| 78 | 0.021836 | 0.023598 | 0.025426 | 0.029265 | 0.033322 |
| 79 | 0.021690 | 0.023457 | 0.025291 | 0.029143 | 0.033215 |
| 80 | 0.021548 | 0.023321 | 0.025161 | 0.029026 | 0.033112 |
| 81 | 0.021410 | 0.023188 | 0.025034 | 0.028912 | 0.033012 |
| 82 | 0.021276 | 0.023059 | 0.024911 | 0.028803 | 0.032916 |
| 83 | 0.021145 | 0.022934 | 0.024792 | 0.028696 | 0.032823 |
| 84 | 0.021018 | 0.022812 | 0.024676 | 0.028593 | 0.032733 |
| 85 | 0.020894 | 0.022694 | 0.024563 | 0.028493 | 0.032647 |
| 86 | 0.020773 | 0.022578 | 0.024454 | 0.028396 | 0.032563 |
| 87 | 0.020656 | 0.022466 | 0.024347 | 0.028303 | 0.032482 |
| 88 | 0.020541 | 0.022357 | 0.024244 | 0.028212 | 0.032404 |
| 89 | 0.020430 | 0.022251 | 0.024144 | 0.028124 | 0.032328 |
| 90 | 0.020321 | 0.022148 | 0.024046 | 0.028038 | 0.032256 |
| 91 | 0.020215 | 0.022047 | 0.023951 | 0.027955 | 0.032185 |
| 92 | 0.020112 | 0.021949 | 0.023859 | 0.027875 | 0.032117 |
| 93 | 0.020011 | 0.021853 | 0.023769 | 0.027797 | 0.032051 |
| 94 | 0.019913 | 0.021760 | 0.023681 | 0.027721 | 0.031987 |
| 95 | 0.019817 | 0.021669 | 0.023596 | 0.027648 | 0.031926 |
| 96 | 0.019723 | 0.021581 | 0.023513 | 0.027577 | 0.031866 |
| 97 | 0.019632 | 0.021495 | 0.023432 | 0.027507 | 0.031809 |
| 98 | 0.019543 | 0.021411 | 0.023354 | 0.027440 | 0.031753 |
| 99 | 0.019456 | 0.021329 | 0.023277 | 0.027375 | 0.031699 |
| 100 | 0.019371 | 0.021249 | 0.023203 | 0.927312 | 0.931647 |

**Table 7 (continued)**

| $n$ | $3\frac{1}{2}\%$ | $4\%$ | $4\frac{1}{2}\%$ | $5\%$ | $5\frac{1}{2}\%$ |
|---|---|---|---|---|---|
| 1 | 1.035000 | 1.040000 | 1.045000 | 1.050000 | 1.055000 |
| 2 | 0.526401 | 0.530196 | 0.533998 | 0.537805 | 0.541618 |
| 3 | 0.356934 | 0.360349 | 0.363773 | 0.367209 | 0.370654 |
| 4 | 0.272251 | 0.275490 | 0.278744 | 0.282012 | 0.285294 |
| 5 | 0.221481 | 0.224627 | 0.227792 | 0.230975 | 0.234176 |
| 6 | 0.187668 | 0.190762 | 0.193878 | 0.197017 | 0.200179 |
| 7 | 0.163544 | 0.166610 | 0.169701 | 0.172820 | 0.175964 |
| 8 | 0.145477 | 0.148528 | 0.151610 | 0.154722 | 0.157864 |
| 9 | 0.131446 | 0.134493 | 0.137574 | 0.140690 | 0.143839 |
| 10 | 0.120241 | 0.123291 | 0.126379 | 0.129505 | 0.132668 |
| 11 | 0.111092 | 0.114149 | 0.117248 | 0.120389 | 0.123571 |
| 12 | 0.103484 | 0.106552 | 0.109666 | 0.112825 | 0.116029 |
| 13 | 0.097062 | 0.100144 | 0.103275 | 0.106456 | 0.109684 |
| 14 | 0.091571 | 0.094669 | 0.097820 | 0.101024 | 0.104279 |
| 15 | 0.086825 | 0.089941 | 0.093114 | 0.096342 | 0.099626 |
| 16 | 0.082685 | 0.085820 | 0.089015 | 0.092270 | 0.095583 |
| 17 | 0.079043 | 0.082199 | 0.085418 | 0.088699 | 0.092042 |
| 18 | 0.075817 | 0.078993 | 0.082237 | 0.085546 | 0.088920 |
| 19 | 0.072940 | 0.076139 | 0.079407 | 0.082745 | 0.086150 |
| 20 | 0.070361 | 0.073582 | 0.076876 | 0.080243 | 0.083679 |
| 21 | 0.068037 | 0.071280 | 0.074601 | 0.077996 | 0.081465 |
| 22 | 0.065932 | 0.069199 | 0.072546 | 0.075971 | 0.079471 |
| 23 | 0.064019 | 0.067309 | 0.070682 | 0.074137 | 0.077670 |
| 24 | 0.062273 | 0.065587 | 0.068987 | 0.072471 | 0.076036 |
| 25 | 0.060674 | 0.064012 | 0.067439 | 0.070952 | 0.074549 |
| 26 | 0.059205 | 0.062567 | 0.066021 | 0.069564 | 0.073193 |
| 27 | 0.057852 | 0.061239 | 0.064719 | 0.068292 | 0.071952 |
| 28 | 0.056603 | 0.060013 | 0.063521 | 0.067123 | 0.070814 |
| 29 | 0.055445 | 0.058880 | 0.062415 | 0.066046 | 0.069769 |
| 30 | 0.054371 | 0.057830 | 0.061392 | 0.065051 | 0.068805 |
| 31 | 0.053372 | 0.056855 | 0.060443 | 0.064132 | 0.067917 |
| 32 | 0.052442 | 0.055949 | 0.059563 | 0.063280 | 0.067095 |
| 33 | 0.051572 | 0.055104 | 0.058745 | 0.062490 | 0.066335 |
| 34 | 0.050760 | 0.054315 | 0.057982 | 0.061755 | 0.065630 |
| 35 | 0.049998 | 0.053577 | 0.057270 | 0.061072 | 0.064975 |
| 36 | 0.049284 | 0.052887 | 0.056606 | 0.060434 | 0.064366 |
| 37 | 0.048613 | 0.052240 | 0.055984 | 0.059840 | 0.063800 |
| 38 | 0.047982 | 0.051632 | 0.055402 | 0.059284 | 0.063272 |
| 39 | 0.047388 | 0.051061 | 0.054856 | 0.058765 | 0.062780 |
| 40 | 0.046803 | 0.050523 | 0.054343 | 0.058278 | 0.062320 |
| 41 | 0.046298 | 0.050017 | 0.053862 | 0.057822 | 0.061891 |
| 42 | 0.045798 | 0.049540 | 0.053409 | 0.057395 | 0.061489 |
| 43 | 0.045325 | 0.049090 | 0.052982 | 0.056993 | 0.061113 |
| 44 | 0.044878 | 0.048665 | 0.052581 | 0.056616 | 0.060761 |
| 45 | 0.044453 | 0.048262 | 0.052202 | 0.056262 | 0.060431 |
| 46 | 0.044051 | 0.047882 | 0.051845 | 0.055928 | 0.060122 |
| 47 | 0.043669 | 0.047522 | 0.051507 | 0.055614 | 0.059831 |
| 48 | 0.043306 | 0.047181 | 0.051189 | 0.055318 | 0.059559 |
| 49 | 0.042962 | 0.046857 | 0.050887 | 0.055040 | 0.059302 |
| 50 | 0.042634 | 0.046550 | 0.050602 | 0.054777 | 0.059061 |

| $n$ | $3\frac{1}{2}\%$ | $4\%$ | $4\frac{1}{2}\%$ | $5\%$ | $5\frac{1}{2}\%$ |
|---|---|---|---|---|---|
| 51 | 0.042322 | 0.046259 | 0.050332 | 0.054529 | 0.058835 |
| 52 | 0.042024 | 0.045982 | 0.050077 | 0.054294 | 0.058622 |
| 53 | 0.041741 | 0.045719 | 0.049835 | 0.054073 | 0.058421 |
| 54 | 0.041471 | 0.045469 | 0.049605 | 0.053864 | 0.058232 |
| 55 | 0.041213 | 0.045231 | 0.049388 | 0.053667 | 0.058055 |
| 56 | 0.040967 | 0.045005 | 0.049181 | 0.053480 | 0.057887 |
| 57 | 0.040732 | 0.044789 | 0.048985 | 0.053303 | 0.057729 |
| 58 | 0.040508 | 0.044584 | 0.048799 | 0.053136 | 0.057580 |
| 59 | 0.040294 | 0.044388 | 0.048622 | 0.052978 | 0.057440 |
| 60 | 0.040089 | 0.044202 | 0.048454 | 0.052828 | 0.057307 |
| 61 | 0.039892 | 0.044024 | 0.048295 | 0.052686 | 0.057182 |
| 62 | 0.039705 | 0.043854 | 0.048143 | 0.052552 | 0.057064 |
| 63 | 0.039525 | 0.043692 | 0.047998 | 0.052424 | 0.056953 |
| 64 | 0.039353 | 0.043538 | 0.047861 | 0.052304 | 0.056847 |
| 65 | 0.039188 | 0.043390 | 0.047730 | 0.052189 | 0.056748 |
| 66 | 0.039030 | 0.043249 | 0.047606 | 0.052081 | 0.056654 |
| 67 | 0.038879 | 0.043115 | 0.047488 | 0.051978 | 0.056565 |
| 68 | 0.038734 | 0.042986 | 0.047375 | 0.051880 | 0.056482 |
| 69 | 0.038595 | 0.042863 | 0.047267 | 0.051787 | 0.056402 |
| 70 | 0.038461 | 0.042745 | 0.047165 | 0.051699 | 0.056328 |
| 71 | 0.038333 | 0.042633 | 0.047068 | 0.051616 | 0.056257 |
| 72 | 0.038210 | 0.042525 | 0.046975 | 0.051536 | 0.056190 |
| 73 | 0.038092 | 0.042422 | 0.046886 | 0.051461 | 0.056127 |
| 74 | 0.037978 | 0.042323 | 0.046802 | 0.051390 | 0.056067 |
| 75 | 0.037869 | 0.042229 | 0.046721 | 0.051322 | 0.056010 |
| 76 | 0.037765 | 0.042139 | 0.046644 | 0.051257 | 0.055956 |
| 77 | 0.037664 | 0.042052 | 0.046571 | 0.051196 | 0.055906 |
| 78 | 0.037567 | 0.041969 | 0.046501 | 0.051138 | 0.055858 |
| 79 | 0.037474 | 0.041890 | 0.046434 | 0.051082 | 0.055812 |
| 80 | 0.037385 | 0.041814 | 0.046371 | 0.051030 | 0.055769 |
| 81 | 0.037299 | 0.041741 | 0.046310 | 0.050980 | 0.055729 |
| 82 | 0.037216 | 0.041671 | 0.046252 | 0.050932 | 0.055690 |
| 83 | 0.037137 | 0.041605 | 0.046197 | 0.050887 | 0.055654 |
| 84 | 0.037060 | 0.041541 | 0.046144 | 0.050844 | 0.055619 |
| 85 | 0.036987 | 0.041479 | 0.046093 | 0.050803 | 0.055587 |
| 86 | 0.036916 | 0.041420 | 0.046045 | 0.050764 | 0.055556 |
| 87 | 0.036848 | 0.041364 | 0.045999 | 0.050727 | 0.055527 |
| 88 | 0.036782 | 0.041310 | 0.045955 | 0.050692 | 0.055499 |
| 89 | 0.036719 | 0.041258 | 0.045913 | 0.050659 | 0.055473 |
| 90 | 0.036658 | 0.041208 | 0.045873 | 0.050627 | 0.055448 |
| 91 | 0.036599 | 0.041160 | 0.045835 | 0.050597 | 0.055424 |
| 92 | 0.036543 | 0.041114 | 0.045798 | 0.050568 | 0.055402 |
| 93 | 0.036488 | 0.041070 | 0.045763 | 0.050541 | 0.055381 |
| 94 | 0.036436 | 0.041028 | 0.045730 | 0.050515 | 0.055361 |
| 95 | 0.036385 | 0.040987 | 0.045698 | 0.050490 | 0.055342 |
| 96 | 0.036337 | 0.040949 | 0.045667 | 0.050466 | 0.055324 |
| 97 | 0.036290 | 0.040911 | 0.045638 | 0.050444 | 0.055307 |
| 98 | 0.036245 | 0.040875 | 0.045610 | 0.050423 | 0.055291 |
| 99 | 0.036201 | 0.040841 | 0.045584 | 0.050402 | 0.055276 |
| 100 | 0.036159 | 0.040808 | 0.045558 | 0.050383 | 0.055261 |

**Table 7 (continued)**

| n | 6% | 6½% | 7% | 7½% | 8% |
|---|---|---|---|---|---|
| 1 | 1.060000 | 1.065000 | 1.070000 | 1.075000 | 1.080000 |
| 2 | 0.545437 | 0.549262 | 0.553092 | 0.556928 | 0.560769 |
| 3 | 0.374110 | 0.377576 | 0.381052 | 0.384538 | 0.388034 |
| 4 | 0.288591 | 0.291903 | 0.295228 | 0.298568 | 0.301921 |
| 5 | 0.237396 | 0.240635 | 0.243891 | 0.247165 | 0.250456 |
| 6 | 0.203363 | 0.206568 | 0.209796 | 0.213045 | 0.216315 |
| 7 | 0.179135 | 0.182331 | 0.185553 | 0.188800 | 0.192072 |
| 8 | 0.161036 | 0.164237 | 0.167468 | 0.170727 | 0.174015 |
| 9 | 0.147022 | 0.150238 | 0.153486 | 0.156767 | 0.160080 |
| 10 | 0.135868 | 0.139105 | 0.142378 | 0.145686 | 0.149029 |
| 11 | 0.126793 | 0.130055 | 0.133357 | 0.136697 | 0.140076 |
| 12 | 0.119277 | 0.122568 | 0.125902 | 0.129278 | 0.132695 |
| 13 | 0.112960 | 0.116283 | 0.119651 | 0.123064 | 0.126522 |
| 14 | 0.107585 | 0.110940 | 0.114345 | 0.117797 | 0.121297 |
| 15 | 0.102963 | 0.106353 | 0.109795 | 0.113287 | 0.116830 |
| 16 | 0.098952 | 0.102378 | 0.105858 | 0.109391 | 0.112977 |
| 17 | 0.095445 | 0.098906 | 0.102425 | 0.106000 | 0.109629 |
| 18 | 0.092357 | 0.095855 | 0.099413 | 0.103029 | 0.106702 |
| 19 | 0.089621 | 0.093156 | 0.096753 | 0.100411 | 0.104128 |
| 20 | 0.087185 | 0.090756 | 0.094393 | 0.098092 | 0.101852 |
| 21 | 0.085005 | 0.088613 | 0.092289 | 0.096029 | 0.099832 |
| 22 | 0.083046 | 0.086691 | 0.090404 | 0.094187 | 0.098032 |
| 23 | 0.081278 | 0.084961 | 0.088714 | 0.092535 | 0.096422 |
| 24 | 0.079679 | 0.083398 | 0.087189 | 0.091050 | 0.094978 |
| 25 | 0.078227 | 0.081981 | 0.085811 | 0.089711 | 0.093679 |
| 26 | 0.076904 | 0.080695 | 0.084561 | 0.088500 | 0.092507 |
| 27 | 0.075697 | 0.079523 | 0.083426 | 0.087402 | 0.091448 |
| 28 | 0.074593 | 0.078453 | 0.082392 | 0.086405 | 0.090489 |
| 29 | 0.073580 | 0.077474 | 0.081449 | 0.085498 | 0.089619 |
| 30 | 0.072649 | 0.076577 | 0.080586 | 0.084671 | 0.088827 |
| 31 | 0.071792 | 0.075754 | 0.079797 | 0.083916 | 0.088107 |
| 32 | 0.071002 | 0.074997 | 0.079073 | 0.083226 | 0.087451 |
| 33 | 0.070273 | 0.074299 | 0.078408 | 0.082594 | 0.086852 |
| 34 | 0.069598 | 0.073656 | 0.077797 | 0.082015 | 0.086304 |
| 35 | 0.068974 | 0.073062 | 0.077234 | 0.081483 | 0.085803 |
| 36 | 0.068395 | 0.072513 | 0.076715 | 0.080994 | 0.085345 |
| 37 | 0.067857 | 0.072005 | 0.076237 | 0.080545 | 0.084924 |
| 38 | 0.067358 | 0.071535 | 0.075795 | 0.080132 | 0.084539 |
| 39 | 0.066894 | 0.071099 | 0.075387 | 0.079751 | 0.084185 |
| 40 | 0.066462 | 0.070694 | 0.075009 | 0.079400 | 0.083860 |
| 41 | 0.066059 | 0.070318 | 0.074660 | 0.079077 | 0.083561 |
| 42 | 0.065683 | 0.069968 | 0.074336 | 0.078778 | 0.083287 |
| 43 | 0.065333 | 0.069644 | 0.074036 | 0.078502 | 0.083034 |
| 44 | 0.065006 | 0.069341 | 0.073758 | 0.078247 | 0.082802 |
| 45 | 0.064700 | 0.069060 | 0.073500 | 0.078011 | 0.082587 |
| 46 | 0.064415 | 0.068797 | 0.073260 | 0.077794 | 0.082390 |
| 47 | 0.064148 | 0.068553 | 0.073037 | 0.077592 | 0.082208 |
| 48 | 0.063898 | 0.068325 | 0.072831 | 0.077405 | 0.082040 |
| 49 | 0.063664 | 0.068112 | 0.072639 | 0.077232 | 0.081886 |
| 50 | 0.063444 | 0.067914 | 0.072460 | 0.077072 | 0.081743 |

| n | 6% | 6½% | 7% | 7½% | 8% |
|---|---|---|---|---|---|
| 51 | 0.063239 | 0.067729 | 0.072294 | 0.076924 | 0.081611 |
| 52 | 0.063046 | 0.067556 | 0.072139 | 0.076787 | 0.081490 |
| 53 | 0.062866 | 0.067394 | 0.071995 | 0.076659 | 0.081377 |
| 54 | 0.062696 | 0.067243 | 0.071861 | 0.076541 | 0.081274 |
| 55 | 0.062537 | 0.067101 | 0.071736 | 0.076432 | 0.081178 |
| 56 | 0.062388 | 0.066969 | 0.071620 | 0.076330 | 0.081090 |
| 57 | 0.062247 | 0.066846 | 0.071512 | 0.076236 | 0.081008 |
| 58 | 0.062116 | 0.066730 | 0.071411 | 0.076148 | 0.080932 |
| 59 | 0.061992 | 0.066622 | 0.071317 | 0.076067 | 0.080862 |
| 60 | 0.061876 | 0.066520 | 0.071229 | 0.075991 | 0.080798 |
| 61 | 0.061766 | 0.066426 | 0.071147 | 0.075921 | 0.080738 |
| 62 | 0.061664 | 0.066337 | 0.071071 | 0.075856 | 0.080683 |
| 63 | 0.061567 | 0.066254 | 0.071000 | 0.075796 | 0.080632 |
| 64 | 0.061476 | 0.066176 | 0.070934 | 0.075740 | 0.080585 |
| 65 | 0.061391 | 0.066103 | 0.070872 | 0.075688 | 0.080541 |
| 66 | 0.061310 | 0.066033 | 0.070814 | 0.075639 | 0.080501 |
| 67 | 0.061235 | 0.065970 | 0.070760 | 0.075594 | 0.080464 |
| 68 | 0.061163 | 0.065910 | 0.070710 | 0.075553 | 0.080429 |
| 69 | 0.061096 | 0.065854 | 0.070663 | 0.075514 | 0.080397 |
| 70 | 0.061033 | 0.065801 | 0.070620 | 0.075478 | 0.080368 |
| 71 | 0.060974 | 0.065752 | 0.070579 | 0.075444 | 0.080340 |
| 72 | 0.060918 | 0.065705 | 0.070541 | 0.075413 | 0.080315 |
| 73 | 0.060865 | 0.065662 | 0.070505 | 0.075384 | 0.080292 |
| 74 | 0.060815 | 0.065621 | 0.070472 | 0.075357 | 0.080270 |
| 75 | 0.060769 | 0.065583 | 0.070441 | 0.075332 | 0.080250 |
| 76 | 0.060725 | 0.065547 | 0.070412 | 0.075304 | 0.080231 |
| 77 | 0.060683 | 0.065513 | 0.070385 | 0.075287 | 0.080214 |
| 78 | 0.060644 | 0.065482 | 0.070359 | 0.075267 | 0.080198 |
| 79 | 0.060607 | 0.065452 | 0.070336 | 0.075248 | 0.080183 |
| 80 | 0.060573 | 0.065424 | 0.070314 | 0.075231 | 0.080170 |
| 81 | 0.060540 | 0.065398 | 0.070293 | 0.075215 | 0.080157 |
| 82 | 0.060509 | 0.065374 | 0.070274 | 0.075200 | 0.080146 |
| 83 | 0.060480 | 0.065351 | 0.070256 | 0.075186 | 0.080135 |
| 84 | 0.060453 | 0.065329 | 0.070239 | 0.075173 | 0.080125 |
| 85 | 0.060427 | 0.065309 | 0.070223 | 0.075161 | 0.080116 |
| 86 | 0.060402 | 0.065290 | 0.070209 | 0.075150 | 0.080107 |
| 87 | 0.060380 | 0.065272 | 0.070195 | 0.075139 | 0.080099 |
| 88 | 0.060358 | 0.065256 | 0.070182 | 0.075129 | 0.080092 |
| 89 | 0.060338 | 0.065240 | 0.070170 | 0.075120 | 0.080085 |
| 90 | 0.060318 | 0.065225 | 0.070159 | 0.075112 | 0.080079 |
| 91 | 0.060300 | 0.065212 | 0.070149 | 0.075104 | 0.080073 |
| 92 | 0.060283 | 0.065199 | 0.070139 | 0.075097 | 0.080067 |
| 93 | 0.060267 | 0.065186 | 0.070130 | 0.075090 | 0.080062 |
| 94 | 0.060252 | 0.065175 | 0.070121 | 0.075084 | 0.080058 |
| 95 | 0.060238 | 0.065164 | 0.070113 | 0.075078 | 0.080053 |
| 96 | 0.060224 | 0.065154 | 0.070106 | 0.075072 | 0.080050 |
| 97 | 0.060211 | 0.065145 | 0.070097 | 0.075067 | 0.080046 |
| 98 | 0.060199 | 0.065136 | 0.070092 | 0.075063 | 0.080042 |
| 99 | 0.060188 | 0.065128 | 0.070086 | 0.075058 | 0.080039 |
| 100 | 0.060177 | 0.065120 | 0.070081 | 0.075054 | 0.080036 |

# Table 8

$$\frac{1}{s_{\overline{n}|r}}$$

$r$ = interest rate per payment period; $n$ = number of payment periods

| $n$ | $\frac{1}{4}\%$ | $\frac{1}{2}\%$ | $\frac{3}{4}\%$ | $1\%$ | $1\frac{1}{4}\%$ |
|---|---|---|---|---|---|
| 1 | 1.000000 | 1.000000 | 1.000000 | 1.000000 | 1.000000 |
| 2 | 0.499376 | 0.498753 | 0.498132 | 0.497512 | 0.496894 |
| 3 | 0.332502 | 0.331672 | 0.330846 | 0.330022 | 0.329201 |
| 4 | 0.249065 | 0.248133 | 0.247205 | 0.246281 | 0.245361 |
| 5 | 0.199003 | 0.198010 | 0.197022 | 0.196040 | 0.195062 |
| 6 | 0.165628 | 0.164595 | 0.163569 | 0.162548 | 0.161534 |
| 7 | 0.141789 | 0.140729 | 0.139675 | 0.138628 | 0.137589 |
| 8 | 0.123910 | 0.122829 | 0.121756 | 0.120690 | 0.119633 |
| 9 | 0.110005 | 0.108907 | 0.107819 | 0.106740 | 0.105671 |
| 10 | 0.098880 | 0.097771 | 0.096671 | 0.095582 | 0.094503 |
| 11 | 0.089778 | 0.088659 | 0.087551 | 0.086454 | 0.085368 |
| 12 | 0.082194 | 0.081066 | 0.079951 | 0.078849 | 0.077758 |
| 13 | 0.075776 | 0.074642 | 0.073522 | 0.072415 | 0.071321 |
| 14 | 0.070275 | 0.069136 | 0.068011 | 0.066901 | 0.065805 |
| 15 | 0.065508 | 0.064364 | 0.063236 | 0.062124 | 0.061026 |
| 16 | 0.061336 | 0.060189 | 0.059059 | 0.057945 | 0.056847 |
| 17 | 0.057656 | 0.056506 | 0.055373 | 0.054258 | 0.053160 |
| 18 | 0.054384 | 0.053232 | 0.052098 | 0.050982 | 0.049885 |
| 19 | 0.051457 | 0.050303 | 0.049167 | 0.048052 | 0.046955 |
| 20 | 0.048823 | 0.047666 | 0.046531 | 0.045415 | 0.044320 |
| 21 | 0.046439 | 0.045282 | 0.044145 | 0.043031 | 0.041937 |
| 22 | 0.044273 | 0.043114 | 0.041977 | 0.040864 | 0.039772 |
| 23 | 0.042295 | 0.041135 | 0.039998 | 0.038886 | 0.037797 |
| 24 | 0.040481 | 0.039321 | 0.038185 | 0.037073 | 0.035987 |
| 25 | 0.038813 | 0.037652 | 0.036516 | 0.035407 | 0.034322 |
| 26 | 0.037273 | 0.036112 | 0.034977 | 0.033869 | 0.032787 |
| 27 | 0.035847 | 0.034686 | 0.033552 | 0.032446 | 0.031367 |
| 28 | 0.034523 | 0.033362 | 0.032229 | 0.031124 | 0.030049 |
| 29 | 0.033291 | 0.032129 | 0.030997 | 0.029895 | 0.028822 |
| 30 | 0.032141 | 0.030979 | 0.029848 | 0.028748 | 0.027679 |
| 31 | 0.031065 | 0.029903 | 0.028774 | 0.027676 | 0.026609 |
| 32 | 0.030056 | 0.028895 | 0.027766 | 0.026671 | 0.025608 |
| 33 | 0.029108 | 0.027947 | 0.026820 | 0.025727 | 0.024668 |
| 34 | 0.028216 | 0.027056 | 0.025931 | 0.024840 | 0.023784 |
| 35 | 0.027375 | 0.026215 | 0.025092 | 0.024004 | 0.022951 |
| 36 | 0.026581 | 0.025422 | 0.024300 | 0.023214 | 0.022165 |
| 37 | 0.025830 | 0.024671 | 0.023551 | 0.022468 | 0.021423 |
| 38 | 0.025118 | 0.023960 | 0.022842 | 0.021761 | 0.020720 |
| 39 | 0.024443 | 0.023286 | 0.022169 | 0.021092 | 0.020054 |
| 40 | 0.023802 | 0.022646 | 0.021530 | 0.020456 | 0.019421 |
| 41 | 0.023192 | 0.022036 | 0.020923 | 0.019851 | 0.018821 |
| 42 | 0.022611 | 0.021456 | 0.020345 | 0.019276 | 0.018249 |
| 43 | 0.022057 | 0.020903 | 0.019793 | 0.018727 | 0.017705 |
| 44 | 0.021529 | 0.020375 | 0.019268 | 0.018204 | 0.017186 |
| 45 | 0.021023 | 0.019871 | 0.018765 | 0.017705 | 0.016690 |
| 46 | 0.020540 | 0.019389 | 0.018285 | 0.017228 | 0.016217 |
| 47 | 0.020078 | 0.018927 | 0.017825 | 0.016771 | 0.015764 |
| 48 | 0.019634 | 0.018485 | 0.017385 | 0.016334 | 0.015331 |
| 49 | 0.019209 | 0.018061 | 0.016963 | 0.015915 | 0.014916 |
| 50 | 0.018801 | 0.017654 | 0.016558 | 0.015513 | 0.014518 |

| $n$ | $\frac{1}{4}\%$ | $\frac{1}{2}\%$ | $\frac{3}{4}\%$ | $1\%$ | $1\frac{1}{4}\%$ |
|---|---|---|---|---|---|
| 51 | 0.018409 | 0.017263 | 0.016169 | 0.015127 | 0.014136 |
| 52 | 0.018032 | 0.016887 | 0.015795 | 0.014756 | 0.013769 |
| 53 | 0.017669 | 0.016525 | 0.015435 | 0.014400 | 0.013417 |
| 54 | 0.017320 | 0.016177 | 0.015089 | 0.014057 | 0.013078 |
| 55 | 0.016983 | 0.015841 | 0.014756 | 0.013726 | 0.012751 |
| 56 | 0.016659 | 0.015518 | 0.014435 | 0.013408 | 0.012437 |
| 57 | 0.016345 | 0.015206 | 0.014125 | 0.013102 | 0.012135 |
| 58 | 0.016043 | 0.014905 | 0.013826 | 0.012806 | 0.011843 |
| 59 | 0.015751 | 0.014614 | 0.013537 | 0.012520 | 0.011562 |
| 60 | 0.015469 | 0.014333 | 0.013258 | 0.012244 | 0.011290 |
| 61 | 0.015196 | 0.014061 | 0.012989 | 0.011978 | 0.011028 |
| 62 | 0.014931 | 0.013798 | 0.012728 | 0.011720 | 0.010774 |
| 63 | 0.014676 | 0.013543 | 0.012476 | 0.011471 | 0.010529 |
| 64 | 0.014428 | 0.013297 | 0.012231 | 0.011230 | 0.010292 |
| 65 | 0.014188 | 0.013058 | 0.011995 | 0.010997 | 0.010063 |
| 66 | 0.013955 | 0.012826 | 0.011765 | 0.010771 | 0.009841 |
| 67 | 0.013729 | 0.012602 | 0.011543 | 0.010551 | 0.009626 |
| 68 | 0.013510 | 0.012384 | 0.011327 | 0.010339 | 0.009417 |
| 69 | 0.013297 | 0.012172 | 0.011118 | 0.010133 | 0.009215 |
| 70 | 0.013090 | 0.011967 | 0.010915 | 0.009933 | 0.009019 |
| 71 | 0.012889 | 0.011767 | 0.010717 | 0.009739 | 0.008829 |
| 72 | 0.012694 | 0.011573 | 0.010526 | 0.009550 | 0.008645 |
| 73 | 0.012504 | 0.011384 | 0.010339 | 0.009367 | 0.008466 |
| 74 | 0.012319 | 0.011201 | 0.010158 | 0.009189 | 0.008292 |
| 75 | 0.012139 | 0.011022 | 0.009982 | 0.009016 | 0.008123 |
| 76 | 0.011964 | 0.010848 | 0.009810 | 0.008848 | 0.007959 |
| 77 | 0.011793 | 0.010679 | 0.009643 | 0.008684 | 0.007800 |
| 78 | 0.011627 | 0.010514 | 0.009481 | 0.008525 | 0.007644 |
| 79 | 0.011465 | 0.010354 | 0.009322 | 0.008370 | 0.007493 |
| 80 | 0.011307 | 0.010197 | 0.009168 | 0.008219 | 0.007347 |
| 81 | 0.011153 | 0.010044 | 0.009018 | 0.008072 | 0.007204 |
| 82 | 0.011003 | 0.009896 | 0.008871 | 0.007929 | 0.007064 |
| 83 | 0.010856 | 0.009750 | 0.008728 | 0.007789 | 0.006929 |
| 84 | 0.010713 | 0.009609 | 0.008589 | 0.007653 | 0.006797 |
| 85 | 0.010574 | 0.009470 | 0.008453 | 0.007520 | 0.006668 |
| 86 | 0.010437 | 0.009335 | 0.008320 | 0.007391 | 0.006543 |
| 87 | 0.010304 | 0.009203 | 0.008191 | 0.007264 | 0.006420 |
| 88 | 0.010174 | 0.009074 | 0.008064 | 0.007141 | 0.006301 |
| 89 | 0.010046 | 0.008948 | 0.007941 | 0.007021 | 0.006185 |
| 90 | 0.009922 | 0.008825 | 0.007820 | 0.006903 | 0.006071 |
| 91 | 0.009800 | 0.008705 | 0.007702 | 0.006788 | 0.005961 |
| 92 | 0.009681 | 0.008587 | 0.007587 | 0.006676 | 0.005853 |
| 93 | 0.009564 | 0.008472 | 0.007474 | 0.006567 | 0.005747 |
| 94 | 0.009450 | 0.008360 | 0.007364 | 0.006460 | 0.005644 |
| 95 | 0.009339 | 0.008249 | 0.007256 | 0.006355 | 0.005544 |
| 96 | 0.009230 | 0.008141 | 0.007150 | 0.006253 | 0.005445 |
| 97 | 0.009123 | 0.008036 | 0.007047 | 0.006153 | 0.005349 |
| 98 | 0.009018 | 0.007932 | 0.006946 | 0.006055 | 0.005256 |
| 99 | 0.008915 | 0.007831 | 0.006847 | 0.005959 | 0.005164 |
| 100 | 0.008814 | 0.007732 | 0.006750 | 0.005866 | 0.005074 |

**Table 8 (continued)**

| n | 1½% | 1¾% | 2% | 2½% | 3% |
|---|---|---|---|---|---|
| 1 | 1.000000 | 1.000000 | 1.000000 | 1.000000 | 1.000000 |
| 2 | 0.496278 | 0.495663 | 0.495050 | 0.493827 | 0.492611 |
| 3 | 0.328383 | 0.327567 | 0.326755 | 0.325137 | 0.323530 |
| 4 | 0.244445 | 0.243532 | 0.242624 | 0.240818 | 0.239027 |
| 5 | 0.194089 | 0.193121 | 0.192158 | 0.190247 | 0.188355 |
| 6 | 0.160525 | 0.159523 | 0.158526 | 0.156550 | 0.154598 |
| 7 | 0.136556 | 0.135531 | 0.134512 | 0.132495 | 0.130506 |
| 8 | 0.118584 | 0.117543 | 0.116510 | 0.114467 | 0.112456 |
| 9 | 0.104610 | 0.103558 | 0.102515 | 0.100457 | 0.098434 |
| 10 | 0.093434 | 0.092375 | 0.091327 | 0.089259 | 0.087231 |
| 11 | 0.084294 | 0.083230 | 0.082178 | 0.080106 | 0.078077 |
| 12 | 0.076680 | 0.075614 | 0.074560 | 0.072487 | 0.070462 |
| 13 | 0.070240 | 0.069173 | 0.068118 | 0.066048 | 0.064030 |
| 14 | 0.064723 | 0.063656 | 0.062602 | 0.060537 | 0.058526 |
| 15 | 0.059944 | 0.058877 | 0.057825 | 0.055766 | 0.053767 |
| 16 | 0.055765 | 0.054700 | 0.053650 | 0.051599 | 0.049611 |
| 17 | 0.052080 | 0.051016 | 0.049970 | 0.047928 | 0.045953 |
| 18 | 0.048806 | 0.047745 | 0.046702 | 0.044670 | 0.042709 |
| 19 | 0.045878 | 0.044821 | 0.043782 | 0.041761 | 0.039814 |
| 20 | 0.043246 | 0.042191 | 0.041157 | 0.039147 | 0.037216 |
| 21 | 0.040865 | 0.039815 | 0.038785 | 0.036787 | 0.034872 |
| 22 | 0.038703 | 0.037656 | 0.036631 | 0.034647 | 0.032747 |
| 23 | 0.036731 | 0.035688 | 0.034668 | 0.032696 | 0.030814 |
| 24 | 0.034924 | 0.033886 | 0.032871 | 0.030913 | 0.029047 |
| 25 | 0.033263 | 0.032230 | 0.031220 | 0.029276 | 0.027428 |
| 26 | 0.031732 | 0.030703 | 0.029699 | 0.027769 | 0.025938 |
| 27 | 0.030315 | 0.029291 | 0.028293 | 0.026377 | 0.024564 |
| 28 | 0.029001 | 0.027982 | 0.026990 | 0.025088 | 0.023293 |
| 29 | 0.027779 | 0.026764 | 0.025778 | 0.023891 | 0.022115 |
| 30 | 0.026639 | 0.025630 | 0.024650 | 0.022788 | 0.021019 |
| 31 | 0.025574 | 0.024570 | 0.023596 | 0.021739 | 0.019999 |
| 32 | 0.024577 | 0.023578 | 0.022611 | 0.020768 | 0.019047 |
| 33 | 0.023641 | 0.022648 | 0.021687 | 0.019859 | 0.018156 |
| 34 | 0.022762 | 0.021774 | 0.020819 | 0.019007 | 0.017322 |
| 35 | 0.021934 | 0.020951 | 0.020002 | 0.018206 | 0.016539 |
| 36 | 0.021152 | 0.020175 | 0.019233 | 0.017452 | 0.015804 |
| 37 | 0.020414 | 0.019443 | 0.018507 | 0.016741 | 0.015112 |
| 38 | 0.019716 | 0.018750 | 0.017821 | 0.016070 | 0.014459 |
| 39 | 0.019055 | 0.018094 | 0.017171 | 0.015436 | 0.013844 |
| 40 | 0.018427 | 0.017472 | 0.016556 | 0.014836 | 0.013262 |
| 41 | 0.017831 | 0.016882 | 0.015972 | 0.014268 | 0.012712 |
| 42 | 0.017264 | 0.016321 | 0.015417 | 0.013729 | 0.012192 |
| 43 | 0.016725 | 0.015787 | 0.014890 | 0.013217 | 0.011698 |
| 44 | 0.016210 | 0.015278 | 0.014388 | 0.012730 | 0.011230 |
| 45 | 0.015720 | 0.014793 | 0.013910 | 0.012268 | 0.010785 |
| 46 | 0.015251 | 0.014330 | 0.013453 | 0.011827 | 0.010363 |
| 47 | 0.014803 | 0.013888 | 0.013018 | 0.011407 | 0.009961 |
| 48 | 0.014375 | 0.013466 | 0.012602 | 0.011006 | 0.009578 |
| 49 | 0.013965 | 0.013061 | 0.012204 | 0.010623 | 0.009213 |
| 50 | 0.013572 | 0.012674 | 0.011823 | 0.010258 | 0.008865 |

| 1½% | 1¾% | 2% | 2½% | 3% | n |
|---|---|---|---|---|---|
| 0.013195 | 0.012303 | 0.011459 | 0.009909 | 0.008534 | 51 |
| 0.012833 | 0.011947 | 0.011109 | 0.009574 | 0.008217 | 52 |
| 0.012485 | 0.011605 | 0.010774 | 0.009254 | 0.007915 | 53 |
| 0.012151 | 0.011277 | 0.010452 | 0.008948 | 0.007626 | 54 |
| 0.011830 | 0.010961 | 0.010143 | 0.008654 | 0.007349 | 55 |
| 0.011521 | 0.010658 | 0.009847 | 0.008372 | 0.007084 | 56 |
| 0.011223 | 0.010366 | 0.009561 | 0.008102 | 0.006831 | 57 |
| 0.010937 | 0.010085 | 0.009287 | 0.007842 | 0.006588 | 58 |
| 0.010660 | 0.009814 | 0.009022 | 0.007593 | 0.006356 | 59 |
| 0.010393 | 0.009553 | 0.008768 | 0.007353 | 0.006133 | 60 |
| 0.010136 | 0.009302 | 0.008523 | 0.007123 | 0.005919 | 61 |
| 0.009888 | 0.009059 | 0.008286 | 0.006901 | 0.005714 | 62 |
| 0.009647 | 0.008825 | 0.008058 | 0.006688 | 0.005517 | 63 |
| 0.009415 | 0.008598 | 0.007839 | 0.006482 | 0.005328 | 64 |
| 0.009191 | 0.008380 | 0.007626 | 0.006285 | 0.005146 | 65 |
| 0.008974 | 0.008168 | 0.007421 | 0.006094 | 0.004971 | 66 |
| 0.008764 | 0.007964 | 0.007223 | 0.005910 | 0.004803 | 67 |
| 0.008560 | 0.007766 | 0.007032 | 0.005733 | 0.004642 | 68 |
| 0.008363 | 0.007575 | 0.006847 | 0.005562 | 0.004486 | 69 |
| 0.008172 | 0.007389 | 0.006668 | 0.005397 | 0.004337 | 70 |
| 0.007987 | 0.007210 | 0.006494 | 0.005238 | 0.004193 | 71 |
| 0.007808 | 0.007036 | 0.006327 | 0.005084 | 0.004054 | 72 |
| 0.007634 | 0.006867 | 0.006165 | 0.004936 | 0.003921 | 73 |
| 0.007465 | 0.006704 | 0.006007 | 0.004792 | 0.003792 | 74 |
| 0.007301 | 0.006546 | 0.005855 | 0.004654 | 0.003668 | 75 |
| 0.007141 | 0.006392 | 0.005708 | 0.004520 | 0.003548 | 76 |
| 0.006987 | 0.006243 | 0.005564 | 0.004390 | 0.003433 | 77 |
| 0.006836 | 0.006098 | 0.005426 | 0.004265 | 0.003322 | 78 |
| 0.006690 | 0.005957 | 0.005291 | 0.004143 | 0.003215 | 79 |
| 0.006548 | 0.005821 | 0.005161 | 0.004026 | 0.003112 | 80 |
| 0.006410 | 0.005688 | 0.005034 | 0.003912 | 0.003012 | 81 |
| 0.006276 | 0.005559 | 0.004911 | 0.003803 | 0.002916 | 82 |
| 0.006145 | 0.005434 | 0.004792 | 0.003696 | 0.002823 | 83 |
| 0.006018 | 0.005312 | 0.004676 | 0.003593 | 0.002733 | 84 |
| 0.005894 | 0.005194 | 0.004563 | 0.003493 | 0.002647 | 85 |
| 0.005773 | 0.005078 | 0.004454 | 0.003396 | 0.002563 | 86 |
| 0.005656 | 0.004966 | 0.004347 | 0.003303 | 0.002482 | 87 |
| 0.005541 | 0.004857 | 0.004244 | 0.003212 | 0.002404 | 88 |
| 0.005430 | 0.004751 | 0.004144 | 0.003124 | 0.002328 | 89 |
| 0.005321 | 0.004648 | 0.004046 | 0.003038 | 0.002256 | 90 |
| 0.005215 | 0.004547 | 0.003951 | 0.002955 | 0.002185 | 91 |
| 0.005112 | 0.004449 | 0.003859 | 0.002875 | 0.002117 | 92 |
| 0.005011 | 0.004353 | 0.003769 | 0.002797 | 0.002051 | 93 |
| 0.004913 | 0.004260 | 0.003681 | 0.002721 | 0.001987 | 94 |
| 0.004817 | 0.004169 | 0.003596 | 0.002648 | 0.001926 | 95 |
| 0.004723 | 0.004081 | 0.003513 | 0.002577 | 0.001866 | 96 |
| 0.004632 | 0.003995 | 0.003432 | 0.002507 | 0.001809 | 97 |
| 0.004543 | 0.003911 | 0.003354 | 0.002440 | 0.001753 | 98 |
| 0.004456 | 0.003829 | 0.003277 | 0.002375 | 0.001699 | 99 |
| 0.004371 | 0.003749 | 0.003203 | 0.002312 | 0.001647 | 100 |

**Table 8 (continued)**

| n | 3½% | 4% | 4½% | 5% | 5½% |
|---|---|---|---|---|---|
| 1 | 1.000000 | 1.000000 | 1.000000 | 1.000000 | 1.000000 |
| 2 | 0.491401 | 0.490196 | 0.488998 | 0.487805 | 0.486618 |
| 3 | 0.321934 | 0.320349 | 0.318773 | 0.317209 | 0.315654 |
| 4 | 0.237251 | 0.235490 | 0.233744 | 0.232012 | 0.230294 |
| 5 | 0.186481 | 0.184627 | 0.182792 | 0.180975 | 0.179176 |
| 6 | 0.152668 | 0.150762 | 0.148878 | 0.147017 | 0.145179 |
| 7 | 0.128544 | 0.126610 | 0.124701 | 0.122820 | 0.120964 |
| 8 | 0.110477 | 0.108528 | 0.106610 | 0.104722 | 0.102864 |
| 9 | 0.096446 | 0.094493 | 0.092574 | 0.090690 | 0.088839 |
| 10 | 0.085241 | 0.083291 | 0.081379 | 0.079505 | 0.077668 |
| 11 | 0.076092 | 0.074149 | 0.072248 | 0.070389 | 0.068571 |
| 12 | 0.068484 | 0.066552 | 0.064666 | 0.062825 | 0.061029 |
| 13 | 0.062062 | 0.060144 | 0.058275 | 0.056456 | 0.054684 |
| 14 | 0.056571 | 0.054669 | 0.052820 | 0.051024 | 0.049279 |
| 15 | 0.051825 | 0.049941 | 0.048114 | 0.046342 | 0.044626 |
| 16 | 0.047685 | 0.045820 | 0.044015 | 0.042270 | 0.040583 |
| 17 | 0.044043 | 0.042199 | 0.040418 | 0.038699 | 0.037042 |
| 18 | 0.040817 | 0.038993 | 0.037237 | 0.035546 | 0.033920 |
| 19 | 0.037940 | 0.036139 | 0.034407 | 0.032745 | 0.031150 |
| 20 | 0.035361 | 0.033582 | 0.031876 | 0.030243 | 0.028679 |
| 21 | 0.033037 | 0.031280 | 0.029601 | 0.027996 | 0.026465 |
| 22 | 0.030932 | 0.029199 | 0.027546 | 0.025971 | 0.024471 |
| 23 | 0.029019 | 0.027309 | 0.025682 | 0.024137 | 0.022670 |
| 24 | 0.027273 | 0.025587 | 0.023987 | 0.022471 | 0.021036 |
| 25 | 0.025674 | 0.024012 | 0.022439 | 0.020952 | 0.019549 |
| 26 | 0.024205 | 0.022567 | 0.021021 | 0.019564 | 0.018193 |
| 27 | 0.022852 | 0.021239 | 0.019719 | 0.018292 | 0.016952 |
| 28 | 0.021603 | 0.020013 | 0.018521 | 0.017123 | 0.015814 |
| 29 | 0.020445 | 0.018880 | 0.017415 | 0.016046 | 0.014769 |
| 30 | 0.019371 | 0.017830 | 0.016392 | 0.015051 | 0.013805 |
| 31 | 0.018372 | 0.016855 | 0.015443 | 0.014132 | 0.012917 |
| 32 | 0.017442 | 0.015949 | 0.014563 | 0.013280 | 0.012095 |
| 33 | 0.016572 | 0.015104 | 0.013745 | 0.012490 | 0.011335 |
| 34 | 0.015760 | 0.014315 | 0.012982 | 0.011755 | 0.010630 |
| 35 | 0.014998 | 0.013577 | 0.012270 | 0.011072 | 0.009975 |
| 36 | 0.014284 | 0.012887 | 0.011606 | 0.010434 | 0.009366 |
| 37 | 0.013613 | 0.012240 | 0.010984 | 0.009840 | 0.008800 |
| 38 | 0.012982 | 0.011632 | 0.010402 | 0.009284 | 0.008272 |
| 39 | 0.012388 | 0.011061 | 0.009856 | 0.008765 | 0.007780 |
| 40 | 0.011827 | 0.010523 | 0.009343 | 0.008278 | 0.007320 |
| 41 | 0.011298 | 0.010017 | 0.008862 | 0.007822 | 0.006891 |
| 42 | 0.010798 | 0.009540 | 0.008409 | 0.007395 | 0.006489 |
| 43 | 0.010325 | 0.009090 | 0.007982 | 0.006993 | 0.006113 |
| 44 | 0.009878 | 0.008665 | 0.007581 | 0.006616 | 0.005761 |
| 45 | 0.009453 | 0.008262 | 0.007202 | 0.006262 | 0.005431 |
| 46 | 0.009051 | 0.007882 | 0.006845 | 0.005928 | 0.005122 |
| 47 | 0.008669 | 0.007522 | 0.006507 | 0.005614 | 0.004831 |
| 48 | 0.008306 | 0.007181 | 0.006189 | 0.005318 | 0.004559 |
| 49 | 0.007962 | 0.006857 | 0.005887 | 0.005040 | 0.004302 |
| 50 | 0.007634 | 0.006550 | 0.005602 | 0.004777 | 0.004061 |

| n | 3½% | 4% | 4½% | 5% | 5½% |
|---|---|---|---|---|---|
| 51 | 0.007322 | 0.006259 | 0.005332 | 0.004529 | 0.003835 |
| 52 | 0.007024 | 0.005982 | 0.005077 | 0.004294 | 0.003622 |
| 53 | 0.006741 | 0.005719 | 0.004835 | 0.004073 | 0.003421 |
| 54 | 0.006471 | 0.005469 | 0.004605 | 0.003864 | 0.003232 |
| 55 | 0.006213 | 0.005231 | 0.004388 | 0.003667 | 0.003055 |
| 56 | 0.005967 | 0.005005 | 0.004181 | 0.003480 | 0.002887 |
| 57 | 0.005732 | 0.004789 | 0.003985 | 0.003303 | 0.002729 |
| 58 | 0.005508 | 0.004584 | 0.003799 | 0.003136 | 0.002580 |
| 59 | 0.005294 | 0.004388 | 0.003622 | 0.002978 | 0.002440 |
| 60 | 0.005089 | 0.004202 | 0.003454 | 0.002828 | 0.002307 |
| 61 | 0.004892 | 0.004024 | 0.003295 | 0.002686 | 0.002182 |
| 62 | 0.004705 | 0.003854 | 0.003143 | 0.002552 | 0.002064 |
| 63 | 0.004525 | 0.003692 | 0.002998 | 0.002424 | 0.001953 |
| 64 | 0.004353 | 0.003538 | 0.002861 | 0.002304 | 0.001847 |
| 65 | 0.004188 | 0.003390 | 0.002730 | 0.002189 | 0.001748 |
| 66 | 0.004030 | 0.003249 | 0.002606 | 0.002081 | 0.001654 |
| 67 | 0.003879 | 0.003115 | 0.002488 | 0.001978 | 0.001565 |
| 68 | 0.003734 | 0.002986 | 0.002375 | 0.001880 | 0.001482 |
| 69 | 0.003595 | 0.002863 | 0.002267 | 0.001787 | 0.001402 |
| 70 | 0.003461 | 0.002745 | 0.002165 | 0.001699 | 0.001328 |
| 71 | 0.003333 | 0.002633 | 0.002068 | 0.001616 | 0.001257 |
| 72 | 0.003210 | 0.002525 | 0.001975 | 0.001536 | 0.001190 |
| 73 | 0.003092 | 0.002422 | 0.001886 | 0.001461 | 0.001127 |
| 74 | 0.002978 | 0.002323 | 0.001802 | 0.001390 | 0.001067 |
| 75 | 0.002869 | 0.002229 | 0.001721 | 0.001322 | 0.001010 |
| 76 | 0.002765 | 0.002139 | 0.001644 | 0.001257 | 0.000956 |
| 77 | 0.002664 | 0.002052 | 0.001571 | 0.001196 | 0.000906 |
| 78 | 0.002567 | 0.001969 | 0.001501 | 0.001138 | 0.000858 |
| 79 | 0.002474 | 0.001890 | 0.001434 | 0.001082 | 0.000812 |
| 80 | 0.002385 | 0.001814 | 0.001371 | 0.001030 | 0.000769 |
| 81 | 0.002299 | 0.001741 | 0.001310 | 0.000980 | 0.000729 |
| 82 | 0.002216 | 0.001671 | 0.001252 | 0.000932 | 0.000690 |
| 83 | 0.002137 | 0.001605 | 0.001197 | 0.000887 | 0.000654 |
| 84 | 0.002060 | 0.001541 | 0.001144 | 0.000844 | 0.000619 |
| 85 | 0.001986 | 0.001479 | 0.001093 | 0.000803 | 0.000587 |
| 86 | 0.001916 | 0.001420 | 0.001045 | 0.000764 | 0.000556 |
| 87 | 0.001848 | 0.001364 | 0.000999 | 0.000727 | 0.000527 |
| 88 | 0.001782 | 0.001310 | 0.000955 | 0.000692 | 0.000499 |
| 89 | 0.001719 | 0.001258 | 0.000913 | 0.000659 | 0.000473 |
| 90 | 0.001658 | 0.001208 | 0.000873 | 0.000627 | 0.000448 |
| 91 | 0.001599 | 0.001160 | 0.000835 | 0.000597 | 0.000424 |
| 92 | 0.001543 | 0.001114 | 0.000798 | 0.000568 | 0.000402 |
| 93 | 0.001488 | 0.001070 | 0.000763 | 0.000541 | 0.000381 |
| 94 | 0.001436 | 0.001028 | 0.000730 | 0.000515 | 0.000361 |
| 95 | 0.001385 | 0.000987 | 0.000698 | 0.000490 | 0.000342 |
| 96 | 0.001337 | 0.000949 | 0.000667 | 0.000466 | 0.000324 |
| 97 | 0.001291 | 0.000911 | 0.000638 | 0.000444 | 0.000307 |
| 98 | 0.001245 | 0.000875 | 0.000610 | 0.000423 | 0.000291 |
| 99 | 0.001201 | 0.000841 | 0.000584 | 0.000402 | 0.000276 |
| 100 | 0.001159 | 0.000808 | 0.000558 | 0.000383 | 0.000261 |

**Table 8 (continued)**

| n | 6% | 6½% | 7% | 7½% | 8% |
|---|---|---|---|---|---|
| 1 | 1.000000 | 1.000000 | 1.000000 | 1.000000 | 1.000000 |
| 2 | 0.485437 | 0.484262 | 0.483092 | 0.481928 | 0.480769 |
| 3 | 0.314110 | 0.312576 | 0.311052 | 0.309538 | 0.308034 |
| 4 | 0.228591 | 0.226903 | 0.225228 | 0.223568 | 0.221921 |
| 5 | 0.177396 | 0.175635 | 0.173891 | 0.172165 | 0.170456 |
| 6 | 0.143363 | 0.141568 | 0.139796 | 0.138045 | 0.136315 |
| 7 | 0.119135 | 0.117331 | 0.115553 | 0.113800 | 0.112072 |
| 8 | 0.101036 | 0.099237 | 0.097468 | 0.095727 | 0.094015 |
| 9 | 0.087022 | 0.085238 | 0.083486 | 0.081767 | 0.080080 |
| 10 | 0.075868 | 0.074105 | 0.072378 | 0.070686 | 0.069029 |
| 11 | 0.066793 | 0.065055 | 0.063357 | 0.061697 | 0.060076 |
| 12 | 0.059277 | 0.057568 | 0.055902 | 0.054278 | 0.052695 |
| 13 | 0.052960 | 0.051283 | 0.049651 | 0.048064 | 0.046522 |
| 14 | 0.047585 | 0.045940 | 0.044345 | 0.042797 | 0.041297 |
| 15 | 0.042963 | 0.041353 | 0.039795 | 0.038287 | 0.036830 |
| 16 | 0.038952 | 0.037378 | 0.035858 | 0.034391 | 0.032977 |
| 17 | 0.035445 | 0.033906 | 0.032425 | 0.031000 | 0.029629 |
| 18 | 0.032357 | 0.030855 | 0.029413 | 0.028029 | 0.026702 |
| 19 | 0.029621 | 0.028156 | 0.026753 | 0.025411 | 0.024128 |
| 20 | 0.027185 | 0.025756 | 0.024393 | 0.023092 | 0.021852 |
| 21 | 0.025005 | 0.023613 | 0.022289 | 0.021029 | 0.019832 |
| 22 | 0.023046 | 0.021691 | 0.020406 | 0.019187 | 0.018032 |
| 23 | 0.021278 | 0.019961 | 0.018714 | 0.017535 | 0.016422 |
| 24 | 0.019679 | 0.018398 | 0.017189 | 0.016050 | 0.014978 |
| 25 | 0.018227 | 0.016981 | 0.015811 | 0.014711 | 0.013679 |
| 26 | 0.016904 | 0.015695 | 0.014561 | 0.013500 | 0.012507 |
| 27 | 0.015697 | 0.014523 | 0.013426 | 0.012402 | 0.011448 |
| 28 | 0.014593 | 0.013453 | 0.012392 | 0.011405 | 0.010489 |
| 29 | 0.013580 | 0.012474 | 0.011449 | 0.010498 | 0.009619 |
| 30 | 0.012649 | 0.011577 | 0.010586 | 0.009671 | 0.008827 |
| 31 | 0.011792 | 0.010754 | 0.009797 | 0.008916 | 0.008107 |
| 32 | 0.011002 | 0.009997 | 0.009073 | 0.008226 | 0.007451 |
| 33 | 0.010273 | 0.009299 | 0.008408 | 0.007594 | 0.006852 |
| 34 | 0.009598 | 0.008656 | 0.007797 | 0.007015 | 0.006304 |
| 35 | 0.008974 | 0.008062 | 0.007234 | 0.006483 | 0.005803 |
| 36 | 0.008395 | 0.007513 | 0.006715 | 0.005994 | 0.005345 |
| 37 | 0.007857 | 0.007005 | 0.006237 | 0.005545 | 0.004924 |
| 38 | 0.007358 | 0.006535 | 0.005795 | 0.005132 | 0.004539 |
| 39 | 0.006894 | 0.006099 | 0.005387 | 0.004751 | 0.004185 |
| 40 | 0.006462 | 0.005694 | 0.005009 | 0.004400 | 0.003860 |
| 41 | 0.006059 | 0.005318 | 0.004660 | 0.004077 | 0.003561 |
| 42 | 0.005683 | 0.004968 | 0.004336 | 0.003778 | 0.003287 |
| 43 | 0.005333 | 0.004644 | 0.004036 | 0.003502 | 0.003034 |
| 44 | 0.005006 | 0.004341 | 0.003758 | 0.003247 | 0.002802 |
| 45 | 0.004700 | 0.004060 | 0.003500 | 0.003011 | 0.002587 |
| 46 | 0.004415 | 0.003797 | 0.003260 | 0.002794 | 0.002390 |
| 47 | 0.004148 | 0.003553 | 0.003037 | 0.002592 | 0.002208 |
| 48 | 0.003898 | 0.003325 | 0.002831 | 0.002405 | 0.002040 |
| 49 | 0.003664 | 0.003112 | 0.002639 | 0.002232 | 0.001886 |
| 50 | 0.003444 | 0.002914 | 0.002460 | 0.002072 | 0.001743 |

| n | 6% | 6½% | 7% | 7½% | 8% |
|---|---|---|---|---|---|
| 51 | 0.003239 | 0.002729 | 0.002294 | 0.001924 | 0.001611 |
| 52 | 0.003046 | 0.002556 | 0.002139 | 0.001787 | 0.001490 |
| 53 | 0.002866 | 0.002394 | 0.001995 | 0.001659 | 0.001377 |
| 54 | 0.002696 | 0.002243 | 0.001861 | 0.001541 | 0.001274 |
| 55 | 0.002537 | 0.002101 | 0.001861 | 0.001432 | 0.001178 |
| 56 | 0.002388 | 0.001969 | 0.001620 | 0.001330 | 0.001090 |
| 57 | 0.002247 | 0.001846 | 0.001512 | 0.001236 | 0.001008 |
| 58 | 0.002116 | 0.001730 | 0.001411 | 0.001148 | 0.000932 |
| 59 | 0.001992 | 0.001622 | 0.001317 | 0.001067 | 0.000862 |
| 60 | 0.001876 | 0.001520 | 0.001229 | 0.000991 | 0.000798 |
| 61 | 0.001766 | 0.001426 | 0.001147 | 0.000921 | 0.000738 |
| 62 | 0.001664 | 0.001337 | 0.001071 | 0.000856 | 0.000683 |
| 63 | 0.001567 | 0.001254 | 0.001000 | 0.000796 | 0.000632 |
| 64 | 0.001476 | 0.001176 | 0.000934 | 0.000740 | 0.000585 |
| 65 | 0.001391 | 0.001103 | 0.000872 | 0.000688 | 0.000541 |
| 66 | 0.001310 | 0.001034 | 0.000814 | 0.000639 | 0.000501 |
| 67 | 0.001235 | 0.000970 | 0.000760 | 0.000594 | 0.000464 |
| 68 | 0.001163 | 0.000910 | 0.000710 | 0.000553 | 0.000429 |
| 69 | 0.001096 | 0.000854 | 0.000663 | 0.000514 | 0.000397 |
| 70 | 0.001033 | 0.000801 | 0.000620 | 0.000478 | 0.000368 |
| 71 | 0.000974 | 0.000752 | 0.000579 | 0.000444 | 0.000340 |
| 72 | 0.000918 | 0.000705 | 0.000541 | 0.000413 | 0.000315 |
| 73 | 0.000865 | 0.000662 | 0.000505 | 0.000384 | 0.000292 |
| 74 | 0.000815 | 0.000621 | 0.000472 | 0.000357 | 0.000270 |
| 75 | 0.000769 | 0.000583 | 0.000441 | 0.000332 | 0.000250 |
| 76 | 0.000725 | 0.000547 | 0.000412 | 0.000309 | 0.000231 |
| 77 | 0.000683 | 0.000513 | 0.000385 | 0.000287 | 0.000214 |
| 78 | 0.000644 | 0.000482 | 0.000359 | 0.000267 | 0.000198 |
| 79 | 0.000607 | 0.000452 | 0.000336 | 0.000248 | 0.000183 |
| 80 | 0.000573 | 0.000424 | 0.000314 | 0.000231 | 0.000170 |
| 81 | 0.000540 | 0.000398 | 0.000293 | 0.000215 | 0.000157 |
| 82 | 0.000509 | 0.000374 | 0.000274 | 0.000200 | 0.000146 |
| 83 | 0.000480 | 0.000351 | 0.000256 | 0.000186 | 0.000135 |
| 84 | 0.000453 | 0.000329 | 0.000239 | 0.000173 | 0.000125 |
| 85 | 0.000427 | 0.000309 | 0.000223 | 0.000161 | 0.000116 |
| 86 | 0.000402 | 0.000290 | 0.000209 | 0.000150 | 0.000107 |
| 87 | 0.000380 | 0.000272 | 0.000195 | 0.000139 | 0.000099 |
| 88 | 0.000358 | 0.000256 | 0.000182 | 0.000129 | 0.000092 |
| 89 | 0.000338 | 0.000240 | 0.000170 | 0.000120 | 0.000085 |
| 90 | 0.000318 | 0.000225 | 0.000159 | 0.000112 | 0.000079 |
| 91 | 0.000300 | 0.000212 | 0.000149 | 0.000104 | 0.000073 |
| 92 | 0.000283 | 0.000199 | 0.000139 | 0.000097 | 0.000067 |
| 93 | 0.000267 | 0.000186 | 0.000130 | 0.000090 | 0.000062 |
| 94 | 0.000252 | 0.000175 | 0.000121 | 0.000084 | 0.000058 |
| 95 | 0.000238 | 0.000164 | 0.000113 | 0.000078 | 0.000053 |
| 96 | 0.000224 | 0.000154 | 0.000106 | 0.000072 | 0.000050 |
| 97 | 0.000211 | 0.000145 | 0.000099 | 0.000067 | 0.000046 |
| 98 | 0.000199 | 0.000136 | 0.000092 | 0.000063 | 0.000042 |
| 99 | 0.000188 | 0.000128 | 0.000086 | 0.000058 | 0.000039 |
| 100 | 0.000177 | 0.000120 | 0.000081 | 0.000054 | 0.000036 |

**Table 9**
Binomial Probabilities $b(n,k;p)$

| n | k | .05 | .10 | .15 | .20 | .25 | .30 | .35 | .40 | .45 | .50 |
|---|---|------|------|------|------|------|------|------|------|------|------|
| 1 | 0 | .9500 | .9000 | .8500 | .8000 | .7500 | .7000 | .6500 | .6000 | .5500 | .5000 |
|   | 1 | .0500 | .1000 | .1500 | .2000 | .2500 | .3000 | .3500 | .4000 | .4500 | .5000 |
| 2 | 0 | .9025 | .8100 | .7225 | .6400 | .5625 | .4900 | .4225 | .3600 | .3025 | .2500 |
|   | 1 | .0950 | .1800 | .2550 | .3200 | .3750 | .4200 | .4550 | .4800 | .4950 | .5000 |
|   | 2 | .0025 | .0100 | .0225 | .0400 | .0625 | .0900 | .1225 | .1600 | .2025 | .2500 |
| 3 | 0 | .8574 | .7290 | .6141 | .5120 | .4219 | .3430 | .2746 | .2160 | .1664 | .1250 |
|   | 1 | .1354 | .2430 | .3251 | .3840 | .4219 | .4410 | .4436 | .4320 | .4084 | .3750 |
|   | 2 | .0071 | .0270 | .0574 | .0960 | .1406 | .1890 | .2389 | .2880 | .3341 | .3750 |
|   | 3 | .0001 | .0010 | .0034 | .0080 | .0156 | .0270 | .0429 | .0640 | .0911 | .1250 |
| 4 | 0 | .8145 | .6561 | .5220 | .4096 | .3164 | .2401 | .1785 | .1296 | .0915 | .0625 |
|   | 1 | .1715 | .2916 | .3685 | .4096 | .4219 | .4116 | .3845 | .3456 | .2995 | .2500 |
|   | 2 | .0135 | .0486 | .0975 | .1536 | .2109 | .2646 | .3105 | .3456 | .3675 | .3750 |
|   | 3 | .0005 | .0036 | .0115 | .0256 | .0469 | .0756 | .1115 | .1536 | .2005 | .2500 |
|   | 4 | .0000 | .0001 | .0005 | .0016 | .0039 | .0081 | .0150 | .0256 | .0410 | .0625 |
| 5 | 0 | .7738 | .5905 | .4437 | .3277 | .2373 | .1681 | .1160 | .0778 | .0503 | .0312 |
|   | 1 | .2036 | .3280 | .3915 | .4096 | .3955 | .3602 | .3124 | .2592 | .2059 | .1562 |
|   | 2 | .0214 | .0729 | .1382 | .2048 | .2637 | .3087 | .3364 | .3456 | .3369 | .3125 |
|   | 3 | .0011 | .0081 | .0244 | .0512 | .0879 | .1323 | .1811 | .2304 | .2757 | .3125 |
|   | 4 | .0000 | .0004 | .0022 | .0064 | .0146 | .0284 | .0488 | .0768 | .1128 | .1562 |
|   | 5 | .0000 | .0000 | .0001 | .0003 | .0010 | .0024 | .0053 | .0102 | .0185 | .0312 |
| 6 | 0 | .7351 | .5314 | .3771 | .2621 | .1780 | .1176 | .0754 | .0467 | .0277 | .0156 |
|   | 1 | .2321 | .3543 | .3993 | .3932 | .3560 | .3025 | .2437 | .1866 | .1359 | .0938 |
|   | 2 | .0305 | .0984 | .1762 | .2458 | .2966 | .3241 | .3280 | .3110 | .2780 | .2344 |
|   | 3 | .0021 | .0146 | .0415 | .0819 | .1318 | .1852 | .2355 | .2765 | .3032 | .3125 |
|   | 4 | .0001 | .0012 | .0055 | .0154 | .0330 | .0595 | .0951 | .1382 | .1861 | .2344 |
|   | 5 | .0000 | .0001 | .0004 | .0015 | .0044 | .0102 | .0205 | .0369 | .0609 | .0938 |
|   | 6 | .0000 | .0000 | .0000 | .0001 | .0002 | .0007 | .0018 | .0041 | .0083 | .0156 |
| 7 | 0 | .6983 | .4783 | .3206 | .2097 | .1335 | .0824 | .0490 | .0280 | .0152 | .0078 |
|   | 1 | .2573 | .3720 | .3960 | .3670 | .3115 | .2471 | .1848 | .1306 | .0872 | .0547 |
|   | 2 | .0406 | .1240 | .2097 | .2753 | .3115 | .3177 | .2985 | .2613 | .2140 | .1641 |
|   | 3 | .0036 | .0230 | .0617 | .1147 | .1730 | .2269 | .2679 | .2903 | .2918 | .2734 |
|   | 4 | .0002 | .0026 | .0109 | .0287 | .0577 | .0972 | .1442 | .1935 | .2388 | .2734 |
|   | 5 | .0000 | .0002 | .0012 | .0043 | .0115 | .0250 | .0466 | .0774 | .1172 | .1641 |
|   | 6 | .0000 | .0000 | .0001 | .0004 | .0013 | .0036 | .0084 | .0172 | .0320 | .0547 |
|   | 7 | .0000 | .0000 | .0000 | .0000 | .0001 | .0002 | .0006 | .0016 | .0037 | .0078 |
| 8 | 0 | .6634 | .4305 | .2725 | .1678 | .1001 | .0576 | .0319 | .0168 | .0084 | .0039 |
|   | 1 | .2793 | .3826 | .3847 | .3355 | .2670 | .1977 | .1373 | .0896 | .0548 | .0312 |
|   | 2 | .0515 | .1488 | .2376 | .2936 | .3115 | .2965 | .2587 | .2090 | .1569 | .1094 |
|   | 3 | .0054 | .0331 | .0839 | .1468 | .2076 | .2541 | .2786 | .2787 | .2568 | .2188 |
|   | 4 | .0004 | .0046 | .0185 | .0459 | .0865 | .1361 | .1875 | .2322 | .2627 | .2734 |
|   | 5 | .0000 | .0004 | .0026 | .0092 | .0231 | .0467 | .0808 | .1239 | .1719 | .2188 |
|   | 6 | .0000 | .0000 | .0002 | .0011 | .0038 | .0100 | .0217 | .0413 | .0703 | .1094 |
|   | 7 | .0000 | .0000 | .0000 | .0001 | .0004 | .0012 | .0033 | .0079 | .0164 | .0312 |
|   | 8 | .0000 | .0000 | .0000 | .0000 | .0000 | .0001 | .0002 | .0007 | .0017 | .0039 |

**Table 9 (continued)**

| n | k | .05 | .10 | .15 | .20 | .25 | .30 | .35 | .40 | .45 | .50 |
|---|---|-----|-----|-----|-----|-----|-----|-----|-----|-----|-----|
| 9 | 0 | .6302 | .3874 | .2316 | .1342 | .0751 | .0404 | .0207 | .0101 | .0046 | .0020 |
|   | 1 | .2985 | .3874 | .3679 | .3020 | .2253 | .1556 | .1004 | .0605 | .0339 | .0176 |
|   | 2 | .0629 | .1722 | .2597 | .3020 | .3003 | .2668 | .2162 | .1612 | .1110 | .0703 |
|   | 3 | .0077 | .0446 | .1069 | .1762 | .2336 | .2668 | .2716 | .2508 | .2119 | .1641 |
|   | 4 | .0006 | .0074 | .0283 | .0661 | .1168 | .1715 | .2194 | .2508 | .2600 | .2461 |
|   | 5 | .0000 | .0008 | .0050 | .0165 | .0389 | .0735 | .1181 | .1672 | .2128 | .2461 |
|   | 6 | .0000 | .0001 | .0006 | .0028 | .0087 | .0210 | .0424 | .0743 | .1160 | .1641 |
|   | 7 | .0000 | .0000 | .0000 | .0003 | .0012 | .0039 | .0098 | .0212 | .0407 | .0703 |
|   | 8 | .0000 | .0000 | .0000 | .0000 | .0001 | .0004 | .0013 | .0035 | .0083 | .0176 |
|   | 9 | .0000 | .0000 | .0000 | .0000 | .0000 | .0000 | .0001 | .0003 | .0008 | .0020 |
| 10 | 0 | .5987 | .3487 | .1969 | .1074 | .0563 | .0282 | .0135 | .0060 | .0025 | .0010 |
|   | 1 | .3151 | .3874 | .3474 | .2684 | .1877 | .1211 | .0725 | .0403 | .0207 | .0098 |
|   | 2 | .0746 | .1937 | .2759 | .3020- | .2816 | .2335 | .1757 | .1209 | .0763 | .0439 |
|   | 3 | .0105 | .0574 | .1298 | .2013 | .2503 | .2668 | .2522 | .2150 | .1665 | .1172 |
|   | 4 | .0010 | .0112 | .0401 | .0881 | .1460 | .2001 | .2377 | .2508 | .2384 | .2051 |
|   | 5 | .0001 | .0015 | .0085 | .0264 | .0584 | .1029 | .1536 | .2007 | .2340 | .2461 |
|   | 6 | .0000 | .0001 | .0012 | .0055 | .0162 | .0368 | .0689 | .1115 | .1596 | .2051 |
|   | 7 | .0000 | .0000 | .0001 | .0008 | .0031 | .0090 | .0212 | .0425 | .0746 | .1172 |
|   | 8 | .0000 | .0000 | .0000 | .0001 | .0004 | .0014 | .0043 | .0106 | .0229 | .0439 |
|   | 9 | .0000 | .0000 | .0000 | .0000 | .0000 | .0001 | .0005 | .0016 | .0042 | .0098 |
|   | 10 | .0000 | .0000 | .0000 | .0000 | .0000 | .0000 | .0000 | .0001 | .0003 | .0010 |
| 11 | 0 | .5688 | .3138 | .1673 | .0859 | .0422 | .0198 | .0088 | .0036 | .0014 | .0005 |
|   | 1 | .3293 | .3835 | .3248 | .2362 | .1549 | .0932 | .0518 | .0266 | .0125 | .0054 |
|   | 2 | .0867 | .2131 | .2866 | .2953 | .2581 | .1998 | .1395 | .0887 | .0513 | .0269 |
|   | 3 | .0137 | .0710 | .1517 | .2215 | .2581 | .2568 | .2254 | .1774 | .1259 | .0806 |
|   | 4 | .0014 | .0158 | .0536 | .1107 | .1721 | .2201 | .2428 | .2365 | .2060 | .1611 |
|   | 5 | .0001 | .0025 | .0132 | .0388 | .0803 | .1321 | .1830 | .2207 | .2360 | .2256 |
|   | 6 | .0000 | .0003 | .0023 | .0097 | .0268 | .0566 | .0985 | .1471 | .1931 | .2256 |
|   | 7 | .0000 | .0000 | .0003 | .0017 | .0064 | .0173 | .0379 | .0701 | .1128 | .1611 |
|   | 8 | .0000 | .0000 | .0000 | .0002 | .0011 | .0037 | .0102 | .0234 | .0462 | .0806 |
|   | 9 | .0000 | .0000 | .0000 | .0000 | .0001 | .0005 | .0018 | .0052 | .0126 | .0269 |
|   | 10 | .0000 | .0000 | .0000 | .0000 | .0000 | .0000 | .0002 | .0007 | .0021 | .0054 |
|   | 11 | .0000 | .0000 | .0000 | .0000 | .0000 | .0000 | .0000 | .0000 | .0002 | .0005 |
| 12 | 0 | .5404 | .2824 | .1422 | .0687 | .0317 | .0138 | .0057 | .0022 | .0008 | .0002 |
|   | 1 | .3413 | .3766 | .3012 | .2062 | .1267 | .0712 | .0368 | .0174 | .0075 | .0029 |
|   | 2 | .0988 | .2301 | .2924 | .2835 | .2323 | .1678 | .1088 | .0639 | .0339 | .0161 |
|   | 3 | .0173 | .0852 | .1720 | .2362 | .2581 | .2397 | .1954 | .1419 | .0923 | .0537 |
|   | 4 | .0021 | .0213 | .0683 | .1329 | .1936 | .2311 | .2367 | .2128 | .1700 | .1208 |
|   | 5 | .0002 | .0038 | .0193 | .0532 | .1032 | .1585 | .2039 | .2270 | .2124 | .1934 |
|   | 6 | .0000 | .0005 | .0040 | .0155 | .0401 | .0792 | .1281 | .1766 | .2124 | .2256 |
|   | 7 | .0000 | .0000 | .0006 | .0033 | .0115 | .0291 | .0591 | .1009 | .1489 | .1934 |
|   | 8 | .0000 | .0000 | .0001 | .0005 | .0024 | .0078 | .0199 | .0420 | .0762 | .1208 |
|   | 9 | .0000 | .0000 | .0000 | .0001 | .0004 | .0015 | .0048 | .0125 | .0277 | .0537 |
|   | 10 | .0000 | .0000 | .0000 | .0000 | .0000 | .0002 | .0008 | .0025 | .0068 | .0161 |
|   | 11 | .0000 | .0000 | .0000 | .0000 | .0000 | .0000 | .0001 | .0003 | .0010 | .0029 |
|   | 12 | .0000 | .0000 | .0000 | .0000 | .0000 | .0000 | .0000 | .0000 | .0001 | .0002 |

**Table 9 (continued)**

| n | k | .05 | .10 | .15 | .20 | .25 | .30 | .35 | .40 | .45 | .50 |
|---|---|-----|-----|-----|-----|-----|-----|-----|-----|-----|-----|
| 13 | 0 | .5133 | .2542 | .1209 | .0550 | .0238 | .0097 | .0037 | .0013 | .0004 | .0001 |
|  | 1 | .3512 | .3672 | .2774 | .1787 | .1029 | .0540 | .0259 | .0113 | .0045 | .0016 |
|  | 2 | .1109 | .2448 | .2937 | .2680 | .2059 | .1388 | .0836 | .0453 | .0220 | .0095 |
|  | 3 | .0214 | .0997 | .1900 | .2457 | .2517 | .2181 | .1651 | .1107 | .0660 | .0349 |
|  | 4 | .0028 | .0277 | .0838 | .1535 | .2097 | .2337 | .2222 | .1845 | .1350 | .0873 |
|  | 5 | .0003 | .0055 | .0266 | .0691 | .1258 | .1803 | .2154 | .2214 | .1989 | .1571 |
|  | 6 | .0000 | .0008 | .0063 | .0230 | .0559 | .1030 | .1546 | .1968 | .2169 | .2095 |
|  | 7 | .0000 | .0001 | .0011 | .0058 | .0186 | .0442 | .0833 | .1312 | .1775 | .2095 |
|  | 8 | .0000 | .0000 | .0001 | .0011 | .0047 | .0142 | .0336 | .0656 | .1089 | .1571 |
|  | 9 | .0000 | .0000 | .0000 | .0001 | .0009 | .0034 | .0101 | .0243 | .0495 | .0873 |
|  | 10 | .0000 | .0000 | .0000 | .0000 | .0001 | .0006 | .0022 | .0065 | .0162 | .0349 |
|  | 11 | .0000 | .0000 | .0000 | .0000 | .0000 | .0001 | .0003 | .0012 | .0036 | .0095 |
|  | 12 | .0000 | .0000 | .0000 | .0000 | .0000 | .0000 | .0000 | .0001 | .0005 | .0016 |
|  | 13 | .0000 | .0000 | .0000 | .0000 | .0000 | .0000 | .0000 | .0000 | .0000 | .0001 |
| 14 | 0 | .4877 | .2288 | .1028 | .0440 | .0178 | .0068 | .0024 | .0008 | .0002 | .0001 |
|  | 1 | .3593 | .3559 | .2539 | .1539 | .0832 | .0407 | .0181 | .0073 | .0027 | .0009 |
|  | 2 | .1229 | .2570 | .2912 | .2501 | .1802 | .1134 | .0634 | .0317 | .0141 | .0056 |
|  | 3 | .0259 | .1142 | .2056 | .2501 | .2402 | .1943 | .1366 | .0845 | .0462 | .0222 |
|  | 4 | .0037 | .0349 | .0998 | .1720 | .2202 | .2290 | .2022 | .1549 | .1040 | .0611 |
|  | 5 | .0004 | .0078 | .0352 | .0860 | .1468 | .1963 | .2178 | .2066 | .1701 | .1222 |
|  | 6 | .0000 | .0013 | .0093 | .0322 | .0734 | .1262 | .1759 | .2066 | .2088 | .1833 |
|  | 7 | .0000 | .0002 | .0019 | .0092 | .0280 | .0618 | .1082 | .1574 | .1952 | .2095 |
|  | 8 | .0000 | .0000 | .0003 | .0020 | .0082 | .0232 | .0510 | .0918 | .1398 | .1833 |
|  | 9 | .0000 | .0000 | .0000 | .0003 | .0018 | .0066 | .0183 | .0408 | .0762 | .1222 |
|  | 10 | .0000 | .0000 | .0000 | .0000 | .0003 | .0014 | .0049 | .0136 | .0312 | .0611 |
|  | 11 | .0000 | .0000 | .0000 | .0000 | .0000 | .0002 | .0010 | .0033 | .0093 | .0222 |
|  | 12 | .0000 | .0000 | .0000 | .0000 | .0000 | .0000 | .0001 | .0005 | .0019 | .0056 |
|  | 13 | .0000 | .0000 | .0000 | .0000 | .0000 | .0000 | .0000 | .0001 | .0002 | .0009 |
|  | 14 | .0000 | .0000 | .0000 | .0000 | .0000 | .0000 | .0000 | .0000 | .0000 | .0001 |
| 15 | 0 | .4633 | .2059 | .0874 | .0352 | .0134 | .0047 | .0016 | .0005 | .0001 | .0000 |
|  | 1 | .3658 | .3432 | .2312 | .1329 | .0668 | .0305 | .0126 | .0047 | .0016 | .0005 |
|  | 2 | .1348 | .2669 | .2856 | .2309 | .1559 | .0916 | .0476 | .0219 | .0090 | .0032 |
|  | 3 | .0307 | .1285 | .2184 | .2501 | .2252 | .1700 | .1110 | .0634 | .0318 | .0139 |
|  | 4 | .0049 | .0428 | .1156 | .1876 | .2252 | .2186 | .1792 | .1268 | .0780 | .0417 |
|  | 5 | .0006 | .0105 | .0449 | .1032 | .1651 | .2061 | .2123 | .1859 | .1404 | .0916 |
|  | 6 | .0000 | .0019 | .0132 | .0430 | .0917 | .1472 | .1906 | .2066 | .1914 | .1527 |
|  | 7 | .0000 | .0003 | .0030 | .0138 | .0393 | .0811 | .1319 | .1771 | .2013 | .1964 |
|  | 8 | .0000 | .0000 | .0005 | .0035 | .0131 | .0348 | .0710 | .1181 | .1647 | .1964 |
|  | 9 | .0000 | .0000 | .0001 | .0007 | .0034 | .0116 | .0298 | .0612 | .1048 | .1527 |
|  | 10 | .0000 | .0000 | .0000 | .0001 | .0007 | .0030 | .0096 | .0245 | .0515 | .0916 |
|  | 11 | .0000 | .0000 | .0000 | .0000 | .0001 | .0006 | .0024 | .0074 | .0191 | .0417 |
|  | 12 | .0000 | .0000 | .0000 | .0000 | .0000 | .0001 | .0004 | .0016 | .0052 | .0139 |
|  | 13 | .0000 | .0000 | .0000 | .0000 | .0000 | .0000 | .0001 | .0003 | .0010 | .0032 |
|  | 14 | .0000 | .0000 | .0000 | .0000 | .0000 | .0000 | .0000 | .0000 | .0001 | .0005 |
|  | 15 | .0000 | .0000 | .0000 | .0000 | .0000 | .0000 | .0000 | .0000 | .0000 | .0000 |

**Table 9** (continued)

| n | k | .05 | .10 | .15 | .20 | .25 | .30 | .35 | .40 | .45 | .50 |
|---|---|-----|-----|-----|-----|-----|-----|-----|-----|-----|-----|
| 16 | 0 | .4401 | .1853 | .0743 | .0281 | .0100 | .0033 | .0010 | .0003 | .0001 | .0000 |
|    | 1 | .3706 | .3294 | .2097 | .1126 | .0535 | .0228 | .0087 | .0030 | .0009 | .0002 |
|    | 2 | .1463 | .2745 | .2775 | .2111 | .1336 | .0732 | .0353 | .0150 | .0056 | .0018 |
|    | 3 | .0359 | .1423 | .2285 | .2463 | .2079 | .1465 | .0888 | .0468 | .0215 | .0085 |
|    | 4 | .0061 | .0514 | .1311 | .2001 | .2252 | .2040 | .1553 | .1014 | .0572 | .0278 |
|    | 5 | .0008 | .0137 | .0555 | .1201 | .1802 | .2099 | .2008 | .1623 | .1123 | .0667 |
|    | 6 | .0001 | .0028 | .0180 | .0550 | .1101 | .1649 | .1982 | .1983 | .1684 | .1222 |
|    | 7 | .0000 | .0004 | .0045 | .0197 | .0524 | .1010 | .1524 | .1889 | .1969 | .1746 |
|    | 8 | .0000 | .0001 | .0009 | .0055 | .0197 | .0487 | .0923 | .1417 | .1812 | .1964 |
|    | 9 | .0000 | .0000 | .0001 | .0012 | .0058 | .0185 | .0442 | .0840 | .1318 | .1746 |
|    | 10 | .0000 | .0000 | .0000 | .0002 | .0014 | .0056 | .0167 | .0392 | .0755 | .1222 |
|    | 11 | .0000 | .0000 | .0000 | .0000 | .0002 | .0013 | .0049 | .0142 | .0337 | .0667 |
|    | 12 | .0000 | .0000 | .0000 | .0000 | .0000 | .0002 | .0011 | .0040 | .0115 | .0278 |
|    | 13 | .0000 | .0000 | .0000 | .0000 | .0000 | .0000 | .0002 | .0008 | .0029 | .0085 |
|    | 14 | .0000 | .0000 | .0000 | .0000 | .0000 | .0000 | .0000 | .0001 | .0005 | .0018 |
|    | 15 | .0000 | .0000 | .0000 | .0000 | .0000 | .0000 | .0000 | .0000 | .0001 | .0002 |
|    | 16 | .0000 | .0000 | .0000 | .0000 | .0000 | .0000 | .0000 | .0000 | .0000 | .0000 |
| 17 | 0 | .4181 | .1668 | .0631 | .0225 | .0075 | .0023 | .0007 | .0002 | .0000 | .0000 |
|    | 1 | .3741 | .3150 | .1893 | .0957 | .0426 | .0169 | .0060 | .0019 | .0005 | .0001 |
|    | 2 | .1575 | .2800 | .2673 | .1914 | .1136 | .0581 | .0260 | .0102 | .0035 | .0010 |
|    | 3 | .0415 | .1556 | .2359 | .2393 | .1893 | .1245 | .0701 | .0341 | .0144 | .0052 |
|    | 4 | .0076 | .0605 | .1457 | .2093 | .2209 | .1868 | .1320 | .0796 | .0411 | .0182 |
|    | 5 | .0010 | .0175 | .0668 | .1361 | .1914 | .2081 | .1849 | .1379 | .0875 | .0472 |
|    | 6 | .0001 | .0039 | .0236 | .0680 | .1276 | .1784 | .1991 | .1839 | .1432 | .0944 |
|    | 7 | .0000 | .0007 | .0065 | .0267 | .0668 | .1201 | .1685 | .1927 | .1841 | .1484 |
|    | 8 | .0000 | .0001 | .0014 | .0084 | .0279 | .0644 | .1134 | .1606 | .1883 | .1855 |
|    | 9 | .0000 | .0000 | .0003 | .0021 | .0093 | .0276 | .0611 | .1070 | .1540 | .1855 |
|    | 10 | .0000 | .0000 | .0000 | .0004 | .0025 | .0095 | .0263 | .0571 | .1008 | .1484 |
|    | 11 | .0000 | .0000 | .0000 | .0001 | .0005 | .0026 | .0090 | .0242 | .0525 | .0944 |
|    | 12 | .0000 | .0000 | .0000 | .0000 | .0001 | .0006 | .0024 | .0081 | .0215 | .0472 |
|    | 13 | .0000 | .0000 | .0000 | .0000 | .0000 | .0001 | .0005 | .0021 | .0068 | .0182 |
|    | 14 | .0000 | .0000 | .0000 | .0000 | .0000 | .0000 | .0001 | .0004 | .0016 | .0052 |
|    | 15 | .0000 | .0000 | .0000 | .0000 | .0000 | .0000 | .0000 | .0001 | .0003 | .0010 |
|    | 16 | .0000 | .0000 | .0000 | .0000 | .0000 | .0000 | .0000 | .0000 | .0000 | .0001 |
|    | 17 | .0000 | .0000 | .0000 | .0000 | .0000 | .0000 | .0000 | .0000 | .0000 | .0000 |
| 18 | 0 | .3972 | .1501 | .0536 | .0180 | .0056 | .0016 | .0004 | .0001 | .0000 | .0000 |
|    | 1 | .3763 | .3002 | .1704 | .0811 | .0338 | .0126 | .0042 | .0012 | .0003 | .0001 |
|    | 2 | .1683 | .2835 | .2556 | .1723 | .0958 | .0458 | .0190 | .0069 | .0022 | .0006 |
|    | 3 | .0473 | .1680 | .2406 | .2297 | .1704 | .1046 | .0547 | .0246 | .0095 | .0031 |
|    | 4 | .0093 | .0700 | .1592 | .2153 | .2130 | .1681 | .1104 | .0614 | .0291 | .0117 |
|    | 5 | .0014 | .0218 | .0787 | .1507 | .1988 | .2017 | .1664 | .1146 | .0666 | .0327 |
|    | 6 | .0002 | .0052 | .0301 | .0816 | .1436 | .1873 | .1941 | .1655 | .1181 | .0708 |
|    | 7 | .0000 | .0010 | .0091 | .0350 | .0820 | .1376 | .1792 | .1892 | .1657 | .1214 |
|    | 8 | .0000 | .0002 | .0022 | .0120 | .0376 | .0811 | .1327 | .1734 | .1864 | .1669 |
|    | 9 | .0000 | .0000 | .0004 | .0033 | .0139 | .0386 | .0794 | .1284 | .1694 | .1855 |
|    | 10 | .0000 | .0000 | .0001 | .0008 | .0042 | .0149 | .0385 | .0771 | .1248 | .1669 |
|    | 11 | .0000 | .0000 | .0000 | .0001 | .0010 | .0046 | .0151 | .0374 | .0742 | .1214 |
|    | 12 | .0000 | .0000 | .0000 | .0000 | .0002 | .0012 | .0047 | .0145 | .0354 | .0708 |
|    | 13 | .0000 | .0000 | .0000 | .0000 | .0000 | .0002 | .0012 | .0045 | .0134 | .0327 |
|    | 14 | .0000 | .0000 | .0000 | .0000 | .0000 | .0000 | .0002 | .0011 | .0039 | .0117 |
|    | 15 | .0000 | .0000 | .0000 | .0000 | .0000 | .0000 | .0000 | .0002 | .0009 | .0031 |
|    | 16 | .0000 | .0000 | .0000 | .0000 | .0000 | .0000 | .0000 | .0000 | .0001 | .0006 |
|    | 17 | .0000 | .0000 | .0000 | .0000 | .0000 | .0000 | .0000 | .0000 | .0000 | .0001 |
|    | 18 | .0000 | .0000 | .0000 | .0000 | .0000 | .0000 | .0000 | .0000 | .0000 | .0000 |

**Table 9 (continued)**

| n | k | .05 | .10 | .15 | .20 | .25 | .30 | .35 | .40 | .45 | .50 |
|---|---|-----|-----|-----|-----|-----|-----|-----|-----|-----|-----|
| 19 | 0 | .3774 | .1351 | .0456 | .0144 | .0042 | .0011 | .0003 | .0001 | .0000 | .0000 |
|    | 1 | .3774 | .2852 | .1529 | .0685 | .0268 | .0093 | .0029 | .0008 | .0002 | .0000 |
|    | 2 | .1787 | .2852 | .2428 | .1540 | .0803 | .0358 | .0138 | .0046 | .0013 | .0003 |
|    | 3 | .0533 | .1796 | .2428 | .2182 | .1517 | .0869 | .0422 | .0175 | .0062 | .0018 |
|    | 4 | .0112 | .0798 | .1714 | .2182 | .2023 | .1491 | .0909 | .0467 | .0203 | .0074 |
|    | 5 | .0018 | .0266 | .0907 | .1636 | .2023 | .1916 | .1468 | .0933 | .0497 | .0222 |
|    | 6 | .0002 | .0069 | .0374 | .0955 | .1574 | .1916 | .1844 | .1451 | .0949 | .1518 |
|    | 7 | .0000 | .0014 | .0122 | .0443 | .0974 | .1525 | .1844 | .1797 | .1443 | .0961 |
|    | 8 | .0000 | .0002 | .0032 | .0166 | .0487 | .0981 | .1489 | .1797 | .1771 | .1442 |
|    | 9 | .0000 | .0000 | .0007 | .0051 | .0198 | .0514 | .0980 | .1464 | .1771 | .1762 |
|    | 10 | .0000 | .0000 | .0001 | .0013 | .0066 | .0220 | .0528 | .0976 | .1449 | .1762 |
|    | 11 | .0000 | .0000 | .0000 | .0003 | .0018 | .0077 | .0233 | .0532 | .0970 | .1442 |
|    | 12 | .0000 | .0000 | .0000 | .0000 | .0004 | .0022 | .0083 | .0237 | .0529 | .0961 |
|    | 13 | .0000 | .0000 | .0000 | .0000 | .0001 | .0005 | .0024 | .0085 | .0233 | .0518 |
|    | 14 | .0000 | .0000 | .0000 | .0000 | .0000 | .0001 | .0006 | .0024 | .0082 | .0222 |
|    | 15 | .0000 | .0000 | .0000 | .0000 | .0000 | .0000 | .0001 | .0005 | .0022 | .0074 |
|    | 16 | .0000 | .0000 | .0000 | .0000 | .0000 | .0000 | .0000 | .0001 | .0005 | .0018 |
|    | 17 | .0000 | .0000 | .0000 | .0000 | .0000 | .0000 | .0000 | .0000 | .0001 | .0003 |
|    | 18 | .0000 | .0000 | .0000 | .0000 | .0000 | .0000 | .0000 | .0000 | .0000 | .0000 |
|    | 19 | .0000 | .0000 | .0000 | .0000 | .0000 | .0000 | .0000 | .0000 | .0000 | .0000 |
| 20 | 0 | .3585 | .1216 | .0388 | .0115 | .0032 | .0008 | .0002 | .0000 | .0000 | .0000 |
|    | 1 | .3774 | .2702 | .1368 | .0576 | .0211 | .0068 | .0020 | .0005 | .0001 | .0000 |
|    | 2 | .1887 | .2852 | .2293 | .1369 | .0669 | .0278 | .0100 | .0031 | .0008 | .0002 |
|    | 3 | .0596 | .1901 | .2428 | .2054 | .1339 | .0716 | .0323 | .0123 | .0040 | .0011 |
|    | 4 | .0133 | .0898 | .1821 | .2182 | .1897 | .1304 | .0738 | .0350 | .0139 | .0046 |
|    | 5 | .0022 | .0319 | .1028 | .1746 | .2023 | .1789 | .1272 | .0746 | .0365 | .0148 |
|    | 6 | .0003 | .0089 | .0454 | .1091 | .1686 | .1916 | .1712 | .1244 | .0746 | .0370 |
|    | 7 | .0000 | .0020 | .0160 | .0545 | .1124 | .1643 | .1844 | .1659 | .1221 | .0739 |
|    | 8 | .0000 | .0004 | .0046 | .0222 | .0609 | .1144 | .1614 | .1797 | .1623 | .1201 |
|    | 9 | .0000 | .0001 | .0011 | .0074 | .0271 | .0654 | .1158 | .1597 | .1771 | .1602 |
|    | 10 | .0000 | .0000 | .0002 | .0020 | .0099 | .0308 | .0686 | .1171 | .1593 | .1762 |
|    | 11 | .0000 | .0000 | .0000 | .0005 | .0030 | .0120 | .0336 | .0710 | .1185 | .1602 |
|    | 12 | .0000 | .0000 | .0000 | .0001 | .0008 | .0039 | .1036 | .0355 | .0727 | .1201 |
|    | 13 | .0000 | .0000 | .0000 | .0000 | .0002 | .0010 | .0045 | .0146 | .0366 | .0739 |
|    | 14 | .0000 | .0000 | .0000 | .0000 | .0000 | .0002 | .0012 | .0049 | .0150 | .0370 |
|    | 15 | .0000 | .0000 | .0000 | .0000 | .0000 | .0000 | .0003 | .0013 | .0049 | .0148 |
|    | 16 | .0000 | .0000 | .0000 | .0000 | .0000 | .0000 | .0000 | .0003 | .0013 | .0046 |
|    | 17 | .0000 | .0000 | .0000 | .0000 | .0000 | .0000 | .0000 | .0000 | .0002 | .0011 |
|    | 18 | .0000 | .0000 | .0000 | .0000 | .0000 | .0000 | .0000 | .0000 | .0000 | .0002 |
|    | 19 | .0000 | .0000 | .0000 | .0000 | .0000 | .0000 | .0000 | .0000 | .0000 | .0000 |
|    | 20 | .0000 | .0000 | .0000 | .0000 | .0000 | .0000 | .0000 | .0000 | .0000 | .0000 |

**Table 10**
Normal Curve Table
$Z = Z - \text{score}$

An entry in the table is the proportion under the curve between $Z = 0$ and a positive value of $Z$. Areas for negative values of $Z$ are obtained by symmetry.

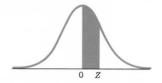

| Z | 0.00 | 0.01 | 0.02 | 0.03 | 0.04 | 0.05 | 0.06 | 0.07 | 0.08 | 0.09 |
|---|------|------|------|------|------|------|------|------|------|------|
| 0.0 | 0.0000 | 0.0040 | 0.0080 | 0.0120 | 0.0160 | 0.0199 | 0.0239 | 0.0279 | 0.0319 | 0.0359 |
| 0.1 | 0.0398 | 0.0438 | 0.0478 | 0.0517 | 0.0557 | 0.0596 | 0.0636 | 0.0675 | 0.0714 | 0.0753 |
| 0.2 | 0.0793 | 0.0832 | 0.0871 | 0.0910 | 0.0948 | 0.0987 | 0.1026 | 0.1064 | 0.1103 | 0.1141 |
| 0.3 | 0.1179 | 0.1217 | 0.1255 | 0.1293 | 0.1331 | 0.1368 | 0.1406 | 0.1443 | 0.1480 | 0.1517 |
| 0.4 | 0.1554 | 0.1591 | 0.1628 | 0.1664 | 0.1700 | 0.1736 | 0.1772 | 0.1808 | 0.1844 | 0.1879 |
| 0.5 | 0.1915 | 0.1950 | 0.1985 | 0.2019 | 0.2054 | 0.2088 | 0.2123 | 0.2157 | 0.2190 | 0.2224 |
| 0.6 | 0.2257 | 0.2291 | 0.2324 | 0.2357 | 0.2389 | 0.2422 | 0.2454 | 0.2486 | 0.2517 | 0.2549 |
| 0.7 | 0.2580 | 0.2611 | 0.2642 | 0.2673 | 0.2703 | 0.2734 | 0.2764 | 0.2794 | 0.2823 | 0.2852 |
| 0.8 | 0.2881 | 0.2910 | 0.2939 | 0.2967 | 0.2995 | 0.3023 | 0.3051 | 0.3078 | 0.3106 | 0.3133 |
| 0.9 | 0.3159 | 0.3186 | 0.3212 | 0.3238 | 0.3264 | 0.3289 | 0.3315 | 0.3340 | 0.3365 | 0.3389 |
| 1.0 | 0.3413 | 0.3438 | 0.3461 | 0.3485 | 0.3508 | 0.3531 | 0.3554 | 0.3577 | 0.3599 | 0.3621 |
| 1.1 | 0.3642 | 0.3665 | 0.3686 | 0.3708 | 0.3729 | 0.3749 | 0.3770 | 0.3790 | 0.3810 | 0.3830 |
| 1.2 | 0.3849 | 0.3869 | 0.3888 | 0.3907 | 0.3925 | 0.3944 | 0.3962 | 0.3980 | 0.3997 | 0.4015 |
| 1.3 | 0.4032 | 0.4049 | 0.4066 | 0.4082 | 0.4099 | 0.4115 | 0.4131 | 0.4147 | 0.4162 | 0.4177 |
| 1.4 | 0.4192 | 0.4207 | 0.4222 | 0.4236 | 0.4251 | 0.4265 | 0.4279 | 0.4292 | 0.4306 | 0.4319 |
| 1.5 | 0.4332 | 0.4345 | 0.4357 | 0.4370 | 0.4382 | 0.4394 | 0.4406 | 0.4418 | 0.4429 | 0.4441 |
| 1.6 | 0.4452 | 0.4463 | 0.4474 | 0.4484 | 0.4495 | 0.4505 | 0.4515 | 0.4525 | 0.4535 | 0.4545 |
| 1.7 | 0.4554 | 0.4564 | 0.4573 | 0.4582 | 0.4591 | 0.4599 | 0.4608 | 0.4616 | 0.4625 | 0.4633 |
| 1.8 | 0.4641 | 0.4649 | 0.4656 | 0.4664 | 0.4671 | 0.4678 | 0.4686 | 0.4693 | 0.4699 | 0.4706 |
| 1.9 | 0.4713 | 0.4719 | 0.4726 | 0.4732 | 0.4738 | 0.4744 | 0.4750 | 0.4756 | 0.4761 | 0.4767 |
| 2.0 | 0.4772 | 0.4778 | 0.4783 | 0.4788 | 0.4793 | 0.4798 | 0.4803 | 0.4808 | 0.4812 | 0.4817 |
| 2.1 | 0.4821 | 0.4826 | 0.4830 | 0.4834 | 0.4838 | 0.4842 | 0.4846 | 0.4850 | 0.4854 | 0.4857 |
| 2.2 | 0.4861 | 0.4864 | 0.4868 | 0.4871 | 0.4875 | 0.4878 | 0.4881 | 0.4884 | 0.4887 | 0.4890 |
| 2.3 | 0.4893 | 0.4896 | 0.4898 | 0.4901 | 0.4904 | 0.4906 | 0.4909 | 0.4911 | 0.4913 | 0.4916 |
| 2.4 | 0.4918 | 0.4920 | 0.4922 | 0.4925 | 0.4927 | 0.4929 | 0.4931 | 0.4932 | 0.4934 | 0.4936 |
| 2.5 | 0.4938 | 0.4940 | 0.4941 | 0.4943 | 0.4945 | 0.4946 | 0.4948 | 0.4949 | 0.4951 | 0.4952 |
| 2.6 | 0.4953 | 0.4955 | 0.4956 | 0.4957 | 0.4959 | 0.4960 | 0.4961 | 0.4962 | 0.4963 | 0.4964 |
| 2.7 | 0.4965 | 0.4966 | 0.4967 | 0.4968 | 0.4969 | 0.4970 | 0.4971 | 0.4972 | 0.4973 | 0.4974 |
| 2.8 | 0.4974 | 0.4975 | 0.4976 | 0.4977 | 0.4977 | 0.4978 | 0.4979 | 0.4979 | 0.4980 | 0.4981 |
| 2.9 | 0.4981 | 0.4982 | 0.4982 | 0.4983 | 0.4984 | 0.4984 | 0.4985 | 0.4985 | 0.4986 | 0.4986 |
| 3.0 | 0.4987 | 0.4987 | 0.4987 | 0.4988 | 0.4988 | 0.4989 | 0.4989 | 0.4989 | 0.4990 | 0.4990 |

**Table 11**
Partial Table of Values of $e^x$ and $e^{-x}$

| $x$ | $e^x$ | $e^{-x}$ | $x$ | $e^x$ | $e^{-x}$ | $x$ | $e^x$ | $e^{-x}$ | $x$ | $e^x$ | $e^{-x}$ |
|---|---|---|---|---|---|---|---|---|---|---|---|
| 0.0 | 1.000 | 1.000 | 2.5 | 12.18 | 0.082 | 5.0 | 148.4 | 0.0067 | 7.5 | 1,808.0 | 0.00055 |
| 0.1 | 1.105 | 0.905 | 2.6 | 13.46 | 0.074 | 5.1 | 164.0 | 0.0061 | 7.6 | 1,998.2 | 0.00050 |
| 0.2 | 1.221 | 0.819 | 2.7 | 14.88 | 0.067 | 5.2 | 181.3 | 0.0055 | 7.7 | 2,208.3 | 0.00045 |
| 0.3 | 1.350 | 0.741 | 2.8 | 16.44 | 0.061 | 5.3 | 200.3 | 0.0050 | 7.8 | 2,440.6 | 0.00041 |
| 0.4 | 1.492 | 0.670 | 2.9 | 18.17 | 0.055 | 5.4 | 221.4 | 0.0045 | 7.9 | 2,697.3 | 0.00037 |
| 0.5 | 1.649 | 0.607 | 3.0 | 20.09 | 0.050 | 5.5 | 244.7 | 0.0041 | 8.0 | 2,981.0 | 0.00034 |
| 0.6 | 1.822 | 0.549 | 3.1 | 22.20 | 0.045 | 5.6 | 270.4 | 0.0037 | 8.1 | 3,294.5 | 0.00030 |
| 0.7 | 2.014 | 0.497 | 3.2 | 24.53 | 0.041 | 5.7 | 298.9 | 0.0033 | 8.2 | 3,641.0 | 0.00027 |
| 0.8 | 2.226 | 0.449 | 3.3 | 27.11 | 0.037 | 5.8 | 330.3 | 0.0030 | 8.3 | 4,023.9 | 0.00025 |
| 0.9 | 2.460 | 0.407 | 3.4 | 29.96 | 0.033 | 5.9 | 365.0 | 0.0027 | 8.4 | 4,447.1 | 0.00022 |
| 1.0 | 2.718 | 0.368 | 3.5 | 33.12 | 0.030 | 6.0 | 403.4 | 0.0025 | 8.5 | 4,914.8 | 0.00020 |
| 1.1 | 3.004 | 0.333 | 3.6 | 36.60 | 0.027 | 6.1 | 445.9 | 0.0022 | 8.6 | 5,431.7 | 0.00018 |
| 1.2 | 3.320 | 0.301 | 3.7 | 40.45 | 0.025 | 6.2 | 492.8 | 0.0020 | 8.7 | 6,002.9 | 0.00017 |
| 1.3 | 3.669 | 0.273 | 3.8 | 44.70 | 0.022 | 6.3 | 544.6 | 0.0018 | 8.8 | 6,634.2 | 0.00015 |
| 1.4 | 4.055 | 0.247 | 3.9 | 49.40 | 0.020 | 6.4 | 601.8 | 0.0017 | 8.9 | 7,332.0 | 0.00014 |
| 1.5 | 4.482 | 0.223 | 4.0 | 54.60 | 0.018 | 6.5 | 665.1 | 0.0015 | 9.0 | 8,103.1 | 0.00012 |
| 1.6 | 4.953 | 0.202 | 4.1 | 60.34 | 0.017 | 6.6 | 735.1 | 0.0014 | 9.1 | 8,955.3 | 0.00011 |
| 1.7 | 5.474 | 0.183 | 4.2 | 66.69 | 0.015 | 6.7 | 812.4 | 0.0012 | 9.2 | 9,897.1 | 0.00010 |
| 1.8 | 6.050 | 0.165 | 4.3 | 73.70 | 0.014 | 6.8 | 897.8 | 0.0011 | 9.3 | 10,938 | 0.00009 |
| 1.9 | 6.686 | 0.150 | 4.4 | 81.45 | 0.012 | 6.9 | 992.3 | 0.0010 | 9.4 | 12,088 | 0.00008 |
| 2.0 | 7.389 | 0.135 | 4.5 | 90.02 | 0.011 | 7.0 | 1,096.6 | 0.0009 | 9.5 | 13,360 | 0.00007 |
| 2.1 | 8.166 | 0.122 | 4.6 | 99.48 | 0.010 | 7.1 | 1,212.0 | 0.0008 | 9.6 | 14,765 | 0.00007 |
| 2.2 | 9.025 | 0.111 | 4.7 | 109.95 | 0.009 | 7.2 | 1,339.4 | 0.0007 | 9.7 | 16,318 | 0.00006 |
| 2.3 | 9.974 | 0.100 | 4.8 | 121.51 | 0.008 | 7.3 | 1,480.3 | 0.0007 | 9.8 | 18,034 | 0.00006 |
| 2.4 | 11.023 | 0.091 | 4.9 | 134.29 | 0.007 | 7.4 | 1,636.0 | 0.0006 | 9.9 | 19,930 | 0.00005 |

# Answers to Selected Problems

1. $A = \{6,7,8,9\}$    $A = \{x \,|\, 6 \leqq x \leqq 9 \text{ and } x \text{ is a digit}\}$
5. $\notin$
8. $\notin$
10. $R = \{x \,|\, x \text{ is a rational number}\}$ or $P = \{x \,|\, x \text{ is a prime integer}\}$.
11. Any random selection such as $S = \{1, 1/2, \sqrt{2}, \pi, -5, 6\}$.

1. (a) $-13$     (h) $7/8$
   (c) $-20$     (j) $2$
   (e) $32/21$   (l) $9$
   (g) $1/2$

2. (a) $.25$     (d) $.571$
   (c) $.6$      (f) $.5625$

1. $3x + 5 \leqq 2$
   $3x \leqq -3$
   $x \leqq -1$
   $X = \{x \,|\, x \leqq -1\}$

3. $-3x + 5 \leqq 2$
   $-3x \leqq -3$
   $x \geqq 1$
   $X = \{x \,|\, x \geqq 1\}$

5. $14x - 21x + 16 \leqq 3x - 2$
   $-7x + 16 \leqq 3x - 2$
   $16 \leqq 10x - 2$
   $18 \leqq 10x$
   $9/5 \leqq x$
   $X = \{x \mid x \geqq 9/5\}$

2. $A = (4, 2)$    $E = (-2, -3)$    $H = (5, 0)$
   $C = (5, 3)$    $F = (3, -2)$

3. (b) $\dfrac{f_2 - c_2}{f_1 - c_1} = \dfrac{-2 - 3}{3 - 5} = \dfrac{-5}{-2} = \dfrac{5}{2}$

4. (a) $d = \sqrt{(3 - 3)^2 + (1 - (-4))^2} = \sqrt{0 + (5)^2} = \sqrt{25} = 5$
   (c) $d = \sqrt{(2 - 1/2)^2 + (1 - 0)^2} = \sqrt{9/4 + 1} = \sqrt{13/4} = \sqrt{13}/2$

5. (b) $d(P_1, P_2) = \sqrt{(6 - (-1))^2 + (2 - 4)^2} = \sqrt{49 + 4} = \sqrt{53}$
   $d(P_1, P_3) = \sqrt{(4 - (-1))^2 + (-5 - 4)^2} = \sqrt{25 + 81} = \sqrt{106}$
   $d(P_2, P_3) = \sqrt{(4 - 6)^2 + (-5 - 2)^2} = \sqrt{4 + 49} = \sqrt{53}$
   Since $(\sqrt{53})^2 + (\sqrt{53})^2 = (\sqrt{106})^2$, the triangle is a right triangle.
   It is also isosceles.

6. (b) $y = 2x - 3$
   If $x = 0$,  $y = 2(0) - 3 = -3$.
   If $x = 2$,  $y = 2(2) - 3 = 1$.

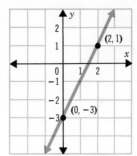

1. (a) $m = \dfrac{1 - 3}{0 - 2} = \dfrac{-2}{-2} = 1$

   (f) $m = \dfrac{-2 - (-2)}{6 - (-3)} = \dfrac{0}{9} = 0$

   (c) $m = \dfrac{-4 - 0}{-5 - (-3)} = \dfrac{-4}{-2} = 2$

2. (a) $y - 3 = 1(x - 2)$
   $y = x + 1$
   (f) $y = -2$

   (a) $y = x + 1$

   (f) $y = -2$

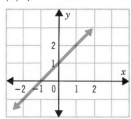

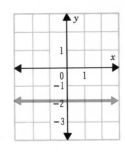

3. (a) $y - 3 = \frac{1}{2}(x - (-2))$
$y - 3 = \frac{1}{2}x + 1$
$y = \frac{1}{2}x + 4$

(f) $y - 0 = 3(x - (-\frac{1}{2}))$
$y = 3x + \frac{3}{2}$

(d) $m = \dfrac{1-3}{1-0} = -2$

$y - 3 = -2(x - 0)$
$y = -2x + 3$

4. (c)

| $x$ | $\frac{1}{2}$ | 4 | $\frac{9}{2}$ | 2 | $\frac{3}{2}$ | $-4$ |
|---|---|---|---|---|---|---|
| $y$ | $-5$ | 2 | 3 | $-2$ | $-3$ | $-14$ |

5. (a) $3x - 2y = 6$
$-2y = -3x + 6$
$y = \frac{3}{2}x - 3$
$m = \frac{3}{2}, \quad b = -3$

(f) $2x - 2y = 1$
$-2y = -2x + 1$
$y = x - \frac{1}{2}$
$m = 1, \quad b = -\frac{1}{2}$

(a)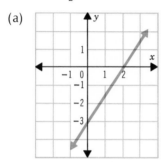

(f)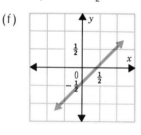

7. $C = 0.50x + 0.50$

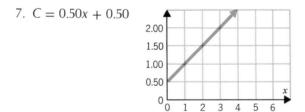

8. $F = \frac{9}{5}C + 32$

9. (a) $P(0) = 3100(0) + 75{,}000 = \$75{,}000$
(b) $P(6) = 3100(6) + 75{,}000 = \$93{,}600$

1.6
Exercise
(page 32)

1. (a) $L$ and $M$ are parallel since the slope of each line is 2/3 and each $y$-intercept is different.

(c) $3x_0 - 3y_0 + 10 = 0 \qquad x_0 + y_0 - 2 = 0$
$y_0 = x_0 + \frac{10}{3} \qquad\qquad y_0 = -x_0 + 2$
$\qquad\qquad x_0 + 10/3 = -x_0 + 2$
$\qquad\qquad\qquad 2x_0 = -4/3$
$\qquad\qquad\qquad x_0 = -2/3$
$\qquad\qquad y_0 = -2/3 + 10/3 = 8/3$
Hence, $P = (-2/3, 8/3)$.

(e) $P = (1, 1)$.

(a)

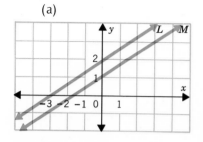

(c)

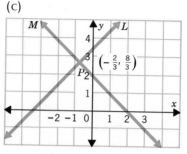

(e)

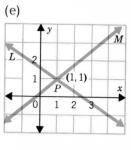

3. $x$ = amount in AAA bonds; $y$ = amount in Savings and Loan
$y = \$50{,}000 - x$ and $.09x + .07y = 4000$
$(.09)x + (.07)(50{,}000 - x) = 4{,}000$
$(.09)x + 3{,}500 - (.07)x = 4{,}000$
$(.02)x = 500$

$$x = \frac{500}{.02} = 25{,}000$$

$x = 25{,}000$ in AAA bonds
$y = 25{,}000$ in the Savings and Loan

5. $x$ = pounds of cashews; $y$ = pounds of pecans
$y = 60 - x$ and $1.5x + 1.8y + 40(.8) = 1.25(100)$
$x(1.5) + (60 - x)(1.8) + (40)(.8) = 125$
$(1.5)x - (1.8)x = -15$
$.3x = 15$
$x = 50$ pounds of cashews; $y = 10$ pounds of pecans

7. $x$ = amount of $\$.75$ per pound coffee; $y$ = amount of $\$1.00$ per pound coffee.
$y = 100 - x$ and $.75x + y = .9(100)$
$(.75)x + (100 - x) = (.90)(100)$
$10 = .25x$
$40 = x$
$x = 40$ pounds of $\$.75$ per pound coffee
$y = 60$ pounds of $\$1.00$ per pound coffee

9. $x$ = amount at 8%, $y$ = amount at 18%
$y = 10{,}000 - x$ and $.08x + .18y = 1000$
$(.08)x + (.18)(10{,}000 - x) = 1{,}000$
$800 = .1x$
$8{,}000 = x$
$x = \$8{,}000$ at 8%; $y = \$2{,}000$ at 18%

11. $x$ = total distance; $y$ = speed
$1/3x = y \cdot 1$; $x = 3y$

$$\frac{x}{2} + 18 = 2y; \quad \frac{3y}{2} + 18 = 2y; \quad 3y + 36 = 4y$$

$36 = y$; $x = 3 \cdot 36 = 108$
Distance is 108 miles; Speed is 36 miles per hour; Time is 3 hours.

1. (a)

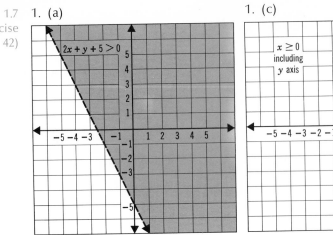

1. (c)

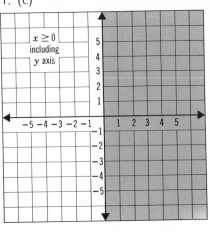

2. (b)

2. (e)

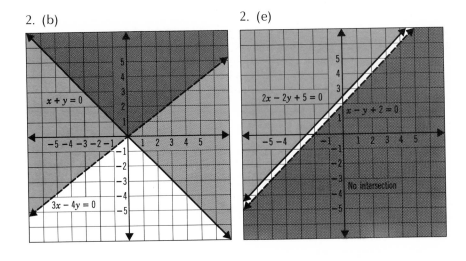

2. (g)

2. (k)

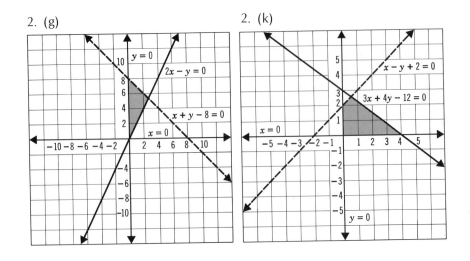

Review Exercises
(page 43)

1. (a) $x = 17/12$

   (i) $(2x)^4 = 2^4$
$$2x = 2$$
$$x = 1$$

(c) $x = 1/8$

   (k) $-2x \geqq -2$
$$x \leqq 1$$

(e) $2x - 4 + 4 \leqq 8 + 4$
$$2x \leqq 12$$
$$x \leqq 6$$

   (m) $4 + 3 \leqq 3x + 6x$
$$7 \leqq 9x$$
$$x \geqq 7/9$$

2. (a)

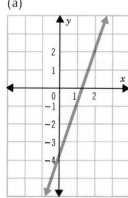

(b)

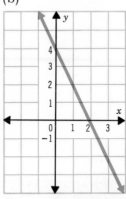

3. (a) $-4y = -3x - 12$
$$y = \tfrac{3}{4}x + 3$$
$$m = \tfrac{3}{4}, \quad b = 3$$

(c) $2y = -4x + 9$
$$y = -2x + 9/2$$
$$m = -2, \quad b = 9/2$$

4. (a) $y - 2 = 2(x - 1)$
$$y - 2 = 2x - 2$$
$$y = 2x$$

(c) $y = -3x + 4$

5. (a) $P = (-6/11, 26/11)$

(d) $3x - y + 5 = 0 \qquad y = 3x - 2$
$$y = 3x + 5$$

Since both lines have slope $m = 3$, but different $y$-intercepts, the lines are parallel.

6. (b) $x_0 = 4; \; y_0 = 6$

7. $x$ = amount in A-rated bond; $y$ = amount in bank
$y = \$70{,}000 - x$ and $.09x + .04y = 5000$
$$(.09)x + (.04)(70{,}000 - x) = 5{,}000$$
$$(.09x) - (.04)x + 2{,}800 = 5{,}000$$
$$(.05)x = 2{,}200$$
$$x = \$44{,}000 \text{ in A-rated bonds}$$
$$y = \$26{,}000 \text{ in bank}$$

CHAPTER 2
2.1
Exercise
(page 53)

1. (a) $f(3) = 3(3) - 2 = 7$    (c) $f(0) = 3(0) - 2 = -2$

2. (a) $f(1) = 3(1)^4 + 1 = 4$    (b) $f(h) = 3(h)^4 + 1 = 3h^4 + 1$

(d) $f(h + 1) = 3(h + 1)^4 + 1$

3. (I) (a) $f(x + h) = 2(x + h) + 5 = 2x + 2h + 5$

(I) (b) $f(x + h) - f(x) = 2x + 2h + 5 - (2x + 5) = 2h$

(III) (a) $f(x + h) = \dfrac{1}{x + h + 3}$

4. (a) Not a function since two values of $y$ are associated with each value of $x$.

(c) $D = \{x \mid x \in R^{\#}\}$

(e) $D = \{x \mid x \geqq -1\}$

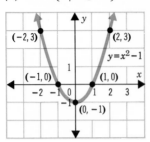

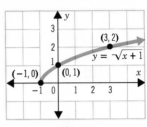

5. (a) $D = \{x \mid x < 5\}$     5. (c) $D = \{x \mid x \in R^{\#}\}$

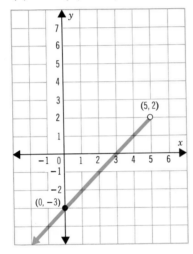

1. (a) opens up vertex: $x = -1/4$
$$y = f(-1/4) = 2(-1/4)^2 - 1/4 - 3 = -25/8$$
$x$-intercepts: $(2x + 3)(x - 1) = 0$
$$x_1 = -3/2, x_2 = 1$$
$y$-intercept: $y = -3$

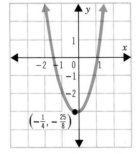

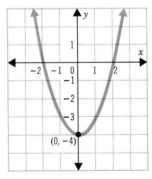

(c) opens up vertex: $x = 0$
$$y = f(0) = -4$$
$x$-intercepts: $(x + 2)(x - 2) = 0$
$$x_1 = -2, x_2 = 2$$
$y$-intercept: $y = -4$

(g) opens down vertex: $x = 0$
$$y = f(0) = 1$$
x-intercepts: $(-x + 1)(x + 1) = 0$
$$x_1 = -1, x_2 = 1$$
y-intercept: $y = 1$

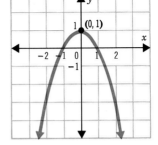

(h) opens up vertex: $x = -1$
$$y = f(-1) = 0$$
x-intercept: $(x + 1)^2 = 0$
$$x = -1$$
y-intercept: $y = 1$

2. (a), (b), and (c) are polynomial functions.
3. (a) $D = \{x \mid x \neq -2\}$
   (c) $D = \{x \mid x \neq -1/3 \text{ and } x \neq 2\}$
5. (b)

(c)

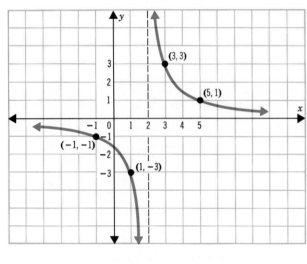

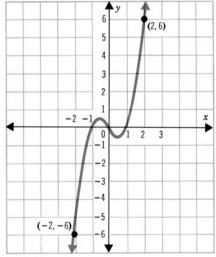

1. (b) $D = \{x \mid x \in R^{\#}\}$     (d) $D = \{x \mid x > 1\}$
2. (a) $f(x + h) = 3x + 3h + 4$
   $$f(x + h) - f(x) = 3h$$
   $$\frac{f(x + h) - f(x)}{h} = 3, \quad h \neq 0$$

3. (b) $D = \{x \mid x \geqq -1\}$.
4. (b)            (d)            (e)

Review Exercises
(page 61)

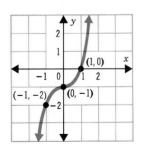

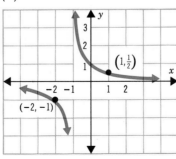

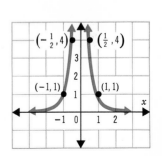

2. Let $x$ = number of hours worked and $y$ = take-home pay. Then,

$$y = .81(6.50)x = 5.265x$$

If $y = 200$, then $x = \dfrac{200}{5.265} = 38$ hours.

3. Let $x$ = mileage and $C$ = cost of transportation. Then, $(100, 5)$ and $(700, 28.5)$ are points on the line. The slope is

$$\frac{28.5 - 5}{700 - 100} = \frac{23.5}{600} = .039$$

The relationship is

$$C - 5 = .039\,(x - 100)$$

If $x = 200$,

$$C - 5 = .039\,(100)$$
$$C = \$8.90$$

5. (a) $C = \$10x + \$600, R = \$30x$
$$10x + 600 = 30x$$
$$600 = 20x$$
$$30 = x$$

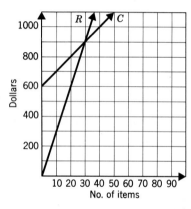

6. $C = \$0.75x + 300, R = \$1 \cdot x$
$$0.75x + 300 = x$$
$$300 = .25x$$
$$1200 = x$$

8. $S = 0.7p + 0.4, D = -0.5p + 1.6$
$$0.7p + 0.4 = -0.5p + 1.6$$
$$7p + 4 = -5p + 16$$
$$12p = 12$$
$$p = \$1$$
$$S = 0.7 \cdot 1 + 0.4 = 1.1$$

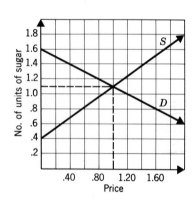

The coordinates of the point of intersection are (market price, quantity demanded).

1. $P$ = (rent per unit) (number of units rented) $-$ 6(number of units rented)
$$P = (120 + 3x)(50 - x) - 6(50 - x) = 5700 + 36x - 3x^2$$

Maximum profit occurs at the vertex:

$$x = \frac{-36}{-6} = 6$$

$P(6) = 5700 + 36(6) - 3(6)^2 = 5916 - 108 = \$5808$

Monthly rental $= 120 + 3(6) = \$138$.

2. (a) $P = R - C = 18x - 2x^2 - 6x = 12x - 2x^2$

(b) This occurs at the vertex: $x = \dfrac{-12}{-4} = 3$

(c) $P(3) = 12(3) - 2(3)^2 = 18$

5. $90\sqrt{2x} = 3x + 1200$

$30\sqrt{2x} = x + 400$

$900(2x) = x^2 + 800x + 160{,}000$

$x^2 - 1000x + 160{,}000 = 0$

$(x - 800)(x - 200) = 0$

$x = 200, x = 800$

There are two break-even points. Profits occur for $200 < x < 800$.

Review Exercises
(page 82)

1. Let $x =$ number of items and $C =$ daily cost. Then

$$C = 1200 + 1.5x$$

3. (a) $P = R - C = (12 - 4x)x - 4x = -4x^2 + 8x$

(b) The vertex is at $x = \dfrac{-8}{-8} = 1$

(c) $P(1) = -4 + 8 = 4$

CHAPTER 4

4.2
Exercise
(page 99)

1. See graphs on following page.

(a) $f = 5x + 7y$ has no maximum under these conditions.

(d) The vertices are: $(0, 2), (0, 4), (2, 0), (4, 0), (24/7, 12/7)$. Testing these in the function $f = 5x + 7y$ we get:

$f = 5 \cdot 0 + 7 \cdot 2 = 14$

$f = 5 \cdot 0 + 7 \cdot 4 = 28$

$f = 5 \cdot 2 + 7 \cdot 0 = 10$

$f = 5 \cdot 4 + 7 \cdot 0 = 20$

$$f = 5\left(\frac{24}{7}\right) + 7\left(\frac{12}{7}\right) = 29\frac{1}{7}$$

The maximum is $29\frac{1}{7}$

(f) The vertices are $(0, 2), (0, 5), (2, 0), (8, 0), (6, 2)$.

Testing these in the function $f = 5x + 7y$ we get

$f = 5 \cdot 0 + 7 \cdot 2 = 14$

$f = 5 \cdot 0 + 7 \cdot 5 = 35$

$f = 5 \cdot 2 + 7 \cdot 0 = 10$

$f = 5 \cdot 8 + 7 \cdot 0 = 40$

$f = 5 \cdot 6 + 7 \cdot 2 = 44$

The maximum is 44 at $(6, 2)$.

1. (a)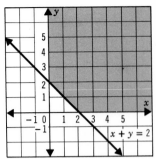

1. (d)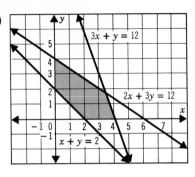

1. (f)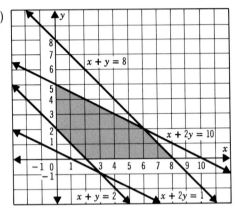

2. (a) The minimum is 0 at $(0,0)$.

(b) See graph of 1.(a) above.
The vertices are $(0,2), (2,0)$.
Testing these in the function $f = 2x + 3y$ we get
$f = 2 \cdot 0 + 3 \cdot 2 = 6$
$f = 2 \cdot 2 + 3 \cdot 0 = 4$
The minimum is 4 at $(2,0)$.

(c) See graph of 1.(d) above.
The vertices are $(0,2), (0,4), (2,0), (4,0), (24/7, 12/7)$.
Testing these in the function $f = 2x + 3y$ we get
$f = 2 \cdot 0 + 3 \cdot 2 = 6$
$f = 2 \cdot 0 + 3 \cdot 4 = 12$
$f = 2 \cdot 2 + 3 \cdot 0 = 4$
$f = 2 \cdot 4 + 3 \cdot 0 = 8$
$f = 2 \cdot 24/7 + 3 \cdot 12/7 = 12$
The minimum is 4 at $(2,0)$.

(f) See graph of 1.(f) above.
The vertices are $(0,2), (0,5), (2,0), (8,0), (6,2)$.
Testing these in the function $f = 2x + 3y$ we get
$f = 2 \cdot 0 + 3 \cdot 2 = 6$
$f = 2 \cdot 0 + 3 \cdot 5 = 15$
$f = 2 \cdot 2 + 3 \cdot 0 = 4$
$f = 2 \cdot 8 + 3 \cdot 0 = 16$
$f = 2 \cdot 6 + 3 \cdot 2 = 18$
The minimum is 4 at $(2,0)$.

3. The vertices are $(10, 0)$, $(0, 10)$, $(10/3, 10/3)$.

   (a) $f = 10 + 0 = 10$     maximum, anywhere along the line
                          $x + y = 10$
     $f = 0 + 10 = 10$     from $(0, 10)$ to $(10, 0)$.
     $f = 10/3 + 10/3 = 20/3$, minimum

   (c) $f = 3 \cdot 10 + 4 \cdot 0 = 30$
     $f = 3 \cdot 0 + 4 \cdot 10 = 40$, maximum
     $f = 3 \cdot 10/3 + 4 \cdot 10/3 = 23\ 1/3$, minimum

   (e) $f = 5 \cdot 10 + 2 \cdot 0 = 50$, maximum
     $f = 5 \cdot 0 + 2 \cdot 10 = 20$, minimum
     $f = 5 \cdot 10/3 + 2 \cdot 10/3 = 23\ 1/3$

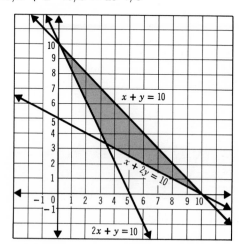

4. $P = (\$0.30)x + (\$0.40)y$
   $P_1 = (\$0.30) \cdot 0 + (\$0.40) \cdot 0 = \$0.00$
   $P_2 = (\$0.30) \cdot 0 + (\$0.40) \cdot 150 = \$60.00$
   $P_3 = (\$0.30) \cdot 160 + (\$0.40) \cdot 0 = \$48.00$
   $P_4 = (\$0.30) \cdot 90 + (\$0.40) \cdot 105 = \$27.00 + \$42.00 = \$69.00$
   90 packages of the low-grade mixture
   105 packages of the high-grade mixture

6. $P = \$4x + \$3y$
   $P_1 = \$4 \cdot 0 + \$3 \cdot 0 = 0$
   $P_2 = \$4 \cdot 0 + \$3 \cdot 30 = \$90$
   $P_3 = \$4 \cdot 40 + \$3 \cdot 0 = \$160$
   $P_4 = \$4 \cdot 20 + \$3 \cdot 20 = \$80 + \$60 = \$140$
   40 standard models should be produced and no deluxe models

9. $x =$ ounces of supplement I; $y =$ ounces of supplement II
   The problem is to minimize
   $C = (\$0.03) \cdot x + \$(0.04) \cdot y$
   Subject to
   $x \geqq 0, y \geqq 0$
   $5x + 25y \geqq 50$ or $x + 5y \geqq 10$
   $25x + 10y \geqq 100$ or $5x + 2y \geqq 20$
   $10x + 10y \geqq 60$ or $x + y \geqq 6$
   $35x + 20y \geqq 180$ or $7x + 4y \geqq 36$

The vertices are: $(0, 10)$, $(10, 0)$, $(5, 1)$, $(4, 2)$, $(4/3, 20/3)$.

$C_1 = (\$0.03) \cdot 0 + (\$0.04) \cdot 10 = \$0.40$

$C_2 = (\$0.03) \cdot 10 + (\$0.04) \cdot 0 = \$0.30$

$C_3 = (\$0.03) \cdot 5 + (\$0.04) \cdot 1 = \$0.15 + \$0.04 = \$0.19$

$C_4 = (\$0.03) \cdot 4 + (\$0.04) \cdot 2 = \$0.12 + \$0.08 + \$0.20$

$C_5 = (\$0.03) \cdot 4/3 + (\$0.04) \cdot 20/3 \doteq \$0.04 + \$0.27 = \$0.31$

He should add 5 ounces of Supplement I and 1 ounce of Supplement II to each 100 ounces of feed.

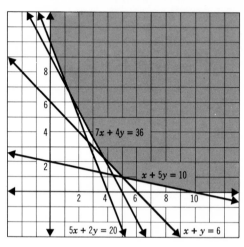

10. $x = $ acres of crop $A$; $y = $ acres of crop $B$

The problem is to maximize

$P = \$40 \cdot x + \$120 \cdot y$

Subject to

$x \geqq 0, y \geqq 0$

$\$10x + \$40y \leqq \$1100$ or $x + 4y \leqq 110$     $2x + 3y \leqq 160$

See graph following.

The vertices are: $(0, 0)$, $(0, 55/2)$, $(80, 0)$, $(62, 12)$.

$P_1 = \$40 \cdot 0 + \$120 \cdot 0 = \$0$

$P_2 = \$40 \cdot 0 + \$120 \cdot 55/2 = \$3300$

$P_3 = \$40 \cdot 80 + \$120 \cdot 0 = \$3200$

$P_4 = \$40 \cdot 62 + \$120 \cdot 12 = \$2480 + \$1440 = \$3920$

62 acres of crop A should be planted and 12 acres of crop B should be planted; 74 acres of land are used leaving 26 acres idle.

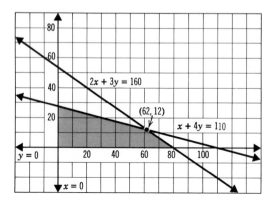

12. $f = 2x + y + 3z$

$L_1: x + 2y + z \leqq 25$     $L_2: 3x + 2y + 3z \leqq 30$

$L_3: x \geqq 0$     $L_4: y \geqq 0$     $L_5: z \geqq 0$

(a) $L_1, L_2, L_3$ give $x_0 = 0$

$2y + z = 25$     $2y + 3z = 30$

$$-z_0 + 25 = -3z_0 + 30$$
$$2z_0 = 5$$
$$z_0 = 5/2$$

$2y_0 + 5/2 = 25$

$$y_0 = \frac{-5}{4} + \frac{25}{2} = \frac{-5 + 50}{4} = \frac{45}{4} \qquad (0, 45/4, 5/2)$$

(b) $L_1, L_2, L_4$ give $y_0 = 0$

$x + z = 25, 3x + 3z = 30$

$$x + z = 10$$

No solution

(c) $L_1, L_2, L_5$ give: $z_0 = 0$

$x + 2y = 25, 3x + 2y = 30$

$$x_0 - 25 = 3x_0 - 30$$
$$5 = 2x_0$$
$$5/2 = x_0$$

$5/2 + 2y_0 = 25$

$$y_0 = \frac{-5}{4} + \frac{25}{2} = \frac{-5}{4} + \frac{50}{4} = \frac{45}{4}$$

$(5/2, 45/4, 0)$

(d) $L_1, L_3, L_4$ give: $x_0 = 0, y_0 = 0, z_0 = 25$
but $(0, 0, 25)$ does not satisfy $L_2$.

(e) $L_1, L_3, L_5$ give: $x_0 = 0, z_0 = 0$

$2y_0 = 25$

$y_0 = 25/2$

$(0, 25/2, 0)$

(f) $L_1, L_4, L_5$ give: $y_0 = 0, z_0 = 0, x_0 = 25$
$(25, 0, 0)$ does not satisfy $L_2$.

(g) $L_2, L_3, L_4$ give: $x_0 = 0, y_0 = 0$

$3z_0 = 30$

$z_0 = 10, (0, 0, 10)$

(h) $L_2, L_3, L_5$ give: $x_0 = 0, z_0 = 0$

$2y_0 = 30$

$y_0 = 15$ $(0, 15, 0)$ does not satisfy $L_1$.

(i) $L_2, L_4, L_5$ give: $y_0 = 0, z_0 = 0$

$3x_0 = 30$

$x_0 = 10, (10, 0, 0)$

(j) $L_3, L_4, L_5$ give: $(0, 0, 0)$

The points in the set of feasible solutions are: $(0, 45/4, 5/2)$,
$(5/2, 45/4, 0)$, $(0, 25/2, 0)$, $(0, 0, 10)$, $(10, 0, 0)$, $(0, 0, 0)$.

$f_1 = 2 \cdot 0 + 45/4 + 3 \cdot 5/2 = 75/4 = 18 \ 3/4$

$f_2 = 2 \cdot 5/2 + 45/4 + 3 \cdot 0 = 65/4 = 16 \ 1/4$

$f_3 = 2 \cdot 0 + 25/2 + 3 \cdot 0 = 25/2 = 12 \ 1/2$

$f_4 = 2 \cdot 0 + 0 + 3 \cdot 10 = 30$

$f_5 = 2 \cdot 10 + 0 + 3 \cdot 0 = 20$
$f_6 = 2 \cdot 0 + 0 + 3 \cdot 0 = 0$
The maximum is $f = 30$ at $(0, 0, 10)$.

Review Exercises
(page 102)

1. (a) $f = 15x + 20y$
    The vertices are: $(0, 0), (0, 3), (4, 0)$.
    $f_1 = 15 \cdot 0 + 20 \cdot 0 = 0$
    $f_2 = 15 \cdot 0 + 20 \cdot 3 = 60$
    $f_3 = 15 \cdot 4 + 20 \cdot 0 = 60$
    Maximum is 60 at any point on the
    line $3x + 4y = 12$ between
    $(0, 3)$ and $(4, 0)$. Minimum is 0
    at $(0, 0)$.

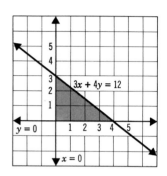

(c) $f = 15x + 20y$
    The vertices are: $(0, 0), (0, 9),$
    $(4, 5), (6, 0)$.
    $f_1 = 15 \cdot 0 + 20 \cdot 0 = 0$
    $f_2 = 15 \cdot 0 + 20 \cdot 9 = 180$
    $f_3 = 15 \cdot 4 + 20 \cdot 5 = 160$
    $f_4 = 15 \cdot 6 + 20 \cdot 0 = 90$
    Maximum is 180 at $(0, 9)$.
    Minimum is 0 at $(0, 0)$.

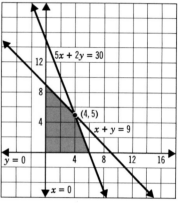

3. $x$ = pounds of food A
   $y$ = pounds of food B
   $C$ = cost of the foods per month = $\$1.30x + \$0.80y$
   $x \geqq 0, y \geqq 0$
   $5x + 2y \geqq 60 \qquad 3x + 2y \geqq 45 \qquad 4x + 1y \geqq 30$
   The vertices are $(0, 30), (15/2, 45/4), (15, 0)$.
   $C_1 = \$1.30 \cdot 0 + \$0.80 \cdot 30 = \$24.00$

   $C_2 = \$1.30 \cdot \dfrac{15}{2} + \$0.80 \cdot \dfrac{45}{4} = \$18.75$

   $C_3 = \$1.30 \cdot 15 + \$0.80 \cdot 0 = \$19.50$
   She should buy 7 1/2 pounds of A and 11 1/4 pounds of B.

CHAPTER 5

5.1
Exercise
(page 108)

1. (a) $2 \times 3$     (c) $1 \times 3$     (f) $1 \times 1$

3.

|  | Katy | Mike | Danny |
|---|---|---|---|
| gum | 5 | 2 | 1 |
| ice cream | 2 | 0 | 1 |
| jelly beans | 10 | 15 | 0 |
| candy bars | 0 | 2 | 4 |

or

| | gum | ice cream | jelly beans | candy bars |
|---|---|---|---|---|
| Katy | 5 | 2 | 10 | 0 |
| Mike | 2 | 0 | 15 | 2 |
| Danny | 1 | 1 | 0 | 4 |

5. $A = \begin{pmatrix} x+y & 2 \\ 4 & 0 \end{pmatrix}$   $B = \begin{pmatrix} 6 & x-y \\ 4 & z \end{pmatrix}$

$x + y = 6 \quad x - y = 2 \quad z = 0$
$\quad 2x = 8 \quad\quad x = 4 \quad y = 2$

$A = \begin{pmatrix} 6 & 2 \\ 4 & 0 \end{pmatrix} = B$

1. (a) $\begin{pmatrix} 2 & -1/2 & -1/3 \\ 6 & 4 & 2/3 \end{pmatrix} + \begin{pmatrix} -2 & 6 & 0 \\ 3 & -1 & 2/3 \end{pmatrix} = \begin{pmatrix} 0 & 11/2 & -1/3 \\ 9 & 3 & 4/3 \end{pmatrix}$

5.2
Exercise
(page 112)

(d) $\begin{pmatrix} 2 & -1/2 & -1/3 \\ 6 & 4 & 2/3 \end{pmatrix} - \begin{pmatrix} -2 & 6 & 0 \\ 3 & -1 & 2/3 \end{pmatrix} = \begin{pmatrix} 4 & -13/2 & -1/3 \\ 3 & 5 & 0 \end{pmatrix}$

2. $2 + x = 6; \quad x = 4$
$3 + y = -8; \quad y = -11$
$-4 + z = 2 \quad z = 6$

1. (a) $\begin{pmatrix} 1 & -1 & 1 \\ 2 & 0 & 1 \\ 3 & -1 & 1 \end{pmatrix} \begin{pmatrix} 1 & 2 \\ -1 & 1 \\ 1 & 3 \end{pmatrix} = \begin{pmatrix} 3 & 4 \\ 3 & 7 \\ 5 & 8 \end{pmatrix}$

5.3
Exercise
(page 122)

3. $\begin{pmatrix} a & b \\ c & d \end{pmatrix} \begin{pmatrix} 0 & 1 \\ 2 & -1 \end{pmatrix} = \begin{pmatrix} 2 & 1 \\ -1 & 0 \end{pmatrix}$   $\begin{aligned} 2b &= 2; & b &= 1 \\ a - b &= 1; & a &= 2 \\ 2d &= 1; & d &= -1/2 \\ c - d &= 0; & c &= -1/2 \end{aligned}$

7. $\begin{pmatrix} 2 \\ 1 \\ 0 \end{pmatrix} + \begin{pmatrix} a_1 \\ a_2 \\ a_3 \end{pmatrix} = \begin{pmatrix} 2 \\ -1 \\ 3 \end{pmatrix}$   $\begin{aligned} 2 + a_1 &= 2; & a_1 &= 0 \\ 1 + a_2 &= -1; & a_2 &= -2 \\ 0 + a_3 &= 3; & a_3 &= 3 \end{aligned}$

9. $\begin{pmatrix} a & b \\ c & d \end{pmatrix} \begin{pmatrix} 1 & 1 \\ -1 & 1 \end{pmatrix} = \begin{pmatrix} 1 & 1 \\ -1 & 1 \end{pmatrix} \begin{pmatrix} a & b \\ c & d \end{pmatrix};$   $\begin{aligned} a - b &= a + c \\ a + b &= b + d & a &= d \\ c - d &= -a + c & c &= -b \\ c + d &= -b + d \end{aligned}$

14. $A \cdot A = \begin{pmatrix} a & 1-a \\ 1+a & -a \end{pmatrix} \begin{pmatrix} a & 1-a \\ 1+a & -a \end{pmatrix}$

$= \begin{pmatrix} a^2 + (1-a^2) & a(1-a) - a(1-a) \\ a(1+a) - a(1+a) & (1-a^2) + a^2 \end{pmatrix} = \begin{pmatrix} 1 & 0 \\ 0 & 1 \end{pmatrix}$

$= I_2$

15. $(x_1 \quad x_2) \begin{pmatrix} 1/2 & 1/2 \\ 1/4 & 3/4 \end{pmatrix} = (x_1 \quad x_2)$

$1/2x_1 + 1/4x_2 = x_1.$
$1/2x_1 + 3/4x_2 = x_2'$
$1/4x_2 = 1/2x_1$
$x_2 = 2x_1, \qquad x_1 + x_2 = 1$
$3x_1 = 1$
$x_1 = 1/3, \qquad x_2 = 2/3$

19.

|  | Mike | Danny |
|---|---|---|
| pants | 6 | 2 |
| shirts | 8 | 5 |
| jackets | 2 | 3 |

$(5 \quad 3 \quad 9) \begin{pmatrix} 6 & 2 \\ 8 & 5 \\ 2 & 3 \end{pmatrix} = (72 \quad 52)$

Mike spent $72.00. Danny spent $52.00.

**5.4.1
Exercise
(page 131)**

1. (a) $r_1' = r_1 - r_2$

2. (a) $\begin{pmatrix} 1 & 2 & 3 & 8 \\ 0 & 5 & -2 & 1 \\ -2 & 0 & -3 & 4 \\ 2 & 2 & 2 & 2 \end{pmatrix} \approx \begin{pmatrix} 1 & 2 & 3 & 8 \\ 0 & 5 & -2 & 1 \\ 0 & 4 & 3 & 20 \\ 0 & -2 & -4 & -14 \end{pmatrix} \approx \begin{pmatrix} 1 & 2 & 3 & 8 \\ 0 & -2 & -4 & -14 \\ 0 & 4 & 3 & 20 \\ 0 & 5 & -2 & 1 \end{pmatrix}$

$\approx \begin{pmatrix} 1 & 2 & 3 & 8 \\ 0 & 1 & 2 & 7 \\ 0 & 4 & 3 & 20 \\ 0 & 5 & -2 & 1 \end{pmatrix} \approx \begin{pmatrix} 1 & 0 & -1 & -6 \\ 0 & 1 & 2 & 7 \\ 0 & 0 & -5 & -8 \\ 0 & 0 & -12 & -34 \end{pmatrix} \approx \begin{pmatrix} 1 & 0 & -1 & -6 \\ 0 & 1 & 2 & 7 \\ 0 & 0 & 1 & 1.6 \\ 0 & 0 & 12 & 34 \end{pmatrix}$

$\approx \begin{pmatrix} 1 & 0 & 0 & -4.4 \\ 0 & 1 & 0 & 3.8 \\ 0 & 0 & 1 & 1.6 \\ 0 & 0 & 0 & 14.8 \end{pmatrix} \approx \begin{pmatrix} 1 & 0 & 0 & 0 \\ 0 & 1 & 0 & 0 \\ 0 & 0 & 1 & 0 \\ 0 & 0 & 0 & 1 \end{pmatrix}$   Rank is 4.

(e) $\begin{pmatrix} 2 & 4 & 5 & 2 \\ 3 & 4 & 5 & 4 \\ 4 & 4 & 5 & 3 \\ 1 & 4 & 5 & 1 \end{pmatrix} \approx \begin{pmatrix} 1 & 4 & 5 & 1 \\ 3 & 4 & 5 & 4 \\ 4 & 4 & 5 & 3 \\ 2 & 4 & 5 & 2 \end{pmatrix} \approx \begin{pmatrix} 1 & 4 & 5 & 1 \\ 0 & -8 & -10 & 1 \\ 0 & -12 & -15 & -1 \\ 0 & -4 & -5 & 0 \end{pmatrix} \approx \begin{pmatrix} 1 & 0 & 0 & 1 \\ 0 & 0 & 0 & 1 \\ 0 & 0 & 0 & -1 \\ 0 & -4 & -5 & 0 \end{pmatrix}$

$\approx \begin{pmatrix} 1 & 0 & 0 & 1 \\ 0 & -4 & -5 & 0 \\ 0 & 0 & 0 & -1 \\ 0 & 0 & 0 & 1 \end{pmatrix} \approx \begin{pmatrix} 1 & 0 & 0 & 0 \\ 0 & -4 & -5 & 0 \\ 0 & 0 & 0 & -1 \\ 0 & 0 & 0 & 0 \end{pmatrix} \approx \begin{pmatrix} 1 & 0 & 0 & 0 \\ 0 & 1 & 5/4 & 0 \\ 0 & 0 & 0 & 1 \\ 0 & 0 & 0 & 0 \end{pmatrix}$   Rank is 3.

3. (a) $\begin{pmatrix} 1 & 1 & 1 \\ 3 & 2 & -1 \\ 3 & 1 & 2 \end{pmatrix} \approx \begin{pmatrix} 1 & 1 & 1 \\ 0 & -1 & -4 \\ 0 & -2 & -1 \end{pmatrix} \approx \begin{pmatrix} 1 & 1 & 1 \\ 0 & 1 & 4 \\ 0 & -2 & -1 \end{pmatrix} \approx \begin{pmatrix} 1 & 0 & -3 \\ 0 & 1 & 4 \\ 0 & 0 & 7 \end{pmatrix}$

$\approx \begin{pmatrix} 1 & 0 & 0 \\ 0 & 1 & 0 \\ 0 & 0 & 1 \end{pmatrix}$   Rank is 3.

5.4.2
Exercise
(page 142)

1. (a) coefficient matrix $A = \begin{pmatrix} 2 & 3 & -1 \\ 1 & 1 & 1 \\ 0 & 2 & -1 \end{pmatrix}$

augmented matrix $A|B = \begin{pmatrix} 2 & 3 & -1 & 8 \\ 1 & 1 & 1 & 7 \\ 0 & 2 & -1 & 3 \end{pmatrix}$

rank $A = 3$; rank $A|B = 3$; number of unknowns $= 3$. The set of solutions is unique.

$$A|B = \begin{pmatrix} 2 & 3 & -1 & 8 \\ 1 & 1 & 1 & 7 \\ 0 & 2 & -1 & 3 \end{pmatrix} \approx \begin{pmatrix} 1 & 1 & 1 & 7 \\ 2 & 3 & -1 & 8 \\ 0 & 2 & -1 & 3 \end{pmatrix} \approx \begin{pmatrix} 1 & 1 & 1 & 7 \\ 0 & 1 & -3 & -6 \\ 0 & 2 & -1 & 3 \end{pmatrix}$$

$$\approx \begin{pmatrix} 1 & 0 & 4 & 13 \\ 0 & 1 & -3 & -6 \\ 0 & 0 & 5 & 15 \end{pmatrix} \approx \begin{pmatrix} 1 & 0 & 4 & 13 \\ 0 & 1 & -3 & -6 \\ 0 & 0 & 1 & 3 \end{pmatrix} \approx \begin{pmatrix} 1 & 0 & 0 & 1 \\ 0 & 1 & 0 & 3 \\ 0 & 0 & 1 & 3 \end{pmatrix}$$

Solution is $x_1 = 1, x_2 = 3, x_3 = 3$.

3. Let $A = \begin{pmatrix} x_1 & x_2 \\ x_3 & x_4 \end{pmatrix}$.

Then $\begin{pmatrix} 1 & 2 \\ 3 & 4 \end{pmatrix}\begin{pmatrix} x_1 & x_2 \\ x_3 & x_4 \end{pmatrix} = \begin{pmatrix} 9 & 1 \\ 0 & 7 \end{pmatrix}$

$x_1 + 2x_3 = 9$
$x_2 + 2x_4 = 1$
$3x_1 + 4x_3 = 0$
$3x_2 + 4x_4 = 7$

The coefficient matrix is

$$\begin{pmatrix} 1 & 0 & 2 & 0 \\ 0 & 1 & 0 & 2 \\ 3 & 0 & 4 & 0 \\ 0 & 3 & 0 & 4 \end{pmatrix}$$

The augmented matrix is

$$\begin{pmatrix} 1 & 0 & 2 & 0 & 9 \\ 0 & 1 & 0 & 2 & 1 \\ 3 & 0 & 4 & 0 & 0 \\ 0 & 3 & 0 & 4 & 7 \end{pmatrix}$$

The rank of the coefficient matrix is 4 and the rank of the augmented matrix is 4. The solution exists and is unique.

$$\begin{pmatrix} 1 & 0 & 2 & 0 & 9 \\ 0 & 1 & 0 & 2 & 1 \\ 3 & 0 & 4 & 0 & 0 \\ 0 & 3 & 0 & 4 & 7 \end{pmatrix} \approx \begin{pmatrix} 1 & 0 & 0 & 0 & -18 \\ 0 & 1 & 0 & 0 & 5 \\ 0 & 0 & 1 & 0 & 27/2 \\ 0 & 0 & 0 & 1 & -2 \end{pmatrix}$$

Thus,

$$A = \begin{pmatrix} -18 & 5 \\ 27/2 & -2 \end{pmatrix}$$

5. $\begin{pmatrix} 0.06 & 0.07 & 0.08 & 358 \\ 0.06 & 0.07 & -0.08 & 70 \\ 1 & 1 & 1 & 5000 \end{pmatrix} \approx \begin{pmatrix} 6 & 7 & 8 & 35800 \\ 6 & 7 & -8 & 7000 \\ 1 & 1 & 1 & 5000 \end{pmatrix} \approx \begin{pmatrix} 1 & 1 & 1 & 5000 \\ 6 & 7 & 8 & 35800 \\ 0 & 0 & 16 & 28800 \end{pmatrix}$

$$\approx \begin{pmatrix} 1 & 1 & 1 & | & 5000 \\ 0 & 1 & 2 & | & 5800 \\ 0 & 0 & 1 & | & 1800 \end{pmatrix} \approx \begin{pmatrix} 1 & 0 & -1 & | & -800 \\ 0 & 1 & 2 & | & 5800 \\ 0 & 0 & 1 & | & 1800 \end{pmatrix} \approx \begin{pmatrix} 1 & 0 & 0 & | & 1000 \\ 0 & 1 & 0 & | & 2200 \\ 0 & 0 & 1 & | & 1800 \end{pmatrix}$$

Hence, $x_1 = \$1000,$     $x_2 = \$2200,$     $x_3 = \$1800.$

**5.5**
**Exercise**
**(page 146)**

1. (a) $\begin{pmatrix} 0 & 0 & 1 & | & 1 & 0 & 0 \\ 0 & 1 & 0 & | & 0 & 1 & 0 \\ 1 & 0 & 0 & | & 0 & 0 & 1 \end{pmatrix} \approx \begin{pmatrix} 1 & 0 & 0 & | & 0 & 0 & 1 \\ 0 & 1 & 0 & | & 0 & 1 & 0 \\ 0 & 0 & 1 & | & 1 & 0 & 0 \end{pmatrix}$ $A^{-1} = \begin{pmatrix} 0 & 0 & 1 \\ 0 & 1 & 0 \\ 1 & 0 & 0 \end{pmatrix}$

(c) $\begin{pmatrix} 2 & 3 & -1 & | & 1 & 0 & 0 \\ 1 & 1 & 1 & | & 0 & 1 & 0 \\ 0 & 2 & -1 & | & 0 & 0 & 1 \end{pmatrix} \approx \begin{pmatrix} 1 & 0 & 0 & | & 3/5 & -1/5 & -4/5 \\ 0 & 1 & 0 & | & -1/5 & 2/5 & 3/5 \\ 0 & 0 & 1 & | & -2/5 & 4/5 & 1/5 \end{pmatrix}$

3. $I_2 - A = \begin{pmatrix} 0 & -2 \\ -7 & -8 \end{pmatrix}$ $\quad \begin{pmatrix} 0 & -2 & | & 1 & 0 \\ -7 & -8 & | & 0 & 1 \end{pmatrix} \approx \begin{pmatrix} 1 & 0 & | & 4/7 & -1/7 \\ 0 & 1 & | & -1/2 & 0 \end{pmatrix}$

$(I_2 - A)^{-1} = \begin{pmatrix} 4/7 & -1/7 \\ -1/2 & 0 \end{pmatrix}$

**5.6.1**
**Exercise**
**(page 151)**

1. The system of equations is
$$x_1 = .3x_1 + .3x_2 + .3x_3 + .2x_4$$
$$x_2 = .2x_1 + .3x_2 + .3x_3 + .2x_4$$
$$x_3 = .2x_1 + .1x_2 + .1x_3 + .2x_4$$
$$x_4 = .3x_1 + .3x_2 + .3x_3 + .4x_4$$
which we may write as
$$-.7x_1 + .3x_2 + .3x_3 + .2x_4 = 0$$
$$.2x_1 + (-.7)x_2 + .3x_3 + .2x_4 = 0$$
$$.2x_1 + .1x_2 + (-.9x_3) + .2x_4 = 0$$
$$.3x_1 + .3x_2 + .3x_3 + (-.6x_4) = 0$$
we reduce the coefficient matrix of this system:

$$\begin{pmatrix} -.7 & .3 & .3 & .2 \\ .2 & -.7 & .3 & .2 \\ .2 & .1 & -.9 & .2 \\ .3 & .3 & .3 & -.6 \end{pmatrix} \approx \begin{pmatrix} -7 & 3 & 3 & 2 \\ 2 & -7 & 3 & 2 \\ 2 & 1 & -9 & 2 \\ 3 & 3 & 3 & -6 \end{pmatrix} \approx \begin{pmatrix} 1 & 1 & 1 & -2 \\ 2 & -7 & 3 & 2 \\ 2 & 1 & -9 & 2 \\ -7 & 3 & 3 & 2 \end{pmatrix}$$

$$\approx \begin{pmatrix} 1 & 1 & 1 & -2 \\ 0 & -9 & 1 & 6 \\ 0 & -1 & -11 & 6 \\ 0 & 10 & 10 & -12 \end{pmatrix} \approx \begin{pmatrix} 1 & 1 & 1 & -2 \\ 0 & 1 & 11 & -6 \\ 0 & -9 & 1 & 6 \\ 0 & 10 & 10 & -12 \end{pmatrix} \approx \begin{pmatrix} 1 & 0 & -10 & 4 \\ 0 & 1 & 11 & -6 \\ 0 & 0 & 100 & -48 \\ 0 & 0 & -100 & 48 \end{pmatrix}$$

$$\approx \begin{pmatrix} 1 & 0 & 0 & -4/5 \\ 0 & 1 & 0 & -18/25 \\ 0 & 0 & 1 & -12/25 \\ 0 & 0 & 0 & 0 \end{pmatrix}$$

Hence $x_1 = 4/5x_4,$ $x_2 = 18/25x_4,$ $x_3 = 12/25x_4$ and the incomes are in the ratio $25: 18: 12: 20.$

Review Exercises
(page 159)

3. $(t_1 \quad t_2) \begin{pmatrix} 1/4 & 3/4 \\ 2/3 & 1/3 \end{pmatrix} = (t_1 \quad t_2), t_1 + t_2 = 1$

$1/4t_1 + 2/3t_2 = t_1; \ 3/4t_1 + 1/3t_2 = t_2$
$3/4t_1 = 2/3t_2 \quad \text{or} \quad 9t_1 = 8t_2$
$\qquad\qquad t_1 + t_2 = 1$
$\qquad\qquad 8/9t_2 + t_2 = 1$
$\qquad\qquad\qquad 17/9t_2 = 1$

$t_2 = 9/17, t_1 = 8/17$

6. coefficient matrix $A = \begin{pmatrix} 2 & -1 & 1 \\ 1 & 1 & -1 \\ 3 & -1 & 1 \end{pmatrix}$ augmented matrix $A|B = \begin{pmatrix} 2 & -1 & 1 & 1 \\ 1 & 1 & -1 & 2 \\ 3 & -1 & 1 & 0 \end{pmatrix}$

rank $A = 2$; rank $A|B = 3$; number of unknowns $= 3$. This system has no solution.

CHAPTER 6

6.1
Exercise
(page 165)

1. $5x_1 + 2x_2 + x_3 + x_4 = 20 \qquad x_4 \geqq 0$
$6x_1 + x_2 + 4x_3 + x_5 = 24 \qquad x_5 \geqq 0$
$x_1 + x_2 + 4x_3 + x_6 = 16 \qquad x_6 \geqq 0$
2. $2.2x_1 + 1.8x_2 + x_3 = 5 \qquad x_3 \geqq 0$
$0.8x_1 + 1.2x_2 + x_4 = 2.5 \qquad x_4 \geqq 0$
$-x_1 - x_2 + x_5 = -.1 \qquad x_5 \geqq 0$
3. $x_1 + x_2 + x_3 + x_4 = 50 \qquad x_4 \geqq 0$
$-3x_1 - 2x_2 - x_3 + x_5 = -10 \qquad x_5 \geqq 0$

6.2
Exercise
(page 167)

1.
$\begin{array}{cccc} x_1 & x_2 & x_3 & x_4 \end{array}$
$\begin{pmatrix} 1 & ② & 1 & 0 & | & 300 \\ 3 & 2 & 0 & 1 & | & 480 \end{pmatrix} \begin{array}{c} x_3 \\ x_4 \end{array}$

$\begin{pmatrix} 1/2 & 1 & 1/2 & 0 & | & 150 \\ 3 & 2 & 0 & 1 & | & 480 \end{pmatrix}$

$\begin{array}{cccc} x_1 & x_2 & x_3 & x_4 \end{array}$
$\begin{pmatrix} 1/2 & 1 & 1/2 & 0 & | & 150 \\ 2 & 0 & -1 & 1 & | & 180 \end{pmatrix} \begin{array}{c} x_2 \\ x_4 \end{array}$

6.3
Exercise
(page 172)

1.
$\begin{array}{cccc} x_1 & x_2 & x_3 & x_4 \end{array}$
$\begin{pmatrix} 2 & ③ & 1 & 0 & | & 12 \\ 3 & 1 & 0 & 1 & | & 12 \\ \hline -5 & -7 & 0 & 0 & | & 0 \end{pmatrix} \begin{array}{c} x_3 \\ x_4 \\ \phantom{x} \end{array}$

$\begin{array}{cccc} x_1 & x_2 & x_3 & x_4 \end{array}$
$\begin{pmatrix} 2/3 & 1 & 1/3 & 0 & | & 4 \\ ⑦/③ & 0 & -1/3 & 1 & | & 8 \\ \hline -1/3 & 0 & 7/3 & 0 & | & 28 \end{pmatrix} \begin{array}{c} x_2 \\ x_4 \\ \phantom{x} \end{array}$

$\begin{array}{cccc} x_1 & x_2 & x_3 & x_4 \end{array}$
$\begin{pmatrix} 0 & 1 & 5/21 & -2/7 & | & 12/7 \\ 1 & 0 & -1/7 & 3/7 & | & 24/7 \\ \hline 0 & 0 & 16/7 & 1/7 & | & 204/7 \end{pmatrix} \begin{array}{c} x_2 \\ x_1 \\ \phantom{x} \end{array}$

$P = 204/7, \qquad x_1 = 24/7, \qquad x_2 = 12/7$

2.
$\begin{array}{cccc} x_1 & x_2 & x_3 & x_4 \end{array}$
$\begin{pmatrix} 2 & 1 & 1 & 0 & | & 10 \\ 1 & ② & 0 & 1 & | & 10 \\ \hline -1 & -5 & 0 & 0 & | & 0 \end{pmatrix} \begin{array}{c} x_3 \\ x_4 \\ \phantom{x} \end{array}$

$\begin{array}{cccc} x_1 & x_2 & x_3 & x_4 \end{array}$
$\begin{pmatrix} 3/2 & 0 & 1 & -1/2 & | & 5 \\ 1/2 & 1 & 0 & 1/2 & | & 5 \\ \hline 3/2 & 0 & 0 & 5/2 & | & 25 \end{pmatrix} \begin{array}{c} x_3 \\ x_2 \\ \phantom{x} \end{array}$

$P = 25, \qquad x_1 = 0, \qquad x_2 = 5$

3.

$$\begin{array}{ccccc} x_1 & x_2 & x_3 & x_4 & x_5 \end{array}$$

$$\left(\begin{array}{ccccc|c} -2 & 1 & -2 & 1 & 0 & 4 \\ ① & -2 & 1 & 0 & 1 & 2 \\ \hline -2 & -1 & -1 & 0 & 0 & 0 \end{array}\right) \begin{array}{c} x_4 \\ x_5 \\ \\ \end{array}$$

$$\begin{array}{ccccc} x_1 & x_2 & x_3 & x_4 & x_5 \end{array}$$

$$\left(\begin{array}{ccccc|c} 0 & -3 & 0 & 1 & 2 & 8 \\ 1 & -2 & 1 & 0 & 1 & 2 \\ \hline 0 & -5 & 1 & 0 & 2 & 4 \end{array}\right) \begin{array}{c} x_4 \\ x_1 \\ \\ \end{array}$$

No solution since all ratios for the $x_2$ column are negative.

6.

$$\begin{array}{ccccc} x_1 & x_2 & x_3 & x_4 & x_5 \end{array}$$

$$\left(\begin{array}{ccccc|c} 2 & 2 & 3 & 1 & 0 & 30 \\ ② & 2 & 1 & 0 & 1 & 12 \\ \hline -6 & -6 & -2 & 0 & 0 & 0 \end{array}\right) \begin{array}{c} x_4 \\ x_5 \\ \\ \end{array}$$

$$\begin{array}{ccccc} x_1 & x_2 & x_3 & x_4 & x_5 \end{array}$$

$$\left(\begin{array}{ccccc|c} 0 & 0 & 2 & 1 & -1 & 18 \\ 1 & 1 & 1/2 & 0 & 1/2 & 6 \\ \hline 0 & 0 & 1 & 0 & 3 & 36 \end{array}\right) \begin{array}{c} x_4 \\ x_1 \\ \\ \end{array}$$

$P = 36, \qquad x_1 = 6, \qquad x_2 = 0, \qquad x_3 = 0$

Note that $x_1$ and $x_2$ are interchangeable in this problem.

6.4
Exercise
(page 178)

1. The augmented matrix of the system is

$$\begin{array}{cc} x_1 & x_2 \end{array}$$

$$\left(\begin{array}{cc|c} 1 & 1 & 4 \\ 3 & 4 & 12 \\ \hline 6 & 3 & 0 \end{array}\right)$$

Interchanging rows and columns we obtain

$$\left(\begin{array}{cc|c} 1 & 3 & 6 \\ 1 & 4 & 3 \\ \hline 4 & 12 & 0 \end{array}\right)$$

The simplex tableaux and solution are:

$$\begin{array}{cccc} y_1 & y_2 & y_3 & y_4 \end{array}$$

$$\left(\begin{array}{cccc|c} 1 & 3 & 1 & 0 & 6 \\ 1 & ④ & 0 & 1 & 3 \\ \hline -4 & -12 & 0 & 0 & 0 \end{array}\right) \begin{array}{c} y_3 \\ y_4 \\ \\ \end{array}$$

$$\left(\begin{array}{cccc|c} 1/4 & 0 & 1 & -3/4 & 15/4 \\ ⑴/4 & 1 & 0 & 1/4 & 3/4 \\ \hline -1 & 0 & 0 & 3 & 9 \end{array}\right) \begin{array}{c} y_3 \\ y_2 \\ \\ \end{array}$$

$$
\begin{array}{cccc}
y_1 & y_2 & y_3 & y_4 \\
\end{array}
$$

$$
\left(
\begin{array}{cccc|c}
0 & -1 & 1 & -1 & 3 \\
1 & 4 & 0 & 1 & 3 \\
\hline
0 & 4 & 0 & 4 & 12
\end{array}
\right)
\begin{array}{c}
y_3 \\
y_1 \\
\\
\end{array}
$$

Thus, $C = 12$, $\quad x_1 = 0$, $\quad x_2 = 4$.

3. The augmented matrix of the system is

$$
\left(
\begin{array}{ccc|c}
1 & -3 & 4 & 12 \\
3 & 1 & 2 & 10 \\
-1 & 1 & 1 & 8 \\
\hline
1 & 2 & 1 & 0
\end{array}
\right)
$$

Interchanging rows and columns we obtain

$$
\left(
\begin{array}{ccc|c}
1 & 3 & -1 & 1 \\
-3 & 1 & 1 & 2 \\
4 & 2 & 1 & 1 \\
\hline
12 & 10 & 8 & 0
\end{array}
\right)
$$

The simplex tableau and solution are:

$$
\begin{array}{cccccc}
y_1 & y_2 & y_3 & y_4 & y_5 & y_6
\end{array}
$$

$$
\left(
\begin{array}{cccccc|c}
1 & 3 & -1 & 1 & 0 & 0 & 1 \\
-3 & 1 & 1 & 0 & 1 & 0 & 2 \\
④ & 2 & 1 & 0 & 0 & 1 & 1 \\
\hline
-12 & -10 & -8 & 0 & 0 & 0 & 0
\end{array}
\right)
\begin{array}{c}
y_4 \\
y_5 \\
y_6 \\
\\
\end{array}
$$

$$
\begin{array}{cccccc}
y_1 & y_2 & y_3 & y_4 & y_5 & y_6
\end{array}
$$

$$
\left(
\begin{array}{cccccc|c}
0 & 5/2 & -5/4 & 1 & 0 & -1/4 & 3/4 \\
0 & 5/2 & 7/4 & 0 & 1 & 3/4 & 11/4 \\
1 & 1/2 & ①/4 & 0 & 0 & 1/4 & 1/4 \\
\hline
0 & -4 & -5 & 0 & 0 & 3 & 3
\end{array}
\right)
\begin{array}{c}
y_4 \\
y_5 \\
y_1 \\
\\
\end{array}
$$

$$
\begin{array}{cccccc}
y_1 & y_2 & y_3 & y_4 & y_5 & y_6
\end{array}
$$

$$
\left(
\begin{array}{cccccc|c}
5 & 5 & 0 & 1 & 0 & 1 & 2 \\
-7 & -1 & 0 & 0 & 1 & -1 & 1 \\
4 & 2 & 1 & 0 & 0 & 1 & 1 \\
\hline
20 & 6 & 0 & 0 & 0 & 8 & 8
\end{array}
\right)
\begin{array}{c}
y_4 \\
y_5 \\
y_3 \\
\\
\end{array}
$$

Thus, $P = C = 8$, $\quad x_1 = 0$, $\quad x_2 = 0$, $\quad x_3 = 8$.

1. Let $x_1$ = amount of Food I.
   Let $x_2$ = amount of Food II.
   Let $x_3$ = amount of Food III.
   Minimize

$$
C = 2x_1 + x_2 + 3x_3
$$

6.5
Exercise
(page 190)

Subject to

$$2x_1 + 3x_2 + 4x_3 \geqslant 20$$
$$4x_1 + 2x_2 + 2x_3 \geqslant 15$$

The augmented matrix of the system is

$$
\begin{array}{ccc}
x_1 & x_2 & x_3
\end{array}
$$
$$
\left(
\begin{array}{ccc|c}
2 & 3 & 4 & 20 \\
4 & 2 & 2 & 15 \\
\hline
2 & 1 & 3 & 0
\end{array}
\right)
$$

The matrix of the corresponding dual program is

$$
\left(
\begin{array}{cc|c}
2 & 4 & 2 \\
3 & 2 & 1 \\
4 & 2 & 3 \\
\hline
20 & 15 & 0
\end{array}
\right)
$$

The simplex tableaux and solution are:

$$
\begin{array}{ccccc}
y_1 & y_2 & y_3 & y_4 & y_5
\end{array}
$$
$$
\left(
\begin{array}{ccccc|c}
2 & 4 & 1 & 0 & 0 & 2 \\
③ & 2 & 0 & 1 & 0 & 1 \\
4 & 2 & 0 & 0 & 1 & 3 \\
\hline
-20 & -15 & 0 & 0 & 0 & 0
\end{array}
\right)
\begin{array}{l}
y_3 \\
y_4 \\
y_5
\end{array}
$$

$$
\begin{array}{ccccc}
y_1 & y_2 & y_3 & y_4 & y_5
\end{array}
$$
$$
\left(
\begin{array}{ccccc|c}
0 & 8/3 & 1 & -2/3 & 0 & 4/3 \\
1 & ②/③ & 0 & 1/3 & 0 & 1/3 \\
0 & -2/3 & 0 & -4/3 & 1 & 5/3 \\
\hline
0 & -5/3 & 0 & 20/3 & 0 & 20/3
\end{array}
\right)
\begin{array}{l}
y_3 \\
y_1 \\
y_5
\end{array}
$$

$$
\begin{array}{ccccc}
y_1 & y_2 & y_3 & y_4 & y_5
\end{array}
$$
$$
\left(
\begin{array}{ccccc|c}
-4 & 0 & 1 & -2 & 0 & 0 \\
3/2 & 1 & 0 & 1/2 & 0 & 1/2 \\
1 & 0 & 0 & -1 & 1 & 2 \\
\hline
5/2 & 0 & 0 & 15/2 & 0 & 15/2
\end{array}
\right)
\begin{array}{l}
y_3 \\
y_2 \\
y_5
\end{array}
$$

$$C = \$7.50, \qquad x_1 = 0, \qquad x_2 = 7.5, \qquad x_3 = 0$$

3. Let $x_1$ = number of Crying Dolls
$\qquad x_2$ = number of Laughing and Crying Dolls
Maximize $\quad P = 8x_1 + 12x_2 \qquad$ subject to $1/4x_1 + 1/2x_2 \leqq 10$
or $\quad x_1 + 2x_2 \leqq 40 \qquad$ and $\quad x_1 + 2x_2 \leqq 50$
The second constraint may be disregarded.
The simplex tableaux and solution are:

$$
\begin{array}{ccc}
x_1 & x_2 & x_3
\end{array}
$$
$$
\left(
\begin{array}{ccc|c}
1 & ② & 1 & 40 \\
\hline
-8 & -12 & 0 & 0
\end{array}
\right)
\begin{array}{l}
x_3
\end{array}
\qquad
\begin{array}{ccc}
x_1 & x_2 & x_3
\end{array}
\left(
\begin{array}{ccc|c}
①/② & 1 & 1/2 & 20 \\
\hline
-2 & 0 & 6 & 240
\end{array}
\right)
\begin{array}{l}
x_2
\end{array}
\qquad
\begin{array}{ccc}
x_1 & x_2 & x_3
\end{array}
\left(
\begin{array}{ccc|c}
1 & 2 & 1 & 40 \\
\hline
0 & 4 & 8 & 320
\end{array}
\right)
\begin{array}{l}
x_1
\end{array}
$$

Thus 40 Crying Dolls should be produced with a profit of $320.

Review Exercises
(page 191)

1. $3x_1 + 5x_2 + x_3 = 12$
   $x_1 + 7x_2 + x_4 = 8$
   $x_1 + 2x_2 + x_5 = 5$

2. Maximize $P = 40x_1 + 60x_2 + 50x_3$
   subject to

   $x_1 + x_2 + x_3 + x_4 = 30$
   $-x_1 + 2x_3 + x_5 = 0$
   $-x_1 + x_2 - x_3 + x_6 = 0$

$$
\begin{array}{cccccc}
x_1 & x_2 & x_3 & x_4 & x_5 & x_6 \\
\end{array}
$$

$$
\left(
\begin{array}{cccccc|c}
1 & \textcircled{1} & 1 & 1 & 0 & 0 & 30 \\
-1 & 0 & 2 & 0 & 1 & 0 & 0 \\
-1 & 1 & -1 & 0 & 0 & 1 & 0 \\
\hline
-40 & -60 & -50 & 0 & 0 & 0 & 0
\end{array}
\right)
\begin{array}{c}
x_4 \\
x_5 \\
x_6 \\
\\
\end{array}
$$

$$
\begin{array}{cccccc}
x_1 & x_2 & x_3 & x_4 & x_5 & x_6 \\
\end{array}
$$

$$
\left(
\begin{array}{cccccc|c}
1 & 1 & 1 & 1 & 0 & 0 & 30 \\
-1 & 0 & 2 & 0 & 1 & 0 & 0 \\
-2 & 0 & -2 & -1 & 0 & 1 & -30 \\
\hline
20 & 0 & 10 & 60 & 0 & 0 & 1800
\end{array}
\right)
\begin{array}{c}
x_2 \\
x_5 \\
x_6 \\
\\
\end{array}
$$

$P = 1800, \qquad x_1 = 0, \qquad x_2 = 30, \qquad x_3 = 0$

CHAPTER 7

7.2
Exercise
(page 202)

1. (a) $\lim\limits_{x \to a} f(x)$ does not exist because $\lim\limits_{x \to a^-} f(x) \neq \lim\limits_{x \to a^+} f(x)$.

   (c) Only $\lim\limits_{x \to a^+} f(x)$ exists.

   (e) $\lim\limits_{x \to a^-} f(x) = \lim\limits_{x \to a^+} f(x) = \lim\limits_{x \to a} f(x)$

2. (a) $\lim\limits_{x \to 2^-} f(x) = \lim\limits_{x \to 2^+} f(x)$        (c) $\lim\limits_{x \to 1^-} f(x) = \lim\limits_{x \to 1^+} f(x)$

   $\qquad = \lim\limits_{x \to 2} f(x) = 9$        $\qquad = \lim\limits_{x \to 1} f(x) = 2$

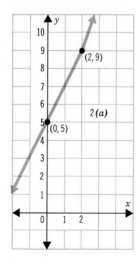

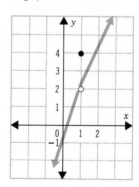

(f) $\lim\limits_{x \to 1^-} f(x) = 2,$ $\lim\limits_{x \to 1^+} f(x) = 3$

$\lim\limits_{x \to 1} f(x)$ does not exist.

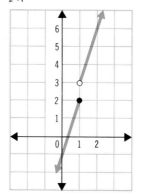

(h) $\lim\limits_{x \to -1^-} f(x) = 1,$ $\lim\limits_{x \to -1^+} f(x) = 5$

$\lim\limits_{x \to -1} f(x)$ does not exist.

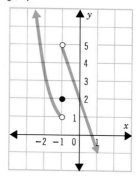

4. (a)

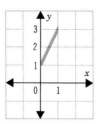

(b) $\lim\limits_{x \to 0^+} f(x) = 1,$ (c) $\lim\limits_{x \to 1^-} f(x) = 3$

(d) $f(x)$ is not defined for values of $x$ such that $x < 0$ or $x > 1$.

5. $\lim\limits_{x \to 3} x^2 = 9$

| $x$ | 2.8 | 2.9 | 2.99 | 3.01 | 3.1 | 3.2 |
|---|---|---|---|---|---|---|
| $x^2$ | 7.84 | 8.41 | 8.9401 | 9.0601 | 9.61 | 10.24 |

6. (a) $\lim\limits_{x \to 0} \dfrac{1}{x^2} = +\infty$

| $x$ | $-0.2$ | $-0.1$ | $-0.01$ | 0.01 | 0.1 | 0.2 |
|---|---|---|---|---|---|---|
| $\dfrac{1}{x^2}$ | 25 | 100 | 10,000 | 10,000 | 100 | 25 |

(c) $\lim\limits_{x \to 2} \dfrac{1}{x - 2}$ does not exist.

| $x$ | 1.8 | 1.9 | 1.99 | 2.01 | 2.1 | 2.2 |
|---|---|---|---|---|---|---|
| $\dfrac{1}{x - 2}$ | $-5$ | $-10$ | $-100$ | 100 | 10 | 5 |

(f) $\lim\limits_{x \to -\infty} \dfrac{2}{x} = 0$

| $x$ | $-10$ | $-100$ | $-500$ | $-1000$ |
|---|---|---|---|---|
| $\dfrac{2}{x}$ | $-0.2$ | $-0.02$ | $-0.004$ | $-0.002$ |

1. (a) $\lim\limits_{x\to 6}(6x^2+1) = \lim\limits_{x\to 6}6x^2 + \lim\limits_{x\to 6}1$ (III)

$$= \lim\limits_{x\to 6}6 \cdot \lim\limits_{x\to 6}x^2 + \lim\limits_{x\to 6}1 \quad \text{(IV)}$$

$$= 6\cdot 6^2 + 1 \qquad \text{(V, I)}$$

$$= 217$$

(e) $\lim\limits_{x\to 5}\left(x^3 - \dfrac{1}{x^3}\right) = \lim\limits_{x\to 5}x^3 - \lim\limits_{x\to 5}\dfrac{1}{x^3}$ (III)

$$= \lim\limits_{x\to 5}x^3 - \dfrac{\lim\limits_{x\to 5}1}{\lim\limits_{x\to 5}x^3} \qquad \text{(VI)}$$

$$= 5^3 - \dfrac{1}{5^3} = 124.992 \quad \text{(V)}$$

(g) $\lim\limits_{x\to 3}4 = 4$ (I)

2. (a) $\lim\limits_{x\to 3}\left(\dfrac{x^2-9}{x-3}\right) = \lim\limits_{x\to 3}\left(\dfrac{(x+3)(x-3)}{(x-3)}\right) = \lim\limits_{x\to 3}(x+3) = 6$

(b) $\lim\limits_{x\to -4}\dfrac{x^2+7x+12}{x^2+6x+8} = \lim\limits_{x\to -4}\dfrac{(x+3)(x+4)}{(x+2)(x+4)} = \lim\limits_{x\to -4}\dfrac{x+3}{x+2} = \dfrac{-4+3}{-4+2} = \dfrac{1}{2}$

(e) $\lim\limits_{x\to 0}\dfrac{3x}{x^3-x} = \lim\limits_{x\to 0}\dfrac{3x}{x(x^2-1)} = \lim\limits_{x\to 0}\dfrac{3}{x^2-1} = -3$

3. (a) $\lim\limits_{x\to +\infty}\dfrac{x+1}{x-1} = \lim\limits_{x\to +\infty}\dfrac{1+1/x}{1-1/x} = \dfrac{1+0}{1-0} = 1$

(c) $\lim\limits_{x\to +\infty}\dfrac{x}{x^2+1} = \lim\limits_{x\to +\infty}\dfrac{1/x}{1+1/x^2} = \dfrac{0}{1} = 0$

4. (a) $\lim\limits_{x\to 3}\dfrac{f(x)-f(3)}{x-3} = \lim\limits_{x\to 3}\dfrac{x^2-9}{x-3} = \lim\limits_{x\to 3}\dfrac{(x+3)(x-3)}{(x-3)} = \lim\limits_{x\to 3}(x+3) = 6$

(b) $\lim\limits_{x\to a}\dfrac{f(x)-f(a)}{x-a} = \lim\limits_{x\to a}\dfrac{x^2-a^2}{x-a} = \lim\limits_{x\to a}\dfrac{(x+a)(x-a)}{x-a} = \lim\limits_{x\to a}(x+a) = 2a$

5. $\lim\limits_{x\to a}\dfrac{f(x)-f(a)}{x-a} = \lim\limits_{x\to a}\dfrac{\dfrac{1}{x}-\dfrac{1}{a}}{x-a} = \lim\limits_{x\to a}\dfrac{\dfrac{-(x-a)}{ax}}{x-a} = \lim\limits_{x\to a}\dfrac{-1}{ax} = -\dfrac{1}{a^2}$

7. $\lim\limits_{x\to a}\dfrac{x^n-a^n}{x-a} = \lim\limits_{x\to a}(x^{n-1}+ax^{n-2}+\cdots+a^{n-1})$

$$= \underbrace{a^{n-1}+a\cdot a^{n-2}+\cdots+a^{n-2}\cdot a+a^{n-1}}_{n \text{ terms}} = na^{n-1}$$

1. (a) $f(x)$ is continuous at $x=0$ since
$\lim\limits_{x\to 0}f(x) = \lim\limits_{x\to 0}(3x-1) = -1 = f(0)$

(b) Not continuous at $x=1$ since
$\lim\limits_{x\to 1^-}f(x) = \lim\limits_{x\to 1^-}(3x-1) = 2$

$\lim\limits_{x\to 1^+}f(x) = \lim\limits_{x\to 1^+}(2x+1) = 3$

(c)

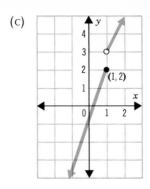

3. (a) $f(x)$ is continuous at $x = 0$ since

$$\lim_{x \to 0^-} f(x) = \lim_{x \to 0^-} (2x + 1) = 1,$$

$$\lim_{x \to 0^+} f(x) = \lim_{x \to 0^+} (x^2 + 1) = 1$$

and $f(0) = 2 \cdot 0 + 1 = 1$

(b)

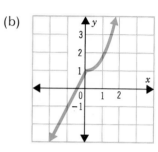

4. (a) $f(x)$ is continuous on the interval $[-3, 2]$ except at $x = 0$.

(b)

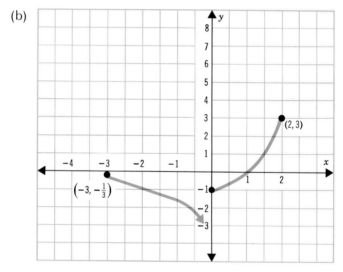

5. (a) $f(1)$ does not exist.
6. (b) One such function is given in problem 5(a).
7. (a)
$$C(x) = \begin{cases} 3x, & 1 \leq x \leq 5 \\ 2.5x, & 5 < x < 10 \\ 2.25x, & 10 \leq x < 20 \\ 2x, & 20 \leq x \end{cases}$$

(c) $x = 5, \quad x = 10, \quad x = 20$

8. (a)
$$C(x) = \begin{cases} 0.5x + 500 & 0 < x \leq 10{,}000 \\ 0.5x + 1000 & 10{,}000 < x \leq 20{,}000 \\ 0.5x + 1500 & 20{,}000 < x \leq 30{,}000 \\ 0.5x + 2000 & 30{,}000 < x \leq 40{,}000 \end{cases}$$

(b) $D = \{0 < x \leq 40{,}000\}$
(c) $x = 10{,}000, x = 20{,}000,$
$\qquad x = 30{,}000$

1. (a) $\lim\limits_{x\to 3} (3x - 4) = 5$

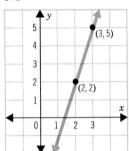

(d) $\lim\limits_{x\to 1} 5 = 5$

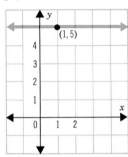

(e) $\lim\limits_{x\to +\infty} \dfrac{1}{x} = 0$

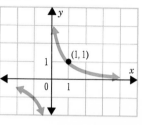

2. (a) $\lim\limits_{x\to 3} 2x = 6$

| $x$ | 2 | 2.9 | 2.99 | 3.01 | 3.1 | 4 |
|---|---|---|---|---|---|---|
| $2x$ | 4 | 5.8 | 5.98 | 6.02 | 6.2 | 8 |

(d) $\lim\limits_{x\to 1} \dfrac{1}{(x - 1)^2} = +\infty$

| $x$ | 0.5 | 0.9 | 0.99 | 1.01 | 1.1 | 1.5 |
|---|---|---|---|---|---|---|
| $f(x)$ | 4 | 100 | 10,000 | 10,000 | 100 | 4 |

3. (a) $\lim\limits_{x\to -2} \dfrac{x^2 + 4x + 4}{x^2 - 4} = \lim\limits_{x\to -2} \dfrac{x + 2}{x - 2} = \dfrac{\lim\limits_{x\to -2}(x + 2)}{\lim\limits_{x\to -2}(x - 2)} = \dfrac{0}{-4} = 0$

(c) $\lim\limits_{x\to 1} \dfrac{x^3 - 1}{x - 1} = \lim\limits_{x\to 1}(x^2 + x + 1) = 3$

(e) $\lim\limits_{x\to 0} \dfrac{1}{x^2 - 2x + 1} = \dfrac{\lim\limits_{x\to 0} 1}{\lim\limits_{x\to 0} x^2 - 2\lim\limits_{x\to 0} x + \lim\limits_{x\to 0} 1} = \dfrac{1}{0 - 0 + 1} = 1$

4. (a) $\lim\limits_{x\to 1} f(x)$ does not exist because $\lim\limits_{x\to 1^-} f(x) = -\infty$ and $\lim\limits_{x\to 1^+} f(x) = +\infty$

(b) $\lim\limits_{x\to -1} f(x) = \lim\limits_{x\to -1} \dfrac{(x + 1)(x + 1)}{(x - 1)(x + 1)} = \dfrac{0}{-2} = 0$

(d) $\lim\limits_{x\to -\infty} f(x) = \lim\limits_{x\to -\infty} \dfrac{1 + 2/x + 1/x^2}{1 - 1/x^2} = \dfrac{1 + 0}{1 - 0} = 1$

(f) $\lim\limits_{x\to 4} f(x) = \lim\limits_{x\to 4} \dfrac{x^2 + 2x + 1}{x^2 - 1} = \dfrac{25}{15} = \dfrac{5}{3}$

5. (a) Yes, since $\lim\limits_{x\to 1^-} f(x) = \lim\limits_{x\to 1^+} f(x) = f(1) = 3$

(c) No, since $\lim\limits_{x\to 1^-} f(x) = \lim\limits_{x\to 1^-} \dfrac{1}{(x - 1)^2} = +\infty$

(c)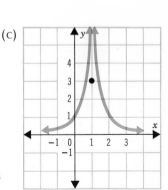

6. (a) $\lim\limits_{x\to 4} \dfrac{4x - 16}{x - 4} = \lim\limits_{x\to 4} \dfrac{4(x - 4)}{(x - 4)} = \lim\limits_{x\to 4} 4 = 4$

(b) $\lim\limits_{x\to 4} \dfrac{x^2 - 16}{x - 4} = \lim\limits_{x\to 4} \dfrac{(x + 4)(x - 4)}{x - 4} = \lim\limits_{x\to 4}(x + 4) = 8$

1. (a) $\Delta y = f(4) - f(0) = 18 - (-2) = 20$

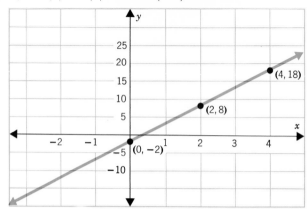

(c) $\Delta x = 4 - 0 = 4, \quad \dfrac{\Delta y}{\Delta x} = \dfrac{20}{4} = 5$

(e) The average rate of change is the constant 5. The graph is a straight line which has a constant slope.

3. (a) $\Delta y = f(1) - f(-1) = 1 - (-1) = 2$

(b) $\Delta y = f(4) - f(0) = 64 - 0 = 64$

(d) $\Delta x = 4 - 0 = 4 \quad \dfrac{\Delta y}{\Delta x} = \dfrac{64}{4} = 16$

(c) $\Delta x = 1 - (-1) = 2, \quad \dfrac{\Delta y}{\Delta x} = \dfrac{2}{2} = 1$

(e) $m = \dfrac{\Delta y}{\Delta x} = \dfrac{f(2) - f(-2)}{2 - (-2)} = \dfrac{16}{4} = 4$

4. (a) From $(0, f(0))$ to $(1, f(1))$, $m = \dfrac{f(1) - f(0)}{1 - 0} = \dfrac{0 - 1}{1} = -1$

5. From \$700 to \$2200,

$$\dfrac{\Delta y}{\Delta x} = \dfrac{21{,}700 - 12{,}700}{2200 - 700}$$

$$= \dfrac{9000}{1500} = 6$$

From \$1000 to \$1400,

$$\dfrac{\Delta y}{\Delta x} = \dfrac{17{,}100 - 13{,}100}{1400 - 1000}$$

$$= \dfrac{4000}{400} = 10$$

From \$1000 to \$1200,

$$\dfrac{\Delta y}{\Delta x} = \dfrac{14{,}700 - 13{,}100}{1200 - 1000}$$

$$= \dfrac{1600}{200} = 8$$

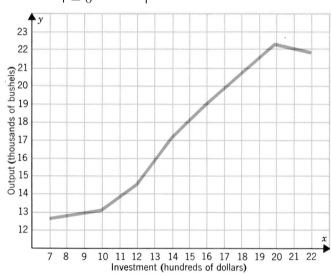

7. From 0 to 16 hours, $\dfrac{\Delta s}{\Delta t} = \dfrac{s(16) - s(0)}{16 - 0} = \dfrac{4}{16} = 0.25$ miles per hour.

From 1 to 4 hours, $\dfrac{\Delta s}{\Delta t} = \dfrac{s(4) - s(1)}{4 - 1} = \dfrac{1}{3} = 0.33$ miles per hour.

From 1 to 2 hours, $\dfrac{\Delta s}{\Delta t} = \dfrac{s(2) - s(1)}{2 - 1} = \dfrac{0.41}{1} = 0.41$ miles per hour.

8. (b) $m = \dfrac{x^2 + 4 - (0 + 4)}{x - 0}$

$= \dfrac{x^2}{x} = x$

(d) $m = \dfrac{x^3 + 8 - (0 + 8)}{x - 0}$

$= \dfrac{x^3}{x} = x^2$

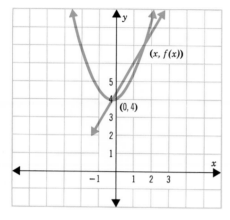

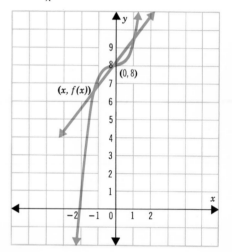

(f) $m = \dfrac{1/(x + 1) - 1/1}{x - 0}$

$= \dfrac{-x/(x + 1)}{x}$

$= -\dfrac{1}{x + 1}$

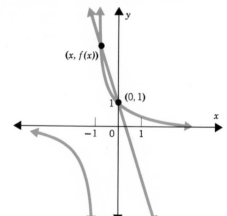

1. (a) $\quad m = \lim\limits_{x \to 3} \dfrac{f(x) - f(3)}{x - 3}$

$= \lim\limits_{x \to 3} \dfrac{x^2 - 9}{x - 3}$

$= \lim\limits_{x \to 3} (x + 3)$

$= 6$

$y - 9 = 6(x - 3)$

$y = 6x - 9$

8.3
Exercise
(page 238)

(c) $\quad m = \lim\limits_{x \to -1} \dfrac{f(x) - f(-1)}{x - (-1)}$

$= \lim\limits_{x \to -1} \dfrac{x^2 + 2x + 1 - 0}{x + 1}$

$= \lim\limits_{x \to -1} (x + 1) = 0$

$y - 0 = 0(x - (-1)) \qquad$ or $\qquad y = 0$

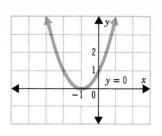

(e) $\quad m = \lim\limits_{x \to 1} \dfrac{f(x) - f(1)}{x - 1}$

$= \lim\limits_{x \to 1} \dfrac{1/x - 1}{x - 1}$

$= \lim\limits_{x \to 1} \dfrac{(1 - x)/x}{x - 1}$

$= \lim\limits_{x \to 1} -\dfrac{1}{x} = -1$

$y - 1 = -1(x - 1) \qquad$ or $\qquad y = -x + 2$

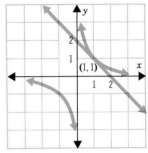

2. (a) $f'(3) = \lim\limits_{x \to 3} \dfrac{f(x) - f(3)}{x - 3} = \lim\limits_{x \to 3} \dfrac{5 - 5}{x - 3} = 0$

(c) $f'(2) = \lim\limits_{x \to 2} \dfrac{3x - 5 - 1}{x - 2} = \lim\limits_{x \to 2} \dfrac{3x - 6}{x - 2} = \lim\limits_{x \to 2} 3 = 3$

(e) $f'(2) = \lim\limits_{x \to 2} \dfrac{1/x^2 - 1/4}{x - 2} = \lim\limits_{x \to 2} \dfrac{-(x + 2)}{4x^2} = -\dfrac{1}{4}$

3. $f'(a) = \lim\limits_{x \to a} \dfrac{f(x) - f(a)}{x - a} = \lim\limits_{x \to a} \dfrac{mx + b - (ma + b)}{x - a} = \lim\limits_{x \to a} \dfrac{m(x - a)}{x - a} = m.$

5. (a) $f(x)$ is continuous at $x = 0$ since $\lim\limits_{x \to 0^-} f(x) = \lim\limits_{x \to 0^+} f(x) = f(0) = 0.$

(b) $\left.\begin{array}{l} \lim\limits_{x \to 0^-} \dfrac{f(x) - f(0)}{x - 0} = \lim\limits_{x \to 0^-} \dfrac{x^3 - 0}{x} = 0 \\[2ex] \lim\limits_{x \to 0^+} \dfrac{f(x) - f(0)}{x - 0} = \lim\limits_{x \to 0^+} \dfrac{x^2 - 0}{x} = 0 \end{array}\right\}$ Hence, $f'(0) = 0.$

7. (a) Average cost $= \dfrac{\Delta C}{\Delta x} = \dfrac{C(10) - C(0)}{10 - 0} = \dfrac{1002 - 2}{10} = 100$

(b) $MC = C'(10) = \lim\limits_{x \to 10} \dfrac{x^3 + 2 - 1002}{x - 10} = \lim\limits_{x \to 10} \dfrac{x^3 - 1000}{x - 10}$

$= \lim\limits_{x \to 10} (x^2 + 10x + 10^2) = 300$

(c) Average cost $= \dfrac{\Delta C}{\Delta x} = \dfrac{C(a) - C(0)}{a - 0} = \dfrac{2 + a^3 - (2)}{a} = a^2$

(d) $MC = C'(a) = \lim\limits_{x \to a} \dfrac{(2 + x^3 - 2 - a^3)}{x - a} = 3a^2$

9. (a) Average speed $= \dfrac{\Delta s}{\Delta t} = \dfrac{s(30) - s(0)}{30 - 0} = \dfrac{960}{30} = 32$ miles per second

(b) $s'(a) = \lim\limits_{t \to a} \dfrac{s(t) - s(a)}{t - a} = \lim\limits_{t \to a} \dfrac{t^2 + 2t - (a^2 + 2a)}{t - a}$

$\quad\quad = \lim\limits_{t \to a} \dfrac{(t - a)(t + a + 2)}{t - a} = \lim\limits_{t \to a} (t + a + 2) = 2a + 2$

$\quad s'(10) = 2(10) + 2 = 22$
$\quad s'(15) = 2(15) + 2 = 32$
$\quad s'(25) = 2(25) + 2 = 52$

(c) $s(t) = t^2 + 2t = 8$
$\quad t^2 + 2t - 8 = 0$
$\quad (t + 4)(t - 2) = 0$
$\quad t = -4 \quad$ or $\quad t = 2$

Hence, 2 seconds are required for the wave to travel 8 miles.
The speed of the shock wave is given by the derivative $s'(t)$;
hence, $s'(2) + 2(2) + 2 = 6$ miles per second.

10. (a) $\Delta A = \pi(r + \Delta r)^2 - \pi r^2 = 2\pi r \Delta r + \pi \Delta r^2 = \pi \Delta r(2r + \Delta r)$

(b) $\Delta C = 2\pi(r + \Delta r) - 2\pi r = 2\pi \Delta r$

(c) $\dfrac{\Delta A}{\Delta r} = \dfrac{\pi \Delta r(2r + \Delta r)}{\Delta r} = \pi(2r + \Delta r)$

(d) $\dfrac{\Delta C}{\Delta r} = \dfrac{2\pi \Delta r}{\Delta r} = 2\pi$

(e) $A'(r) = \lim\limits_{\Delta r \to 0} \dfrac{\Delta A}{\Delta r} = \lim\limits_{\Delta r \to 0} \pi(2r + \Delta r) = 2\pi r$

(f) $C'(r) = \lim\limits_{\Delta r \to 0} \dfrac{\Delta C}{\Delta r} = \lim\limits_{\Delta r \to 0} 2\pi = 2\pi$

13. (b) $\lim\limits_{x \to 0^-} (x^2 - 1) = -1$

$\lim\limits_{x \to 0^+} \sqrt{x} = 0$

$f(x)$ is not continuous and has no
derivative at $x = 0$.

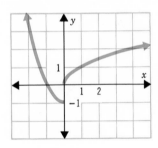

13. (c) $\lim\limits_{x \to 1} f(x) = 2, f(1) = 0$

$f(x)$ is not continuous at $x = 1$
and has no derivative there.

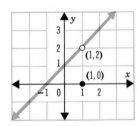

1. (a) $f'(x) = 4x^3, \quad f'(2) = 4 \cdot 2^3 = 32$

(c) $f'(x) = -1 \cdot x^{-2} = -\dfrac{1}{x^2}; \quad f'(2) = -\dfrac{1}{4}$

8.4
Exercise
(page 243)

(d) $f'(x) = \frac{2}{3}x^{-1/3} = \frac{2}{3\sqrt[3]{x}};$  $f'(8) = \frac{2}{3\sqrt[3]{8}} = \frac{1}{3}$

(f) $f'(x) = -\frac{1}{2}x^{-3/2} = -\frac{1}{2\sqrt{x^3}};$  $f'(3) = -\frac{1}{6\sqrt{3}}$

2. (a) $f'(x) = 4x^3;$ $m = f'(1) = 4$

$y - 1 = 4(x - 1)$

$y = 4x - 3$

(d) $f'(x) = -2x^{-3} = -\frac{2}{x^3}$

$m = f'(3) = -\frac{2}{27}$

$y - \frac{1}{9} = -\frac{2}{27}(x - 3)$

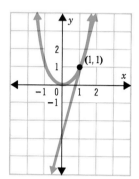

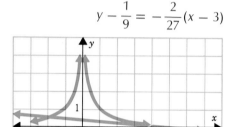

3. (a) Yes, $\lim_{x \to 0^-} f(x) = \lim_{x \to 0^+} f(x) = f(0) = 0$

(b) No, since $\lim_{x \to 0} \frac{f(x) - f(0)}{x - 0} = \lim_{x \to 0} \frac{f(x)}{x}$ does not exist;

$\lim_{x \to 0^-} \frac{f(x)}{x} = 1$, and $\lim_{x \to 0^+} \frac{f(x)}{x} = 0$.

(c) For $x < 0, f'(x) = 1;$  $f'(-1) = 1$

(d) For $x > 0, f'(x) = 2x;$  $f'(1) = 2 \cdot 1 = 2$

5. $s(t) = t^{3/2};$  $s'(t) = \frac{3}{2}t^{1/2}$

$s'(1) = \frac{3}{2} \cdot 1 = 1.5$ feet per second

If $s(t) = 8 = t^{3/2},$

$t^3 = 64$

$t = 4$ is time required for the child to hit the ground.

$s'(4) = \frac{3}{2}\sqrt{4} = 3$ feet per second

8.5
Exercise
(page 250)

1. (b) $\frac{d}{dx}(\sqrt{x} - x) = \frac{1}{2\sqrt{x}} - 1$

(d) $\frac{d}{dx}(3x^2 + 9) = 6x$

(f) $\frac{d}{dx}f(x) = 5x^4 - 6x + 2$

(h) $\frac{d}{dx}(x^3(\sqrt{x} + 1)) = x^3 \cdot \frac{d}{dx}(\sqrt{x} + 1) + (\sqrt{x} + 1)\frac{d}{dx}(x^3)$

$= x^3 \cdot \frac{1}{2\sqrt{x}} + (\sqrt{x} + 1) \cdot 3x^2 = \frac{1}{2}x^{5/2} + 3x^{5/2} + 3x^2 = \frac{7}{2}x^{5/2} + 3x^2$

(j) $\frac{d}{dx}\left(\frac{x^2 + 2x + 1}{x - 1}\right) = \frac{(x - 1)(2x + 2) - (x^2 + 2x + 1) \cdot 1}{(x - 1)^2}$

$= \frac{x^2 - 2x - 3}{(x - 1)^2} = \frac{(x + 1)(x - 3)}{(x - 1)^2}$

2. (a) $f'(x) = \dfrac{(x + 1)(3x^2) - x^3(1)}{(x + 1)^2} = \dfrac{x^2(2x + 3)}{(x + 1)^2}$     $m = f'(0) = 0$

(b) $f'(x) = \sqrt{x}(2x) + (x^2 + 2)\left(\dfrac{1}{2\sqrt{x}}\right) = \dfrac{5x^2 + 2}{2\sqrt{x}}$     $m = f'(1) = \dfrac{5 \cdot 1 + 2}{2 \cdot 1} = \dfrac{7}{2}$

(e) $f'(x) = 10x + 2;\ m = f'(2) = 10 \cdot 2 + 2 = 22$

3. (a) $f'(x) = 6x - 12$     (c) $f'(x) = 3x^2 - 3$
   $6x - 12 = 0$     $3x^2 - 3 = 0$
   $x = 2$     $3(x^2 - 1) = 0$
        $x = -1$     or     $x = 1.$

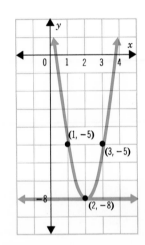     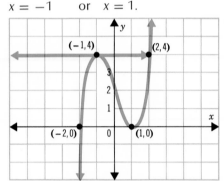

4. (a) $R(x) = xp(x) = 1000x - .005x^2$
   (b) $MR = R'(x) = 1000 - .01x$
       $R'(20) = 1000 - .2 = 999.8$
5. (a) $P(x) = R(x) - C(x) = -.505x^2 + 996.87x - 500$
   (b) $P(20) = \$19{,}235.40$
   (c) $P'(x) = -1.01x + 996.87$
   (d) $1000 - .01x = x + 3.13;\ x = 987$
6. (a) $R(x) = xp(x) = 18000x - 2000x^2$
   (b) $C(x) = 2000x$
   (c) $P(x) = R(x) - C(x) = 16000x - 2000x^2$
   (d) $MR = R'(x) = 18000 - 4000x$
   (e) $MC = C'(x) = 2000$
   (f) $18000 - 4000x = 2000;\ x = 4$
       $P(4) = 16000(4) - 2000(4)^2$
       $= \$32{,}000.$
8. $A'(t) = 3a_3t^2 + 2a_2t + a_1$

14. $\dfrac{d}{dx}\dfrac{1}{f(x)} = \dfrac{f(x) \cdot 0 - 1 \cdot f'(x)}{(f(x))^2} = -\dfrac{f'(x)}{(f(x))^2}$

8.6
Exercise
(page 255)

1. (a) $\dfrac{dy}{dx} = 3(2x^2 + x + 1)^2 \cdot (4x + 1)$

(c) $\dfrac{dy}{dx} = \tfrac{1}{2}(3x^2 + 1)^{-1/2} \cdot 6x = \dfrac{3x}{(3x^2 + 1)^{1/2}}$

3. $f'(x) = x \cdot \frac{1}{2}(1 - x^2)^{-1/2}(-2x) + (1 - x^2)^{1/2} \cdot 1$

$$= \frac{-x^2}{(1 - x^2)^{1/2}} + \frac{1 - x^2}{(1 - x^2)^{1/2}} = \frac{1 - 2x^2}{\sqrt{1 - x^2}}$$

$f'(x) = 0 \Rightarrow 1 - 2x^2 = 0; \; x = \pm\dfrac{\sqrt{2}}{2}$

$f'(x)$ does not exist for $x = \pm 1$.

5. $s(t) = \sqrt{(52 - 8t)^2 + (12t)^2} = 4\sqrt{13t^2 - 52t + 169}$

$$s'(t) = \frac{1}{2} \cdot 4(13t^2 - 52t + 169)^{-1/2}(26t - 52) = \frac{52(t - 2)}{\sqrt{13(t^2 - 4t + 13)}}$$

$$s'(1) = \frac{52(1 - 2)}{\sqrt{13(1 - 4 + 13)}} = -\frac{52}{\sqrt{130}} = -4.56$$

$$s'(4) = \frac{52(4 - 2)}{\sqrt{13(16 - 16 + 13)}} = \frac{104}{\sqrt{13^2}} = \frac{104}{13} = 8$$

Since $8 > 0$, the ships are receding at 10 P.M.

$s'(t) = 0 \Rightarrow t - 2 = 0; \; t = 2$

Hence, they are closest at 8 P.M.

7. $A'(t) = 3(t^{1/4} + 3)^2 \cdot \frac{1}{4}t^{-3/4} = \dfrac{\frac{3}{4}(t^{1/4} + 3)^2}{\sqrt[4]{t^3}}$

$$A'(16) = \frac{\frac{3}{4}(16^{1/4} + 3)^2}{\sqrt[4]{16^3}} = \frac{\frac{3}{4}(5)^2}{8} = \frac{75}{32} = 2.34$$

**8.7**
**Exercise**
**(page 258)**

1. (a) $f'(x) = 3x^2 - 6x \qquad f''(x) = 6x - 6$

(d) $f'(x) = \dfrac{1}{2}(x + 5)^{-1/2} = \dfrac{1}{2\sqrt{x + 5}}$

$$f''(x) = -\frac{1}{4}(x + 5)^{-3/2} = \frac{-1}{4(x + 5)^{3/2}}$$

(e) $f'(x) = \frac{1}{2}(x^2 + 4)^{-1/2} \cdot 2x = x(x^2 + 4)^{-1/2} = \dfrac{x}{(x^2 + 4)^{1/2}}$

$$f''(x) = \frac{(x^2 + 4)^{1/2} \cdot 1 - x(x^2 + 4)^{-1/2} \cdot x}{x^2 + 4} = \frac{4}{(x^2 + 4)^{3/2}}$$

(g) $f'(x) = \frac{3}{2}(x^2 - 1)^{1/2} \cdot 2x = 3x(x^2 - 1)^{1/2}$

$f''(x) = 3x \cdot \frac{1}{2}(x^2 - 1)^{-1/2} \cdot 2x + (x^2 - 1)^{1/2} \cdot 3$

$$= \frac{3x^2}{(x^2 - 1)^{1/2}} + \frac{3x^2 - 3}{(x^2 - 1)^{1/2}} = \frac{6x^2 - 3}{(x^2 - 1)^{1/2}}$$

2. (a) $3x^2 - 6x = 0 \qquad\qquad$ (c) $2x - 2 = 0$

$x = 0 \quad$ or $\quad x = 2 \qquad\qquad\qquad x = 1$

$f''(2) = 6 \cdot 2 - 6 = 6 \qquad\qquad f''(1) = 2$

$f''(0) = 6 \cdot 0 - 6 = -6$

(e) $\dfrac{x}{(x^2 + 4)^{1/2}} = 0 \qquad x = 0 \qquad f''(0) = \dfrac{4}{(0 + 4)^{3/2}} = \dfrac{4}{8} = \dfrac{1}{2}$

(g) $3x(x^2 - 1)^{1/2} = 0$

$\quad$ $x = -1$ or $x = 1$ $\qquad$ ($x = 0$ is not in the domain of $f(x)$)

$\quad$ $f''(-1)$ and $f''(1)$ are not defined.

3. $s'(t) = 80 - 32t$

$\quad$ $s'(2) = 80 - 32 \cdot 2 = 16$ feet per second

$\quad$ $s'(t) = 0 \Rightarrow 32t = 80$ or $t = 2.5$ seconds

$\quad$ $s(2.5) = 6 + 80(\frac{5}{2}) - 16(\frac{5}{2})^2 = 106$ feet

$\quad$ $s''(t) = -32$ feet/sec$^2$ is the acceleration at any time $t$

4. $s'(t) = 0 - 3(2 - t)^2 \cdot (-1) = 3(2 - t)^2$

$\quad$ $s'(1) = 3 \cdot 1^2 = 3$ meters per second

$\quad$ $s'(t) = -6(2 - t)$ $\quad 0 \leq t \leq 2$, is the acceleration at any time $t$

Review Exercises
(page 258)

1. $f(x) = x^2 + 1$

(a) $\dfrac{\Delta y}{\Delta x} = \dfrac{f(1) - f(0)}{1 - 0} = \dfrac{2 - 1}{1} = 1$

(b) $m = \dfrac{\Delta y}{\Delta x} = \dfrac{f(3) - f(0)}{3 - 0} = \dfrac{10 - 1}{3} = 3$

(c) $\quad$ $f'(x) = 2x$; $f'(1) = 2$ $\quad$ (d) $f'(3) = 6$ $\quad$ (e) $f'(0) = 0$

(f) $\quad$ From part (c), $m = 2$

$\qquad$ $\therefore y - 2 = 2(x - 1)$ $\qquad$ or $\qquad$ $y = 2x$

(g) $\quad$ $f'(x) = 2x$ $\quad$ (h) $f''(x) = 2$

(i) $\quad$ $f'(x) = 2x = 0 \Rightarrow x = 0$; point $(0, 1)$, $f''(x) = 2 \neq 0$.

3. $f(x) = x^3$

(a) $\dfrac{\Delta y}{\Delta x} = \dfrac{1 - 0}{1 - 0} = 1$ $\quad$ (b) $m = \dfrac{\Delta y}{\Delta x} = \dfrac{27 - 0}{3 - 0} = 9$

(c) $f'(x) = 3x^2$ $\quad$ $f'(1) = 3$ $\quad$ (d) $f'(3) = 27$ $\quad$ (e) $f'(0) = 0$

(f) $f(1) = 1$, $m = 3$, $y - 1 = 3(x - 1)$ $\qquad$ or $\qquad$ $y = 3x - 2$

(g) $f'(x) = 3x^2$ $\quad$ (h) $f''(x) = 6x$

(i) $f'(x) = 0$ $\quad$ at $\quad$ $x = 0$; point $(0, 0)$

$\quad$ $f''(x) = 0$ at $x = 0$; point $(0, 0)$

6. (a) $f'(x) = \frac{1}{2}x(x + 1)^{-1/2} + (x + 1)^{1/2} \cdot 1 = \dfrac{\frac{3}{2}x + 1}{(x + 1)^{1/2}} = \dfrac{3x + 2}{2(x + 1)^{1/2}}$

(b) $f''(x) = \dfrac{2(x + 1)^{1/2} \cdot 3 - (3x + 2) \cdot \frac{1}{2} \cdot 2(x + 1)^{-1/2}}{4(x + 1)}$

$\qquad = \dfrac{6(x + 1) - (3x + 2)}{4(x + 1)^{3/2}} = \dfrac{3x + 4}{4(x + 1)^{3/2}}$

(c) $f'(x) = 0 \Rightarrow 3x + 2 = 0 \Rightarrow x = -\frac{2}{3}$

(d) $f''(-\frac{2}{3}) = \dfrac{3(-\frac{2}{3}) + 4}{4(-\frac{2}{3} + 1)^{3/2}} = \dfrac{2}{.4(\frac{1}{3})^{3/2}} \approx \dfrac{1}{.385} \approx 2.6$

8. (a) $f'(x) = \frac{3}{2}x^{1/2} = \frac{3}{2}\sqrt{x}$ $\quad$ (b) $f''(x) = \frac{1}{2} \cdot \frac{3}{2}x^{-1/2} = \frac{3}{4}x^{-1/2} = \dfrac{3}{4\sqrt{x}}$

(c) $f'(x) = 0 \Rightarrow x = 0$; $\quad$ point $(0, 0)$ $\quad$ (d) $f''(0)$ is not defined.

9. (a) $f'(x) = \frac{1}{2}(x^2 + 9)^{-1/2} \cdot 2x = \dfrac{x}{(x^2 + 9)^{1/2}}$

(b) $f''(x) = \dfrac{(x^2 + 9)^{1/2} \cdot 1 - x \cdot \frac{1}{2}(x^2 + 9)^{-1/2} \cdot 2x}{(x^2 + 9)} = \dfrac{x^2 + 9 - x^2}{(x^2 + 9)^{3/2}} = \dfrac{9}{(x^2 + 9)^{3/2}}$

(c) $f'(x) = 0 \Rightarrow x = 0$;  point $(0, 3)$   (d) $f''(0) = \dfrac{9}{(0 + 9)^{3/2}} = \dfrac{9}{27} = \dfrac{1}{3}$

10. $f'(x) = \lim\limits_{x \to 0} \dfrac{2x^2 - x + 4 - (0 - 0 + 4)}{x - 0} = \lim\limits_{x \to 0} \dfrac{2x^2 - x}{x} = \lim\limits_{x \to 0} \dfrac{x(2x - 1)}{x}$

$= \lim\limits_{x \to 0} (2x - 1) = -1$

1. (a) $x > -2$                                (b) $x < 0$    and    $x > 1$
      Critical values are $-2$ and 1.          Critical values are 0 and 1.

   (c) $x > \frac{1}{2}$
      Critical values are 0 and $\frac{1}{2}$.

2. (a) $f'(x) = 3x^2 - 6x = 3x(x - 2),$
      for $x < 0$, $f'(x) > 0$; $f(x)$ is increasing.
      for $0 < x < 2$, $f'(x) < 0$; $f(x)$ is decreasing.
      for $x > 2$, $f'(x) > 0$; $f(x)$ is increasing.
      Critical values: $x = 0$ and $x = 2$
      $(0, 0)$ is a relative maximum.
      $(2, -4)$ is a relative minimum.

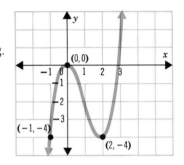

   (d) $f'(x) = -\dfrac{1}{x^2} < 0$

      $f(x)$ is decreasing for all $x \neq 0$.
      No critical points.

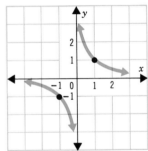

   (f) $f'(x) = 4x^3 - 4x = 4x(x + 1)(x - 1)$
      $x < -1$, $f(x)$ is decreasing.
      $-1 < x < 0$, $f(x)$ is increasing.
      $0 < x < 1$, $f(x)$ is decreasing.
      $x > 1$, $f(x)$ is increasing.
      Critical values: $x = -1$, $x = 0$, $x = 1$
      $(-1, 0)$ and $(1, 0)$ are relative minima.
      $(0, 1)$ is a relative maximum.

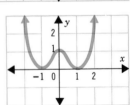

3. (a) $f''(x) = 6x - 6$
      at $x = 0$, $f''(0) = -6 \Rightarrow (0, 0)$ is a relative maximum.
      at $x = 2$, $f''(2) = 6 \Rightarrow (2, -4)$ is a relative minimum.
      See 2(a) above for the graph.

   (d) $f''(x) = \dfrac{2}{x^3}$. There are no critical values, so the second derivative

      test is not applicable. See 2(d) above for the graph.

(f) $f''(x) = 12x^2 - 4$.

$f''(-1) = 8 \Rightarrow (-1, 0)$ is a relative minimum.

$f''(0) = -4 \Rightarrow (0, 1)$ is a relative maximum.

$f''(1) = 8 \Rightarrow (1, 0)$ is a relative minimum.

See 2(f) above for the graph.

4. (a) $f'(x) = x^{1/3} - 1$; Critical value: $x = 1$

$f''(x) = \frac{1}{3}x^{-2/3}$; $f''(1) = \frac{1}{3}$

Critical point $(1, -\frac{1}{4})$ is a relative minimum.

(c) $f'(x) = x + \frac{1}{x^2}$; Critical value: $x = -1$.

$f''(x) = 1 - \frac{2}{x^3}$; $f''(-1) = 3$

Critical point $(-1, \frac{3}{2})$ is a relative minimum.

5. $s(t) = \sqrt{(12t)^2 + (30 - 6t)^2} = 6\sqrt{5t^2 - 10t + 25}$

$s'(t) = \frac{1}{2} \cdot 6(10t - 10)(5t^2 - 10t + 25)^{-1/2} = \frac{30(t - 1)}{\sqrt{5t^2 - 10t + 25}}$

$s'(t) = 0 \Rightarrow t = 1$ (11 A.M.)

$s(1) = 6\sqrt{20} \approx 26.8$ miles.

7. $P(x) = 30x - (25 + 2x + .01x^2) = -.01x^2 + 28x - 25$

$P'(x) = -.02x + 28$

$-.02x + 28 = 0$; $x = 1400$ units

$P(1400) = -.01(1400)^2 + 28(1400) - 25 = \$19{,}575$.

8. Time with no wind: $t = \dfrac{d}{r} = \dfrac{3000}{500} = 6$ hours

(a) $t = \dfrac{3000}{500 + 25} \approx 5$ hours 43 minutes

(b) $t = \dfrac{3000}{500 - 50} = 6$ hours 40 minutes

Time saved = 17 minutes

Time lost = 40 minutes

(c) $C(500) = 100 + \dfrac{500}{10} + \dfrac{36000}{500} = \$222$

(d) $C(525) = 100 + \dfrac{525}{10} + \dfrac{36000}{525} \approx \$221.07$

(e) $C(450) = 100 + \dfrac{450}{10} + \dfrac{36000}{450} = \$225$

(f) $C'(x) = \dfrac{1}{10} - \dfrac{36000}{x^2}$

$C'(x) = 0 \Rightarrow x^2 = 360{,}000$; $x = 600$ miles per hour

(g) $C(600) = 100 + \dfrac{600}{10} + \dfrac{36000}{600} = \$220$

12. (a) $f'(x_0) = 4x_0 - 2 = 0 \Rightarrow x_0 = \frac{1}{2}$

$f(\frac{1}{2}) = 2(\frac{1}{2})(\frac{1}{2} - 1) = -\frac{1}{2}$     Hence, $(x_0, f(x_0)) = (\frac{1}{2}, -\frac{1}{2})$

(c) $f'(x_0) = 4x_0^3 - 4x_0 = 0 \Rightarrow x_0 = 0, x_0 = 1$, or $x_0 = -1$

$f(0) = -8$

$f(1) = 1 - 2 - 8 = -9$

$f(-1) = 1 - 2 - 8 = -9$

Hence, there are three such points, $(0, -8)$, $(1, -9)$, and $(-1, -9)$.

1. $f(x) = x^3 - 3x^2, [-1, 4]$
$f'(x) = 3x^2 - 6x = 0 \Rightarrow x = 0$ or $x = 2$
$f(0) = 0; f(2) = 8 - 12 = -4$
$f(-1) = -4; f(4) = 64 - 48 = 16$
Hence, the absolute maximum is 16 and the absolute minimum is $-4$.

3. $f(x) = x^3 - 9x^2 + 27x - 27; [-2, 2]$
$f'(x) = 3x^2 - 18x + 27 = 3(x - 3)^2 = 0 \Rightarrow x = 3$. Hence there are no
critical values in the domain.
$f(-2) = -125; f(2) = -1$
Therefore, $-125$ is the absolute minimum and $-1$ the absolute maximum.

4. $f(x) = \dfrac{1}{x}, [1, 3]$

$f'(x) = -\dfrac{1}{x^2} \neq 0$ for any $x$, so there are no critical values.

$f(1) = \frac{1}{1} = 1; f(3) = \frac{1}{3}$

Therefore, $\frac{1}{3}$ and 1 are the absolute minimum and maximum, respectively.

6. $f(x) = x^4 - 2x^2 + 1, [-2, 3]$
$f'(x) = 4x^3 - 4x = 0 \Rightarrow x = 0, x = -1$, or $x = 1$
$f(0) = 1; f(-1) = 1 - 2 + 1 = 0; f(1) = 1 - 2 + 1 = 0$
$f(-2) = 16 - 8 + 1 = 9; f(3) = 81 - 18 + 1 = 64$
Hence, the absolute minimum is 0, the absolute maximum is 64.

7. $f(x) = x^{2/5}, [-1, 32]$

$f'(x) = \frac{2}{5}x^{-3/5} = \dfrac{2}{5x^{3/5}}; f'(x) \neq 0$, for any $x$ so there are no critical values.

However, $f'(x)$ does not exist for $x = 0$. Thus, we test
$f(0) = 0; f(-1) = (-1)^{2/5} = 1; f(32) = (32)^{2/5} = 4.$
Hence, the absolute minimum is 0; the absolute maximum is 4.

1. $f'(x) = 3x^2 - 18x$
$f''(x) = 6x - 18 = 0 \Rightarrow x = 3$
$x < 3, f''(x) < 0 \Rightarrow$ concave down
$x > 3, f''(x) > 0 \Rightarrow$ concave up
$f(3) = 3^3 - 9(3)^2 + 2 = -52$
Hence, $(3, -52)$ is an inflection point.

2. $f'(x) = 5x^4$
$f''(x) = 20x^3 = 0 \Rightarrow x = 0$
$x < 0, f''(x) < 0 \Rightarrow$ concave down
$x > 0, f''(x) > 0 \Rightarrow$ concave up
$f(0) = -1$
Hence $(0, -1)$ is an inflection point.

3. $f'(x) = 4x^3 - 12x^2$
$f''(x) = 12x^2 - 24x = 0 \Rightarrow x = 0$ or $x = 2$.
$x < 0, f''(x) > 0 \Rightarrow$ concave up
$0 < x < 2, f''(x) < 0 \Rightarrow$ concave down
$x > 2, f''(x) > 0 \Rightarrow$ concave up
$f(0) = 10$

$f(2) = 2^4 - 4(2)^3 + 10 = -6$

Hence, $(0, 10)$ and $(2, -6)$ are inflection points.

8. $f'(x) = 1 - \dfrac{1}{x^2}$

$f''(x) = \dfrac{2}{x^3}$

Since $f''(x) \neq 0$ for any value of $x$, there are no inflection points.

9. $f'(x) = -4(2x)(x^2 + 4)^{-2} = \dfrac{-8x}{(x^2 + 4)^2}$

$f''(x) = \dfrac{-8(x^2 + 4)^2 - (-8x)(2)(2x)(x^2 + 4)}{(x^2 + 4)^4} = \dfrac{8(3x^2 - 4)}{(x^2 + 4)^3}$

$f''(x) = 0 \Rightarrow 3x^2 - 4 = 0, x = \pm\dfrac{2\sqrt{3}}{3}$

$x < -\dfrac{2\sqrt{3}}{3}, f''(x) > 0 \Rightarrow$ concave up

$-\dfrac{2\sqrt{3}}{3} < x < \dfrac{2\sqrt{3}}{3}, f''(x) < 0 \Rightarrow$ concave down

$x > \dfrac{2\sqrt{3}}{3}, f''(x) > 0 \Rightarrow$ concave up

$f\left(-\dfrac{2\sqrt{3}}{3}\right) = f\left(\dfrac{2\sqrt{3}}{3}\right) = \dfrac{3}{4}$

Hence, $\left(-\dfrac{2\sqrt{3}}{3}, \dfrac{3}{4}\right)$ and $\left(\dfrac{2\sqrt{3}}{3}, \dfrac{3}{4}\right)$ are inflection points.

11. $f'(x) = 3x^2 - 18x \Rightarrow x = 0$ or $x = 6$ are critical values.

$f''(x) = 6x - 18$

$f''(0) = -18 \Rightarrow (0, 2)$ is a relative maximum.

$f''(6) = 18 \Rightarrow (6, -106)$ is a relative minimum.

For inflection points, see Problem 1 above.

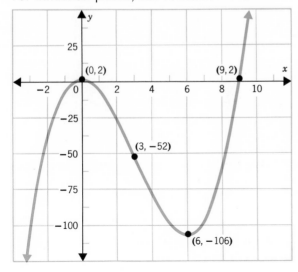

12. $f'(x) = 4x^3 - 12x^2 = 0 \Rightarrow x = 0$ or $x = 3$ are critical values.
$f''(x) = 12x^2 - 24x$.
$f''(3) = 36 \Rightarrow (3, -17)$ is a relative minimum.
$(0, 10)$ is an inflection point. (See problem 3 above.)

13. $f'(x) = 5x^4 - 5 = 0 \Rightarrow x = -1$ or $x = 1$ are critical values.
$f''(x) = 20x^3$.
$f''(-1) = -20 \Rightarrow (-1, 4)$ is a relative maximum.
$f''(1) = 20 \Rightarrow (1, -4)$ is a relative minimum.
$f''(x) = 0 \Rightarrow x = 0$
$x < 0, f''(x) < 0 \Rightarrow$ concave down.
$x > 0, f''(x) > 0 \Rightarrow$ concave up.
Hence $(0, 0)$ is an inflection point.

12.

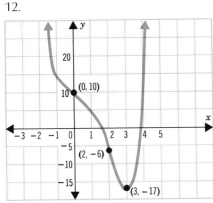

13

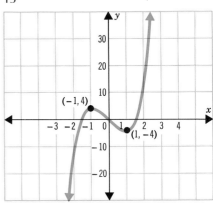

16. $C'(x) = .003x^2 - .6x + 30$
$C''(x) = .006x - .6 = 0 \Rightarrow x = 100$
For $x < 100$, $C''(x) < 0 \Rightarrow$ concave down.
For $x > 100$, $C''(x) > 0 \Rightarrow$ concave up.
Hence, $(100, 1042)$ is an inflection point.
The cost rate at $(100, 1042)$ changes from decreasing to increasing.

9.5
Exercise
(page 289)

1. $C(x) = .005x + \dfrac{4500}{x}$

$C'(x) = .005 - \dfrac{4500}{x^2} = \dfrac{.005x^2 - 4500}{x^2} = 0 \Rightarrow .005x^2 = 4500$

or $x = 300\sqrt{10} \approx 948$

$C''(x) = \dfrac{9000}{x^3}$, $C''(300\sqrt{10}) > 0$ and $x = 300\sqrt{10}$ is a minimum.

2. Let $x$ be one number. The other number is $18 - x$.
$f(x) = x(18 - x) = 18x - x^2$
$f'(x) = 18 - 2x = 0 \Rightarrow x = 9$
Since $f''(x) = -2$, there is a maximum at $x = 9$
Hence, the numbers are 9 and 9.

4. $S = 2\pi r^2 + 2\pi rh$

For $V = \pi r^2 h = 10$, $h = \dfrac{10}{\pi r^2}$ and $S = 2\pi r^2 + \dfrac{10}{\pi r^2}(2\pi r) = 2\pi r^2 + \dfrac{20}{r}$

$C(x) = 2(2\pi r^2) + 1.5\left(\dfrac{20}{r}\right) = 4\pi r^2 + \dfrac{30}{r}$

$C'(x) = 8\pi r - \dfrac{30}{r^2} = 0 \Rightarrow \dfrac{8\pi r^3 - 30}{r^2} = 0 \Rightarrow r = \sqrt[3]{\dfrac{15}{4\pi}} \doteq 1.061$

$h = \dfrac{10}{\pi r^2} \approx \dfrac{10}{3.535} \approx 2.829$

6. Let $x =$ cars not rented
   The number of cars rented $= 200 - x$; income per car $= 180 + 10x$
   Total income $I(x) = (180 + 10x)(200 - x) = 36000 + 1820x - 10x^2$
   $I'(x) = 1820 - 20x = 0 \Rightarrow x = 91$, and $I''(x) = -20$, so $I''(91) < 0$.
   Hence, $x = 91$ is maximum thus, he should charge \$1090.

7. For an increase of $x$ members.
   $R(x) = (60 + x)(200 - 2x) = 12000 + 80x - 2x^2$
   $R'(x) = 80 - 4x = 0 \Rightarrow x = 20$. $R''(20) = -4$, so $x = 20$ is a maximum.
   Hence, 80 members gives a maximum income.

9. The diameter of the circle (6 in.) must equal the diagonal of the
   rectangle. By the Pythagorean theorem, if one side is $x$, the other
   must be $\sqrt{36 - x^2}$, and the area $A = x(36 - x^2)^{1/2}$ with $0 < x < 6$.

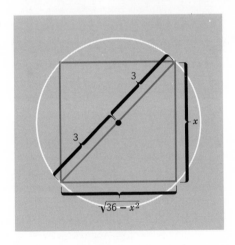

$A'(x) = \dfrac{36 - 2x^2}{(36 - x^2)^{1/2}} = 0 \Rightarrow 2x^2 = 36$ or $x = 3\sqrt{2}$

$\sqrt{36 - 18} = 3\sqrt{2}$, so the area is maximized when the rectangle is
a square with sides $3\sqrt{2}$.

11. Let the dimensions of the page be $x$ and $y$. (See Figure on next page.)
    Then $(x - 4)(y - 2) = 50$. The quantity to be minimized is the area
    $A = x \cdot y$. Thus,

    $A(x) = x\left[\dfrac{50}{x - 4} + 2\right]$

$$A'(x) = \frac{50}{x - 4} + 2 + x\left[\frac{-50}{(x - 4)^2}\right] = \frac{50x - 200 + 2(x - 4)^2 - 50x}{(x - 4)^2}$$

$A'(x) = 0 \Rightarrow 200 = 2(x - 4)^2 \Rightarrow (x - 4)^2 = 100 \Rightarrow x - 4 = 10 \Rightarrow x = 14$

The dimensions of the page are 14 in. by 7 in.

1. $R(x) = xp = 20x - .03x^2$
   $P(x) = R(x) - C(x) = -.03x^2 + 19.98x - 3$
   $P'(x) = -.06x + 19.98 = 0 \Rightarrow x = 333$ units
2. (a) $MR = R'(x) = 8 - 2x$
   (b) $R'(3) = 8 - 2(3) = 2$ (million dollars)
      $R'(4) = 8 - 2(4) = 0$
   (c) $MC = C'(x) = 2$ (million dollars)
   (d) Fixed cost $= 5$ (million dollars)
   (e) Variable cost $= 2x$; $2(4) = 8$ (million dollars)
   (f) $8x - x^2 = 2x + 5$; $x^2 - 6x + 5 = 0, x = 5, x = 1$
   (g) $P(x) = R(x) - C(x) = -x^2 + 6x - 5$
   (h) $P'(x) = -2x + 6 = 0 \Rightarrow x = 3$ (thousand units)
   (i) $P(3) = -(3)^2 + 6(3) - 5 = 4$ (million dollars)
   (j) $R'(3) = 2$ (million dollars)
   (k) $R(3) = 8(3) - (3)^2 = 15$ (million dollars)
   (l) Variable cost $= 2(3) = 6$ (million dollars)
4. $C(x) = 10x$
   $R(x) = xp = 90x - .02x^2$
   $P(x) = R(x) - C(x) = 80x - .02x^2$
   (a) $P'(x) = 80 - .04x = 0 \Rightarrow x = 2000$
   (b) $p = 90 - .02(2000) = \$50$
   (c) $P(2000) = 80(2000) - .02(2000)^2 = \$80,000$
6. $R(x) = xp = 19000x - 2x^2$
   $P(x) = R(x) - C(x) = -5x^2 + 9000x - 1,000,000$
   $P'(x) = -10x + 9000 = 0$; $x = 900$

1. $C(t) = \dfrac{10k}{t} + \dfrac{250}{t} = \dfrac{10t^{4/3}}{t} + \dfrac{250}{t} = 10t^{1/3} + \dfrac{250}{t}$

$C'(t) = \tfrac{10}{3}t^{-2/3} - \dfrac{250}{t^2} = \dfrac{\tfrac{10}{3}t^{4/3} - 250}{t^2}$

$C'(t) = 0 \Rightarrow \dfrac{10}{3}t^{4/3} - 250 = 0 \Rightarrow t = (75)^{3/4} = 25.49$ years

2. $t = 18 - 3x^2$
   $R(x) = xt = 18x - 3x^3$
   $R'(x) = 18 - 9x^2 = 0 \Rightarrow x = \sqrt{2} \approx 1.41$
   $R(1.41) \approx 16.97$ (maximum revenue)
   $t = 18 - 3(1.41)^2 = 12\%$

1. (a) $f'(x) = 3x^2 - 6x + 3 = 3(x - 1)^2 \geqq 0$
       $f$ is increasing
       $f'(x) = 0 \Rightarrow x = 1$
       $f''(x) = 6x - 6$
       $f''(x) = 0 \Rightarrow x = 1$
       For $x < 1, f''(x) < 0 \Rightarrow$ concave down
       For $x > 1, f''(x) > 0 \Rightarrow$ concave up
       Hence, $(1, 0)$ is an inflection point.

   (c) $f'(x) = \dfrac{1}{2}(x - 2)^{-1/2} = \dfrac{1}{2(x - 2)^{1/2}}$

       Since $f'(x) > 0$ for all $x > 2$, $f$ is increasing everywhere on its domain $\{x \mid x \geqq 2\}$, and there are no critical values.
       At the point $(2, 0)$ the function has a vertical tangent.

       $f''(x) = -\dfrac{1}{4}(x - 2)^{-3/2} = -\dfrac{1}{4(x - 2)^{3/2}}$

       Since $f''(x) < 0$, for all $x > 2$, the function is concave down with no inflection points.

   (e) The domain of $f$ is $\{x \mid x \neq 0\}$.

       $f'(x) = \dfrac{x(2x) - 1(x^2 + 1)}{x^2} = \dfrac{x^2 - 1}{x^2}$

       $f'(x) = 0 \Rightarrow x = -1$ \quad or \quad $x = 1$

       $f''(x) = \dfrac{x^2(2x) - 2x(x^2 - 1)}{x^4} = \dfrac{2}{x^3}$

       For $x = -1, f''(x) < 0 \Rightarrow (-1, -2)$ is a relative maximum.
       For $x = 1, f''(x) > 0 \Rightarrow (1, 2)$ is a relative minimum.
       Since $f''(x) \neq 0$, there are no inflection points.
       For $x < -1$, $f$ is increasing.
       For $-1 < x < 0$, $f$ is decreasing.
       For $0 < x < 1$, $f$ is decreasing.
       For $x > 1$, $f$ is increasing.
       For $x > 0$, $f$ is concave up; for $x < 0$, $f$ is concave down.

(e)

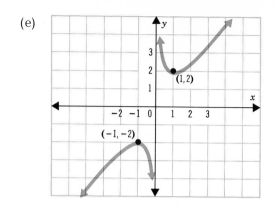

(h) $f(x) = \sqrt{\dfrac{1}{x}} = x^{-1/2}$

(h)

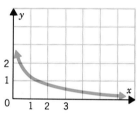

The domain of $f$ is $\{x \mid x > 0\}$

$$f'(x) = -\tfrac{1}{2}x^{-3/2} = -\frac{1}{2\sqrt{x^3}}$$

$$f''(x) = \tfrac{3}{4}x^{-5/2} = \frac{3}{4\sqrt{x^5}}$$

Since $f'(x) < 0$, $f$ is decreasing and there are no critical values. Since $f''(x) > 0$, the function is concave up with no inflection point.

2. (a) $f'(x) = 3x^2 - 6x + 3 = 3(x^2 - 2x + 1) = 3(x - 1)^2$
   Thus $x = 1$ is a critical value.
   $f(1) = 0$
   $f(-10) = -1331$
   $f(10) = 729$
   Hence, $-1331$ is the absolute minimum and $729$ is the absolute maximum.

   (c) $f(x) = (x^2 + 4)^{1/3}$

   $$f'(x) = \tfrac{1}{3}(2x)(x^2 + 4)^{-2/3} = \frac{2x}{3(x^2 + 4)^{2/3}}$$

   $f'(x) = 0 \Rightarrow x = 0$
   $f(0) = (4)^{1/3} \approx 1.6$
   $f(-2) = 8^{1/3} = 2$
   $f(\sqrt{23}) = 27^{1/3} = 3$
   Therefore $1.6$ is the absolute minimum and $3$ is the absolute maximum.

3. $P'(x) = 120 - 6x$
   $P'(x) = 0 \Rightarrow x = 20$ (thousand dollars).

5. $R(x) = xp = 2402.5x - 0.5x^3$
   $P(x) = R(x) - C(x) = 2400x - 0.5x^3 - 1500$
   $P'(x) = 2400 - 1.5x^2$
   $P'(x) = 0 \Rightarrow x = 40$.

6. Let $x$ = the number of $15 reductions
$R(x) = (1500 + 200x)(300 - 15x) = 450,000 + 37,500x - 3000x^2$
$R'(x) = 37500 - 6000x$
$R'(x) = 0 \Rightarrow x = 6.25$
Hence, the price should be $300 - 6.25(15) = \$206.25$.

1. (c)

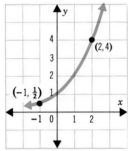

(f)

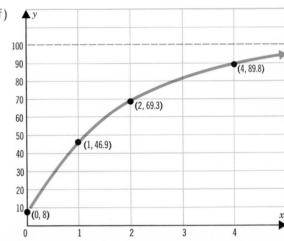

2. $B(x) = (1 + .07)^x \cdot 1000$
$B(5) = (1.07)^5 \cdot 1000 = \$1402.55$

3. Let $x$ = time in years and $P(x)$ denote earnings after $x$ years. If $P_0$ denotes earnings at time $x = 0$, then $P(x) = (1 + 0.10)^x P_0 = (1.10)^x P_0$.

5. First year:   $P = \$22,500$      6. $f(2) = 90\%$
   Third year: $P \approx \$13,125$      $f(3) = 96.7\%$
   Fifth year: $P \approx \$10,781.25$      $f(5) = 99.6\%$

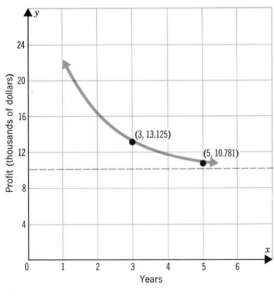

7. (a) $f(x + 1) = a^{x+1} = a^x \cdot a^1 = af(x)$

1. (a)

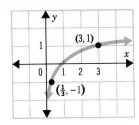

(c)

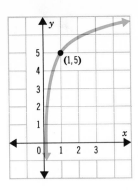

2. (a) $\log_2 2 = 1$
   (c) $\log_{10} 10^4 = 4 \log_{10} 10 = 4 \cdot 1 = 4$
   (e) $\log_2 32 = \log_2 2^5 = 5 \cdot \log_2 2 = 5 \cdot 1 = 5$
   (f) $\log_{1/2} 32 = \log_{1/2} (\frac{1}{2})^{-5} = -5 \cdot \log_{1/2} \frac{1}{2} = -5 \cdot 1 = -5$

3. (a) $\log_{10} 12 = \log_{10} (2^2 \cdot 3) = \log_{10} 2^2 + \log_{10} 3 = 2 \cdot \log_{10} 2 + \log_{10} 3$
   $= 2 \cdot .3010 + .4771 = 1.0791$

   (d) $\log_{10} (\frac{1}{8}) = \log_{10} \frac{1}{2^3} = \log_{10} 1 - 3 \log_{10} 2 = 0 - 3 \cdot .3010 = -.9030$

   (f) $\log_{10} 12.5 = \log_{10} \left(\frac{5^2}{2}\right) = 2 \log_{10} 5 - \log_{10} 2 = 2 \cdot .6990 - .3010 = 1.0970$

   (h) $\log_{10} (\frac{1}{2}) = \log_{10} 1 - \log_{10} 2 = -.3010$

5. Let $x$ = number of quarters. For an investment $P$ to double,
   $$2P = P(1 + .03)^x$$
   $$2 = (1.03)^x$$

   $$x = \log_{1.03} 2 = \frac{\log_{10} 2}{\log_{10} 1.03} = \frac{.3010}{.0128} = 23.5 \text{ quarters}$$

   Time = 5.9 years

7. (b) $1 - e^{-.05(10)} = 1 - e^{-.5} \approx 1 - .6065 = .3935$ or $39.35\%$

8. $f(x + h) - f(x) = \log_a (x + h) - \log_a (x) = \log_a \left(\frac{x + h}{x}\right) = \log_a \left(1 + \frac{h}{x}\right)$

1. (a) $\dfrac{d}{dx} e^{x^2} = e^{x^2} \dfrac{d}{dx} x^2 = 2xe^{x^2}$

   (c) $\dfrac{d}{dx} e^{-x} = e^{-x} \dfrac{d}{dx} (-x) = -e^{-x}$

   (e) $\dfrac{d}{dx} \left(\dfrac{1}{3}\right)^x = \left(\ln \dfrac{1}{3}\right) \left(\dfrac{1}{3}\right)^x$     (g) $\dfrac{d}{dx} \log_3 x = \dfrac{1}{(\ln 3)x}$

2. (a) $f'(x) = x^3 e^x + 3x^2 e^x = x^2 e^x (x + 3)$
   $f'(0) = 0$
   Hence, $y = 0$ is the equation of the tangent line.

   (b) $f'(x) = x \cdot \dfrac{1}{x} + \ln x = \ln x + 1$

   $f'(1) = \ln 1 + 1 = 0 + 1 = 1$
   $y - f(1) = y - 0 = 1(x - 1)$     or     $y = x - 1$

(c)  $f'(x) = \dfrac{-e^x}{(1 + e^x)^2}$

$f'(0) = \dfrac{-1}{(1 + 1)^2} = -\tfrac{1}{4}$

$y - \tfrac{1}{2} = -\tfrac{1}{4}(x - 0)$   or   $y = -\tfrac{1}{4}x + \tfrac{1}{2}$

3. (a) $f'(x) = e^{x^4}\dfrac{d}{dx}(x^4) = 4x^3 e^{x^4}$

(b) $f'(x) = e^{x^{1/2}}\dfrac{d}{dx}(x^{1/2}) = \tfrac{1}{2}x^{-1/2}e^{x^{1/2}} = \dfrac{e^{\sqrt{x}}}{2\sqrt{x}}$

(d) $f'(x) = \dfrac{4x + 2}{2x^2 + 2x + 1}$

4. (a) $f'(x) = x^2 e^x + 2xe^x$

$f''(x) = x^2 e^x + 2xe^x + 2xe^x + 2e^x = x^2 e^x + 4xe^x + 2e^x$

$f'''(x) = x^2 e^x + 2xe^x + 4xe^x + 4e^x + 2e^x = x^2 e^x + 6xe^x + 6e^x$

(c) $f'(x) = ae^{ax};\ f''(x) = a^2 e^{ax};\ f'''(x) = a^3 e^{ax}$

(d) $f'(x) = x \cdot \dfrac{1}{x} + 1 \cdot \ln x = 1 + \ln x$     $f''(x) = \dfrac{1}{x};\ f'''(x) = -\dfrac{1}{x^2}$

5. $MC = C'(x) = \dfrac{1}{x + 1}$

6. $MR = R'(x) = .1$

For maximum profit, $MC = MR$, or

$\dfrac{1}{x + 1} = .1$

$x + 1 = 10$     $x = 9$ units

7. (d) $f'(x) = xe^x + e^x = e^x(x + 1)$

$f'(x) \neq 0$ on the interval $[0, 4]$; hence there are no critical values to be tested.

$f(0) = 0$, absolute minimum

$f(4) = 4e^4 \approx 218$, absolute maximum

8. (b) $f'(x) = \dfrac{1}{x} = 1 \cdot x^{-1};\ f''(x) = -1x^{-2};\ f'''(x) = (-1)(-2)x^{-3}$

$f^n(x) = \dfrac{(-1)^{n-1}(n - 1)!}{x^n}$

9. (a) $\ln y = \ln (x^2 + 1) + \ln (x + 2)^{1/2}$

$\dfrac{1}{y}\dfrac{dy}{dx} = \dfrac{2x}{x^2 + 1} + \dfrac{\tfrac{1}{2}(x + 2)^{-1/2}}{(x + 2)^{1/2}} = \dfrac{2x}{x^2 + 1} + \dfrac{1}{2(x + 2)}$

$\dfrac{dy}{dx} = 2x\sqrt{x + 2} + \tfrac{1}{2}(x^2 + 1)(x + 2)^{-1/2}$

1. (a) $y\text{-intercept} = \dfrac{5000}{1 + 5 \cdot e^0} = \dfrac{5000}{6} \approx 833.33$

$\lim\limits_{x \to -\infty} f(x) = \lim\limits_{x \to -\infty} \dfrac{5000}{1 + 5e^{-x}} = 0$

10.5
Exercise
(page 328)

$$\lim_{x\to+\infty} f(x) = \lim_{x\to+\infty} \frac{5000}{1+5e^{-x}} = \frac{5000}{1+5\cdot 0} = 5000$$

$$f'(x) = \frac{5000}{(1+5e^{-x})^2}\cdot 5e^{-x} = \frac{25{,}000e^{-x}}{(1+5e^{-x})^2}$$

Since $f'(x) > 0$, $f(x)$ is increasing for all $x$.

$$f''(x) = 25{,}000\frac{d}{dx}[e^{-x}(1+5e^{-x})^{-2}]$$

$$= 25{,}000[-e^{-x}(1+5e^{-x})^{-2} + 2e^{-x}\cdot 5e^{-x}(1+5e^{-x})^{-3}]$$

$$= 25{,}000e^{-x}\left(\frac{5e^{-x}-1}{(1+5e^{-x})^3}\right)$$

Inflection point at $5e^{-x} - 1 = 0$ since $f''(x) < 0$ for $e^{-x} < \frac{1}{5}$ and $f''(x) > 0$ for $e^{-x} > \frac{1}{5}$. For $e^{-x} = \frac{1}{5}$, we have $x \approx 1.61$. The inflection point is $(1.61, 2500)$.

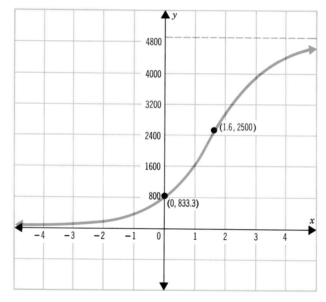

2. The rate of spreading of flu is

$$N'(t) = \frac{99{,}990{,}000e^{-t}}{(1+9999e^{-t})^2} \text{ which reaches a maximum when}$$

$$N''(t) = 99{,}990{,}000e^{-t}\left(\frac{9999e^{-t}-1}{(1+9999e^{-t})^3}\right) = 0, \text{ or}$$

$9999e^{-t} = 1$; $e^t = 9999$; $t \approx 9.21$ days

3. $f'(x)$ reaches a maximum for

$$ae^{-bx} = 1; \ e^{bx} = a; \ bx = \ln a; \ x = \frac{\ln a}{b}$$

Review Exercises
(page 329)

3. (a) $f'(x) = e^{x^3}\cdot 3x^2 = 3x^2 e^{x^3}$  (c) $f'(x) = \frac{d}{dx}\ln x^{-1} = \frac{-x^{-2}}{x^{-1}} = -\frac{1}{x}$

(e) $f'(x) = \frac{3x^2-3}{x^3-3x+4}$  (f) $f'(x) = e^{x+2}\cdot 1 = e^{x+2}$

1. (a) $F(x) = \dfrac{4x^6}{6} + K = \dfrac{2x^6}{3} + K$   (c) $F(x) = \dfrac{x^{3/2}}{\frac{3}{2}} + K = \dfrac{2}{3}x^{3/2} + K$

(e) $F(x) = \dfrac{x^{7/2}}{\frac{7}{2}} + K = \dfrac{2}{7}x^{7/2} + K$

(g) $F(x) = \dfrac{2x^{-1}}{-1} + K = -2x^{-1} + K$

2. (a) $F(x) = x^4 - x^3 + x + K$   (c) $F(x) = \dfrac{4x^{5/2}}{\frac{5}{2}} - x + K = \dfrac{8}{5}x^{5/2} - x + K$

(e) $F(x) = K$   (g) $F(x) = \dfrac{x^{29}}{29} + x + K$

3. $F(x) = \dfrac{2x^2}{2} - x + K = x^2 - x + K$

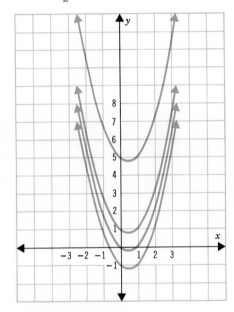

4. Since $MC = C'(x)$,

$C(x) = 1000x - \dfrac{20x^2}{2} + \dfrac{x^3}{3} + K$, where $K = C(0) = 9000$, the fixed cost.

Hence, $C(x) = 9000 + 1000x - 10x^2 + \frac{1}{3}x^3$.

5. (a) $R(x) = 3400x$
   (b) $P(x) = R(x) - C(x) = 2400x + 10x^2 - \frac{1}{3}x^3 - 9000$
   (c) $P'(x) = 2400 + 20x - x^2$
   $P'(x) = 0 \Rightarrow x^2 - 20x - 2400 = 0; \ x = 60$
   (d) $P(60) = \$99,000$

1. $\displaystyle\int 6\, dx = 6x + K$

3. $\displaystyle\int x^{-4}\, dx = \dfrac{x^{-3}}{-3} + K = -\frac{1}{3}x^{-3} + K$

5. $\int (4x^3 + 3x^2 - 4)\, dx = x^4 + x^3 - 4x + K$

7. $\int (3\sqrt{x} + x)\, dx = \dfrac{3x^{3/2}}{\frac{3}{2}} + \dfrac{x^2}{2} + K = 2x^{3/2} + \frac{1}{2}x^2 + K$

9. $\int (4x^{3/2} + x^{1/2})\, dx = \dfrac{4x^{5/2}}{\frac{5}{2}} + \dfrac{x^{3/2}}{\frac{3}{2}} + K = \frac{8}{5}x^{5/2} + \frac{2}{3}x^{3/2} + K$

11. $\int \dfrac{3x^5 + 1}{x^2}\, dx = \int (3x^3 + x^{-2})\, dx = \frac{3}{4}x^4 - x^{-1} + K$

13. $\int \dfrac{x^3 - 8}{x - 2}\, dx = \int (x^2 + 2x + 4)\, dx = \frac{1}{3}x^3 + x^2 + 4x + K$

16. $R(x) = \int (50x - x^2)\, dx = \frac{50}{2}x^2 - \frac{1}{3}x^3 + K$

Since $R(0) = 0$, $K = 0$, and $R(x) = 25x^2 - \frac{1}{3}x^3$
Maximum revenue occurs at
$R'(x) = 50x - x^2 = 0$; $50 - x = 0$; $x = 50$

18. $C(x) = \int (14x - 280)\, dx = \frac{14}{2}x^2 - 280x + K$

Since the fixed cost is 4300, $K = C(0) = 4300$
Hence $C(x) = 7x^2 - 280x + 4300$
The minimum cost occurs for $C'(x) = 14x - 280 = 0$; $x = 20$; $C(20) = 1500$

1. (a) $\int (3x - 1)^3\, dx = \frac{1}{3}\int (3x - 1)^3\, 3dx = \dfrac{1}{3}\dfrac{(3x - 1)^4}{4} + K$

$= \frac{1}{12}(3x - 1)^4 + K$

(c) $\int (x^2 + 2)^6\, 4x\, dx = 2\int (x^2 + 2)^6\, 2x\, dx = 2\dfrac{(x^2 + 2)^7}{7} + K$

$= \frac{2}{7}(x^2 + 2)^7 + K$

(e) $\int \dfrac{dx}{(3 + 5x)^2} = \frac{1}{5}\int (3 + 5x)^{-2}\, 5\, dx = -\frac{1}{5}(3 + 5x)^{-1} + K$

(g) $\int \dfrac{(x^{1/3} - 1)^6}{x^{2/3}}\, dx = 3\int (x^{1/3} - 1)^6\, \frac{1}{3}x^{-2/3}\, dx = \frac{3}{7}(x^{1/3} - 1)^7 + K$

(i) $\int \dfrac{(x + 1)\, dx}{(x^2 + 2x + 3)^{1/4}} = \frac{1}{2}\int (x^2 + 2x + 3)^{-1/4}(2x + 2)\, dx$

$= \dfrac{1}{2}\dfrac{(x^2 + 2x + 3)^{3/4}}{\frac{3}{4}} + K = \frac{2}{3}(x^2 + 2x + 3)^{3/4} + K$

2. $f(x) = \int \dfrac{dx}{(x + 1)^{1/2}} = \dfrac{(x + 1)^{1/2}}{\frac{1}{2}} + K = 2(x + 1)^{1/2} + K$

$f(0) = 2(0 + 1)^{1/2} + K = 1$; $2 + K = 1$; $K = -1$
$f(x) = 2(x + 1)^{1/2} - 1$

4. $C(x) = \int x\sqrt{3x^2 + 1}\, dx = \frac{1}{6}\int (3x^2 + 1)^{1/2}\, 6x\, dx$

$= \dfrac{1}{6}\dfrac{(3x^2 + 1)^{3/2}}{\frac{3}{2}} + K = \frac{1}{9}(3x^2 + 1)^{3/2} + K$

$C(0) = \frac{1}{9}(1)^{3/2} + K = 20$

$\frac{1}{9} + K = 20$

$K = \frac{179}{9}$

$C(x) = \frac{1}{9}(3x^2 + 1)^{3/2} + \frac{179}{9}$

1. $\int \frac{dx}{x + 1} = \ln|x + 1| + K$

11.5
Exercise
(page 346)

3. $\int \frac{x + 1}{x^2 + 2x + 2}\, dx = \frac{1}{2}\int \frac{2x + 2}{x^2 + 2x + 2}\, dx = \frac{1}{2}\ln|x^2 + 2x + 2| + K$

5. $\int e^{-x}\, dx = -\int e^{-x}(-dx) = -e^{-x} + K$

7. $\int \frac{e^x}{e^x + 1}\, dx = \ln|e^x + 1| + K$

8. $\int (e^x + e^{-x})\, dx = e^x - e^{-x} + K$

11. $\int \frac{e^{\sqrt{x}}}{\sqrt{x}}\, dx = 2\int e^{x^{1/2}} \cdot \frac{1}{2}x^{-1/2}\, dx = 2e^{\sqrt{x}} + K$

1. Let $\ u = x \qquad dv = e^{2x}\, dx$

$\qquad du = dx \qquad v = \frac{1}{2}e^{2x}$

11.6
Exercise
(page 349)

$\int xe^{2x}\, dx = x \cdot \frac{1}{2}e^{2x} - \int \frac{1}{2}e^{2x}\, dx = \frac{1}{2}xe^{2x} - \frac{1}{4}\int 2e^{2x}\, dx = \frac{1}{2}xe^{2x} - \frac{1}{4}e^{2x} + K$

3. Let $\ u = \ln x \quad dv = \ln x\, dx$

$\qquad du = \frac{dx}{x} \quad v = x(\ln x - 1)$

$\int (\ln x)^2\, dx = x\ln x\,(\ln x - 1) - \int x\,(\ln x - 1)\frac{1}{x}\, dx$

$\qquad = x\ln x\,(\ln x - 1) - \int (\ln x - 1)\, dx$

$\qquad = x\ln x\,(\ln x - 1) - \int \ln x\, dx + \int dx$

$\qquad = x\ln x\,(\ln x - 1) - x\,(\ln x - 1) + x + K$

$\qquad = x\,(\ln x)^2 - 2x\ln x + 2x + K$

5. Let $\ u = (\ln x)^2 \qquad dv = x\, dx$

$\qquad du = \frac{2\ln x}{x}\, dx \qquad v = \frac{x^2}{2}$

$\int x\,(\ln x)^2\, dx = \frac{x^2}{2}(\ln x)^2 - \int \frac{x^2}{2} \cdot \frac{2\ln x}{x}\, dx$

$\qquad = \frac{x^2}{2}(\ln x)^2 - \int x\ln x\, dx$

$\qquad = \frac{x^2}{2}(\ln x)^2 - \frac{x^2}{2}(\ln x - \frac{1}{2}) + K$ (from Example 6.2)

1. (a) $\int (x^{1/3} - \sqrt{x})\,dx = \int x^{1/3}\,dx - \int x^{1/2}\,dx = \frac{3}{4}x^{4/3} - \frac{2}{3}x^{3/2} + K$

(c) $\int (1 + x)^{-1/2}\,dx = \dfrac{(1 + x)^{1/2}}{\frac{1}{2}} + K = 2(1 + x)^{1/2} + K$

(e) $\int x\sqrt{x^2 - 1}\,dx = \frac{1}{2}\int (x^2 - 1)^{1/2}\,2x\,dx = \dfrac{1}{2}\dfrac{(x^2 - 1)^{3/2}}{\frac{3}{2}} + K = \frac{1}{3}(x^2 - 1)^{3/2} + K$

2. $F(x) = \int (4x + 1)\,dx = 2x^2 + x + K$

3. (a) $\int x^2(x - 1)\,dx = \int (x^3 - x^2)\,dx$

$\qquad = \frac{1}{4}x^4 - \frac{1}{3}x^3 + K$

(b) $\int \sqrt{3x - 2}\,dx = \dfrac{(3x - 2)^{3/2}}{3 \cdot \frac{3}{2}} + K = \frac{2}{9}(3x - 2)^{3/2} + K$

(c) $\int (x^4 + 1)^{-3/2}x^3\,dx = \frac{1}{4}\int (x^4 + 1)^{-3/2}4x^3\,dx = \dfrac{1}{4}\dfrac{(x^4 + 1)^{-1/2}}{-\frac{1}{2}} + K$

$\qquad = -\frac{1}{2}(x^4 + 1)^{-1/2} + K$

5. $R(x) = \int (64x - x^2)\,dx = 32x^2 - \dfrac{x^3}{3} + K$

Since $R(0) = 0$, $K$ must be zero; hence,

$R(x) = 32x^2 - \dfrac{x^3}{3}$

Maximum revenue occurs when
$R'(x) = 64x - x^2 = 0;\ x = 64$

6. (a) $\int \dfrac{dx}{3x + 2} = \frac{1}{3}\int \dfrac{3}{3x + 2}\,dx = \frac{1}{3}\ln |3x + 2| + K$

(d) $\int e^{-1/2x}\,dx = -2\int e^{-1/2x}(-\frac{1}{2}\,dx) = -2e^{-1/2x} + K$

(e) $\int \dfrac{x^{3/2}\,dx}{x^{5/2} + 2} = \frac{2}{5}\int \dfrac{\frac{5}{2}x^{3/2}}{x^{5/2} + 2}\,dx = \frac{2}{5}\ln |x^{5/2} + 2| + K.$

1. (a) $\displaystyle\int_0^3 x^2\,dx = \dfrac{x^3}{3}\bigg|_0^3 = \frac{27}{3} - 0 = 9$

(c) $\displaystyle\int_1^3 4t^3\,dt = t^4\bigg|_1^3 = 81 - 1 = 80$

(e) $\displaystyle\int_{-1}^3 (x^3 - 2)\,dx = \left(\dfrac{x^4}{4} - 2x\right)\bigg|_{-1}^3 = (\frac{81}{4} - 6) - (\frac{1}{4} + 2) = 12$

(g) $\displaystyle\int_2^3 (2x^2 - x + 1)\,dx = (\frac{2}{3}x^3 - \frac{1}{2}x^2 + x)\bigg|_2^3 = (18 - \frac{9}{2} + 3) - (\frac{16}{3} - 2 + 2) = \frac{67}{6}$

2. (a) $\displaystyle\int_0^1 e^{-x}\,dx = -e^{-x}\bigg|_0^1 = -e^{-1} + e^0 = -\dfrac{1}{e} + 1 = -.3679 + 1 = .6321$

(d) $\displaystyle\int_0^1 x^2 e^{x^3}\,dx = \frac{1}{3}\int_0^1 e^{x^3}\,3x^2\,dx = \frac{1}{3}(e^{x^3})\bigg|_0^1 = \frac{1}{3}(e - 1) = \frac{1}{3}(1.7183) = .5728$

(f) $\int_2^3 \dfrac{dx}{x \ln x} = \int_2^3 \dfrac{\frac{1}{x} dx}{\ln x} = \ln (\ln x) \Big|_2^3 = \ln (\ln 3) - \ln (\ln 2)$

3. (a) $\int_1^3 xe^{2x} dx = (\frac{1}{2}xe^{2x} - \frac{1}{4}e^{2x}) \Big|_1^3 = e^{2x}(\frac{1}{2}x - \frac{1}{4}) \Big|_1^3 = e^6(\frac{3}{2} - \frac{1}{4}) - e^2(\frac{1}{2} - \frac{1}{4})$

$$= \tfrac{5}{4}(403.4) - \tfrac{1}{4}(7.389) = 504.25 - 1.847 = 502.4$$

(c) $\int_1^5 \ln x \, dx = x (\ln x - 1) \Big|_1^5 = 5 (\ln 5 - 1) - 1 (\ln 1 - 1) = 5 \ln 5 - 4$

(e) Integrate by parts, letting $u = \ln x, \quad dv = x^2 \, dx$

$$du = \frac{1}{x} dx, \quad v = \frac{x^3}{3}$$

$$\int x^2 \ln x \, dx = \frac{x^3}{3} \ln x - \int \frac{x^2}{3} dx = \frac{x^3}{3} \ln x - \frac{x^3}{9} + K$$

Then $\int_1^3 x^2 \ln x \, dx = \dfrac{x^3}{3} (\ln x - \tfrac{1}{3}) \Big|_1^3 = 9(\ln 3 - \tfrac{1}{3}) - \tfrac{1}{3}(0 - \tfrac{1}{3})$

$$= 9 \ln 3 - \frac{26}{9}$$

1. $\int_2^6 (3x + 2) \, dx = (\tfrac{3}{2}x^2 + 2x) \Big|_2^6 = (54 + 12) - (6 + 4) = 56.$

12.3
Exercise
(page 368)

3. $\int_1^4 \dfrac{1}{x^2} dx = -x^{-1} \Big|_1^4 = -\tfrac{1}{4} - (-1) = \tfrac{3}{4}.$

5. $\int_0^1 xe^{-x} dx = (-xe^{-x} - e^{-x}) \Big|_0^1 = (-e^{-1} - e^{-1}) - (-1) = -2e^{-1} + 1$

$$= -.7358 + 1 = .2642$$

7. $\int_0^2 e^{3x} dx = \tfrac{1}{3} \int_0^2 e^{3x}3 \, dx = \tfrac{1}{3}e^{3x} \Big|_0^2 = \tfrac{1}{3}(e^6 - 1) = \tfrac{1}{3}(403.4 - 1) = 134.14$

8. Points of intersection: $4 - x^2 = x + 2$
$$x^2 + x - 2 = (x + 2)(x - 1) = 0$$
Thus the curves intersect at $(-2, 0)$ and $(1, 3)$.
For $-2 \leq x \leq 1, f(x) \geq g(x) \geq 0.$

$A = \int_{-2}^1 (f(x) - g(x)) \, dx$

$= \int_{-2}^1 [4 - x^2 - (x + 2)] \, dx$

$= \int_{-2}^1 (-x^2 - x + 2) \, dx$

$= \left(-\dfrac{x^3}{3} - \dfrac{x^2}{2} + 2x\right) \Big|_{-2}^1$

$= \tfrac{7}{6} - (-\tfrac{10}{3}) = 4.5$

10. Points of intersection:
$$2 + x - x^2 = -x - 1$$
$$x^2 - 2x - 3 = (x + 1)(x - 3) = 0$$
$$x = -1 \quad \text{or} \quad x = 3$$
Thus the curves intersect at $(-1, 0)$ and $(3, -4)$.

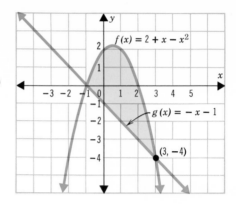

For $-1 \leqq x \leqq 2$, $f(x) \geqq 0$ and $g(x) \leqq 0$

Hence, the area from $x = -1$ to $x = 2$ will be $\int_{-1}^{2} (f(x) - g(x))\, dx$.

For $2 \leqq x \leqq 3$, $g(x) \leqq f(x) \leqq 0$
Hence, the area from $x = 2$ to $x = 3$ will be

$$\int_{2}^{3} (-g(x))\, dx - \int_{2}^{3} (-f(x))\, dx = \int_{2}^{3} (f(x) - g(x))\, dx.$$

Thus the total area $A = \int_{-1}^{2} (f(x) - g(x))\, dx + \int_{2}^{3} (f(x) - g(x))\, dx$

$$= \int_{-1}^{3} (f(x) - g(x))\, dx = \int_{-1}^{3} (2 + x - x^2 - (-x - 1))\, dx$$

$$= \int_{-1}^{3} (-x^2 + 2x + 3)\, dx = \left( -\frac{x^3}{3} + x^2 + 3x \right) \Big|_{-1}^{3}$$

$$= (-9 + 9 + 9) - (\tfrac{1}{3} + 1 - 3) = 10\tfrac{2}{3}$$

11. For $1 \leqq x \leqq 2$,

$$\text{Area} = \int_{1}^{2} (f(x) - h(x))\, dx$$

For $2 \leqq x \leqq 5$,

$$\text{Area} = \int_{2}^{5} (f(x) - g(x))\, dx$$

Thus,

$$A = \int_{1}^{2} (f(x) - h(x))\, dx + \int_{2}^{5} (f(x) - g(x))\, dx$$

$$= \int_{1}^{2} (\tfrac{9}{2}x - \tfrac{9}{2})\, dx + \int_{2}^{5} (-\tfrac{3}{2}x + \tfrac{15}{2})\, dx$$

$$= \tfrac{9}{2} \int_{1}^{2} (x - 1)\, dx + \tfrac{3}{2} \int_{2}^{5} (-x + 5)\, dx$$

$$= \frac{9}{2} \left( \frac{x^2}{2} - x \right) \Big|_{1}^{2} + \frac{3}{2} \left( -\frac{x^2}{2} + 5x \right) \Big|_{2}^{5}$$

$$= \tfrac{9}{2}(0 - (-\tfrac{1}{2})) + \tfrac{3}{2}(\tfrac{25}{2} - 8)$$

$$= \tfrac{9}{4} + \tfrac{27}{4} = 9$$

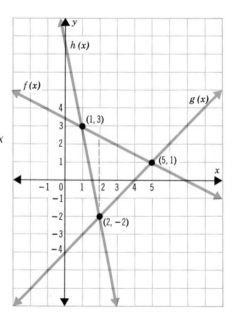

12. $S = \int_0^5 (1340 - 850e^{-x}) \, dx = (1340x + 850e^{-x}) \Big|_0^5 = 1340 \cdot 5 + 850e^{-5} - 850$

$= 5850 + 850(.0067) = 5855.7$

14. (a) $c^2(1 - 0) = \int_0^1 x^2 \, dx$

$c^2 = \dfrac{x^3}{3} \Big|_0^1 = \tfrac{1}{3}$    or    $c = \dfrac{\sqrt{3}}{3} \approx .577$

1. $\int_{35}^{60} 1000x^{-0.5} \, dx = 2000x^{1/2} \Big|_{35}^{60} = 2000(7.746 - 5.916) = 3660$ hours    12.4.1<br>Exercise<br>(page 371)

3. The direct labor required approaches a constant value irrespective of the number of units produced.

1. $20 - 5x = 4x + 8;\ 9x = 12;\ x^* = \tfrac{4}{3}$    12.4.2<br>Exercise<br>(page 374)

$p^* = D(x^*) = D(\tfrac{4}{3}) = \tfrac{40}{3}$

$CS = \int_0^{4/3} (20 - 5x) \, dx - \tfrac{40}{3} \cdot \tfrac{4}{3} = (20x - \tfrac{5}{2}x^2) \Big|_0^{4/3} - \tfrac{160}{9} = \tfrac{200}{9} = \tfrac{160}{9} = \tfrac{40}{9} = \$4.44$

$PS = \tfrac{40}{3} \cdot \tfrac{4}{3} - \int_0^{4/3} (4x + 8) \, dx = \tfrac{160}{9} - (2x^2 + 8x) \Big|_0^{4/3} = \tfrac{160}{9} - \tfrac{128}{9} = \tfrac{32}{9} = \$3.56$

1.    $R'(t) = C'(t)$    12.4.3<br>Exercise<br>(page 377)

$19 - t^{1/2} = 3 + 3t^{1/2}$

$4t^{1/2} = 16$

$t^{1/2} = 4$

$t^* = 16$

The operation should continue for 16 years.

$P(t^*) = \int_0^{16} (R'(t) - C'(t) \, dt = \int_0^{16} [(19 - t^{1/2}) - (3 + 3t^{1/2})] \, dt$

$= \int_0^{16} (16 - 4t^{1/2}) \, dt = \left(16t - \dfrac{4t^{3/2}}{\frac{3}{2}}\right) \Big|_0^{16} = 256 - \tfrac{512}{3} \approx 85.33$ (millions of dollars)

1. (a) $A = \int_3^6 (2x - 5) \, dx = (x^2 - 5x) \Big|_3^6 = 6 - (-6) = 12$    Review Exercises<br>(page 377)

(c) $A = -\int_2^{5/2} f(x) \, dx + \int_{5/2}^4 f(x) \, dx$

$= -(x^2 - 5x) \Big|_2^{5/2} + (x^2 - 5x) \Big|_{5/2}^4 = \tfrac{1}{4} + 2\tfrac{1}{4} = 2\tfrac{1}{2}$

2. Points of intersection $x^3 = x^2$

$x^3 - x^2 = x^2(x - 1) = 0$

Thus the curves intersect at $(0,0)$ and $(1,1)$.

For $0 \leqq x \leqq 1$, $f(x) \geqq g(x) \geqq 0$

$$A = \int_0^1 (x^2 - x^3)\,dx = \left(\frac{x^3}{3} - \frac{x^4}{4}\right)\bigg|_0^1 = \tfrac{1}{3} - \tfrac{1}{4} = \tfrac{1}{12}$$

5. Since $f(x) \geqq 0$ for $x \geqq 0$,

$$A = \int_0^1 xe^{3x^2}\,dx = \tfrac{1}{6}\int_0^1 e^{3x^2} 6x\,dx = \tfrac{1}{6}(e^{3x^2})\bigg|_0^1 = \tfrac{1}{6}(20.086 - 1) = \tfrac{1}{6}(19.086) = 3.181$$

7. Points of intersection: $x^2 = \sqrt{x}$

$$x^4 = x$$
$$x(x^3 - 1) = 0$$
$$x = 0 \quad \text{or} \quad x = 1$$

Thus the curves intersect at $(0,0)$ and $(1,1)$.

For $0 \leqq x \leqq 1$, $g(x) \geqq f(x) \geqq 0$.

$$A = \int_0^1 (x^{1/2} - x^2)\,dx = \left(\tfrac{2}{3}x^{3/2} - \frac{x^3}{3}\right)\bigg|_0^1 = \tfrac{2}{3} - \tfrac{1}{3} = \tfrac{1}{3}$$

CHAPTER 13      1. none of these
3. $\sim$

13.2      6. none of these
Exercise      9. $\sim, =, \subseteq$
(page 384)      12. For a set with $n$ elements, there are $2^n$ subsets.
(a) $\{a, b, c, d\}$, $\{a, b, c\}$, $\{a, c, d\}$, $\{a, b, d\}$, $\{b, c, d\}$, $\{a, b\}$ $\{a, c\}$, $\{a, d\}$, $\{b, c\}$, $\{b, d\}$ $\{c, d\}$, $\{a\}$, $\{b\}$, $\{c\}$, $\{d\}$, $\varnothing$
13. $C \subseteq A, C \subseteq B, A \neq B$

13.3      1. (a) $A$      (c) $U$      (d) $A$
Exercise      2. (c) $\overline{A \cap B} = \{5\}$
(page 389)      3. (f) $\overline{A \cup B} = \overline{\{1, 2, 3, 5\}} = \{4\}$
4. (a) $A \cap E = \{x \mid x$ is a customer of IBM and is a member of the Board of Directors of IBM$\}$
(c) $B \cap D = \{x \mid x$ is a secretary employed by IBM and is a stock-holder of IBM$\}$

5. (a) 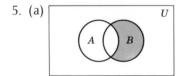      (e)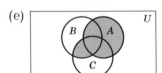

(c) 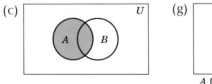      (g)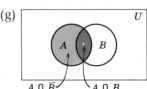

$A \cap \overline{B}$      $A \cap B$

6. (a)

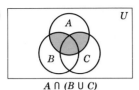

$A \cap (B \cup C)$

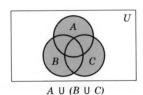

$(A \cap B) \cup (A \cap C)$

(e)

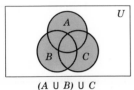

$(A \cup B) \cup C$

$A \cup (B \cup C)$

7. (c) $(A \cup B) \cap C = \{3, 5\}$    (g) $(A \cap B) \cap C = \{3\}$
8. (a) $\bar{A} \cup \bar{B} = U = \{1, 2, 3, 4, 5, 7\}$    (c) $\bar{A} \cap \bar{B} = \emptyset$
   (e) $\overline{U \cap B} = \bar{B} = \{1, 3, 5, 7\}$    (g) $\overline{C \cap A} = \{2, 4, 5, 7\}$
9. (a) $A = B$    (b) $A \subseteq B$
10. (a) $A = \{1, 3, 5, 6\}$
    (b) If $B = \{2\}$, then $A = \{1, 3, 4, 5\}$.
       If $B = \{1, 2\}$, then $A = \{3, 4, 5\}$.
       If $B = \{2, 3\}$, then $A = \{1, 4, 5\}$.
       If $B = \{1, 2, 3\}$, then $A = \{4, 5\}$.

1. (a) $c(D) = 10$          4. $c(A \cap B) = 0$          13.4
2. (c) $c(A \cap B) = 0$    6. $c(B) = 24$              Exercise
3. (a) $c[A \cup (B \cap C)] = 4$    8. 452              (page 392)
   (d) $c[(A \cap B) \cup C] = 2$    9. (a) 536

1. 8 different bloods    2. (i) 42    (iv) 2    5. 68    13.5
                            (ii) 9    (v) 44              Exercise
                            (iii) 5   (vi) 31             (page 395)

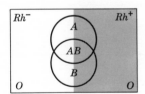

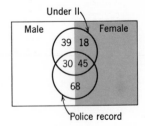

1. (a) $P(6, 4) = 6 \cdot 5 \cdot 4 \cdot 3 = 360$    2. (a) $x = 5$    (b) $x = 2$    13.6
   (e) $P(8, 7) = 8 \cdot 7 \cdot 6 \cdot 5 \cdot 4 \cdot 3 \cdot 2$    5. $(3)(2)(4) = 24$    Exercise
              $= 40{,}320$                                 6. $(3)(6) = 18$    (page 404)
   (f) $P(6, 6) = 6! = 720$

7. $\dfrac{8!}{2!2!} = \dfrac{8 \cdot 7 \cdot 6 \cdot 5 \cdot 4 \cdot 3 \cdot 2}{2 \cdot 2} = 10{,}080$

8. $4^{10} \cdot 2^{15} = 2^{35}$

11. $(12)(3) = 36$

13.7
Exercise
(page 409)

1. (a) $C(6, 4) = 15$    (b) $C(7, 2) = 21$    (d) $C(5, 4) = 5$

2. (a) $x = 5$    (b) $x = 3$ or $x = 4$

7. $C(6, 2) = 15$

8. $\dbinom{2}{1}\dbinom{3}{2}\dbinom{7}{2} = 2 \cdot 3 \cdot 21 = 126$    10. $\dbinom{1352}{641}\dbinom{711}{234}\dbinom{477}{477}$

9. $\dbinom{3}{1}\dbinom{2}{1}\dbinom{5}{2} = 3 \cdot 2 \cdot 10 = 60$    11. $C(17, 4) = 2380$

12. $\dbinom{52}{13}$    13. $\dfrac{100!}{22!13!10!5!16!17!17!}$    14. $\dbinom{10}{3}\dbinom{7}{3}\dbinom{4}{4}$

Review Exercises
(page 412)
Part A

2. c, d    4. g    8. c, d
10. e    12. b
14. g    16. b

Part B

3. $A = \{1, 2, 3\}, A = \{1, 2\}, A = \{1, 3\}, A = \{1\}$

6. (a) 165
(b) 40

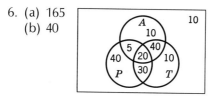

8. (a) $P(4, 2) = 4 \cdot 3 = 12$
(b) $C(4, 2) = 6$

10. $\dbinom{16}{4}\dbinom{10}{3}$

13. (a) $(31)(31) = 961$
(b) $P(31, 2) = (31)(30) = 930$
(c) $C(31, 2) = (31)(15) = 465$

14. (a) $P(6, 3) = 6 \cdot 5 \cdot 4 = 120$

(b) $C(6, 3) = \dfrac{120}{6} = 20$

15. Let $A, B, C, D, E$ be the five people and let $X = AB$ be the ones that can't stand each other. There are 5! ways of arranging $A$, $B$, $C$, $D$, $E$ and 4! ways to rearrange $X$, $C$, $D$, $E$. But $A$ and $B$ are next to each other in $2 \cdot 4!$ ways since neither $X = AB$ nor $X = BA$ are desirable. Thus, in all, the number of ways is

$$5! - 2 \cdot 4! = 3 \cdot 4! = 72$$

16. One path from $A$ to $B$ is $R\,R\,R\,R\,R\,R\,U\,U\,U\,U\,U\,U$. All paths from $A$ to $B$ are exactly 12 moves of which exactly 6 are to the right ($R$). Thus, in all, there are $\binom{12}{6}$ paths from $A$ to $B$.

1. By the Fundamental Principle of Counting, the number of ways is $5 \cdot 6 \cdot 8 = 240$.
2. The number of names is $\quad 100 + 100 \cdot 99 + 100 \cdot 99 \cdot 98$
3. Consider the number of ways of obtaining the team consisting of 1 boy and 3 girls. The boy can be chosen in $C(3, 1) = 3$ ways and the three girls in $C(5, 3) = 10$ ways. By the Fundamental Principle of Counting, such a team can be made in $3 \cdot 10 = 30$ ways.
4. There are 5! ways of ordering the speakers. $A$ will precede $B$ the same number of times that $B$ precedes $A$ so 1/2 of the arrangements must be eliminated. Therefore we have $\dfrac{5!}{2} = \dfrac{5 \cdot 4 \cdot 3 \cdot 2 \cdot 1}{2} = 60$ ways of ordering the speakers.
5. If $AB = X$ then we have $X$, $C$, $D$, $E$ to order. We have $4! = 4 \cdot 3 \cdot 2 \cdot 1 = 24$ ways to order the speakers.
6. There are $26 \cdot 10^4$ licenses with one letter and $26^2 \cdot 10^4$ licenses with two letters. Thus, there are at most $26 \cdot 10^4 + 26^2 \cdot 10^4$ different licenses.

## CHAPTER 14

1. (a) $S = \{TTTTT,\ TTTTH,\ TTTHT,\ TTTHH,\ TTHTT,\ TTHTH,\ TTHHT,$
$TTHHH,\ THTTT,\ THTTH,\ THTHT,\ THTHH,\ THHTT,\ THHTH,$
$THHHT,\ THHHH,\ HTTTT,\ HTTTH,\ HTTHT,\ HTTHH,\ HTHTT,$
$HTHTH,\ HTHHT,\ HTHHH,\ HHTTT,\ HHTTH,\ HHTHT,$
$HHTHH,\ HHHTT,\ HHHTH,\ HHHHT,\ HHHHH\},\ 32$

   (b) $S = \{H,\ TH,\ TTH,\ TTTH, \ldots\}$, infinite
   (c) $S$ is the same as in problem 1a.
   (e) $S = \{(1, 1),\ (1, 2),\ (1, 3),\ (1, 4),\ (1, 5),\ (2, 1),\ (2, 2),\ (2, 3),\ (2, 4),$
$(2, 5), (3, 1), (3, 2), (3, 3), (3, 4), (3, 5), (4, 1), (4, 2), (4, 3), (4, 4),$
$(4, 5),\ (5, 1),\ (5, 2),\ (5, 3),\ (5, 4),\ (5, 5)\},\ 25$

2. (a) $\binom{52}{5} = 2{,}598{,}960$ \qquad (b) $\binom{11}{5} = 462$

3. The model is the sample space $S$ and the probability assignment.
   (1a) One assignment is $P(\text{each simple event}) = 1/32$.
   Another assignment is $P(HHHHH) = 1$; $P(\text{other simple events}) = 0$.
   Other assignments are possible.
4. $S = \{[(H), (Gabcd)], [(Ha), (Gbcd)], [(Hb), (Gacd)], [(Hc), (Gabd)],$
$[(Hd), (Gabc)], [(Hab), (Gcd)], [(Hac), (Gbd)], [(Had), (Gbc)],$
$[(Hbc), (Gad)], [(Hbd), (Gac)], [(Hcd), (Gab)], [(Habc), (Gd)],$
$[(Habd), (Gc)], [(Hacd), (Gb)], [(Hbcd), (Ga)], [(Habcd), (G)]\}$
   Free competition:
   $\{[(Hab), (Gcd)], [(Hac), (Gbd)], [(Had), (Gbc)], [(Hbc), (Gad)],$
$[(Hbd), (Gac)],\ [(Hcd), (Gab)]\}$

5. (b)

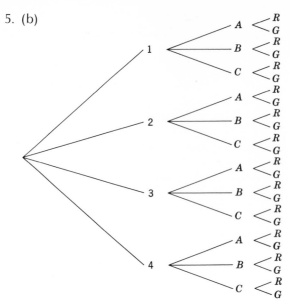

$4 \cdot 3 \cdot 2 = 24$ outcomes

6. (c) $\bar{A} \cap \bar{B}$

  (e) $(A \cap \bar{B}) \cup (\bar{A} \cap B)$

  (h) $(A \cap \bar{B}) \cup (\bar{A} \cap B)$

8. (b) $P(F) = \dfrac{1}{4} + \dfrac{1}{4} = \dfrac{1}{2}$ for the first assignment

$P(F) = \dfrac{1}{6} + \dfrac{1}{4} = \dfrac{5}{12}$ for the second assignment

9. (a) The number on the red die is three times the number on the green die $\{(3,1),(6,2)\}$.

  (c) The number on the red die is smaller or the same as the number on the green die.

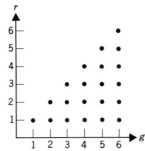

11. (a) Let
$$x = P(\{e_1\}).$$
Since
$$P(\{e_1\}) + \cdots + P(\{e_7\}) = 1$$
$$x + x + 1/2x + 1/4x + 1/4x + x + 1/2x = 1$$
$$9/2x = 1 \qquad x = 2/9$$
$P(\{e_1\}) = 2/9 \qquad P(\{e_2\}) = 2/9 \qquad P(\{e_3\}) = 1/9 \qquad P(\{e_4\}) = 1/18$
$P(\{e_5\}) = 1/18 \qquad P(\{e_6\}) = 2/9 \qquad P(\{e_7\}) = 1/9$

1. $E = \{4\}$, $F = \{2,4,6\}$, $E \cap F = \{4\}$
   $E$ and $F$ are not mutually exclusive since $E \cap F \neq \emptyset$.
3. (a) Sum of the probabilities exceeds one.
   (c) $P(A \cup B) \neq P(A) + P(B)$
4. Approximately 1 for Senators; exactly 1 for Representatives.
5. For a group of two people;
   $1 - (12)(11)/12^2 = 1/12 = .083$
   For a group of four people:
   $1 - (12)(11)(10)(9)/12^4 = 1 - (990)/1728 = (738)/1728 = .427$
8. $.8 = .4 + .6 - P(E \cap M)$
   $P(E \cap M) = .2$
10. 1 to 5, 1 to 17, 2 to 7
11. $P(A \cup B) = 1/6 + 1/4 = 5/12$; 5 to 7
15. (a) $P(A \cup B) = .85$
    (b) $P(\overline{A \cup B}) = .15$
18. $P(A \cup B \cup C) = P(A \cup B) + P(C) - P[(A \cup B) \cap C]$
    $\qquad = P(A) + P(B) - P(A \cap B) + P(C) - P[(A \cup B) \cap C]$
    $\qquad = P(A) + P(B) + P(C) - P(A \cap B) - P[(A \cap C) \cup (B \cap C)]$
    $\qquad = P(A) + P(B) + P(C) - P(A \cap B) - P(A \cap C)$
    $\qquad\quad - P(B \cap C) + P[(A \cap C) \cap (B \cap C)]$
    $\qquad = P(A) + P(B) + P(C) - P(A \cap B) - P(A \cap C)$
    $\qquad\quad - P(B \cap C) + P(A \cap B \cap C)$

14.3
Exercise
(page 438)

1. $1/18, 1/12, 1/18$    3. $1/4, 1/2$    5. $2/9$    6. $.433$
7. $A \cap B = \{(1,2), (1,4), (1,6), (2,1), (4,1), (6,1)\}$
   $P(A \cap B) = 1/6$
   $A \cup B = \{(1,1), (1,2), (1,3), (1,4), (1,5), (1,6), (2,1), (3,1), (4,1),$
   $\qquad\qquad (5,1), (6,1), (2,3), (2,5), (3,2), (5,2), (3,4), (3,6), (4,3),$
   $\qquad\qquad (6,3), (4,5), (5,4), (5,6), (6,5)\}$
   $P(A \cup B) = 23/26$
   $A \cap \overline{B} = \{(2,3), (2,5), (3,2), (5,2), (3,4), (3,6), (4,3), (6,3), (4,5),$
   $\qquad\qquad (5,4), (5,6), (6,5)\}$
   $P(A \cap \overline{B}) = 1/3$
8. (a) $.00000283$
9.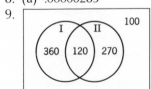
   (a) $.36$    (c) $.10$
   (b) $.27$    (d) $.15$

10. $\dfrac{\binom{13}{5}\binom{13}{4}\binom{13}{3}\binom{13}{1}}{\binom{52}{13}}$

11. (a) $\dfrac{4}{\binom{52}{5}} = .0000015$    (b) $\dfrac{32}{\binom{52}{5}} = .0000123$

14.4
Exercise
(page 444)

(c) $\dfrac{13 \cdot 12 \cdot 4}{\binom{52}{5}} = .0024$  (d) $\dfrac{\binom{4}{3} \cdot 13 \cdot \binom{4}{2} \cdot 12}{\binom{52}{2}} = .0014$

(e) $.0020 + .0039 + .0014 + .00024 + .0000123 + .0000015 = .0076$

12. $\dfrac{P(8,5)}{8^5} = \dfrac{\frac{8!}{3!}}{8^5} = \dfrac{8 \cdot 7 \cdot 6 \cdot 5 \cdot 4}{8^5} = \dfrac{840}{8^4} = \dfrac{840}{4096} = .205$

1. $P(E|F) = .5$
2. $P(F) = .5$
3. (a) The probability that the person is an executive, given that he or she earns over \$25,000 per year.
4. (b) $P(F|I) = 5/9$  (d) $P(D|M) = 5/11$  (f) $P(I|M) = 2/11$
7. $R = \{\text{Republicans}\}, D = \{\text{Democrats}\}$
   $V = \{\text{People who voted Democratic}\}$
   $P(R) = 3/4, P(D) = 1/4, P(V) = 5/9$
   $P(V) = P(V \cap R) + P(V \cap D)$
   $5/9 = P(V \cap R) + 1/4$
   $P(V \cap R) = 5/9 - 1/4 = 11/36$

   $P(R|V) = \dfrac{P(R \cap V)}{P(V)} = \dfrac{\frac{11}{36}}{\frac{5}{9}} = \dfrac{11}{20} = .55$

8. $2/11$
9. $P(\{0 \text{ children}\}) = .25$   $P(\{5 + \text{children}\}) = .08$
   $P(\{1 \text{ child}\}) = .25$   $G = \{\text{at least one child}\}$
   $P(\{2 \text{ children}\}) = .18$   $P(G) = 1 - .25 = .75$
   $P(\{3 \text{ children}\}) = .16$   $H = \{\text{more than 2 children}\}$
   $P(\{4 \text{ children}\}) = .08$   $P(H) = .16 + .08 + .08 = .32$

   $P(H|G) = \dfrac{P(H \cap G)}{P(G)} = \dfrac{P(H)}{P(G)} = \dfrac{32}{75}$

11. $M = \{\text{men}\}, W = \{\text{women}\}, U = \{\text{under 160 lbs.}\}$
    Assume 200 people

    $P(W|U) = \dfrac{P(W \cap U)}{P(U)} = \dfrac{70/200}{105/200}$

    $= 70/105 = 2/3$

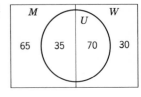

12. $M = \{\text{couples where man votes}\}$ $W = \{\text{couples where woman votes}\}$
    $P(M) = .5$   $P(W) = .6$   $P(W|M) = .9$
    (a) $P(M \cap W) = P(M) \cdot P(W|M) = (.5)(.9) = .45$

    (b) $P(M|M \cup W) = \dfrac{P(M \cap (M \cup W))}{P(M \cup W)} = \dfrac{P(M)}{P(M) + P(W) - P(M \cap W)}$

    $= \dfrac{.50}{.50 + .60 - .45} = \dfrac{.50}{.65} = \dfrac{10}{13} = .77$

13. $A = \{\text{students with an } A \text{ average}\}$ $P(A) = .24$
$R = \{\text{students who attended private schools}\}$ $P(R) = .40$
$U = \{\text{students who attended public schools}\}$ $P(U) = .60$
$P(A|R) = .30$

$$P(R|A) = \frac{P(R \cap A)}{P(A)} = \frac{P(A|R) \cdot P(R)}{P(A)} = \frac{(.4)(.3)}{.24} = \frac{1}{2}$$

Venn diagram solution: Assume 100 people

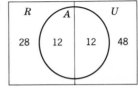

$$P(R|A) = \frac{P(R \cap A)}{P(A)} = \frac{.12}{.24} = \frac{1}{2}$$

14.6
Exercise
(page 455)

3. $S = \{RRR, RRL, RLR, LRR, RLL, LRL, RLL, LLL\}$
$E = \{RRL, LRR\}$ $\quad$ $F = \{LLL\}$
$E \cap F = \emptyset, P(E \cap F) = 0$
$P(E) = 1/4, P(F) = 1/8, P(E) \cdot P(F) = 1/32$
$P(E \cap F) \neq P(E) \cdot P(F)$
$E$ and $F$ are not independent.

5. $S = \{BB, BG, GB, GG\}$
$E = \{BG, GB, GG\}$ $\quad$ $P(E) = 3/4$
$F = \{BG, GB)$ $\quad$ $P(F) = 1/2$
$E \cap F = \{BG, GB\}$ $\quad$ $P(E \cap F) = 1/2$

$$P(E) \cdot P(F) = \frac{3}{4} \cdot \frac{1}{2} = \frac{3}{8} \neq \frac{1}{2} = P(E \cap F)$$

$E$ and $F$ are not independent.

8. $P(A \cap B) = P(\{2\}) = 1/4$ $\qquad$ $P(B \cap C) = P(\{3\}) = 1/4$

$$P(A) \cdot P(B) = \frac{1}{2} \cdot \frac{1}{2} = \frac{1}{4} \qquad P(B) \cdot P(C) = \frac{1}{2} \cdot \frac{1}{2} = \frac{1}{4}$$

$P(A \cap B) = P(A) \cdot P(B)$ $\qquad$ $P(B \cap C) = P(B) \cdot P(C)$
$P(A \cap C) = P(\{1\}) = 1/4$

$$P(A) \cdot P(C) = \frac{1}{2} \cdot \frac{1}{2} = \frac{1}{4}$$

$P(A \cap C) = P(A) \cdot P(C)$

10. $P(E) = .70$ $\qquad$ $P(F) = .60$
$P(\bar{E}) = .30$ $\qquad$ $P(\bar{F}) = .40$
(a) $P(E \cap F) = .52$ $\qquad$ $P(E) \cdot P(F) = (.70) \cdot (.60) = .42$
$E$ and $F$ are not independent.

12. $P(E) \cdot P(F) = P(E \cap F)$
$P(\bar{E}) = 1 - P(E)$ $\qquad$ $P(\bar{F}) = 1 - P(F)$
$P(\bar{E}) \cdot P(\bar{F}) = (1 - P(E)) \cdot (1 - P(F)) = 1 - P(E) - P(F) + P(E) \cdot P(F)$
$\qquad = 1 - [P(E) + P(F) - P(E \cap F)] = 1 - P(E \cup F)$
$\qquad = P(\overline{E \cup F}) = P(\bar{E} \cap \bar{F})$ by De-Morgan's Law

14. $P(E) = 1/6, P(F) = 1/6, P(G) = 1/6$
$P(E \cap F) = 1/36, P(E \cap G) = 1/36$
$P(F \cap G) = 1/36$

$$P(E) \cdot P(F) = \frac{1}{6} \cdot \frac{1}{6} = \frac{1}{36} = P(E \cap F)$$

$$P(E) \cdot P(G) = \frac{1}{6} \cdot \frac{1}{6} = \frac{1}{36} = P(E \cap G)$$

$$P(F) \cdot P(G) = \frac{1}{6} \cdot \frac{1}{6} = \frac{1}{36} = P(F \cap G)$$

$$P(E \cap F \cap G) = 0$$

$$P(E) \cdot P(F) \cdot P(G) = \frac{1}{6} \cdot \frac{1}{6} \cdot \frac{1}{6} = \frac{1}{216}$$

$P(E \cap F \cap G) \neq P(E) \cdot P(F) \cdot P(G)$ therefore $E$, $F$, and $G$ are not independent.

15. (a) $E$: at least one ace

F: no ace

$P(E) = 1 - P(F) = 1 - .4823 = .5177$

(b) $G$: at least one pair of aces

H: no pairs of aces

$P(G) = 1 - P(H) = 1 - .509 = .491$

16. $\dfrac{9}{10} \cdot \dfrac{8}{9} \cdot \dfrac{7}{8} \cdot \dfrac{6}{7} \cdot \dfrac{1}{6} = \dfrac{1}{10}$

14.7
Exercise
(page 465)

2. $E$: item is defective      $A_2$: item is from machine II

$A_1$: item is from machine I      $A_3$: item is from machine III

$$P(A_1|E) = \frac{(0.2)(.4)}{(.02)(.4) + (.04)(.5) + (.01)(.1)} = \frac{8}{29}$$

$$P(A_2|E) = \frac{(.04)(.5)}{.029} = \frac{20}{29} \qquad P(A_3|E) = \frac{(.01)(.1)}{.029} = \frac{1}{29}$$

4. $P(A_2|E) = 0 \qquad P(A_3|E) = .065$

5. $P(A_1|E) = \dfrac{(.05)(.98)}{(.05)(.98) + (.95)(.15)} = \dfrac{.049}{.049 + .1425} = .256$

6. $P(U_I|E) = \dfrac{P(E|U_I)}{P(E|U_1) + P(E|U_2) + P(E|U_3)}$

$$= \frac{5/14}{5/14 + 1/4 + 7/16} = \frac{.357}{.357 + .25 + .437} = .342$$

$P(U_{II}|E) = \dfrac{P(E|U_{II})}{1.044} = \dfrac{.25}{1.044} = .239 \qquad P(U_{III}|E) = \dfrac{P(E|U_{III})}{1.044} = \dfrac{.437}{1.044} = .419$

7. $A$: a person has tuberculosis

B: test is positive

$$P(A|B) = \frac{P(B|A)P(A)}{P(B|A) \cdot P(A) + P(B|\bar{A}) \cdot P(\bar{A})}$$

$$= \frac{(.90)(.11)}{(.90)(.11) + (.3)(.89)} = .27$$

8. $P(I) = .67 \qquad P(D|I) = .02 \qquad$ (a priori)

$P(II) = .33 \qquad P(D|II) = .01$

$$P(I|D) = \frac{(.02)(.67)}{(.02)(.67) + (.33)(.01)} = .80 \qquad \text{(a posteriori)}$$

10. $R$ = soil is rock; $C$ = soil is clay; $S$ = soil is sand
    $A$ = test is positive
    $P(R) = .53 \qquad P(A|R) = .35$
    $P(C) = .21 \qquad P(A|C) = .48$
    $P(S) = .26 \qquad P(A|S) = .75$

$$P(R|A) = \frac{(.53)(.35)}{(.53)(.35) + (.21)(.48) + (.26)(.75)} = .39$$

$$P(C|A) = \frac{.1008}{.4813} = .21 \qquad P(S|A) = \frac{.1950}{.4813} = .41$$

11. $P(A_j|E) = \dfrac{P(A_j \cap E)}{P(E)} = \dfrac{P(A_j \cap E)}{P(A_1 \cap E) + P(A_2 \cap E) + \cdots + P(A_n \cap E)}$

$$= \frac{P(A_j)P(E|A_j)}{P(A_1) \cdot P(E|A_1) + P(A_2)P(E|A_2) + \cdots + P(A_n) \cdot P(E|A_n)}$$

14.8
Exercise
(page 471)

1. (a) .0250     (d) .0811     (f) .0005
2. (a) .0165     (c) .2326

3. $b\left(5, 2; \dfrac{1}{6}\right) = \dbinom{5}{2}\left(\dfrac{1}{6}\right)^2\left(\dfrac{5}{6}\right)^3 = \dfrac{5!}{2!3!} \cdot \dfrac{1}{36} \cdot \dfrac{125}{216} = .16$

4. (a)

(b) $\left(\dfrac{3}{4} \cdot \dfrac{3}{4} \cdot \dfrac{1}{4} \cdot \dfrac{1}{4}\right) \cdot 6 = \dfrac{6 \cdot 9}{256} = \dfrac{27}{128} = .2109$

(c) $b\left(4, 2; \dfrac{1}{4}\right) = .2109$

6. (a) $b\left(6, 2; \dfrac{1}{2}\right) = .2344$

(b) $E$: exactly two heads are obtained
$F$: at least one head is obtained
$G$: no heads are obtained

$$P(E \mid F) = \frac{P(E \cap F)}{P(F)} = \frac{P(E)}{1 - P(G)} = \frac{\dfrac{15}{64}}{1 - \dfrac{1}{64}} = \frac{\dfrac{15}{64}}{\dfrac{63}{64}} = \frac{15}{63} = .24$$

8. $b(4, 2; .25) + b(4, 3; .25) + b(4, 4; .25) = .2109 + .0469 + .0039 = .2617$
$1 - b(4, 0; .25) = 1 - .3164 = .6836$

10. $b(7, 4; .35) + b(7, 5; .35) + b(7, 6; .35) + b(7, 7; .35) = .1998$

11. (a) $b\left(6, 5; \dfrac{1}{2}\right) + b\left(6, 6; \dfrac{1}{2}\right) = .0938 + .0156 = .1094$

12. $1 - b\left(n, 0; \dfrac{1}{2}\right) \geqq .98 \qquad b\left(n, 0; \dfrac{1}{2}\right) \leqq .02$

$n$ must be 6 or more

13. The probability that any month will have a birthday is $6/12 = 1/2$.

$b\left(10, 2; \dfrac{1}{2}\right) = .0439$

14. $1 - \left[b\left(500, 0; \dfrac{1}{500}\right) + b\left(500, 1; \dfrac{1}{500}\right) + b\left(500, 2; \dfrac{1}{500}\right)\right]$

The indicated solution above is sufficient.
For the interested student, the answer is 0.08.

15. Investigate the binomial for $n = 5, 6, 7$, $x = 1, 2, 3$, and $p = 1/3$.
When $n = 5$ there is a dual maximum for 1 or 2 successes.
When $n = 6$ there is a singular maximum at 2 successes.
When $n = 7$ there is a singular maximum at 2 successes. We are looking for the smallest $n$ that has a singular maximum at 2 successes.
Thus $n = 6$.

**Review Exercises
(page 473)**

1. $S = \{BB, GB, BG, GG\}$

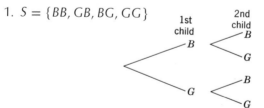

2. (a) $S = \{HHH, HHT, HTH, HTT, THH, THT, TTH, TTT\}$
Let $E$ be a simple event in $S$, $P(E) = 1/8$.
(b) (i) 1/2, (ii) 1/2, (iii) 3/4, (iv) 7/8, (v) 1/2, (vi) 1/8

4. There are 16 different paths he might take each with probability 1/16.
Four paths lead to station $G$. The probability of ending at $G$ is
$4 \cdot 1/16 = 4/16 = 1/4$.

5. (a) No.
(b) $(0, 0, 0)$ has the highest probability; $(1, 1, 1)$ has the lowest probability.

(c) $F = \{(0, 1, 2), (0, 2, 1), (1, 2, 0), (1, 0, 2), (2, 0, 1), (2, 1, 0)\}$
Each simple event in $F$ has probability $12/512$.

$$P(F) = 6\frac{12}{512} = \frac{72}{512} = \frac{9}{64}$$

8.

| Envelope | Possible arrangements of letters | | | | | |
|----------|---|---|---|---|---|---|
| $E_1$ | 1 | 1 | 2 | 2 | 3 | 3 |
| $E_2$ | 2 | 3 | 1 | 3 | 1 | 2 |
| $E_3$ | 3 | 2 | 3 | 1 | 2 | 1 |

Four out of the six possible ways of mailing the letters are such that
at least one letter gets to the correct person; therefore the probability
is $4/6 = 2/3$.

12. $\{HH, HT, TH, TT\}$
$P\{HH\} = 1/16, P\{HT\} = 3/16, P\{TH\} = 3/16$
$P\{TT\} = 9/16$
$E = \{HH, HT\}$ $\quad P(E) = 1/4$
$F = \{HT, TT\}$ $\quad P(F) = 3/4$
$E \cap F = \{HT\}$ $\quad P(E \cap F) = 3/16$

$$P(E) \cdot P(F) = \frac{1}{4} \cdot \frac{3}{4} = 3/16$$

$P(E \cap F) = P(E) \cdot P(F)$ $\quad$ $E$ and $F$ are independent.

16. $C$: have cancer $\quad$ $D$: test detects cancer
$P(C) = .018$ $\quad P(\bar{C}) = .982$ $\quad P(D|C) = .85$ $\quad P(D|\bar{C}) = .08$

$$P(C|D) = \frac{P(D|C) \cdot P(C)}{P(D|C) \cdot P(C) + P(D|\bar{C}) \cdot P(\bar{C})} = \frac{(.85)(.018)}{(.85) \cdot (.018) + (.08) \cdot (.982)}$$

$$= \frac{.0153}{.09386} = .163$$

19. $1 - b\left(5, 0; \frac{1}{20}\right) = 1 - \binom{5}{0}\left(\frac{1}{20}\right)^0\left(\frac{19}{20}\right)^5 = 1 - \left(\frac{19}{20}\right)^5 = 1 - .774 = .226$

CHAPTER 15

15.1
Exercise
(page 482)

1. (a) $E = 1.2$
2. $E = 1 \cdot 1/6 + 2 \cdot 1/6 + 3 \cdot 1/6 + 4 \cdot 1/6 + 5 \cdot 1/6 + 6 \cdot 1/6 = 21/6$
$\quad = \$3.50$
5. $E = 44{,}560$
6. $E = 2.058$
10. $E_1 = 15{,}000 \cdot 2/3 - 3000 \cdot 1/3 = 10{,}000 - 1000 = 9000$
$\quad E_2 = 20{,}000 \cdot 1/3 - 6000 \cdot 2/3 = 6667 - 2000 = 4667$
$\quad$ Location 1
11. $E = 30 \cdot 1/2 = 15$ right answers; Score is 0.
14. $S = \{H, TH, TTH, TTTH, TTTT\}$
$\quad P(\{H\}) = 1/4$
$\quad P(\{TH\}) = 3/4 \cdot 1/4 = 3/16$
$\quad P(\{TTH\}) = 3/4 \cdot 3/4 \cdot 1/4 = 9/64$
$\quad P(\{TTTH\}) = 3/4 \cdot 3/4 \cdot 3/4 \cdot 1/4 = 27/256$
$\quad P(\{TTTT\}) = 3/4 \cdot 3/4 \cdot 3/4 \cdot 3/4 = 81/256$
$\quad E = 1 \cdot 1/4 + 2 \cdot 3/16 + 3 \cdot 9/64 + 4 \cdot 27/256$
$\quad\quad + 4 \cdot 81/256$
$\quad\quad = 175/64 = 2.73$ tosses

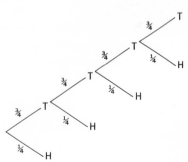

15. $E = 1 \cdot \dfrac{\binom{3}{1} \cdot \binom{9}{4}}{\binom{12}{5}} + 2 \cdot \dfrac{\binom{3}{2} \cdot \binom{9}{3}}{\binom{12}{5}} + 3 \cdot \dfrac{\binom{3}{3} \cdot \binom{9}{2}}{\binom{12}{5}} = 1.25$

16. $E_1 = m_1 p_1 + m_2 p_2 + \cdots + m_n p_n.$
Multiplying each value by $c$ we get:
$E_2 = cm_1 p_1 + cm_2 p_2 + \cdots + cm_n p_n = c[m_1 p_1 + m_2 p_2 + \cdots + m_n p_n] = c \cdot E_1$
Thus we can see that the expected value of the new experiment, $E_2$, is $c$ times the original expected value $E_1$.
Add to each outcome used in figuring $E_1$ the constant $k$. The new expected value is:
$E_3 = (m_1 + k)p_1 + (m_2 + k)p_2 + \cdots + (m_n + k)p_n$
$= m_1 p_1 + kp_1 + m_2 p_2 + kp_2 + \cdots + m_n p_n + kp_n$
$= m_1 p_1 + m_2 p_2 + \cdots + m_n p_n + kp_1 + kp_2 + \cdots + kp_n$
$= E_1 + k(p_1 + p_2 + \cdots + p_n)$
Since $p_1 + p_2 + \cdots + p_n = 1$ we get $E_3 = E_1 + k$
Thus we see that the expected value of the new experiment, $E_3$, is the expected value of the original experiment, $E_1$, plus $k$.

15.2
Exercise
(page 488)

2.

| Group Size | Expected Tests Saved Per Component | Percent Saving |
|---|---|---|
| 2 | $p^2 - \frac{1}{2} = .64 - .5 = .14$ | 14 |
| 3 | $p^3 - \frac{1}{3} = .512 - .333 = .179$ | 17.9 |
| 4 | $p^4 - \frac{1}{4} = .409 - .25 = .159$ | 15.9 |
| 5 | $p^5 - \frac{1}{5} = .327 - .20 = .127$ | 12.7 |
| 6 | $p^6 - \frac{1}{6} = .262 - .166 = .096$ | 9.6 |

15.3.1
Exercise
(page 492)

1. Let positive numbers denote Tami's winnings and negative numbers denote Laura's winnings.

Laura

  I     II

Tami $\begin{matrix} I \\ II \end{matrix} \begin{pmatrix} -10 & 10 \\ 10 & -10 \end{pmatrix}$    entries are in cents.

4. (a) strictly determined, value is $-1$

(b) strictly determined, value is 2

(c) not strictly determined
(d) not strictly determined

(e) not strictly determined

(f) strictly determined, value is 0

(g) strictly determined, value is 0

(h) not strictly determined
(i) strictly determined, value is 2

15.3.2
Exercise
(page 496)

1. $P = (.3 \quad .7) \qquad Q = \begin{pmatrix} .4 \\ .6 \end{pmatrix}$

$E = (.3 \quad .7) \begin{pmatrix} 6 & 0 \\ -2 & 3 \end{pmatrix} \begin{pmatrix} .4 \\ .6 \end{pmatrix} = (.4 \quad 2.1) \begin{pmatrix} .4 \\ .6 \end{pmatrix} = .16 + 1.26 = 1.42$

2. (a) $E = (1/2 \quad 1/2)\begin{pmatrix} 4 & 0 \\ 2 & 3 \end{pmatrix}\begin{pmatrix} 1/2 \\ 1/2 \end{pmatrix} = (3 \quad 3/2)\begin{pmatrix} 1/2 \\ 1/2 \end{pmatrix} = 3/2 + 3/4 = 9/4$

3. (a) $E = (2/3 \quad 1/3)\begin{pmatrix} 4 & 0 \\ -3 & 6 \end{pmatrix}\begin{pmatrix} 1/3 \\ 2/3 \end{pmatrix} = (5/3 \quad 2)\begin{pmatrix} 1/3 \\ 2/3 \end{pmatrix} = 5/9 + 4/3 = 17/9$

1. (a) $\begin{pmatrix} 1 & 2 \\ 4 & 1 \end{pmatrix} p_1 = \dfrac{1-4}{1+1-2-4} = -3/-4 = 3/4; \; p_2 = 1/4$

15.3.3
Exercise
(page 502)

$\quad\quad q_1 = \dfrac{1-2}{1+1-2-4} = -1/-4 = 1/4; \; q_2 = 3/4$

$\quad\quad V = (3/4 \quad 1/14)\begin{pmatrix} 1 & 2 \\ 4 & 1 \end{pmatrix}\begin{pmatrix} 1/4 \\ 3/4 \end{pmatrix} = (7/4 \quad 7/4)\begin{pmatrix} 1/4 \\ 3/4 \end{pmatrix} = 28/16$

(c) $\begin{pmatrix} 2 & -1 \\ -1 & 4 \end{pmatrix} p_1 = \dfrac{4-(-1)}{2+4+1+1} = 5/8; \; p_2 = 3/8$

$\quad\quad q_1 = \dfrac{4+1}{8} = 5/8; \; q_2 = 3/8$

$\quad\quad V = (5/8 \quad 3/8)\begin{pmatrix} 2 & -1 \\ -1 & 4 \end{pmatrix}\begin{pmatrix} 5/8 \\ 3/8 \end{pmatrix} = (7/8 \quad 7/8)\begin{pmatrix} 5/8 \\ 3/8 \end{pmatrix} = 7/8$

2. $\begin{pmatrix} 4 & -1 \\ 0 & 3 \end{pmatrix} p_1 = \dfrac{3-0}{4+3+1} = 3/8; \; p_2 = \dfrac{4+1}{8} = 5/8$

$\quad\quad q_1 = \dfrac{3+1}{8} = 1/2; \; q_2 = \dfrac{4}{8} = 1/2$

$\quad\quad V = (3/8 \quad 5/8)\begin{pmatrix} 4 & -1 \\ 0 & 3 \end{pmatrix}\begin{pmatrix} 1/2 \\ 1/2 \end{pmatrix} = (3/2 \quad 3/2)\begin{pmatrix} 1/2 \\ 1/2 \end{pmatrix} = 1.5$

The game favors the Democrats.

1. (a) $\begin{pmatrix} 8 & 3 & 8 \\ 6 & 5 & 4 \\ -2 & 4 & 1 \end{pmatrix}$ row three is dominated by row two, the reduced matrix is:

15.3.4
Exercise
(page 513)

$\begin{pmatrix} 8 & 3 & 8 \\ 6 & 5 & 4 \end{pmatrix}$ column 1 is dominated by column two, the reduced matrix is:

$\begin{pmatrix} 3 & 8 \\ 5 & 4 \end{pmatrix} p_1 = \dfrac{4-5}{3+4-8-5} = -1/-6 = 1/6; \; p_2 = 5/6$

$\quad\quad q_1 = \dfrac{4-8}{-6} = -4/-6 = 2/3; \; q_2 = 1/3$

$\quad\quad V = (1/6 \quad 5/6)\begin{pmatrix} 3 & 8 \\ 5 & 4 \end{pmatrix}\begin{pmatrix} 2/3 \\ 1/3 \end{pmatrix} = (14/3 \quad 14/3)\begin{pmatrix} 2/3 \\ 1/3 \end{pmatrix} = 14/3$

(b) $\begin{pmatrix} 2 & 1 & 0 & 6 \\ 3 & -2 & 1 & 2 \end{pmatrix}$ column three dominates columns one and four; the reduced matrix is:

$\begin{pmatrix} 1 & 0 \\ -2 & 1 \end{pmatrix} p_1 = \dfrac{1+2}{1+1+2} = 3/4; \; p_2 = 1/4 \quad\quad q_1 = 1/4; \; q_2 = 3/4$

$\quad\quad V = (3/4 \quad 1/4)\begin{pmatrix} 1 & 0 \\ -2 & 1 \end{pmatrix}\begin{pmatrix} 1/4 \\ 3/4 \end{pmatrix} = (1/4 \quad 1/4)\begin{pmatrix} 1/4 \\ 3/4 \end{pmatrix} = 1/4$

(c) $\begin{pmatrix} 6 & -4 & 2 & -3 \\ -4 & 6 & -5 & 7 \end{pmatrix}$   Column three dominates column one
Column two dominates column four; the
reduced matrix is:

$\begin{pmatrix} -4 & 2 \\ 6 & -5 \end{pmatrix} p_1 = \dfrac{-5-6}{-4-5-2-6} = 11/17; p_2 = 6/17$

$q_1 = \dfrac{-5-2}{-17} = \dfrac{7}{17}; q_2 = 10/17$

$V = (11/7 \quad 6/17) \begin{pmatrix} -4 & 2 \\ 6 & -5 \end{pmatrix} \begin{pmatrix} 7/17 \\ 10/17 \end{pmatrix}$

$\quad = (-8/17 \quad -8/17) \begin{pmatrix} 7/17 \\ 10/17 \end{pmatrix}$

$\quad = -136/289$

(d) $\begin{pmatrix} 4 & -5 & 5 \\ -6 & 3 & 3 \\ 2 & -6 & 3 \end{pmatrix}$   row one dominates row three, the reduced
matrix is:

$\begin{pmatrix} 4 & -5 & 5 \\ -6 & 3 & 3 \end{pmatrix}$   column two dominates column three, the reduced matrix is:

$\begin{pmatrix} 4 & -5 \\ -6 & 3 \end{pmatrix} p_1 = \dfrac{3+6}{4+3+5+6} = 9/18 = 1/2; p_2 = 1/2$

$q_1 = \dfrac{3+5}{18} = 8/18 = 4/9; q_2 = 5/9$

$V = (1/2 \quad 1/2) \begin{pmatrix} 4 & -5 \\ -6 & 3 \end{pmatrix} \begin{pmatrix} 4/9 \\ 5/9 \end{pmatrix} = (-1 \quad -1) \begin{pmatrix} 4/9 \\ 5/9 \end{pmatrix} = -1$

Review Exercises
(page 515)

1. $E = 1/6 \cdot (.80) + 1/3(.30) + 1/2(.10) = \$.28$
The game is not fair to the player.
3. (a) strictly determined, value is 3.
(b) strictly determined, value is 15.
(c) strictly determined, value is 50.

4. (a) $V = (1/3 \quad 2/3) \begin{pmatrix} -1 & 1 \\ 1 & -1 \end{pmatrix} \begin{pmatrix} 1 \\ 0 \end{pmatrix} = (1/3 \quad -1/3) \begin{pmatrix} 1 \\ 0 \end{pmatrix} = 1/3$

(b) $V = (0 \quad 1) \begin{pmatrix} -1 & 1 \\ 1 & -1 \end{pmatrix} \begin{pmatrix} 1/2 \\ 1/2 \end{pmatrix} = (1 \quad -1) \begin{pmatrix} 1/2 \\ 1/2 \end{pmatrix} = 0$

7. (a) $\begin{pmatrix} 4 & 6 & 3 \\ 1 & 2 & 5 \end{pmatrix}$   Column one dominates column two, the reduced
matrix is:

$\begin{pmatrix} 4 & 3 \\ 1 & 5 \end{pmatrix} p_1 = \dfrac{5-1}{4+5-3-1} = 4/5; p_2 = 1/5$

$q_1 = \dfrac{5-3}{5} = 2/5; q_2 = 3/5$

$V = (4/5 \quad 1/5) \begin{pmatrix} 4 & 3 \\ 1 & 5 \end{pmatrix} \begin{pmatrix} 2/5 \\ 3/5 \end{pmatrix} = (17/5 \quad 17/5) \begin{pmatrix} 2/5 \\ 3/5 \end{pmatrix} = 17/5$

## CHAPTER 16

1.

| x = Number of Heads Obtained in Two Flips | Probability |
|---|---|
| 0 | 1/4 |
| 1 | 1/2 |
| 2 | 1/4 |

4.

| x = Number Right Minus Number Wrong | Probability |
|---|---|
| 3 | 1/8 |
| 1 | 3/8 |
| −1 | 3/8 |
| −3 | 1/8 |

5. Discrete and infinite.
7. Continuous.

1. (a) $P(X \leq 5) = f(0) + f(1) + f(2) + f(3) + f(4) + f(5)$
$$= e^{-6} + 6e^{-6} + 18e^{-6} + 36e^{-6} + 54e^{-6} + 64.8e^{-6}$$
$$= 179.8e^{-6} = .4495$$

(d) $P(1 < X < 4) = f(2) + f(3) = 54e^{-6} = .1350$

3. $n = 5000$
$p = \frac{8}{100,000}$
$np = \frac{8}{20} = .40$
Let $X$ denote a Poisson random variable.
$P(X > 3) = 1 - P(X \leq 3) = 1 - [f(0) + f(1) + f(2) + f(3)] = .001$

5. (a) $P(X < 5) = f(0) + f(1) + f(2) + f(3) + f(4)$
$$= e^{-7} + 7e^{-7} + \tfrac{49}{2}e^{-7} + 57.2e^{-7} + 100e^{-7} = 189.7e^{-7} = .171$$

1. (a) $\int_0^3 \frac{4}{3} \frac{dx}{(x+1)^2} = \frac{4}{3}\left(\frac{-1}{x+1}\right)\Big|_0^3 = \frac{4}{3}\left(\frac{-1}{4} + 1\right) = 1$
and $f(x) \geq 0$ on $[0, 3]$.

2. (a) $\int_0^5 kf(x)\,dx = 1 \qquad k\int_0^5 (10x - x^2)\,dx = 1$

$k\left(5x^2 - \frac{x^3}{3}\right)\Big|_0^5 = 1 \qquad k(125 - \tfrac{125}{3}) = 1 \qquad k(125)(\tfrac{2}{3}) = 1 \qquad k = \tfrac{3}{250}$

3. $P(T \geq .6) = 1 - P(T < 6) = 1 - \int_0^6 .5e^{-.5t}\,dt$

$$= 1 + e^{-.5t}\Big|_0^6 = 1 + (e^{-3} - 1) = e^{-3} = .050$$

5. $P(T < 5) = \int_0^5 .4e^{-.4t}\,dt = \frac{.4e^{-.4t}}{-.4}\Big|_0^5 = 1 - e^{-2} = .865$

6. $0 \leq t \leq 50;\ P(T \geq 30) = \int_{30}^{50} \tfrac{1}{50}\,dt = \tfrac{1}{50}t\Big|_{30}^{50} = .4$

16.6.1
Exercise
(page 542)

3. $Z = \dfrac{7 - 13.1}{9.3} = -.6559$ $\qquad$ $Z = \dfrac{29 - 13.1}{9.3} = 1.7097$

4. (a) $.89 \rightarrow .3133$ $\qquad$ (d) $3.00 \rightarrow .4987$ $\qquad$ (f) $-2.31 \rightarrow .4896$

5. $A \rightarrow 5.48\%$ $\qquad$ $B \rightarrow 21.95\%$ $\qquad$ $C \rightarrow 34.36\%$ $\qquad$ $D \rightarrow 30.13\%$ $\qquad$ $F \rightarrow 8.08\%$

6. (a) $\dfrac{142 - 130}{5.2} = 2.31$ $\qquad$ $.5000 - .4896 = .0104 = 1.04\%$

$\quad$ (b) $124.59 - 135.41$

10. $C: Z = \dfrac{76 - 82}{7} = -.86$ $\qquad$ $M: Z = \dfrac{89 - 93}{2} = -2$ $\qquad$ $K: Z = \dfrac{21 - 24}{9} = -.33$

$\qquad$ Kathleen has the highest relative standing.

16.6.2
Exercise
(page 546)

1. $m = 2.0$; $\sigma = .011$

$$Z = \frac{1.98 - 2.0}{.011} = \frac{-.02}{.011} = -1.818$$

$$Z = \frac{2.02 - 2.0}{.011} = \frac{.02}{.011} = 1.818$$

$P(-1.82 < Z < 1.82) = 2(.4656) = .9312$

3. $m = 176$; $\sigma = 22$

$$Z = \frac{150 - 176}{22} = \frac{-26}{22} = -1.182$$

$$Z = \frac{250 - 176}{22} = \frac{74}{22} = 3.36$$

$P(-1.182 < Z < 3.36) = .3810 + .5 = .8810$

8. $m = 24$; $\sigma = 2$; $Z = \dfrac{x - 24}{2} = 1.04$

$x = 24 + 2.08 = 26.08$ inches

Review Exercises
(page 547)

1. (a) Discrete and finite $\qquad$ (b) Discrete and finite

4. $\displaystyle\int_{20}^{100} \frac{3}{688,000}(-x^2 + 200x - 5000)\, dx$

$$= \frac{3}{688,000}\left(\frac{-x^3}{3} + 100x^2 - 5000x\right)\Bigg|_{20}^{100}$$

$$= \frac{3}{688,000}\left[\frac{-100(10,000)}{3} + 100(10,000) - 5000(100)\right.$$

$$\left. + \frac{20(400)}{3} - 100(400) + 5000(20)\right]$$

$$= \frac{3}{688,000}\left[\frac{10,000(100)2}{3} - 5000(80) - 400\left(\frac{280}{3}\right)\right]$$

$$= \frac{3}{688}\left[\frac{20(100)}{3} - 400 - \frac{4(28)}{3}\right] = \frac{3}{688}\left[\frac{1}{3}\right][2000 - 1200 - 112]$$

$$= \frac{800 - 112}{688} = \frac{688}{688} = 1$$

6. $Z = \dfrac{-14 + 10.33}{1.25} = -2.94$

About .16% will die before 10 years, 4 months.

1. (a) $I = Prt = (\$420)(.06)\left(\dfrac{1}{4}\right) = \$6.30; \ A = P + I = \$426.30.$

   (d) $I = (\$400)(.05)(10) = \$200; \ A = \$600.$

2. (a) $A = P + PI = P(1 + rt); \ P = \dfrac{A}{(1 + rt)}$

   (c) $P = \dfrac{\$183.68}{(1 + .1867)} = \$154.78$

3. (b) (1) $A = P(1 + r)^n = (\$3250)(1 + .03)^5$
   $= (3250)(1.159274) = \$3,767.64$
   $I = A - P = 3,767.64 - 3,250 = \$517.64$
   (2) $A = P(1 + r)^n = (\$3250)(1 + .015)^{10}$
   $= (3250)(1.160541) = \$3,771.76$
   $I = A - P = 3,771.76 - 3250 = \$521.76$

4. (1) Use a principal of $100.00 or $1000.00.
   $A = (\$100)(1 + .03)^2 = \$106.09$ effective rate is 6.09%

5. (d) (1) $P = A_n(1 + r)^{-n} = (300)(1 + .045)^{-3}$
   $= (300)(.876297) = \$262.89$
   (2) $P = A^n(1 + r)^{-n} = (300)(1 + .015)^{-9}$
   $= (300)(.874592) = \$262.38$

7. $A = P + I$
   $I = Prt$

   $50 = 500\left(\dfrac{20}{12}\right)r$

   $12 = 200r \quad$ or $\quad r = \dfrac{12}{200} = 6\%$

9. $2P = P(1 + r)^{10}$
   $2 = (1 + r)^{10}$
   $\sqrt[10]{2} = 1 + r$
   $1.071773 = 1 + r; \ .071773 = r$
   $.143546 = 2r$
   rate of interest $= 14.35\%$

12. (a) $2P = P(1 + .03)^n$
   $2 = (1.03)^n$

   $n = \log_{1.03} 2 = \dfrac{\log_{10} 2}{\log_{10} 1.03} = \dfrac{.3010}{.0128} = 23.51$ quarterly periods $= 5.87$ years

1. (a) $A = P \cdot s_{\overline{n}|r} = 1500 \cdot s_{\overline{15}|.06} = (1500)(23.275970) = 34,913.96$
   $V = P \cdot a_{\overline{n}|r} = 1500a_{\overline{15}|.06} = (1500)(9.712249) = 14,568.37$

2. (c) $V = P \cdot a_{\overline{n}|r}; \ P = V\left(\dfrac{1}{a_{\overline{n}|r}}\right) = \dfrac{6000}{a_{\overline{10}|.05}} = (6000)(.129505) = 777.03$

3. $A = P \cdot s_{\overline{n}|r} = 10s_{\overline{60}|.005} = (10)(69.770034) = 697.70.$
5. $V = P \cdot a_{\overline{n}|r} = 200a_{\overline{76}|.015} = (200)(45.164138) = 9032.83$

**17.3**
**Exercise**
**(page 565)**

1. $P = A\left(\dfrac{1}{a_{\overline{n}|r}}\right) = 10,000\left(\dfrac{1}{a_{\overline{40}|.02}}\right) = (10,000)(.036556)$

3. (a) Equity after 4 years $= 25,000 - [(402.23)(a_{\overline{36}|.0075})]$
$= 25,000 - [(402.23)(31.446804)] = 25,000 - 12,648.85 = 12,351.15.$
(b) Equity after 6 years $= 25,000 - [(402.23)(a_{\overline{12}|.0075})]$
$= 25,000 - [(402.23)(11.434912)] = 25,000 - 4599.46 = 20,400.54.$

6. $P = (30,000)\left(\dfrac{1}{a_{\overline{40}|.02}}\right) = (30,000)(.036556) = 1,096.68$ over 10 years

$P = (30,000)\left(\dfrac{1}{a_{\overline{80}|.02}}\right) = (30,000)(.02561) = 754.83$ over 20 years.

8. $P = (5,000,000)\left(\dfrac{1}{s_{\overline{20}|.05}}\right) = (5,000,000)(.030243) = 151,215.00$

**Review Exercises**
**(page 566)**

3. $A = P(1 + r)^n = 100(1.02)^9 = 100(1.195093) = \$119.51$
6. $2P = P(1 + r)^{10}$
$2 = (1 + r)^{10}$
$\sqrt[10]{2} - 1 = r$ or $.071773 = r$ or $r = 7.18\%$
7. (a) $I = Prt = (3000)(3)(.18) = \$1620.00$
(b) $A = P(1 + r)^n = (3000)(1.04)^{12} = (3000)(1.601032) = \$4803.09;$
$4803.09 - 3000 = 1803.09 = I$
The simple interest loan costs least.
9. $P = A(1 + r)^{-n} = 75(1 + .005)^{-6} = 75(.970518)$
11. $P = A\left(\dfrac{1}{s_{\overline{n}|r}}\right) = 500\left(\dfrac{1}{s_{\overline{24}|.015}}\right) = 500(.034924) = 17.46$
14. $V = Pa_{\overline{n}|r} = 50 \cdot a_{18.01} = 50(16.398268) = 819.91$
15. $P = V\left(\dfrac{1}{a_{\overline{n}|r}}\right) = 25,000\left(\dfrac{1}{a_{\overline{5}|.08}}\right) = (25,000)(.250456) = 6261.40$

20. $.1x + x\left(\dfrac{1}{s_{\overline{15}|.07}}\right) = 25,000$

$.1x + x(.039795) = 25,000$
$x(.139795) = 25,000$
$x = 178,833.29$

**APPENDIX**

**A.1**
**Exercise**
**(page 571)**

1. $3^3 = 27.$    3. $2^{-3} = \dfrac{1}{2^3} = \dfrac{1}{8}$    5. $(\frac{1}{2})^3 = \frac{1}{8}.$

7. $(343)^{1/3} = 7$   since $7^3 = 343.$
9. $(-243)^{1/5} = -3$   since $(-3)^5 = -243$    11. $2^{-1} + 4^{-1} = \frac{1}{2} + \frac{1}{4} = \frac{3}{4}$

13. $(3^{-2})(3^4) = 3^{-2+4} = 3^2 = 9$    15. $\dfrac{(2^{-2})(2^4)}{2^5} = 2^{-2+4-5} = 2^{-3} = \frac{1}{8}$

17. $(\sqrt{2})(\sqrt[4]{32}) = 2^{1/2} \cdot 2^{5/4} = 2^{1/2+5/4} = 2^{7/4}$

19. $\sqrt{81/16} = \frac{9}{4}$     21. $\frac{2^3 x^2}{x^5} = 8x^{2-5} = 8x^{-3} = \frac{8}{x^3}$

23. $\frac{(2x)^3}{(3x)^2} = \frac{2^3 x^3}{3^2 x^2} = \frac{8}{9} x^{3-2} = \frac{8x}{9}$     25. $\sqrt{x^3} \cdot \sqrt{x} = x^{3/2} \cdot x^{1/2} = x^{3/2+1/2} = x^2$

27. $\left(\frac{1}{\sqrt{x}}\right)^{-2} = (\sqrt{x})^2 = x$     29. $4x^0 + x^{-1} = 4 + \frac{1}{x} = \frac{4x+1}{x}$

1. $(x + 1)^2 = x^2 + 2x + 1$
3. $(x + 6)(x + 1) = x^2 + 6x + x + 6 = x^2 + 7x + 6$
5. $(x + \sqrt{2})(x - \sqrt{2}) = x^2 - (\sqrt{2})^2 = x^2 - 2$
7. $(4x + 1)(x - 3) = 4x^2 + x - 12x - 3 = 4x^2 - 11x - 3$
9. $(x + 1)^3 = x^3 + 3(x^2)(1) + 3(x)(1^2) + 1^3 = x^3 + 3x^2 + 3x + 1$
11. $(x - 1)(x^2 + x + 1) = x^3 - 1.$
13. $(2x - 3)^3 = (2x)^3 - 3(2x)^2(3) + 3(2x)(3^2) - 3^3 = 8x^3 - 36x^3 + 54x - 21$
15. $(x - 3)^2$
17. $(x + \sqrt{5})(x - \sqrt{5})$
19. $(2x + 5)(3x - 1)$
21. $(3x + 2)^2$
23. $(2x - 1)(4x^2 + 2x + 1)$
25. $(3x + 1)(9x^2 - 3x + 1)$
27. (a) $(x + h)^2 - x^2 = x^2 + 2xh + h^2 - x^2 = 2xh + h^2$
    (b) $(x + h)^3 - x^3 = x^3 + 3x^2h + 3xh^2 + h^3 - x^3 = 3x^2h + 3xh^2 + h^3$
29. (III) $(x + a)(x + b) = (x + a)x + (x + a)b = x^2 + ax + bx + ab$
                        $= x^2 + (a + b)x + ab$

1. $2x + 8 = 0$
   $2x = -8$
   $\frac{1}{2}(2x) = \frac{1}{2}(-8)$
   $x = -4$

3. $2(2x - 3) = 5$
   $4x - 6 = 5$
   $4x = 11$
   $\frac{1}{4}(4x) = \frac{1}{4}(11)$
   $x = \frac{11}{4}$

5. $\frac{x}{2} + \frac{1}{3} = \frac{4}{3}$

   $\frac{x}{2} = \frac{4}{3} - \frac{1}{3}$

   $\frac{x}{2} = 1$

   $2\left(\frac{x}{2}\right) = 2(1)$

   $x = 2$

6. $4 + \frac{x}{3} = 1 - x$

   $\frac{x}{3} + x = 1 - 4$

   $\frac{4}{3}x = -3$

   $(\frac{3}{4})\frac{4}{3}x = -3(\frac{3}{4})$

   $x = -\frac{9}{4}$

11. $x^2 - 16 = 0$
    $(x + 4)(x - 4) = 0$
    $x + 4 = 0$    or    $x - 4 = 0$
    $x = -4$    or    $x = 4$

10. $x^2 + 7x - 8 = 0$
    $(x + 8)(x - 1) = 0$
    $x + 8 = 0$    or    $x - 1 = 0$     $x = -8$    or    $x = 1$

14. $2x^5 = 64$
$\frac{1}{2}(2x^5) = \frac{1}{2}(64)$
$x^5 = 32$
$(x^5)^{1/5} = (32)^{1/5}$
$x = 2.$

15. $x^2 - x - 12 = 0$
$(x + 3)(x - 4) = 0$
$x + 3 = 0 \quad$ or $\quad x - 4 = 0$
$x = -3 \quad$ or $\quad x = 4$

**A.4**
**Exercise**
(page 577)

1. (a) $\dfrac{2}{3x - 3} + \dfrac{x + 1}{x^2} = \dfrac{2}{3(x - 1)} + \dfrac{x + 1}{x^2} = \dfrac{2x^2 + 3(x - 1)(x + 1)}{3x^2(x - 1)}$

$= \dfrac{2x^2 + 3x^2 - 3}{3x^2(x - 1)} = \dfrac{5x^2 - 3}{3x^2(x - 1)}$

(c) $\dfrac{7}{x + h} - \dfrac{7}{x} = \dfrac{7x - 7(x + h)}{x(x + h)} = \dfrac{7x - 7x - 7h}{x(x + h)} = \dfrac{-7h}{x(x + h)}$

2. (b) $\dfrac{\sqrt{x + 4} - \sqrt{x}}{2} \cdot \dfrac{\sqrt{x + 4} + \sqrt{x}}{\sqrt{x + 4} + \sqrt{x}} = \dfrac{x + 4 - x}{2(\sqrt{x + 4} + \sqrt{x})} = \dfrac{2}{(\sqrt{x + 4} + \sqrt{x})}$

3. (b) $\sqrt{2x + 3} - \dfrac{1}{\sqrt{2x + 3}} = \dfrac{(\sqrt{2x + 3})^2 - 1}{\sqrt{2x + 3}} = \dfrac{2x + 3 - 1}{\sqrt{2x + 3}} = \dfrac{2(x + 1)}{\sqrt{2x + 3}}$

(c) $\dfrac{1}{(x + h)^2} - \dfrac{1}{x^2} = \dfrac{x^2 - (x + h)^2}{x^2(x + h)^2} = \dfrac{x^2 - x^2 - 2xh - h^2}{x^2(x + h)^2} = \dfrac{-h(2x + h)}{x^2(x + h)^2}$

**A.5**
**Exercise**
(page 580)

1. (a) $-5 < x < 5$    (d) $-4 \leqq x \leqq 4$

2. (d) $\qquad -10 \leqq 3x - 7 \leqq 10$
$\qquad -10 + 7 \leqq 3x - 7 + 7 \leqq 10 + 7$
$\qquad -3 \leqq 3x \leqq 17$
$\qquad (1/3)(-3) \leqq (1/3)3x \leqq (1/3)17$
$\qquad -1 \leqq x \leqq 17/3$
$\qquad \{x \mid -1 \leqq x \leqq 17/3\}$

# Index